Scotland

The lush Scottish countryside is graced by mountains and glens, lochs, and heather-covered moors. © Dewitt Jones/Robert Holmes Photography.

Gloriously illuminated at night, Edinburgh Castle rises above the city at the western end of the Royal Mile. This castle, where Mary Queen of Scots gave birth to James VI of Scotland, is filled with history, legend, and lore. See chapter 4. © Kindra Clineff Photography.

Old Town's Royal Mile stretches from Edinburgh Castle all the way to the Palace of Holyroodhouse and bears four names along its length—Castlehill, Lawnmarket, High Street, and Canongate. See chapter 4. © Catherine Karnow Photography.

The oldest (1128) and probably largest of the Borders abbeys, Kelso Abbey has lain in ruins since the late 16th century, when it suffered its last and most devastating attack by the English. See chapter 5. © Andrea Pistolesi/The Image Bank.

With more than 440 courses, Scotland is synonymous with golf. The famous golfing center/sports complex at Gleneagles boasts several 18-hole courses: The King's and Queen's are among the best in the country. See chapters 3 and 9. © Macduff Everton Photography.

Loch Awe is Scotland's longest lake. Along it's banks are many ruins, including those of Kilchurn castle, once a stronghold of the Campbells of Glen Orchy and still spectacularly intact. See chapter 7. © John Lawrence/Tony Stone Images.

Near Callander is Balquhidder Church, containing the 8th-century St. Angus Stone, a 17th-century bell, and some Gaelic Bibles. But most people come here to see the grave of Robert "Rob Roy" MacGregor. See chapter 8. © Catherine Karnow Photography.

The first Saturday of September brings the Royal Highland Gathering to Braemar. The highlights are bagpiping and dancing competitions and performances of great strength like the hammer throw. See chapter 9. © Churchill & Klehr Photography.

The lochs and moors of the West Highlands are irresistibly beautiful spots where you'll want to linger and shoot a few rolls of film. This is Rannoch Moor off Loch Laidon, as viewed from A82. See chapter 10. © Kindra Clineff Photography.

Near Kyle of Lochalsh is Eilean Donan Castle, built in 1214 as a defense against the Danes. In ruins for 200 years, it was restored in 1932 by Colonel MacRae of Clan MacRae and is now a memorial/museum. See chapter 11. © Catherine Karnow Photography.

On Skye and the other Hebridean Islands are thatch-roofed "black houses," built without mortar. Though some houses have chimneys, the smoke from the fires inside passes through the thatch, making it "black." See chapter 11. © Art Wolfe Photography.

George Grant, Chairman of the Glenfarclas Distillery at Ballindalloch. The Grant family has been producing whisky at Glenfarclas since 1836. See chapter 9. © Catherine Karnow Photography.

When should I travel to get the best airfare?
Where do I go for answers to my travel questions?
What's the best and easiest way to plan and book my trip?

frommers.travelocity.com

Frommer's, the travel guide leader, has teamed up with **Travelocity.com**, the leader in online travel, to bring you an in-depth, easy-to-use resource designed to help you plan and book your trip online.

At **frommers.travelocity.com**, you'll find free online updates about your destination from the experts at Frommer's plus the outstanding travel planning and purchasing features of Travelocity.com. Travelocity.com provides reservations capabilities for 95 percent of all airline seats sold, more than 47,000 hotels, and over 50 car rental companies. In addition, Travelocity.com offers more than 2,000 exciting vacation and cruise packages. Travelocity.com puts you in complete control of your travel planning with these and other great features:

Expert travel guidance from Frommer's - over 150 writers reporting from around the world!

Best Fare Finder - an interactive calendar tells you when to travel to get the best airfare

Fare Watcher - we'll track airfare changes to your favorite destinations

Dream Maps - a mapping feature that suggests travel opportunities based on your budget

Shop Safe Guarantee - 24 hours a day / 7 days a week live customer service, and more!

Whether traveling on a tight budget, looking for a quick weekend getaway, or planning the trip of a lifetime, Frommer's guides and Travelocity.com will make your travel dreams a reality. You've bought the book, now book the trip!

A New Star-Rating System & Other Exciting News from Frommer's!

In our continuing effort to publish the savviest, most up-to-date, and most appealing travel guides available, we've added some great new features.

Frommer's guides now include a new **star-rating system.** Every hotel, restaurant, and attraction is rated from 0 to 3 stars to help you set priorities and organize your time.

We've also added **seven brand-new features** that point you to the great deals, in-the-know advice, and unique experiences that separate travelers from tourists. Throughout the guide look for:

Finds	Special finds—those places only insiders know about
Fun Fact	Fun facts—details that make travelers more informed and their trips more fun
Kids	Best bets for kids—advice for the whole family
Moments	Special moments—those experiences that memories are made of
Overrated	Places or experiences not worth your time or money
Tips	Insider tips—some great ways to save time and money
Value	Great values—where to get the best deals

We've also added a **"What's New"** section in every guide—a timely crash course in what's hot and what's not in every destination we cover.

Other Great Guides for Your Trip:

Frommer's England

Frommer's England from $75 a Day

Frommer's London

Frommer's Ireland

Frommer's Best-Loved Driving Tours: Scotland

Scotland

7th Edition

by Darwin Porter & Danforth Prince

Here's what the critics say about Frommer's:

"Amazingly easy to use. Very portable, very complete."
—*Booklist*

"The only mainstream guide to list specific prices. The Walter Cronkite of guidebooks—with all that implies."
—*Travel & Leisure*

"Complete, concise, and filled with useful information."
—*New York Daily News*

"Hotel information is close to encyclopedic."
—*Des Moines Sunday Register*

Best-Selling Books • Digital Downloads • e-Books • Answer Networks
e-Newsletters • Branded Web Sites • e-Learning
New York, NY • Cleveland, OH • Indianapolis, IN

About the Authors

Darwin Porter has covered Scotland since the beginning of his travel-writing career as author of *Frommer's England & Scotland*. Since 1982, he has been joined in his efforts by **Danforth Prince,** formerly of the Paris bureau of the *New York Times*. Together, they've written numerous best-selling Frommer's guides—notably to England, France, and Italy.

Published by:

Hungry Minds, Inc.

909 Third Avenue
New York, NY 10022

ISBN 0-7645-6510-9
ISSN 1055-5390

Editor: Leslie Shen
Production Editor: Tammy Ahrens
Photo Editor: Richard Fox
Cartographer: Nicholas Trotter
Production by Hungry Minds Indianapolis Production Services

Front cover photo: Eilean Donan Castle in Dornie (near Kyle of Lochalsh)
Back cover photo: Standing Stones of Callanish on the Isle of Lewis

Special Sales

For general information on Hungry Minds' products and services, please contact our Customer Care department; within the U.S. at 800-762-2974, outside the U.S. at 317-572-3993 or fax 317-572-4002. For sales inquiries and reseller information, including discounts, bulk sales, customized editions, and premium sales, please contact our Customer Care department at 800-434-3422.

Manufactured in the United States of America

5 4 3 2

Contents

5 The Borders & Galloway Regions   116

6 Glasgow & the Strathclyde Region   156

7 Argyll & the Southern Hebrides   204

List of Maps

An Invitation to the Reader

In researching this book, we discovered many wonderful places—hotels, restaurants, shops, and more. We're sure you'll find others. Please tell us about them, so we can share the information with your fellow travelers in upcoming editions. If you were disappointed with a recommendation, we'd love to know that, too. Please write to:

Frommer's Scotland, 7th Edition
Hungry Minds, Inc. • 909 Third Avenue • New York, NY 10022

An Additional Note

Please be advised that travel information is subject to change at any time—and this is especially true of prices. We therefore suggest that you write or call ahead for confirmation when making your travel plans. The authors, editors, and publisher cannot be held responsible for the experiences of readers while traveling. Your safety is important to us, however, so we encourage you to stay alert and be aware of your surroundings. Keep a close eye on cameras, purses, and wallets, all favorite targets of thieves and pickpockets.

New! Frommer's Star Ratings & Icons

Every hotel, restaurant, and attraction listing in this guide has been ranked for quality, value, service, amenities, and special features using a star-rating scale. In country, state, and regional guides, we also rate towns and regions to help you narrow down your choices and budget your time accordingly. Hotels and restaurants in the Very Expensive and Expensive categories are rated on a scale of one (highly recommended) to three stars (exceptional). Those in the Moderate and Inexpensive categories rate from zero (recommended) to two stars (very highly recommended). Attractions, towns, and regions are rated according to the following scale: zero stars (recommended), one star (highly recommended), two stars (very highly recommended), and three stars (must-see).

In addition to the rating system, we also use seven icons to highlight insider information, useful tips, special bargains, hidden gems, memorable experiences, kid-friendly venues, places to avoid, and other useful information:

| Finds | Fun Fact | Kids | Moments | Overrated | Tips | Value |

The following abbreviations are used for credit cards:

AE	American Express	DISC	Discover	V	Visa
DC	Diners Club	MC	MasterCard		

FROMMERS.COM

Now that you have the guidebook to a great trip, visit our website at **www.frommers.com** for travel information on nearly 2,000 destinations. With features updated regularly, we give you instant access to the most current trip-planning information available. At Frommers.com, you'll also find the best prices on airfares, accommodations, and car rentals—and you can even book travel online through our travel booking partners. At Frommers.com, you'll also find the following:

- Daily Newsletter highlighting the best travel deals
- Hot Spot of the Month/Vacation Sweepstakes & Travel Photo Contest
- More than 200 Travel Message Boards
- Outspoken Newsletters and Feature Articles on travel bargains, vacation ideas, tips & resources, and more!

What's New in Scotland

With its own Parliament in place, Scotland hasn't achieved independence from England, but it is forging ahead to carve a niche for itself in the 21st century. Here are some of the latest developments:

PLANNING YOUR TRIP Orient Express Trains & Cruises (© 800/524-2420 in the U.S.; www.orient-express.com) has launched its fifth train in Britain, the *Northern Belle*. It carries 252 passengers and feeds them in six stately dining rooms evocative of a country home in Scotland.

The best way to see the Highlands is aboard the *Lord of the Glens* riverboat (© 020/7616-1000; www.vjv.co.uk), running between Inverness and Oban. It's the first luxury passenger boat to take on overnight passengers for the 200-mile (322km) jaunt that allows you to view some of the most dramatic scenery of Scotland. For Nessie watchers, it even crosses Loch Ness. See "Getting There," in chapter 2 for details.

EDINBURGH Accommodations The latest development shaking Edinburgh is that Hilton has acquired the capital's most staid and traditional hotel, the **Caledonian**, Princes St. (© 0131/222-8888; www.hilton.com). The news has gone over with locals as though the Japanese had just announced the acquisition of the White House in Washington. Hilton plans many improvements, but—to prevent rioting in the streets—tradition will be respected.

One of the most delightful hotels to open in all of Scotland is **The Scotsman**, 20 N. Bridge St. (© 0131/556-5565; www.thescotsmanhotel.com). Its name comes from the building's former role as the headquarters of one of Scotland's most famous newspapers. A 1904 baronial limestone pile, it is one of the most charming of the city's first-class hotels, and is giving the old dragons big competition.

A real discovery is **Newington Cottage**, 15 Blacket Place (© 0131/668-1935; www.scotland2000.com/newington). It contains only three bedrooms, but they're of the quality of a government-rated five-star hotel at only a fraction of the price.

Edinburgh continues to see the opening of small, affordable guesthouses. One of the latest is **Barony House**, 23 Mayfield Gardens (© 0131/667-5806; www.baronyhouse.co.uk), on the south side of the city. It's run with a real personal touch.

Dining The hot new restaurant generating local excitement is **The Tower**, at the top of the Museum of Scotland on Chambers Street (© 0131/225-3003), which artfully uses local ingredients to create some of the capital's tastiest fare.

Also garnering raves is **Martin Wishart**, 54 The Shore, in Leith in the northern regions of Edinburgh (© 0131/553-3557), hailed by several gourmet associations as "the Scottish restaurant of the year." The namesake of the restaurant is one of the most talented chefs in Britain. Gourmets are beating a path to his door.

Seeing the Sights The Millennium Dome at Greenwich outside London may have gone bust, but the new millennium museum for Scotland is packing in the crowds in 2001. **Dynamic Earth,** Holyrood Road (© 0131/550-7800), not far from the Palace of Holyroodhouse, tells the story of Earth itself in all its diversity. You can also see replicas of the slimy green primordial soup where life began, along with a series of specialized aquariums that re-create primordial life forms. All 11 galleries have stunning special effects. See chapter 4 for more information on Edinburgh.

THE BORDERS A real find, **Clint Lodge Hotel,** in the old village of St. Boswells (© 01835/822-027; www.tasteofscotland.co.uk/clint_lodge.html), is a restored former sports lodge dating from the 18th century. Turned into a small hotel of charm and grace, it features panoramic views and a "taste of Scotland" menu. See chapter 5 for details.

GLASGOW Accommodations One of the city's most stylish hotels has opened in the Education Department's former headquarters. **The ArtHouse,** 129 Bath St. (© 0141/221-6789), overcomes that institutional look, however. Ranald MacColl has brought zip and glamour to architect Henry E. Clifford's neoclassical interiors. The gilded Scottish lions and the stained-glass windows are still here, but everything else, including the bedrooms and state-of-the-art bathrooms, is modernized. Even the staff members in their unisex suits are hip.

Dining Glasgow is now vying with Edinburgh for the title of gastronomic capital of Scotland. One of the trendiest restaurants to open is **The ArtHouse Grill,** in The ArtHouse hotel (see above).

Chef Ferrier Richardson is creating excitement among foodies at his **Eurasia,** 150 St. Vincent St. (© 0141/204-1150), with a fusion cuisine greatly influenced by Asia but filled with Scottish delights from field and stream as well.

With its global cuisine, **Stravaigin,** 26 Gibson St., Hillhead (© 0141/334-2665), celebrates the regional bounty of Scotland but also roams the world for inspiration, from the Caribbean to China.

See chapter 6 for more information on Glasgow.

INVERNESS & THE WEST HIGHLANDS The far north's most modern hotel, **The New Weigh Inn & Lodges,** Burnside, Thurso (© 01847/893-722; www.weighinn.co.uk/frmain.htm), has opened in the most northerly town on the Scottish mainland. It overlooks Pentland Firth, and in the distance is a panoramic view of the Orkney Islands. It's not distinguished architecturally, but is most comfortable and was built to high standards after a landmark inn, which stood on these grounds burned in 1997. It offers accommodations in a wide range of styles, from self-catering chalets to family rooms, small singles to luxurious units with four-posters. See chapter 10 for details.

The Best of Scotland

Scotland is permeated with legend and romance. Its ruined castles standing amid fields of heather and bracken speak of a past full of heroism and struggle and events that still ring across the centuries. Its two great cities—the ancient seat of Scottish royalty, Edinburgh, and the even more ancient Glasgow, boasting Victorian splendor—are among Europe's most dynamic centers. The country's other side is its awesomely beautiful outdoors, with highlands, mountains, lochs, salmon-filled rivers, incomparable golf courses, and more.

1 The Best Travel Experiences

- **Checking Out the Local Pub:** You're in a Scottish pub, talking to the bartender and choosing from a dizzying array of single-malt whiskies. Perhaps the wind is blowing fitfully outside, causing the wooden sign to creak above the battered door, and a fire is flickering against the blackened bricks of the old fireplace. If you head here to ward off the chill of a cold, damp night, you certainly won't be alone. As the evening wanes and you've established common ground with the locals, you'll realize you're having one of your most authentic Scottish experiences. We list our favorite pubs in the destination chapters that follow.

- **Visiting Edinburgh at Festival Time:** The Edinburgh International Festival has become one of Europe's most prestigious arts festivals. During 3 weeks in August, a host of performers descends on the city, infusing it with a kind of manic creative energy. If you're planning to sample the many offerings, get your tickets well in advance, and make your hotel and flight reservations early. Call

© **0131/473-2001** or go to www. eif.co.uk to check schedules and purchase tickets. See chapter 4.

- **Sailing off the Coast of Argyll:** Eons ago, glaciers carved the west coast of Scotland into one of Europe's most spectacularly jagged shorelines. Warmed by the Gulf Stream and dotted with sheltered estuaries and channels, it offers challenging sailing and rugged scenery. If you're a qualified sailor, you can rent a vessel from virtually any fisherman along the coast for a watery overview of terrain made famous by the Lowland clans. Or you can rent a boat from the **Linnhe Marine Watersports Centre,** Lettershuna, Appin (© **01631/730-401**). See chapter 7.

- **Horseback Trekking Through the Highlands & Argyll:** There's nothing like riding one of the country's sturdy ponies through the Highlands' lichen-covered rocks and fragrant heather. One of Scotland's biggest stables is the **Highland Riding Centre,** Drumnadrochit (© **01456/450-220**); see chapter 10. For scenic equestrian treks across the Argyll area's

Scotland

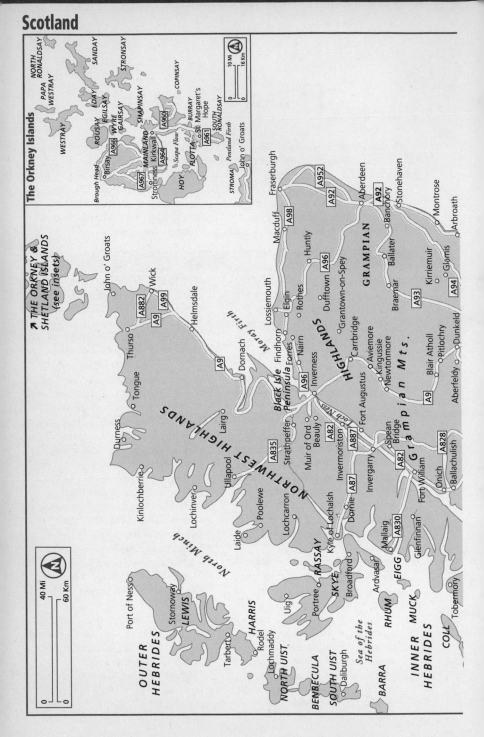

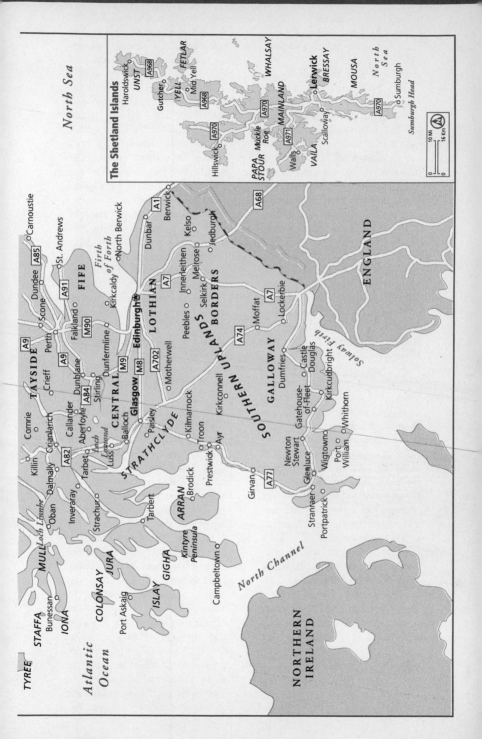

The Shetland Islands

North Sea

Haroldswick
Gutcher
UNST
YELL
FETLAR
Mid Yell
WHALSAY
A968
A968
A970
A970
MAINLAND
Lerwick
BRESSAY
MOUSA
A971
Scalloway
VAILA
Walls
Mackie
Roe
PAPA
STOUR
A970
Hillswick
North Sea
Sumburgh
Sumburgh Head

10 MI
16 KM
0
0

North Sea

TYREE
STAFFA
Bunessan
IONA
Atlantic Ocean
MULL
Loch Linnhe
Oban
Dalmally
Inveraray
Strachur
COLONSAY
JURA
Port Askaig
ISLAY
GIGHA
Campbeltown
North Channel
Kintyre Peninsula
Tarbert
ARRAN
Brodick
STRATHCLYDE
Paisley
Troon
Prestwick
Ayr
Girvan
A77
Stranraer
Portpatrick
Glenluce
Newton Stewart
Wigtown
Port William
Whithorn
GALLOWAY
Gatehouse-of-Fleet
Kirkcudbright
Castle Douglas
Dumfries
Solway Firth
A74
SOUTHERN UPLANDS
Kirkconnell
BORDERS
Moffat
Lockerbie
A7
A74
A702
Peebles
Selkirk
Melrose
Innerleithen
A7
LOTHIAN
Edinburgh
M8
M9
Glasgow
Balloch
Luss
Loch Lomond
Tarbet
A82
Callander
Aberfoyle
A84
Stirling
Dunblane
CENTRAL
Killin
Comrie
Crianlarich
Crieff
A9
TAYSIDE
A9
Perth
Scone
Dundee
A85
Carnoustie
St. Andrews
A91
FIFE
Falkland
M90
Dunfermline
Kirkcaldy
Firth of Forth
North Berwick
Dunbar
Berwick
A1
Kelso
Jedburgh
A68
A7
ENGLAND
NORTHERN IRELAND

moors, highlands, and headlands, try the **Ardfern Riding Centre**, Loch Gilphead (℃ **01852/500-632**). See chapter 7.

• **Cruising Along the Caledonian Canal:** In 1822, a group of enterprising Scots connected three of the Highlands' longest lakes (Lochs Ness, Lochy, and Oich) with a canal linking Britain's east and west coasts. Since then, barges have hauled everything from grain to building supplies without having to negotiate the wild storms off Scotland's northernmost tips. If you'd like a waterborne view of the countryside tamed centuries ago by the Camerons, the Stewarts, and the MacDonalds, you can rent a cabin cruiser. **Caley Cruisers,** based in Inverness (℃ **01463/236-328;** www.caley cruisers.co.uk), maintains Scotland's largest inventory of 60-horsepower diesel-powered cruisers. See chapter 10.

• **Attending a Highland Game:** Unlike any other sporting event, a Highland Game emphasizes clannish traditions rather than athletic dexterity, and the centerpiece is usually an exhibition of brute strength (tossing logs and the like). Most visitors show up for the men in kilts, the bagpipe playing, the pomp and circumstance, and the general celebration of all things Scottish. The best-known (and most widely televised) of the events is the **Braemar Royal Highland Gathering,** held near Balmoral Castle in late August or early September. For details, call the local tourist office at ℃ **013397/742-208.** See chapter 10.

• **Ferrying to the Isle of Iona:** It's an otherworldly rock, one of Europe's most evocative holy places, anchored solidly among the Hebrides off Scotland's western coast. St. Columba established it as a Christian center in A.D. 563 and used it as a base for converting Scotland. You'll find a ruined Benedictine nunnery and a fully restored cathedral where 50 Scottish kings opted to be buried during the early Middle Ages. Hundreds of Celtic crosses once adorned the island; today, only three of the originals remain. The island, now part of the National Trust, is home to the Iona Community, an ecumenical group dedicated to the perpetuation of Christian ideals. Reaching the island requires a 10-minute ferry ride from the hamlet of Fionnphort, on the island of Mull. See chapter 11.

• **Exploring the Orkneys:** Archaeologists say the Orkneys, an archipelago with some 70 islands, contain the richest trove of prehistoric monuments in the British Isles—an average of three sites per square mile. Ornithologists claim that about 16% of all winged animals in the United Kingdom reside here, and linguists document an ancient dialect still using Viking terms. Northwest of the Scottish mainland, closer to Oslo than to faraway London, these islands are on the same latitude as St. Petersburg but much more exposed to the raging gales of the North Sea. The sunsets here during late spring and the aurora borealis have been called mystical, and in midsummer the sun remains above the horizon for 18 hours per day. In winter, the islands are plunged into an equivalent twilight or total darkness. Only 19 of the Orkneys are inhabited; the others seem to float above primordial seas, drenched with rains and the weak sunlight of these northern climes. See chapter 12.

2 The Best Golf

For full details about golfing in Scotland, see chapter 3.

- **Turnberry Hotel Golf Courses** (Ayrshire; ℂ **01655/331-000**): Established in 1902, this is one of the world's most sought-after courses. It's not for the faint of heart—although some of the links are verdant, others are uncomfortably paired with the sands, the salt-resistant tough grasses, and the powerful winds blasting in from the nearby sea. See chapter 6.
- **Royal Troon Golf Club** (Ayrshire; ℂ **01292/311-555**): Laid out along lines paralleling the Firth of Clyde, this club fills a flat lowland terrain whose fairways are almost breathtakingly green despite their foundations on sandy soil. This is Lowland Scotland at its most seductive, a 7,097-yard (6,458m) course (one of Scotland's longest) with a par of 71. See chapter 6.
- **The Old Course** (St. Andrews; ℂ **01334/466-666**): Sometime during the late 14th century, a group of bored aristocrats started batting a ball around the nearby meadows. By the time their activities were officially recorded in

1552, the bylaws of the game were well on the way to being part of Scotland's lore. The Old Course is the world's most legendary temple of golf, one whose difficulty is shaped by nature and the long-ago paths of grazing sheep. See chapter 8.
- **Carnoustie Golf Links** (Tayside; ℂ **01241/853-789**): Site of six British Opens, Carnoustie is much more difficult than most players anticipate at first glance. U.S. champions Tom Watson and Gary Player have referred to it as their favorite, and much of the town of Carnoustie was built because of the stream of world-class golfers who migrated here. See chapter 9.
- **Royal Dornoch Golf Club** (Sutherland; ℂ **01862/810-219**): This is the most northerly of the world's great golf courses, only 6° south of the Arctic Circle. Despite its northern isolation, Royal Dornoch enjoys a microclimate more akin to the fens around Norfolk, England, than to the Arctic. See chapter 10.

3 The Best Fishing

For more details about fishing in Scotland, see chapter 3.

- **The Borders & Galloway Regions:** Sea fishing is pure heaven in the Solway Firth; it's best near Port William and Portpatrick villages, in the vicinity of Loch Ryan, and along the shore of the Isle of Whithorn. The elusive salmon is best pursued along the River Tweed, and the lesser-known hill lochans are ideal for trout fishermen. Local tourist offices distribute two helpful guides: *A Comprehensive Guide to*

Scottish Borders Angling and *Castabout Anglers Guide to Dumfries and Galloway.* See chapter 5.
- **Argyll & the Southern Hebrides:** This much-visited area in western Scotland is split in two by the long peninsula of Kintyre. It's definitely a northern Atlantic ecology, filled with open sea and loch and separated by the Firth of Clyde from the islands of the Inner Hebrides. There are some 50 prime sites on rivers and lochs for freshwater fishing, and some two dozen villages with fantastic sea fishing. See chapter 7.

- **Tayside:** The northeast section of Scotland is filled with major rivers—the Don, Dee, Ythan, and Deverson—plus smaller rivers like the Ugie, all ideal for salmon fishing. When estuary and loch fishing are considered, this becomes one of the country's best areas for game fishing. Local tourist offices keep abreast of all the details about boat rentals and permit prices, and some country hotels offer fishing packages. See chapter 9.
- **The Great Glen:** From all over the world, anglers flock to the Great Glen, with its many lochs and rivers, to cast their flies in search of Scottish trout and salmon. Sea angling from boat or shore is also permitted. Salmon season runs from February to September; brown trout season is mid-March to early October. Anglers can catch rainbow trout here year-round. See chapter 10.
- **Northern Highlands:** There are endless possibilities for fishing here, since Sutherland is riddled with lochs. Trout fishing is the big lure, and local tourist offices will tell you all about boats and permits. Not only is the fishing great, but your hotel cook may also prepare your catch for you. See chapter 10.
- **The Orkney Islands:** These far northern islands are major fishing grounds. At least seven outfitters offer charters, and you can rent fishing equipment. Loch fishing is also a popular pastime in the Orkneys, especially in Loch of Stenness and Loch of Harray, where hopeful anglers go after salmon, trout, sea trout, and salmon trout, although porbeagle shark, cod, halibut, bass, hake, skate, and turbot also turn up. See chapter 12.

4 The Best Countryside Drives

- **The Valley of the Tweed:** The waters originate in Scotland, define the border with England for part of their length, and are noted for some of Britain's best salmon fishing. Ruins of once-wealthy abbeys dot the landscape like beacons of long-lost power and prestige. Most travelers begin in Kelso and move west through Dryburgh, Selkirk, Melrose, Innerleithen, and Peebles. Although the total distance is less than 50 miles (80.5km), with a bit of backtracking en route, the many historic sites call for at least a full day's exploration. See chapter 5.
- **The Isle of Arran:** Anchored off Scotland's southwestern edge, Arran combines radically different climates and topographies into a relatively small space. You'll find a rich trove of prehistoric monuments, a red-sandstone pile beloved by medievalists, nostalgic ruins, and sweeping panoramas as far away as Northern Ireland. Its southern tier, warmed by the Gulf Stream, contains lush, temperate vegetation, while the moors and hills of its northern edge are as wild and craggy as the Highlands. Allow half a day, not including stopover times, for the 56-mile (90km) circumnavigation of the island's coastal road. See chapter 7.
- **The Lochs & Mountains South of Oban:** This area is lonely, but its drama includes views of the longest freshwater lake (Loch Awe), one of the longest saltwater fjords (Loch Fyne), some of the most historic buildings (Kilchurn Castle, Carnasserie Castle, and the Kilmartin Church), and one of

the most crucial battlefields (the slopes of Ben Cruachan) in Scotland. Locals refer to it as the Hinterlands near Oban, but the 87-mile (140km) route follows an excellent network of highways along the jagged coast. Major towns you'll traverse en route are Dalmally, Inveraray, Lochgilphead, and Oban. See chapter 7.

- **The Trossachs:** At the narrowest point of the mainland, just north of Glasgow, the Trossachs have been famous for their scenery since Queen Victoria decreed them lovely in 1869. Mystery seems to shroud the waters of Lochs Lomond and Katrine. According to legend, the region's highest mountain, Ben Venue, is the traditional meeting point for Scotland's goblins. Ruled for generations by the MacGregor clan, this is the countryside of Sir Walter Scott's *Rob Roy* and *The Lady of the Lake*. A tour through the region, beginning at Callander and meandering through Aberfoyle, Stronachlacher, and Inversnaid, should take about half a day. Expect lots of traffic in summer, often from tour buses. See chapter 8.

- **The Road to the Isles (Hwy. A830):** It begins in Fort William, western terminus of the Caledonian Canal, and ends at Mallaig, the departure point for ferries servicing several offshore islands, including Mull, 46 miles (74km) northwest. En route, it passes the highest mountains in Britain. Along the way, you can see one of the Victorian Age's most dramatic engineering triumphs—Neptune's Staircase, a network of eight locks that raise the level of the canal 64 feet (19m) in less than 500 yards (455m). Although summer traffic can be dense, services en route are scarce, so start with a full tank of gas. See chapters 10 and 11.

5 The Best Bike Rides

For details on biking around the country, see chapter 3.

- **The Galloway Region:** Scotland's southwestern region is one of the least visited but one of the most beautiful. A land of fields, verdant forests, and mist-shrouded hills, Galloway offers endless biking possibilities. All tourist offices in the area carry *Cycling in Dumfries and Galloway,* which describes the best routes. A free leaflet published by the Scottish Forest Enterprise gives trail routes through the various forests. See chapter 5.

- **The Isle of Arran:** The largest of the Clyde Islands, Arran has been called "Scotland in miniature." If you don't have time to see the whole country, you can get a preview of its various regions by biking this island. The northern part is mountainous like the Highlands, but the southern part is more typically Lowland, like the scenery in the Borders. The full circuit around the island takes about 9 hours. The tourist office distributes the free *Cycling on Arran,* giving the best routes. See chapter 7.

- **The Trossachs:** Scotland's most beautiful stretch for biking is the Trossachs (also the loveliest for driving or country walks), famed as Rob Roy MacGregor country. The best spot for biking is along Loch Katrine, 10 miles (16km) long and 2 miles (3km) at its widest. See chapter 8.

- **Glencoe:** Site of a famous 1692 massacre, Glencoe features stark and grandiose mountain scenery. Rent a bike in the village and set out on an adventure, although you're likely to get rained on, as some 100 inches of rain a year are recorded. But as one local said, "Biking through Glencoe in the rain is when it's at its most mystical—we Scots have done that for years." See chapter 10.

- **The Isle of Skye:** One of the most evocative of the Hebrides, Skye is the land of the Cuillins, a brooding

mountain range you'll see at every turn as you pedal along. The most unusual place to bike is the 20-mile (32km) Trotternish Peninsula. It's known for its odd rock formations, and its coastal road passes an area of beautiful but often rocky seascapes, opening onto Loch Snizort and the Sound of Raasay. See chapter 11.

6 The Best Hikes

- **The Southern Upland Way:** Rivaling the West Highland Way (see below), this is the second of Scotland's great walks. The footpath begins at Portpatrick and runs 212 miles (341km) on the southwest coast to Cockburnspath on the eastern coast. Along the way, it passes through some of the most dramatic scenery in the Borders, including Galloway Forest Park. Contact the **Scottish Tourist Board,** 23 Ravelston Terrace, Edinburgh (© **0131/332-2433**). See chapter 5.

- **East Neuk:** Directly south of St. Andrews lie some of Scotland's loveliest fishing villages, collectively known as East Neuk. The most enchanting walk is between the villages of Pittenweem and Anstruther. The day is likely to be breezy, with wind from the sea, so dress accordingly. The path begins at the bottom of West Braes, a cul-de-sac off the main road in Anstruther. See chapter 8.

- **The Trossachs:** The Trossachs Trail stretches from Loch Lomond in the west to Callander in the east and also from Doune to Aberfoyle and the Lord Ard Forest to the south. In the north, it's bounded by the Crianlarich Hills and Balquhidder, the site of Rob Roy's grave. Ever since Sir Walter Scott published *The Lady of the Lake* and *Rob Roy,* the area has attracted hikers in search of its unspoiled

natural beauty. Our favorite start for walks is the village of Brig o' Turk, between Lochs Achray and Venachar at the foot of Glen Finglas. From here you can set out in all directions, including one signposted to the Achray Forest. There's also the Glen Finglas circular walk, and many hikers leave Brig o' Turk heading for Balquhidder via Glen Finglas. See chapter 8.

- **The West Highland Way:** This is one of Scotland's great walks. Beginning north of Glasgow in Milngavie, the footpath stretches for 95 miles (153km) north along Loch Lomond, going through Glencoe to Fort William and eventually to Ben Nevis, Britain's highest mountain. Even if you walk only part of this path, you need to make plans in advance. Contact the **Scottish Tourist Board,** 23 Ravelston Terrace, Edinburgh (© **0131/332-2433**). See chapters 8 and 10.

- **Ben Nevis:** Four miles (6km) southeast of the town of Fort William looms Ben Nevis, Britain's highest mountain at 4,406 feet (1,336.5m). The snow-capped granite mass dominates this entire region of Scotland. This trip can be done in a day, but you'll need to massage your feet in the evening at a local pub. See chapter 10.

7 The Best Castles & Palaces

• **Edinburgh Castle** (Edinburgh): Few other buildings symbolize the grandeur of an independent Scotland as clearly as this one. Begun around A.D. 1000 on a hilltop high above the rest of Edinburgh, it witnessed some of the bloodiest and most treacherous events in Scottish history, including its doomed 1573 defense by Scottish patriot Grange in the name of Mary Queen of Scots. See chapter 4.

• **Palace of Holyroodhouse** (Edinburgh): Throughout the clan battles for independence from England, this palace served as a pawn between opposing forces. In its changing fortunes, it has housed a strange assortment of monarchs involved in traumatic events: Mary Queen of Scots, Bonnie Prince Charlie, James VII (before his ascendancy to the throne), and French king Charles X (on his forced abdication after an 1830 revolution). The building's present form dates from the late 1600s, when it was rebuilt in a dignified neo-Palladian style. Today, Holyroodhouse is one of Queen Elizabeth's official residences. See chapter 4.

• **Drumlanrig Castle** (Dumfries): Begun in 1679, this castle required 12 years to build and so much money that its patron, the third earl and first duke of Queensbury, complained to anyone who would listen how deeply he resented its existence. Later, it was embroiled in dynastic inheritance scandals worthy of a gothic novel. One of the most prestigious buildings in Scotland, it contains the antiques and artwork of four illustrious families. See chapter 5.

• **Culzean Castle** (near Maybole): Designed for comfort and prestige, this castle was built in the late 1700s by Scotland's most celebrated architect, Robert Adam, as a replacement for a dark, dank tower that had stood for longer than anyone could remember. It was donated to the National Trust for Scotland just after World War II. A suite was granted to General Eisenhower for his lifetime use, in gratitude for his role in staving off a foreign invasion of Britain. See chapter 6.

• **Stirling Castle** (Stirling): Stirling is a triumph of Renaissance ornamentation, a startling contrast to the severe bulk of many other Scottish castles. Despite its beauty, after its completion in 1540 the castle was one of the most impregnable fortresses in the British Isles, thanks partly to its position on a rocky crag. See chapter 8.

• **Scone Palace** (Scone): As early as A.D. 900, Scottish kings were crowned here, on a lump of granite so permeated with ancient magic the English hauled it off to Westminster Abbey in the 13th century, where it remained until 1995. The building you see today was rebuilt in 1802 from ruins that incorporated a 1580 structure and stones laid during the dim early days of Scottish and Pictish union. See chapter 9.

• **Glamis Castle** (Glamis): This castle's core was built for defense against rival clans during the 1400s, but over the centuries it evolved into a luxurious dwelling. The seat of the same family since 1372, Glamis is said to be haunted by the ghost of one of its former owners, Lady Glamis, who James V had burnt as a witch when she resisted his annexation of her castle. It figured into the ambitions of Macbeth, thane of Glamis, as well. See chapter 9.

- **Crathes Castle & Gardens** (Grampian): Crathes evokes the severe luxury of a 15th- and 16th-century Scottish laird. The style focuses on high heraldry, with frequent references to the persistent Scottish hope of an enduring independence. The gardens contain massive yew hedges originally planted in 1702. See chapter 9.
- **Balmoral Castle** (Ballater): Scotland offers far greater castles to explore, but Balmoral, the rebuilt castle of Prince Albert and Queen Victoria, draws the visiting hordes, hoping to get a glimpse of Prince William, no doubt. That's because it's still the Scottish residence of the queen. Although you can visit only its ballroom, the sprawling manicured grounds

and gardens also await you. See chapter 9.
- **Braemar** (Grampian): Built by the earl of Mar in 1628 as a hunting lodge, Braemar was burned to the ground, and then rebuilt by Farquharson of Invercauld, the ancestor of the present owner. It's often photographed as a symbol of Scottish grandeur and the well-upholstered aristocratic life. See chapter 9.
- **Cawdor Castle** (Cawdor): From its heavily fortified origins in the 1300s, Cawdor evolved into the Campbell clan's luxurious seat. According to legend and Shakespearean plot lines, three witches promised this castle to Macbeth to tempt him into the deeds that led to his destruction. See chapter 10.

8 The Best Cathedrals

- **Melrose Abbey** (the Borders): If it weren't for the abbey's location in the frequently devastated Borders, this would be one of the world's most spectacular ecclesiastical complexes. Founded in the 1100s, Melrose acquired vast wealth and was the target of its covetous enemies; it was burned and rebuilt several times before the Protestant takeover of Scotland. Today, it's one of the world's most beautiful ruins, a site immortalized by Robert Burns, who advised people to visit it only by moonlight. See chapter 5.
- **Cathedral of St. Kentigern** (Glasgow): In the 7th century, St. Mungo built a wooden structure here, intending it as his headquarters and eventual tomb. It burned down but was rebuilt in the 1300s. St. Kentigern is mainland Scotland's only complete medieval cathedral, with a form based extensively on the pointed arch. In the 1600s, the Calvinists stripped

it of anything hinting at papist idolatry, although a remarkable set of sculptures atop its stone nave screen, said to be unique in Scotland, still represent the seven deadly sins. See chapter 6.
- **Dunfermline Abbey** (Fife): During the 1100s, in its role as Scotland's Westminster Abbey, Dunfermline became one of Europe's wealthiest churches. Three kings of Scotland were born here, and 22 members of the Scottish royal family were buried here. In the early 1800s, its ruined premises were partially restored to what you see today. Several years later, a different kind of benefactor, Andrew Carnegie, was born within the cathedral's shadow. See chapter 8.
- **Dunblane Cathedral** (Fife): Partly because the site had been holy since the days of the Celts, David I founded a church here in 1150. Despite later alterations and additions, Dunblane is still one of

the country's best examples of Gothic architecture from the 1200s. See chapter 8.

- **St. Magnus Cathedral** (the Orkney Islands): The most spectacular medieval building in the Orkneys, St. Magnus features an odd imposition of the Norman Gothic style on a territory administered during the time of its construction (the 1100s) by the Norwegians. The bodies of St. Magnus, patron saint of the Orkneys, and his nephew Earl Rognvald, the church's builder, are buried inside. See chapter 12.

9 The Best Ruins

- **Linlithgow Palace** (Lothian): These ruins brood over an island in a loch, an unhappy vestige of what was the most glamorous royal residence during Scotland's golden age of independence in the early 1500s. Mary Queen of Scots was born here, but tragedy seemed to permeate the palace, as roofs collapsed from lack of maintenance and early deaths in the royal family hastened an inevitable union of Scotland with England. In 1745, after it was occupied by Bonnie Prince Charlie and his troops, a mysterious fire swept over it. See chapter 4.
- **Dryburgh Abbey** (the Borders): Begun in 1150 against a meandering curve of the River Tweed, Dryburgh was once home to thousands of monks who transformed the surrounding forests into arable fields and drained many local swamps. The abbey's position astride the much-troubled border with England resulted in its destruction in three episodes (1322, 1385, and 1544), the last of which included the burning of the nearby village (Dryburgh) as well. Today, the red-sandstone rocks are dim reminders of a long-ago monastic age. See chapter 5.
- **Kildrummy Castle** (Aberdeen): Built in the 1200s, this castle was one of northern Scotland's most important strongholds, mingling architectural principles of France with those developed in England and Wales. In 1715, after centuries of playing a decisive role in Scottish history, it was demolished by its enemies and dismantled stone by stone. Thus humbled, it broods as a reminder of former glories. See chapter 9.
- **Elgin Cathedral** (Grampian): This cathedral was built during the 1100s, and although many other churches were erected in Scotland at the time, Elgin was believed to have been the most beautiful. Burned and rebuilt twice (1290 and 1370), it deteriorated after the Reformation, along with many other Catholic churches, to the point that the belfry collapsed in 1711, shattering most of the roof and some of the walls. Efforts were begun to repair the damage, yet the place remains an evocative ruin. See chapter 9.
- **Skara Brae** (the Orkney Islands): Last occupied around 2500 B.C. and far humbler than the feudal castles you'll find on the Scottish mainland, this cluster of fortified stone buildings is the best-preserved Neolithic village in northwestern Europe. Buried beneath sand for thousands of years, they were uncovered by a storm as recently as 1850. See chapter 12.

10 The Best Museums

- **National Gallery of Scotland** (Edinburgh): This museum boasts a small but choice collection whose presence in Edinburgh is firmly entwined with the city's self-image as Scotland's cultural capital. (Glaswegians will happily dispute that idea.) Highlights include works by Velázquez, Zurbarán, Verrocchio, del Sarto, and Cézanne. See chapter 4.

- **Museum of Scotland** (Edinburgh): In 1998, the collections of the Royal Museum of Scotland and the National Museum of Antiquities were united into a coherent whole. Here you'll find everything you ever wanted to know about Scotland, from prehistory to the Industrial Age, as represented by the unsparing views of life in the Saltmarket District of Glasgow. It's all here, from a milk bottle once carried by Sean Connery when he was a milkman to a rock that's 2.9 billion years old from the Isle of South Uist. See chapter 4.

- **Burrell Collection** (Glasgow): The contents of this collection were accumulated through the exclusive efforts of Sir William Burrell (1861–1958), an industrialist who devoted the last 50 years of his life to spending his fortune on art. Set in a postmodern building in a suburb of Glasgow, it's one of Scotland's most admired museums, with a strong focus on medieval art, 19th-century French paintings, and Chinese ceramics. See chapter 6.

- **Hunterian Art Gallery** (Glasgow): This museum owns much of the artistic estate of James McNeill Whistler, as well as a recreation of the home of Scotland's most famous designer, Charles Rennie Mackintosh. On display are grand oils by Whistler, Reubens, and Rembrandt, as well as one of the country's best collections of 19th-century Scottish paintings. See chapter 6.

- **Glasgow Art Gallery & Museum** (Glasgow): This is Britain's finest municipally funded museum, a source of pride for Glaswegians everywhere. It contains a superb collection of arms and armor, as well as paintings by Whistler and seemingly everyone else, from Millet to Giorgione, Rembrandt to Dalí. See chapter 6.

- **Aberdeen Art Gallery** (Aberdeen): A treasure trove of world art, this prestigious gallery has exhibits ranging from the 1700s to the present, from Hogarth and Reynolds to Picasso. The museum is also home to the most important temporary exhibits in northeast Scotland. See chapter 9.

11 The Best Luxury Hotels

- **Howard Hotel** (Edinburgh; © 0131/557-3500): Three adjacent Georgian-style town houses in an upscale neighborhood have undergone millions of pounds' worth of renovations, creating the most alluring accommodations in a city filled with fine hotels. A restaurant in one of the cellars serves meals inspired by Scotland's traditions. See chapter 4.

- **Holyrood Hotel** (Edinburgh; © 0131/550-4500): This deluxe charmer launched itself into the millennium when it was proclaimed "Hotel of the Year in Scotland." Near the new Scottish Parliament, it is a bastion of comfort with luxury furnishings. See chapter 4.

- **The Malmaison** (Leith, outside Edinburgh; ☎ 0131/555-6868): Malmaison is at the port of Leith, about a 15-minute ride northeast of Edinburgh's center. Named after Joséphine's mansion outside Paris, it celebrates the Auld Alliance of France and Scotland and was created from a 1900 Victorian building. Malmaison once housed indigent seamen, but today is an oasis of chic. See chapter 4.

- **Greywalls Hotel** (East Lothian; ☎ 01620/842-144): Although Sir Edward Lutyens designed dozens of opulent Edwardian homes throughout Britain, this is one of the few that's been converted into a hotel. Built in 1901 in what architects praise as perfect harmony with its setting, Greywalls features walled gardens designed by the doyenne of eccentric turn-of-the-20th-century landscape architects, Gertrude Jekyll. This national treasure, representing the Empire's most ostentatious days, is eccentric but eminently comfortable. See chapter 4.

- **Knockinaam Lodge** (Portpatrick; ☎ 01776/810-471): Memories of Winston Churchill's clandestine meetings with General Eisenhower, a beacon of hope during the darkest days of World War II, pervade the Knockinaam. Today, the late-Victorian country house is as well upholstered and wryly sedate as you'd expect from a top-notch hotel with such a pedigree. Its restaurant is always included in critics' lists of the best of Scotland. See chapter 5.

- **One Devonshire Gardens** (Glasgow; ☎ 0141/339-2001): This is the best-groomed building in a neighborhood filled with similar sandstone-fronted town houses.

Ring the doorbell and an Edwardian-costumed maid will answer, curtsy, and usher you inside as if you're an extra in a Merchant-Ivory film. This re-creation of a high-bourgeois, very proper Scottish home from the early 1900s boasts antique furnishings and discreetly concealed modern comforts. See chapter 6.

- **Airds Hotel** (Port Appin; ☎ 01631/730-236): The Airds's stucco-sheathed exterior resembles that of hundreds of other Scottish waterside buildings. Inside, however, this Relais & Châteaux member is unexpectedly luxurious, offering an award-winning cuisine and a tradition of hospitality dating back to 1760. See chapter 7.

- **Rufflets Country House Hotel** (St. Andrews; ☎ 01334/472-594): Set on 10 acres (4.1 hectares) near Scotland's most prestigious golf course, this house has won virtually every hotel award possible and offers predominantly Queen Anne–style furnishings along with lovely gardens. See chapter 8.

- **Auchterarder House** (Auchterarder; ☎ 01764/663-646): Scholars refer to the Auchterarder's design as a perfect example of the Scots Jacobean Revival as interpreted by 1830s builders. Guests refer to it as a supremely comfortable hotel with well-appointed accommodations, a worthy dining room, and a polite, hardworking staff. Afternoon tea, plus a sampling of the bar's inventory of single malts, is part of the experience. See chapter 9.

- **Kinnaird** (Dunkeld; ☎ 01796/482-440): An 18th-century hunting lodge for the duke of Atholl, Kinnaird dominates an enormous estate—9,000 acres (3,645 hectares) of moor, mountain, and forest. You'll find all the accoutrements of a British country house in high-Edwardian style. The supremely comfortable interiors contrast dramatically with the tempests of the great outdoors, and the dining room is among the finest in the country. See chapter 9.

- **Raemoir House** (Banchory; ℂ 01330/824-884): A perfect retreat from the modern world, this 18th-century mansion is set on a 3,500-acre (1,417.5-hectare) estate. Tudor four-posters, rich brocades, paneled walls, and museum-caliber antiques transport you into an elegant past. See chapter 9.

- **Inverlochy Castle** (near Fort William; ℂ 01397/702-177): This castle was built in 1863 by Lord Abinger in a style that set into stone the most high-blown hopes of Scottish Romantics. Today, lovers can follow in the footsteps of Queen Victoria amid the frescoed walls of this Scottish baronial hideaway. See chapter 10.

- **Culloden House** (Inverness; ℂ 01463/790-461): If you'd like to sleep where Bonnie Prince Charlie did, head for this Adam-style Georgian mansion on 40 acres (16.2 hectares) of parkland. Scottish tradition appears at every turn, from the grand lounge to the sound of a bagpiper on the grounds. Dinner in the Adam Room is an elegant affair, with French culinary skills applied to the finest Scottish produce. See chapter 10.

- **Carnegie Club at Skibo Castle** (Dornoch; ℂ 01862/894-600): Andrew Carnegie called his glorious Highland castle and estate Heaven on Earth, and so it is. A private residential golf and sporting club, it stands on a 7,000-acre (2,835-hectare) estate in one of Europe's last great wilderness areas. It was owned by the Carnegie family until the early 1980s and is one of the few places left where you can see how the privileged of the Gilded Age lived. See chapter 10.

12 The Best Moderately Priced Hotels

- **Kew Guest House** (Edinburgh; ℂ 0131/313-0700): This is one of the most elegant guest houses in Edinburgh, even better than some first-class hotels. Its welcoming and attractively furnished bedrooms retain much of their original Victorian character. See chapter 4 .

- **Lodge Hotel** (Edinburgh; ℂ 0131/337-3682): One of the city's best Georgian town-house hotels, this gem was converted from an 1836 manse. Elegantly and sumptuously decorated, it is remarkably affordable for what it offers. See chapter 4.

- **Malmaison** (Glasgow; ℂ 0141/572-1000): Linked to a hotel

with the same name in Edinburgh (see above), this Malmaison dates from the 1830s, when it was built as a Greek Orthodox church. Now converted into one of the best of Glasgow's moderately priced hotels (though its prices are creeping up into the expensive range), it welcomes visitors with Scottish hospitality and houses them with quite a bit of style. See chapter 6.

- **The ArtHouse** (Glasgow; ℂ 0141/221-6789): Unique to Glasgow, this stunner was converted from a 1911 Edwardian school building. Dramatically recycled, it offers first-class comfort and affordable prices, all part of a striking design. See chapter 6.

• **Inn at Lathones** (St. Andrews; ℭ 01334/840-494): In the golf capital of Scotland is this 2-century-old manor that has been lovingly restored with excellent accommodations. Scottish hospitality and tradition permeate the place, also known for its "Taste of Scotland" menu. See chapter 8.

• **Polmaily House Hotel** (Drumnadrochit; ℭ 01456/450-343): While you search for Nessie, the Loch Ness Monster, you can lodge comfortably at this inn. The building dates from the 18th century and offers tasteful Edwardian-style living on an 18-acre (7.3-hectare) farm of mixed gardens and woodland. See chapter 10.

• **Cuillin Hills Hotel** (Portree, Isle of Skye; ℭ 01478/612-003): Built in the 1820s as a hunting lodge for the MacDonald clan, this manor house has been skillfully converted into a small hotel. It attracts nature lovers to its nearby hills of heath and heather and offers lovely rooms and great food using some of the best Highland produce. See chapter 11.

13 The Best Restaurants

• **The Tower** (Edinburgh; ℭ 0131/225-3003): The town's hot new dining ticket lies on the top floor of the Museum of Scotland, an unlikely venue for one of Edinburgh's best restaurants. Featuring fresh seafood and an innovative modern British cuisine, The Tower serves some of the city's tastiest fare based on the freshest of ingredients. See chapter 4.

• **Martin Wishart** (Edinburgh; ℭ 0131/553-3557): Many food critics hail this newcomer as the best restaurant in Scotland. If not that, it ranks among the top five. Out in the port-bordering town of Leith in Greater Edinburgh, it serves a modern French cuisine— dishes composed with quality products and filled with flavor. See chapter 4.

• **Airds Hotel** (Port Appin; ℭ 01631/730-236): Around 1700, these premises were used to feed and house travelers after a ferry transit. Today, Airds is a citadel of Scottish cuisine, elevating dishes like Loch Fyne kippers to something with a cult following. Its haunch of venison with rowanberry jam is also notable. See chapter 7.

• **Ostlers Close** (Cupar, near St. Andrews; ℭ 01334/655-574): Chef Jimmy Graham is one of the finest in the St. Andrews area, and he's known to pick his own wild mushrooms. Golfers with discriminating palates flock to this modestly appointed place, which makes the best use of fish and seafood from the Fife Coast and ducks from a local free-range supplier. Everything is delectable. See chapter 8.

• **The Georgian Room, in the DeVere Cameron House** (Balloch; ℭ 01389/755-565): The setting is lavishly Victorian and the food an award-winning blend of Scottish and French. Indulge in a rabbit-and-hare terrine encased in a sheathing of leeks. See chapter 8.

• **The Cross** (Kingussie; ℭ 01540/661-166): Housed in a cleverly converted 19th-century tweed mill, The Cross is a lot more chic than you'd imagine. The menu items are a celebration of Scottish ingredients, prepared with modern international palates in mind. An example is the West Coast seafood salad with ultrafresh monkfish, scallops, prawns, and asparagus. See chapter 9.

- **Inverlochy Castle** (near Fort William; ✆ **01397/702-177**): Cherubs cavort across frescoed ceilings and chandeliers drip with Venetian crystal in a dining room

created in the 1870s for a mogul. A Relais & Châteaux member, Inverlochy is likely to draw aristocrats and movie stars with a cuisine focusing on flavorful and natural interpretations of Scottish delicacies. See chapter 10.

14 The Best Pubs

- **Café Royal Circle Bar** (Edinburgh; ✆ **0131/556-1884**): The Café Royal Circle stands out in a city famous for its pubs. This longtime favorite, boasting lots of atmosphere and Victorian trappings, attracts a sea of drinkers, locals as well as visitors. See chapter 4.
- **Deacon Brodie's Tavern** (Edinburgh; ✆ **0131/225-6531**): This is the best spot for a wee dram or a pint along Edinburgh's Royal Mile. It perpetuates the memory of Deacon Brodie, good citizen by day and robber by night, the prototype for Robert Louis Stevenson's *Dr. Jekyll and Mr. Hyde*. It's been around since 1806 and has a cocktail-lounge bar and a large, rowdy tavern. See chapter 4.
- **Globe Inn** (Dumfries; ✆ **01387/252-335**): In the Borders, this was Robert Burns's favorite *howff* (small, cozy room). Today, you can imbibe as he did in a pub that's been in business since 1610. He liked the place so much that he had a child with the barmaid. A small museum is devoted to Burns. See chapter 5.
- **Corn Exchange** (Glasgow; ✆ **0141/248-5380**): There was a time when it took a bit of courage or a foolish heart to enter a Glasgow pub. Those bad old days are long forgotten at this reliable pub in the center. In the mid-1800s, the Corn Exchange was here (hence the name), but today it's a watering hole with good drinks

and modestly priced bar platters. See chapter 6.

- **Rabbie's Bar** (Ayr; ✆ **01292/262-112**): Robert Burns didn't confine his drinking to Dumfries. Ayr was also one of his hangouts, and this favorite pub is a nostalgic reminder of another era. Bits of pithy verse by Burns adorn the walls, and the collection of imported beers is the best in the area. See chapter 6.
- **Dreel Tavern** (Anstruther; ✆ **01333/310-727**): This 16th-century wood-and-stone coaching inn is now a pub where old salts from the harbor and other locals gather to unwind on windy nights. Try the Orkney Dark Island on hand pump. Anstruther, 46 miles (74km) northeast of Edinburgh, is a gem of a Scottish seaside town. See chapter 8.
- **Ship Inn** (Elie; ✆ **01333/330-246**): Down at the harbor in this little port town, the Ship Inn is one of the best places for a pint along the east coast. The building dates from 1778, and the pub from 1830. In summer, you can enjoy your pint outside with a view over the water, but on blustery winter days, the blazing fireplace is the attraction. Stick around for dinner—the menu ranges from pheasant to venison to fresh seafood, not your typical pub grub. See chapter 8.
- **Prince of Wales** (Aberdeen; ✆ **01224/640-597**): Furnished with church pews and antiques, the Prince of Wales features the

city's longest bar counter. Oilmen from the North Sea join the regulars to ask for tap beers like Courage Directors and sample the chef's Guinness pie. You'll find real flavor and authentic atmosphere; it's a good place to mingle with the locals in a mellow setting. See chapter 9.

15 The Best Shopping

- **Celtic Jewelry:** Modern reproductions of Celtic jewelry are one of Scotland's most creative craft forms. Some pieces reflect early Christian themes, like the Gaelic cross so often displayed in Presbyterian churches. Others are pure pagan, and sometimes Nordic, rich with symbols like dragons, intertwined ovals, and geometrics that would gladden the heart of a Celtic lord. Another common theme commemorates the yearnings for a politically independent country (Luckenbooths, entwined hearts surmounted by a monarch's crown). Clan brooches, kilt pins, and other jewelry are often adorned with the Highland thistle and sometimes rendered in fine gold, silver, or platinum.
- **Sheepskins:** Some of the rocky districts of Scotland contain more sheep than people. Tanned sheepskins are for sale in hundreds of shops, usually accompanied by advice from the sales staff on what to do with them once you return home. *Note:* Black sheepskins are much rarer than white ones.
- **Sweaters, Tartans & Fabrics:** Sweaters come in every style and design, from bulky fishermen's pullovers to silky cashmere cardigans. Some factories pride themselves on duplicating the tartans of every Scottish clan; others stick to 50 or so of the more popular designs. A meter of fine tartan fabric sells for around £35 ($52.50). For a more authentic experience, buy your garment directly from whomever sewed or knitted it. You'll find ample opportunities at crofts and crafts shops around the countryside.
- **Liquor:** One of the most famous liquors in the world is named after the country that produces it: Scotch whisky (spelled without the "e") is distilled and aged throughout the country. Use your trip to Scotland as an opportunity to try new single malts (Laphroig and MacCallan are our favorites) and bring a bottle or two home.

2

Planning Your Trip
to Scotland

This chapter is devoted to the where, when, and how of your trip—the advance planning required to get it together and take it on the road. Because you may not know exactly where in Scotland you want to go or what surrounds the major city you want to see, we begin with a quick rundown on the various regions.

1 The Regions in Brief

Scotland is Great Britain's oldest geological formation, and is divided into three major regions: the **Southern Uplands,** smooth, rolling moorland broken with low crags and threaded with rivers and valleys, between the central plain and the English border; the **Central Lowlands,** where three valleys and the estuaries (firths) of the Clyde, Forth, and Tay rivers make up a fertile belt from the Atlantic Ocean to the North Sea; and the granite **Highlands,** with lochs, glens, and mountains, plus the hundreds of islands to the west and north. Each of these regions is then made up of smaller regions (see below).

Consult the map on p. 4–5 to visualize the areas described below.

EDINBURGH & THE LOTHIAN REGION

This area includes not only the country's capital but also West Lothian, most of Midlothian, and East Lothian. Half medieval and half Georgian, **Edinburgh** is at its liveliest every August at the International Arts Festival, but you can visit Edinburgh Castle and Holyroodhouse and walk the Royal Mile year-round. This is one of Europe's most beautiful capitals, and in 3 days you can do it royally, taking in the highlights of the Old Town and

the New Town, which include some of the country's major museums. Edinburgh is surrounded by major attractions like the village of **Cramond,** the ancient town of **Linlithgow,** and **Dirleton,** the "prettiest village in Scotland."

THE BORDERS & GALLOWAY REGIONS

Witness to a turbulent history, the Borders and Galloway regions between England and Scotland are rich in castle ruins and Gothic abbeys.

Home of the cashmere sweater and the tweed suit, **Borders** proved a rich mine for the fiction of Sir Walter Scott. Highlights are **Kelso,** which Scott found "the most beautiful," and **Melrose,** site of the ruined Melrose Abbey and Scott's former home of Abbotsford. Ancient monuments include Jedburgh Abbey and Dryburg Abbey, Scott's burial place. At Floors Castle, outside Kelso, you can see one of the great mansions designed by William Adam.

Southwestern Scotland is known as the **Galloway region.** It incorporates much of the former stamping ground of Robert Burns and includes centers like **Dumfries, Castle Douglas,** and **Moffat.** Highlights are the artists' colony of **Kidcudbright,** the baronial

Threave Garden, Sweetheart Abbey outside Dumfries (the ruins of a Cisterian abbey from 1273), and the Burns Mausoleum at Dumfries.

GLASGOW & THE STRATHCLYDE REGION

A true renaissance has come to the once-grimy industrial city of **Glasgow,** and we recommended you spend at least 2 days in "the greatest surviving example of a Victorian city." Of course, part of the fun of going to Glasgow is meeting Glaswegians and, if only temporarily, becoming part of their life. But there are plenty of museums and galleries, too, notably the Burrell Collection, a wealthy shipowner's gift of more than 8,000 items from the ancient world to the modern; the Hunterian Art Gallery, with its array of masterpieces by everybody from Rembrandt to Whistler; and the Art Gallery and Museum at Kelvingrove, home of Britain's finest civic collection of British and European paintings.

Glasgow is at the doorstep of one of the most historic regions of Scotland. You can explore Robert Burns Country in the **Strathclyde region,** especially the district around Ayr and Prestwick, or visit a string of famous seaside resorts (including Turnberry, which boasts some of the country's greatest golf courses). An especially worthwhile destination in this region is **Culzean Castle,** overlooking the Firth of Clyde and designed by Robert Adam in the 18th century.

ARGYLL & THE SOUTHERN HEBRIDES

Once the independent kingdom of Dalriada, the **Argyll Peninsula** of western Scotland is centered at **Oban,** a bustling port town and one of Scotland's leading coastal resorts. Ace attractions here are **Argyll Forest Park,** actually three forests—Benmore,

Ardgartan, and Glenbranter—covering some 60,000 acres (24,300 hectares). You can also visit **Loch Awe,** a natural moat that protected the Campbells of Inveraray from their enemies to the north, and explore some of Scotland's most interesting islands, including the **Isle of Arran,** called "Scotland in miniature." The **Isle of Islay** is the southernmost of the Inner Hebrides, with lonely moors, lochs, tranquil bays, and windswept cliffs. The **Isle of Jura,** the fourth largest of the Inner Hebrides, is known for its red deer, and it was on this remote island that George Orwell wrote his masterpiece *1984.* Finally, you can visit **Kintyre,** the longest peninsula in Scotland, more than 60 miles (97km) of beautiful scenery, sleepy villages, and sandy beaches.

FIFE & THE CENTRAL HIGHLANDS

The "kingdom" of **Fife** is one of the most history-rich parts of Scotland, evocative of the era of romance and pageantry during the reign of the early Stuart kings. Its most enchanting stretch is a series of villages called **East Neuk.** And **Culross,** renovated by the National Trust, could well be the most beautiful village in Scotland. Opening onto the North Sea, **St. Andrews,** the "Oxford of Scotland," is the capital of golf and boasts many great courses. The area is rich in castles and abbeys, notably Dunfermline Abbey, burial place of 22 royal personages, and Falkland Palace and Gardens, where Mary Queen of Scots came for hunting and hawking. You can also visit **Stirling,** dominated by its castle, where Mary Queen of Scots lived as an infant monarch. **Loch Lomond,** largest of the Scottish lakes, is fabled for its "bonnie bonnie banks," and the **Trossachs** is perhaps the most beautiful area in Scotland, famed for its moors, mountains, and lakes.

ABERDEEN & THE TAYSIDE & GRAMPIAN REGIONS

Carved from the old counties of Perth and Angus, **Tayside** takes its name from its major river, the Tay, running for 119 miles (192km). One of the loveliest regions, it's known for salmon and trout fishing. Major centers are **Perth,** former capital of Scotland, standing where the Highlands meet the Lowlands; **Dundee,** an old seaport and royal burgh on the north shore of the Firth of Tay; and **Pitlochry,** a popular resort that's an ideal base for touring the Valley of the Tummel. The area abounds in castles and palaces, including Glamis, linked to British royalty for 10 centuries, and Scone, an art-filled palace from 1580. The great city of the north, **Aberdeen** is called Scotland's "granite city" and ranks third in population. It's the best center for touring "castle country." **Braemar** is known for its scenery as well as for being the site of every summer's Royal Highland Gathering, and Balmoral Castle at Ballater was the "beloved paradise" of Queen Victoria and is still home to the royal family. Finally, you can follow the **Whisky Trail** to check out some of Scotland's most famous distilleries, including Glenlivet and Glenfiddich.

INVERNESS & THE WEST HIGHLANDS

Land of rugged glens and majestic mountain landscapes, the Highlands is one of the great meccas of the United Kingdom. The capital is **Inverness,** one of the oldest inhabited localities in Scotland; another city of great interest is **Nairn,** old-time royal burgh and seaside resort. Top attractions are **Loch Ness,** home of the legendary "Nessie," and **Cawdor Castle,** the most romantic in the Highlands, linked with Macbeth. The **Caledonian Canal,** launched in 1803, stretches for 60 miles (97km) of man-made canal, joining the natural lochs. As you proceed to the north you can visit the **Black Isle,** a historic peninsula, before heading for such far northern outposts as **Ullapool,** an 18th-century fishing village on the shores of Loch Broom (and for some, a gateway to the Outer Hebrides), and **John o' Groats,** the most distant point to which you can drive, near the northernmost point of mainland Britain, **Dunnet Head.**

THE HEBRIDEAN ISLANDS

The chain of the Inner Hebrides lies just off the west coast of the mainland. The major center is the **Isle of Skye,** a mystical island and subject of the Scottish ballad "Over the Sea to Skye." If you have time to visit only one island, make it Skye—it's the most beautiful and intriguing. However, the **Isle of Mull,** third largest of the Inner Hebrides, is also rich in legend and folklore, including ghosts, monsters, and the "wee folk." **Iona,** off the coast of Mull, is known as the "Grave of Kings," with an abbey dating from the 13th century. Those with time remaining can also explore the Outer Hebrides, notably **Lewis,** the largest and most northerly. Along with the island of **Harris,** Lewis stretches for a combined length of some 95 miles (153km). This is relatively treeless land of marshy peat bogs and ancient relics.

THE ORKNEY & SHETLAND ISLANDS

These northern outposts of British civilization are archipelagos consisting of some 200 islands, about 40 of which are inhabited. With a rich Viking heritage, they reward visitors with scenery and antiquities. Major centers of the Orkneys are **Kirkwall,** established by Norse invaders and the capital of the Orkneys for 9 centuries, and **Stromness,** the main port of the archipelago and once the last port of call before the New World. **Lerwick** is the capital of the Shetlands and has been since the 17th century. All these islands are filled with ancient monuments: The most outstanding are Midhower Broch and Tombs on Rousay, dating from the Iron Age and called the "great ship of death"; Quoyness Chambered Tomb, on Sanday, a spectacular chambered cairn from 2900 B.C.; the Ring of Brodgar between Loch and Stennes, a stone circle of some 36 stones dating from 1560 B.C. and called the "Stonehenge of Scotland"; and Skara Brae, a Neolithic village joined by covered passages, last occupied about 2500 B.C.

2 Visitor Information

Before you go, you can get information from the **British Tourist Authority** (www.visitbritain.com). In the **United States:** 551 Fifth Ave., Suite 701, New York, NY 10176-0799 (℗ **800/462-2748,** or 212/986-2200 in New York), or 625 North Michigan Ave., 10th floor, in Chicago (same toll-free number as for the New York office). In **Canada:** 111 Avenue Rd., Suite 450, Toronto, ON M5R 3J8 (℗ **888/VISIT-UK** in Canada, or 905/405-1840 in Toronto). In **Australia:** Level 16, Gateway, 1 Macquarie Place, Sydney, NSW 200 (℗ **02/9377-4400**). In **New Zealand:** Suite 305, Dilworth Building, Customs and Queen streets, Auckland 1 (℗ **09/303-1446**).

If you're in London and are contemplating a trip north, you can visit the **Scottish Tourist Board,** 19 Cockspur St., London SW1 Y5BL (℗ **020/7930-8661**); it's open Monday through Friday from 9:30am to 5:30pm and Saturday from noon to 4pm. Once you're in Scotland, you can stop by the **Edinburgh and Scotland Information Centre,** Waverley Market, 3 Princes St., Edinburgh EH2 2QP (℗ **0131/473-3800**). July and August, it's open Monday through Saturday from 9am to 8pm and Sunday from 10am to 8pm. May, June, and September, hours are Monday through Saturday from 9am to 7pm and Sunday from 10am to 7pm. From October to April, hours are Monday through Saturday from 9am to 6pm and Sunday from 10am to 6pm.

There are more than 170 **tourist centers** in Scotland, all well signposted in their cities or towns; some are closed in winter, however.

3 Entry Requirements & Customs

ENTRY REQUIREMENTS
All Americans, Canadians, Australians, and New Zealanders must have a **passport** with at least 2 months remaining validity. No visa is required. The immigration officer may also want proof of your intention to return home (usually a round-trip ticket). If your passport is lost or stolen while traveling, head to your consulate as soon as possible for a replacement.

If you're planning to fly from the United States or Canada to the United Kingdom and then on to a country that requires a visa (India, for example), you should secure that visa before you arrive in Britain.

Your valid **driver's license** and at least 1 year of driving experience is required to drive personal or rented cars.

CUSTOMS
WHAT YOU CAN BRING INTO SCOTLAND For visitors, goods fall into two basic categories: purchases made in a non–European Union (EU) country (or bought tax free in the EU) and purchases on which tax was paid in the EU. In the former category,

limits on imports by individuals (17 and older) include 200 cigarettes, 50 cigars, or 250 grams (8.8 oz.) of loose tobacco; 2 liters (2.1 qt.) of still table wine, 1 liter of liquor (over 22% alcohol content), or 2 liters of liquor (under 22%); and 2 fluid ounces of perfume. In the latter category, limits are much higher: An individual may import 800 cigarettes, 200 cigars, and 1 kilogram (2.2 lb.) of loose tobacco; 90 liters (23.4 gal.) of wine, 10 liters (2.6 gal.) of alcohol (over 22%), and 110 liters (28.6 gal.) of beer; plus unlimited amounts of perfume. Customs will also allow you to bring in whatever sporting equipment you'll need—within reason, of course. This includes tennis, golfing, fishing, and skiing equipment. Be sure to check with your airline to determine baggage restrictions.

WHAT YOU CAN BRING HOME
Returning **United States** citizens who have been away for 48 hours or more are allowed to bring back, once every 30 days, $400 worth of merchandise duty free. You'll be charged a flat rate of 10% duty on the next $1,000 worth of purchases. Be sure to have your receipts handy. On gifts, the duty-free limit is $100 (one parcel per day per address). You can't bring fresh foodstuffs into the States; tinned foods, however, are allowed. For more information, contact the **U.S. Customs Service,** 1301 Constitution Ave. (P.O. Box 7407), Washington, DC 20044 (© **202/927-6724**), and request the free pamphlet *Know Before You Go.* It's also available at **www.customs.ustreas.gov.**

Citizens of **Canada** can visit the comprehensive website of the **Canada Customs and Revenue Agency** (**www.ccra-adrc.gc.ca**).

Citizens of **Australia** should request the helpful Australian Customs brochure *Know Before You Go,* available by calling © **02/9213-2000** from within Australia, or 61-2/6275-6666 from abroad. For additional information, go online to **www.customs.gov.au** and click on "Hints for Australian Travellers."

For **New Zealand** information, contact the New Zealand Customs Service at © **09/359-6655,** or go online to **www.customs.govt.nz.**

4 Money

CURRENCY

The currency of Britain is the **pound sterling (£),** made up to 100 **pence (p).** Scotland issues its own pound notes, but English and Scottish money are interchangeable. Pence come in 1p, 2p, 5p, 10p, 20p, 50p, and £1 coins. Notes are issued in £1, £5, £10, £20, and £50 denominations.

For the moment at least, Britain has decided not to join the rest of the European Community in the switch to the euro, the new single European currency; the traditional British pound sterling will remain the coin of the realm.

Although exchange rates are more favorable at the point of arrival, it's always wise to exchange at least some money before going abroad. This way, you avoid delays and the lousy rates at the airport exchange booths. When exchanging money, you're likely to get a better rate for traveler's checks than for cash.

Time Out recently did a survey of exchange facilities, and American Express came out on top, with the lowest commission charged on dollar transactions. **American Express** is at 139 Princes St., Edinburgh (© **800/221-7282** or 0131/718-2501), and other locations throughout the city. It charges no commission when cashing traveler's checks; however, a flat rate of £2 ($3) is charged when exchanging

The U.S. Dollar & the British Pound
At this writing, the price conversions in this book have been computed at the rate of $1 U.S. equals 67p (or £1 = $1.50). Bear in mind that exchange rates always fluctuate for a variety of reasons, so it's important to check the latest quotes before your trip. Go online at **www.x-rates.com**.

the dollar to the pound. Most other agencies tend to charge a percentage rate commission (usually 2%) with a £2 to £3 ($3 to $4.50) minimum charge.

ATMs
ATMs are linked to a national network that most likely includes your home bank. **Cirrus** (© 800/424-7787; www.mastercard.com/card holderservices/atm/) and **PLUS** (© 800/843-7587; www.visa.com) are the two most popular networks; check the back of your ATM card to see which network your bank belongs to. Use the toll-free numbers or websites to locate ATMs in your destination.

ATMs are commonly available in all Scottish cities and towns, even in many villages. Of course, for the latter you should always check to be sure.

Make sure the PINs on your ATM cards and credit cards will work in Scotland. You'll need a **four-digit code** (six digits won't work), so if you have a six-digit code you'll have to get a new PIN for your trip. If you're unsure about this, contact Cirrus or PLUS. Be sure to check the daily withdrawal limit at the same time.

CREDIT CARDS
Credit cards are invaluable when traveling. They're a safe way to carry money and provide a convenient record of all your expenses. You can also withdraw cash advances from your credit cards at any bank (but you'll start paying hefty interest on the

advance the moment you receive the cash and won't get frequent-flyer miles on an airline credit card). At most banks, you don't even need to go to a teller; you can get a cash advance at the ATM if you know your PIN.

TRAVELER'S CHECKS
You can get traveler's checks at almost any bank. **American Express** offers checks in denominations of $10, $20, $50, $100, $500, and $1,000. You'll pay a service charge ranging from 1% to 4%. You can also get American Express traveler's checks over the phone by calling © 800/221-7282 or 800/721-9768, or you can buy checks online at **www.americanexpress.com**. Amex gold or platinum cardholders can avoid paying the fee by ordering over the phone; platinum cardholders can also purchase checks fee-free in person at Amex Travel Service locations (check the website for the office nearest you). American Automobile Association members can get checks fee-free at most AAA offices.

Visa offers traveler's checks at Citibank branches and other financial institutions nationwide; call © 800/227-6811 to find a location near you. **MasterCard** also offers traveler's checks through **Thomas Cook Currency Services;** call © 800/223-9920 for a location near you.

If you carry traveler's checks, be sure to keep a record of their serial numbers (separately from the checks, of course), so you're ensured a refund in case they're lost or stolen.

5 When to Go

The cheapest time to travel to Scotland is off-season: **November 1 to December 12 and December 26 to March 14.** In the past few years, airlines have been offering irresistible fares during these periods. And weekday flights are cheaper than weekend fares, often by 10% or more.

Rates generally increase **March 14 to June 5** and in **October,** and then hit their peak in the high seasons from **June 6 to September 30** and **December 13 to 24.** July and August are when most Britons take their holidays, so besides the higher prices, you'll have to deal with crowds and limited availability of accommodations.

Sure, in winter Scotland may be rainy and cold—but it doesn't shut down when the tourists leave. In fact, the winter season gives visitors a more honest view of Scottish life. Additionally, many hotel prices drop by 20%, and cheaper accommodations offer weekly rates (unheard of during peak travel times). By arriving after the winter holidays, you can take advantage of post-Christmas sales to buy your fill of woolens, china, crystal, silver, fashion, handicrafts, and curios.

In short, spring offers the countryside at its greenest, autumn brings the bright colors of the northern Highlands, and summer's warmth gives rise to the many outdoor music and theater festivals. But winter offers savings across the board and a chance to see Britons going about their everyday lives largely unhindered by tourist invasions.

WEATHER

Weather is of vital concern in Scotland. It can seriously affect your travel plans. The Lowlands usually have a moderate year-round temperature. In spring, the average temperature is 53°F (11.6°C), rising to about 65°F (18.3°C) in summer. By the time the crisp autumn has arrived, the temperatures have dropped to spring levels. In winter, the average temperature is 43°F (6°C). Temperatures in the north of Scotland are lower, especially in winter, and you should dress accordingly. It rains a lot in Scotland, but perhaps not as much as age-old myths would have it: The rainfall in Edinburgh is exactly the same as that in London. September can be the sunniest month.

HOLIDAYS

The following holidays are celebrated in Scotland: New Year's Day (January 1 and 2), Good Friday and Easter Monday, May Day (May 1), spring bank holiday (last Monday in May), summer bank holiday (first Monday in August), Christmas Day (December 25), and Boxing Day (December 26).

SCOTLAND CALENDAR OF EVENTS

You can get details of specific events at many of the festivals below by going to **www.go-edinburgh.co.uk**.

January

Celtic Connections, Glasgow. During this celebration of the Celtic roots that combined with other cultures to form modern Scotland, concerts are staged in churches, auditoriums, and meeting halls throughout the city. A prime venue is the Old Fruit Market on Albion Street, drawing dance troupes from throughout Scotland, Wales, and Ireland. For tickets and details, call © **0141/287-5511.** Throughout January.

Burns Night, Ayr (near his birthplace), Dumfries, and Edinburgh. Naturally, during the celebrations to honor Robert Burns, there's much toasting with scotch and eating of haggis, whose arrival is announced by a bagpipe. For details, call © **01292/443-700** in

Ayr, **0131/473-3800** in Edinburgh, or **01387/253-862** in Dumfries. January 25.

Up Helly Aa, Lerwick, in the Shetland Islands. The most northerly town in Great Britain still clings to tradition by staging an ancient Norse fire festival whose aim is to encourage the return of the sun after the pitch-dark days of winter. Its highlight is the burning of a replica of a Norse longboat. Call ℂ **01595/693-434.** Last Tuesday in January.

February

Aberdeen Angus Cattle Show, Perth. This show draws the finest cattle raised in Scotland. Sales are lively. Call ℂ **01738/474-170.** Early February.

March

Whuppity Scourie, Lanark. Residents of the Strathclyde get so tired of winter that they stage this traditional ceremony to chase it away. Call ℂ **01555/661-661.** March 1.

Annual Drama Festival, Tobermory. This cultural event draws some of Britain's finest theatrical talent to the Isle of Mull. Call ℂ **01688/302-182.** Mid- to late March.

April

Edinburgh Folk Festival, at various venues, Edinburgh. For details on this feast of Scottish folk tunes, call ℂ **0131/473-3800.** Generally April 1.

Exhibitions at the Royal Scottish Academy, Edinburgh. Changing exhibits of international interest are offered here annually. Call ℂ **0131/473-3800.** Mid-April.

Kate Kennedy Procession & Pageant, St. Andrews. This historic university pageant is staged annually in the university city of St. Andrews, in eastern Scotland. Call ℂ **01334/472-021.** April.

May

Scottish Motorcycle Trials, Fort William. The trials are run for 6 days at the beginning of the month, drawing aficionados from all over Europe. Call ℂ **01397/703-781.** Early May.

Highland Games & Gatherings, at various venues throughout the country, including Aberfeldy, Perth, Crieff, Ballater, Oban, and Portree on the Isle of Skye. Details are available from the Edinburgh and Scotland Information Centre (see "Visitor Information," earlier in this chapter). Early May to mid-September.

Pitlochry Festival Theatre, Pitlochry. Scotland's "theater in the hills" launches its season in mid-May. Call ℂ **01796/472-215.** Mid-May to October.

June

Promenade Concerts, Glasgow. These concerts by the Scottish National Orchestra are given at the Glasgow Royal Concert Hall. Call ℂ **0141/353-8000.** Throughout June (sometimes into July).

Lanimer Day, Lanark. This week of festivities features a ritual procession around the town's boundaries, the election of a Lanimer Queen and a Cornet King, and a parade with floats, along with Highland dances and bagpipe playing. Call ℂ **01555/661-661.** The Thursday between June 6 and 12.

Guid Nychtburris (Good Neighbors), Dumfries. This age-old festival is an event similar to (but less impressive than) the Selkirk Common Riding (see below). Call ℂ **01387/253-862.** Mid-June.

Royal Highland Show, at the Ingliston Showground, outskirts of Edinburgh. This show is devoted to agriculture and commerce. For details, call ℂ **0131/473-3800.** Mid- to late June.

Selkirk Common Riding, Selkirk. This is Scotland's most elaborate display of horsemanship, remembering Selkirk's losses in the 1560 Battle of Flodden—only one Selkirk soldier returned alive from the battle to warn the town before dropping dead in the marketplace. Some 400 horses and riders parade through the streets, and a young unmarried male is crowned at the sound of the cornet, representing the soldier who sounded the alarm. Call ✆ **01750/219-54.** Mid-June.

Beltane Day, Peebles. A town "Cornet" rides around to see the boundaries are safe from the "invading" English, a young girl is elected Festival Queen, and her court is filled with courtiers, sword-bearers, guards, and attendants. Children of the town dress in costumes for parade floats through the streets. Call ✆ **01721/720-138.** Mid-June.

Gay Pride, Edinburgh or Glasgow. Scotland's annual gay pride celebration alternates between Edinburgh and Glasgow. You'll see a quirky, boisterous parade through the heart of Glasgow or along Princes Street in Edinburgh. For details, call Glasgow's Gay Switchboard (✆ **0141/332-8372)** or Edinburgh's Gay Switchboard (✆ **0131/556-4049).** Sometime in June; Glasgow will play host in 2002.

July

Glasgow International Jazz Festival, Glasgow. Jazz musicians from all over the world come together to perform at various venues around the city. Call ✆ **0141/204-4400.** First week in July.

August

Lammas Fair, St. Andrews. Although there's a dim medieval origin to this 2-day festival, it's not particularly obvious. Temporary Ferris wheels and whirligigs are

hauled in, cotton candy and popcorn are sold, palm readers describe your past and your future, and flashing lights and recorded disco music create something akin to Blackpool-in-the-Highlands. There's even an opportunity for bungee-jumping. Call ✆ **01334/472-021.** Second Monday and Tuesday of August.

World Pipe Band Championships, Glasgow. For this relatively new event (it's only 5 or 6 years old), bagpipe bands from around the world gather on the parklike Glasgow Green in the city's East End. From 11am to about 6pm, there's a virtual orgy of bagpiping, as kilted participants strut their stuff in musical and military precision. Call ✆ **0141/204-4400.** Mid-August.

Edinburgh International Festival, Edinburgh. Scotland's best-known festival is held for 3 weeks (see chapter 4, "Edinburgh & the Lothian Region" for more information). Called an "arts bonanza," it draws major talent from around the world, with more than a thousand shows presented and a million tickets sold. Book, jazz, and film festivals are also staged at this time, but nothing tops the Military Tattoo against the backdrop of spot-lit Edinburgh Castle. Contact the Festival Society, 21 Market St., Edinburgh, Scotland EH1 1BW (✆ **0131/473-2001).** Three weeks in August.

September

Ben Nevis Mountain Race, Fort William, in the Highlands. A tradition since 1895, when it was established by a member of the MacFarlane clan, it assembles as many as 500 runners who compete for the coveted MacFarlane Cup, a gold medal, and a prize of £50 ($75). Runners congregate at the base of Ben Nevis (Britain's highest peak) to tackle a course that takes them up narrow footpaths to the summit and back. Bagpipes rise in crescendos at the beginning and end of the experience. Call ℂ **01397/704-189.** First Saturday in September.

Highland Games & Gathering, Braemar. The queen and many members of the royal family often show up for this annual event, with its massed bands, piping and dancing competitions, and performances of great strength by a tribe of gigantic men. Contact the tourist office in Braemar, The Mews, Mar Road, Braemar, Aberdeenshire, AB35 5YP (ℂ **013397/416-00**). First Saturday in September.

Ayr Festival, Ayr. This is the major cultural event on the Ayr calendar, offering an array of film, theater, and music concerts. For exact dates, call ℂ **01292/288-688.**

Hamilton Flat Races, Hamilton, near Glasgow. The races take place over a period of 2 to 3 days. Call the Hamilton race course at ℂ **01698/ 283-806.**

October
Highland Autumn Cattle Show, Oban, in western Scotland. Since the days of Rob Roy, Oban has been a marketplace for the long-haired tawny cattle whose elongated horns have been associated with the toughness of the Highlands. For this show, buyers and sellers from Britain, as well as such cold-weather climes as Sweden,

Norway, and Canada, come to buy cattle (either for stud or for beef purposes). Everything is rather businesslike (but still colorful) in the industrial-looking Caledonian Auction Mart, 3 miles (5km) south of Oban. Call ℂ **01631/563-122.** Mid-October.

November
Winter Antiques Fair, Edinburgh. This fair draws dealers and buyers from all over Europe and America. Call ℂ **0131/473-3800.** Third week in November.

Christmas Shopping Festival, Aberdeen. For those who want to shop early for Christmas. Call ℂ **01224/522-000.** Third week of November to December.

St. Andrews Week, St. Andrews. This annual festival of exhibits, concerts, sporting events, fireworks displays, and local foods takes place over the week leading up to St. Andrews Day on November 30. Call ℂ **01334/472-021.** The week ending November 30.

December
Flambeaux Procession, Comrie, Tayside. This torchlight parade takes place on New Year's Eve. For details, call ℂ **01764/652-578** in Crieff. December 31.

Hogmanay, Edinburgh. Hogmanay begins on New Year's Eve and merges into New Year's Day festivities. Events include a torchlight procession, a fire festival along Princes Street, a carnival, and a street theater spectacular. Call ℂ **0131/473-3800.** December 31.

6 Health & Insurance

STAYING HEALTHY
You'll encounter few health problems while in Scotland. The tap water is safe to drink, the milk is pasteurized, and health services are good. The mad-cow crisis is over, but caution is

always advised. (For example, it's been suggested that it's safer to eat British beef cut from the bone instead of on the bone.)

If you need a doctor, your hotel can recommend one, or you can contact your embassy or consulate. *Note:* U.S. visitors who become ill while in England are eligible for free emergency care only. For other treatment, including follow-up care, you'll be asked to pay.

If you worry about getting sick away from home, you may want to consider **medical travel insurance** (see "Insurance," below). In most cases, however, your existing health plan will provide all the coverage you need. Be sure to carry your identification card in your wallet.

If you suffer from a chronic illness, consult your doctor before your departure. For conditions like epilepsy, diabetes, or heart problems, wear a **Medic Alert Identification Tag** (© 888/633-4298; www. medicalert.org), which will immediately alert doctors to your condition and give them access to your records through Medic Alert's 24-hour hotline.

Pack prescription medications in your carry-on luggage. Bring written prescriptions in generic, not brand-name, form, and dispense all prescription medications from their original labeled vials. If you wear contact lenses, pack an extra pair in case you lose one.

The **International Association for Medical Assistance to Travelers,** or **IAMAT** (© 716/754-4883 or 416/652-0137; www.sentex.net/~iamat), offers tips on travel and health concerns in the countries you'll be visiting and lists many local English-speaking doctors. In Canada, call © 519/836-0102.

INSURANCE

There are three kinds of travel insurance: trip-cancellation, medical, and lost-luggage coverage. Trip-cancellation insurance is a good idea if you have paid a large portion of your vacation expenses up front (say, by purchasing a package deal). Make sure you buy it from an outside vendor, though, and not from your tour operator; you don't want to put all your eggs in one basket.

Check your existing policies before you buy any additional coverage you may not need. Your existing health insurance should cover you if you get sick while on vacation—but if you belong to an HMO, you should check to see whether you are fully covered when away from home. For independent travel health-insurance providers, see below.

Your homeowner's or renter's insurance should cover lost or stolen luggage. The airlines are responsible for only a very limited amount if they lose your luggage on an overseas flight, so if you plan to carry anything really valuable, keep it in your carry-on bag.

The differences between travel assistance and insurance are often blurred, but in general, the former offers on-the-spot assistance and 24-hour hotlines (mostly oriented toward medical problems), while the latter reimburses you for travel problems (medical, travel, or otherwise) after you have filed the paperwork. The coverage you should consider depends on how much protection is already in your existing health insurance or other policies. Some credit and charge card companies may insure you against travel accidents if you buy plane, train, or bus tickets with their cards. Before purchasing additional insurance, read your policies and agreements carefully. Call your insurers or credit card companies if you have any questions.

If you do require additional insurance, try one of the companies listed below, but don't pay for more than you need. If you need only trip-cancellation insurance, don't buy coverage for lost or stolen property, which should be covered by your homeowner's or renter's policy. Trip-cancellation insurance costs approximately 6% to 8% of the total value of your vacation.

Among the reputable issuers of travel insurance are **Access America** (℡ 800/284-8300; www.access america.com) and **Travel Guard International** (℡ 800/826-1300; www.noelgroup.com). One company specializing in accident and medical care is **Travel Assistance International** (Worldwide Assistance Services; ℡ 800/821-2828 or 202/828-5894).

Travelers from Australia and New Zealand can receive free medical care as long as they are in possession of their Medicare card and photo identification. Canadian travelers are protected by their home province's health insurance plan for up to 90 days after leaving Canada.

7 Tips for Travelers with Special Needs

FOR TRAVELERS WITH DISABILITIES

Many Scottish hotels, museums, restaurants, and sights have wheelchair ramps. Persons with disabilities are often granted special discounts at attractions and, in some cases, nightclubs. These are called "concessions" in Britain. It always pays to ask.

Moss Rehab ResourceNet (www.mossresourcenet.org) is a great source for information and resources relating to accessible travel. You'll find links to a number of travel agents who specialize in planning trips for disabled travelers here and through **Access-Able Travel Source** (www.access-able.com), another excellent online source. You'll also find relay and voice numbers for hotels, airlines, and car-rental companies on Access-Able's user-friendly site, as well as links to accessible accommodations, attractions, transportation, tours, local medical resources and equipment repairers, and much more.

You can join the **Society for Accessible Travel & Hospitality (SATH)**, 347 Fifth Ave., Suite 610, New York, NY 10016 (℡ 212/447-7284; fax 212-725-8253; www.sath.org), to gain access to its vast network of connections in the travel industry. It provides information sheets on destinations and referrals to tour operators that specialize in traveling with disabilities. Its quarterly magazine, *Open World,* is full of information.

A World of Options, a 658-page book of resources for disabled travelers, covers everything from biking trips to scuba outfitters. It costs $35 ($30 for members) and is available from **Mobility International USA** (℡ 541/343-1284, voice and TDD; www.miusa.org). Annual membership for Mobility International is $35, which includes its quarterly newsletter, *Over the Rainbow.*

You may want to join a tour catering to travelers with disabilities. One of the best operators is **Flying Wheels Travel** (℡ 800/535-6790; www.flyingwheelstravel.com), offering various escorted tours and cruises, with an emphasis on sports, as well as private tours in minivans with lifts. Other reputable operators are **Accessible Journeys** (℡ 800/TINGLES or 610/521-0339; www.disabilitytravel.com), for slow walkers and wheelchair travelers; **The Guided Tour** (℡ 215/782-1370); and **Directions Unlimited** (℡ 800/533-5343).

For British travelers, the **Royal Association for Disability and Rehabilitation (RADAR),** Unit 12, City Forum, 250 City Rd., London EC1V 8AF (℡ 020/7250-3222; www.radar.org.uk), publishes three holiday "fact packs" for £2 ($3) each or £5 ($7.50) for all three. The first provides general info, including planning and booking a holiday, insurance, and finances; the second outlines transportation available when going abroad and equipment for rent; and the third deals with specialized accommodations. Another good resource is the **Holiday Care Service,** Imperial Building, 2nd Floor, Victoria Road, Horley, Surrey RH6 7PZ (© **01293/774-535;** fax 01293/784-647), a national charity advising on accessible accommodations for the elderly and persons with disabilities. Annual membership is £30 ($45).

FOR GAY & LESBIAN TRAVELERS

Bars, clubs, restaurants, and hotels catering to gays are confined almost exclusively to Edinburgh, Glasgow, and Inverness. Call the **Edinburgh Gay and Lesbian Switchboard** (© **0131/556-4049**) or the **Glasgow Gay and Lesbian Switchboard** (© **0141/332-8372**) for information on local events.

Scotland doesn't boast much of a gay scene. Gay-bashing happens, especially in the grimy industrial sections of Glasgow, where neo-Nazi skinheads hang out. Although it's a crime, it's rarely punished. Open displays of affection between same-sex couples usually invite scorn in rural Scotland, although there's none of the fanatical homophobia so prevalent among the lunatic fringe in the United States.

The best guide is *Spartacus Britain and Ireland.* Although the second edition of *Frommer's Gay & Lesbian Europe* doesn't include Scotland, it does include London, Brighton, and Manchester, in case you're heading to England before or after Scotland. For up-to-the-minute activities in Britain, we recommend *Gay Times* (London). These books and others are available from **Giovanni's Room,** 345 S. 12th St., Philadelphia, PA 19107 (© **215/923-2960**).

If you want help planning your trip, the **International Gay & Lesbian Travel Association,** or IGLTA (© **800/448-8550** or 954/776-2626; www.iglta.org), can link you up with the appropriate gay-friendly service

organization or tour specialist. With around 1,200 members, it offers quarterly newsletters, marketing mailings, and a membership directory that's updated quarterly. Members are kept informed of gay and gay-friendly hoteliers, tour operators, and airline and cruise-line representatives.

Out and About (© **800/929-2268** or 415/229-1793; www.outandabout.com) has been hailed for its "straight" reporting about gay travel. It offers a monthly newsletter packed with information on the global gay and lesbian scene. *Out and About's* guidebooks are available at most major bookstores.

General U.S. gay and lesbian travel agencies include **Above and Beyond Tours** (© **800/397-2681**). In the United Kingdom, try **Alternative Holidays** (© **020/7701-7040;** fax 020/7708-5668; www.alternative holidays.com).

FOR SENIORS

One of the benefits of age is that travel often costs less. Always bring an ID card, especially if you've kept your youthful glow. Also mention that you're a senior when you first make your reservations, because many airlines and hotels offer discount programs for senior travelers.

Seniors over 60 receive 10% discounts on **British Airways** through its Privileged Traveler program. They also qualify for reduced restrictions on APEX cancellations. Discounts are also granted for BA tours and for intra-Britain air tickets if booked in North America.

Members of the **American Association of Retired Persons,** or AARP (© **800/424-3410;** www.aarp.org), get discounts on hotels, airfares, and car rentals. The AARP offers members a wide range of benefits, including *Modern Maturity* magazine and a monthly newsletter. If you're not already a member, do yourself a favor and join.

SAGA International Holidays, 222 Berkeley St., Boston, MA 02116 (© 800/343-0273; www.saga holidays.com), offers inclusive tours and cruises for those 50 and older. SAGA also sponsors the more substantial **Road Scholar Tours** (© 800/621-2151), which are fun-loving but with an educational bent.

If you want something more than the average vacation or guided tour, try **Elderhostel** (© 877/426-8056; www.elderhostel.org) or the University of New Hampshire's **Interhostel** (© 800/733-9753), both variations on the same theme: educational travel for senior citizens. On these escorted tours, the days are packed with seminars, lectures, and field trips, and the sightseeing is all led by academic experts. The courses in both programs are ungraded, involve no homework, and often focus on the liberal arts. They're not luxury vacations, but are fun and fulfilling.

FOR FAMILIES

Several books on the market offer tips to help you travel with kids. *Family Travel* (Lanier Publishing International) and *How to Take Great Trips with Your Kids* (Harvard Common Press) are full of good general advice

that can apply to travel anywhere. Another reliable tome, with a worldwide focus, is *Adventuring with Children* (Foghorn Press).

Family Travel Times is published six times a year by TWYCH (Travel with Your Children; © 888/822-4322 or 212/477-5524), and includes a weekly call-in service for subscribers. Subscriptions are $40 a year. Call for a free publication list and a sample issue.

The University of New Hampshire runs **Familyhostel** (© 800/733-9753), an intergenerational alternative to standard guided tours. You live on a European college campus for the 2- or 3-week program, attend lectures and seminars, go on lots of field trips, and do all the sightseeing—guided by a team of experts and academics. It's designed for children 8 to 15, parents, and grandparents.

FOR STUDENTS

The best resource for students is the **Council on International Educational Exchange,** or CIEE (© 212/822-2700; www.ciee.org). It can set you up with an ID card (see below), and its travel branch, **Council Travel Service** (© 888/COUNCIL; www.counciltravel.com), is the world's

---

Tips Farmhouse Holidays

One way to understand the agricultural roots of Scotland is overnighting on a Scottish farm. **Scottish Farmhouse Holidays,** Drumtenant, Ladybank, Fife KY15 7UG (© 0189/075-1830; fax 01337/831-301), will find you an appropriate croft. The company was begun in 1982 by Scots-born Jane Buchanan, who describes herself as a farmer's daughter, a farmer's wife, a businesswoman steeped in both agriculture and tourism, and a former exchange student with 4-H programs in Michigan and Utah.

Only family-managed working farms are selected for the program, most within easy driving distance of at least a handful of historic sites. Many of the farmhouses are a century or so old and have been in the same family for several generations. Rates for bed-and-breakfast in rooms without a bathroom are £18 to £30 ($27–$45); rates for dinner, bed, and breakfast run £19.50 to £42 ($29.25–$63). Occupants of single rooms usually pay a £10 ($15) supplement.

biggest student travel agency operation. It can get you discounts on plane
tickets, railpasses, and the like. Ask for
a list of CTS offices in major cities so
you can keep the discounts flowing
(and aid lines open) as you travel.
From CIEE you can get the student
traveler's best friend, the $18 **Interna-
tional Student Identity Card (ISIC).**
It's the only officially acceptable form
of student ID, good for cut rates on
railpasses and plane tickets and other
discounts. It also provides you with
basic health and life insurance and a
24-hour help line. If you're no longer
a student but are still under 26, you

can get from the same organization a
GO 25 card, which will get you the
insurance and some of the discounts
(but not student admission prices in
museums).
In Canada, **Travel CUTS,** 200
Ronson St., Suite 320, Toronto,
Ontario M9W 5Z9 (© 800/
667-2887 or 416/614-2887; www.
travelcuts.com), offers similar services.
USIT Campus, 52 Grosvenor Gardens, London SW1W 0AG (© 0870/
240-1010; www.usitcampus.co.uk),
opposite Victoria Station, is Britain's
leading specialist in student and youth
travel.

8 Getting There

BY PLANE
The national carrier of Britain,
British Airways (© 800/247-9297
in the U.S. and Canada, 0345/222-
111 in England, or 01/610-666 in
Ireland; www.british-airways.com),
operates the greatest number of flights
into all parts of the country, including
Scotland. This airline is the only non-
U.S. carrier with its own terminal at
New York's JFK.
BA serves at least 20 North American cities with nonstop flights at least
once a day into London's most convenient airport, Heathrow. From
Heathrow, BA offers 22 nonstop
flights daily to both Edinburgh and
Glasgow. Some Scotland-bound passengers opt for flights into Manchester
in England—it's closer than London
to Scotland's Highlands and islands.
BA offers frequent flights into Manchester, many nonstop, from various
parts of the United States.
American Airlines (© 800/
433-7300; www.aa.com) is the U.S.
carrier with the most routes into London. From May 5 to November 1,
American offers a daily nonstop flight
to Glasgow from Chicago; the rest of
the year, you'll make at least one transfer. In addition, the airline has seven
daily nonstops from New York to

London and one nonstop from
Chicago to Manchester, England.
American also offers at least one daily
nonstop to London from Chicago,
Dallas/Fort Worth, Los Angeles,
Boston, and Miami.
United Airlines (© 800/538-
2929; www.ual.com) offers daily
nonstop service to London from New
York, Newark, Washington, D.C., San
Francisco, and Los Angeles.
Northwest Airlines (© 800/225-
2525; www.nwa.com) operates nonstop flights between Boston and Glasgow daily in summer, somewhat less
frequently in winter. It also offers daily
nonstops from Minneapolis and
Detroit to London. Thanks to Northwest's partnership with Holland's
national airline, KLM, it also offers
easy connections through Amsterdam
to Britain and most of the other countries of Europe.
Delta Air Lines (© 800/241-
4141; www.delta.com) has daily nonstop flights to London from Atlanta
and Cincinnati.
Virgin Atlantic Airways (© 800/
862-8621; www.virgin-atlantic.com)
flies to London's Gatwick from
Boston, Orlando, and Miami and to
London's Heathrow from Los Angeles,
Newark, and New York. Depending

on the point of origin, flights leave four to seven times a week.

For travelers departing from Canada, **Air Canada** (✆ 888/247-2262; www.aircanada.ca) flies daily to London nonstop from Vancouver, Montréal, and Toronto. There are frequent direct services from Calgary and Ottawa. Air Canada also offers daily flights from Toronto to Manchester. An add-on to Glasgow or Edinburgh can be arranged when the initial flight is booked. From Canada, **British Airways** (✆ 800/247-9297; www.british-airways.com) has direct flights to London from Toronto, Montréal, and Vancouver.

For travelers departing from the United Kingdom, **British Airways** (✆ 0345/222-111) flies from Heathrow to both Edinburgh and Glasgow, with frequent daily flights. **KLM UK** (✆ 0990/074-074) flies from Stansted and London City airports to both Edinburgh and Glasgow daily. **Rynair** (✆ 0541/569-569) flies from Stansted outside London to Prestwick on the west coast of Scotland, and **British Midland** (✆ 0345/554-554) flies from Heathrow to both Edinburgh and Glasgow.

For travelers departing from Australia, **British Airways** (✆ 02/8904-8800; www.british-airways.com) has flights to London from Sydney, Melbourne, Perth, and Brisbane. **Qantas** (✆ 008/112-121) offers direct flights with stopovers from Sydney and Melbourne to London. Both airlines have the bonus of a free stopover in Bangkok or Singapore.

For travelers departing from New Zealand, **Air New Zealand** (✆ 0800/737-000) has direct flights to London from Auckland. These flights depart Wednesday, Saturday, and Sunday.

Aer Lingus (✆ 800/223-6537, or 01/844-4711 in Ireland; www.aerlingus.ie) flies daily from Dublin to both Glasgow and Edinburgh. Direct flights are also available through **Ryan Air** (✆ 0541/569-569 in England), which flies several times a day from Dublin to Glasgow.

FLY FOR LESS: TIPS FOR GETTING THE BEST AIRFARES

- **Take advantage of APEX fares.** Advance-purchase booking or APEX fares are often the key to getting the lowest price. You generally must be willing to make your plans and buy your tickets as far ahead as possible: The **21-day APEX** is seconded only by the **14-day APEX,** with a stay in Scotland of 7 to 30 days. Because the number of seats allocated to APEX fares is sometimes fewer than 25% of plane capacity, the early bird gets the low-cost seat. There's often a surcharge for flying on a weekend, and cancellation and refund policies can be strict.

- **Watch for sales.** You'll almost never see them during July and August or the Thanksgiving or Christmas seasons, but at other times, you can get great deals. In the past couple of years, there have been amazing deals on winter flights to Europe. If you already hold a ticket when a sale breaks, it may even pay to exchange it, which usually incurs a $50 to $75 charge. Note, however, that the lowest-priced fares are often non-refundable, require advance purchase of 1 to 3 weeks and a certain length of stay, and carry penalties for changing dates of travel. So, when you're quoted a fare, make sure you know exactly what the restrictions are before you commit.

- **Stay an extra day, or fly midweek.** If your schedule is flexible, ask if you can secure a cheaper fare this way. (Many airlines won't volunteer this information.)

• **Check with consolidators** (also known as bucket shops), a good place to find low fares, often below even the airlines' discounted rates. There's nothing shady about the reliable ones—basically, they're just big travel agents that get discounts for buying in bulk and pass some of the savings on to you. Before you pay, however, ask for a confirmation number from the consolidator and then call the airline itself to confirm your seat. Be prepared to book your ticket with a different consolidator—there are many to choose from—if the airline can't confirm your reservation. Also be aware that consolidator tickets are usually nonrefundable or come with stiff cancellation penalties.

We've gotten great deals from **Cheap Tickets** (© **800/377-1000;** www.cheaptickets.com). **Council Travel** (© **800/226-8624;** www.counciltravel.com) and **STA Travel** (© **800/781-4040;** www.statravel.com) cater especially to young travelers, but their bargain-basement prices are available to people of all ages. Other reliable consolidators include **Lowestfare.com** (© **888/278-8830;** www.lowestfare.com), **1-800-AIRFARE** (www.1800airfare.com), **Cheap Seats** (© **800/451-7200;** www.cheapseatstravel.com), and **1-800-FLY-CHEAP** (www.flycheap.com).

• **Search the Internet** for cheap fares—but it's still best to compare your findings with the research of a dedicated travel agent, if you're lucky enough to have one, especially when you're booking more than just a flight. Two of the better-respected virtual travel agents are **Travelocity (www. travelocity.com)** and **Microsoft Expedia (www.expedia.com)**. The latest buzz in the online travel world is about **Orbitz (www. orbitz.com)**, a site launched by United, Delta, Northwest, American, and Continental airlines. It shows all possible fares for your desired trip, offering fares lower than those available through travel agents. (Stay tuned: At press time, travel-agency associations were waging an antitrust battle against this site.) **Qixo (www.qixo.com)** is another powerful search engine that allows you to search for flights 20 other travel-planning sites at once.

Smarter Living (www.smarter living.com) is a great source for last-minute deals. Take a moment to register, and every week you'll get an e-mail summarizing the discount fares available from your departure city. The site also features concise lists of links to hotel, car-rental, and other hot travel deals.

BY TRAIN

From England, two main rail lines link London to Scotland. The most popular and fastest route is **King's Cross Station** in London to Edinburgh, going by way of Newcastle and Durham. Trains cross from England into Scotland at Berwick-upon-Tweed. Fifteen trains a day leave London for Edinburgh between 8am and 6pm; night service is more limited, and you must reserve sleepers. Three of these trains go on to Aberdeen.

If you're going on to the western Highlands and islands, Edinburgh makes a good gateway, with better train connections to those areas than Glasgow.

If you're going via the west coast, trains leave **Euston Station** in London for Glasgow, by way of Rugby, Crewe, Preston, and Carlisle, with nearly a train per hour during the day. Most of these trains take about 5 hours to reach Glasgow. You can also take the *Highland Chieftain,* going direct to Stirling and Aviemore and terminating in Inverness, capital of the Highlands. There's overnight sleeper service from Euston Station to Glasgow, Perth, Stirling, Aviemore, Fort William, and Inverness. It's possible to book a family compartment.

Scotland is served by other trains from England, including regular service from such cities as Birmingham, Liverpool, Manchester, Southampton, and Bristol. If you're in Penzance (Cornwall), you can reach Glasgow or Edinburgh directly by train without having to return to London.

Orient Express Trains & Cruises has launched its fifth train in Britain, the *Northern Belle*. You get great luxury, except for one oversight: There are no berths. Making about 20 departures a week, the *Northern Belle* carries 252 passengers and feeds them in six stately dining rooms evocative of a country home in Scotland. In addition to its runs in England, the train features weekend jaunts up to Scotland, with departures from Liverpool, Manchester, and York. What about taking a bath? Stays in hotels will be part of the plan. For reservations, call © **020/7805-5100** in the U.K., or 800/524-2420 in the United States. You can also go to **www.orient express.com**.

See "Getting Around," below, for information on railpasses.

BY BUS (COACH)

Long-distance buses, called "motor-coaches" in Britain, are the least expensive means of reaching Scotland from England. Some 20 coach companies run services, mainly from London to Edinburgh or Glasgow. The major operators are **National Express, Scottish Omnibuses, Western SMT, Stagecoach,** and **Eastern Scottish.** It takes 8 to 8½ hours to reach Edinburgh or Glasgow from London.

It's estimated that coach fares are about one-third of the rail charges for comparable trips to Scotland. Most coaches depart from London's **Victoria Coach Station.** If you're visiting between June and August, it's wise to make seat reservations at least 3 days in advance (4 or 5 days if possible). For timetables, available from London to Edinburgh, call **National Express** (© **0990/808-080** in London) or **Scottish Omnibuses** (© **01847/893-123**), or check on all other companies by calling © **08705/505-050.** Travel centers and travel agents also have details. Most travel agents in London sell coach seats and can make reservations for you.

BY CAR

If you're driving north to Scotland from England, it's fastest to take the **M1 motorway** north from London. You can reach M1 by driving to the ring road from any point in the British capital. Southeast of Leeds, you'll need to connect with **A1** (not a motorway), which you take north to Scotch Corner. Here **M1** resumes, ending south of Newcastle-upon-Tyne. Then you can take **A696,** which becomes **A68,** for its final run north into Edinburgh.

If you're in the west of England, go north along **M5,** which begins at Exeter (Devon). Eventually this will merge with **M6.** Continue north on M6 until you reach a point north of Carlisle. From Carlisle, cross into Scotland near Gretna Green. Continue north along **A74** via Moffat. A74 will eventually connect with **M74** heading toward Glasgow. If your goal is Edinburgh, not Glasgow, various roads will take you east to the Scottish capital, including **M8,** which goes part of the way, as do **A702, A70,** and **A71** (all these routes are well signposted).

BY PACKAGE TOUR

Another option is booking your flight as part of an escorted or a package tour. What you lose in freedom and adventure, you'll gain in time and money saved on accommodations,

Active Vacation Tours

See chapter 3, "The Active Vacation Planner," for tour operators specializing in active outdoor vacations, like walking and biking tours.

and even food and entertainment, along with your airline ticket.

The best place to start searching is the travel section of your local Sunday newspaper and the ads in the back of national travel magazines. **Liberty Travel** (© 888/271-1585; www. libertytravel.com) has the most branches. One of the biggest packagers in the Northeast, Liberty usually boasts a full-page ad in Sunday papers. **American Express Travel** (© 800/446-6234; www.americanexpress.com) is another option.

Another good resource is the airlines themselves, which often package their flights together with accommodations. Among the airline packagers, options include **American Airlines Vacations** (© 800/321-2121; www. aavacations.com), **Delta Vacations** (© 800/872-7786; www.deltavacations.com), and **Northwest Airlines** (© 800/225-2525; www.nwa.com). Some of the airline offerings are escorted tours; others are independent fly-drive packages.

British Airways (© 877/428-2228; www.british-airways.com) offers a full spectrum of what it calls "designer holidays," constructed for a wide range of people. Offerings range from tightly scheduled motorcoach tours for those who want the greatest amount of guidance to tours designed for independent souls needing no more than discounted car-rental vouchers and reserved rooms at specific types of hotels (ranging from simple inns to fine baronial mansions).

Other companies offering escorted trips include **CIE Tours** (book through any travel agency, not through CIE directly); **Travoca** (© 800/992-2825), which offers upscale escorted tours by deluxe

motorcoach; and **Trafalgar Tours** (© 800/854-0103), which offers affordable packages with lodging in unpretentious but comfortable hotels.

A RAIL TOUR **Abercrombie & Kent,** 1520 Kensington Rd., Oak Brook, IL 60521 (© 800/323-7308; fax 630/954-2944; www.abercrombiekent.com), offers the most glamorous rail tours in Europe. A & K is the only U.S. sales agent for an elegant train known as the *Royal Scotsman.* Passengers board the luxury train in Edinburgh and can enjoy either a 4-night Scotland tour or a new 2-night tour of the east or west coasts of Scotland. The food rivals that served in the finest restaurants, and the package includes bus trips and tours of castles, manor houses, gardens, and historic sites, many of which are not open to the public. The train stops every evening in a quiet place to guarantee passengers a good night's sleep. Two-night tours begin at $2,450 per person for a twin or single cabin. Call for information on 4-night tours.

CRUISES   No area of Scotland is far from a loch, an estuary, or the wide-open sea, a fact that has greatly affected the country's history. One of the best ways to visit its far-flung islands is by ship, offering a luxury and convenience difficult to duplicate any other way.

One company geared for this kind of travel is **Hebridean Island Cruises,** Acorn Park, Skipton, North Yorkshire BD23 2UE (© 800/659-2648 in the U.S. and Canada, or 01756/704-704; www.hebridean.co.uk). It operates the *Hebridean Princess,* a shallow-draft, much-refitted and -retooled remake (1990) of an older vessel. Outfitted with 30 staterooms and a crew of 38, it can carry up to 50 passengers in cozy circumstances to some of the most remote and inaccessible regions of Scotland. The ship is equipped with beach landing craft, especially useful during explorations of the fragile ecosystems and bird life of the more remote islands.

From March to October, the company offers 12 itineraries that focus on nature and ecology or on the castles, gardens, and archaeology of Scotland. Tours usually depart from Oban and cruise through the Inner and Outer Hebrides and the Orkneys, stopping in places like Saint Kilda's, known for its bird life and tundra. The tours and prices vary enormously depending on the date of travel, but generally range from 4 to 14 nights and cost £1,100 to £16,000 ($1,650 to $24,000). All meals and shore excursions are included, but liquor tabs at the well-stocked bar, wine at dinner, and gratuities are extra.

For more luxurious tours through the islands and lochs of Scotland, contact **Seabourn Cruise Line** (© 800/929-9595; www.seabourn. com), which offers cruises aboard its top-of-the-line yacht *Seabourn Sun,* often as part of longer itineraries around the British Isles.

If you can afford it, the best way to see the Highlands is aboard the 50-passenger *Lord of the Glens* riverboat running between Inverness, capital of the Highlands, and Oban, a port city on the west coast of Scotland. This 150-foot vessel is the first luxury passenger boat to carry overnight passengers on the 200-mile jaunt that takes in some of the most dramatic scenery of Scotland Great Glen. For Nessie watchers, it even crosses Loch Ness. A 10-night package, starting at $4,595 (£3,063), includes 2 nights at Edinburgh's Balmoral Hotel and a night at Loch Lomond's Cameron House. For arrangements, contact **Voyages Jules Verne,** Travel Promotions Ltd., 21 Dorset Square, London NWL 6QE (© 020/7616-1000; fax 020/7723-8629; www.vjv.co.uk).

9 Getting Around

BY PLANE

The **British Airways Europe Airpass** allows travel in a continuous loop to between 3 and 12 cities on BA's European and domestic routes. Passengers must end their journey at the same point they began. If you book such a ticket (say, London to Manchester to Glasgow to Aberdeen to the Shetland Islands, with an eventual return to London), each segment of the itinerary costs about 40% to 50% less than if you'd booked it individually. The pass is available for travel to about a dozen of the most visited cities and regions of Britain, with discounted add-ons available to most of BA's destinations in Europe. It must be booked and paid for at least 7 days before departure from the States, and all sectors of the itinerary must be booked simultaneously. Some changes are permitted in flight dates (but not in the cities visited) after the ticket is issued. Check with BA (© 800/247-9297, or 0345/222-111 in the U.K.; www.british-airways.com) for full details.

Scotland's relatively small scale makes flights between many cities inconvenient and impractical. Although **British Airways** (see above) offers regular flights between Glasgow and Edinburgh, the excellent rail and highway connections usually deter most passengers from flying that route—unless their plane just happens to stop en route to other, more distant, points in Scotland. Frankly, except for visits to the far-distant

Shetlands and Orkneys, we prefer to drive to all but the most inaccessible points. However, British Airways is by far the largest intra-Britain carrier since its recent merger with regional carriers Logan Airways and British Express. Aboard BA from Edinburgh, you can arrange flights to Inverness, Wick, Kirkwall (the Orkneys), and Lerwick (the Shetlands). Aboard **British Midlands** (© **0870/607-0555**), you can fly from London to Edinburgh and Glasgow, but it doesn't offer any other routes in Scotland.

BY TRAIN

The cost of rail travel in Scotland can be quite low. Trains are generally punctual, carrying you across the country or at least to ferry terminals if you're exploring the islands. Timetables are available at all stations, and free timetables covering only certain regions are available at various stations. For £18 ($27), a **young person's rail card** (ages 16 to 25) is sold at major stations. Two passport-size photos are needed. It's estimated this card reduces all fares by one-third for 1 year.

If you plan to travel a great deal on the European railroads, it's worth securing a copy of the *Thomas Cook European Timetable of European Passenger Railroads*. It's available from **Forsyth Travel Library,** 44 S. Broadway, White Plains, NY 10604 (© **800/FORSYTH**), for $27.95 plus $4.95 priority airmail postage in the United States or plus $2 (U.S.) for shipments to Canada. You can also find the timetable at major travel bookstores.

For information on rail travel in Scotland, contact **ScotRail,** P.O. Box 49, Cardiff CF1 5YU, Scotland (© **0845/755-0033**).

BRITRAIL PASSES The **BritRail Pass** permits unlimited rail travel in England, Scotland, and Wales on all British Rail routes (it's not valid on

ships between the U.K. and the Continent, the Channel Islands, or Ireland). An 8-day pass costs $400 first-class and $265 standard, a 15-day pass $600 and $400, a 22-day pass $760 and $505, and a 1-month pass $900 and $600. Kids 5 to 15 are charged half fare, and children under 5 travel free.

Youth passes (ages 16 to 25), all standard, are $215 for 8 days, $280 for 15 days, $355 for 22 days, and $420 for 1 month. If you choose to go first class, you pay full adult fare. **Seniors** (60 and over) qualify for rates of $340 for 8 days, $510 for 15 days, $645 for 22 days, and $765 for 1 month. All BritRail senior rates are for first-class travel.

Note: Prices for BritRail passes are higher for Canadian travelers because of the different conversion rate for Canadian dollars.

BritRail passes can't be obtained in Britain and should be secured before leaving North America either through a travel agent or by contacting **BritRail Travel International,** 500 Mamaroneck Ave., Suite 314, Harrison, NY 10528 (© **888/BRITRAIL** or 800/677-8585 in the U.S., 800/555-2748 in Canada; www.raileurope.com).

BRITRAIL FLEXIPASSES The **BritRail Flexipass** lets you travel anywhere on British Rail but limits travel to 4, 8, or 15 days within a 60-day period. The 4-day Flexipass costs $350 in first class and $235 in standard; seniors pay $300 for a first-class pass, students (ages 16 to 25) pay $185 for a standard pass. The 8-day pass is $510 in first class, $340 in standard, $435 for seniors, and $240 for students. The 15-day Flexipass (15 days of travel in a 2-month period) is $770 in first class and $515 in standard; seniors pay $655. Students are charged $360 for a 15-day pass, but can spread their travel over a 2-month period.

The Flexipass must be purchased from your travel agent or from BritRail Travel International in North America (see address above).

TRAVELPASSES FOR SCOTLAND

If you plan to tour throughout the United Kingdom, one of the above BritRail passes might be appropriate. If you focus intensively on Scotland, however, a BritRail pass might not be adequate. The Scottish Tourist Authorities offer the **Freedom of Scotland Travelpass,** with unlimited transportation on trains and most ferries throughout Scotland and discounts for bus travel. It includes access to obscure bus routes to almost forgotten hamlets, free rides on ferries operated by Caledonian MacBrayne, and discounted fares with P&O Scottish Lines. The ferries connect to the Western Islands, the islands of the Clyde, and the historic Orkneys.

The Travelpass covers all the Scottish rail network and is usable from Carlisle on the western border of England and Scotland and from Berwick-upon-Tweed on the eastern Scottish border. In addition, if you have to fly into London and want to go straight to Scotland from there, a reduced rate is available for a round-trip ticket between London and Edinburgh or Glasgow for Travelpass holders.

The Travelpass is available for 4 days' travel over an 8-day period for $137; 8 days' travel over a 15-day period for $189; and 12 days' travel over a 15-day period for $206. When you validate the pass at the beginning of the journey, you'll get a complete packet of rail, bus, and ferry schedules. For more information, contact **BritRail Travel International,** 500 Mamaroneck Ave., Suite 314, Harrison, NY 10528 (© **888/BRITRAIL**

or 800/677-8585 in the U.S., 800/555-2748 in Canada; www.raileurope.com), or the Manager of Public Affairs, British Rail–Scottish Region, **ScotRail,** P.O. Box 49, Cardiff CF1 5YU, Scotland (© **0845/755-0033**).

BY BUS (COACH)

No doubt about it, the cheapest means of transport from London to Scotland is the bus (coach). It's also the least expensive means of travel within Scotland.

All major towns have a **local bus service,** and every tourist office can provide details about half- or full-day bus excursions to scenic highlights. If you want to explore a particular area, you can often avail yourself of an economical bus pass. If you're planning to travel extensively in Scotland, see the Freedom of Scotland Travelpass, described above.

Many adventurous travelers like to explore the country on one of the **postal buses,** which carry not only mail but also a limited number of passengers to rural areas. Ask at any local post office for details. A general timetable is available at the head post office in Edinburgh.

Scottish CityLink Coaches are a good bet. They link the major cities (Glasgow and Edinburgh) with the two most popular tourist centers, Inverness and Aviemore. Travel is fast and prices are low. For example, it takes only 3 hours to reach Aviemore from Edinburgh, and Inverness is just 3½ hours from Edinburgh. A direct Scottish CityLink overnight coach makes the run from London to Aviemore and Inverness at reasonable fares.

Coaches offer many other popular runs, including links between Glasgow

Eurailpass Warning

Note that your Eurailpass is *not* valid on trains in Great Britain.

and Fort William, Inverness and Ullapool, and Glasgow and Oban. For details, contact **Highland Bus and Coach,** Farralane Park, Inverness (© 01463/233-371), or **Scottish CityLink,** Buchanan Street Bus Station, Glasgow (© 0141/332-7133).

BY CAR

Scotland has many excellent roads, often "dual carriageways" (divided highways), as well as fast trunk roads, linking the Lowlands to the Highlands. In more remote areas, especially the islands of western Scotland, single-lane roads exist. Here caution in driving is most important. Passing places are provided.

However, many of the roads are unfenced, and livestock can be a serious problem when you're driving, either day or night. Drive slowly when you're passing through areas filled with sheep.

CAR RENTALS It's best to shop around, compare prices, and have a clear idea of your needs before you reserve a car. All companies give the best rates to those who reserve at least 2 business days in advance before leaving home and who agree to return the car to its point of origin, and some require drivers be at least 23 years old (in some cases 21). It's also an advantage to keep the car for at least a week, as opposed to 3 or 4 days. Be warned that all car rentals in the United Kingdom are slapped with a whopping 17.5% government tax known as VAT.

To rent a car in Scotland, you must present your passport and driver's license along with your deposit. No special British or international license is needed.

The three major rental companies are **Avis** (© 800/331-2112; www. avis.com), **Budget** (© 800/527-0700; www.budgetrentacar.com), and **Hertz** (© 800/654-3131; www.hertz. com). We've often found the cheapest rates through Budget, but it's worth

noting that frequent flyers on British Airways may be eligible for discounts on Hertz rentals if they make their reservations through the airline. Good deals are also available at **EuroDollar Rent-a-Car** (© 800/800-6000) and **Alamo** (© 800/522-9696; www. goalamo.com).

Other companies specializing in European car rentals are **Auto Europe** (© 800/223-5555; www.autoeurope. com), **Europe by Car** (© 800/223-1516, 800/252-9401 in California, or 212/581-3040 in New York; www. europebycar.com), and **Kemwel** (© 800/678-0678; www.kemwel. com).

Another bargain option is a car-rental reservations network based in Florida: **I.T.S. of Broward County** (© 800/521-0643, 800/227-8990, or 800/248-4350), which represents two of Britain's largest rental companies, Kenning and Town & Country. I.T.S. usually offers prices up to 40% lower than those available at most car-rental kiosks. Prepayment isn't required, but a printed confirmation will be faxed or mailed to those who reserve a car in advance. A week's rental of a Rover Mini or Fiat 1.0 costs £80.70 ($121.05) with unlimited mileage and tax; optional collision insurance is around £12.50 ($18.75) per day. Pickup for cars can be arranged at any of the major U.K. airports. Be warned, however, that pickups at certain off-the-beaten-path places might require a phone call on your arrival before an I.T.S. representative arrives. If you're flexible, you might save enough money on the rental to make the inconvenience worthwhile.

In some cases, slight discounts are offered to members of the American Automobile Association (AAA) or the American Association of Retired Persons (AARP). Be sure to ask.

Each company offers a collision-damage waiver (CDW) at $15 to $25 per day (depending on the car's value).

Getting Your VAT Refund

You can get a VAT refund if you shop at stores that participate in the Retail Export Scheme. (Signs are posted in the window.) When you make a purchase, show your passport and request a Retail Export Scheme form (VAT 407) and a stamped, pre-addressed envelope. Show the VAT form and your sales receipt to British Customs when you leave the country—they may also ask to see the merchandise. After Customs has stamped it, mail the form back to the shop in the envelope provided *before you leave the country.* Your VAT refund will be mailed to you.

Remember: Keep your VAT forms with your passport; pack your purchases in a carry-on bag so you'll have them handy; and allow yourself enough time at your departure point to find a mailbox.

Several readers have reported a VAT refund scam. You must get the refund forms from the retailer on the spot. (Don't leave the store without one.) Some merchants allegedly tell customers they can get a refund form at the airport on their way out of the country. *This is not true.* The form must be completed by the retailer on the spot, or you won't get a refund later.

This extra protection will cover all or part of the repair-related costs if you have an accident. (In some cases, even if you buy the CDW, you'll pay $200 to $300 per accident. Ask questions before you sign.) Check your existing auto insurance and what's available through your credit cards first. (Note that credit cards may cover collision but will usually not cover liability.)

GASOLINE   There are plenty of gas ("petrol") stations in the environs of Glasgow and Edinburgh. However, in remote areas they're often few and far between, and many are closed on Sunday. If you're planning a lot of Sunday driving in remote parts, always make sure your tank is full on Saturday.

Note that gasoline costs more in Britain than in North America, and to encourage energy saving the government has imposed a new 25% tax on gas. The price of a liter of gas (about ¼ gallon) is typically 64p (95¢), including taxes.

DRIVING RULES & REQUIRE-MENTS   In Scotland, you drive on the left and pass on the right. Road signs are clear and the international symbols unmistakable. To drive a car in Scotland, U.S. visitors need a passport and driver's license (no special British license is needed). Wearing seat belts is mandatory in the British Isles.

A word of warning: Pedestrian crossings are marked by striped lines (zebra striping) on the road and flashing orange curbside lights. Drivers must stop and yield the right of way if a pedestrian has stepped into the zebra zone to cross the street.

ROAD MAPS   The best road map, especially if you're trying to locate some obscure village, is *The Ordnance Survey Motor Atlas of Great Britain,* revised annually and published by Temple Press. It's available at most bookstores in Scotland. If you're in London and plan to head north to Scotland, go to W. & G. Foyle Ltd.,

113 and 119 Charing Cross Rd. (© 020/7440-3225).

Other excellent maps include the *AAA Road Map of Scotland*, the *Collins Touring Map of Scotland*, and *Frommer's Road Atlas.*

BREAKDOWNS Membership in one of the two major auto clubs can be helpful: the **Automobile Association (AA)** at Norfolk House, Priestly Road, Basingstoke, Hampshire RG24 9NY (© 0990/500-600), or the **Royal Automobile Club (RAC)**, P.O. Box 700, Bristol, Somerset BS99 1RB (© 08705/722-722). You can join these clubs through your car-rental agent. (Members of AAA in the U.S. can enjoy reciprocity overseas.) There are roadside emergency telephone boxes about every mile along the motorways. If you don't see one, walk down the road for a bit to the blue-and-white marker with an arrow that points to the nearest box. The 24-hour number to call for the AA is © 0800/887-766; for the RAC, it's © 0800/828-282. In addition, you can call a police traffic unit that will contact either of the auto clubs on your behalf.

BY FERRY

You can use a variety of special excursion fares to reach Scotland's islands. For the Clyde and Western Isles, contact **Caledonian MacBrayne** (© 01475/650-100, or 01475/650-288 for brochures); for the Orkneys and Shetlands, contact **P&O Scottish Ferries** (© 01224/572-615).

Caledonian MacBrayne, operating 30 ferries in all, sails to 23 Hebridean and all Clyde Islands. The fares, times of departure, and even accommodation suggestions are in a special book, *Ferry Guide to 23 Scottish Islands.* There are reasonably priced fares for vehicles and passengers through a "Go As You Please" plan, a kind of island hopscotch program offering a choice of 24 preplanned routes at a discount off the cost of individual tickets. Tickets are valid for 1 month and can be used in either direction for one trip on each leg of the tour. Cyclists can take their bikes aboard free on some routes.

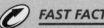 **FAST FACTS: Scotland**

American Express There's an office at 139 Princes St. in Edinburgh (© 0131/718-2505); hours are Monday through Friday from 9am to 5:30pm and Saturday from 9am to 4pm. Another office is at 115 Hope St. in Glasgow (© 0141/222-1405); it's open Monday through Friday from 8:30am to 5:30pm, Saturday from 9am to noon (9am to 4pm in June and July).

Auto Clubs Call the **Automobile Association** (© 800/AAA-HELP) or the **Royal Automobile Club** (© 0141/248-4444).

Business Hours Most banks are open Monday through Thursday from 9:30am to 12:30pm and 1:30 to 3:30pm; Friday hours are often 9:30am to 1:30pm. Bar and pub hours are Monday through Saturday from 11am to 11pm, but this can vary widely; Sunday hours are usually 12:30 to 2:30pm and 6:30 to 11pm, but some pubs are closed Sunday. Office hours are Monday through Friday from 9am to 5pm; the lunch break lasts an hour, but most places stay open all day. Post offices are open Monday through Friday from 9am to 5pm and Saturday from 9am to noon. Stores are generally open Monday through Saturday from 9am to 5:30 or 6pm. Most stores close early on Tuesday or Wednesday afternoon.

Drug Laws Great Britain is becoming increasingly severe in enforcing drug laws. People arrested for possession of even tiny quantities of marijuana have been deported, forced to pay stiff fines, or sentenced to jail for 2 to 7 years. Possession of drugs like heroin and cocaine carries even more stringent penalties.

Drugstores In Great Britain they're called "chemist" shops. Every police station has a list of emergency chemists; dial "0" (zero) and ask the operator for the local police. Emergency drugs are normally available at most hospitals, but you'll be examined to see if the drugs you request are really necessary.

Electricity The electricity is 240 volts AC (50Hz). Some international hotels are specially wired to allow North Americans to plug in their appliances, but you usually need a transformer plus an adapter for your electric razor or hair dryer.

Embassies & Consulates All embassies are in London. There's a **U.S. Consulate** in Edinburgh at 3 Regent Terrace (© **0131/556-8315**), open Monday through Friday from 1 to 4pm. All other nationals have to use London to conduct their business: The **Canadian High Commission** is at MacDonald House, 1 Grosvenor Sq., London W1K 4AB (© **020/ 7258-6600**), open Monday through Friday from 8am to 4pm. The **Australian High Commission** is at the Strand, London WC2B 4LI (© **020/ 7379-4334**), open Monday through Friday from 9:30am to 3:30pm. The **New Zealand High Commission** is at New Zealand House, 80 Haymarket at Pall Mall, London SW1Y 4TQ (© **020/7930-8422**), open Monday through Friday from 9am to 5pm. The **Irish Embassy** is at 17 Grosvenor Place, London SW1X 7HR (© **020/7235-2171**), open Monday through Friday from 9:30am to 1pm and 2:15 to 5pm.

Emergencies For police, fire, or ambulance, dial © **999**. Give your name, address, phone number, and the nature of the emergency. Misuse of the 999 service will result in a heavy fine (cardiac arrest, yes; dented fender, no).

Legal Aid Your consulate, embassy, or high commission (see above) will give you advice if you run into trouble. They can advise you of your rights and even provide a list of attorneys (for which you'll have to pay if services are used), but they can't interfere on your behalf in the legal processes of Great Britain. For questions about American citizens arrested abroad, including ways of getting money to them, call the **Citizens Emergency Center of the Office of Special Consulate Services,** in Washington, D.C. (© **202/647-5225**). Other nationals can go to their nearest consulate or embassy.

Liquor Laws The legal drinking age is 18. Children under 16 aren't allowed in pubs, except in certain rooms, and then only when accompanied by a parent or guardian. Don't drink and drive; the penalties are stiff. Basically, you can get a drink from 11:30am to 11pm, but this can vary widely, depending on the discretion of the local tavern owner. Not all pubs are open on Sunday; those that are generally stay open from noon to 3pm and 7 to 10:30 or 11pm. Restaurants are allowed to serve liquor during these hours, but only to people who are dining on the premises. The law allows 30 minutes for "drinking-up time." A meal, incidentally, is defined as "substantial refreshment." And you have to eat and drink sitting down. In hotels, liquor may be served from 11am to 11pm to both guests and nonguests; after 11pm, only guests may be served.

Mail Sending an airmail letter to North America costs 44p (65¢) and postcards require a 38p (55¢) stamp. British mailboxes are painted red and carry a royal coat-of-arms.

Newspapers & Magazines Each major Scottish city publishes its own newspaper. All newsagents (newsstands) carry the major London papers as well. In summer, you can generally pick up a copy of the *International Herald Tribune*, published in Paris, along with the European editions of *USA Today*, *Time*, and *Newsweek*.

Pets Great Britain has finally eased a 100-year-old mandatory pet quarantine, but rigid requirements are still in place. Now pets need no longer fear a long separation from their Britain-bound families if they pass several tests and can wait long enough. The animal must also be coming from a country that is approved by Britain. All countries in the European Union such as Germany, Switzerland, Austria, Spain, Italy, and France are participants in the PETS program, but the United States is not. For information, check out www.defra.gov.uk/animalh/quarantine/index.htm.

Police The best source of help and advice in emergencies is the police. For non-life-threatening situations, dial "0" (zero) and ask for the police, or 999 for emergencies. If the local police can't assist, they'll have the address of a person who can. Losses, thefts, and other crimes should be reported immediately.

Restrooms Public toilets are clean and often have an attendant. Hotels can be used, but they discourage nonguests. Garages (filling stations) don't always have facilities for the use of customers. There's no need to tip, except to a hotel attendant.

Safety Although crime isn't a serious problem for the average visitor, many areas in and around Glasgow are dangerous, with dozens of muggings reported weekly. Caution should always be taken. Never leave your car unlocked and always protect your valuables.

Taxes There's no local sales tax. However, Great Britain imposes a standard value-added tax (VAT) of 17.5%. Hotel rates and meals in restaurants are taxed 17.5%; the extra charge will show up on your bill unless otherwise stated. This can be refunded if you shop at stores that participate in the Retail Export Scheme; (Signs are posted in the window.) see "Getting Your VAT Refund," above.

The departure tax for leaving Britain is £20 ($30) for passengers flying worldwide, including the United States, and £10 ($15) for flights within Britain and the European Union. This tax is accounted for in your ticket.

As part of an energy-saving scheme, the British government has also added a special 25% tax on gasoline ("petrol").

Telephone & Fax Consult "Directory Enquiries" ("Information") to aid you; dial ⓒ **153**, give the operator the town where you want the number, the subscriber's name, and then the address.

Pay phones accept all British coins except 1p. A local call costs 10p (15¢). Phone books contain detailed instructions on how to make a call in the British Isles. You can also dial the operator for assistance. There are special phone booths that accept phonecards only.

To call from one U.K. city to another: Dial the entire city code, including the initial 0 and the 1 that's now an integral part of each British city code. Then dial the local phone number. **To dial direct internationally,** dial 00, then the country code (the United States and Canada 1, Ireland 353, Australia 61, and New Zealand 64), the area code, and then the local phone number.

Unless you activate one of the direct-access codes below, try to make international calls from a public pay phone, preferably with a phonecard (see below), because hotels almost invariably charge high markups on international calls. Calls dialed directly from any public phone are usually billed on the basis of the call's duration, not on any supplemental add-on charges. A reduced rate applies to domestic long-distance and international calls placed between 11pm and 8am Monday through Saturday and all day Sunday. Know in advance that direct-dial calls from the United States to anywhere in the United Kingdom are usually much cheaper than equivalent calls placed from Britain to North America; in many cases, it's worthwhile to place a short call to your designated party and then give them a phone number where they can call you back.

If you don't know the phone number of the party you want to call, you can dial **National Directory Enquiries** at ✆ 192; the call is free. You can access **International Directory Enquiries** at ✆ 192, but it will cost 25p (40¢) a shot.

Phonecards are available in denominations of £5 ($7.50), £10 ($15), £20 ($30), and £50 ($75). They're sold at thousands of outlets around Britain, including newspaper kiosks, tobacco shops, and cafes. Depending on the phone where you place your call, you either insert your phonecard directly into the phone box or key in the numbers that appear on the face of the card.

Many travelers find the most convenient way to place international calls is making **collect or calling card calls** directly from their hotel room or from any public phone in Britain. To do this, if the phone requires it, drop 20p (30¢) into the coin slot. (Don't worry, the call is free, and you'll get your coins refunded before you complete the call.) Then dial the direct-access code of any of the U.S.-based long-distance carriers below and you'll be connected to an English-speaking operator who can assist you with the call, regardless of the country you're trying to reach. The following calling card numbers work all over Britain: To access **AT&T,** dial ✆ 0800/890-0011; to access **World Phone,** dial ✆ 0800/890-222; and to access **Sprint,** dial ✆ 0800/890-877.

To place **collect calls** from Britain to a country beside the United States or Canada, dial ✆ 155, and then tell the operator you intend to make a collect call.

Time Britain is based on Greenwich mean time (GMT), 5 hours ahead of the U.S. East Coast, with British summer time (BST, or GMT plus 1 hour) used roughly from April to October. When it's noon in Edinburgh or

Calling Scotland

To call Scotland from the United States, dial the **international prefix, 011;** then Scotland's **country code, 44;** then the **city code** (for example, **131** for Edinburgh and **141** for Glasgow—minus the initial zero, which is used only if you're dialing from within the United Kingdom); then dial the actual **phone number.**

Glasgow, it's 7am in New York, 6am in Chicago, 5am in Denver, and 4am in Los Angeles.

Tipping For **cab drivers,** add about 10% to 15% to the fare as shown on the meter. If the driver personally unloads or loads your luggage, add 35p (40¢) per bag.

Hotel **porters** get 75p ($1.10) per bag even if you have only one small suitcase. Hall porters are tipped only for special services. **Maids** receive £1 ($1.50) per day. In top-ranked hotels, the **concierge** often submits a separate bill, showing charges for newspapers and the like; if he or she has been particularly helpful, tip extra.

Hotels often add a **service charge** of 10% to 15% to bills. In smaller B&Bs, the tip isn't likely to be included. Therefore, tip for special services, such as the waiter who serves you breakfast. If several people have served you in a B&B, a 10% to 15% charge will be added to the bill and divided among the staff.

In **restaurants** and **nightclubs,** a 15% service charge is added to the bill. To that, add another 3% to 5%, depending on the quality of the service. **Waiters** in deluxe restaurants and clubs are accustomed to the extra 5%, which means you'll end up tipping 20%. If that seems excessive, remember that the initial service charge reflected in the fixed price is distributed among all the help. **Sommeliers** (wine stewards) get about £1 ($1.50) per bottle of wine served. Tipping in **pubs** is not common, although in cocktail bars the waiter or barmaid usually gets about £1 ($1.50) per round of drinks.

Barbers and **hairdressers** expect 10% to 15%. **Tour guides** expect £2 ($3), but it's not mandatory. **Petrol station attendants** are rarely tipped. **Theater ushers** also don't expect tips.

Water Tap water is considered safe to drink throughout Scotland.

3

The Active Vacation Planner

If you're headed to Scotland to enjoy the outdoors, you can get guidance from the **Scottish Sports Council,** Caledonian House, South Gyle, Edinburgh EH12 9DQ (© **0131/317-7200;** fax 0131/317-7202), open Monday through Friday from 9am to 5pm. It can supply names of nature areas, playing fields, prices, and facilities, as well as send a copy of *Arena,* a bulletin packed with advice on sporting programs and facilities.

1 Teeing Off: Golfing in Scotland

Although golf has become Scotland's pride, don't think the sport was always well received. Monks around St. Andrews weren't applauded when they diverted themselves from a schedule of felling trees and praying to play *gowff,* and James I and James II rather churlishly issued edicts prohibiting its practice. Despite that, by the mid-1700s the game was firmly entrenched in Scotland and viewed as a bucolic oddity by Englishmen chasing after the hounds in the milder climes to the south.

Scotland has more than 440 golf courses, many of them municipal courses open to everyone. Some are royal and ancient (such as St. Andrews), others modern and hip. An example of a well-received newcomer is the Loch Lomond course in the Trossachs, established as a private club in 1993. Although they lie as far north as Sutherland, only 6 degrees south of the Arctic Circle, most courses are in the Central Belt, stretching from Stirling down to Edinburgh and Glasgow.

A beginner doesn't need to lug a complete set of golf clubs across the Atlantic because many courses rent full or half sets. If you're female or plan on playing golf with someone who is, be aware that some courses are restricted to men only, banning women completely or limiting them to designated days. Despite this tradition-bound holdover from another era, women's golf thrives in Scotland, with about 33,000 members in the Scottish Ladies Golfing Association. The Ladies British Open Amateur Championship was first held in 1893. (The U.S. equivalent was first held in 1895.) Contact Mrs. L. H. Park, Secretary, **Scottish Ladies Golfing Association** (information on tournaments or finding women golf partners), or Ian Hume, Esq., Secretary, at the **Scottish National Golf Centre,** Drumoig, Leuchars, St. Andrews, Fife KY16 0DW, Scotland (© **01382/549-500;** fax 01382/549-510). Sharing offices with the Scottish Ladies Golfing Association is the **Scottish Golf Union,** established in 1920 to foster and maintain a high standard of amateur golf in Scotland.

Any serious golfer who will be in Scotland for a long stay should consider joining a local club. Membership makes it easier to get coveted tee times, and attending or competing in a local club's tournaments can be both fun and sociable. If you won't be staying long, you might not bother, but remember to bring a letter from a golf club in your home country—it can open a lot of doors otherwise closed to the general public.

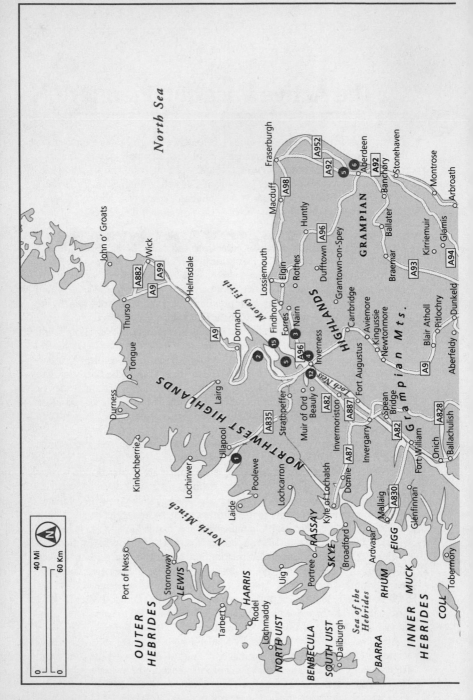

North Sea

North Minch

North Uist

Moray Firth

Loch Ness

Sea of the Hebrides

GRAMPIAN

HIGHLANDS

Grampian Mts.

NORTHWEST HIGHLANDS

OUTER HEBRIDES

INNER HEBRIDES

LEWIS

HARRIS

NORTH UIST

BENBECULA

SOUTH UIST

BARRA

RHUM

EIGG

MUCK

COLL

SKYE

RAASAY

John o' Groats
Wick
A882
A99
A9
Helmsdale
Thurso
Tongue
Durness
Lairg
Dornach
A9
Kinlochberrie
Lochinver
Ullapool
A835
Strathpeffer
Poolewe
Lochcarron
Laide
Kyle of Lochalsh
Dornie
A87
Kinlochmoddy
Tarbert
Rodel
Port of Ness
Stornoway
Uig
Portree
Broadford
Ardvasar
Mallaig
Glenfinnan
A830
Fort William
Onich
Ballachulish
A828
Spean Bridge
Invergarry
A82
Invermoriston
A887
Fort Augustus
Beauly
Muir of Ord
A82
Inverness
A96
Nairn
Findhorn
Forres
Elgin
Lossiemouth
Rothes
A98
Macduff
Fraserburgh
A952
A92
Aberdeen
Stonehaven
Banchory
A92
Montrose
Arbroath
Glamis
A94
Kirriemuir
Ballater
Braemar
A93
Aberfeldy
Dunkeld
Pitlochry
Blair Atholl
A9
Newtonmore
Kingussie
Aviemore
Carrbridge
Grantown-on-Spey
Dufftown
A96
Huntly
Tongue
Tomore

Durness

40 Mi
60 Km

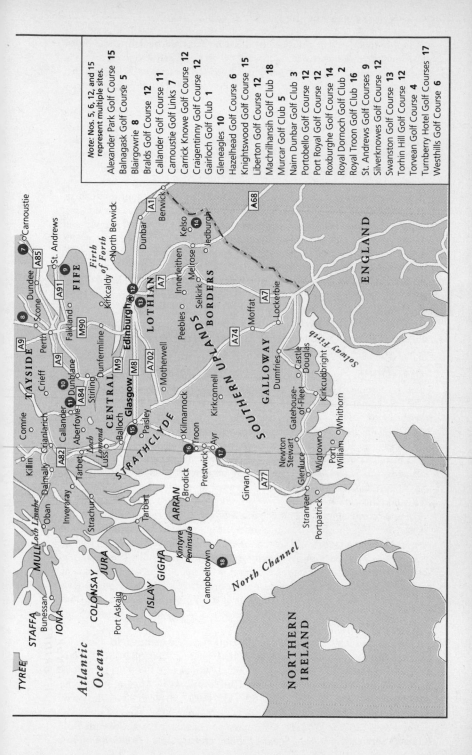

Note: Nos. 5, 6, 12, and 15 represent multiple sites.

Alexander Park Golf Course **15**
Balnagask Golf Course **5**
Blairgowrie **8**
Braids Golf Course **12**
Callander Golf Course **11**
Carnoustie Golf Links **7**
Carrick Knowe Golf Course **12**
Craigentinny Golf Course **12**
Gairloch Golf Club **1**
Gleneagles **10**
Hazelhead Golf Course **6**
Knightswood Golf Course **15**
Liberton Golf Course **12**
Machrihansih Golf Club **18**
Murcar Golf Club **5**
Nairn Dunbar Golf Club **3**
Portobello Golf Course **12**
Port Royal Golf Course **12**
Roxburghe Golf Course **14**
Royal Dornoch Golf Club **2**
Royal Troon Golf Club **16**
St. Andrews Golf Courses **9**
Silverknowes Golf Course **12**
Swanston Golf Course **13**
Torhin Hill Golf Course **12**
Torvean Golf Course **4**
Turnberry Hotel Golf Courses **17**
Westhills Golf Course **6**

Access to many private clubs can be dicey, however, particularly those boasting so much tradition that waiting lists for tee-off times can stretch on for up to a year in advance. You can always stay in a hotel (Gleneagles or Turnberry) that has its own course, thereby guaranteeing the availability of tee times, Or you can arrange a golf tour (see below).

Abandon forever any hope of balmy tropical weather, azure skies, and lush fairways. Don't anticipate the sprinklers that flood many warm-weather courses in other countries. Scotland's rains and fogs produce an altogether different kind of golf-related aesthetic, one buffeted by coastal winds, sometimes torn by gales and storms, and (in some places) accented only with salt-tolerant tough grasses and wind-blown stunted trees and shrubs like gorse and heather.

Knowing a term or two in advance might help in picking your golf course. The Scots make a strong distinction between their two types of courses: links and upland. **Links courses** nestle into the sandy terrain of coastal regions, and although years of cultivation have rendered their fairways and putting greens emerald colored, there's a vague sense that eons ago the terrain was submerged beneath the water. Links courses are among the famous names in Scotland and include Royal Troon, Turnberry, Prestwick, North Berwick, and Glasgow Gailes. All links courses are on or near the sea. **Upland courses,** by contrast, are based inland and invariably consist of hilly terrain. They're usually drier and less windy than links courses, Nonetheless, it rains a lot in Scotland, so a sweater and raingear are recommended for *all* courses. Examples of upland courses are Gleneagles, Loch Lomond, and Pitlochry.

GOLF TOURS

Access for nonmembers to the country's maze of golf courses hasn't always been possible. All that changed in 1988, however, with the establishment of **Golf International,** 14 E. 38th St., New York, NY 10016 (© **800/833-1389** or 212/986-9176; www.golfinternational.com), which maintains a branch office in St. Andrews, the ivy-clad *sanctum sanctorum* of the golfing world. The company caters to golfers from moderate to advanced levels and, against hitherto impossible odds, will guarantee its clients starting times at 40 or so of Scotland's most sought-after courses, including St. Andrews, Carnoustie, Royal Troon, Prestwick, and Gullane.

Potential clients, in self-organized groups of 2 to 12, produce a wish list of the courses they'd like to play. Starting times are prearranged (sometimes rigidly) with an ease that an individual traveler or even a travel agent would find impossible. Packages can be arranged for anywhere from 7 to 14 days (the average is about 7 days) and can include as much or as little golf, at as many courses, as you want. Weekly prices, including hotels, breakfasts, car rentals, greens fees, and the services of a greeter and helpmate at the airport on arrival, range from $2,295 to $4,995 (£1,538 to £3,347) per person. Discounted airfares to Scotland can also be arranged.

Other companies specializing in golf tours are **Adventures in Golf,** 11 Northeastern Blvd., Suite 360, Nashua, NH 03062 (© **603/882-8367**); **Classic Golf & Leisure,** 75706 McLachlin Circle, Palm Desert, CA 92211 (© **760/772-2560;** www.classic-golf.com); **ITC Golf Tours,** 4134 Atlantic Ave., Suite 205, Long Beach, CA 90807 (© **800/257-4981** or 562/595-6905; www.itcgolf.com); **Perry Golf,** 8302 Dunwoody Place, Suite 305, Atlanta, GA 30350 (© **800/344-5257** or 770/641-9696; www.perrygolf.com); and **Scottish Golf & Travel Service,** 12 Rutland Square, Edinburgh EH1 2BB (© **800/847-8064** in U.S.).

THE CLASSIC COURSES

For more details on these fabled golf courses, refer to "The Best Golf" in chapter 1. In addition to the big names below, many additional courses are listed in the appropriate destination chapters that follow.

The **Carnoustie Golf Links,** Links Parade, Carnoustie, Tayside (© **01241/ 853-789;** fax 01241/852-720), has a par of 72. This 6,941-yard (6,316m) championship course requires the use of a caddy, costing £30 ($45) for 18 holes. As with most championship courses, electric golf carts aren't allowed, but you can rent a trolley for £3 ($4.50) per round. Greens fees are £75 ($112.50), and club rentals, available at Simpson's Golf Shop, 6 Links Parade (© **01241/ 854-477),** or David Low's, 7 Links Ave. (© **01241/853-439),** cost £10 to £15 ($15 to $22.50).

The par-72 **Old Course, St. Andrews,** Golf Place, St. Andrews, Fife (© **01334/466-666),** is a 6,566-yard (5,975km) 18-hole course. Golf was first played here around 1400, and it's billed as the Home of Golf. This fabled course hosted the 2000 British Open, and witnessed history when Tiger Woods became the youngest golfer to complete a grand slam (and only the fifth golfer to ever perform the feat). Greens fees are £10 to £85 ($15 to $127.50), a caddy costs £30 ($45) plus tip, and clubs rent for £20 to £30 ($30 to $45) per round. There are no electric carts allowed, and you can rent a trolley on afternoons only between May and September for £3 ($4.50). Reservations must be made in advance.

The 18-hole **Royal Dornoch Golf Club,** Dornoch, Sutherland (© **01862/ 810-219),** 40 miles (64.5km) north of Inverness, has a par of 70. At this 6,185-yard (5,628m) course, the greens fees are £60 ($90) Monday through Saturday and £70 ($105) on Sunday (members only). Golf club and trolley rentals are £20 to £30 ($30 to $45) and £3 ($4.50), respectively. Caddy service is available for £30 ($45) plus tip.

The par-71 **Royal Troon Golf Club,** Craigend Road, Troon, Ayrshire (© **01292/311-555;** fax 01292/318-204), has one of the largest courses in Scotland, with 7,097 yards (6,458m) of playing area. The greens fees of £95 to £135 ($142.50 to $202.50) for a day include a buffet lunch and two 18-hole sets. For one round of play, a trolley rents for £4 ($6) and a caddy £30 ($45); club rental is £25 ($37.50) per round or £35 ($52.50) per day.

The **Turnberry Hotel Golf Courses,** Ayrshire (© **01655/331-000;** fax 01655/331-706), gives priority at its 6,971yard (6,344m) par-70 course to guests of the hotel. The greens fees—£95 ($142.50) for guests and £120 to £150 ($180 to $225) for nonguests—include 18 holes on the Ailsa course and an 18-hole round on the less-desirable Arran course. For one round, clubs rent for £35 ($52.50) and caddy service costs £25 ($37.50) plus tip. If you're not staying here, call in the morning to check on any unclaimed tee times—but it's a long shot.

A Beginner's Warning

Neophytes unfamiliar with the rules of the game aren't just allowed to play the country's most legendary golf courses. Many courses will want evidence of your familiarity with the game before you're allowed on the links. Depending on the setting and the season, this could include a letter from your club back home citing your ability and experience, or visual proof you've mastered a basically sound swing and an understanding of golf-related etiquette.

2 Fishing

Anglers consider Scotland a paradise. Its fast-flowing rivers harbor Atlantic salmon (the king of all game fish). The rivers and numerous pristine *lochs* (lakes) allow you to enjoy some of Europe's most beautiful scenery, along with the marvelous hospitality extended by its innkeepers. Note that permits for fishing (often arranged by your hotel) can be expensive. For one of the grand beats on the River Tay, a week's permit could run into hundreds of pounds. However, there are many lesser-known rivers where a club ticket costs only pounds a day.

The **Tweed** and the **Tay** are just two of the famous Scottish salmon rivers. In Perthshire, the Tay is the broadest and longest river in the country. The **Dee** is the famous salmon-fishing river of Aberdeenshire. The royal family fishes this river, and the queen herself has been seen casting from these banks. Other anglers prefer to fish the **Spey,** staying at one of the inns along the Malt Whisky Trail. Certain well-heeled fishermen travel every year to Scotland to fish in the lochs and rivers of the **Outer Hebrides.**

In general, Scotland's season for salmon fishing runs from late February until late October, but these dates vary from region to region.

TYPES OF FISHING

Here's a breakdown of terms you're likely to hear even before you cast your first line into the country's glittering waters:

COARSE FISHING   This means going after any species of freshwater fish except salmon and trout. Especially prized trophies, known for putting up a spirited fight, are carp, tench, pike, bream, roach, and perch. Because few lochs actually freeze during winter, the sport can be practiced throughout the year. Local tourist boards all over the country can provide advice.

GAME FISHING   Salmon and trout (brown, rainbow, or sea) are the most desired of the game fish and the ones that have inspired the image of a fly fisherman whipping a lure and line in serpentine arcs above a loch. Many vacationers dream of donning bulky rubber waders up to their waists and trying their luck in streams and freshwater lochs. Fly-fishing for salmon and trout is subject to seasonal controls and sometimes requires a permit. For details on game fishing, contact the **Salmon & Trout Association (Scottish Branch),** 10 Great Stuart St., Edinburgh EH3 7TN (© **0131/558-3644;** fax 0131/557-6269; www.salmon-trout.org).

SEA FISHING   This simply means fishing from a beach, a rocky shoreline, or a pier. Inshore fishing involves dropping a line into ocean waters within 3 miles (5km) of any Scottish coastline; deep-sea fishing is off a boat more than 3 miles (5km) offshore in a style made popular by cigar-chomping tycoons and Hemingway clones. Offshore waters have produced several species of shark, including porbeagle, thresher, mako, and blue shark. For information on what to expect from deep offshore waters, contact the **Scottish Tourist Board,** 23 Ravelston Terrace, Edinburgh EH14 3TP (© **0131/332-2433**).

FISHING CLUBS

Getting permits and information on worthwhile places to fish is easier if you join one of the more than 380 fishing clubs headquartered in Scotland. (The oldest angling club in the world, the Ellem Fishing Club, was founded in Scotland in 1829.) Each of its activities is supervised by the **Scottish Anglers**

National Association (© 0131/339-8808), which firmly believes that new-comers should learn at the side of the more experienced. Courses and reunions are offered in the fine art of fishing in or around Scotland. For details, contact the Scottish Tourist Board (see above).

3 Biking, Walking & Other Outdoor Pursuits

BIKING

Scotland is one of the most gorgeous settings in Europe for a bike trip, but note that bicycles are forbidden on most highways and trunk roads and on what the British call dual carriageways (divided highways). May, June, and September are the best months for cycling in spite of the often bad weather. Many of the nar-row and scenic roads are likely to be overcrowded with cars in July and August. For the best biking routes, see chapter 1.

Your first source of information should be the **Scottish Cyclists Union,** which provides an annual handbook and a regular newsletter for members. It's also one of the most potent lobbying groups in Scotland for the inauguration and preservation of cyclists' byways. It distributes maps showing worthwhile bike routes and supports the publication of technical material of interest to cyclists. Nonmembers are welcome for a small fee. Contact Jim Riach, Execu-tive Office, Scottish Cyclists Union, The Velodrome, Meadowbrook Stadium, London Road, Edinburgh EH7 6AD (© **0131/652-0187;** fax 0131/661-0474; www.scuweb.com).

Although based in England, the **Cyclists Tourist Club,** Cotterell House, 69 Meadrow, Godalming, Surrey GU7 3HS (© **01483/417-217;** fax 01483/426-994; www.ctc.org.uk), offers details on cycling holidays in Scotland. Mem-bership is £25 ($37.50) a year for adults and £15 ($22.50) for those 17 and under. A family with three or more members can get a membership for £40 ($60). This organization will give advice on where to rent or buy a bike; it also offers free legal advice to members involved in cycle-related accidents and advice on available medical insurance for members.

It's possible to take your bike without restrictions on car and passenger ferries in Scotland. There's almost no case where it's necessary to make arrangements in advance. However, the transport of your bike is likely to cost £1 to £6 ($1.50 to $9), plus the cost of your own passage.

The best biking trips in Scotland are offered by **Bespoke Highland Tours,** The Bothy, Camusdarach, Inverness PH39 4NT (© **01687/450-272**), and **Scottish Border Trails,** Drummore, Venlaw High Road, Peebles EH45 8RL (© **01721/720-336;** fax 01721/723-004).

U.S.-based **Backroads,** 801 Cedar St. Berkeley, CA 94710 (© **800/ GO-ACTIVE** [462-2848] or 510/527-1555; www.backroads.com), offers a couple of week-long biking tours through Scotland. Accommodations are in charming inns along the way, and fine food, all equipment, and van support are included.

Local rental shops offer a wide range of bicycles, from three-speeds to moun-tain bikes, and may offer organized trips, ranging from tours of several hours to full-fledged week-long itineraries. We've listed the best local rental shops, with their rates, in the destination chapters that follow.

BIRD-WATCHING

The moors and Highlands of Scotland, partly because of their low population density, attract millions of birds. For reasons not fully understood by ornithologists, the Orkneys shelter absolutely staggering numbers of birds. Bird-watchers cite the Orkneys as even richer in native species than the more isolated Shetlands, with species like the hen harrier, short-eared owl, and red-throated diver (a form of Arctic loon) not frequently seen in the Shetlands.

Any general tour of the Orkneys will bring you into contact with thousands of birds, as well as Neolithic burial sites, cromlechs, dolmens, and other items with intriguing backgrounds and histories. A worthy tour operator is **Wild About,** 5 Clouston Corner, Stenness, Orkney KW17 3LD (© **01856/ 851-011**). Minivans will help in spotting birds whose breeding and mating habits will be discussed on the tours. The per-person cost is £17.50 ($26.25) for a full day, £11.50 ($17.25) for a half day. In summer, reserve in advance.

A bird-watching specialist is **Orkney Island Wildlife,** Shapinsay 12, Orkney KW17 2DY (© **01856/711-373**). Between May and November, it leads 5-day bird-watching tours that include full board, housing, and exposure to the fields, moors, and wetlands of Shapinsay and Orkney. Tours are conducted from a rustic croft that was upgraded and enlarged into a streamlined modern format in 1990. Your hosts are Paul and Louise Hollinrake, both qualified wardens at the Mill Dam Wetlands Reserve and accredited by the Royal Society for the Protection of Birds. Tours depart every morning around 9am (allowing participants to either sleep late or embark on sunrise expeditions of their own). Lunches are box-lunch affairs. Touring is by minivan or by inflatable boat, allowing close-up inspection of offshore skerries (small islets without vegetation) and sea caves. No more than six participants are allowed on any tour. All-inclusive rates are £550 to £660 ($825 to $990) per person for the 5-day/6-night experience.

During winter and early spring, the entire Solway shoreline, Loch Ryan, Wigtown Bay, and Auchencairn Bay areas are excellent locations for observing wintering wildfowl and waders. Inland, Galloway has a rich and varied range of bird life, including British barn owls, kestrels, tawnies, and merlins. Bird-watching fact sheets are available at tourist offices in Galloway.

CANOEING

Several canoe clubs offer instruction and advice. Supervising their activities is the **Scottish Canoe Association (SCA),** Caledonia House, South Gyle, Edinburgh EH12 9DH (© **0131/317-7314**). It coordinates all competitive canoeing events in Scotland, including slaloms, polo games, and white-water races. It also offers a handbook and a range of other publications, plus promotional material like its own magazine, *Scottish Paddler.* (An equivalent magazine published in England is *Canoe Focus.*)

HIKING & WALKING

Scotland is Valhalla for those who like to walk and hike across mountain and dale, coming to rest on the bonnie, bonnie banks of a loch.

In all Scotland, there are no finer long-distance footpaths than the **West Highland Way** and the **Southern Upland Way,** both previewed in chapter 1. One begins north of Glasgow in the town of Milngavie, the other in Portpatrick in Galloway. Information on these paths is provided by the **Scottish Tourist Board,** 23 Ravelston Terrace, Edinburgh EH4 3EU (© **0131/332-2433**). Nearly all bookstores in Scotland sell guides documenting these paths.

The **Borders** (see chapter 5, "The Borders & Galloway Regions") is one of the greatest places for walks. All tourist boards in the area provide a free guide, *Walking in the Scottish Borders,* detailing half-day scenic walks around the various towns. As mentioned, Scotland's longest footpath, the 212-mile (341km) **Southern Upland Way,** also extends through the Borders.

The magnificent coastline of **Galloway,** southwest of the Borders, is ideal for walks. Tourist offices distribute a free guide to 30 walks, *Walking in Dumfries and Galloway.* They also offer a helpful pamphlet called *Ranger-Led Walks and Events,* outlining scenic hikes through the forests of the southwest.

In central Scotland, the **Cairngorm region** offers the major concentration of ski resorts in the country, including Ben Macdui, the second highest peak in Britain at nearly 4,300 feet (1,304m). In the Cairngorm Ski Area, Cairngorm Rangers offer guided walks through the forest to both skilled and beginning hikers. The **Glenmore Forest Park Visitors Centre** (© 1479/861-220) dispenses information on great walks in the area. It's open daily from 9am to 5pm.

The best self-led tours of the Scottish Highlands and islands is offered by **Bespoke Highland Tours,** 14 Belmont Crescent, Glasgow (© 0141/ 334-9017). It has devised a series of treks, lasting from 3 to 12 days, including the **West Highland Way,** that take in the finest scenery in Scotland. Their tours are reasonably priced, ranging from £80 to £390 ($120 to $585).

John Fisher, The Old Inn, Strachur, Argyll (© 01369/860-712), specializes in guided walking and hiking holidays. Most of them last 6 days, with 7 nights' accommodation at a cost of £550 to £650 ($825 to $975). Groups are small, usually between four and eight persons. Highlights of these tours include treks across the isles of Mull and Iona. And with **North-West Frontiers,** 18A Braes, Ullapool (© 01854/612-628), you can explore remote glens, magnificent mountains and lochs, and isolated islands and beaches. You're likely to see seals, deer, and many species of birds, including divers and golden eagles. Unlike Bespoke (see above), these tours are led by experienced hikers who know the countryside like their backyard.

Some of the most memorable walks in Scotland are along **Loch Lomond** and the **Trossachs.** At tourist centers and various bookstores in Scotland, you can purchase a copy of *Walk Loch Lomond and the Trossachs* to guide you on your way.

An organization that can put you in touch with like-minded hikers is the **Ramblers Association (Scotland),** Crusader House, Haig Business Park, Markinch, Fife KY7 6AQ (© 01577/861-222). To book a rambling tour before you go to Scotland, contact the **English Lakeland Ramblers,** 18 Stuyvesant Oval, Suite 1A, New York, NY 10009 (© 212/505-1020; www.ramblers.com).

Offering guided walking and hiking tours on a daily basis from Edinburgh, **Walkabout Scotland,** 2 Rossie Place, Edinburgh (© 0131/661-7168; www.walkaboutscotland.com), specializes in jaunts through the Highlands. A different tour for each day of the week is offered, tackling different grades of walks. From backpackers to millionaires, the ages of clients range from 16 to 69. Longer walking holidays throughout Scotland can also be booked, including to such fabled spots as Glen Nevis, Glen Coe, Loch Lomond, and the Isle of Arran.

HORSEBACK RIDING & PONY TREKKING

Horseback riding and trekking through the panoramic countryside—from the Lowlands to the Highlands and through all the in-between lands—can be enjoyed by most everyone, from novices to experienced riders.

Although more adventurous riders prefer the hillier terrain of the Highlands, the Borders in the southeast (see chapter 5) is the best for horseback riding—in fact, it's often called Scotland's horse country. Its equivalent in the United States would be Kentucky. On the western coastline, Argyll (see chapter 7, "Argyll & the Southern Hebrides") is another great center for riding, taking in dramatic scenery. The Argyll Forest Park, stretching almost to Loch Fyne, encompasses 60,000 acres (24,300 hectares) and contains some of the lushest scenery in Scotland. It's a favorite for trails leading through forests to sea lochs cut deep into the park, evoking the fjords of Norway.

Pony trekking across moors and dales is reason enough to come to Scotland. Pony trekking originated as a job for Highland ponies that weren't otherwise engaged in toting dead deer off the hills during deer-stalking season. Most treks last from 2½ hours to a full day, and most centers have ponies suitable for most age groups. You'll find operators in Kirkudbright and on Shetland, plus several in the Hebrides.

MOUNTAINEERING

Mountain climbing can range from fair-weather treks over heather-clad hilltops to demanding climbs up rock faces in wintry conditions of snow and ice.

The **Southern Uplands,** the **offshore islands,** and the **Highlands** of Scotland contain the best mountaineering sites. Regardless of your abilities, treat the landscape with respect. The weather can turn foul during any season with almost no advance notice, creating dangerous conditions. If you're climbing rock faces, you should be familiar with basic techniques and the use of such specialized equipment as carabiners, crampons, ice axes, and ropes. Don't even consider climbing without proper instruction and equipment.

Ben Nevis is the highest (but by no means the most remote) peak in Scotland. Despite its loftiness at 4,406 feet (1,336m), it has attracted some daredevils who have driven cars and motorcycles to points near its top; one eccentric even arranged the transport of a dining table with formal dinner service and a grand piano.

If you want to improve your rock-climbing skills, consider joining a club or signing on for a mountaineering course at a climbing center maintained by the Scottish Sports Council. Also contact the **Mountaineering Council of Scotland,** Perth (© **01738/638-227;** www.mountaineering-scotland.org.uk). Membership allows overnight stays at the club's climbing huts on the island of Skye (in Glen Brittle), in the Cairngorms (at Glen Feshie), and near the high-altitude mountain pass at Glencoe. True rock-climbing aficionados looking to earn certification might contact the **Scottish Mountain Leader Training Board,** at Glenmore, Aviemore, Inverness-shire PH22 1QU (© **01479/861-248;** www.ukmtb.org).

SAILING & WATERSPORTS

Wherever you travel in Scotland, you're never far from the water. Windsurfing, canoeing, water-skiing, and sailing are just some of the activities available at a number of sailing centers and holiday parks. You'll find it easy to rent boats and equipment at any of the major resorts along Scotland's famous lakes.

4

Edinburgh & the Lothian Region

Edinburgh ✸✸✸ (pronounced *Edin*-burra) has been called one of Europe's fairest cities, the Athens of the North, and the gateway to central Scotland. You can use it as a base for excursions to the Borders, the Trossachs (Scotland's Lake District), the silver waters of Loch Lomond, and the Kingdom of Fife on the opposite shore of the Firth of Forth.

Edinburgh is filled with historic and literary association: John Knox, Mary Queen of Scots, Robert Louis Stevenson, Sir Arthur Conan Doyle, Alexander Graham Bell, Sir Walter Scott, and Bonnie Prince Charlie are all part of its past.

In modern times, the city has become famous as the scene of the ever-growing **Edinburgh International Festival,** with its action-packed list of cultural events. But remember the treasures of this ancient seat of Scottish royalty are available all year—in fact, when the festival-hoppers have gone home, the pace is more relaxed, the prices are lower, and the people themselves, under less pressure, return to their traditional hospitable nature.

Built on extinct volcanoes atop an inlet from the North Sea (the Firth of Forth) and enveloped by rolling hills, lakes (*lochs*), and forests, Edinburgh is a city made for walking. Its Old Town and New Town sport elegant streets, cobbled alleys, lovely squares, and enough circuses and crescents to rival Bath in England; from every hilltop, another panoramic view unfolds. Edinburgh's sunsets are spectacularly romantic—Scots call the fading evening light the "gloaming."

Edinburgh was once the cultural capital of the north, but it has lost that position to Glasgow. However, the lively capital is trying its best to regain its old reputation. In fact, if you could visit only two cities in all Great Britain, we'd say make it London first and Edinburgh second. But you may want to budget some time for side trips, too. Notable attractions on the doorstep of Edinburgh are the royal burgh of Linlithgow, where Mary Queen of Scots was born at Linlithgow Palace; the port of North Berwick (today a holiday resort); and lovely Dirleton, with its 13th-century castle ruins.

1 Essentials

ARRIVING

BY PLANE   Edinburgh is about an hour's flying time from London, 393 miles (633km) south. **Edinburgh Airport** (© **0131/333-1000**) is 6 miles (10km) west of the center, receiving flights from within the British Isles and the rest of Europe. Before heading into town, you might want to stop at the information and accommodations desk (© **0131/473-3800**). An Airlink bus makes the trip from the airport to the city center every 10 minutes, letting you off near

Waverley Bridge; the fare is £3.30 ($4.95) one-way or £5 ($7.50) round-trip, and the trip takes about 25 minutes. A taxi into the city will cost £14 ($21) or more, depending on traffic, and the ride will be about 25 minutes.

BY TRAIN   InterCity trains that link London with Edinburgh are fast and efficient, providing restaurant and bar service as well as air-conditioning. Trains from London's Kings Cross Station arrive in Edinburgh at **Waverley Station,** at the east end of Princes Street (© **0345/484-950** in London for information). Trains depart London every hour or so, taking about 4½ hours and costing £76 to £86 ($114 to $129) round-trip. Overnight trains have a sleeper berth, which you can rent for an extra £30 ($45).

BY BUS   The least expensive way to go from London to Edinburgh is by bus, but it's an 8-hour journey. It costs only about £20 ($30) one-way or £30 ($45) round-trip. **Scottish CityLink** coaches depart from London's Victoria Coach Station, delivering you to Edinburgh's **St. Andrew Square Bus Station,** St. Andrew Square (© **0990/808-080** for information).

BY CAR   Edinburgh is 46 miles (74km) east of Glasgow and 105 miles (169km) north of Newcastle-upon-Tyne in England. No express motorway links London and Edinburgh. The M1 from London takes you part of the way north, but you'll have to come into Edinburgh along secondary roads: A68 or A7 from the southeast, A1 from the east, or A702 from the north. The A71 or A8 comes in from the west, A8 connecting with M8 just west of Edinburgh; A90 comes down from the north over the Forth Road Bridge. Allow 8 hours or more for the drive north from London.

VISITOR INFORMATION

Edinburgh & Scotland Information Centre, Waverley Shopping Centre, 3 Princes St., at the corner of Princes Street and Waverley Bridge (© **0131/ 473-3800;** fax 0131/473-3881; www.edinburgh.org; Bus: 3, 7, 14, 31, 69), can give you sightseeing information and also help find lodgings. The center sells bus tours, theater tickets, and souvenirs of Edinburgh. It's open July and August, Monday through Saturday from 9am to 8pm and Sunday from 10am to 8pm; May, June, and September, Monday through Saturday from 9am to 7pm and Sunday from 10am to 7pm; and October to April, Monday through Saturday from 9am to 6pm and Sunday from 10am to 6pm. There's also an information and accommodations desk at Edinburgh Airport.

CITY LAYOUT

Edinburgh is divided into a New Town and an Old Town. Chances are, you'll find lodgings in the New Town and visit the Old Town only for dining, drinking, shopping, and sightseeing.

The **New Town,** with its world-famous **Princes Street,** came about in the 18th century in the Golden Age of Edinburgh. Everybody from Robert Burns to James Boswell visited in that era. The first building went up here in 1767, and by the end of the century, classical squares, streets, and town houses had been added. Princes Street is known for its shopping and also for its beauty, as it opens onto the Princes Street Gardens with panoramic views of the Old Town.

North of and running parallel to Princes Street is the New Town's second great street, **George Street.** It begins at Charlotte Square and runs east to St. Andrew Square. Directly north of George Street is another impressive thoroughfare, **Queen Street,** opening onto Queen Street Gardens on its north side.

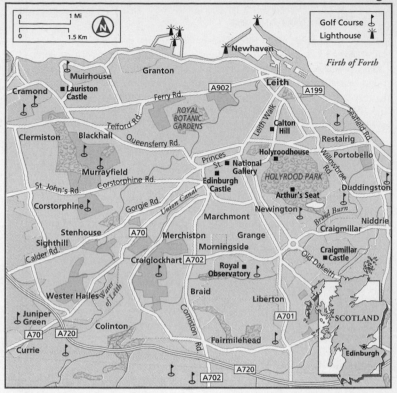

You'll also hear a lot about **Rose Street,** directly north of Princes Street—it boasts more pubs per square block than any other place in Scotland and is filled with shops and restaurants.

Seemingly everyone has heard of the **Royal Mile,** the main thoroughfare of the **Old Town,** beginning at Edinburgh Castle and running all the way to the Palace of Holyroodhouse. A famous street to the south of the castle is **Grass-market,** where convicted criminals were once hanged on the dreaded gallows.

THE NEIGHBORHOODS IN BRIEF

The Old Town This area is where Edinburgh began. Its backbone is the **Royal Mile,** a medieval thoroughfare stretching for about a mile from Edinburgh Castle running downhill to the Palace of Holyroodhouse. It's composed of four connected streets: Castlehill, Lawnmarket, High Street, and Canongate. "This is perhaps the largest, longest, and finest street for buildings and number of inhabitants in the world," or so wrote English author Daniel Defoe. The same might be said of the street today.

The New Town Lying below the Old Town, the New Town burst into full bloom between 1766 and 1840 and became one of the largest Georgian developments in the world. It takes in most of the northern half of the heart of the city, covering some 790 acres (320 hectares). With about 25,000

Tips **Finding an Address**

Edinburgh's streets often follow no pattern whatsoever, and both names and house numbers seem to have been created purposely to confuse. First, the city is checkered with innumerable squares, terraces, circuses, wynds, and closes, which will jut into or cross or overlap or interrupt whatever street you're trying to follow, usually without the slightest warning.

Then the house numbers run in sequences of odds or evens or run clockwise or counterclockwise as the wind blows—that is, when they exist at all. Many establishments don't use street numbers. (This is even truer when you leave Edinburgh and go to provincial towns.) Even though a road might run for a mile, some buildings on the street will be numbered and others will say only "Kings Road" or whatever, giving no number. Before heading out, get a detailed map of Edinburgh and ask for a location to be pinpointed; locals are generally glad to assist a bewildered foreigner. If you're looking for an address, try to get the name of the nearest cross street.

---

residents, it's the largest conservation area in all Britain. The New Town is made up of a network of squares, streets, terraces, and circuses, reaching from Haymarket in the west to Abbeyhill in the east. The New Town also goes from Canonmills on the northern perimeter down to Princes Street, its main artery, along the southern tier.

Marchmont About a mile south of High Street, this suburb borders a public park, the Meadows. It was constructed between 1869 and 1914 as a massive building program of new housing for people who could no longer afford to live in the New Town.

Bruntsfield This suburb to the west is named for Bruntsfield Links. Now a residential district, it was the ground on which James IV gathered the Scottish army he marched to its defeat at Flodden in 1513. Plague victims were once brought here for burial; now suburban gardens have grown over those graves. Many low-cost B&Bs are found in this area.

Churchill Churchill is known as "holy corner" because of the wide array of Scottish churches within its borders at the junctions of Colinton, Chamberlain, and Bruntsfield roads. These churches are primarily for local worshipers and not of artistic interest.

Leith The Port of Leith lies only a few miles north of Princes Street and is the city's major harbor, opening onto the Firth of Forth. The area is currently being gentrified, and visitors come here for the restaurants and pubs, many of which specialize in seafood. The port isn't what it used to be in terms of maritime might; its glory days were back when stevedores unloaded cargoes by hand.

Newhaven Newhaven is the fishing village adjacent to Leith. Founded in the 1400s, this former little harbor with its bustling fish market was greatly altered in the 1960s. Many of its "bow-tows" (a nickname for closely knit, clannish residents) were uprooted, like the Leithers, in a major gentrification program. Now many of the old houses have been restored, and the fishwife no longer goes from door to door hawking fish from her basket. The harbor is today mostly filled with pleasure craft instead of fishing boats. If your time is limited, you can skip this area, as its attractions are limited.

2 Getting Around

Because of its narrow lanes, wynds, and closes, you can only explore the Old Town in any depth on foot. Edinburgh is fairly convenient for the visitor who likes to walk, as most of the attractions are along the Royal Mile, Princes Street, or one of the major streets of the New Town.

BY BUS   The bus will probably be your chief method of transport. Exact change is required if you're paying your fare on the bus. The fare depends on the distance you ride, with a minimum fare of 80p ($1.20) for three stages or less and a maximum fare of £1.70 ($2.55) for 44 or more stages. (A stage isn't a stop, but a distance of about half a mile.) Children 5 to 15 are charged a flat rate of 50p (75¢), but teenagers 13 to 15 must carry a **teen card** (available where bus tickets are sold) as proof of age. A **family ticket** for two adults and four children goes for £6 ($9) a day; another for £1.60 ($2.40) operates from 6:30pm onward. The **Edinburgh Freedom Ticket** allows 1 day of unlimited travel on city buses at a cost of £1.50 to £2.20 ($2.25 to $3.30) for adults and £1.60 ($2.40) for children. A **RideCard** season ticket allows unlimited travel on all buses. For adults, the price is £10.50 ($15.75) for 1 week and £30.50 ($45.75) for 4 weeks; tickets for children are £6.50 ($9.75) for 1 week and £18 ($27) for 4 weeks. Travel must begin on a Sunday.

You can get these tickets and further information at the **Waverley Bridge Transport Office,** Waverley Bridge (© 0131/554-4494; Bus: 3, 31), open daily from 6:30am to 10:30pm; or at the Hanover Street office (Bus: 3, 31), open daily from 9am to 7pm. For timetables, call © 0131/555-6363.

BY TAXI   You can hail a taxi or pick one up at a taxi stand. Meters begin at £1.80 ($2.70) and increase at 20p (30¢) every 52 seconds. Taxi ranks are at Hanover Street, North Street, Andrew Street, Waverley Station, Haymarket Station, and Lauriston Place. Fares are displayed on the meter and charges posted, including extra charges for night drivers or destinations outside the city limits. To call for a taxi, try **City Cabs** (© 0131/228-1211).

BY CAR   Don't think about driving in Edinburgh—it's a tricky business, even for natives. Parking is expensive and difficult to find. Metered parking is available, but you'll need the right change and have to watch out for traffic wardens who issue tickets. Some zones are marked PERMIT HOLDERS ONLY—your vehicle will be towed if you have no permit. A yellow line along the curb indicates no parking. Major parking lots (car parks) are at Castle Terrace, convenient for Edinburgh Castle and the west end of Princes Street; at Lothian Road, near the west end of Princes Street; at St. John Hill, convenient to the Royal Mile, the

---

Tips Look Both Ways!

Remember, you're in Great Britain, and cars drive on the left. Always look both ways before stepping off a curb. Lots of new arrivals practically commit suicide crossing the street because they forget which way to look for traffic.

west end of Princes Street, and Waverley Station; and at St. James Centre (entrance from York Place), close to the east end of Princes Street.

You may want a rental car for touring the countryside or for heading onward. Many agencies grant discounts to those who reserve in advance (see chapter 2, "Planning Your Trip to Scotland," for more information). Most will accept your U.S. or Canadian driver's license, provided you've held it for more than a year and are over 21. The major car rental companies maintain offices at the Edinburgh Airport. Call **Avis** (© **0131/333-1866**), **Hertz** (© **0131/344-3260**), or **Europcar** (© **0131/333-2588**) for information.

BY BICYCLE   Biking isn't a good idea for most visitors because the city is constructed on a series of high ridges and terraces. You may, however, want to rent a bike for exploring the flatter countryside around the city. Try **Central Cycle Hire,** 13 Lochrin Place (© **0131/228-6333;** Bus: 10), off Home Street in Tollcross, near the Cameo Cinema. Charges range from £10 to £18 ($15 to $27) per day. A deposit of £50 to £100 ($75 to $150) is imposed. The shop is open June to September, Monday through Saturday from 9:30am to 6pm and Sunday from noon to 7pm; and October to May, Monday through Saturday from 10am to 5:30pm. **Edinburgh Cycle Hire and Safaris,** 29 Blackfriars St. (© **0131/556-5560**), offers day rentals from £15 ($22.50) and weekly rentals from £35 to £70 ($52.50 to $105). It's open daily from 10am to 7pm (later in summer) and requires a credit card for a deposit. City and Highland tours can be arranged.

ⓔ *FAST FACTS:* Edinburgh

American Express The office is at 139 Princes St. (© **0131/225-7881;** Bus: 3, 39, 69), 5 blocks from Waverley Station. It's open Monday through Friday from 9am to 5:30pm and Saturday from 9am to 4pm; on Thursday, the office opens at 9:30am.

Babysitters The most reliable services are provided by Guardians Baby Sitting Service, 13 Eton Terrace (© **0131/337-4150**), and Care Connections, 45 Barclay Place (© **01506/856-106**).

Business Hours In Edinburgh, banks are usually open Monday through Wednesday from 9:30am to 3:45pm and Thursday and Friday from 9:30am to 5 or 5:30pm. Shops are generally open Monday through Saturday from 10am to 5:30 or 6pm; on Thursday, stores are open to 8pm. Offices are open Monday through Friday from 9am to 5pm.

Currency Exchange Try the **Clydesdale Bank** at 5 Waverley Bridge and at Waverley Market.

Dentists If you have a dental emergency, go to the **Edinburgh Dental Institute,** 39 Lauriston Place (© **0131/536-4900;** Bus: 23, 41), open Monday through Friday from 9am to 3pm.

Doctors You can seek help from the **Edinburgh Royal Infirmary,** 1 Lauriston Place (© **0131/536-1000;** Bus: 23, 41). Medical attention is available 24 hours.

Embassies & Consulates See "Fast Facts: Scotland," in chapter 2.

Emergencies Call © **999** in an emergency to summon the police, an ambulance, or firefighters.

Hospitals See "Doctors," above.

Internet Access The **International Telecom Centre**, 52 High St. (© **0131/559-7114**; Bus: 1, 6), charges £1 ($1.50) for 15 minutes. Open daily from 9am to 10pm.

Laundry/Dry Cleaning Try **Capital Launderette & Drycleaners**, 208 Dalkeith Rd. (© **0131/667-0825**; Bus: 14, 21, 33, 82), open Monday through Friday from 8:30am to 5pm and Saturday from 8:30am to 4pm. For your dry cleaning needs, go to **Johnson's Cleaners**, 23 Frederick St. (© **0131/225-8095**; Bus: 23, 41), open Monday through Friday from 8am to 5:30pm and Saturday from 8am to 4pm.

Luggage Storage/Lockers You can store luggage in lockers at **Waverley Station**, at Waverley Bridge (© **0131/550-2333**), open Monday through Saturday from 7am to 11pm and Sunday from 8am to 11pm.

Newspapers Published since 1817, *The Scotsman* is a quality daily newspaper. Along with national and international news, it's strong on the arts.

Pharmacies There are no 24-hour drugstores (called chemists or pharmacies) in Edinburgh. The major drugstore is **Boots**, 48 Shandwick Place (© **0131/225-6757**; Bus: 3, 31), open Monday through Friday from 8am to 9pm, Saturday from 8am to 7pm, and Sunday from 10am to 4pm.

Police See "Emergencies," above.

Post Office The Edinburgh Branch Post Office, St. James's Centre, is open Monday through Friday from 9am to 5:30pm and Saturday from 9am to noon. For postal information and customer service, call © **0131/550-8232**.

Restrooms These are found at rail stations, terminals, restaurants, hotels, pubs, and department stores. Don't hesitate to use the system of public toilets, often marked wc, at strategic corners and squares throughout the city. They're perfectly safe and clean, but likely to be closed late in the evening.

Safety Edinburgh is generally safer than Glasgow—in fact, it's one of Europe's safest capitals for a visitor to stroll at any time of day or night. But that doesn't mean crimes, especially muggings, don't occur. They do, largely because of Edinburgh's shockingly large drug problem.

Weather For weather forecasts and road conditions, call © **0891/505-322**. This number also provides weather information for Lothian, the Borders, Tayside, and Fife.

3 Accommodations

Edinburgh offers a full range of accommodations throughout the year. However, it should come as no surprise that during the 3-week period of the Edinburgh International Festival in August, the hotels fill up; if you're coming at that time, be sure to reserve far in advance.

Edinburgh & Scotland Information Centre, Waverley Shopping Centre, 3 Princes St., at the corner of Princes Street and Waverley Bridge (© **0131/473-3800**; fax 0131/473-3881; www.edinburgh.org; Bus: 3, 7, 14, 31, 69), compiles a list of small hotels, guesthouses, and private homes with rates of as little as £18 ($27) per person. A £4 ($6) booking fee and a 10% deposit are

Edinburgh Accommodations & Dining

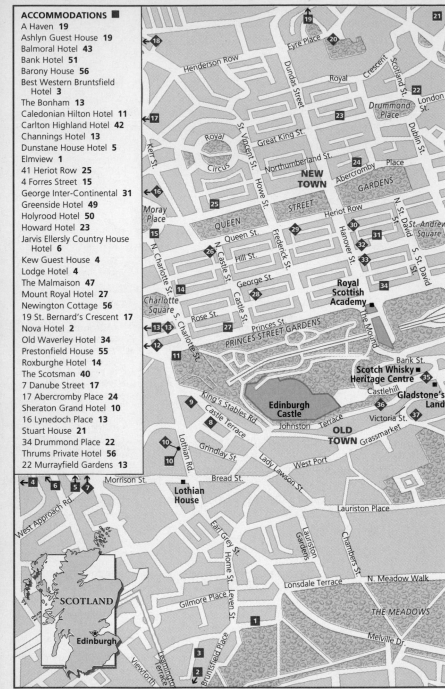

ACCOMMODATIONS ■

A Haven **19**
Ashlyn Guest House **19**
Balmoral Hotel **43**
Bank Hotel **51**
Barony House **56**
Best Western Bruntsfield Hotel **3**
The Bonham **13**
Caledonian Hilton Hotel **11**
Carlton Highland Hotel **42**
Channings Hotel **13**
Dunstane House Hotel **5**
Elmview **1**
41 Heriot Row **25**
4 Forres Street **15**
George Inter-Continental **31**
Greenside Hotel **49**
Holyrood Hotel **50**
Howard Hotel **23**
Jarvis Ellersly Country House Hotel **6**
Kew Guest House **4**
Lodge Hotel **4**
The Malmaison **47**
Mount Royal Hotel **27**
Newington Cottage **56**
19 St. Bernard's Crescent **17**
Nova Hotel **2**
Old Waverley Hotel **34**
Prestonfield House **55**
Roxburghe Hotel **14**
The Scotsman **40**
7 Danube Street **17**
17 Abercromby Place **24**
Sheraton Grand Hotel **10**
16 Lynedoch Place **13**
Stuart House **21**
34 Drummond Place **22**
Thrums Private Hotel **56**
22 Murrayfield Gardens **13**

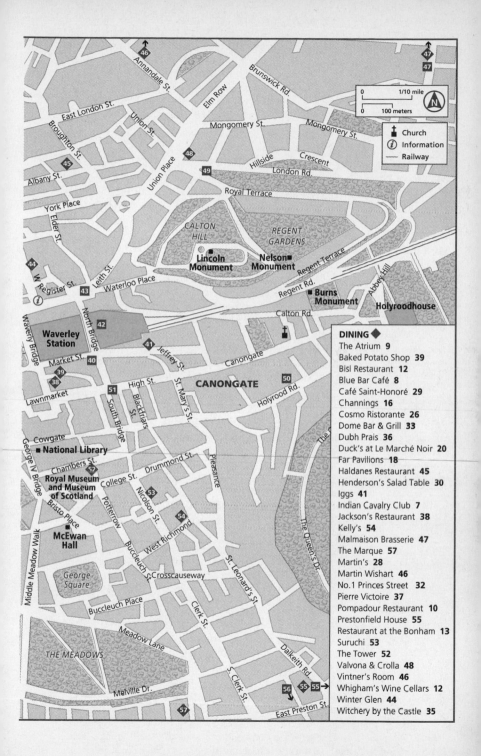

DINING ◆

The Atrium **9**
Baked Potato Shop **39**
Bisl Restaurant **12**
Blue Bar Café **8**
Café Saint-Honoré **29**
Channings **16**
Cosmo Ristorante **26**
Dome Bar & Grill **33**
Dubh Prais **36**
Duck's at Le Marché Noir **20**
Far Pavilions **18**
Haldanes Restaurant **45**
Henderson's Salad Table **30**
Iggs **41**
Indian Cavalry Club **7**
Jackson's Restaurant **38**
Kelly's **54**
Malmaison Brasserie **47**
The Marque **57**
Martin's **28**
Martin Wishart **46**
No.1 Princes Street **32**
Pierre Victoire **37**
Pompadour Restaurant **10**
Prestonfield House **55**
Restaurant at the Bonham **13**
Suruchi **53**
The Tower **52**
Valvona & Crolla **48**
Vintner's Room **46**
Whigham's Wine Cellars **12**
Winter Glen **44**
Witchery by the Castle **35**

charged. Allow about 4 weeks' notice, especially in summer and during the festival weeks.

If you have an early flight out and need a hotel convenient to the airport, consider the 259-unit **Swallow Royal Scot,** 111 Glasgow Rd. (© **0131/334-9191**),
off A8 on Edinburgh's western outskirts. It offers doubles for £145 to £185
($217.50 to $277.50), including breakfast. Facilities include an indoor pool,
gym, sauna, and restaurant.

IN OR NEAR THE CENTER
VERY EXPENSIVE
Balmoral Hotel 🎔🎔🎔   This legendary place opened in 1902 as the grandest
hotel in the north of Britain. After a $35-million restoration, it reopened in
1991 under a new name, the Balmoral. Almost directly above the Waverley Rail
Station, it features a soaring clock tower many locals consider one of their city's
landmarks. Kilted doormen and a bagpiper supply the Scottish presence. Furnished with reproduction pieces, the guest rooms are distinguished and rather
large—a graceful reminder of Edwardian sprawl. Each unit comes with a com-
modious bathroom with combination tub/shower. Dining options include the
elegant No. 1 Princes Street (see "Dining," later in this chapter) and the more
convivial brasserie Hadrian's. Afternoon tea is served in the high-ceilinged Palm
Court. Foremost among the several bar areas is N.B.'s, a Scottish pub with an
entrance directly on Princes Street.

Princes St., Edinburgh EH2 2EQ. © **800/225-5843** in the U.S., or 0131/556-2414. Fax 0131/557-3747. www.
rfhotels.com. 188 units. Apr–Oct £260 ($390) double, from £430 ($645) suite; off-season £230 ($345)
double, from £430 ($645) suite year-round. AE, DC, MC, V. Valet parking £15 ($22.50). Bus: 50. **Amenities:**
Restaurant, bar; pool; health club; room service. *In room:* A/C, TV, minibar, hair dryer.

The Bonham 🎔🎔   One of Edinburgh's newest and most stylish hotels occupies three connected town houses that functioned since the 19th century as a
nursing home and as dorms for the local university. In 1998, all that changed
when a team of entrepreneurs poured millions of pounds into its refurbishment,
pumped up the style level, and outfitted each high-ceilinged guest room in a hip
blend of old and new. Each has an individual theme, plush upholsteries, and a
TV with a keyboard hooked up to the Internet—the first setup of its kind in
Europe. Bathrooms are cutting edge, with checkered floors, Molton Brown toiletries, and combination tub/showers. The Restaurant at the Bonham is
reviewed under "Dining," later in this chapter.

35 Drumsheugh Gardens, Edinburgh EH3 7RN. © **0131/623-6060.** Fax 0131/226-6080. www.thebonham.
com. 48 units. £165–£295 ($247.50–$442.50) double; £255–£295 ($382.50–$442.50) suite. AE, MC, V. Bus:
41 or 42. **Amenities:** Restaurant, bar; room service; babysitting; laundry/dry cleaning. *In room:* TV, DVD, CD
player, dataport, minibar, coffeemaker, hair dryer, iron.

Caledonian Hilton Hotel 🎔🎔   Completely renovated in 1991, the hotel
remains one of the city's landmarks and offers commanding views over Edinburgh Castle and the Princes Street Gardens. The public rooms are reminiscent
of Edwardian splendor, and the guest rooms (many of which are exceptionally
spacious) are conservatively styled with reproduction furniture. The fifth-floor
rooms are the smallest. Bathrooms come with combination tub/showers.
Although the accommodations are superior to those of many first-class hotels in
Edinburgh, the Caledonian lacks the leisure facilities of its major competitor, the
Balmoral. The hotel contains a traditional pub, Henry J. Beans, and Chisholms
Bar. More formal meals are served in Pompadour Restaurant (see "Dining," later
in this chapter). A traditional tea is featured in the high-ceilinged lounge.

Princes St., Edinburgh EH1 2AB. © **0131/222-8888.** Fax 0131/222-8889. www.hilton.com. 249 units. From £235 ($352.50) double; from £360 ($540) suite. Children under 16 stay free in parents' room. AE, DC, DISC, MC, V. Parking £7.50 ($11.25). Bus: 33. **Amenities:** 3 restaurants, 2 bars; pool; health club; spa; Jacuzzi; sauna; concierge; room service; laundry/dry cleaning. *In room:* TV, minibar, coffeemaker, hair dryer, iron.

Carlton Highland Hotel ⍟ *(Kids*

A century ago, this was one of Edinburgh's leading department stores, with 4 of its 10 stories below sidewalk level. In 1984, the baronial pile was converted into a plush hotel. Its Victorian turrets, Flemish gables, and severe gray stonework rise from a corner on the Royal Mile, near Waverley Station. The interior is a surprisingly bright and airy modern space— each guest room has a kind of Scandinavian simplicity, most with matching tartan drapes and spreads. Though adequate, the bathrooms tend to be small. The restaurant is designed like a 19th-century library and offers an international and Scottish menu. A pianist entertains in the lounge, and the coffee bar called Central Perk is based on the cafe in the sitcom *Friends.* The hotel is especially inviting to families.

19 North Bridge, Edinburgh EH1 1SD. © **0131/556-7277.** Fax 0131/556-2691. 197 units. £193–£240 ($289.50–$360) double, £270 ($405) suite. Rates include breakfast. Children under 15 stay free in parents' room. AE, DC, MC, V. Parking £6 ($9). Bus: 55 or 80. **Amenities:** Restaurant, bar; pool; gym; solarium; 2 squash courts; Jacuzzi; aerobics studio. *In room:* TV, coffeemaker, hair dryer.

George Inter-Continental ⍟

Designed by famed architect Robert Adam and only yards from St. Andrew Square, the city's financial center, the George opened in 1755, housed the trading room of the Caledonian Insurance Company in 1845, and was enlarged and graced with a new facade in 1881. A new wing was added in 1972, and the place has thrived ever since as a member of the Inter-Continental hotel group. The public rooms have retained the style, elegance, and old-fashioned comfort of a country house. The guest rooms come in various sizes and have undergone frequent refurbishments. The best units, opening onto views, are those on the fourth floor and above in the new wing. Bathrooms contain combination tub/showers. The Carver's Table, with some of Adam's design still intact, has for almost a century fed diners on prime Scottish beef, lamb, and pork. Le Chambertin is the choice for gourmet French fare.

19–21 George St., Edinburgh EH2 2PB. © **800/327-0200** in the U.S., or 0131/225-1251. Fax 0131/226-5644. www.interconti.com. 195 units. £199–£230 ($298.50–$345) double; £499–£675 ($748.50–$1,012.50) suite. AE, DC, MC, V. Bus: 41 or 42. **Amenities:** 2 restaurants, bar; concierge; room service; dry cleaning. *In room:* TV, minibar, coffeemaker, hair dryer.

The Howard ⍟⍟

These three Georgian terrace houses (ca. 1770–825) combine to form one of Edinburgh's finest hotels. The decor is a mix of traditional and modern, with antiques and reproductions. The spacious guest rooms have top-notch Georgian-style furnishings and elaborate bathrooms with combination tub/showers. The elegant No. 36 restaurant specializes in smoked Scottish salmon and pan-fried Scottish sirloin.

34 Great King St., Edinburgh EH3 6QH. © **0131/557-3500.** Fax 0131/557-6515. www.thehoward.com. 15 units. £225–£280 ($337.50–$420) double; £335 ($502.50) suite. Rates include breakfast. AE, DC, MC, V. Bus: 13, 23, 27, or C5. **Amenities:** Restaurant, bar; concierge; room service; babysitting; laundry/dry cleaning. *In room:* TV, hair dryer.

The Scotsman ⍟⍟⍟

Located on the historic North Bridge, only minutes from the Royal Mile and Princes Street, this is one of the brightest and most stylish hotels to open in Edinburgh in many a year. Its name honors the famous newspaper that was published here for nearly a century. One reviewer noted when it opened: "Think native son Sir Arthur Conan Doyle getting a reverent makeover from Gucci's Tom Ford." Traditional styling and cutting-edge design are harmoniously wed in the 1904 baronial limestone pile, a city landmark since it was first constructed. Guest rooms, in honor of their former roles as newspaper offices, are categorized by size and given masthead ranks such as assistant editor, editor, or publisher. They include state-of-the-art bathrooms with combination tub/showers and such extras as two-way service closets, which means your laundry is picked up virtually unnoticed. Our favorite retreat here is Room 399, a cozy bar named for its number of single-malt whiskies.

20 N. Bridge St., Edinburgh EH1 1XT. © 0131/556-5565. Fax 0131/652-3652. www.thescotsmanhotel.com. 68 units. £149–£275 ($223.50–$412.50) double; from £300 ($450) suite. AE, MC, V. Bus: 7, 8, 21, 31, or 33. **Amenities:** 2 restaurants, bar; pool; health spa; exercise room; salon; room service; massage; babysitting; laundry/dry cleaning. *In room:* TV, minibar, hair dryer, safe.

Sheraton Grand Hotel ☆☆
This former railway siding, a short walk from Princes Street, is now a six-story postmodern structure housing a glamorous hotel and an office complex. The hotel is elegant, with soaring public rooms and carpeting in tones of thistle and mauve. Boasting a central location and a well-chosen staff, this is the most appealing modern hotel in the capital. The spacious, well-furnished guest rooms have double-glazed windows; glamorous suites are available, as are rooms for nonsmokers and travelers with disabilities. The castle-view rooms on the top three floors are the best. Bathrooms contain combination tub/showers. The main restaurant, with views of the Festival Square Fountain, presents well-prepared meals and a lavish Sunday buffet. The plushly modern cocktail bar is a favorite rendezvous for locals.

1 Festival Sq., Edinburgh EH3 9SR. © 800/325-3535 in the U.S. and Canada, or 0131/229-9131. Fax 0131/228-4510. www.sheraton.com. 278 units. June–Sept £240–£260 ($360–$390) double, from £350 ($525) suite; off-season £220 ($330) double, £315 ($472.50) suite. Children under 17 stay free in parents' room. AE, DC, MC, V. Parking £8 ($12). Bus: 4, 15, or 44. **Amenities:** 2 restaurants, bar; leisure center with pool; gym; Jacuzzi; sauna; concierge; business center; room service; babysitting; laundry/dry cleaning. *In room:* A/C, TV, dataport, minibar, coffeemaker, hair dryer.

EXPENSIVE

Bank Hotel ☆ (Value)
This simple hotel offers better value than many of its competitors in this congested neighborhood beside the Royal Mile. Until around 1990, it was a branch of the Royal Bank of Scotland, and the past is still evident in its bulky, no-nonsense design. High ceilings, simple furnishings, and king-size beds provide comfort; all guest rooms have shower-only bathrooms.

Royal Mile at 1–3 S. Bridge St., Edinburgh EH1 1LL. © 0131/556-9043. Fax 0131/558-1362. www.festival-inns.co.uk. 9 units. £120 ($180) double. Rates include breakfast. AE, DC, MC, V. Nearby parking £6 ($9). Bus: 4, 15, 31, or 100. **Amenities:** Bar; laundry service. *In room:* TV, coffeemaker, hair dryer.

Channings ☆☆
Five Edwardian terrace houses combine to create this hotel, 7 blocks north of Dean Village in a tranquil residential area. Although it's a 5-minute drive from the city center, it maintains the atmosphere of a Scottish country house, with oak paneling, ornate fireplaces, molded ceilings, and antiques. The guest rooms are in a modern style; the front units get the views, but the rear ones get the quiet. The most desirable rooms are the "Executives," most of which have bay windows and wingback chairs. Even if you're not a guest, consider a meal here, as Channings offers some of the best hotel food in Edinburgh (see "Dining," later in this chapter).

15 S. Learmonth Gardens, Edinburgh EH4 1EZ. © 0131/332-3232. Fax 0131/332-9631. www.channings. co.uk. 46 units. £175–£240 ($262.50–$360) double; £235 ($352.50) garden suite. Rates include breakfast. Children under 15 stay free in parents' room. AE, DC, MC, V. Bus: 41 or 42. **Amenities:** Restaurant, bar; concierge; room service; babysitting; dry cleaning. *In room:* TV, dataport, coffeemaker, hair dryer.

Holyrood Hotel ✦✦✦ We prefer this deluxe charmer to the grand palace hotels of Edinburgh. Holyrood launched itself into the millennium by being proclaimed "Hotel of the Year for Scotland" by Automobile Association. This impressive and exceedingly stylish hotel stands near the Scottish Parliament, the Palace of Holyroodhouse, and Dynamic Earth, and is only 5 minutes from Princes Street. Bedrooms are luxurious, with deluxe furnishings, elegant toiletries, and combination tub/showers. The Club Floor is one of the best retreats in Edinburgh for luxury-minded guests: It has its own private elevator, lounge, and library along with butler and business services.

Holyrood Rd., Edinburgh EH8 6AE. ℂ 0131/550-4500. Fax 0131/550-4545. www.macdonaldhotels.co.uk/holyrood-hotel. 157 units. £90–£116 ($135–$174) double. AE, DC, MC, V. Bus: 25. **Amenities:** Restaurant, bar; indoor pool; gym; solarium; Jacuzzi; sauna; beauty treatment rooms. *In room:* A/C, TV, minibar, hair dryer, safe.

Mount Royal Hotel ✦ The Mount Royal, a remake of an 1860s hotel, is right in the middle of Princes Street. A modern world emerges as you climb the spiral staircase or take an elevator to the second floor, with its reception rooms and lounges and floor-to-ceiling windows opening onto views of the Old Town and the castle. There aren't a lot of frills, but the comfort is genuine in the streamlined guest rooms. Bathrooms contain combination tub/showers. Be aware this is a tour-group favorite. The lounge, with views of the Scott Memorial and Princes Street, provides a wide range of savory and sweet snacks and beverages throughout the day.

53 Princes St., Edinburgh EH2 2DG. ℂ 0131/225-7161. Fax 0131/220-4671. 158 units. £145–£165 ($217.50–$247.50) double; £170–£185 ($255–$277.50) triple or family room. AE, DC, MC, V. Bus: 15 or 100. **Amenities:** Restaurant, bar; room service; laundry/dry cleaning. *In room:* TV, coffeemaker, hair dryer.

Old Waverley Hotel ✦ Opposite Waverley Station, the Old Waverley dates from 1848, when the seven-floor structure was built to celebrate the then-newfangled railroads. The lounges have been given a contemporary look. The recently refurbished guest rooms are well maintained and comfortable; some look onto Princes Street and the castle. Each unit comes with a combination tub/shower. The hotel also has a good carvery-style restaurant.

43 Princes St., Edinburgh EH2 2BY. ℂ 0131/556-4648. Fax 031/557-6316. oldwaverlyreservations@paramount-hotels.co.uk. 66 units. £160 ($240) double. Rates include breakfast. AE, DC, MC, V. Parking £6 ($9) for 12 hrs. Bus: 15 or 100. **Amenities:** Restaurant, bar; room service; dry cleaning. *In room:* TV, hair dryer.

Prestonfield House ✦✦ The Prestonfield, rising in Jacobean splendor above 13 acres (5.3 hectares) of grounds and a 15-minute drive from the center, is more celebrated as a restaurant than as a hotel. It was designed by Sir William Bruce, who also designed Holyroodhouse. Guests appreciate the traditional atmosphere and 1680s architecture as well as the peacocks and Highland cattle that strut and stroll across the grounds. The spacious bedrooms are decorated in country-house style and open onto a view of Arthur's Seat, a golf course, and the gardens. In 1997, the five rooms in the main house were supplemented by a three-story annex that matches the original structure; these up-to-date rooms get lots of sun thanks to the large windows. Each unit comes with a combination tub/shower. The hotel has one of the city's finest dining rooms (see "Dining," later in this chapter).

Priestfield Rd., Edinburgh EH16 5UT. ℂ 0131/668-3346. Fax 0131/668-3976. www.prestonfieldhouse.com. 31 units. £145–£225 ($217.50–$337.50) double; £290 ($435) suite. Rates include breakfast. AE, DC, MC, V. Free parking. Bus: 21 or 33. **Amenities:** Restaurant, two bars; concierge; room service; babysitting; laundry/dry cleaning. *In room:* TV, coffeemaker, hair dryer.

Roxburghe Hotel ⓕ   The heart of the Roxburghe is a stately gray-stone–Robert Adam town house on a tree-filled square, a short walk from Princes Street. The atmosphere is traditional, reflected in the drawing room with its ornate ceiling and woodwork, antique furnishings, and tall arched windows. In 1999, the hotel was enlarged into two neighboring buildings, tripling the original number of guest rooms, which vary in size. The largest are in the original building and maintain features like their imposing fireplaces. The new rooms have more recent furnishings and more up-to-date plumbing. All come with a combination tub/shower. The elegant Consort Restaurant is a good place to congregate for drinks.

38 Charlotte Sq. (at George St.), Edinburgh EH2 4HG. ⓒ 0131/225-3921. Fax 0131/220-2518. 197 units. £149–£195 ($223.50–$292.50) double; from £250 ($375) suite. Children under 14 stay free in parents' room. AE, DC, MC, V. Parking £4.50 ($6.75). Bus: 100. **Amenities:** 2 restaurants, 2 bars; pool; gym; sauna; room service; babysitting; laundry/dry cleaning. *In room:* TV, minibar, coffeemaker, hair dryer.

17 Abercromby Place   Run by the popular Eirlys Lloyd, this is one of the city's most upmarket B&Bs, set a 5-minute walk north of Princes Street. The gray-stone terrace house was the 1820s home of William Playfair, who designed many of Edinburgh's landmarks. While some of the guest rooms are bigger than others, they're all of an acceptable size, painted in distinct colors and furnished with antiques. Bathrooms come with combination tub/showers. Evening meals can be arranged with prior notice. No smoking is permitted.

17 Abercromby Place, Edinburgh EH3 6LB. ⓒ 0131/557-8036. Fax 0131/558-3453. www.abercrombyhouse. com. 10 units. £90–£120 ($135–$180) double. Rates include breakfast. MC, V. Free parking. Bus: 15 or 100. *In room:* TV, coffeemaker, hair dryer.

MODERATE
A Haven   A Haven is a semi-detached gray-stone Victorian, a 15-minute walk or a 5-minute bus ride north of the rail station in an up-and-coming neighborhood. The guest rooms are of various sizes (the biggest on the second floor) and outfitted with traditional furnishings and shower-only bathrooms. Some units in back overlook the Firth of Forth, and those in front open onto views of Arthur's Seat. Ronnie Murdock extends a Scottish welcome in this family-type place. He has a licensed bar, but breakfast is the only meal served.

180 Ferry Rd., Edinburgh, EH6 4NS. ⓒ 0131/554-6559. Fax 0131/554-5252. www.a-haven.co.uk. 14 units. £60–£99 ($90–$148.50) double. Rates include breakfast. AE, MC, V. Free parking. Bus: 1, 6, 7, 11, 14, 25, C3, 17, 14A, 25A, or 55. **Amenities:** Bar. *In room:* TV, dataport, hair dryer, coffeemaker, iron.

41 Heriot Row   This stone-fronted town house was built in 1817 on what was then one of Edinburgh's most prestigious residential streets. Today, it's the home of Erlend and Hélène Clouston, who make an event out of breakfasts and are especially proud of the fenced-in park across the street (guests can gain access to it); its decorative pond is said to have inspired Robert Louis Stevenson while he was writing *Treasure Island*. The furnishings are attractive and upscale, with unusual prints, exposed flagstone floors, and antique rugs and furnishings. The guest rooms have brass headboards, unusual books, and small, shower-only bathrooms.

41 Heriot Row, Edinburgh EH3 6ES. ⓒ and fax 0131/225-3113. www.wwwonderful.net. 2 units. £85–£95 ($127.50–$142.50) double with bathroom. Rates include breakfast. No credit cards. Bus: 4. *In room:* Coffeemaker, hair dryer, no phone.

4 Forres Street ⓚ   Behind a granite facade in the commercial heart of town, a 2-minute walk from Princes Street, this cozy B&B dates back to

1825. A sweeping staircase leads up to the Yellow, Cream, and Pink Rooms, high-ceilinged and very large. (The Cream Room has the largest bathroom, with its own Jacuzzi.) Less spacious, but still comfortable, are the Blue and Green Rooms. Unlike many other Edinburgh guesthouses, this one welcomes kids over 10. No smoking is permitted.

4 Forres St., Edinburgh EH3 6BJ. ℂ 0131/220-5073. www.aboutscotland.co.uk/edin/forres.html. 5 units. £80–£100 ($120–$150) double. Rates include breakfast. MC, V. Bus: 82. In room: TV, coffeemaker, hair dryer.

19 St. Bernard's Crescent   One of the city's most appealing guesthouses occupies the grand home of William Balfour, owner of Edinburgh's Theatre School of Dance and Drama. It was built as an architectural showplace in the early 1800s by the son of Sir Henry Raeburn, one of Scotland's most prominent portraitists. It has grand Doric pillars, a magnificent sandstone staircase, and a distinguished collection of 18th- and 19th-century furniture. Guests enjoy access to the salons and sitting rooms (site of a grand piano). The midsize guest rooms are comfortably appointed, often with four-poster beds (most with shower only). No smoking is permitted.

19 St. Bernard's Crescent, Edinburgh EH4 1NR. ℂ and fax 0131/332-6162. www.aboutedinburgh.com/stbernards/index.html. 3 units. £50–£90 ($75–$135) double. Rates include continental or full Scottish breakfast. MC, V. Bus: 24 or 34. In room: No phone.

7 Danube Street ✦   This 1825 B&B, run by Fiona and Colin Mitchell-Rose, is in Stockbridge, a stylish residential neighborhood a 10-minute walk north of the commercial center. It was designed by architect James Milne and was once the home of painter Horatio McCulloch. The public rooms and spacious guest rooms boast artfully draped chintzes. The most desirable room has a four-poster bed and direct access to the garden. All units are well stocked with such sundries as perfumed soaps, adapters, dental floss, and nail files, along with combination tub/showers. A lavish breakfast in the formal dining room may include venison sausages, omelets made from free-range eggs, homemade scones, and jams and marmalades put up by Fiona. No smoking is permitted.

7 Danube St., Edinburgh EH4 1NN. ℂ 0131/332-2755. Fax 0131/343-3648. www.aboutedinburgh.com/danube. 5 units. £95 ($142.50) double. Rates include breakfast. MC, V. Free nearby parking. Bus: 28. In room: TV, coffeemaker, hair dryer, iron.

16 Lynedoch Place   This stone-fronted 1821 Georgian row house, run by affable hosts Andrew and Susie Hamilton, has a flower-filled front garden, unusual for a house of this type. Inside are high ceilings with deep cove moldings, a cantilevered staircase illuminated by a glassed-in cupola, and family antiques. The midsize guest rooms are cozy and decorated with charm (some with shower only). The elaborate breakfasts are served in a formal dining room. Andrew is an expert in planning itineraries through the Highlands, thanks to the time he spent there as a member of the elite Black Watch Infantry.

16 Lynedoch Place, Edinburgh EH3 7PY. ℂ 0131/225-5507. Fax 0131/236-4185. susie.lynedoch@btinternet.com. 5 units. £70–£100 ($105–$150) double. Rates include breakfast. MC, V. Bus: 19. In room: TV, no phone.

Stuart House   At the western end of Claremont Street, in one of the dozens of nearly identical row houses, is this charming B&B. Convenient to the commercial center, it offers modernized, average-size, high-ceilinged rooms that retain many of their original 1830 cove moldings (bathrooms have showers only). No smoking is permitted.

12 E. Claremont St., Edinburgh EH7 4JP. © **0131/557-9030.** Fax 0131/557-0563. www.users.globalnet. co.uk/~stuartho. 7 units. £70–£100 ($105–$150) double. Rates include breakfast. AE, DC, MC, V. Closed 1 week at Christmas. Street parking available. Bus: 8, 9, or 19. *In room:* TV, coffeemaker, hair dryer.

34 Drummond Place (Kids *Finds* Located a 10-minute walk north of Princes Street, the exterior of this B&B is as severe-looking as John Calvin himself, thanks to a raw granite–fronted 1818 design. The interior, however, is whimsical and colorful. Accommodations include the large, bright Master Bedroom and the floral-patterned Family Room, which in a pinch can host up to three. The shower-only bathrooms are well maintained. Views from the front of the house overlook the garden, while the back opens onto the Firth of Forth.

34 Drummond Place, Edinburgh EH3 6PW. © **0131/556-5400.** Fax 0131/556-7707. www.aboutedinburgh. com/drummond/index.html. 3 units. £80–£90 ($120–$135) double; £105 ($157.50) family room for three. Extra person £25 ($37.50). Rates include breakfast. No credit cards. Bus: 13. *In room:* TV, no phone.

INEXPENSIVE

Greenside Hotel Behind a chiseled sandstone facade on the back side of Carlton Hill, this four-story Georgian, although recently renovated, has retained such features as its high ceilings, cove moldings, and elaborate trim. Guests access their rooms via a winding staircase, illuminated by a skylight. The rooms are so large that 10 of them contain a double bed and two singles. All have shower-only bathrooms. The Firth of Forth, the yacht *Britannia,* and the dramatic Forth Road Bridge are visible from the uppermost front floors; a sloping tiered garden, with a patio at the bottom, is visible from the rear windows. Breakfast is served in a formal dining room.

9 Royal Terrace, Edinburgh EH7 5AB. © and fax **0131/557-0022.** www.townhousehotels.co.uk. 15 units. £45–£90 ($67.50–$135) double. Rates include breakfast. AE, DC, DISC, MC, V. Bus: 4, 15, or 44. **Amenities:** Bar; access to nearby health club; babysitting. *In room:* TV, coffeemaker, hair dryer, iron.

Mansfield House Well located in the New Town, this friendly gay guesthouse offers clean, individually decorated rooms of reasonable size. Bathrooms contain showers only. The hotel is within walking distance of all the gay bars, clubs, and restaurants. It's always busy, so early booking is advised.

57 Dublin St., Edinburgh EH3 6NL. © **0131/556-7980.** www.mansfieldguesthouse.com. 9 units, 6 with private bathroom. £50 ($75) double without bathroom; £60–£70 ($90–$105) double with bathroom. Rates include continental breakfast. MC, V. Bus: 19 or 39. *In room:* TV, fridge, coffeemaker, iron, no phone.

(Kids **Family-Friendly Hotels**

Carlton Highland Hotel *(see p. 69)* Of the upmarket hotels of Edinburgh, this is the one that is known as the most family-friendly. Children are not only welcomed and housed free if 14 and under (in their parents' room), but can also enjoy the hotel pool.

Nova Hotel *(see p. 76)* This hotel features five spacious family rooms, each designed for total comfort. It's on a quiet, secluded cul-de-sac.

Thrums Private Hotel *(see p. 77)* This hotel takes its name from J. M. Barrie's fictional name for his hometown of Kirriemuir. Barrie is known to children as the author of *Peter Pan.* Kids are made especially welcome here and are housed in family rooms with their parents.

WEST OF THE CENTER
EXPENSIVE

Jarvis Ellersly Country House Hotel ✪ Within walled gardens, this three-story Edwardian country house offers privacy in a dignified residential area near the Murrayfield rugby grounds, about a 5-minute ride from the center. The well-equipped guest rooms, which vary in size (all with shower only), are in the main house or the less desirable annex. The hotel possesses a well-stocked wine cellar and offers good Scottish and French meals. After a refurbishment, the Jarvis Ellersly is better than ever and the service, first class.

4 Ellersly Rd., Edinburgh EH12 6HZ. © 0131/337-6888. Fax 0131/313-2543. 57 units. £139 ($208.50) double; £154 ($231) suite. AE, DC, MC, V. Free parking. Bus: 2, 2A, 21, 26, 31, 36, or 36A. Take A8 2½ miles (4km) west of the city center. **Amenities:** Restaurant, wine cellar; room service; laundry. *In room:* TV, hair dryer.

MODERATE

Dunstane House Hotel This stone-sided 1850 house sits behind a pleasant garden, a 10-minute walk from Princes Street in the center of New Town. The owner maintains the place in well-scrubbed condition, with respectful awareness of the building's architectural importance. The well-appointed guest rooms contain antiques or reproductions; two have four-poster beds. All have shower-only bathrooms.

4 W. Coates, Edinburgh EH12 5JQ. © 0131/337-6169. Fax 0131/337-6060. www.dunstanehousehotel. co.uk. 16 units. £70–£110 ($105–$165) double; £85–£160 ($127.50–$240) family room. Rates include breakfast. AE, DC, MC, V. Free parking. Bus: 2, 12, 26, 31, or 69. **Amenities:** 2 restaurants, bar; concierge; tour desk. *In room:* Coffeemaker, hair dryer.

Kew Guest House ✪✪ *Finds* This is one of Edinburgh's most refined guesthouses. It doesn't enjoy the rank of a full hotel, yet it is far more sumptuous than many first-class inns. Only a 15-minute walk from the heart of town, the inviting property was converted from buildings dating from 1860. Much of the original Victorian character of the house has been retained. The bedrooms are exceedingly comfortable, filled with a number of amenities and small, shower-only bathrooms. Many welcoming touches abound, such as a decanter of sherry awaiting you along with fresh flowers, chocolates, and shortbreads. Surprisingly for such a small place, the inn also offers a bar and restaurant. No smoking is permitted.

1 Kew Terrace, Murrayfield, EH12 5JE Edinburgh. © 0131/313-0700. Fax 0131/313-0747. www.kewhouse. co.uk/guest.htm. 6 units. £86 ($129) double; £38 ($57) per person in family room. Rates include breakfast. AE, DC, MC, V. Bus: 12, 26, 31, or 86. **Amenities:** Restaurant, bar. *In room:* TV, coffeemaker, hair dryer.

The Lodge Hotel ✪✪ *Finds* Although not widely known, this is one of Edinburgh's finest town-house hotels. A detached 1836 Georgian stone manse, it lies a 15-minute walk from Princes Street on the main A8 Glasgow-Edinburgh road. Each bedroom is well appointed, with canopied beds and midsize bathrooms with showers. Guests enjoy a selection of fine malts in the fire-lit lounge, along with a number of imaginative dishes in the dining room. Thoughtful extras include fresh flowers and a free decanter of sherry for guests. No smoking is permitted.

6 Hampton Terrace, West Coates, EH12 5JD Edinburgh. © 0131/337-3682. Fax 0131/313-1700. www.thelodgehotel.co.uk. 12 units. £75–£98 ($112.50–$147) double. Rates include breakfast. MC, V. Bus: 2, 12, 26, 31, 36, or 69. **Amenities:** Restaurant, bar. *In room:* TV, hair dryer, no phone.

22 Murrayfield Gardens ✪ *Finds* This elegant Victorian house with big bay windows is an undiscovered little gem. Set in a leafy, tranquil suburb of Edinburgh, it's just 1 mile (1.6km) west of the center (10 minutes by bus) and convenient to Waverley Station. The bedrooms are individually outfitted, with luxurious duvets and shower-only bathrooms. Breakfast is served in a sun-drenched room overlooking private gardens; there's also a spacious, rather grand drawing room. Dinners can be arranged on request.

22 Murrayfield Gardens, EH12 6DF Edinburgh. ℂ **0131/337-3569.** Fax 0131/337-3803. www.number22. co.uk. 3 units. £80 ($120) double. 2-night minimum stay in summer. Rates include breakfast. MC, V. Bus: 2 or 2A. *In room:* TV, hair dryer, no phone.

SOUTH OF THE CENTER
EXPENSIVE

Best Western Bruntsfield Hotel ⍟   Bruntsfield's neo-Gothic facade over-looks an expanse of park and is a 15-minute bus ride south of the city heart, opposite what may be the world's oldest golf course, Bruntsfield Links. Like the other 19th-century buildings lining the street, this four-story hotel is built of evenly spaced rows of honey-colored stones. Inside, all is neat and stylish, from the French-inspired armchairs to the recently refurbished guest rooms (some with shower only). Some are equipped for travelers with disabilities.

69–74 Bruntsfield Place, Edinburgh EH10 4HH. ℂ **800/528-1234** in the U.S. and Canada, or 0131/229-1393. Fax 0131/229-5634. www.thebruntsfield.co.uk. 75 units. £115–£155 ($172.50–$232.50) double. AE, DC, MC, V. Free parking. Bus: 11, 15, 16, 17, or 23. **Amenities:** Restaurant, bar; concierge; room service; babysitting; dry cleaning. *In room:* TV, dataport, coffeemaker, hair dryer, iron.

MODERATE

Elmview   One of the best things about this stone-fronted row house is the view it provides over the putting greens of Scotland's oldest golf course, Brunts-field Links. Half a mile (1km) southwest of Princes Street, it was built in the late 19th century and today functions as a highly personalized, small-scale guest-house. The high-ceilinged bedrooms are spacious and comfortable, with floral fabrics and homey charm (all with shower only). The garden provides a pleasant spot for breakfast. This is a no-smoking establishment.

15 Glengyle Terrace, Edinburgh EH3 9LN. ℂ **0131/228-1973.** Fax 0131/229-7296. www.elmview.co.uk. 4 units. £75–£95 ($112.50–$142.50) double. Rates include breakfast. MC, V. Bus: 11, 16, 17, 19, or 23. *In room:* TV, dataport, fridge, coffeemaker, hair dryer, iron, safe.

Newington Cottage ⍟⍟ *Finds*   This is one of the most inviting little inns in Edinburgh, filled with thoughtful extras like fresh flowers, fresh fruit, and com-plimentary sherry. Close to historic Old Town, the hotel, a classic 1832 build-ing, was awarded the Scottish Tourist Board's five-star rating—but it offers the comforts of a five-star city hotel at a fraction of the cost. The spacious bedrooms are exceedingly comfortable, and each roomy bathroom contains a shower, deluxe toiletries, and even a candle fixture, should you be in the mood for a romantic candlelit bath.

15 Blacket Place, Edinburgh EH9 1RJ. ℂ **0131/668-1935.** Fax 0131/667-4644. www.scotland2000.com/ newington. 3 units. £90–£100 ($135–$150). Rates include breakfast. MC, V. Bus 7, 8, or 31. **Amenities:** Lounge; laundry. *In room:* TV, hair dryer, iron, no phone.

Nova Hotel *Kids*   The Nova, an 1875 Victorian, is on a quiet cul-de-sac a 10-minute ride from the center, with a view over Bruntsfield Links in front and the Pentland Hills in back. It's within walking distance of the Royal Mile and Princes Street. You'll find its guest rooms large and well appointed, with mod-ern, shower-only bathrooms. Some are large enough for families.

5 Bruntsfield Crescent, Edinburgh EH10 4EZ. ℂ **0131/447-6437.** Fax 0131/452-8126. www.novahotel.f9. co.uk/home.htm. 13 units. £60–£80 ($90–$120) double; £90–£120 ($135–$180) family room. AE, DC, MC, V.

Street parking available. Bus: 11, 15, 16, 17. **Amenities:** 2 restaurants, 2 bars; concierge; car-rental desk; business center; room service; laundry/dry cleaning. *In room:* TV, minibar, coffeemaker, hair dryer, iron, safe.

Thrums Private Hotel *(Kids*   About a mile (1.6km) south of Princes Street, Thrums is a pair of connected antique buildings, one a two-story 1820 Georgian and the other a small inn (ca. 1900). The hotel contains high-ceilinged guest rooms with contemporary (in the inn) or reproduction antique (in the Georgian) furnishings. Each comes with a shower-only bathroom. The Thrums restaurant serves set-price menus of British food; there's also a bar and a peaceful garden.

14–15 Minto St., Edinburgh EH9 1RQ. ℂ **0131/667-5545.** Fax 0131/667-8707. 15 units. £70–£85 ($105–$127.50) double; £90–£115 ($135–$172.50) family room. Rates include breakfast. MC, V. Free parking. Bus: 3, 7, 8, 31, 81, 87. **Amenities:** Restaurant, bar; laundry service. *In room:* TV, coffeemaker, hair dryer.

INEXPENSIVE
Barony House *(Kids*   This restored Victorian villa on the south side, only a mile) (1.6km) from Waverley Station, is one of the city's better small guesthouses. Its new owner, Susie Berkengoff, has imbued the place with a personal touch, as evidenced by the tasteful furnishings and the comfort of her traditionally furnished bedrooms, each with combination tub/shower. Many of the units are large enough for families.

23 Mayfield Gardens, Edinburgh EH9 2BX. ℂ **0131/667-5806.** Fax 0131/667-6833. www.baronyhouse. co.uk. 9 units. £50–£90 ($75–$135) double; £90–£150 ($135–$225) family room. Rates include breakfast. No credit cards. Bus: 3, 7, 31, or 86. **Amenities:** Laundry/dry cleaning. *In room:* TV, hair dryer, no phone.

NORTH OF THE CENTER
INEXPENSIVE
Ashlyn Guest House   Near the Botanic Garden, a 5-minute ride from the center, this is a small, family-operated guesthouse, duplicating for many visitors the comforts of a private home. The rather elegant Georgian town house offers bedrooms that are most inviting. One unit is large enough for families. Five of the standard-size rooms come with private, shower-only bathrooms.

42 Inverleith Row, Edinburgh EH3 5PY. ℂ **0131/552-2954.** www.edinburgh.org. 8 units, 5 with private bathroom. £50 ($75) double without bathroom; £70 ($105) double with bathroom. Rates include breakfast. No credit cards. **Amenities:** Lounge; babysitting. *In room:* TV, coffeemaker, hair dryer, no phone.

IN LEITH
The satellite neighborhood of Leith was once run-down, but it's now a hip, up-and-coming area.

EXPENSIVE
The Malmaison *(Kids*   This is the most interesting hotel in Edinburgh's dockyard district, a few steps from Leith Water. It was converted from an 1883 seamen's mission/dorm and is capped by a stately stone clock tower. Its owners have created a hip, unpretentious place with a minimalist decor. The color schemes vary by floor; the purple-and-beige floor has been favored by rock bands who have stayed here during concert tours. Rooms are average in size but well equipped, each with a combination tub/shower. The facilities are sparse, but you'll find the Malmaison Brasserie (see "Dining," later in this chapter) and a cafe and wine bar favored by locals.

1 Tower Place, Leith, Edinburgh EH6 7DB. ℂ **0131/555-6868.** Fax 0131/468-5002. www.malmaison. com. 60 units. £115 ($172.50) double; £165 ($247.50) suite. AE, DC, MC, V. Free parking. Bus: 16 or 22. **Amenities:** Restaurant, bar. *In room:* TV, CD player, minibar, coffeemaker, hair dryer.

4 Dining

Rivaled only by Glasgow, Edinburgh boasts the finest restaurants in Scotland, and the choice is more diverse now than ever before. Even if you don't care for some of the more exotic regional fare, like haggis (spicy intestines), you'll find an array of top French dining rooms along with other foreign cuisines, especially Indian. And you'll find more and more restaurants catering to vegetarians. But we advise you go native and sample many of the dishes Edinburgh is known for doing best, like fresh salmon and seafood, game from Scottish fields, and Aberdeen Angus steaks. What's the rage at lunch? Stuffed potatoes (baked potatoes with a variety of stuffings). Many Scots make a lunch out of just one of these.

Some restaurants have sections reserved for nonsmokers; others don't. If smoking and dining (or nonsmoking and dining) are very important to you, inquire when making your reservation.

Note: For the locations of the restaurants below, see the "Edinburgh Accommodations & Dining" map, on p. 66–67.

IN THE CENTER: THE NEW TOWN
EXPENSIVE
The Atrium ⊕ MODERN SCOTTISH/INTERNATIONAL   Since 1993, this has been one of the most emulated restaurants in Edinburgh. No more than 60 diners can be accommodated in the "deliberately moody" atmosphere that's a fusion of Argentinean hacienda and stylish Beverly Hills bistro. Flickering oil lamps create shadows on the dark-colored walls while patrons enjoy dishes prepared with taste and flair. Although offerings vary according to the inspiration of the chef, our favorites include grilled salmon and roasted sea bass, the latter with Dauphinois potatoes, baby spinach, charcoal-grilled eggplant, and baby fennel. The desserts are equally superb, especially the lemon tart with berry soulis and crème fraîche.

10 Cambridge St. (beneath Saltire Court). ⓒ 0131/228-8882. Reservations recommended. Fixed-price meal £14–£18 ($21-$27) at lunch; main courses £13.50–£18.50 ($20.25–$27.75) at dinner. AE, DC, MC, V. Mon–Fri noon–2pm and 6:30–10pm; Sat 6:30–10pm. Closed 1 week at Christmas.

Channings ⊕ SCOTTISH/INTERNATIONAL   This is the main dining room of an Edwardian charmer of a hotel, offering traditional decor and elegant service from a well-trained staff. The exemplary cuisine allows the natural flavors of the superior-quality Scottish ingredients to shine through. The chefs know, for example, to go to the "Baines of Tarves" for his free-range Aberdeen chickens, or to Iain Mellis for his cheese. For dinner, you might opt for the terrine of seared tuna, potatoes, and slow-roasted tomatoes. To finish, try the hot banana and butterscotch soufflé with honeycomb ice cream. The restaurant is proud of its extensive wine list, which incorporates the old standards and newer, more exciting choices.

A less formal brasserie, with a log fireplace and a casual atmosphere, serves bar meals, light lunches, and dinners.

In Channings Hotel, 15 S. Learmonth Gardens. ⓒ 0131/315-2225. Reservations recommended. Fixed-price lunch £12 ($18) for 2 courses, £15 ($22.50) for 3 courses; fixed-price dinner £19.50 ($29.25) for 2 courses, £24.50 ($36.75) for 3 courses. AE, MC, V. Mon–Sat 12:30–2pm and 6:30–10pm. Closed Dec 26–29. Bus 41 or 42.

Cosmo Ristorante ⊕ ITALIAN   Even after more than 30 years in business, Cosmo is still one of the most popular Italian restaurants in town, where courtesy, efficiency, and good cooking draw in the crowds. The soups and pastas are always reliable. The kitchen is known for its *saltimbocca* (veal with ham) and Italian-inspired preparations of fish. This isn't the greatest Italian dining in Britain, but you'll certainly have a good, filling meal.

58A N. Castle St. ℭ 0131/226-6743. Reservations required. Main courses £14–£20 ($21–$30). AE, MC, V. Mon–Fri 12:30–2:15pm; Mon–Sat 7–10:45pm. Bus: 31 or 33.

Dome Bar & Grill ✸ INTERNATIONAL In a restored Georgian building with an elaborate domed ceiling, this bar and grill is part of the Dome entertainment complex. Throughout are elaborate columns, pedimental sculptures, and marble mosaic floors. The menu is ambitious and creative, with dishes like duck liver paté with Cumberland sauce and oat cakes, mullet with horseradish mash, and vegetable risotto.

14 George St. ℭ 0131/624-8624. Reservations required for lunch and dinner. Main courses £8–£15 ($12–$22.50) at lunch; £8.50–£18.50 ($12.75–$27.75) at dinner; fixed-price dinner menu £30 ($45). AE, DC, MC, V. Restaurant daily noon–10pm; bar Sun–Thurs noon–11:30pm, Fri–Sat noon–1am. Bus: 3, 21, 26, 31, or 85.

Duck's at Le Marché Noir ✸ SCOTTISH/FRENCH Set in a wood house whose exterior and interior are decorated in shades of dark green, this place's cuisine is more stylish, and more tuned to the culinary sophistication of London, than many other restaurants in Edinburgh. A handful of dishes honor the traditions of Scotland—for example, the baked haggis in phyllo pastry on a bed of turnip purée. More modern dishes include roasted rack of lamb, served with thyme juice and roasted vegetables, and grilled red snapper with wild rice and lime-marinated sweet potato pickles.

2–4 Eyre Place. ℭ 0131/558-1608. Reservations recommended. Set-price lunch £13.50 ($20.25) for 2 course, £15.50 ($23.25) for 3 courses; dinner main courses £17.50–£20.50 ($26.25–$30.75). AE, DC, MC, V. Mon–Sat noon–2pm and 7–9:30pm. Bus: 23, 27.

Haldanes Restaurant ✸ SCOTTISH Set in the cellar of the Albany Hotel building, in a pair of royal blue and gold dining rooms, Haldanes serves dinners that are conducted like meals in a private country house, with polite and deferential service. In nice weather, you can sit in the verdant garden. The chef applies a light touch to innovative dishes. Menu items include haggis in phyllo pastry with tatties (roasted turnips) and whisky sauce; pan-fried crab cakes with a tomato and spring onion salsa; and a pavé of lamb with mint-flavored herb crust, wild mushrooms, and zucchini.

39A Albany St. ℭ 0131/556-8407. Reservations recommended. Set-price lunch £10.50–£15 ($15.75–$22.50); dinner main courses £16.25–£22 ($24.40–$33). AE, DC, MC, V. Daily noon–1:30pm and 6–9:30pm. Bus: 15.

Martin's ✸ SCOTTISH Owners Gay and Martin Irons and their trio of top chefs are deeply committed to wild and organically grown foods and include them on the menu when they can. Although the setting is unlikely, off Edinburgh's pub street and down an unpromising alley, the restaurant's celadon-green rooms are now a landmark. The menu changes daily to take advantage of the freshest ingredients, and Martin's father provides herbs from his own garden. The best of the country's venison, fish (especially salmon), and shellfish appear regularly; wild mushrooms are a particular favorite. You might try breast of guinea fowl with burgundy jus, phyllo parcels filled with langoustines and organic leeks in basil dressing, or a charcoal-grilled tuna steak with Scottish shitake mushrooms and avocado-and-tomato compote. Many of the cheeses are

---

Oh, Give It a Try!

Haggis, the much-maligned national dish of Scotland, is certainly an acquired taste. But you've come all this way—why not be brave and give it a try? **Macsween of Edinburgh Haggis** is a long-established family business specializing in haggis. Macsween haggis includes lamb, beef, oatmeal, onions, and a special blend of seasonings and spices cooked together. There's also an all-vegetarian version. Both are sold in vacuum-packed plastic bags that require only reheating in a microwave or regular oven. You can find this company's product at food stores and supermarkets throughout Edinburgh. Two central distributors are **Peckham's Delicatessen**, 155–159 Bruntsfield Place ((C) **0131/229-7054**), open daily from 8am to 8pm, and **Jenner's Department Store**, 2 East Princes St. ((C) **0131/260-2242**), open Monday through Saturday from 9am to 6pm and Sunday from noon to 5pm.

---

unpasteurized farmhouse delights. End your meal with a delectable fruit tart or a homemade sorbet like basil, lime, and elderflower.

70 Rose St., North Lane. (C) **0131/225-3106.** Reservations required. Lunch main courses £9–£12.50 ($13.50–$18.75), 2-course lunch £12.50 ($18.75); dinner main courses £18–£21 ($27–$31.50), 3-course dinner £25 ($37.50). AE, DC, MC, V. Tues–Fri noon–2pm; Tues–Sat 7–10pm. During festival in Aug Mon–Sat 6:30–11pm. Closed Dec 24–Jan 23, 1 week in May/June, and 1 week in Sept/Oct. Bus: 2, 4, 15, 21, or 44. No children under 8 allowed.

No. 1 Princes Street (✿ SCOTTISH/CONTINENTAL This is the Balmoral's premier restaurant, an intimate, crimson-colored enclave whose walls are studded with Scottish memorabilia. You can sample the likes of pan-seared Isle of Skye monkfish with saffron mussel broth, or perhaps roulade of Dover sole with langoustine, oyster, and scallop garnish. Dessert brings a variety of sorbets, cheeses, and more exotic choices like mulled wine parfait with a cinnamon sauce. There's a separate vegetarian menu and a wide-ranging wine list with celestial tariffs.

In the Balmoral Hotel, 1 Princes St. (C) **0131/556-2414.** Reservations recommended. Main courses £20–£35 ($30–$52.50); fixed-price lunch £18.50 ($27.75) for 2 courses; fixed-price dinner £37.50 ($56.25) for 3 courses, £50 ($75) for 6 courses. AE, DC, MC, V. Sun–Thurs 7–10pm; Fri–Sat 7–10:30pm.

Pompadour Restaurant (✿ SCOTTISH/FRENCH On the mezzanine of the Caledonian hotel, the Pompadour is one of Edinburgh's best. The restaurant has been refurbished in a Louis XV decor. The chef blends cuisine moderne with traditional menus, and his daily offerings reflect the best available from the market, with Scottish salmon, venison, and other game often included. The menu also features fresh produce from local and French markets—items like goose liver with wild mushrooms, lamb with spinach and rosemary, and charlotte of marinated salmon filled with seafood. The wine list is lethally expensive.

In the Caledonian Hilton, Princes St. (C) **0131/459-9988.** Reservations required. Fixed-price lunches £15.50–£18.50 ($23.25–$27.75); main courses £14–£24 ($21–$36). AE, DC, MC, V. Tues–Sat 12:30–2pm and 7–10pm. Bus: 4, 15, or 44.

Winter Glen (✿ SCOTTISH The name alone holds a certain romantic Scottish aura; inside, this basement restaurant close to New Town has an elegant atmosphere, with luxurious draperies and tastefully set tables. The changing menu might include spiced crab cake flavored with cumin and coriander;

smoked-salmon sausage served on mashed olives; and grilled halibut steak, marinated in olive oil and coriander. Desserts include such delights as an old-fashioned, cinnamon-laced rice pudding.

3A1 Dundas St. © 0131/477-7060. Reservations required. Main courses £14–£20 ($21–$30); fixed-price menus £24–£26 ($36–$39). AE, MC, V. Mon–Fri noon–2pm; Mon–Sat 6:30–10pm. Closed first week of Jan. Bus: 23.

Witchery by the Castle ⍟ SCOTTISH/FRENCH   This place bills itself as the oldest, most haunted restaurant in town, and the Hellfire Club was supposed to have met here during the Middle Ages. The building has been linked with witchcraft since the period between 1470 and 1722, when more than 1,000 people were burned alive on Castlehill; one of the victims is alleged to haunt the Witchery. The chef uses creative flair to create unfussy Scottish food, such as Skye prawns, Tay salmon, and venison Wellington in a sauce of figs and chocolate. Some 550 wines and 40 malt whiskies are available.

352 Castlehill, Royal Mile. © 0131/225-5613. Reservations recommended. Main courses £16–£22 ($24–$33). AE, DC, MC, V. Daily noon–4pm and 5:30–11pm. Bus: 1 or 6.

MODERATE

Bisi Restaurant (Value) ITALIAN   You'll find fresh pasta—lasagna, rigatoni, fusilli, and so on—at great prices here. The menu changes every few weeks and may include sauces like *matriciana*, with Italian bacon and onions, and *puttanesca*, with black olives, kippers, anchovies, and tomatoes. The assortment of Italian desserts includes tiramisu and *torta amoretta*.

10 Randolph Place. © 0131/225-6060. Reservations recommended. Main courses £6.25–£13.95 ($9.40–$20.95). AE, DC, MC, V. Mon–Sat noon–2:30pm and 5:30–10pm (Fri–Sat until 10:30pm). Bus: 3, 34, or 35.

Blue Bar Café INTERNATIONAL   In the building containing the Traverse Theatre, this attractive bistro is the less expensive sibling of the Atrium (see above). You'll find a mostly white, minimalist decor (with touches of blue); solid oaken tables; and a cheerful staff. The sophisticated menu might include delectable crabmeat spring rolls; succulent breast of duck with a compote of figs and apple jus; and a perfect charcoal-grilled tuna with basil-flavored noodles.

10 Cambridge St. © 0131/221-1222. Reservations recommended. Set-price lunch £9–£12 ($13.50–$18); main courses £10–£13.50 ($15–$20.25). AE, DC, MC, V. Daily noon–3pm and 6–11pm. Bus: 10, 11, 16, or 27.

Tea for Two

If you're looking for a bit of refreshment while sightseeing, try **Clarinda's Tea Room**, 69 Canongate (© **0131/557-1888**), for the very British experience of afternoon tea. This cubbyhole of a tearoom is only steps from Holyroodhouse and decorated in the manner you'd expect, with lace tablecloths, bone china, and antique Wedgwood plates on the walls. A long list of tempting sweets is offered, plus homemade soup, lasagna, baked potatoes, and salads. Open Monday through Saturday from 9am to 4:45pm and Sunday from 10am to 4:45pm. Another choice is **Ryan's Bar**, 2 Hope St. (© **0131/226-6669**), near the northwestern corner of the West Princes Street Gardens. It serves tea daily from 10:30am to 10pm. If you want a more formal tea ceremony, try the Palm Court at the **Balmoral Hotel**, Princes Street (© **0131/556-2414**), serving tea daily from noon to 5pm.

Café Saint-Honoré FRENCH/SCOTTISH   This French-inspired bistro is a deliberately rapid-paced place at lunchtime, then becomes much more formal at dinner. The menu is completely revised each day, based on what's fresh and what the chefs feel inspired to cook. An upbeat and usually enthusiastic staff serves a combination of Scottish and French cuisine that includes venison with juniper berries and wild mushrooms, local pheasant in wine and garlic sauce, or lamb kidneys with broad beans.

34 NW Thistle St. Lane (between Frederick and Hanover Sts.). (**C**) **0131/226-2211**. Reservations recommended. Lunch main courses £7.50–£12.50 ($11.25–$18.75); fixed-price dinners £13.75–£17.25 ($20.65–$25.90). AE, DC, MC, V. Mon–Fri noon–2:15pm and 5:30–7pm (pre-theater dinner); Mon–Sat 7–10pm. Bus: 3, 16, 17, 23, 27, or 31.

The Marque 🍴 SCOTTISH/INTERNATIONAL   The Marque is ideally located for the theater and offers reasonably priced pre- and post-theater dinners. Owned by Lara Kearney, John Rutter, and Glyn Stevens, all formerly of the Atrium, this is a fast-growing, popular place. The bold yellow walls and black-and-white floor give this converted antiques shop a unique, contemporary look. The cuisine is ambitious and seductive. Main courses include halibut roasted in olive oil, chargrilled tuna, and chicken and fois gras terrine with onion jam. The rhubarb crumble with tamarind ice cream is a great way to end an enjoyable meal.

19–21 Causewayside. (**C**) **0131/229-9859**. Reservations recommended. Main courses £11.50–£16.95 ($17.25–$25.45); set-price lunch and pre- and post-theater dinner £10 ($15) for 2 courses. AE, MC, V. Tues–Thurs 11:45am–2pm and 5:45–10pm; Fri 11:45am–2pm and 5:45–11pm; Sat 12:30–2pm and 5:45–11pm; Sun 12:30–2pm and 5:45–10pm. Bus 42.

Restaurant at the Bonham 🍴🍴 SCOTTISH/CONTINENTAL   The setting at one of Edinburgh's most charming restaurants marries 19th-century oak paneling and deep ceiling coves with modern paintings and oversized mirrors. Chef Michel Bouyer has greatly improved the cuisine here, creating a stimulating menu in his own style. Though classically trained in Paris, he adds his own creative touches to favorites such as char-grilled tuna with a lime and mint couscous; wild mushroom, lentil, and tarragon ravioli with a green bean and artichoke salad; and pan-fried halibut with a carrot and cumin purée and candied lemons.

In the Bonham Hotel, 35 Drumsheugh Gardens. (**C**) **0131/623-9319**. Reservations recommended. Main courses £11.50–£17 ($17.25–$25.50); fixed-price lunches £12.50–£15 ($18.75–$22.50). AE, DC, MC, V. Daily 12:30–2:30pm and 6:30–10pm. Bus: 19, 40, 41.

The Tower 🍴🍴 SEAFOOD/MODERN BRITISH   This is the town's hot new dining ticket, set at the top of the Museum of Scotland. The chef uses local ingredients to create some of the capital's tastiest fare. The inventive kitchen will regale you with hearty portions of steak, roast beef, and excellent seafood. We still remember fondly the smoked haddock risotto with a poached egg and shavings of Parmesan cheese. The sea bass was perfectly seasoned and grilled, and there's even sushi on the menu.

In the Museum of Scotland, Chambers St. (**C**) **0131/225-3003**. Reservations required. Main courses £10–£14 ($15–$21) at lunch, £13–£25 ($19.50–$37.50) at dinner. AE, DC, MC, V. Daily noon–11pm. Bus: 3, 7, 21, 30, 31, 53, 69, or 80.

INEXPENSIVE

Far Pavilions INDIAN/CONTINENTAL   Established in 1987, this Indian restaurant offers finely tuned service. You might appreciate a drink in the bar before confronting the long menu, with dishes from the former Portuguese colony of Goa and the northern Indian province of Punjab. Highly recommended is the house specialty, Murgi Massala, concocted with tandoori chicken that falls off the bone thanks to slow cooking in a garlic-based butter sauce.

10 Craighleith Rd., Comely Bank. © 0131/332-3362. Reservations recommended. Lunch main courses £8–£17 ($12–$25.50), lunch buffet £6.95 ($10.45) per person; dinner main courses £7–£13 ($10.50–$19.50). AE, MC, V. Mon–Fri noon–2pm; Mon–Sat 5:30–11:30pm. Bus: 19, 39, 55, 81, or X91.

Henderson's Salad Table ☞ *Value* VEGETARIAN   This self-service place is a Shangri-la for health-food lovers. You can pick and choose eggs, carrots, grapes, nuts, yogurt, cheese, potatoes, cabbage, watercress—you name it. Hot dishes such as peppers stuffed with rice and pimiento are served on request, and a vegetarian twist on the national dish of Scotland, haggis, is usually available. Other well-prepared, flavorful dishes include cheese and onion potato croquet, vegetable lasagna, and a broccoli and cheese crumble. The wine cellar offers 30 choices. Live music, ranging from classical to jazz to folk, is featured nightly.

94 Hanover St. © 0131/225-2131. Main courses £3.95–£5 ($5.95–$7.50); fixed-price lunch £7.25 ($10.90); fixed-price dinner £10.95 ($16.45). AE, MC, V. Mon–Sat 8am–10:45pm. Bus: 23 or 27.

Indian Cavalry Club INDIAN   The Indian Cavalry Club is more than your average curry place. The elegant atmosphere evokes the British heyday in India, when Queen Victoria was known as Empress of India. You'll find the classic and tandoori Indian dishes, plus many options based on recipes from Nepal or Burma. Vegetarians flock here, and much of the cuisine is steamed. The restaurant has many seating areas, including the ground-floor Officer's Mess and the marquee-style Club Tent downstairs.

3 Atholl Place. © 0131/228-3282. Reservations required. Main courses £7–£14 ($10.50–$21); 3-course lunch £6.95 ($10.45); 5-course table d'hôte dinner £16.50–£21.50 ($24.75–$32.25). AE, DC, MC, V. Daily noon–2pm and 5:30–11:30pm. Bus: 3, 21, 23, or 26.

Suruchi INDIAN   This intriguing restaurant occupies a gray-stone early-19th-century storefront opposite the Festival Theatre. The dining rooms are showcases for exclusively Indian furniture, artwork, table linens, and artifacts; note the elaborate wall tiles and the rows of miniature paintings from the owner's hometown of Jaipur, in Rajastan. Every month, a culinary festival features the art, music, and cuisine of a different region of India. The menu, written in the Edinburgh dialect, divides the country's cuisine regionally to help you understand the complexities and subtleties. Items include grilled kebabs, vegetarian dishes, lamb, and an unusual version of fresh Scottish trout. The set-price menu changes daily and is always an interesting option. Light jazz is presented Wednesday and Friday evenings.

14A Nicholson St. © 0131/556-6583. Reservations recommended. Main courses £8–£13 ($12–$19.50); fixed-price lunch £4.95–£5.95 ($7.45–$8.95); fixed-price pre-theater dinner (call ahead to check, as it's not always available) £9.95 ($14.95). DC, MC, V. Daily noon–2pm and 5:30–11:30pm. Bus: 30 or 33.

Valvona & Crolla INTERNATIONAL   In 1872, an Italian immigrant opened this restaurant, and it's still going strong today, sharing space with a deli and food emporium selling exotic coffees, Parma ham, Italian cheeses, breads, and takeout sandwiches and casseroles. A satellite room, a few steps down from the main shopping area, contains a cafe and luncheon restaurant where the food is very fresh and prices refreshingly low. You can order three kinds of breakfast (continental, Scottish, or vegetarian); platters of pasta, mixed sausages, and cold cuts; or crostini, risottos, and omelets. Don't expect leisurely dining, as the place caters to office workers and shoppers who dash in for midday sustenance.

(Kids) Family-Friendly Restaurants

Baked Potato Shop *(see p. 85)* Children delight in being taken to this workers' favorite, where they can order flaky baked potatoes with a choice of half a dozen hot fillings along with all sorts of other dishes, including chili and 20 kinds of salads. It's cheap, too.

Henderson's Salad Table *(see p. 83)* Edinburgh's leading vegetarian restaurant has an array of nutritious salads, followed by some of the most delectable homemade desserts in the city.

Mr. Boni's Ice Cream Parlour Mr. Boni's is at 4 Lochrin Bridge (ⓒ **0131/229-5319**). Every kid comes away loving Mr. Boni, who makes the best homemade ice cream in Edinburgh, plus sandwiches, jumbo hot dogs, and burgers with fries.

---

19 Elm Row. ⓒ **0131/556-6066.** Breakfast £4.95 ($7.45); pizzas, pastas, and platters £3–£10 ($4.50–$15). AE, MC, V. Mon–Sat 8:30am–5pm (full lunch service noon–3pm). Bus: 7, 10, 11, 12, or 14.

Whigham's Wine Cellars 🏵 SEAFOOD/VEGETARIAN Whigham's Wine Cellars is in the heart of Edinburgh's financial center. Wine was bottled here in the mid–18th century, and Whigham's used to ship it to the American colonies. Walk across the mellowed stone floors until you find an intimate alcove, where you can make your selection from an assortment of appetizers and *plats du jour*. The smoked fish (not just salmon) and the fresh oysters from Loch Fyne are exceptional. A range of international wines is offered.

13 Hope St. ⓒ **0131/225-8674.** Reservations recommended. Main courses £5.50–£10.50 ($8.25–$15.75). AE, DC, MC, V. Mon–Thurs noon–midnight; Fri–Sat noon–1am. Bus: 2, 4, or 34.

IN THE CENTER: THE OLD TOWN
EXPENSIVE

Dubh Prais 🏵 SCOTTISH Dubh Prais (Gaelic for "The Black Pot") conjures up an image of old-fashioned Scottish recipes bubbling away in a stewpot above a fireplace. In dining rooms adorned with stenciled versions of thistles, you'll be served time-tested and not at all experimental meals that are flavorful nonetheless. Examples include smoked salmon; saddle of venison with juniper sauce; and a suprême of salmon with grapefruit-flavored butter sauce.

123B High St., Royal Mile. ⓒ **0131/557-5732.** Reservations recommended. Main courses £6.50 ($9.75) at lunch; £11.90–£17.50 ($17.85–$26.25) at dinner. AE, MC, V. Tues–Fri noon–2pm; Tues–Sat 6–10:30pm. Bus: 11.

Iggs 🏵 SPANISH/SCOTTISH Just off the Royal Mile in Old Town, this Victorian-style establishment is the domain of a dynamic chef, Andrew McQueen, who is not afraid to experiment but also seems well grounded in the classics. A dinner here is made more charming by the attention from the wait-staff, clad in black polo shirts. Typical choices may include rack of Highland lamb with spring vegetables; if you want to go more exotic, opt for the loin of veal on a truffle and Gruyère risotto given extra flavor by a Madeira sauce. After you think you've had every dessert in the world, along comes a honey-roasted butternut-squash cheesecake with a caramel sauce.

15 Jeffrey St. ⓒ 0131/557-8184. Reservations recommended. Main courses £15.50–£20 ($23.25–$30); fixed-price lunch £15.50 ($23.25); fixed-price dinner £29.50 ($44.25). AE, MC, V. Mon–Sat noon–2:30pm and 6–10:30pm. Bus 1 or 35.

Jackson's Restaurant ⓖ SCOTTISH   Serving a cuisine described as "Scottish with a French flair," this bustling restaurant is in the stone cellar of a 300-year-old building. Choose your drink from almost 40 kinds of Highland malts, and then select from a menu featuring local ingredients. The charming staff will help you translate such items as "beasties of the glen" (haggis with rosemary-and-garlic sauce) and "kilted salmon" pan-fried in green ginger-and-whisky sauce.

209 High St., Royal Mile. ⓒ 0131-225-1793. Reservations recommended. Main courses £13.50–£18 ($20.25–$27); fixed-price dinner £25 ($37.50). AE, DC, MC, V. Daily noon–2:30pm and 6–10:30pm. Bus: 35.

MODERATE
Pierre Victoire FRENCH   This was the original model for the chain of franchises that have sprouted up in recent years. It's an ideal, if chaotic, stop if you're antiques shopping and climbing Victoria Street. It's also a popular evening gathering place. In a bistro setting with crowded tables, you can order grilled mussels in garlic with Pernod butter, salmon with ginger, or roast pheasant with Cassis. Vegetarians will also find selections to suit their taste. Wine specials are posted on the chalkboard.

10–14 Victoria St. ⓒ 0131/225-1721. Reservations recommended. Main courses £7.95–£12.95 ($11.95–$19.40); fixed-price lunch £4.95–£6.90 ($7.45–$10.35). MC, V. Daily noon–3pm and 6–11pm. Bus: 1, 23, 27, 42, 45, 46, 47.

INEXPENSIVE
Baked Potato Shop *Kids* VEGETARIAN/WHOLE FOOD   This is the least expensive restaurant in a very glamorous neighborhood, and it attracts mobs of office workers every day. Place your order at the countertop; it will then be served in ecology-conscious recycled cardboard containers. Only free-range eggs, whole foods, and vegetarian cheeses are used. Vegetarian cakes are a specialty.

56 Cockburn St. ⓒ 0131/225-7572. Reservations not accepted. Food items 60p–£3.20 (90¢–$4.80). No credit cards. Daily 9am–9pm (till 10pm in summer). Bus: 5.

SOUTH OF THE CENTER
EXPENSIVE
Kelly's ⓖ MODERN SCOTTISH/FRENCH   Catering to a crowd of barristers, artists, financiers, and employees of the nearby university, this stylish restaurant is a 20-minute walk south of the center in a residential neighborhood. The place offers an intimate setting decorated with flowers, watercolors, and unusual ceramics. The menu includes such dishes as asado of lamb in olive and herb crust with spicy couscous, roast breast of Barbary duck with black pepper and blueberries, and lobster ravioli with asparagus. Dessert might be a caramelized lemon tart.

46 W. Richmond St. ⓒ 0131/668-3847. Reservations recommended. Main courses £13–£15 ($19.50–$22.50); fixed-price 3-course lunch £11 ($16.50); fixed-price 3-course dinner £27 ($40.50). DC, MC, V. Mon–Sat noon–2pm and 6–10pm. Bus: 11, 12, or 14.

IN LEITH
In the northern regions of Edinburgh, the old port town of Leith opens onto the Firth of Forth. After decades of decay, it has become an arty neighborhood with a collection of restaurants, wine bars, and pubs.

EXPENSIVE

Martin Wishart ✮✮✮ MODERN FRENCH   Several gourmet associations claim this is the "Scottish restaurant of the year." Chef and owner Martin Wishart takes it all in stride and continues to improve the quality of his establishment in a fashionable part of the Leith docklands. The minimalist decor features white walls and modern art. The menu is short but sweet, taking advantage of the best of the season. The gratin of sea bass arrives aromatically with a soft, herby crust. Many dishes are simply prepared, the natural flavors coming through; others show a touch of fantasy, as in the partridge breast with black truffle and foie gras. Where can you get a good pot roast pig's cheek if not here? After eating the glazed lemon tart with praline ice cream on white raspberry coulis, the day is yours.

54 The Shore, Leith. ℂ 0131/553-3557. Reservations required. Main courses £15.50–£20 ($23.25–$30); fixed-price lunch £13.50–£15.50 ($20.25–$23.25). Tues–Fri noon–2pm; Tues–Thurs 6:30–10pm; Fri–Sat 6:30–10:30pm. Bus: 7 or 10.

Vintner's Room ✮ FRENCH/SCOTTISH   This stone-fronted building down by the waterfront was constructed around 1650 as a warehouse for barrels of Bordeaux (claret) and port that came in from Europe's mainland. Near the entrance, beneath a ceiling of venerable oaken beams, a wine bar serves platters and drinks beside a large stone fireplace. Most people, however, head for the dining room, decorated with elaborate Italianate plasterwork and lit with flickering candles. The robust cuisine may include seafood salad with mango mayonnaise, pigeon-and-duck terrine, and venison in a bitter-chocolate sauce.

The Vaults, 87 Giles St., Leith. ℂ 0131/554-6767. Reservations recommended. Table d'hôte meal £11.50–£15 ($17.25–$22.50) at lunch; dinner main courses £15–£32 ($22.50–$48). AE, MC, V. Mon–Sat noon–2pm and 7–10:30pm. Closed 2 weeks at Christmas. Bus: 7 or 10.

MODERATE

Malmaison Brasserie TRADITIONAL FRENCH   In the previously recommended hotel, this unpretentious brasserie is charming enough to merit a trip out from Edinburgh. The setting is simple, with lots of polished wood and wrought iron. The bistro-inspired menu includes fried steak with pommes frites, sea bass with vinaigrette, and sole meunière with rosemary potatoes. Everyone's favorite dessert is the crème brûlée. Regrettably, the restaurant doesn't have a view of the harbor but faces a side street.

In the Malmaison Hotel, 1 Tower Place. ℂ 0131/555-6868. Reservations recommended for dinner. Fixed-price lunches £9.95–£12.95 ($14.95–$19.45) Mon–Sat, £14.95 ($22.45) Sun; fixed-price dinners £11.95–£13.95 ($17.95–$20.95). AE, DC, MC, V. Daily noon–2:30pm and 6–11pm. Bus: 6, 16, or 22A.

IN PRESTONFIELD
EXPENSIVE

Prestonfield House ✮ BRITISH   Hidden amid 13 acres (5.3 hectares) of private parkland and gardens, 3 miles (5km) south of Edinburgh's center, this elegant restaurant often hosts locals celebrating special occasions. It's an old-fashioned choice, certainly, but it still offers the same fine quality as always. Menu items include grilled salmon with braised leeks and gazpacho, baked lamb in phyllo with tomatoes and wild mushrooms, and marinated smoked pigeon with avocado-and-raspberry salad.

In the Prestonfield House Hotel, Priestfield Rd., Edinburgh. ℂ 0131/668-3346. Reservations preferred. Jacket and tie required for men. Main courses £14.50–£19.75 ($21.75–$29.65); table d'hôte lunch £19 ($28.50). AE, DC, MC, V. Daily 12:30–2pm and 7–9:30pm. Bus: 2, 14 or 31.

5 Seeing the Sights

ALONG THE ROYAL MILE

Old Town's **Royal Mile** ✿✿✿ stretches from Edinburgh Castle all the way to the Palace of Holyroodhouse and bears four names along its length: Castlehill, Lawnmarket, High Street, and Canongate. Walking along, you'll see some of the most interesting old structures in the city, with turrets, gables, and towering chimneys. Take bus no. 1, 6, 23, 27, 30, 34, or 36 to reach it.

Edinburgh Castle ✿✿ No place in Scotland is filled with as much history, legend, and lore as Edinburgh Castle, one of the highlights of a visit to this little country. It's believed the ancient city grew up on the seat of a dead volcano, Castle Rock. The early history is vague, but it's known that in the 11th century, Malcolm III (Canmore) and his Saxon queen, later venerated as St. Margaret, founded a castle on this spot. The only fragment left of their castle—in fact, the oldest structure in Edinburgh—is St. Margaret's Chapel, built in the Norman style, the oblong structure dating principally from the 12th century.

You can visit the State Apartments, particularly Queen Mary's Bedroom, where Mary Queen of Scots gave birth to James VI of Scotland (later James I of England). Scottish Parliaments used to convene in the Great Hall. The highlight is the Crown Chamber, housing the Honours of Scotland (Scottish Crown Jewels), used at the coronation of James VI, along with the scepter and sword of state of Scotland. The French Prisons were put to use in the 18th century, and these great storerooms housed hundreds of Napoleonic soldiers in the early 19th century. Many of them made wall carvings you can see today. Among the batteries of cannons that protected the castle is Mons Meg, a 15th-century cannon weighing more than 5 tons.

Castlehill, at the western end of the Royal Mile. © **0131/225-9846**. Admission £7.50 ($11.25) adults, £5.50 ($8.25) seniors, £2 ($3) children under 16. Apr–Sept daily 9:30am–5:15pm; Oct–Mar daily 9:30am–4:15pm. Bus: 1 or 6.

Palace of Holyroodhouse ✿✿ Early in the 16th century, this palace was built by James IV adjacent to an Augustinian abbey David I had established in the 12th century. The nave of the abbey church, now in ruins, still remains, but only the north tower of James's palace is left. Most of what you see today was built by Charles II after Scotland and England were united in the 17th century. The palace suffered long periods of neglect, but it basked in glory at the ball thrown by Bonnie Prince Charlie in the mid–18th century, during the peak of his feverish (and doomed) optimism about uniting the Scottish clans in their struggle against the English. Queen Elizabeth II and Prince Philip stay here whenever they visit Edinburgh; when they're not in residence, the palace is open to visitors.

The old wing was the scene of Holyroodhouse's most dramatic incident. Mary Queen of Scots's Italian secretary, David Rizzio, was stabbed 56 times in front of her eyes by her jealous husband, Lord Darnley, and his accomplices. A plaque marks the spot where he died on March 9, 1566. And one of the more curious exhibits is a piece of needlework done by Mary depicting a cat-and-mouse scene. (Her cousin, Elizabeth I, is the cat.)

Highlights of the palace are the oldest surviving section, King James Tower, where Mary Queen of Scots lived on the second floor, with Lord Darnley's rooms below. Some of the rich tapestries, paneling, massive fireplaces, and antiques from the 1700s are still in place. The Throne Room and other drawing

Edinburgh Attractions

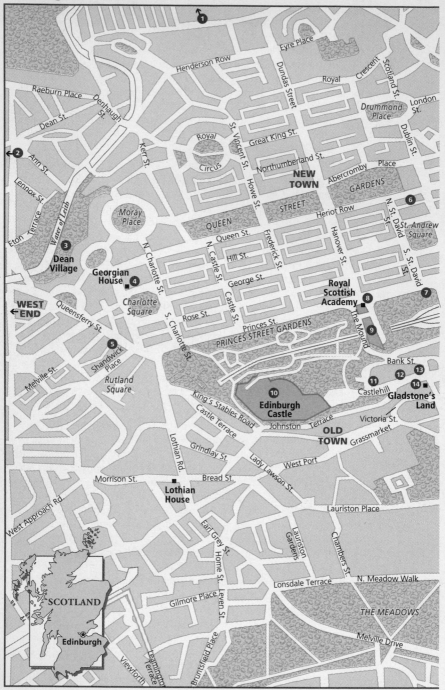

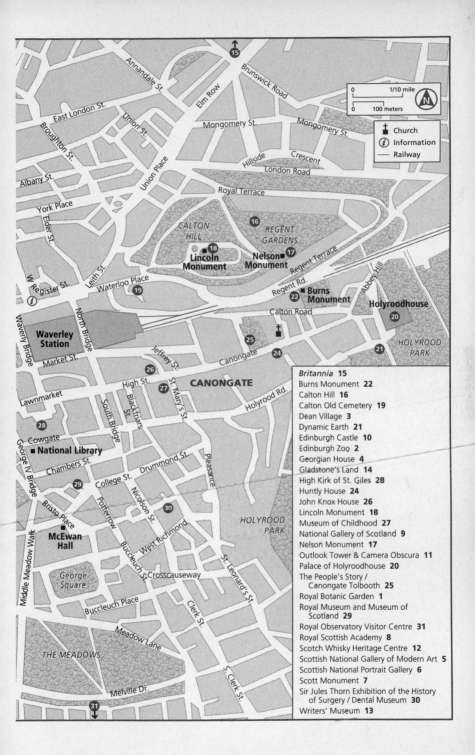

Britannia **15**
Burns Monument **22**
Calton Hill **16**
Calton Old Cemetery **19**
Dean Village **3**
Dynamic Earth **21**
Edinburgh Castle **10**
Edinburgh Zoo **2**
Georgian House **4**
Gladstone's Land **14**
High Kirk of St. Giles **28**
Huntly House **24**
John Knox House **26**
Lincoln Monument **18**
Museum of Childhood **27**
National Gallery of Scotland **9**
Nelson Monument **17**
Outlook Tower & Camera Obscura **11**
Palace of Holyroodhouse **20**
The People's Story /
   Canongate Tolbooth **25**
Royal Botanic Garden **1**
Royal Museum and Museum of
   Scotland **29**
Royal Observatory Visitor Centre **31**
Royal Scottish Academy **8**
Scotch Whisky Heritage Centre **12**
Scottish National Gallery of Modern Art **5**
Scottish National Portrait Gallery **6**
Scott Monument **7**
Sir Jules Thorn Exhibition of the History
   of Surgery / Dental Museum **30**
Writers' Museum **13**

rooms are still used for state occasions. In the rear of the palace is the richly furnished King's Bedchamber. The Picture Gallery boasts many portraits of Scottish monarchs by Dutch artist Jacob De Witt, who in 1684 signed a contract to turn out one potboiler portrait after another at the rate of one a week for 2 years. However, don't take all the portraits too seriously: Some of these royal figures may have never existed, and the likenesses of some aren't known, so the portraits are from the artist's imagination.

Behind Holyroodhouse begins **Holyrood Park,** Edinburgh's largest. With rocky crags, a loch, sweeping meadows, and the ruins of a chapel, it's a wee bit of the Scottish countryside in the city, and a great place for a picnic. If you climb up Holyrood Park, you'll come to 823-foot-high (250m) **Arthur's Seat,** from which the panorama is breathtaking. (The name doesn't refer to King Arthur, as many people assume, but perhaps is a reference to Prince Arthur of Strathclyde or a corruption of *Ard Thor,* Gaelic for "height of Thor." No one knows for sure.) If you visit on a winter morning, you'll think you're in the heart of the Highlands. Arthur's Seat dates from prehistoric times; you can see clusters of cultivated terraces from the Dark Ages, especially on the east flank of the hill, both above and below Queen's Drive.

Canongate, at the eastern end of the Royal Mile. (*C*) 0131/556-7371. Admission £6.50 ($9.75) adults, £5 ($7.50) seniors, £3.30 ($4.95) children under 16, £16.50 ($24.75) per family. Daily 9:30am–4:45pm. Closed 2 weeks in May and 3 weeks in late June and early July (dates vary). Bus: 1 or 6.

Scotch Whisky Heritage Centre   This center is privately funded by a conglomeration of Scotland's biggest distillers. It highlights the economic effect of whisky on both Scotland and the world, and illuminates the centuries-old traditions associated with whisky making. You get to see a 7-minute audiovisual show and ride an electric car past 13 sets showing historic moments in the

---

Frommer's Favorite Edinburgh Experiences

Contemplating the City & Environs from Arthur's Seat. At 823 feet (250m) atop Arthur's Seat (which you reach by climbing up Holyrood Park), you'll see the Highlands in miniature—the view is magical. Scots congregate here to await the solstice.

Visiting Dean Village. About 100 feet (30m) below the level of the rest of the city, Dean Village is an 800-year-old grain-milling town on the Water of Leith. Come here to soak up local color and enjoy a summertime stroll on the path by the river; it makes for great people-watching.

Shopping Along Princes Street. This is the main street of Edinburgh, the local equivalent of New York's Fifth Avenue. Flower-filled gardens stretch along the street's whole south side. When not admiring the flowers, you can browse the country's finest merchandise, everything from kilts to Scottish crystal.

Downing a Pint in an Edinburgh Pub. Sampling a pint of McEwan's real ale or Tennent's lager is a chance to soak up the special atmosphere of Edinburgh. Our favorites are the Abbotsford, Bow Bar, and Kenilworth.

For Fans of Mr. Hyde

Near Gladstone's Land is **Brodie's Close,** a stone-floored alleyway. You can wander into the alley for a view of old stone houses that'll make you think you've stepped into a scene from a BBC production of a Dickens novel. It was named in honor of the notorious Deacon Brodie, a respectable councilor by day and a thief by night (he was the inspiration for Robert Louis Stevenson's *The Strange Case of Dr. Jekyll and Mr. Hyde,* although Stevenson set his story in foggy London town, not in Edinburgh). Brodie was hanged in 1788. The mechanism used for the hangman's scaffolding had previously been improved by Brodie himself—for use on others, of course. Across the street is the most famous pub along the Royal Mile: **Deacon Brodie's Tavern,** 435 Lawnmarket (© 0131/225-6531).

---

whisky industry. A tour entitling you to sample five whiskies and take away a miniature bottle costs £11.95 ($17.95) per person.

354 Castlehill. © **0131/220-0441.** Admission £6.50 ($9.75) adults, £4.25 ($6.40) seniors, £4.50 ($6.75) students, £3.25 ($4.90) children 5–17, £14.50 ($21.75) per family. Daily 10am–5pm.

Outlook Tower and Camera Obscura   The 1853 periscope at the top of the Outlook Tower throws a revolving image of nearby streets and buildings onto a circular table. Guides point out the landmarks and talk about Edinburgh's fascinating history. In addition, there are several entertaining exhibits, all with an optical theme, plus a well-stocked shop selling books, crafts, and CDs.

Castlehill. © **0131/226-3709.** Admission £4.25 ($6.40) adults, £2.70 ($4.05) seniors, £2.10 ($3.15) children. April–Oct Mon–Fri 9:30am–6pm, Sat–Sun 10am–6pm (daily until 7:30pm in July and 7pm in Aug); Nov–March daily 10am–5pm. Bus: 1 or 6.

Writers' Museum   This 1622 house is a treasure trove of portraits, relics, and manuscripts relating to three of Scotland's greatest men of letters: Robert Burns (1759–96), Sir Walter Scott (1771–1832), and Robert Louis Stevenson (1850–94). The Burns collection includes his writing desk, rare manuscripts, portraits, and many other items. Also on display are some of Sir Walter Scott's possessions, including his pipe, chess set, and original manuscripts. The museum holds one of the most significant Stevenson collections anywhere, including personal belongings, paintings, photographs, and early editions.

In Lady Stair's House, off Lawnmarket. © **0131/529-4901.** Free admission. Mon–Sat 10am–5pm.

High Kirk of St. Giles ⊛⊛   Built in 1120 a short walk downhill from Edinburgh Castle, this church is one of the most important architectural landmarks along the Royal Mile. It combines a dark and brooding stone exterior with surprisingly graceful flying buttresses. One of its outstanding features is Thistle Chapel, housing beautiful stalls and notable heraldic stained-glass windows. A particularly severe period in its history occurred between 1560 and 1572, when John Knox, the ultrastrict leader of the Reformation in Scotland, was its minister.

High St. © **0131/225-9442.** Free admission, but £1 ($1.50) donation suggested. Easter–Sept Mon–Fri 9am–7pm, Sat 9am–5pm, Sun 1–5pm; Oct–Easter Mon–Sat 9am–5pm, Sun 1–5pm. Sun services at 8am, 10am, 11:30am, 6pm, and 8pm. Guides are available at all times to conduct tours.

Gladstone's Land ⊛   This 17th-century merchant's house has been furnished and kept in its original style. On the ground floor is a reconstructed shop booth displaying replicas of goods of the period, and an upstairs apartment is furnished as it might have been in the 17th century. It's worth a visit on your journey along the Royal Mile, if only to get the impression of how confined living conditions were, even for the reasonably well off, before the construction of New Town.

477B Lawnmarket. ℂ 0131/226-5856. Admission £3.20 ($4.80) adults, £2.20 ($3.30) children and seniors, £8.60 ($12.90) per family. Apr–Oct Mon–Sat 10am–5pm, Sun 2–5pm.

John Knox House   Even if you're not interested in the reformer who founded the Scottish Presbyterian church, you may want to visit his late-15th-century house, with its timbered gallery, as it's characteristic of the "lands" that used to flank the Royal Mile. The Oak Room is noteworthy for its frescoed ceiling and for its Knox memorabilia. Born into a prosperous East Lothian peasant family, John Knox is acknowledged as the first Moderator of the Presbyterian Church of Scotland, the tenets of which he established in 1560. He's regarded as the prototype Puritan, but actually started his professional life as a Catholic priest and was renowned for his sharp wit and sarcasm. Knox lived at a time of great religious and political upheaval, and although he escaped execution, he spent 2 years as a galley slave in France for agitating against papal authority. On his release, he worked tirelessly with the English crown to ensure Protestant victory in Scotland, and then closely aligned to Catholic France. Knox was also a writer/historian—his *History of the Reformation* was his greatest literary achievement, but he's better known for the inflammatory treatise *The Monstrous Regiment* [Government] *of Women,* largely inspired by his opposition to the reign of Mary Queen of Scots. However, the title did very little to endear him to Mary's cousin Elizabeth I, who insisted his particular brand of crusading zeal remain north of the border.

43–45 High St. ℂ 0131/556-9579. Admission £2.25 ($3.40) adults, £1.75 ($2.65) seniors and students, 75p ($1.10) children. Mon–Sat 10am–4:30pm (July–Sept, also Sun noon–5pm).

Museum of Childhood   The world's first museum devoted solely to the history of childhood stands just opposite the John Knox House. Contents of its four floors range from antique toys to games to exhibits on health, education, and costumes, plus video presentations and an activity area. Not surprisingly, this is usually the noisiest museum in town.

42 High St. ℂ 0131/529-4142. Free admission. Mon–Sat 10am–5pm (July–Aug, also Sun 2–5pm).

The People's Story   If you continue walking downhill along Canongate toward Holyroodhouse (see above), you'll see one of the handsomest buildings on the Royal Mile: Built in 1591, the Canongate Tolbooth was once the courthouse, prison, and center of municipal affairs for the burgh of Canongate. It now contains this museum, which celebrates the social history of the inhabitants of Edinburgh from the late 18th century to the present, with an emphasis on the cultural displacements of the Industrial Revolution.

163 Canongate. ℂ 0131/529-4057. Free admission. Mon–Sat 10am–5pm (Aug, also Sun 2–5pm). Bus 1.

Huntly House   Across from the Canongate Tolbooth (see above) is this fine example of a restored 16th-century mansion, whose builders preferred a bulky, relatively simple design that suited its role as a secular, rather than an ecclesiastical, building. Today, it functions as Edinburgh's principal museum of local history. Inside are faithfully crafted reproductions of rooms inspired by the city's traditional industries, including glassmaking, pottery, wool processing, and cabinetry.

142 Canongate. © 0131/529-4143. Free admission. Mon–Sat 10am–5pm (during the Edinburgh Festival, also Sun 2–5pm). Bus: 1.

THE TOP MUSEUMS & MONUMENTS

National Gallery of Scotland ❋❋❋ In the center of Princes Street Gardens, this gallery is small as national galleries go, but the collection has been chosen with great care and expanded considerably by bequests, gifts, and loans. A recent major acquisition was Giulio Romano's *Vièrge à la Légende*. Other important Italian paintings are Verrocchio's *Ruskin Madonna*, Andrea del Sarto's *Portrait of a Man*, Domenichino's *Adoration of the Shepherds*, and Tiepolo's *Finding of Moses*. There are also works by El Greco and Velázquez.

The duke of Sutherland has lent the museum two Raphaels, Titian's two Diana canvases and *Venus Rising from the Sea*, and Nicolas Poussin's *The Seven Sacraments*. On loan from the queen is an early Netherlandish masterpiece historically linked to Edinburgh, Hugo van der Goess's *Trinity Altarpiece*. Notable also are Rubens's *The Feast of Herod* and *The Reconciliation of Jacob and Esau* and Rembrandt's *Woman in Bed*, as well as superb landscapes by Cuyp and Ruisdael. In 1982, the gallery made one of its most prized acquisitions, Pieter Saenredam's *Interior of St. Bavo's Church, Haarlem*, his largest and arguably finest painting.

The most valuable gift to the gallery since its foundation, the Maitland Collection, includes one of Cézanne's *Mont St-Victoire* series, as well as works by Degas, van Gogh, Renoir, Gauguin, and Seurat. In 1980, two rare works were added: an early Monet, *Shipping Scene—Night Effects*, and a stunning landscape, *Niagara Falls, from the American Side*, by 19th-century American painter Frederic Church. In the new wing (opened in 1978), Henry Raeburn is at his best in the whimsical *The Rev. Robert Walker Skating on Duddingston Loch*.

2 The Mound. © 0131/624-6200. Free admission. Mon–Sat 10am–5pm, Sun noon–5pm; during the Edinburgh Festival, Mon–Sat 10am–6pm, Sun 11am–6pm. Bus: 3, 21, or 26.

Museum of Scotland ❋❋ After being housed (rather awkwardly) in several locations during the 1990s, the Royal Scottish Museum and the National Museum of Antiquities were united in a single headquarters early in 1998. Their newest incarnation, the Museum of Scotland, occupies an 1861 building near the Royal Mile that has been radically upgraded and enlarged with a postmodern wing. Displays include Scotland's most impressive collection of decorative arts, ethnography, natural history, geology, archaeology, technology, and science.

Chambers St. © 0131/225-7534. Free admission. Mon and Wed–Sat 10am–5pm; Tues 10am–8pm; Sun noon–5pm. Walk south from Waverley Station for 10 min. to reach Chambers St., or take bus no. 3, 7, 21, 30, 31, 53, 69, or 80.

Scottish National Gallery of Modern Art ❋ Scotland's national collection of 20th-century art occupies a gallery converted from an 1828 school set on 12 acres (4.9 hectares) of grounds, a 15-minute walk from the west end of Princes Street. The collection is international in scope and quality, despite its modest size. Major sculptures outside include pieces by Henry Moore and Barbara

---

Tips A Note on Museum Hours

Be aware that many museums that are usually closed on Sunday *are* open on Sunday during the Edinburgh Festival. Some museums that open only in summer are also open on public holidays.

The Father of Dr. Jekyll & Mr. Hyde

Robert Louis Stevenson (1850–94) was a complex, often mysterious character. Some saw him as a poet of intellect and sensitivity like Dr. Jekyll, and others as a debauched scoundrel like Mr. Hyde. Born in Edinburgh, he spent much of his life restlessly roaming the world. He has been alternately hailed as Scotland's greatest writer and dismissed as a creator of tall tales for children with limited brain capacity.

Stevenson was the son of Robert Stevenson, the famed Scottish civil engineer. He was a sickly child and, not surprisingly, a big disappointment to his father. When at age 22 he announced he was an agnostic, his father declared, "My son has rendered my whole life a failure." The meager allowance he received from his father drove the promising author to abandon his parents' respectable upper-class neighborhood and live cheaply among Scotland's lowliest dock areas and bordellos. Determined to roam ("I shall be a nomad"), he traveled to France and wrote early works like *An Inland Voyage* (1878) and *Travels with a Donkey in the Cevennes* (1879).

In 1876, he met a married American, Fanny Osborne, who found him an enticing enigma. Fanny divorced her husband by Christmas 1879 and wed Stevenson the following May. She proved a poor critic of his work: She didn't like *The Sea-Cook* (1881), which became the ever-popular *Treasure Island*. That was followed by *Kidnapped* (1886), which Stevenson set in the moorland and wilderness of western Scotland. But his most famous work was *The Strange Case of Dr. Jekyll and Mr. Hyde* (1886). (By the way, Jekyll should be pronounced *Jee*-kill, according to the author.) Fanny's criticism of the first version of this book caused Stevenson to burn it, but he later felt this version was better than the one he published.

Eventually Stevenson and Fanny settled in Samoa, where he bought 300 acres (121.5 hectares), hoping to find a climate that would suit his tuberculosis-damaged lungs. The Samoans loved Stevenson—they called him Tusitala ("Teller of Tales")—but not Fanny. (The Samoan servants labeled her the "Witch Woman of the Mountain.") While here, Stevenson worked on his masterpieces *The Ebb-Tide* (1894) and the unfinished *Weir of Hermiston* (published posthumously in 1896) and translated one of his tales into Samoan. However, his happiness didn't last long, for on December 3, 1894, he suddenly collapsed at only age 43.

More than 200 grieving Samoans dug a road up Mt. Vaea so he could be buried on the mountain he loved. Carved on his grave is his famous requiem:

This be the verse you grave for me:
Here he lies where he longed to be;
Home is the sailor, home from the sea,
And the hunter home from the hill.

Hepworth. Inside, the collection ranges from Braque and Picasso to recent works by Paolozzi. English and Scottish art are strongly represented, and you'll also find artists from Europe and America, notably Matisse, Mir, Kirchner, Ernst, Balthus, Lichtenstein, and Hockney. The cafe sells light refreshments and salads.

Belford Rd. ℂ 0131/556-8921. Free admission, except for some temporary exhibits. Mon–Sat 10am–5pm; Sun noon–5pm. Bus no. 13 stops by the gallery but runs infrequently; nos. 18, 20, and 41 pass along Queensferry Rd., a 5-min. walk up Queensferry Terrace and Belford Rd. from the gallery.

Scottish National Portrait Gallery ℛ   Housed in a red-stone Victorian Gothic building by Rowand Anderson, this portrait gallery gives you a chance to see what the famous people of Scottish history looked like. The portraits, several by Ramsay and Raeburn, include everybody from Mary Queen of Scots to Flora Macdonald to Sean Connery.

1 Queen St. ℂ 0131/624-6200. Free admission, except for some temporary exhibits. Mon–Sat 10am–5pm; Sun noon–5pm. Bus: 18, 20, or 41.

Scott Monument ℛ   Looking more like a church spire than a monument to a writer, the Gothic-inspired Scott Monument is Edinburgh's most famous landmark, completed in the mid–19th century. In the center of the 200-plus-foot (60m) spire is a large seated statue of Sir Walter Scott and his dog, Maida, with Scott's heroes carved as small figures in the monument. You can climb 287 steps to the top for a spectacular view. From here, you can also see the **Burns Monument,** dedicated to Robert Burns and designed by Thomas Hamilton in 1830, clearly visible along Regent Road.

In the East Princes St. Gardens. ℂ 0131/529-4068. Admission £2.50 ($3.75). Mar–May and Oct Mon–Sat 9am–6pm, Sun 10am–6pm; June–Sept Mon–Sat 9am–8pm, Sun 10am–6pm; Nov–Feb Mon–Sat 9am–4pm, Sun 10am–4pm. Bus: 1 or 6.

ADDITIONAL ATTRACTIONS

Dynamic Earth ℛ *Kids*   This former brewery has been converted into a stone amphitheater capped by a futuristic translucent tent. Its galleries celebrate the natural diversity of the physical earth, with emphasis on the seismological and biological processes that led from the Big Bang to the world we know today. The presentation has been called "physical evolution as interpreted by Disney"— audio and video clips; buttons you can push to simulate earthquakes, meteor showers, and views of outer space; replicas of the slimy green primordial soup where life began; time capsules winding their way back through the eons; and a series of specialized aquariums, some with replicas of primordial life forms, some with actual living sharks, dolphins, and coral. You'll wander through simulated terrains like polar ice caps, tundras, deserts, and grasslands. The most dramatic is a tropical rain forest where skies darken at 15-minute intervals, and torrents of rainfall and creepy-crawlies appear underfoot. The most fun part is the exhibit where you can jump up and down on a monitored platform and your movements are amplified to duplicate an earthquake; seismic instruments record what it would have registered on the Richter scale. On the premises are a restaurant, a cafe, a children's play area, and a gift shop. Plan to spend at least 1½ hours here.

Holyrood Rd. ℂ 0131/550-7800. Admission £7.95 ($11.95) adults, £4.95 ($7.45) students, £4.50 ($6.75) seniors and children under 15, £8.50 ($12.75) per family. Apr–Oct daily 10am–6pm; Nov–Mar Wed–Sun 10am–5pm. Bus: 1 or 6.

Britannia: The People's Yacht

In case Queen Elizabeth II never invited you to sail aboard her 412-foot (125m) yacht, you still have a chance to board this famous vessel since the gangplank has been lowered for the public. The luxury *Britannia* 🎖 was launched on April 16, 1953, sailed more than a million miles, and was decommissioned on December 11, 1997. Today, the ship rests at anchor in the port of Leith, 2 miles (3km) from Edinburgh's center. You reach the vessel by going through a visitor center designed by Sir Terence Conran. Once on board, you're guided around all five decks by a 90- to 120-minute audio tour. You can walk the decks where Prince Charles and Princess Diana strolled on their honeymoon, visit the drawing room and the Royal Apartments, and explore the engine room, the galleys, and the captain's cabin.

You must book tickets in advance by calling 📞 **0131/555-5566**. The yacht is open daily except Christmas, with the first tour at 10:30am and the last at 3:50pm. Adults pay £7.75 ($11.65), seniors £5.95 ($8.95), and children 5 to 17 £3.75 ($5.65). A family ticket costs £5.95 ($8.95). From Waverley Bridge, take either city bus (Lothian Transport) X50 or the Guide Friday tour bus marked on its sides with the word BRITANNIA.

Georgian House   Architecturally, the most interesting district of New Town is the north side of Charlotte Square, designed by Robert Adam. Together with his brother, James, he developed a symmetrical but airy style with an elegant reworking of Greek and Roman classical motifs. Their influence was widespread in Britain and the United States, especially in the American South. Georgian House has been refurbished and opened to the public by Scotland's National Trust. The furniture in this Adam house is mainly Hepplewhite, Chippendale, and Sheraton, all from the 18th century. In a ground-floor bedroom is a sturdy old four-poster with an original 18th-century canopy. The dining room table is set with fine Wedgwood china and the kitchen stocked with gleaming copper pots and pans.

7 Charlotte Sq. 📞 **0131/225-2160**. Admission £5 ($7.50) adults; £4 ($6) children, students, and seniors; £14 ($21) per family. Mar–Oct Mon–Sat 10am–4:30pm, Sun 2–4:30pm; Nov–Dec 24 Mon–Sat 11am–3:30pm, Sun 2–3:30pm Bus: 2, 12, 26, or 31.

Royal Observatory Visitor Centre   This center, in a public park on Edinburgh's south side, displays Scotland's largest telescope, antique instruments, and images of astronomical objects. An exhibit called *The Universe* uses photographs, videos, computers, and models to take you on a cosmic whirlwind tour from the beginning of time to the farthest depths of space in a couple of hours. The balcony affords a panoramic view of the city, and the astronomy shop is well stocked.

Blackford Hill. 📞 **0131/668-8405**. Admission £3.50 ($5.25) adults; £2.50 ($3.75) seniors, students, and children 5–16; £8 ($12) per family. Mon–Sat 10am–5pm; Sun noon–5pm. Bus: 40 or 41.

Sir Jules Thorn Exhibition of the History of Surgery/Dental Museum
Edinburgh's rich medical history and associations make the Exhibition of the History of Surgery well worth a visit. On the upper floors of a 19th-century

town house in a tucked-away square, you can chart the development of surgery from 1505 to the 20th century. The sometimes macabre exhibits include such gems as a pocketbook made from the skin of the notorious body snatcher William Burke. The Dental Museum, its gleaming glass cases full of every conceivable dentistry tool, is certainly not for the squeamish or those experiencing dental problems!

9 Hill Sq. (C) 0131/527-1649. Free admission. Mon–Fri 2–4pm. Bus: 31 or 33.

Edinburgh Zoo 🏵🏵 *(Kids)*   This zoo is Scotland's largest animal collection, 10 minutes from Edinburgh's city center on 80 acres (32.4 hectares) of hillside parkland offering unrivaled views from the Pentlands to the Firth of Forth. It contains more than 1,500 animals, including many endangered species: snow leopards, white rhinos, pygmy hippos, and others. The zoo boasts the largest penguin colony in Europe, with four species, plus the world's largest penguin enclosure. From April to September, a penguin parade is held daily at 2pm.

134 Corstorphine Rd. (C) 0131/334-9171. Admission £7 ($10.50) adults, £4.50 ($6.75) seniors, £3.80 ($5.70) children, £20–£24.50 ($30–$36.75) per family. Apr–Sept daily 9am–6pm; Oct–Mar daily 9am–5pm. Parking £2 ($3). Bus: 2, 26, 69, 85, or 86.

THE MONUMENTS ON CALTON HILL

Calton Hill 🏵🏵🏵, rising 350 feet (106m) off Regent Road in the eastern sector, is often credited with giving Edinburgh a look somewhat like that of Athens. It's a hill of monuments; when some of them were created, they were called "instant ruins" by critics. People visit the hill not only to see its monuments but also to enjoy the panoramic views of the Firth of Forth and the city spread beneath it. The "Parthenon" was reproduced in part on this location in 1824. The intention of the builders was to honor the brave Scottish dead killed in the Napoleonic wars. However, the city fathers ran out of money and the monument (often referred to as "Scotland's shame") was never finished.

The **Nelson Monument** ((C) 0131/556-2716), containing relics of the hero of Trafalgar, dates from 1815 and rises more than 100 feet (30m) above the hill. A time ball at the top falls at 1pm Monday through Saturday. The monument is open April to September, Monday from 1 to 6pm and Tuesday through Saturday from 10am to 6pm; and October to March, Monday through Saturday from 10am to 3pm. Admission is £2 ($3). Take bus no. 26, 85, or 86.

For Americans, the curiosity here is the **Lincoln Monument,** which Edinburghers erected in 1893. It was dedicated to the thousands of American soldiers of Scottish descent who lost their lives in America's Civil War. Below Waterloo Place, on the flatter slope of Calton Hill, you can walk through the **Calton Old Cemetery,** dating from the 1700s. Many famous Scots were buried here, often with elaborate tombs honoring their memory (notably the Robert Adam–designed tomb for philosopher David Hume).

DEAN VILLAGE 🏵

Beautiful Dean Village, in a valley about 100 feet (30m) below the level of the rest of Edinburgh, is one of the city's most photographed sights. It's a few minutes from the West End, at the end of Bells Brae off Queensferry Street, on the Water of Leith. The settlement dates from the 12th century, and Dean Village's fame grew as a result of its being a grain-milling center.

You can enjoy a celebrated view by looking downstream under the high arches of Dean Bridge (1833), designed by Telford. The village's old buildings have been restored and converted into apartments and houses. You don't come here for any one particular site but to stroll around, people-watch, and enjoy the village as a whole. You can also walk for miles along the Water of Leith, one of the most tranquil strolls in the greater Edinburgh area.

GARDENS

The **Royal Botanic Garden** ✹✹✹, Inverleith Row (© **0131/552-7171**), is one of the grandest in Great Britain. Sprawling across 70 acres (28.4 hectares), it dates from the late 17th century, when it was originally used for medical studies. In spring, the rhododendrons alone are reason enough to visit Scotland. Admission is by donation. It's open daily: April to August from 9:30am to 7pm, March and September from 9:30am to 6pm, February and October from 9:30am to 5pm, and November to January from 9:30am to 4pm.

As New Town grew, the city fathers decided to turn the area below Edinburgh Castle into the **Princes Street Gardens,** now one of the city's main beauty spots. The area was once Nor Loch, a body of water in the city center, but it was drained to make way for a railway line. (When it was still a bog, the great philosopher David Hume fell into it, couldn't remove himself, and called for help from a passing woman. She recognized him, pronounced him an atheist, and wouldn't offer her umbrella to pull him out of the mire until he recited the Lord's Prayer.)

ORGANIZED TOURS

For a quick introduction to the principal attractions in and around Edinburgh, consider the tours offered from April to late October by **Lothian Region Transport,** 14 Queen St. (© **0131/555-6363**). A curtailed winter program is also offered. You can see most of the major sights by double-decker motorcoach, with guided commentary, at a cost of £7.50 ($11.25) for adults, £6 ($9) for seniors and students, and £2.50 ($3.75) for children. This ticket is valid all day on any LRT Edinburgh Classic Tour bus, allowing you to get on and off at any of the 15 stops. Buses start from the Waverley Bridge near the Scott Monument daily at 9:15am, departing every 15 minutes in summer and about every 30 minutes in winter; if you remain on the bus without getting off, the trip will take about 2 hours.

LRT also operates half- and full-day motorcoach excursions throughout Scotland. White-sided buses identified by their black trim depart from Waverley Station for "Highland Splendour Tours" to such places as Loch Lomond, Loch Katrine, the Trossachs, St. Andrews, the Isle of Arran, and selected sights in Braemar and Deeside. Prices range from £5 to £18 ($7.50 to $27) and sometimes include lunch. Itineraries vary with the day of the week.

You can buy tickets for any of these tours at LRT offices at Waverley Bridge or 27 Hanover St., or at the tourist center in Waverley Market. Advance reservations for the half- and full-day tours are a good idea. For more information, call © **0131/220-2221,** 24 hours.

A former English teacher, **Jackie Queally,** runs the most personalized tours around Edinburgh. She has turned her hobby of exploring legends and landscapes into a business, offering tours of greater Edinburgh that take in cairns, wells, standing stones, groves, chapels, and knights' strongholds. She brings alive personalities such as King Arthur and the wizard Merlin, along with Celtic saints and the mysterious Druids. She has even found local sites linked to the Holy Grail, and she calls Rosslyn Chapel, south of Edinburgh, "the Glastonbury of Scotland." These off-the-beaten-track minibus tours cost £35 ($52.50) per adult and £20 ($30) per child. To book, call © **0131/662-8592.**

6 Special Events

Hogmanay begins on New Year's Eve and merges into New Year's Day festivities. It's celebrated throughout Scotland with the ritual kissing of everyone in sight, followed by the time-honored practice of "first footing" with a lump of coal, a bun, and (needless to say) a drop of the hard stuff. In 1993, the Edinburgh City Council began a 3-day festival that now features street theater, lively processions illuminated by firebrands, and the burning of a long boat. By 1997, the crush to attend Europe's largest winter festival forced the city to limit numbers; you now have to get tickets to enter the city center after 8pm on New Year's Eve. For details, call © **0131/473-3800.**

January 25 is **Burns Night,** *the* night when Scots the world over gather to consume the traditional supper of haggis, neeps (turnips), and tatties (potatoes), accompanied by a wee dram of whisky, while listening to recitals of the works of Scotland's Bard, Robert "Rabbie" Burns, whose birthday is being celebrated. Burns suppers are held all over town.

By far, the highlight of Edinburgh's year comes in the last weeks of August during the **Edinburgh International Festival.** Since 1947, the festival has attracted artists and companies of the highest international standard in all fields of the arts, including music, opera, dance, theater, poetry, and prose. One of the festival's most exciting spectacles is the **Military Tattoo** on the floodlit esplanade in front of Edinburgh Castle, high on its rock above the city. First performed in 1950, the Tattoo features the precision marching of not only the British Army's Scottish regiments but also performers from some 30 countries, including bands, dancers, drill teams, gymnasts, and motorcyclists, even horses, camels, elephants, and police dogs. The music ranges from ethnic to pop and from military to jazz. Schedules are released each year about 6 months before the festival, but they're subject to change. Mail-order bookings are available from the Edinburgh Military Tattoo, Tattoo Office, 32 Market St., Edinburgh EH1 1QB (© **0131/225-1188**). You can check schedules and buy tickets online at **www.eif.co.uk.**

Less predictable in quality but greater in quantity is the **Edinburgh Festival Fringe,** an opportunity for anybody—professional or nonprofessional, an individual, a group of friends, or a whole company—to put on a show wherever they can find an empty stage or street corner. Late-night revues, outrageous contemporary drama, university theater presentations, even full-length opera—Edinburgh gives them all free rein. As if that weren't enough, Edinburgh has a **Film Festival,** a **Jazz Festival,** a **Television Festival,** and a non-annual **Book Festival** at the same time.

Ticket prices vary from £5 to £50 ($7.50 to $75). You can get information from **Edinburgh International Festival,** The Hub, Castle Hill, Edinburgh EH1 7ND (© **0131/473-2000;** fax 0131/473-2003), open Monday through Friday from 9:30am to 5:30pm. Other sources of information are the **Edinburgh Festival Fringe,** 180 High St., Edinburgh EH1 1BW (© **0131/226-5257); Edinburgh Book Festival,** Scottish Book Centre, 137 Dundee St., Edinburgh EH11 1BG (© **0131/228-5444**); and **Edinburgh Film Festival,** 88 Lothian Rd., Edinburgh EH3 9BZ (© **0131/228-4051**).

The most convenient but slightly more expensive way to order tickets for the festival is to purchase them before you leave home from **Global Tickets, Inc.,** 1270 Ave. of the Americas, New York, NY 10020 (© **800/223-6108**).

7 Spectator Sports & Outdoor Pursuits

SPECTATOR SPORTS

HORSE RACING   Place your bets at the **Musselburgh Racecourse,** Musselburgh Park (✆ **0131/665-2859**), about 4 miles (6.5km) east of Edinburgh. In summer, the races are on a flat circular track, but in winter, the more elaborate National Hunt format challenges horses and riders to a series of jumps and obstacle courses of great technical difficulty. Admission is £8 to £13 ($12 to $19.50).

RUGBY   Home of the National Rugby Team of Scotland, **Murrayfield Stadium,** Murrayfield (✆ **0131/346-5000**), is about a mile (1.6km) west of Edinburgh. The sport is played from September to April, usually on Saturdays. Some of the most passionate matches are those among teams from the five-nation bloc comprising Scotland, Wales, England, Ireland, and France. These matches occur only between January and March, when sports enthusiasts in Scotland seem to talk about little else. Ticket prices range from £23 to £35 ($34.50 to $52.50).

SOCCER   You might quickly get swept up in the zeal of Edinburghers for their local soccer (referred to as "football") clubs. Both teams, when not battling each other, challenge other teams from throughout Europe. The home of the Edinburgh Hearts (more formally known as the Heart of Midlothian Football Club) is **Tynecastle Park,** Gorgie Road (✆ **0131/337-7004**); the home of the Hibs (short for the Hibernians) is **Easter Road Park,** Easter Road (✆ **0131/ 661-2159**). The traditional playing times are Saturday afternoons, when games are likely to be televised in pubs throughout Scotland. Tickets range from £10 to £22 ($15 to $33).

OUTDOOR ACTIVITIES

GOLF   Note that none of the following courses has caddy service.

The par-74 **Silverknowes Golf Course,** Silverknowes Parkway (✆ **0131/ 336-3843**), is a 6,202-yard (5,644m) course. Greens fees for 18 holes are £10 ($15) Monday through Friday and £12.50 ($18.75) Saturday and Sunday, with club and cart rentals costing £10.70 ($16.05) and £1.50 ($2.25), respectively.

The par-67 **Craigentinny,** Craigentinny Gold, Fillyside Road (✆ **0131/ 554-7501**), 3 miles (5km) east of Edinburgh, features 5,413 yards (4,926m) of playing area. Clubs rent for £11.25 ($16.90) per round and carts for £1.50 ($2.25). Greens fees for 18 holes are £10 ($15) Monday through Friday and £11.50 ($17.25) Saturday and Sunday.

The par-67, 5,306-yard (4,828m) **Liberton Golf Course,** Kingston Grange, 297 Gilmerton Rd. (✆ **0131/664-8580**), requires 2 days' notice if you want to rent clubs, the price of which is included in the greens fees of £20 ($30) Monday through Friday for 18 holes. On Saturday and Sunday, fees are £35 ($52.50). Carts can be rented for £5 ($7.50).

The par-70 **Braids,** Braid House Golf Course, Approach Road (✆ **0131/ 447-6666**), is 3 miles (5km) south of Edinburgh's city center. The greens fees at this 5,731-yard (5,215m) course are £12 ($18) Monday through Friday and £14 ($21) Saturday and Sunday. Clubs rent for £11.25 ($16.90) including deposit; carts go for £1.50 ($2.25) plus a £20 ($30) deposit per 18 holes of play.

The par-66 **Swanston Golf Course,** Swanston Road (✆ **0131/445-4002**), is an 18-hole, 4,825-yard (4,391m) course located 9 miles (14.5km) southwest of Edinburgh. Clubs go for £7 ($10.50) and trolleys for £2 ($3); greens fees are

£10 ($15) per round Monday through Friday and £15 ($22.50) Saturday and Sunday. The per-day rates are £17.50 to £25 ($26.25 to $37.50).

The **Portobello,** Stanley Street (© **0131/669-4361**), is a 9-hole course with a par of 64. The greens fees at this 2,410-yard (2,193m) course are £4.50 to £9 ($6.75 to $13.50) Monday through Friday and £5 to £10 ($7.50 to $15) Saturday and Sunday. A deposit of £10 ($15) is required for club rental, costing £10.70 ($16.05). Carts go for £1.50 ($2.25) plus a £10 ($15) deposit.

Carrick Knowe, Glen Devon Park (© **0131/557-5457**), is one of Scotland's larger courses, featuring 6,229 yards (5,668m) of playing area. Five miles (8km) west of Edinburgh, this 18-hole, par-71 course was redesigned in 1998 and offers club rentals at £10.65 ($16) and trolleys at £1.55 ($2.35). The greens fees for 18 holes are £9.20 ($13.80) Monday through Friday and £11 ($16.50) Saturday and Sunday.

The par-66 **Torphin Hill Golf Course,** Torphin Road (© **0131/441-1100**), is a 4,648-yard (4,230m), 18-hole course, offering no club rentals or trolleys. The greens fees are £14 ($21) per round Monday through Friday and £20 ($30) per day Saturday and Sunday.

SAILING   Visit the Firth of Forth firsthand by contacting the **Port Edgar Sailing Centre,** Port Edgar, South Queensferry (© **0131/331-3330**), about 9 miles (14.5km) west of the city center. Between Easter and mid-October, it offers instruction in small-craft sailing, canoeing, and powerboating, as well as half-day rentals. The rate for a dinghy, suitable for four adults, is £25.40 ($38.10) for 2 hours. April through September, the center is open daily from 9am to 7:30pm, and boats can be hired to 9pm. In winter, it's open daily from 9am to 5pm.

TENNIS   Reservations are necessary for the courts at the **Craiglockhart Sports Centre,** 177 Colinton Rd. (© **0131/444-1969**), which also has badminton courts and a gym. Indoor courts cost £8.30 to £15 ($12.45 to $22.50) per hour for adults and £8.30 ($12.45) for children; they're available Monday through Thursday from 9am to 9:30pm, Friday from 10am to 9:30pm, and Saturday and Sunday from 9am to 9pm. The outdoor courts cost £4 to £9.10 ($6 to $13.65) per hour for adults and £4 ($6) for children; these are available Saturday through Wednesday from 9am until dark and Friday from 10am until dark (there's no electric lighting). They're closed when the weather turns cold. Racquet rental costs £1.60 ($2.40). More convenient and sometimes more crowded are a handful of concrete-surfaced **public tennis courts** behind George Square, on the north side of the public park known as the Meadows.

8 Shopping

New Town's **Princes Street** is the main shopping artery. **George Street** and Old Town's **Royal Mile** are also major shopping areas. The best buys are in tartans and woolens, along with bone china and Scottish crystal.

Shopping hours are generally Monday through Saturday from 9am to 5 or 5:30pm and Sunday from 11am to 5pm. On Thursdays, many shops remain open to 7 or 8pm.

BOOKS

James Thin, Ltd.   Edinburgh's most respected bookstore is a vast resource for virtually every academic discipline imaginable, yet also stocks a hefty number of counterculture and pop fiction titles, including a section on gay literature. 53 South Bridge. © 0131/556-6743. Bus: 3, 31.

BRASS RUBBINGS
Scottish Stone and Brass Rubbing Centre   You can rub any of the brass or stones on display here to create your own wall hangings, or buy them ready made. Those commemorating King Robert the Bruce are particularly impressive. The brass you choose is covered in white or black paper, silver wax is used to outline the brass, and then you fill it in with different colors of wax. You can visit the center's collection of replicas molded from ancient Pictish stones, rare Scottish brasses, and medieval church brasses. Trinity Apse, Chalmers Close, near the Royal Mile. © 0131/556-4364. Bus: 1.

CRYSTAL
Edinburgh Crystal   Edinburgh Crystal is devoted to handmade crystal glassware. The visitor center (open Mon–Sat 9am–4:30pm, Sun 11am–4:30pm) contains the factory shop where the world's largest collection of Edinburgh Crystal (plus inexpensive factory seconds) is on sale. Although Waterford is the more prestigious name, Edinburgh Crystal is a serious competitor, its most popular design being the thistle, symbolizing Scotland. It can be traced back to the 17th century, when the glassmaking art was brought here by the Venetians. The center also has a gift shop and a coffee shop specializing in home baking. Half-hour tours of the factory to watch glassmakers at work are given Monday through Friday from 9am to 5pm; between April and September, weekend tours are given from 11am to 2:30pm. Tours costs £3 ($4.50) for adults, £2 ($3) for children, and £7.50 ($11.25) per family. Eastfield, Penicuik (10 miles/16km south of Edinburgh, just off A701 to Peebles). © 01968/675-128. Bus: 62 (Lowland), 64 or 65 (green), or 81 or 87 (red) Waverly bus link. A free minibus from Waverley Station leaves on the hour Mon–Fri 10am–4pm, Sat–Sun 11am–2pm.

DEPARTMENT STORES & A MALL
Debenham's   Old reliable Debenham's is still perhaps the best department store in Edinburgh, with a wide array of Scottish and international merchandise displayed in a marble-covered interior. 109–112 Princes St. © 0131/225-1320. Bus: 3, 31, 69.

Jenners   Everyone in Edinburgh has probably been to Jenner's at least once. Its neo-Gothic facade, opposite the Scott Monument, couldn't be more prominent. The store's array of Scottish and international merchandise is astounding. Jenner's sells much the same merchandise as Debenham's, but it boasts a wider selection of china and glassware, and has a well-known food hall with a wide array of products, including heather honey, Dundee marmalade, and a vast selection of Scottish shortbreads and cakes. 48 Princes St. © 0131/225-2442. Bus: 3, 31, 69.

Princes Mall   There's something for everyone at this tri-level mall. You can browse through some 80 shops selling fashions, accessories, gifts, books, jewelry, beauty products, and a wide selection of Scottish arts and crafts. Unique

---

Tips Bring That Passport!
Take along your passport when you go shopping in case you make a purchase that entitles you to a **VAT (value-added tax)** refund. For details, see "Getting Your VAT Refund" under "Fast Facts: Scotland," in chapter 2.

handmade items are sold in the crafts center. The food court has tempting snacks, while the food hall boasts top-quality produce. Next to Waverley Station, Princes St. ℭ 0131/557-3759. Bus: 3, 31, 69.

DOLLS

Doll Hospital (Geraldine's of Edinburgh)   Lined with glass-fronted display cases, this is a basement showroom for Edinburgh's only doll factory, with more than 100 dolls. Each of the heirloom-quality dolls requires about 10 full days' labor to create and has a hand-painted porcelain head and sometimes an elaborate coiffure. Also available are fully jointed, all-mohair teddy bears that your child will love. 35A Dundas St. ℭ 0131/556-4295. Bus: 23, 27.

FASHION

Bill Baber   Ten to 15 highly creative craftspeople work here, creating artfully modernized adaptations of traditional Scottish patterns for both men and women. Expect to find traditional Scottish jacquard-patterned knits spiced up with strands of Caribbean-inspired turquoise or aqua; rugged-looking blazers, jackets, and sweaters suitable for treks or bike rides through the moors; and tailored jackets a woman might feel comfortable wearing to a glamorous cocktail party. 66 Grassmarket, near the Royal Mile. ℭ 0131/225-3249. Bus: 2, 12.

Corniche   Designer Nina Grant operates the most sophisticated boutique in Edinburgh. If it's the latest in Scottish fashion, expect to find it here, even "Anglomania kilts" designed by that controversial lady of fashion herself, Vivienne Westwood. Relative newcomer Jackie Burke has made a splash with her fur-trimmed Harris tweed riding jackets. 2 Jeffrey St. ℭ 0131/556-3707.

Edinburgh Woollen Mill Shop   One of about 30 such shops throughout the United Kingdom, the Edinburgh Woollen Mill Shop sells good Scottish woolens, knitwear, skirts, gifts, and travel rugs. Note, however, that most of the merchandise is made in England. 139 Princes St. ℭ 0131/226-3840. Bus: 3, 31, 69.

Schuh   Schuh has the latest in unique footwear, specializing in the yellow, red, and blue plaid boots made famous by the local rugby team. Expect fierce, funky finds. 6 Frederick St. ℭ 0131/220-0290.

Shetland Connection   Owner Moira-Ann Leask promotes Shetland Island knitwear, and her shop is packed with sweaters, hats, and gloves in colorful Fair Isle designs. She also offers hand-knitted mohair, Aran, and Icelandic sweaters. Items range from fine-ply cobweb shawls to chunky ski sweaters in high-quality wool. A large range of Celtic jewelry and gifts makes this shop a top-priority visit. 491 Lawnmarket. ℭ 0131/225-3525. Bus: 1.

GIFTS

Ness Scotland   Along the Royal Mile, Ness Scotland is filled with whimsical accessories searched out by Gordon MacAulay and Adrienne Wells. They have scoured the country from the Orkney Islands to the Borders for that unique item. You'll see hand-loomed cardigans, tasteful scarves, and charming Dinky bags made during the long winters on the Isle of Lewis. 367 High St. ℭ 0131/226-5227.

JEWELRY

Alistir Tait   This is one of the most charming jewelry stores in Edinburgh, with a reputation for Scottish minerals like agates; Scottish gold; garnets, sapphires, and freshwater pearls; and estate jewelry. Ask to see the artful depictions of Luckenbooths. Fashioned as pendants, usually as two entwined hearts capped

ⓒ Tracing Your Ancestral Roots

If you have a name beginning with Mac (which simply means "son of") or one of the other Scottish names, you may have descended from a clan, a group of kinsmen claiming a common ancestry. Clans and clan societies have their own museums throughout Scotland, and local tourist offices will have details about where to locate them. Bookstores throughout Scotland sell clan histories and maps.

Scotland's densest concentration of genealogical records is at the **General Register Office**, New Register House, 3 W. Register St., Edinburgh EH1 3YT (ⓒ **0131/334-0380**; Bus: 3, 26, 33, 86). Opened in 1863 in a black-brick Victorian headquarters, it contains hundreds of thousands of microfiche and microfilm documents and a computerized system that tells you where to begin looking for whatever records interest you. The strictly self-service system is open Monday through Friday from 9am to 4:30pm; it gets crowded in summer. The fee you pay for a full day's access to the records is £17 ($25.50); if you enter after 1pm, you'll pay £10 ($15).

The house has on record details of every birth, marriage, and death in Scotland since 1855. There are also old parish registers, the earliest dating from 1553, listing baptisms, marriages, and burials, but these older records are far from complete. It also has census returns for every decade from 1841 to 1891 and such data as the foreign marriages of Scots, adopted children's registers, and war registers.

by a royal crest, they're associated with the loves and tragedies of Mary Queen of Scots and often accessorized with a baroque pearl. They come in subtle hues of petal, orange, brown, and (most desirable and rare) purple. Prices for Luckenbooths are £28 to £250 ($42 to $375). 116A Rose St. ⓒ **0131/225-4105.** Bus: 3, 31, 69.

Hamilton & Inches   Since 1866, the prestigious Hamilton & Inches has sold gold and silver jewelry, porcelain and silver, and gift items. You'll find everything you'd want for an upscale wedding present, all sorts of jewelry, and two memorable kinds of silver dishes—weighty plates copied from items found in the Spanish Armada wrecks during Elizabeth I's reign and endearingly folkloric *quaichs.* The quaichs originated in the West Highlands as whisky measures crafted from wood or horn and were later gentrified into something like silver porringers or chafing dishes, each with a pair of lugs (ears) fashioned into Celtic or thistle patterns. 87 George St. ⓒ **0131/225-4898.** Bus: 41, 42.

Robert Anthony   One of Edinburgh's best jewelers, Robert Anthony sells new, antique, and second-hand pieces, as well as gold chains, fine gemstones, and (its specialty) diamonds. Check out the gold bangles and pendants in 9-karat gold. Gold replicas of Scottish pipers and dancers, thistles, and Edinburgh Castle make good souvenirs. 108B Rose St. ⓒ **0131/226-4550.** Bus: 41, 42.

LINENS & BEDS

Linens Fine The danger of popping into the upscale Linens Fine is you might make a much larger investment than you'd intended once you see the fine-textured sheets of Italian, Portuguese, and British cotton. There's also a beautiful collection of ornate brass, iron, and wooden beds you can order and have shipped anywhere. Beds begin at £550 ($825) and go all the way up to £5,000 ($7,500). 30 Dundas St. ℂ 0131/225-6998. Bus: 23, 27.

MUSIC

Virgin Megastore Here you'll find one of the biggest selections of records, CDs, videos, and tapes in Scotland. The shop has a special strength in traditional and Scottish music. The staff is charming and eager to share their love of Scottish music with interested visitors. 125 Princes St. ℂ 0131/220-2230. Bus: 3, 31, 69.

TARTANS & KILTS

Anta Some of the most stylish tartans are found at Anta, where Lachian and Anne Stewart, the creative design team behind Ralph Lauren's home tartan fabrics, present a series of tartans newly invented in unique styles. The woolen blankets with hand-purled fringe are woven on old-style looms. 32 High St. ℂ 0131/557-8300.

Clan Tartan Centre This is one of the leading tartan specialists in Edinburgh, regardless of which clan you claim as your own. If you want help in identifying a particular tartan, the staff will assist you. 70–74 Bangor Rd., Leith. ℂ 0131/553-5100. Bus: 7, 10.

Geoffrey (Tailor) Highland Crafts This is the most famous kiltmaker in the Scottish capital. Its customers have included Sean Connery, Charlton Heston, Dr. Ruth Westheimer, members of Scotland's rugby teams, and Mel Gibson (who favors the tartan design Hunting Buchanan and wore his outfit when he received an award from the Scottish government after filming *Braveheart*). Expect a delay of 4 to 8 weeks before your costume can be completed. The company sets up sales outlets at Scottish reunions and Highland Games around the world and maintains a toll-free number (ℂ 800/566-1467) for anyone who calls from the United States or Canada and wants to be outfitted. It stocks 200 of Scotland's best-known tartan patterns and is revolutionizing the kilt by establishing a subsidiary called 21st Century Kilts, which makes them in fabrics ranging from denim to leather.

Geoffrey is also one of the few kiltmakers to actually weave the object, and you can watch the process at the **Edinburgh Old Town Weaving Company,** 555 Castlehill (ℂ 0131/557-0256; Bus: 1), Monday through Friday from 9am to 5pm. Note that the factory doesn't sell kilts directly to visitors. 57–59 High St. ℂ 0131/557-0256. Bus: 1.

James Pringle Woolen Mill The mill produces a large variety of top-quality wool items, including cashmere sweaters, tartan and tweed ties, travel rugs, tweed hats, and tam o' shanters. In addition, it boasts one of Scotland's best Clan Tartan Centres, with more than 5,000 tartans accessible. A free audiovisual presentation shows the history and development of the tartan. You can visit for free, and there's even a free taxi service to the mill from anywhere in Edinburgh (ask at your hotel). 70–74 Bangor Rd., Leith. ℂ 0131/553-5161. Bus: 7, 10.

Tartan Gift Shops Tartan Gift Shops has a chart indicating the place of origin (in Scotland) of family names, accompanied by a bewildering array of hunt and dress tartans for men and women, sold by the yard. There's also a line of lambswool and cashmere sweaters and all the accessories. 54 High St. ℭ 0131/ 558-3187. Bus: 1.

9 Edinburgh After Dark

Every year in late August, the **Edinburgh International Festival** brings numerous world-class cultural offerings to the city, but year-round there are plenty of choices, whether you prefer theater, opera, ballet, or other diversions. The waterfront district, featuring many jazz clubs and restaurants, is especially lively in summer, and students flock to the pubs and clubs around Grassmarket. Discos are found off High and Princes streets, and in the city's numerous pubs you can often hear traditional Scottish folk music for the price of a pint.

For a thorough list of entertainment options during your stay, pick up a copy of *The List,* a free biweekly paper available at the tourist office. Before you leave home, you might want to check *Time Out* (www.timeout.co.uk) for the latest listings.

THE PERFORMING ARTS

THEATER   Edinburgh has a lively theater scene. In 1994, the **Festival Theatre,** 13–29 Nicolson St. (ℭ 0131/662-1112 for administration, 0131/ 529-6000 for tickets during non-festival times, or 0131/225-5756 for tickets during the festival; Bus: 3, 31, 33), opened in time for some aspects of the Edinburgh Festival. Set on the eastern edge of Edinburgh, near the old campus of the University of Edinburgh, it has since been called "Britain's de facto Dance House" because of its sprung floor, its enormous stage (the largest in Britain), and its suitability for opera presentations of all kinds. Tickets are £5.50 to £45.50 ($8.25 to $68.25).

Another major theater is the **King's Theatre,** 2 Leven St. (ℭ 0131/ 529-6000; Bus: 10, 11), a 1,600-seat Victorian venue offering a wide repertoire of classical entertainment, including ballet, opera, and West End productions.

The **Netherbow Arts Centre,** 43 High St. (ℭ 0131/556-9579; Bus: 1), has been called "informal," and productions here are often experimental and delightful—new Scottish theater at its best. Ask about lunchtime performances.

The resident company of the **Royal Lyceum Theatre,** Grindlay Street (ℭ 0131/248-4848; Bus: 11, 15), also has an enviable reputation; its presentations range from Shakespeare to new Scottish playwrights.

The **Traverse Theatre,** Cambridge Street (ℭ 0131/228-1404; Bus: 11, 15), is one of the few theaters in Britain funded solely to present new plays by British writers and first translations into English of international works. In a modern location, it now offers two theaters under one roof: Traverse 1 seats 250 and Traverse 2 seats 100.

BALLET, OPERA & CLASSICAL MUSIC   The **Scottish Ballet** and the **Scottish Opera** perform at the **Playhouse Theatre,** 18–22 Greenside Place (ℭ 0131/557-0540; Bus: 7, 14), which, with 3,100 seats, is the town's largest theater. The **Scottish Chamber Orchestra** makes its home at the **Queen's Hall,** Clerk Street (ℭ 0131/668-2019; Bus: 3, 33, 31), also a major venue for the Edinburgh International Festival.

FOLK MUSIC & CEILIDHS   Folk music is presented in many clubs and pubs in Edinburgh, but these strolling players tend to be somewhat erratic or irregular in their appearances. It's best to read notices in pubs and talk to the tourist office to see where the ceilidh will be on the night of your visit.

Some hotels regularly feature traditional Scottish music in the evenings. You might check with the **George Hotel,** 19–21 George St. (✆ **0131/225-1251;** Bus: 3, 31, 33). **Jamie's Scottish Evening** is presented at the King James Hotel on Leith Street (✆ **0131/556-0111;** Bus: 7, 14) Tuesday through Sunday at 7pm, costing £41 ($61.50) for a four-course dinner, wine, and show.

THE CLUB & MUSIC SCENE

The Cavendish   This isn't necessarily where you go to hear the next Oasis or Blur, but who knows? A rock legend might be born here every Friday or Saturday, when live bands take the stage. No tennis shoes or jeans. The bar is open Thursday through Saturday from 10pm to 3am. 3 W. Tollcross. ✆ 0131/228-3252. Cover £6 ($9) Fri–Sat. Bus: 11, 15, 23.

Club Mercado   The glamorous Club Mercado, once the headquarters of the Scottish branch of British Rail, hangs suspended over the rail tracks behind the city's main station. On Friday, the action kicks off with no-cover TFIS, which stands for a somewhat saltier version of "Thank God It's Friday"; it runs from 5 to 10pm and caters to youngish workers who indulge in cut-price drinks. Other special nights are alternate-Saturday Viva (eclectic music attracting all sorts from toughs to drag queens) and Eye Candy (basically a rave featuring the latest house music). Open daily from 10pm to 3am. 36–39 Market St. ✆ 0131/226-4224. Cover £3–£10 ($4.50–$15), depending on what's on. Bus: 1.

Po Na Na   Po Na Na is the Edinburgh branch of the most successful chain of clubs in Britain. The theme is a Moroccan casbah, thanks to wall mosaics, brass lanterns, and artifacts shipped in from Marrakech. You'll dance to a mix of house and funk in the cellar of a transformed 19th-century building, beneath a tented ceiling illuminated with strobes. Po Na Na isn't specifically gay, but does draw a strong gay following. Open daily from 8pm to 3am. 43B Frederick St. ✆ 0131/226-2224. Cover £2–£3 ($3–$4.50). Bus: 80.

Revolution   Popular with an under-25 crowd, this is Edinburgh's largest club, with a capacity of 1,500. Mainstream dance music (plus five bars) attracts the crowds, and there are theme and student nights as well. Open Wednesday through Saturday from 10pm to 3am. 31 Lothian Rd. ✆ 0131/229-7670. Cover £3–£7 ($4.50–$10.50). Bus: 11, 15.

Moments   A Wee Dram for Fans of Malt Whisky

It requires a bit of an effort to reach it (take bus 10A, 16, or 17 from Princes Street to Leith), but for fans of malt whisky, the **Scotch Malt Whisky Society** has been called "The Top of the Whisky Pyramid" by distillery-industry magazines in Britain. It's on the second floor of a 16th-century warehouse at 87 Giles St., Leith (✆ **0131/554-3451**), and was originally designed to store Bordeaux and port wines from France and Portugal. All you can order are single-malt whiskies, served neat, usually in a dram (unless you want yours watered down with branch water), and selected from a staggering choice of whiskies from more than 100 distilleries throughout Scotland. Hours are Monday through Wednesday from 8:30am to 5:30pm, Thursday through Saturday from 10am to 11pm.

The Venue   Behind the main post office and Waverley Station is the Venue, the principal stage for live music. Some of the biggest bands in the United Kingdom perform here. 15 Calton Rd. © 0131/557-3073. Bus: 26.

Whynot   In the basement of the Dome Bar & Grill (see "Dining," earlier in this chapter), Whynot is a hot entertainment complex that opened in the former Bank of Scotland building. It has low ceilings with veil-like curtains above the dance floor and lots of seating coves tucked away for privacy. The club swings Thursday through Sunday from 10pm to 3am. On Thursday, there's dancing to the music of the 1960s, 1970s, and 1980s; Friday features mainstream pop; and Saturday brings the best in contemporary dance music. 14 George St. © 0131/624-8633. Cover £3–£7.50 ($4.50–$11.25). Bus: 41, 42.

PUBS & BARS

The Abbotsford   Near the eastern end of Rose Street, a short walk from Princes Street, the Abbotsford has served stiff drinks and oceans of beer since 1887. The gaslight era is alive here, thanks to a careful preservation of the original dark paneling, battered tables, and ornate plaster ceiling. The beers on tap change about once a week, supplementing the roster of single malts. Drinks are served Monday through Saturday from 11am to 11pm. Platters of food are dispensed from the bar Monday through Saturday from noon to 3pm and 5:30 to 10pm. 3 Rose St. © 0131/225-5276. Bus: 3, 31, 33.

Bow Bar   Near Edinburgh Castle, the Victorian Bow Bar is arranged around a series of tall beer pulls, antique phonographs, pendulum clocks, and as many as 140 single-malt whiskies from virtually every corner of the country. The only food offerings are simple snacks like steak or minced pie. Open Monday through Saturday from 11am to 11:30pm and Sunday from 12:30 to 11pm. 80 West Bow. © 0131/226-7667. Bus: 2, 12.

Café Royal Circle Bar   This is Edinburgh's most famous pub. One part is now occupied by the Oyster Bar of the Café Royal, but life in the Circle Bar continues as usual, still with the opulent trappings of the Victorian era. Hours for the bar are Monday through Wednesday from 11am to 11pm, Thursday from 11am to midnight, Friday and Saturday from 11am to 1am, and Sunday from 12:30 to 11pm. The restaurant is open Sunday through Wednesday from noon to 2pm and 7 to 10pm (Thursday to midnight, Friday and Saturday to 1am). 17 W. Register St. © 0131/556-1884. Bus: 3, 31, 33.

Deacon Brodie's Tavern   Opened in 1806, Deacon Brodie's is the neighborhood pub along the Royal Mile. It perpetuates the memory of Deacon Brodie, good citizen by day and robber by night. The tavern and wine cellars offer a traditional pub setting and lots of atmosphere. The tavern is open Sunday through Thursday from 10am to midnight and Friday and Saturday from 10am to 1am. Light meals are served in the bar from 10am to 10pm; in the restaurant upstairs, more substantial food is served from noon to 10pm. 435 Lawnmarket. © 0131/225-6531. Bus: 1.

Drum & Monkey   A block from Princes Street, the Drum & Monkey opened about a century ago and has functioned as both a Japanese restaurant and the local branch of P. J. Clarke's in New York. After a refurbishment of its Victorian-Gothic decor, it has returned to dispensing pints of lager, stiff drinks, and bar fare. At least eight brands of beer are on tap, and the bar platters include haggis, bangers and mash, chicken focaccia, nachos, and burgers. Drinks are served daily from 11:30am to 11pm (Saturday to midnight), with food available

Monday through Friday from 11:30am to 7pm and Saturday from 12:30 to 7pm. 80 Queen St. ✆ 0131/226-9932. Bus: 80.

Guildford Arms   This place got a face-lift back to the mauve era of the 1890s, although a pub has stood here for 200 years. The Victorian Italianesque pub has seven arched windows with etched glass and an ornate ceiling. It's large, bustling, and at times a bit rough, but has plenty of character. Upstairs is a fish-and-chips shop run by the same company. Place your order at the upstairs bar. At festival time, folk music is presented nightly. Open Monday through Wednesday from 11am to 11pm, Thursday through Saturday from 11am to midnight, and Sunday from 12:30 to 11pm. 1–5 W. Register St. ✆ 0131/556-4312. Bus: 3, 31, 33.

GAY BARS & CLUBS

The heart of the gay community is centered on **Broughton Street** around the Playhouse Theatre (take bus 8, 9, or 19). Be sure to check "The Club & Music Scene" (see above) for the heavily gay crowd at **Po Na Na.**

C. C. Bloom's   Named after Bette Midler's character in *Beaches,* C. C. Bloom's is one of Edinburgh's most popular gay spots. The upstairs bar offers drinks and camaraderie; on Thursday and Sunday at 11pm, there's karaoke, and Sunday afternoons heat up with a male stripper. The downstairs club offers dancing to a wide range of music, with no cover. Open Monday through Saturday from 6pm to 3am and Sunday from 3pm to 3am.

Next door is **Habana,** 22 Greenside Place (✆ **0131/556-4349**), drawing a mixed gay crowd daily from noon to 1am. 23–24 Greenside Place. ✆ 0131/556-9331.

New Town Bar   Adjacent to the corner of Queen Street is the New Town Bar, a street-level pub where everyday blokes clad in everything from jeans to suits gather for a pint of lager. It's open daily from noon to 2am. If you're looking for something a bit less conventional and it happens to be Wednesday through Sunday between 10pm and 2am, head into the basement for the Intense Cruise Bar, where the crowd dons its own interpretations of Tom of Finland combat gear, leather, and uniforms. Depending on the crowd, this can be intense, amusing, or both. 26B Dublin St. ✆ 0131/538-7775.

Planet Out   This place hosts a mixed crowd, but attracts more women than most gay bars. It describes itself as a friendly and unpretentious neighborhood bar where you're likely to run into your favorite gay uncle or aunt and share a bit of family gossip, and then meet either the love of your life or a decent building contractor. There's an occasional drag night. Open Monday through Friday from 4pm to 1am and Saturday and Sunday from 12:30pm to 1am. 6 Baxters Place. ✆ 0131/524-0061.

10 Side Trips from Edinburgh: The Best of the Lothian Region

Armed with a good map, you can explore the major attractions of the countryside south of the Firth of Forth enveloping Edinburgh in just a day. Most attractions are no more than an hour's drive from the city. The highlights are Hopetoun House of Robert Adam fame and the impressive ruins of Linlithgow Palace, birthplace of Mary Queen of Scots in 1542.

One of the best day trips from the Scottish capital is to the ancient town of **Dunfermline,** north of Edinburgh. It can easily be visited in a day, which will give you time to see its famous abbey and palace as well as the Andrew Carnegie Birthplace Museum. See chapter 8, "Fife & the Central Highlands," for details.

LINLITHGOW & ITS PALACE

In 1542, Mary Queen of Scots was born in the royal burgh of Linlithgow in West Lothian, 18 miles (29km) west of Edinburgh. You can visit the site of her birth, the roofless Linlithgow Palace. Buses and trains depart daily from Edinburgh for the 20- to 25-minute ride, which costs £6 ($9) round-trip. If you're driving from central Edinburgh, follow A8 toward Glasgow and then merge with M9, following the signs to Linlithgow.

Linlithgow Palace ⊕ Birthplace of Mary Queen of Scots, this was once a favorite residence of Scottish kings and is now one of the country's most poignant ruins. Although the palace is roofless, its pink-ocher walls climb five floors and are supported on the lower edge by flying buttresses. It's most dramatic and evocative when floodlit at night. Many of the former royal rooms are still remarkably preserved, so you can get a clear idea of how grand it used to be. In one of the many tragic events associated with Scottish sovereignty, the palace burned to the ground in 1746, along with many of the hopes and dreams of Scottish independence. The Great Hall is on the first floor, and a small display shows some of the more interesting architectural relics.

On A706, on the south shore of Linlithgow Loch, ½ mile (1km) from Linlithgow Station. ℂ 01506/842-896. Admission £2.80 ($4.20) adults, £2 ($3) seniors, £1 ($1.50) children. Daily 9:30am–6:30pm (last entrance 6pm).

St. Michael's Parish Church   South of the palace stands the medieval kirk of St. Michael the Archangel, site of worship of many a Scottish monarch since its consecration in 1242. Despite being ravaged by the disciples of John Knox (who then chided his followers for their "excesses") and transformed into a stable by Cromwell, this is one of Scotland's best examples of a parish church.

Adjacent to Linlithgow Palace. ℂ 01506/842-188. Free admission. May–Sept daily 10am–4:30pm; Oct–Apr Mon–Fri 10:30am–3pm.

Hopetoun House ⊕ Amid beautifully landscaped grounds laid out along the lines of those at Versailles, Hopetoun is Scotland's greatest Robert Adam mansion and a fine example of 18th-century architecture (note its resemblance to Buckingham Palace). Seven bays extend across the slightly recessed center, and the classical style includes a complicated tympanum, with hood molds, quoins, and straight-headed windows. A rooftop balustrade with urns completes the ensemble. You can wander through splendid reception rooms filled with 18th-century furniture, paintings, statuary, and other artworks and check out the panoramic view of the Firth of Forth from the roof. After touring the house, you can take the nature trail, explore the deer parks, see the Stables Museum, or stroll through the formal gardens. Refreshments are available near the Ballroom Suite.

2 miles (3km) from the Forth Rd. Bridge near South Queensferry, 10 miles (16km) from Edinburgh off A904. ℂ 0131/331-2451. Admission £5.30 ($7.95) adults, £4.70 ($7.05) seniors, £2.70 ($4.05) children, £15 ($22.50) per family. Apr–Sept daily 10am–5:30pm (last entrance 4:30pm). Closed Oct–Mar.

ACCOMMODATIONS

You can also rent rooms at **Champany Inn** (see "Dining," below).

East Bonhard Farm   This isolated B&B is part of the working farm managed by Margaret Linkston, a horse aficionado and dog and cat lover who rents a pair of rooms in her modern stone-and-masonry farmhouse. About 3 miles (5km) north of Linlithgow, it provides more of a direct contact with the Scot soil and rural earthiness than many other recommendations in this guide. The public areas contain mementos of the family's contacts, thanks to horse breeding and

Firth of Forth

SCOTLAND
Edinburgh
Area of Detail

5 Mi
5 Km

North Berwick
Dirleton
Gullane
Haddington
Humbie
Pencaitland
Pathead
Tranent
Cockenzie and Port Seton
Musselburgh
Dalkeith
Gorebridge
Bonnyrigg
North Middleton
Loanhead
Penicuik
Balerno
Wilkieston
Livingston
Broxburn
Winchburgh
Newton
Hopetown
Dalmeny
South Queensferry
North Queensferry
Inverkeithing
Burntisland
Dunfermline
Linlithgow
Edinburgh
Leith

A92
A994
A985
A987
A921
A904
A90
M9
M8
A89
A8
A71
A70
A720
A702
A703
A701
A7
A6094
A68
A198
A702
A68
A7
A6093
A1
A198
A6137

Andrew Carnegie Birthplace Museum **2**
Britannia **6**
Deep Sea World **3**
Dirleton Castle **8**
Dumferline Abbey & Palace **1**
Hopetoun House **4**
Linlithgow Palace **5**
Muirfield Golf Course **7**
Tantallon Castle **9**

111

horse shows, with the royal family. The small guest rooms are cozy and functional. The breakfasts are a showplace for all the bounty of rural Scottish life. No smoking is permitted.

Borrowstoun Rd., Linlithgow, West Lothian EH49 7NT. ✆ 01506/825-047. 2 units. £44 ($66) double. Rates include breakfast. No credit cards. From Linlithgow's center, drive north along A803, following the signs to M9, the hamlet of Borrowstoun, and East Bonhard Farm. *In room:* TV, coffeemaker, hair dryer, no phone.

DINING

Champany Inn 𝕽𝕽 SCOTTISH   You'll find the best steaks in Britain in this converted farmhouse. Owner Clive Davidson is an expert on beef and insists his steaks be 1¼ inches (3cm) thick; his meat is hung for at least 4 weeks, adding greatly to its flavor. He also prepares an assortment of oysters, salmon, and lobsters kept in a pool on the premises. Next door to the main dining room is a chophouse that has less expensive cuts; you can choose your own cut and watch it being grilled. The wine list has won an award for excellence from *Wine Spectator.*

The inn also rents 16 handsomely furnished guest rooms, each with TV, minibar, and phone. The rates of £125 ($187.50) for a double include a full breakfast.

Champany Corner, Linlithgow. ✆ 01506/834-532. Fax 01506/834302. www.champany.com. Reservations required. Main courses £15.50–£30 ($23.25–$45); fixed-price lunch £16.75 ($25.15). AE, DC, MC, V. Mon–Fri 12:30–2pm and 7–10pm. Closed Jan 1–2 and Dec 25. Take M9 until junction 3, then A904 until you reach the restaurant.

Livingston's 𝕽 MODERN SCOTTISH/FRENCH   Chef Julian Wright reigns supreme in this cottagelike restaurant of converted stables with sandstone walls and Black Watch tartan carpets. A conservatory overlooks a neat little garden, and candlelight makes the atmosphere warm and romantic. The chef is inventive and uses quality ingredients imaginatively. The saddle of venison is the most requested dish, and rightly so. It comes in a cassis sauce with glazed shallots and a cassoulet of butter beans. Pigeon pie and brambles often appear on the menu, and perhaps a risotto of wild mushrooms and truffles made all the more delectable by a shaving of Parmesan. Elegant dessert selections may include a chilled soup of strawberries and champagne accompanied by a chocolate mousse. There is an ample wine list, including bottles from California.

52 High St. (opposite the post office), Linlithgow. ✆ 01506/846-565. Reservations recommended. Fixed-price 2-course lunch £13.50 ($20.25); fixed-price dinner £25.50 ($38.25) for 2 courses, £30 ($45) for 3 courses. MC, V. Tues–Sat noon–2:30pm and 6–9pm. Closed first 2 weeks in Jan.

NORTH BERWICK

This royal burgh, created in the 14th century, was once an important Scottish port. In East Lothian, 24 miles (39km) east of Edinburgh, it's now an upmarket holiday resort, drawing visitors to its golf courses, beaches, and harbor life on the Firth of Forth. The town is on a direct rail line from Edinburgh; the trip takes 30 minutes. There's also bus service from Edinburgh, taking 1¼ hours. Both cost £2.25 ($3.40) one way. If you're driving, take A1 in the direction marked THE SOUTH and DUNBAR; then turn onto A198, following the signs to North Berwick.

At the **tourist office,** Quality Street (✆ 01620/892-197), you can get information on how to take boat trips to the offshore islands, including **Bass Rock,** a breeding ground inhabited by about 10,000 gannets. The gannets return from Africa in the spring, usually around April, to nest here until fall. It's possible to see the rock from the harbor, but the viewing is even better at **Berwick Law,** a volcanic lookout point.

Some 2 miles (3km) east of North Berwick and 25 miles (40km) east of Edinburgh on A198 stand the ruins of the 14th-century diked and rose-colored **Tantallon Castle** (✆ **01620/892-727**). This was the ancient stronghold of the Douglases from its construction in the 14th century until its defeat by Cromwell's forces in 1650. Overlooking the Firth of Forth, the ruins are still formidable, with a square five-story central tower and a dovecote, plus the shell of its east tower. It's open April to September, daily from 9:30am to 6:30pm; and October to March, Monday through Wednesday and Saturday from 9:30am to 4pm, Thursday from 9:30am to 4:30pm, and Sunday from 2 to 4:30pm. Admission is £2.80 ($4.20) for adults, £2 ($3) for seniors, and £1 ($1.50) for children.

ACCOMMODATIONS & DINING

The Glebe House   This dignified 18th-century home belongs to Gwen and Jake Scott, who have worked hard to preserve its original character as the residence of the pastor for the nearby Presbyterian Church. Glebe House is near many golf courses and is just a minute's walk south of the town's main street, near the edge of the sea. Each cozy guest room boasts part of Mrs. Scott's collection of hand-painted porcelain, artfully arranged on tabletops, in wall niches, and on hanging shelves. (She'll point out the various manufacturers, which include Quimper, Rouen, and Staffordshire.) Views include 4 acres (1.6 hectares) of field, garden, and horse paddock. The breakfasts are served in a formal, high-ceilinged dining room.

4 Law Rd., North Berwick, East Lothian EH39 4PL. ✆ and fax **01620/892-608**. www.aboutscotland.com/ glebe/house.html. 4 units, 3 with private bathroom. £60–£70 ($90–$105) double with bathroom. Rates include breakfast. No credit cards. *In room:* TV, coffeemaker, hair dryer, no phone.

The Marine   This turreted Victorian commands panoramic views across the West Links Course, some of whose putting greens come close to the hotel's foundations. It's a home for Nicklaus, Trevino, Player, and most of the U.S. Ryder Cup Team during the Open and is in an area with almost 20 golf courses nearby. The hotel feels like an elegant country house. Although its guest rooms vary in size, all are clean and comfortable. The bar is lined with antique golf photos. The dining room is open to nonguests and serves the best food in town: international cuisine, with many Scottish specialties.

18 Cromwell Rd., North Berwick, East Lothian EH39 4LZ. ✆ **800/225-5843** in the U.S., or 01620/892-406. Fax 01620/894-480. 83 units. £60–£150 ($90–$225) double; £120–£220 ($180–$330) suite. AE, DC, MC, V. **Amenities:** Restaurant; bar; pool; putting green; tennis court; sauna; playground; room service. *In room:* TV, coffeemaker, hair dryer.

GULLANE & THE MUIRFIELD GOLF COURSE

Lying 19 miles (30.5km) east of Edinburgh in East Lothian, Gullane, with a population of around 2,000, is an upscale resort with a fine sandy beach and one of Scotland's great country hotels. There's no rail service into Gullane. Buses, including nos. 124 and 125, depart from the St. Andrews Square station in Edinburgh (✆ **0800/23-23-23** for information). They take 20 to 25 minutes and cost £2.45 ($3.70) each way. If you're driving, take A1 in the direction marked THE SOUTH and DUNBAR; then turn onto A198, following the signs to Gullane.

On the western edge of the village, **Gullace Hill** is today a nature reserve and bird sanctuary, with some 200 species of birds spotted here. You can take a small wood footbridge from the car park into the reserve.

What really puts Gullane on the tourist map, other than its fine dining and accommodations, is the 1891 **Muirfield Golf Course** (© **01620/842-123**), ranked 6th among the world's 100 greatest golf courses by the editors of *GolfWeb*. Developed from a boggy piece of low-lying links, Muirfield has hosted 10 open championships and is a par-70, 6,601-yard (6,007m), 18-hole course. A round costs £85 ($127.50).

ACCOMMODATIONS & DINING

Greywalls Hotel ⑂⑂   This is an elegant, exclusive retreat. The Edwardian country house was designed as a private home by the most renowned architect of his day, Sir Edwin Lutyens. It was visited from time to time by Edward VII, who admired the views across the Firth of Forth and south to the Lammermuir Hills. The gardens were laid out by one of England's most respected landscape architects, Gertrude Jekyll. In the paneled library, guests relax on comfortable sofas before a blazing log fire. The guest rooms vary in size; some smaller ones are simply decorated, while the more spacious units are furnished with period pieces. Each comes with a beautifully kept bathroom with a combination tub/shower. Light French-style dishes served in the elegant dining room are made almost as appealing to the eye as to the palate; specialties include fresh seafood.

Muirfield, Duncur Rd., Gullane, East Lothian EH31 2EG. © **01620/842-144.** Fax 01620/842-241. www. greywalls.co.uk. 23 units. £185–£220 ($277.50–$330) double. Rates include Scottish breakfast. AE, DC, MC, V. Closed Oct 15–Apr 15. Follow the signs from A198 about 5 miles (8km) from North Berwick. **Amenities:** Restaurant, bar; access to nearby golf; tennis court; croquet lawn; room service; babysitting; laundry service. *In room:* TV, hair dryer.

DIRLETON: THE PRETTIEST VILLAGE IN SCOTLAND ⑂

Midway between North Berwick and Gullane is the lovely little town of Dirleton. The town plan, drafted in the early 16th century, is essentially unchanged today. Dirleton has two greens shaped like triangles, placed at right angles to a group of cottages. This is a preservation village and subject to careful control of any development. It's on the Edinburgh–North Berwick road (A198); North Berwick is 5 miles (8km) east and Edinburgh 19 miles (31km) west. There's no train service. Buses, including nos. 124 and 125, depart from the St. Andrews Square station in Edinburgh (© **0800/23-23-23** for information). They take 25 minutes and cost £1.60 ($2.40) one way. If you're driving, take A1 in the direction marked THE SOUTH and DUNBAR; then turn onto A198, following the signs to Dirleton.

Dirleton Castle ⑂   A rose-tinted 13th-century castle with surrounding gardens, Dirleton Castle looks like a fairy tale fortification, with towers, arched entries, and an oak ramp similar to the drawbridge that used to protect it. Reputed to have been fully sacked by Cromwell in 1650, the building was in fact only partially destroyed by him and was further torn down by the Nesbitt family, who, after building nearby Archiefield House, desired a romantic ruin on their land. The prison, bakehouse, and storehouses are carved from bedrock. You can see the ruins of the Great Hall and kitchen, as well as what's left of the lord's chamber: windows and window seats, a wall with a toilet and drains, and other household features. The 16th-century main gate has a hole through which boiling tar or water could be poured to discourage unwanted visitors. The castle's country garden and a bowling green are still in use. A 17th-century dovecote with 1,100 nests stands at the east end of the garden. A small gate at the west end leads onto one of the village greens.

Dirleton, East Lothian. 🄒 **01620/850-330**. Admission £2.80 ($4.20) adults, £2 ($3) seniors, £1 ($1.50) children. Apr–Sept Mon–Sat 9:30am–6pm, Sun 10am–6pm; Oct–Mar Mon–Sat 9:30am–4pm, Sun 2–4pm.

ACCOMMODATIONS & DINING

Castle Inn   Opposite the village green and the castle and unspoiled by modernization, this is a most satisfactory village inn, with 10 dormer windows and a pair of entrances. The small guest rooms are pleasant and comfortably furnished. The most desirable units are in the main house, with smaller and more modestly furnished rooms in an adjoining modern annex (all with shower only). Guests are welcome in a lounge with rugged stone walls and a free-standing stone fireplace. During the day, you can order light snacks.

Off A198, Dirleton, East Lothian EH39 5EP. 🄒 **01620/850-221**. 8 units. £60 ($90) double. MC, V. **Amenities:** Restaurant, bar. *In room:* Coffeemaker, no phone.

Open Arms   The Open Arms will receive you with you know what. This old stone hostelry, off A198 overlooking the castle ruins, has been transformed into a handsome hotel that serves the finest food in the area. The average-size guest rooms come with small, shower-only bathrooms. Log fires crackle and blaze, and golfers will find 20 courses within a 20-mile (32km) radius. The owners have built a local reputation for serving Scottish dishes using regional venison, beef, lamb, and freshly caught salmon. The whiskies used in the sauces are of the region, too.

Dirleton, East Lothian EH39 5EG. 🄒 **01620/850-241**. Fax 01620/850-570. openarms@clara.co.uk. 10 units. £140–£180 ($210–$270) double. Rates include Scottish breakfast. MC, V. Free parking. **Amenities:** 2 restaurants, bar; room service; laundry service. *In room:* TV, coffeemaker, hair dryer.

INTO THE DEEP AT DEEP SEA WORLD

Although it's in the Fife region, another popular day trip from Edinburgh is to Deep Sea World. From central Edinburgh, drive 12 miles (19km) west, following the signs to Inverkeithing and the Forth Road Bridge. By train, go to either the Waverley or the Haymarket stations in Edinburgh and take any train stopping at North Queensferry (departing at 35-min. intervals); from the North Queensferry station, follow the signs to Deep Sea World, about a 10-minute walk. Round-trip fare is £5.50 ($8.25).

Deep Sea World 🌟 *Kids*   In the early 1990s, a group of entrepreneurs sealed the edges of an abandoned rock quarry with a sheathing of concrete and positioned a 364-foot (109m) cement-and-acrylic tunnel on the quarry's bottom. They then flooded the quarry with a million gallons of seawater, stocked it with a menagerie of watery creatures, and opened it as Scotland's most comprehensive aquarium. You can either stand on a moving mechanical sideway or walk on a carpeted surface along the tunnel's length. En route, you pass through underwater microclimates featuring views of a kelp forest; sandy underwater flats that shelter bottom-dwelling schools of stingray, turbot, and sole; murky underwater caves favored by conger eels and small sharks; and a scary underwater trench whose sponge-encrusted bottom careens abruptly away from view. Schools of shark and battalions of as many as 5,000 fish stare back at you. On the premises are a cafe, a gift shop, and an audiovisual show. Allow at least 90 minutes for your visit, and try to avoid the weekend crowds.

North Queensferry, in Fife. 🄒 **01383/411-880**. Admission £6.25 ($9.40) adults, £4.50 ($6.75) students, £3.95 ($5.95) children 3–15, £16.95 ($25.45) per family. Apr–June and Sept–Oct daily 10am–6pm; July–Aug daily 10am–6:30pm; Nov–Mar Mon–Fri 11am–5pm, Sat–Sun 10am–6pm.

5

The Borders &
Galloway Regions

The romantic castle ruins and skeletons of Gothic abbeys in the **Borders** region stand as mute reminders of the battles that once raged between England and Scotland. For a long time, the "Border Country" was a no-man's land of plunder and destruction, lying south of the line of the Moorfoot, Pentland, and Lammermuir hill ranges and east of the Annandale Valley and the upper valley of the River Tweed.

The Borders is the land of Sir Walter Scott, master of romantic adventure, who topped the bestseller list in the early 19th century. The remains of the four great mid-12th-century abbeys are here: Dryburgh (where Scott is buried), Melrose, Jedburgh, and Kelso. And because of its abundant sheep-grazing land, the Borders is the home of the cashmere sweater and the tweed suit. Ask at the local tourist office for a *Borders Woollen Trail* brochure, detailing where you can visit woolen mills, shops, and museums and follow the process of weaving from start to finish.

Southwest of the Borders is the often-overlooked **Galloway** region (a.k.a. Dumfries and Galloway), a land of unspoiled countryside, fishing harbors, and romantic ruins. Major centers to visit are the ancient city of Dumfries, perhaps the best base for touring Galloway, and the artists' colony of Kirkcudbright, an ancient burgh filled with color-washed houses. In the far west, Stranraer is a major

terminal for those making the 35-mile (56km) ferry crossing into Northern Ireland. Among the major sights are Sweetheart Abbey, outside Dumfries, and the Burns Mausoleum at Dumfries. If time remains, explore beautiful Threave Garden, outside Castle Douglas.

Edinburgh Airport is about 40 miles (64.5km) northwest of Selkirk in the Borders and **Glasgow Airport** about 75 miles (121km) north of Dumfries in the Galloway region. Trains from Glasgow run south along the coast, toward Stranraer, intersecting with the rail stations at Ayr and Girvan en route. Another rail line from Glasgow extends due south to Dumfries, depositing and picking up passengers before crossing the English border en route to the English city of Carlisle. In direct contrast, southbound trains from Edinburgh almost always bypass most of the Borders towns en route, making direct, usually nonstop, transits for Berwick, in England. Consequently, to reach most of the Borders towns covered here, you'll probably rely on a rental car or on bus service from Edinburgh or Berwick to reach Peebles, Selkirk, Melrose, and Kelso. For train information and schedules, call **National Rail Enquiries (℡ 0345/484-950)**.

If you're coming from England, trains from London's King's Cross Station to Edinburgh's Waverley Station enter Scotland at Berwick-upon-Tweed in 6 hours. From Berwick, a

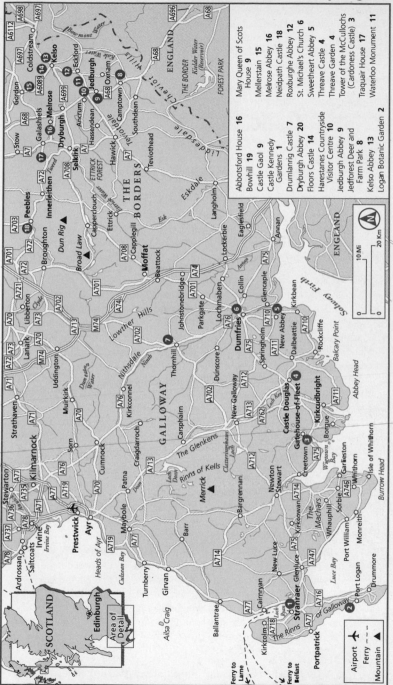

Mary Queen of Scots House **9**
Bowhill **19**
Castle Gaol **9**
Castle Kennedy Gardens **1**
Drumlanrig Castle **7**
Dryburgh Abbey **20**
Floors Castle **14**
Harestanes Countryside Visitor Centre **10**
Jedburgh Abbey **9**
Jedforest Deer and Farm Park **8**
Kelso Abbey **13**
Logan Botanic Garden **2**
Abbotsford House **16**
Mellerstain **15**
Melrose Abbey **16**
Neidpath Castle **18**
Roxburghe Abbey **12**
St. Michael's Church **6**
Sweetheart Abbey **5**
Threave Castle **4**
Threave Garden **4**
Tower of the McCullochs (Cardoness Castle) **3**
Traquair House **17**
Waterloo Monument **11**

Airport ✈
Ferry – – –
Mountain ▲

10 Mi
20 Km

network of local buses runs among the villages and towns. Three rail lines pass through the region from London's Euston Station en route to Glasgow. Dumfries or Stranraer is the best center if you're traveling by rail in the Uplands. Bus travel isn't recommended for reaching the region, but once you get here, you'll find it a reliable means of public transportation because many smaller towns have no rail connections.

1 Jedburgh: Gateway to the Borders ✶

48 miles (77km) SE of Edinburgh, 57 miles (92km) N of Newcastle-upon-Tyne, 13 miles (21km) S of Melrose

The little town of Jedburgh, divided by the River Jed, developed around Jedburgh Abbey on a Roman road called Dere Street. Today the market town gives little hint of the turbulence of its early history as home for royalty in the beleaguered Borders area.

If you have limited time to spend in the region, note that Jedburgh is a typical Borders town and makes a good base: It not only boasts some of the most impressive and evocative abbey ruins around, but is also the home of a fortified town house once inhabited by Mary Queen of Scots. In its environs you can enjoy some of the area's loveliest walks and excursions.

ESSENTIALS

GETTING THERE   There's no direct rail link to Jedburgh. The nearest **rail station** is at Berwick-upon-Tweed (© **0345/484-950** for information and tickets), from which you must take two buses (see below). Depending on the day's schedule, it's sometimes more practical to take a train to Newcastle-upon-Tyne (England), and from there take a bus to Jedburgh (see below).

There are daily **buses** from Edinburgh; a 9:30am bus arrives in Jedburgh at 11:10am and costs £5.50 ($8.25) one-way or £9.25 ($13.90) round-trip. Call © **0990/808-080** for schedules. From England, take the train to Berwick and then the bus (a 75-minute trip) from Berwick to Kelso. In Kelso, transfer to another bus (six to eight per day) that continues to Jedburgh, a 25-minute ride. One-way fares are £2.30 ($3.45). For information, call the Jedburgh tourist office (which has all the schedules) or the Kelso bus station (© **01573/ 224-141**). Two buses a day run from Newcastle-upon-Tyne to Jedburgh, taking 90 minutes and charging £8 to £9.50 ($12 to $14.25) one-way.

If you're **driving,** at Corbridge (England), continue north into Scotland along A68, using Jedburgh as your gateway into the Borders. From Edinburgh, take A7 and then A68, following the signs to Jedburgh. From the center of Edinburgh, expect a driving time of around 75 minutes.

VISITOR INFORMATION   The **Jedburgh Visitor Centre** (© **01835/ 863-435**) is at Murray's Green, near the police station, adjacent to the spot where buses pull in, behind the Town Hall, and very close to the famous abbey. It's open in April and May, Monday through Saturday from 9:30am to 5pm; June, Monday through Saturday from 9:30am to 6pm; July and August, daily from 9am to 8pm; September, Monday through Saturday from 9:30am to 5pm; and October through March, Monday through Saturday from 10am to 4pm.

SEEING THE SIGHTS

Jedburgh Abbey ✶✶   This famous ruined abbey, founded by David I in 1138, is one of Scotland's finest. Under the Augustinian canons from Beauvais, France, it achieved abbey status in 1152 (when enough of its infrastructure was complete to allow a formal endorsement by the Augustinian hierarchies in

Jugglers, dancers and an assortment of acrobats fill the street.

She shoots you a wide-eyed look as a seven-foot cartoon character approaches.

What brought you here was wanting the kids

to see something magical while they still believed in magic.

America Online Keyword: Travel

With 700 airlines, 50,000 hotels and over 5,000 cruise and vaca-

tion getaways, you can now go places you've always dreamed of.

Travelocity.com
A Sabre Company
Go Virtually Anywhere.

"WORLD'S LEADING TRAVEL WEB SITE 5 YEARS IN A ROW" WORLD TRAVEL AWARDS

Rome), and went on to witness much royal pageantry, like the coronation of the founder's grandson, Malcolm IV (1153–65), and the marriage of Alexander III (1249–86) to his second wife, Yolande de Dreux.

The abbey was sacked in 1544 and 1545 by the English during the frequent wars that ravaged the villages along the Scottish and English borders. Its roof was burned, allowing rains to penetrate and further destroy much of the interior detailing. After 1560, the ascendancy of the straitlaced Church of Scotland acted as a disincentive for rebuilding any grand-scale "papist monuments," so no efforts were made to repair the abbey.

For about 300 years, a small section of it was the town's parish church, but in 1875 other premises were found for day-to-day worship. Then teams of architects set to work restoring the place to its original medieval design. The abbey is still roofless but otherwise fairly complete, with most of its exterior stonework still in place. You can view the late-12th-century west front; three pedimented gables remain at the doorway, and the solid buttresses and rounded arches in the Norman style are relatively intact. You can also walk through the nave and the ruins of the former cloister. In a century-old outbuilding is the **Jedburgh Abbey Visitor Centre,** Abbey Place (© **01835/863-925**), open the same hours as the abbey.

Abbey Place. © **01835/863-925.** Admission £3.30 ($4.95) adults, £2.50 ($3.75) seniors, £1.20 ($1.80) children under 16. Apr–Sept daily 9:30am–6:30pm; Oct–Mar Mon–Sat 9:30am–4:30pm, Sun 2–4:30pm. Last entrance 30 min. prior to closing.

Mary Queen of Scots House ✦   Here, in 1566, Mary Stuart spent 6 weeks and almost died of a mysterious ailment after a tiring 40-mile (64.5km) return ride from a visit to her wounded beloved, the earl of Bothwell, at Hermitage Castle (see "Exploring the Countryside," below). In a later lament, commenting on the emotional agonies of the last 20 years of her life, she wrote, "Would that I had died at Jedburgh." The house, in the center of High Street, contains articles dealing with Mary's life, paintings, and engravings. Ancient pear trees still stand on the grounds, a reminder of the days when Jedburgh was famous for its fruit. "Jethard pears" were once hawked in the streets of London.

Queen St. © **01835/863-331.** Admission £2.50 ($3.75) adults, £1.50 ($2.25) seniors and children. Mar–Nov Mon–Sat 10am–4:30pm, Sun 11–4:30pm. Closed Dec–Feb.

Castle Gaol   This museum stands on the site of Jedburgh Castle, a 12th-century royal residence and the scene of many a hunting party because the ancient Jed Forest once surrounded the area. The castle was torn down in the 15th century to keep it from falling under English control. In the 1820s, a Georgian prison was built in its place and became the most modern in the country; its cells even had central heating, a far cry from the typical dungeon prisons of the day.

Castlegate. © **01835/863-254.** Admission £1.50 ($2.25) adults, £1 ($1.50) seniors, children, and students. Easter–Oct Mon–Sat 10am–4:45pm, Sun 1–4pm. Closed Nov to Easter.

EXPLORING THE COUNTRYSIDE

You can rent a bike in the nearby town of Hawick, at the **Hawick Cycle Centre,** 45 N. Bridge St. (© **01450/373-352**), where you'll pay £5 ($7.50) per day or £50 ($75) per week, plus a £50 ($75) deposit. It's open Monday through Thursday from 9am to 7pm, Friday from 9am to 8pm, Saturday from 9am to 5pm, and Sunday from noon to 4pm.

Jedforest Deer and Farm Park *(Finds)* You'll find the area's most interesting walks and nature experiences at this deer and farm park. Eighty acres (32.4 hectares) of this 1,000-acre (405-hectare) farm are open to the public and dotted with unusual species of pigs, chickens, and especially deer. Owner Marion Armitage prides herself on her herds of red fallow and Asian Sika deer (bred for food), which either nuzzle or flee from visitors. You can buy a bag of special deer food for 30p (45¢) and follow one of the two trails along the softly undulating, partially forested terrain. The trail marked with brown signposts requires 30 minutes; the trail marked with green signposts takes an hour. Each is peppered with signs explaining the flora and fauna you'll see en route.

An unusual side attraction in the park is Diana Durman-Walters and her **Birds of Prey Experience.** The staff members exercise the owls, buzzards, eagles, hawks, and falcons at periodic intervals every day, feeding them raw rabbit meat or chicken—but not so much that they lose their incentive to catch rats, rabbits, and field mice during their exercise regimes. If the art of falconry interests you, you can participate in a half-day Hawk Walk for £50 ($75) or a full-day Hawk Walk for £75 ($112.50). Participation requires an advance reservation (call the number below) and is limited to no more than six people. Wear sturdy walking shoes and sensible clothing that won't wilt in a rain shower. If you're willing, you can handle one of these temperamental birds and experience the way it returns to the glove after spotting, catching, and killing a rodent or rabbit.

Camptown, 5 miles (8km) south of Jedburgh along A68. ✆ **01835/840-364.** Admission £3.75 ($5.65) adults, £2.75 ($4.15) children 3–16, £12.50 ($18.75) per family. May–Aug daily 10am–5:30pm; Sept–Oct daily 11am–4pm. Closed Nov–Apr.

Harestanes Countryside Visitor Centre For another experience with nature, head north of Jedburgh (it's signposted) to this visitor center. You can follow marked trails or take guided walks through one of the most beautiful spots in the Borders. The center houses a Discovery Room with displays of wildlife, a gift shop that sells local crafts, and a tearoom.

At the junction of A68 and B6400, Monteviot. ✆ **01835/830-306.** Free admission. Apr–Oct daily 10am–5pm. Closed Nov–Mar.

Hermitage Castle If you want to follow in the footsteps of Mary Queen of Scots, you can drive from Jedburgh to Hermitage Castle. It was to Hermitage that Mary was headed when she made her famous 40-mile (64.5km) ride from Jedburgh to rush to the bedside of her wounded lover, the earl of Bothwell (1535–78), the victim of a raid into Scottish territory by English troops. Still mired in the misty gloom of the Middle Ages, this 1300s castle was restored in the early 1800s. Its original owner, Lord Soulis, was accused of devil worship and boiled alive by the angry townspeople.

On an unclassified road (the castle is signposted) between A7 and B6399, 10 miles (16km) south of Hawick in Liddesdale. ✆ **0131/668-8800.** Admission £2 ($3). Apr–Sept daily 9:30am–6pm. Closed Oct–Mar.

ACCOMMODATIONS
Ancrum Craig Most of this place dates from the 1830s, when a simple 18th-century farmhouse was massively expanded into a red-sandstone Victorian home. Surrounded by landscaped gardens, with views stretching out over the valley of the Teviot, Ancrum Craig is a fine example of baronial, somewhat chilly, Scottish living. The guest rooms are cozy, each with a shower-only bathroom. The largest is the Gold Room, with a bay window boasting a sweeping view. The smallest is the Heather Room, which overlooks the original medieval core, long ago made into an outbuilding. The breakfasts are generous.

Ancrum, Jedburgh, The Borders TD8 6UN. ℭ 01835/830-280. Fax 01835/830259. www.ancrumcraig.co.uk. 3 units. £46–£50 ($69–$75) double. Rates include breakfast. MC, V. Call for directions. *In room:* TV, coffeemaker, hair dryer.

Ferniehirst Mill Lodge Built in 1980, this chalet-inspired modern guesthouse is in a quiet neighborhood away from the town center and attracts those (including hunters and anglers) seeking quiet and rural charm. Its pine-paneled guest rooms are functional but comfortable, each with a private, shower-only bathroom. Horseback riding (for experienced riders only) costs about £25 ($37.50) per hour (minimum of 2 hours), and riders must supply their own riding habits.

Hwy. A68, Jedburgh, The Borders TD8 6PQ. ℭ 01835/863-279. Fax 01835/863-279. http://members.aol. com/ferniemill. 9 units. £23 ($34.50) per person. Rates include breakfast; dinner £14 ($21) extra. Riding packages available for those willing to stay 1 week. MC, V. Free parking. Take A68 2½ miles (4km) south of Jedburgh. **Amenities:** Dining room, bar. *In room:* Coffeemaker.

Glenfriar's Hotel This small private hotel, run by Jenny Bywater, is in a Georgian house on a quiet corner next to St. John's Church. It features antique wooden furnishings, including four-poster beds in two rooms, and well-maintained bathrooms with showers. Since Ms. Bywater cooks, cleans, and books rooms single-handedly, she never accepts more than 10 guests at any one time.

The Friars, Jedburgh, The Borders TD8 6BN. ℭ and fax **01835/862-000**. 6 units. £70–£80 ($105–$120) double. Rates include breakfast. AE, MC, V. **Amenities:** Restaurant, bar. *In room:* TV, coffeemaker, hair dryer.

The Spinney Run by Mr. and Mrs. Fry, this B&B complex includes a main house, a modernized cottage with three doubles, and three pinewood chalets with bathrooms, sitting rooms, and kitchens. Leather and wood furnishings are found throughout the well-maintained guest rooms. The Scottish Tourist Board recently bestowed the guesthouse with a deluxe rating.

Langley, Jedburgh, The Borders TD8 6PB. ℭ 01835/863-525. Fax 01835/864-883. www.smoothhound. co.uk/Jedburgh.html. 3 units, 3 chalets. £23 ($34.50) per person. Rates for regular double rooms include breakfast. MC, V. Take A68 2 miles (3km) south of Jedburgh. *In room:* TV, coffeemaker, hair dryer.

DINING

Carter's Rest SCOTTISH/CONTINENTAL This pub, with a downstairs dining room built of old abbey stones, is the favorite gathering place for locals. Mr. Jonentz, the owner, serves wholesome and hearty food and drink. The simple but tasty menu includes dishes like steaks, scampi, chicken Cordon Bleu, pork or lamb chops, and fresh vegetables in season. The pub also has eight regional beers on tap.

Abbey Place. ℭ 01835/863414. Main courses £5–£12 ($7.50–$18); bar lunches £4.50–£8 ($6.75–$12). MC, V. Restaurant daily noon–2:30pm and 6–9pm; pub Mon–Sat 11am–11pm, Sun 11am–10:30pm.

Simply Scottish SCOTTISH In the heart of town, amid the stripped pinewood floors and heavy pine furniture of what was built around 1900 as a department store, this decent, well-scrubbed restaurant serves savory lunches and dinners, plus countless pots of tea for all the locals who drop by. Menu items, made entirely from Scottish ingredients, are likely to include a salad of smoked chicken and avocado, haggis with white onion sauce, grilled Borders lamb steak with Arran mustard, and roasted salmon with herb-flavored butter sauce. A preferred dessert is summer fruit pudding with fruit compote and honey-flavored ice cream. The restaurant is licensed.

6 High St. ℂ **01835/864-696.** Reservations recommended for dinner. Lunch main courses £4–£7 ($6–$10.50); pot of tea with scones and jam £2 ($3); fixed-price dinner £9.95 ($14.95); dinner main courses £7.95–£11.50 ($11.95–$17.25). MC, V. Daily 10am–9pm.

2 Kelso: Abbey Ruins & Adam Architecture ✶

44 miles (71km) SE of Edinburgh, 12 miles (19km) NE of Jedburgh, 68 miles (109.5km) NW of Newcastle-upon-Tyne, 12 miles (19km) E of Melrose, 23 miles (37km) W of Berwick-upon-Tweed

A typical historic border town like Jedburgh, Kelso lies at the point where the River Teviot meets the River Tweed. Sir Walter Scott called it "the most beautiful, if not the most romantic, village in Scotland." The settlement that grew up here developed into a town around Kelso Abbey.

Kelso today is a flourishing market town, the center of an agricultural district boasting farming and raising livestock. But for visitors, the reasons to come are the ruined abbey and the palatial Floors Castle (by the great architect William Adam) and Mellerstain (begun by William but finished by his son Robert). The town is also one of the best centers for touring the Borders because it's near Jedburgh, Dryburgh Abbey, and Melrose.

ESSENTIALS

GETTING THERE The nearest **rail station** connection is Berwick-upon-Tweed, where you can catch a bus to Kelso (see below). For information, call ℂ **0345/484-950.**

From Edinburgh, board the **bus** to Galashiels, with connecting service to Kelso; the full trip lasts about 80 minutes and costs £5.50 ($8.25) one-way or £10 ($15) round-trip. Phone ℂ **0990/808-080** for information. From Berwick to Kelso, there are between six and eight buses a day. Transit costs £3.75 ($5.65) each way and takes an hour. Because three different bus companies make the run, it's best to call the local tourist office (ℂ **01573/223-464**) for schedules.

If you're **driving** from Jedburgh, follow A6089 northeast to Kelso. From Edinburgh, take A7 and follow the signs to Hawick; then change to A68, follow the signs to Jedburgh, and take A6089 to Kelso.

VISITOR INFORMATION The **tourist office** is at Town House, The Square (ℂ **01573/223-464**). From April to June, it's open Monday through Saturday from 10am to 5pm and Sunday from 10am to 1pm; July and August, Monday through Saturday from 9am to 6pm and Sunday from 10am to 5pm; September, Monday through Saturday from 9:30am to 5pm and Sunday from 10am to 5pm; and October, Monday through Saturday from 9:30am to 4:30pm and Sunday from 10am to 1pm.

SEEING THE SIGHTS

Kelso Abbey ✶ Once a great ecclesiastical center, Kelso Abbey has lain in ruins since the late 16th century, when it suffered its last and most devastating attack by the English, who ripped off its roofs, burned it, and declared it officially defunct. The lands and remaining buildings were given to the earl of Roxburghe. The oldest (1128) and probably largest of the Border abbeys, it was once one of the richest, collecting revenues and rents from granges, fisheries, mills, and manor houses throughout the region. In 1919, the abbey was given to the nation.

Although the remains of this abbey may not be as impressive as those of Jedburgh (see "Jedburgh: Gateway to the Borders," earlier in this chapter), Kelso has had its moments in history, including the crowning of the infant James III.

At the entrance is part of the south recessed doorway, where some of the sculpture on the arches is still fairly intact. The massive west transept tower still suggests its original massive construction, and a trio of building sections with round-headed openings remain. The west front and tower are visible, the whole flanked by buttresses crowned with rounded turrets. A partial cloister here dates from 1933, when it was built as the Roxburghe family vault. Sir Walter Scott knew Kelso Abbey well, as he spent time here studying at Waverley Cottage, which you can see from the abbey's parking area; it was once the Kelso Grammar School, where the famous author learned how to read and write.

Bridge St. Free admission. Apr–Dec Mon–Sat 10am–6:30pm, Sun 2–6:30pm; Jan–Mar by arrangement only.

Floors Castle ⟨★   On the banks of the Tweed, the home of the dukes of Roxburghe was designed in 1721 by William Adam and remodeled in the mid-19th century by William Playfair. Part of the castle contains superb French and English furniture, porcelain, tapestries, and paintings by Gainsborough, Reynolds, and Canaletto. You'll also find a licensed restaurant, a coffee shop, and a gift shop, as well as a walled garden and garden center. You might recognize Floors: It was a major location for the Tarzan film *Greystoke*.

Hwy. A697, 2 miles (3km) north of Kelso. ℂ 01573/223-333. Admission £5 ($7.50) adults, £4.75 ($7.15) seniors, £3.25 ($4.90) children 6–15. Apr–Oct daily 10am–4pm (last admission 3:30pm). Closed Nov–Mar. Follow the signs north from Kelso center.

Mellerstain ⟨★★   Seven miles (11km) northwest of Kelso stands Mellerstain, the seat of the earls of Haddington. This is one of the most famous of the mansions designed by Robert Adam, and one of Scotland's greatest Georgian residences. William Adam built two wings on the house in 1725; the main building was designed by his more famous son, Robert, some 40 years later. (For more details on the Adam family of architectural geniuses, see "Robert Adam: Architect to the King," below.)

Mellerstain is associated with Lady Grisell Baillie (born Grisell Hume). In 1689, at 13 years of age, this Scottish heroine showed great courage by hiding her father in the village church's crypt, bringing him food and supplies in the dead of night, and facing down the English. Hounded by the English, she fled to Holland but returned in triumph with William of Orange (later William I of England) and later married into the Baillie family, scions of Mellerstain. You can see the interior, with its impressive library, paintings, and antique furniture. The garden terrace offers a panoramic view south to the lake, with the Cheviot Hills in the distance. Afternoon tea is served, and souvenir gifts are on sale.

Gordon. ℂ 01573/410-225. Admission £5 ($7.50) adults, £4 ($6) seniors, £2 ($3) children. May–Sept Sun–Fri 12:30–5pm; Oct–Apr by arrangement only. From Edinburgh, follow A68 to Earlston, then follow the signs to Mellerstain for another 5 miles (8km); from Kelso, head northwest along A6089 until you see the signpost turn to the left.

OUTDOOR PURSUITS

The 18-hole **Roxburghe Golf Course** (ℂ 01573/450-331) is the only championship course in the region. This 7,111-yard (6,471m) course was designed by Dave Thomas, one of Britain's leading golf architects. Guests of the hotel (see "Accommodations & Dining," below) get tee times most easily, but the course is open to nonguests as well. Greens fees are £40 ($60) for 18 holes or £60 ($90) for a full day's play.

Our favorite spot for drinking in the scenic countryside is the nearby village of **Kirk Yeetholm,** 7 miles (11km) southeast of Kelso on B6352. This is the northern terminus of the **Pennine Way,** a 250-mile (402.5km) hike that begins

Robert Adam: Architect to the King

In the field of architecture, one Scottish name towers over all the rest: **Robert Adam** (1728–92), whose adaptations of the Italian Palladian style have been admired and duplicated in public and private buildings around the world. He has emerged as Britain's most prestigious neo-classical architect in a century that produced dozens of talented competitors. Today, owning an Adam building is an honor akin to being granted a knighthood by the queen, but (if you happen to be selling the building) infinitely more profitable.

Adam's genius derived from his synthesis of the decorative traditions of the French and Italian Renaissance with the ancient monuments of Greece and Rome. His designs are particularly notable for their lavish use of color, inspired by Grecian vase paintings and by what was being excavated from archaeological digs in places like Pompeii. Almost as important, Adam seemed to have a well-developed business sense and a knack for decorating the right house at the right time, and his money-eyed clients helped propel him into the spotlight.

Throughout much of his career, he collaborated with his capable but less talented younger brother, **James** (1730–94), who handled many of the workaday details of the projects they executed together. And when an English or Scottish lord or lady hired the Adam brothers, they got more than an intensely detailed building—in most cases, the commission included every aspect of the interior decoration and most of the furnishings. The brothers' education in the visual arts began early: Their father, **William Adam** (1689–1748), was the leading Scottish architect of his day and designed dozens of manor houses in what has been called a crude but vigorous Palladian style.

Robert was born in Kirkcaldy, in Fife, but soon emigrated to the source of most of his large commissions, London. He laboriously studied

down in Yorkshire, England. Today, Kirk Yeetholm is filled with tired hikers at the end of the trail, but it was once the Gypsy capital of Scotland—until 1883, a Gypsy queen was crowned here. You can see (at least from the outside) the "Gypsy Palace," really a tiny cottage in the center of the village.

Another place for walking and hiking is around **Smailholm Tower** (© 0131/ **668-8800**), on a ridge 8 miles (13km) west of Kelso and 2 miles (3km) south of Mellerstain (see listing, above), signposted off B6404. A so-called peel tower (fortified tower) from the 1500s, it has been restored and rises 60 feet (18m) above a loch, providing some of the best views of the Borders. April through September, it's open daily from 9:30am to 6:30pm, charging £2 ($3) admission for adults, £1.50 ($2.25) for seniors, and 75p ($1.10) for children. October through March, hours are reduced to Saturday from 9:30am to 4:30pm and Sunday from 2pm to 4:30pm.

ACCOMMODATIONS & DINING
Abbey Bank   This sophisticated B&B started out as the home of a local doctor in 1815. Today, it's owned by Douglas McAdam and his wife, Diah, who

the architecture of imperial Rome under the supervision of then-famous French antiquarian C. L. Clérisseau, with whom he toured widely in Italy and Dalmatia (later part of Yugoslavia). In 1764, he compiled the information he gathered during these tours in the widely acclaimed *The Ruins of the Palace of the Emperor Diocletian at Spalatro.* In 1761, Robert, along with architect William Chambers, was appointed architect of the king's works, at the time the most prestigious post in Britain. In 1773, an illustrated volume, *The Works of Robert and James Adam,* documented his and his brother's vision; they justifiably claimed credit for revolutionizing the principals of English aesthetics.

The Adam style, a richly detailed yet airy interpretation of neoclassicism, was a radical departure from the more ponderous and sometimes ecclesiastical forms that preceded it. Almost immediately, the Adam interpretation of ceiling decorations and mantelpieces was widely copied throughout Britain. And within less than a generation, this vision radically influenced furniture styles throughout Europe and North America, most notably France's Louis XVI style. Looser derivations are the Directoire, Sheraton, and Empire styles.

Adam buildings in Scotland include the **Old Quad** at Edinburgh University and **Mellerstain** in the Borders (described earlier in this chapter). Many more of his works remain in England, especially London, thanks to his careful cultivation of the wealthy English. Examples are **Kenwood House** (1767–69) in London, **Osterly Park** (1761–80) and **Syon House** (1762–69) in Middlesex, and **Luton Hoo** (1768–75) in Bedfordshire. Much more widespread than Adam buildings, however, are examples of their furniture and interior decor (especially chairs, sideboards, and mantelpieces), which are proudly displayed in museums and private homes across the United Kingdom and North America.

have lived in Indonesia and Korea. The house is filled with a mix of British and Oriental furniture. Each sunny guest room has streamlined modern furniture, and most units come with a shower-only bathroom. Because of Diah's familiarity with Indonesian cuisine, you'll be offered *nasi goreng,* the national rice-based dish, as well as a traditional Scottish breakfast of bacon, sausage, eggs, and haggis. A greenhouse contains peach vines and many of the seedlings Douglas nurtures during the coldest months.

The Knowes, Kelso, The Borders TD5 7BH. Ⓒ and fax **01573/226-550.** www.aboutscotland.com/kelso/abbeybank.html. 7 units, 5 with private bathroom. £40 ($60) double without bathroom; £52 ($78) double with bathroom. Rates include breakfast. MC, V. *In room:* TV, no phone.

The Cross Keys Hotel   Facing the cobbled main square of the town, the facade of this hotel is a stately Georgian style from 1769. Since then, guests have included Bonnie Prince Charlie and Beatrix Potter. The public areas are comfortable and busy, vaguely inspired by Scottish Art Nouveau master Charles Rennie MacIntosh. The midsize guest rooms are well upholstered; each has a shower-only bathroom. The restaurant serves lunch and dinner daily, while the cozy Scottish-style bar boasts an impressive collection of single-malt whiskies.

36 The Square, Kelso, The Borders TD5 7HL. © **01573/223-303.** Fax 01573/225-792. www.cross-keys-hotel.co.uk. 28 units. £75.80–£99.80 ($113.70–$149.70) double. Rates include breakfast. AE, MC, V. **Amenities:** Restaurant, bar. *In room:* TV, hair dryer, iron.

Ednam House Hotel 🏰🏰   The Ednam, on the fringe of Kelso, is a conversion of a 1761 Georgian house often referred to as "that lovely place beside the river." In the oldest section is an unusual collection of antiques. The most expensive accommodations, called the "Prince William rooms," are on the third floor and offer a view of the river. The rooms vary in size, but all come with shower or bathtub. For those wanting to chance it with the unreliable Scottish sun, there's a terrace.

Bridge St., Kelso, The Borders TD5 7HT. © **01573/224-168.** Fax 01573/226-319. www.ednamhouse.com. 32 units. £84–£117 ($126–$175.50) double. Rates include breakfast. MC, V. **Amenities:** Restaurant; nearby golf; sauna; babysitting. *In room:* TV, coffeemaker, hair dryer.

The Roxburghe Hotel and Golf Course 🏰🏰   This late-19th-century castle stands on 200 acres of woodland, lawns, and gardens. It was built as the family home of the Roxburghes, who valued its location on the trout-filled Teviot. In 1982, it was converted into a country hotel with well-appointed guest rooms. The old stable block contains six units, while the remainder are in the main house. Amid a subdued but elegant interior, the hotel keeps four log-burning fireplaces going even in summer.

Hwy. A6098, Heiton, Kelso, The Borders TD5 8JZ. © **01573/450-331.** Fax 01573/450-611. www.roxburghe. net. 22 units. £120–£165 ($180–$247.50) double; £200–£205 ($300–$307.50) double with four-poster bed; £255 ($382.50) suite. Rates include breakfast. AE, DC, MC, V. Take A6098 3 miles (5km) southwest of Kelso. **Amenities:** Restaurant, bar; golf course; tennis court; shooting; fishing. *In room:* TV, hair dryer.

A SIDE TRIP TO DRYBURGH ABBEY

Ten miles (16km) west of Kelso and 4 miles (6km) southeast of Melrose (off A68), you'll find the town of **Dryburgh** and its ruined abbey. The adjoining town is **St. Boswells,** an old village on the Selkirk–Kelso road. Near Dryburgh is **Scott's View** 🏰 (take B6356 north) over the Tweed to Sir Walter's beloved Eildon Hills; it's the most glorious vista in the region.

Dryburgh Abbey 🏰🏰   These Gothic ruins are surrounded by gnarled yew trees and cedars of Lebanon, which are said to have been planted by knights returning from the Crusades. It's still a lovely ruin, and its setting in a loop of the Tweed is memorable. The cloister buildings are relatively intact, but not much remains of the church itself, except a few foundation stones. You can see enough fragments to realize the architectural style was transitional, between the Romanesque and the pointed Early English style. Sir Walter Scott is buried here in a pillared side chapel.

Hwy. A68, Dryburgh, Roxburghshire. © **01835/822-381.** Admission £2.50 ($3.75) adults, £1.90 ($2.85) seniors, £1 ($1.50) children 5–15. Apr–Sept daily 9:30am–6:30pm (July–Aug to 7:30pm); Oct–Mar Mon–Sat 9:30am–4:30pm, Sun 2–4:30pm. Drive south from Dryburgh along B6356 (it's signposted); from Edinburgh take A68 to St. Boswells and turn onto B6404 and then left onto B6356.

ACCOMMODATIONS & DINING

Clint Lodge Hotel 🏰 *(Finds)*   This former lodge has been carefully converted into a small guesthouse of charm and grace. In the 18th century, the establishment was a sports lodge, and the setting is still tranquil, with panoramic views over the valley. The midsize bedrooms are comfortable and traditionally furnished, often with a treasure trove of family heirlooms. Each unit comes with a small, shower-only bathroom. The menu features real "taste of Scotland" fare with such dishes as Border lamb with port and red currants, potato pancakes with smoked haddock, and a strawberry and Drambuie cream with homemade shortbread.

St. Boswells, Melrose TD6 ODZ. ✆ **01835/822-027**. Fax. 01835/822-656. www.tasteofscotland.co.uk/clint_lodge.html. 5 units. £60–£100 ($90–$150) double with breakfast; £100–£120 ($150–$180) double with breakfast and dinner. MC, V. At St. Boswells, take B6404, continue 2 miles across Mertoun Bridge, and turn left onto B6356 through Clint Mains village, veering left. This road leads to Clint Lodge, a mile away on the right. **Amenities:** Dining room; lounge. *In room:* TV.

Dryburgh Abbey Hotel ✰✰   Located beside the abbey ruins, this hotel is the best in the area. It was built in 1845 as the home of Lady Grisell Baillie and remained in her family until 1929. It's said to be haunted by the "gray lady," who had an ill-fated affair with a monk that led to his execution and her suicide by drowning. After restoration, the deteriorated property was the first in the Borders to be awarded five crowns by the Scottish Tourist Board. The accommodations include both deluxe rooms with four-poster beds and standard abbey- or river-view rooms. Each unit is equipped with a bathroom with combination tub/shower.

Hwy. B6404, outside St. Boswells, The Borders TD6 0RQ. ✆ **01835/822-261**. Fax 01835/823-945. www.dryburgh.co.uk. 37 units. £80–£118 ($120–$177) double; £120–£158 ($180–$237) suite for 2. Rates include full Scottish breakfast. AE, MC, V. **Amenities:** Restaurant, bar; pool; nearby golf; nearby fishing; room service; babysitting; laundry. *In room:* TV, dataport, coffeemaker, hair dryer, iron, safe.

3 Melrose ✰

37 miles (59.5km) SE of Edinburgh, 70 miles (113km) NW of Newcastle-upon-Tyne, 40 miles (64.5km) W of Berwick-upon-Tweed

Rich in sights, Melrose is one of the highlights of the Borders: It offers one of the most beautiful ruined abbeys in the Borders as well as the region's most widely diversified shopping, and Abbotsford House, former home of Sir Walter Scott, is 2 miles (3km) west. Melrose is also close to the Southern Upland Way, which passes to the north of town. Even if you can follow only part of this trail (see chapter 1, "The Best of Scotland"), take a day hike on the section along the River Tweed outside Melrose—it's one of the most delightful and scenic walks in Scotland.

ESSENTIALS

GETTING THERE   The nearest **rail station** is in Berwick-upon-Tweed, where you can catch a bus to Melrose. From Berwick, about five buses per day travel to Melrose; travel time is about 90 minutes. Fares are about £5 ($7.50) one-way and £9 ($13.50) round-trip. Call the tourist office in Berwick-upon-Tweed at ✆ **01289/330-733** for bus schedules and ✆ **0345/484-950** for train schedules.

Many visitors prefer to take the **bus** into Melrose directly from Edinburgh. Travel time from Edinburgh is 90 minutes, and buses depart every 1½ hours. Phone ✆ **0990/808-080** for information.

If you're **driving** from Edinburgh, you can reach Melrose by going southeast along A7 and following the signs to Galashiels. From Kelso, take A699 west to St. Boswells; at the junction with A6091, head northwest.

VISITOR INFORMATION   The tourist office is at **Abbey House,** Abbey Street (✆ **01896/822-555**). In April, May, and October, it's open Monday through Saturday from 10am to 5pm and Sunday from 10am to 1pm. June and September, hours are Monday through Saturday from 10am to 5:30pm and

Sunday from 10am to 2pm. July and August, hours are Monday through Saturday from 9:30am to 6:30pm and Sunday from 10am to 6pm.

SEEING THE SIGHTS

Melrose Abbey 👁👁 These lichen-covered ruins, among the most beautiful in Europe, are all that's left of the ecclesiastical community established by Cistercian monks in 1136. The complex's pure Gothic lines were made famous by Sir Walter Scott, who was instrumental in getting the decayed remains repaired and restored in the early 19th century. In *The Lay of the Last Minstrel,* Scott wrote, "If thou would'st view fair Melrose aright, go visit in the pale moonlight." You can still view its red-sandstone shell, built in the Perpendicular style and filled with elongated windows and carved capitals with delicate tracery. The heart of Robert the Bruce is supposed to be interred in the abbey, but the location is unknown. Look for the beautiful carvings and the tombs of other famous Scotsmen buried in the chancel.

Abbey St. ✆ **01896/822-562.** Admission £3.30 ($4.95) adults, £2.50 ($3.75) seniors, £1.20 ($1.80) children. Apr–Sept daily 9:30am–6:30pm; Oct–Mar Mon–Sat 9:30am–4:30pm, Sun 2–4:30pm.

Abbotsford House 👁👁 This was the home Sir Walter Scott built and lived in from 1812 until he died. Designed in the Scots baronial style and considered, after his literary works, Scott's most enduring monument, it contains many relics, including artifacts and mementos the famous author collected from the Waterloo battlefield. Other exhibits include his clothes and his death mask. Especially interesting is his study, with his writing desk and chair. In 1935, two secret drawers were found in the desk. One of them contained 57 letters, part of the correspondence between Sir Walter and his wife-to-be.

Scott purchased Cartley Hall farmhouse on the banks of the Tweed in 1812. In 1822, he had the old house demolished and replaced it with the building you see today. Scott was one of Britain's earliest souvenir hunters, scouring the land for artifacts associated with the historical characters he rendered into novel form. One of his proudest possessions was a sword given to the duke of Montrose by English king Charles I for his cooperation (some say collaboration) during the struggles between Scotland and England. The sword is proudly displayed near a gun, sword, dagger, and small knife owned by the sworn enemy of the duke, cattle herder Rob Roy, whose exploits were later crafted by Sir Walter Scott into one of his most enduring dramas. (You may remember the Liam Neeson film from a few years back.) You can see Scott's study, library (with 9,000 rare volumes), drawing room, entrance hall, and armories—even the dining room where he died on September 21, 1832. There are also extensive gardens and grounds to visit, plus the private chapel, added after Scott's death.

Hwy. B6360, Melrose. ✆ **01896/752-043.** Admission £4 ($6) adults, £2 ($3) children. Mar 18–Oct Mon–Sat 9:30am–5pm (Mar–May and Oct, also open Sun 2–5pm). Head just off A7, south of the junction with A72, onto B6360, some 2½ miles (4km) southeast of Galashiels.

Thirlestane Castle 👁 One of Scotland's most imposing country houses, Thirlestane has been owned by the Lauderdale family since 1218. A T-shaped building, the castle has a keep from around the end of the 16th century and was much altered after Queen Victoria took the throne. The interior is known for its ornamental plaster ceilings, the finest in the country from the Restoration period. In the old nurseries is the Historic Toy Collection, and Border Country Life exhibits depict life in the Borders from prehistoric times to the present.

10 miles (16km) north of Melrose, overlooking Leader Water, about half a mile (1km) from Lauder. ✆ **01578/722-430.** Admission £5.20 ($7.80) adults, £3 ($4.50) children, £13 ($19.50) per family. Apr to late Oct Sun–Fri

10:30am–5pm (last admission at 4:15pm). Closed late Oct to Mar. Take A68 to Lauder in Berwickshire, 10 miles (16km) north of Melrose and 28 miles (45km) south of Edinburgh on A68.

Traquair House ⚔⚔   Dating from the 10th century, this is perhaps Scotland's oldest and most romantic house, rich in associations with Mary Queen of Scots and the Jacobite uprisings. The great house is still lived in by the Stuarts of Traquair. One of the most poignant exhibits is an ornately carved oak cradle in the King's Room, in which Mary rocked her infant son, who was to become James VI of Scotland and James I of England. Other treasures here are glass, embroideries, silver, manuscripts, and paintings. Of particular interest is a brew house equipped as it was 2 centuries ago and still used regularly. On the grounds are craft workshops as well as a maze and woodland walks.

Hwy. A72, 16 miles (26km) west of Melrose. © 01896/830-323. Admission £5.30 ($7.95) adults, £4.30 ($6.45) seniors, £2.80 ($4.20) students and children, £15 ($22.50) per family. Easter–May and Sept–Oct daily 12:30–5:30pm (Oct Fri–Sun 12:30–5pm); June–Aug daily 10:30am–5:30pm. Closed Nov–Easter.

SHOPPING

Melrose is one of the best destinations for shopping in the Borders. Most shops are open Monday through Saturday from 9:30am to 5pm and Sunday from noon to around 4pm.

The Country Kitchen, Market Square (© **01896/822-586**), displays a comprehensive choice of English, French, and Scottish cheeses, along with patés and meat products. You can buy them prepackaged or order up gourmet sandwiches and picnic fixings. **Abbey Wines,** Abbey Street (© **01896/823-224**), stocks the town's largest wine selection, plus at least 150 malt whiskies, some from the most obscure distilleries in Scotland.

The town's most complete collection of books is for sale at **Talisman Books,** 9 The Square (© **01896/822-196**), in an old-fashioned Edwardian shop. Gifts,

---

🖉 A Walk Along the Borders

If you're feeling particularly saintly, you can walk in the footsteps of 7th-century St. Cuthbert along the Scotland-England border. The 62½-mile (101km) path stretches from Melrose, 37 miles (59.5km) southwest of Edinburgh, across the border into northeast England to the Holy Island of Lindisfarne on the Northumberland coast. St. Cuthbert began his ministry in Melrose in about A.D. 650 and later was appointed prior at Lindisfarne. The walk passes many places linked to his legend, prehistoric relics, Roman ruins, and historic castles. The high point is Wideopen Hill, 1,430 feet (434m) above sea level. Permission from landowners along the route has been obtained, and the walk is clearly marked. A leaflet suggests distances you can comfortably cover in a day and makes recommendations for overnight stops. Contact Roger Smith, Walking Development Officer, **Scottish Border Enterprise Center,** Bridge Street, Galashiels TB1 ISW (© **01896/758-991;** fax 01896/758-625), for information. To stock up on gear and supplies before you set out, stop in the small town of Galashiels, 3 miles (5km) north of Melrose, and head for **Famous Army Stores,** Unit 8, Douglas Bridge (© **01896/757-964**).

especially impractical-but-charming items in porcelain and china, are available at **Butterfly,** High Street (© **01896/822-045**).

Feeling chilly in the Scottish fog? A meticulously crafted wool or cashmere sweater from **Anne Oliver Knitwear,** 1 Scott's Place (© **01896/822-975**), might provide the extra warmth you'll need. **Lochcarron of Scotland,** The Square (© **01896/823-823**), is larger, but stocks only its own goods. Designers like Calvin Klein, Ralph Lauren, and Jean-Paul Gaultier have ordered bulk amounts here for relabeling and distribution. For tartan and other fabrics, visit **The Fabric Shop,** High Street (© **01896/823-475**), which both high-class couturiers and homegrown dressmakers find appealing.

ACCOMMODATIONS

Burt's Hotel   Within walking distance of the abbey, this family-run inn dates from 1722. It has a traditional three-story town-house design and offers a taste of small-town Scotland. The decor is modern, with an airy and restful feel. All guest rooms are well furnished and equipped with shower-only bathrooms. In the attractive bar, which sports Windsor chairs and a coal-burning fireplace, tasty lunches and suppers are served. The restaurant overlooks a garden.

Market Square, Melrose, The Borders TD6 9PN. © **01896/822-285**. Fax 01896/822-870. www.burtshotel.co. uk. 20 units. £92 ($138) double. Rates include breakfast. AE, DC, MC, V. Free parking. **Amenities:** Restaurant, bar; room service; babysitting; laundry. *In room:* TV, coffeemaker, hair dryer.

King's Arms Hotel   One of Melrose's oldest commercial buildings still in use is this 17th-century coaching inn whose three-story stone-and-brick facade overlooks the pedestrian traffic of the main street. Inside is a series of cozy but slightly dowdy public rooms and half a dozen simple but comfortably furnished small guest rooms, each with a shower only. The restaurant serves an odd mix of international offerings, including Mexican tacos and enchiladas, Indian curries, and British steak pies.

High St., Melrose, The Borders TD6 9BP. © **01896/822-143**. Fax 01896/823-812. www.kingsarmsmelrose. co.uk. 7 units. £57.50 ($86.25) double. MC, V. **Amenities:** Restaurant, bar. *In room:* TV, coffeemaker.

Millars Hotel   This well-maintained, family-owned hotel is in the heart of Melrose and easily recognizable by the colorful window boxes adorning its facade in summer. Most accommodations are rather functionally but comfortably furnished. Bathrooms are equipped with either tub or shower. The most spacious unit comes with a traditional four-poster bed and draperies; honeymooners sometimes stay here and are welcomed in style with a complimentary bottle of champagne, flowers, and chocolates. The dining room offers tasty, reasonably priced fare. Meals are also served in the bar, which boasts a fine assortment of beers and wines.

Market Square, Melrose TD6 9PQ. © **01896/822-645**. Fax 01896/823-474. www.melrose.bordernet. co.uk/traders/millars. 10 units. £75 ($112.50) double; £90 ($135) family room; £100 ($150) four-poster room. Rates include breakfast. MC, V. Closed Christmas. Follow the A68 into Melrose to the center of town. No children under 13 accepted. **Amenities:** Restaurant, bar. *In room:* TV.

Traquair Arms Hotel ❋   This is the area's most tranquil retreat for those seeking a country-house atmosphere. The small hotel was built as a coaching inn around 1780, with later Victorian additions. Open fires in the bar lounge and fresh flowers in the dining room create a pleasant ambience. The cozy guest rooms come with comfortable furnishings, well-maintained tub-and-shower bathrooms, and views over the valley. The hotel is known for fine pub food; vegetarians and others with special dietary needs can be accommodated. The property is within a 5-minute walk of the River Tweed; salmon and trout fishing can be arranged.

Traquair Rd., Innerleithen, The Borders EH44 6PD. (© 01896/830-229. Fax 01896/830-260. traquair.arms@ scottishborders.com. 10 units. £58–£80 ($87–$120) double. Rates include breakfast; dinner £18 ($27) extra. AE, MC, V. Take E69 from Melrose for 14 miles (22.5km). **Amenities:** Restaurant, bar; tour desk. *In room:* TV, coffeemaker.

DINING

Don't miss the pastries at Melrose's best bakery, **Jackie Lunn, Ltd.,** High Street ((© **01896/822-888**).

Two of the town's most likable pubs are the one in the **King's Arms,** High Street ((© **01896/822-143**), where you'll generally find lots of rugby players lifting a pint or two, and the somewhat more sedate one in **Burts Hotel,** The Square ((© **01896/822-285**).

Marmion's Brasserie SCOTTISH Across from the post office in a 150-year-old building, this tasteful restaurant is a cross between a brasserie and a coffee shop. The kitchen likes to use all-Scottish ingredients in its frequently changing menu items, which might include salmon in phyllo with ginger-and-lime sauce; swordfish with butter beans, bacon, and sweet onions; exotic ostrich steak in red-wine sauce; and charcoal-grilled steaks done to perfection.

2 Buccleuch St. (© 01896/822-245. Reservations recommended for dinner. Main courses £2–£8 ($3–$12) at lunch; £6–£14 ($9–$21) at dinner. MC, V. Mon–Sat 9am–10pm.

Melrose Station SCOTTISH/INTERNATIONAL In 1850, an impressive rail station was built in the town center, but a while back, British Rail diverted all service to nearby Berwick-upon-Tweed. Today, the station contains this reliable, conservative restaurant. Lunches are a lot simpler than dinners and may include prawn-and-egg salad with pesto mayonnaise followed by grilled Italian vegetables with brie. The hearty dinners may begin with smoked chicken, avocado, and peach salad in curried mayonnaise sauce, followed by roasted duckling breast in cranberry, port, and orange sauce. The restaurant is licensed for wine and beer.

Palma Place. (© 01896/822-546. Reservations recommended. Main courses £2.95–£6.50 ($4.45–$9.75) at lunch; £3.50–£30.95 ($5.25–$46.45) at dinner. MC, V. Wed–Sun noon–2pm; Thurs–Sat 6–9pm.

4 Selkirk: At the Heart of Scott Country

40 miles (64.5km) SE of Edinburgh, 73 miles (117.5km) SE of Glasgow, 7 miles (11km) S of Galashiels

In the heart of Sir Walter Scott country, Selkirk is a great base if you want to explore many of the region's historic homes, including Bowhill (see below) and Traquair House (see "Melrose," above). Jedburgh and Melrose offer more to see and do, but this ancient royal burgh can easily occupy a morning of your time.

Selkirk was the hometown of the African explorer Mungo Park (1771–1806), whose exploits could have made a great Harrison Ford movie. Park was a doctor, but won fame for exploring the River Niger; he drowned while escaping in a canoe from hostile natives. A statue of him is at the east end of High Street in Mungo Park.

ESSENTIALS

GETTING THERE Berwick-upon-Tweed is the nearest **rail station,** where you can get a connecting bus to Selkirk. The bus ride is just under 2 hours, costing £5 ($7.50) one-way or £8 ($12) round-trip. Call the tourist office in

Berwick-upon-Tweed at ℂ **01289/330-733** for bus schedules or ℂ **0345/ 484-950** for rail information. Most visitors arrive by train from Edinburgh (ℂ **0990/808-080** for information).

Buses running between Newcastle-upon-Tyne and Edinburgh make stops at Selkirk. The trip takes about 2½ hours and costs £7 ($10.50) one-way or £12 ($18) round-trip.

If you're **driving** from Edinburgh, head southeast along A7 to Galashiels, then cut southwest along B6360. The trip takes about an hour. To get here from Melrose, take B6360 southwest to Selkirk; it's a 15-minute drive.

VISITOR INFORMATION   The **tourist office** is at Halliwell's House Museum (ℂ **01750/720-054**). From March to June and September, it's open Monday through Saturday from 10am to 5pm and Sunday from 2 to 4pm; July and August, hours are Monday through Saturday from 10am to 6pm and Sunday from 2 to 5pm; October hours are Monday through Saturday from 10am to 4pm and Sunday from 2 to 4pm.

EXPLORING THE AREA

In Selkirk, the former royal hunting grounds and forests have given way to textile mills along its river banks, but there are many beautiful spots in the nearby countryside—notably **St. Mary's Loch,** 14 miles (22.5km) southwest. Sailors and fishermen love this bucolic body of water, as did literary greats like Thomas Carlyle and Robert Louis Stevenson. One of the most panoramic stretches of the Southern Upland Way, one of Scotland's great backpacking trails (see chapter 1), skirts the east shore of St. Mary's Loch. You can take a day hike on the 8-mile (13km) stretch from the loch to Traquair House (see "Melrose," earlier in this chapter).

Bowhill 𝕬𝕬   This 18th- and 19th-century Border home of the Scotts, the dukes of Buccleuch, contains a rare art collection, French furniture, porcelain, silverware, and mementos of Sir Walter Scott, Queen Victoria, and the duke of Monmouth. Its paintings include works by Canaletto, Claude, Gainsborough, and Reynolds. In the surrounding Country Park, you'll find an Adventure Woodland play area, a Victorian kitchen, an audiovisual presentation, a gift shop, and a tearoom/restaurant. Sotheby's "Works of Art" courses are offered at Bowhill.

Hwy. A708, 3 miles (5km) west of Selkirk. ℂ 01750/222-04. Admission to house £4.50 ($6.75) adults, £4 ($6) seniors, £2 ($3) children; admission to Country Park £2 ($3). House, July daily 1–4:30pm; Country Park, Apr–Aug daily noon–5pm. Closed rest of year.

ACCOMMODATIONS & DINING

Heatherlie House Hotel   An imposing stone-and-slate Victorian mansion with steep gables and turrets, this hotel is set on 2 acres of wooded lands and mature gardens, west from the center along the Green and a short walk from Selkirk. The guest rooms are spotlessly maintained and furnished with reproductions of older pieces. A coal-burning fireplace adds warmth to the lounge, where reasonably priced bar meals are available daily. The high-ceilinged dining room is open for dinner. Golf, fishing, and shooting packages can be arranged, and about half a dozen golf courses are within a reasonable drive.

Heatherlie Park, Selkirk, The Borders TD7 5AL. ℂ 01750/721-200. Fax 01750/720005. www.heatherlie.freeserve.co.uk. 7 units, 6 with private, shower-only bathroom. £64 ($96) double with bathroom. Rates include breakfast. MC, V. **Amenities:** Restaurant, pub. *In room:* TV, coffeemaker, hair dryer.

ⓘ Sir Walter Scott: Master of Romance

Today it's hard to imagine the fame this poet/novelist enjoyed as the best-selling author of his time. His works are no longer so widely read, but in his day, Sir Walter Scott (1771–1832) was considered a master storyteller. He invented a new genre, the romantic adventure in a panoramic setting. He created lively characters and realistic pictures of Scottish life and customs in such works as *The Heart of Midlothian, Rob Roy,* and *Waverley.* He's now best known as the prolific father of the historical novel, a genre that began with *Ivanhoe* and its romantic Jewish heroine, Rebecca (played by Elizabeth Taylor in the popular film), followed by *Kenilworth, The Pirate,* and many others. He was also a popular poet.

Born into an older Border family at Edinburgh on August 14, 1771, Scott became permanently lame after an attack of fever in infancy. All his life he was troubled by ill health, and later by finances as well. He spent his latter years writing to clear his enormous debts. Scott made his country and its scenery fashionable with the English, and even persuaded George IV to wear that once-outlawed tartan during the king's visit to Scotland. Although Scott became the most prominent literary figure in Edinburgh, his heart lay in the Border Country. It was here he chose to live and here he built his house in a style that became known as Scottish baronial, reflecting the nostalgia for medieval days his novels had popularized. Starting with a modest farmhouse, he enlarged Abbotsford into a mansion and fulfilled his ambition to become a *laird* (landlord or property owner). In the economic crash of 1826, he offered the estate to his creditors, who turned it down.

Still heavily in debt and suffering from the effect of several strokes, in 1831 Scott set out on a cruise through the Mediterranean but returned to Abbotsford the following year to die. He was buried at Dryburgh Abbey, sited in a loop of the Tweed 2 miles (3km) from the panoramic view of the river and the Eildon Hills he so admired. It's reported the horses pulling the author's hearse stopped at this spot out of habit, so accustomed were they to Scott's pausing to take in the vista.

Scott's name is also linked to the Trossachs, which he used as a setting for his poem "The Lady of the Lake" and his tale of Rob Roy MacGregor, the 18th-century outlaw. In Edinburgh, the Gothic-inspired Scott Monument is one of the most famous statues in Scotland.

5 Peebles

23 miles (37km) S of Edinburgh, 53 miles (85km) SE of Glasgow, 20 miles (32km) W of Melrose

Peebles, a royal burgh and county town, is a market center in the Tweed Valley, noted for its large woolen mills and fine knitwear shopping. Scottish kings used to come here when they hunted in Ettrick Forest, 22 miles (35km) away. It's one of hundreds of forests scattered throughout the Borders and is very pretty, but no more so than forested patches closer to the town.

Peebles is known as a writer's town. It was home to Sir John Buchan (Baron Tweedsmuir, 1875–1940), a Scottish author who later was appointed governor-general of Canada. He's remembered chiefly for the adventure story *Prester John* and was the author of *The Thirty-Nine Steps,* the first of a highly successful series of secret-service thrillers and later a Hitchcock film. Robert Louis Stevenson lived for a time in Peebles and drew on the surrounding countryside in his novel *Kidnapped* (1886).

ESSENTIALS

GETTING THERE   The nearest **rail station** is in Berwick-upon-Tweed, but bus connections from there into Peebles are quite inconvenient. It's easier to get from Edinburgh to Peebles by a 50-minute **bus** ride. Bus fares from Edinburgh are around £3 ($4.50) one-way. Call ✆ **0345/484-950** for rail and bus information. If you're **driving,** take A703 south from Edinburgh. Continue west along A6091 from Melrose.

VISITOR INFORMATION   The **tourist office** is at the Chamber Institute, 23 High St. (✆ **01721/720-138**). It's open in July and August, Monday through Friday from 9am to 8pm, Saturday from 9am to 7pm, and Sunday from 10am to 6pm; June and September, Monday through Saturday from 9:30am to 5:30pm and Sunday from 10am to 4pm; April and May, Monday through Saturday from 9:30am to 5pm and Sunday from 10am to 2pm; October, Monday through Saturday from 9:30am to 4:30pm and Sunday from 10am to 2pm; and November through March, Monday through Saturday from 9:30am to 4:30pm.

EXPLORING THE TOWN & THE COUNTRYSIDE

The tourist office provides pamphlets describing the best walking tours in the region. The £1 ($1.50) pamphlet *Walks Around Peebles* describes 20 walks, including one along the Tweed. That walk is so popular that a detailed description is available in a pamphlet devoted exclusively to it, priced at 40p (60¢). The **Tweed Walk** begins in the center of Peebles, and takes you downstream along the river, then upstream along the opposite bank for a return to town. You can follow the path for segments of 2½ miles (4km), 4½ miles (7km), or 7½ miles (12km). Regardless of the length of your walk, you'll pass the stalwart walls of Neidpath Castle.

The **Glentress Bicycle Trekking Centre,** Glentress, Peebles (✆ **01721/722-934**), is the place to rent a bike. Daily rates range from £6 to £18 ($9–$27), with a deposit of £50 ($75). Rentals must be arranged in advance. Open daily from 9:30am to 5pm.

Neidpath Castle   Once linked with two of the greatest families in Scotland (the Frasiers and the Hayes), Niedpath, a summer attraction, hasn't been occupied since 1958. Part of the interest here is the way the castle's medieval shell was transformed during the 1600s into a residence, using then-fashionable architectural conceits. Enormous galleries were divided into smaller, cozier spaces, with the exception of the Great Hall, whose statuesque proportions are still visible. The hall's medieval stonework is decorated with 11 batik panels crafted in the mid-1990s by noted artist Monica Hanisch; they depict the life and accomplishments of Mary Queen of Scots. Other parts of the museum are devoted to the role the castle has played in the filming of movies like *The Bruce* (an English film that had the bad luck to be released simultaneously with *Braveheart*), *Merlin, The Quest Begins,* and the courtyard scene in the recent TV miniseries *Joan of Arc,* where the heroine was burnt at the stake. Recently filmed here were new British versions of *Hamlet* and *King Lear.*

Tweeddale, on A72, 1 mile (1.5km) west of Peebles. ℂ **01721/720-333**. Admission £3 ($4.50) adults, £2.50 ($3.75) seniors, £1 ($1.50) children, £7.50 ($11.25) per family. July 1–Sept 10 Mon–Sat 11am–6pm, Sun 1–5pm. Closed mid-Sept to June.

Kailzie Gardens   These 17 acres of formal walled gardens, dating from 1812, include a rose garden, woodlands, and burnside (streamside) walks. Restored over the past 20 years, it provides a stunning array of plants from early spring to late autumn and has a collection of waterfowl and owls. There's also an art gallery, a shop, and a restaurant.

Kailzie on B7062, 2½ miles (4km) southeast of Peebles. ℂ **01721/720-007**. Admission £2.50 ($3.75) adults, 75p ($1.10) children; gardens only £1 ($1.50). Daily dawn to dusk.

Dawyck Botanic Garden   This botanic garden, run by the Royal Botanic Garden in Edinburgh, has a large variety of conifers, some exceeding 100 feet (30m) in height, as well as many species of flowering shrubs. There's also a fine display of early-spring bulbs, plus walks in the woods rich in wildlife interest.

Hwy. B712, 8 miles (13km) southwest of Peebles. ℂ **01721/760-254**. Admission £3 ($4.50) adults, £2.50 ($3.75) seniors and students, £1 ($1.50) children, £7 ($10.50) per family. Mar–Oct daily 9:30am–6pm. Local bus marked BIGGAR.

SHOPPING

Knitwear, crafted from yarn culled from local sheep, is the best buy in Peebles, and easily found as you stroll the High Street. General shopping hours are Monday through Saturday from 9am to 5:30pm. On Sundays, but only in July and August, some shops open from 10am to 5pm.

Woolgathering, 1 Bridge House Terrace (ℂ **01721/720-388**), offers knitwear and all kinds of sweaters. Three sprawling branches of **Castle Warehouse,** at 1 Greenside (ℂ **01721/723-636**), 7–13 Old Town (ℂ **01721/720-348**), and 29–31 Northgate (ℂ **01721/720-814**), sell gift items with a Scottish flavor as well as clothing, such as traditional Scottish garb and anything you might need for a fishing trip.

Caledonian Countrywear, Ltd., 74 High St. (ℂ **01721/723-055**), and **Out & About,** 2 Elcho St. Brae (ℂ **01721/723-590**), are sporting-goods stores with lots of durable clothing and hiking boots.

For Border handcrafts like pinewood furniture, stoneware, and porcelain, go to **Peebles Craft Centre,** 9 Newby Court (ℂ **01721/722-875**), or the **Couchee Righ,** 26 Northgate (ℂ **01721/721-890**).

Fewer than 6 miles (10km) from Walkerburn at Galashiels (head east along A72) is the **Peter Anderson Company,** Nether Mill (ℂ **01896/752-091**). This factory outlet sells more than 750 types of tartan fabrics, all made on the premises on modernized looms. The shop is open Monday through Saturday from 9am to 5pm and Sunday from noon to 5pm. Dozens of other shops are in the nearby textile town of Galashiels.

ACCOMMODATIONS

Castle Venlaw Hotel ⭐   Originally built in 1782 and enlarged in 1854, Castle Venlaw lies among 4 acres (1.6 hectares) of woodlands and offers lovely views of the surrounding countryside. The hotel's round tower and craw-stepped gables are an evocative example of the Scottish baronial style. In 1999, the hotel was completely redecorated, and the heating system and all bathrooms were modernized. Castle Venlaw now has 12 individually decorated rooms equipped with satellite TV and a variety of books and magazines. In the tower at the top of the castle is a spacious family room with a children's den containing bunk beds, games, and a TV/VCR.

Edinburgh Rd., Peebles EH45 8QG. © **01721/720-384.** Fax 01721/724-066. www.venlaw.co.uk. 12 units. £120 ($180) double; £130 ($195) deluxe; £140 ($210) suite. Rates include breakfast. Children under 13 stay in parents' room for £15 ($22.50); children 13–16 pay £20 ($30). MC, V. Free parking. Take A703 to Peebles. **Amenities:** Restaurant, bar; room service; laundry. *In room:* TV.

Cringletie House Hotel ★★★ This imposing 1861 red-sandstone Victorian mansion with towers and turrets is one of the most delightful country-house hotels in the Borders, known for its charming setting and its luxurious rooms. It stands on 28 acres of well-manicured grounds, featuring a superb walled garden that in itself is worth a visit. The tasteful house is immaculately maintained, with public rooms that range from an elegant cocktail lounge to an adjacent conservatory. There's even a small library and, thankfully, an elevator. Each spacious bedroom is individually decorated; several units contain their own original fireplaces. All open onto views of the extensive grounds. The bathrooms, with combination tub/shower, are maintained in state-of-the-art condition and come with luxurious toiletries.

Eddleston, Peebles, The Borders EH45 8PL. © **01721/730-233.** Fax 01721/730-244. www.cringletie.com. 14 units. £150–£220 ($225–$330) double. Rates include breakfast. AE, MC, V. Take A703 for 2½ miles (4km) north of Peebles. **Amenities:** Restaurant; bar; croquet lawn; putting green; fishing can be arranged; room service; babysitting. *In room:* TV, coffeemaker, hair dryer.

The Tontine ★ *Finds* The Tontine was built in 1807 as a private club by a group of hunters who sold their friends shares in its ownership. The construction was executed by French prisoners-of-war during the Napoleonic era; later enlargements were made by the Edwardians. Flower boxes adorn its stone lintels, and a stone lion guards the forecourt fountain. The modestly furnished guest rooms are in an angular modern wing built in back of the 19th-century core. The most expensive units have river views. The Adam-style dining room is one of the town's architectural gems, with tall fan-topped windows and a minstrels' gallery. The Tweeddale Shoot Bar is cozily rustic.

39 High St., Peebles, The Borders EH45 8AJ. © **01721/720-892.** Fax 01721/729-732. 36 units. £68–£76 ($102–$114) double. Rates include breakfast. Children under 15 stay free in parents' room, but pay £5 ($7.50) for breakfast. AE, DC, MC, V. Free parking. **Amenities:** Restaurant, bar. *In room:* TV, coffeemaker, hair dryer.

Whitestone House On the eastern fringe of Peebles, this dignified stone house was built in 1892 to house the pastor of a Presbyterian church that has since been demolished. It's now the genteel domain of Mrs. Margaret Muir. The windows overlook a pleasant garden and the glacial deposits of Whitestone Park, while the comfortable, high-ceilinged guest rooms evoke life in a quiet private home.

Innerleithen Rd., Peebles, The Borders EH45 8BD. © and fax **01721/720-337.** www.aboutscotland.com/ peebles/whitestone.html. 5 units, none with private bathroom. £35–£36 ($52.50–$54) double. Rates include breakfast. No credit cards. *In room:* TV, coffeemaker.

DINING

Horse Shoe Inn SCOTTISH In the center of the nearby village of Eddleston, this country restaurant serves top-quality beef and steaks. Appetizers include everything from the chef's own paté with oat cakes to smoked Shetland salmon with brown bread. House favorites are steak-and-stout pie, Meldon game pie, and vegetable moussaka. The main focus is the food and drink served in the bar, site of most meals. On Friday and Saturday nights and at Sunday lunch, the bar is supplemented by a more formal dining room.

The owners bought the old school next door and converted it into a guesthouse with eight rooms going for £20 to £35 ($30 to $52.50) per person, depending on the season; the rates include breakfast.

Eddleston. (℃ **01721/730-225**. Reservations recommended on Sat. Main courses £6–£14 ($9–$21). AE, DC, MC, V. Easter–Oct Mon–Thurs 11am–11pm, Fri–Sun 11am–midnight; Nov–Easter Mon–Thurs 11am–2:30pm and 5:30–11pm, Fri–Sat 11am–2:30pm and 5:30–midnight, Sun 11am–11pm. Take A701 4½ miles (7km) north of Peebles.

PEEBLES AFTER DARK

Peebles has many options for drinking and dining, and some of the most appealing are in the hotels on the town's edge, even though they may seem rather staid at first glance. On Innerleithen Road, the **Park Hotel** (℃ **01721/720-451**) and the nearby **Hotel Hydro** (℃ **01721/720-602**) contain pubs and cocktail lounges.

For an earthier atmosphere, we highly recommend dropping into the town's oldest pub, at the **Cross Keys Hotel,** 24 Northgate (℃ **01721/724-222**), where you'll find 300-year-old smoke-stained panels, a blazing fireplace, and an evocatively crooked bar. Ask the bartender about the resident ghost. Like the Loch Ness monster, she's taken on an almost mythical identity since her last sighting. No one will be shy about telling you his or her theory, especially if you're buying.

6 Moffat

61 miles (98km) S of Edinburgh, 22 miles (35km) NE of Dumfries, 60 miles (97km) SE of Glasgow

A small town at the head of the Annandale Valley, Moffat thrives as a center of a sheep-farming area, symbolized by a statue of a ram on the wide High Street. It's been a holiday resort since the mid–17th century because of the curative properties of its water, and it was here that Robert Burns composed the drinking song "O Willie Brewd a Peck o' Maut." Today, people visit this town on the banks of the Annan River for its great fishing and golf.

ESSENTIALS

GETTING THERE   The nearest **rail station** is in Lockerbie, 15 miles (24km) south of Moffat. Call ℃ **0345/848-950** for train information. Getting to Lockerbie sometimes requires a change of train in Dumfries, so passengers from Edinburgh or Glasgow often transfer to a **National Express bus** at Dumfries for the 35-minute trip straight to Moffat's High Street, which costs £3 ($4.50) one-way. If you're coming from the Lockerbie rail station, though, you can get a National Express bus to Moffat; they run four times a day, and the fare is £4.05 ($6.05) each way. For bus information, call ℃ **0990/808-080.**

If you're **driving** from Dumfries, head northeast along A701. From Edinburgh, head south along A701; and from Peebles, drive west, following the signs to Glasgow, then turn south on A702 and merge onto M74, following the signs to Moffat.

VISITOR INFORMATION   The **tourist office** is a 5-minute walk south of the town center, at Unit One, Ledyknowe, off Station Road (℃ **01683/ 220-620**). From June to September, it's open Monday through Saturday from 9:30am to 6pm and Sunday from noon to 5pm; April, May, and October, hours are Monday through Friday from 10am to 5pm and Saturday from 10am to 4pm.

OUTDOOR PURSUITS

The region's most famous course is the **Moffat Golf Course,** Coates Hill
(② **01683/220-020**), about a mile (1.6km) southwest of the town center.
Nonmembers can play if they call in advance. The tourist office offers a
brochure called *Golfing in Dumfries & Galloway* for £1.50 ($2.25).

The waters around Moffat team with salmon, trout, and pike. The best source
for fishing is **Mr. John Jack,** owner and manager of the **Ben Mar Esso Garage,**
Station Road (② **01683/220-010**), on the town's southern perimeter. He sells
fishing permits for £10 to £16 ($15 to $24) per day, depending on where you
want to fish. The tourist office sells a brochure called *Fishing in Dumfries & Galloway* for £1.50 ($2.25).

North of Moffat is lots of panoramic hill scenery. Five miles (8km) northwest
is a sheer-sided, 500-foot-deep (152m), 2-mile-wide (3km) hollow in the hills
called the **Devil's Beef Tub,** where cattle thieves (reivers) once hid cattle lifted
in their raids. This hollow is of interest to geologists because of the way it por-
trays Ice Age glacial action, and it makes for a good day hike in the quiet countryside. To reach it, walk north from Moffat along the **Annan Water Valley
Road,** a rural route with virtually no vehicular traffic. In 4 miles (6.5km), the
road will descend a steep slope whose contours form an unusual bowl shape. No
signs mark the site, but you'll know it when you get here.

Northeast along Annan Water, past 2,696-foot-high (818m) White Coomb,
is the **Grey Mare's Tail** ✸✸, a 200-foot (61m) hanging waterfall formed by
the Tail Burn dropping from Loch Skene; it's part of the National Trust for
Scotland.

ACCOMMODATIONS

You can also find accommodations at **Well View Hotel** (see "Dining," below).

Auchen Castle Hotel ✸   About a mile (1.6km) north of the village of Beattock, the area's most luxurious accommodations are at the Auchen, a Victorian
mock-castle. It's really a country house built in 1849 on the site of Auchen Castle, with terraced gardens and a trout-filled loch. Most of the guest rooms are
spacious. Ask for a unit in the main house (which is known as the castle); the
others are in the Cedar Lodge, a less desirable annex built in the late 1970s.

Beattock, Galloway DG10 9SH. ② **01683/300-407.** Fax 01683/300-667. www.auchen-castle-hotel.co.uk. 25
units. £80–£95 ($120–$142.50) double in main house; £110 ($165) suite. AE, DC, MC, V. Take A74 for 2 miles
(3km) north of Moffat. **Amenities:** Restaurant, bar; room service; babysitting; laundry. *In room:* TV.

Beechwood Country House Hotel   This charming country-house hotel was
the 19th-century headquarters of Miss Thompson's Private Adventure Boarding
Establishment and School for Young Ladies. You'll spot its facade of chiseled
stone at the end of a narrow rural lane. A tea lawn, smooth as a putting green,
is the site for outdoor refreshments on sunny days. The guest rooms have a certain amount of homespun charm.

Harthope Place, Moffat, Galloway DG10 9RS. ② **01683/220-210.** Fax 01683/220-889. www.smoothhound.
co.uk/hotelbeechwoo.html. 7 units. £80 ($120) double with breakfast; £123 ($184.50) double with half-
board. AE, MC, V. Free parking. **Amenities:** Restaurant; tennis, golf, fishing, and riding can be arranged; room
service; babysitting; laundry. *In room:* TV, coffeemaker, hair dryer.

Moffat House Hotel   The red- and black-stone Moffat House is one of the
town's most architecturally noteworthy buildings, constructed in 1751 by John
Adam. The modernized guest rooms are comfortable and functional; some are
equipped for travelers with disabilities. The hotel offers some of the best food in
town, especially at night, when the chef prepares an international menu.

High St., Moffat, Galloway DG10 9HL. ☏ **01683/220-039.** Fax 01683/221-288. www.moffathouse.co.uk. 20 units. £70–£90 ($105–$135) double. Rates include breakfast. AE, MC, V. Free parking. **Amenities:** Restaurant, bar; room service. *In room:* TV, coffeemaker, hair dryer.

Star Hotel   With a 17th-century brick facade, this place bears the quirky fame of being the narrowest free-standing hotel in the United Kingdom—it's only 20 feet (6m) wide. The guest rooms are small and unpretentious, with contemporary furnishings and shower-only bathrooms. The food here is popular; menu items are simple and straightforward but savory.

44 High St., Moffat, Galloway DG10 9EF. ☏ **01683/220-156.** Fax 01683/221-524. www.famousstarhotel. com. 8 units. £56 ($84) double. AE, MC, V. **Amenities:** Restaurant, bar; fishing and golf can be arranged; room service; babysitting; pool table. *In room:* TV.

DINING

Other dining options include the restaurants in the hotels listed above.

Well View Hotel ✿✿ BRITISH/CONTINENTAL   Come here for some of the best food in the region. The setting is mid-Victorian, with country-cottage charm and views of the kitchen garden. The fixed-price menus, which vary almost daily, may include roasted breast of Perthshire pigeon with red-wine sauce, roasted saddle of venison with gin-and-juniper sauce, or filet of Aberdeen Angus beef with whole-grain mustard sauce.

Upstairs are six guest rooms, with modern furniture and reproduction antiques, Laura Ashley fabrics, TVs, coffeemakers, and hair dryers. Doubles range from £72 to £96 ($108 to $144).

Ballplay Rd., Moffat DG10 9JU. ☏ **01683/220-184.** www.wellview.co.uk. Reservations recommended. Fixed-price 3-course lunch £14 ($21); fixed-price 6-course dinner £28 ($42). AE, MC, V. Sun–Fri 12:30–1:15pm; daily 7–8:30pm. Closed 2 weeks Jan–Feb. Take A708 ¾ mile (1.2km) east of Moffat.

7 Dumfries: An Ode to Burns ✿

80 miles (129km) SW of Edinburgh, 79 miles (127km) SE of Glasgow, 34 miles (55km) NW of Carlisle

A county town and royal burgh, the Galloway center of Dumfries enjoys associations with national poet Robert Burns and *Peter Pan* author James Barrie. Burns lived in Dumfries from 1791 until his death in 1796 and wrote some of his best-known songs here, including "Auld Lang Syne" and "Ye Banks and Braes of Bonnie Doon." A statue of Burns stands on High Street; you can visit his house, his favorite pub, and his mausoleum. Barrie was a pupil at the Academy here and later wrote that he got the idea for Peter Pan from his games in the nearby garden.

The widest esplanade in Dumfries, Whitesands, flanks the edge of the River Nith. It was once the scene of horse and hiring fairs and is a fine place to park your car and explore this provincial town. The town center is reserved for pedestrians, and on the opposite bank of the Nith, the public Deer Park offers a small-scale manicured version of the wild majesty of Scotland. Allow a morning to visit the city's major sights, but there's even more to see in the surrounding countryside, including Sweetheart Abbey, Ellisland Farm, and the art-filled Drumlanrig Castle at Thornhill.

ESSENTIALS

GETTING THERE   Seven **trains** per day make the run from Glasgow's Central Station, taking 1¾ hours. Tickets cost £9.40 ($14.10) one-way but only £10 to £18.20 ($15 to $27.30) round-trip, depending on time of departure. For information, call ☏ **0345/484-950.**

Stagecoach **buses** depart from Glasgow (from Buchanan Street Station or Anderston Station); the trip is 2 hours and costs £6.50 ($9.75) one-way or £8.50 ($12.75) round-trip. Buses also run to Dumfries from Edinburgh's St. Andrew's Square. The prices are the same as from Glasgow, but the trip is 3 hours. For information, call © **01387/253-496.**

If you're **driving** from Edinburgh, take A701 to Moffat, and then continue southwest to Dumfries. From Glasgow, take M74, which becomes A74 before it approaches Moffat. At Moffat, continue southwest along A701.

VISITOR INFORMATION   The **tourist office** is at 64 Whitesands (© **01387/253-862**), a 2-minute walk from High Street and adjacent to the big car parks. September through March, it's open Monday through Friday from 10am to 5pm and Saturday from 10am to 4pm; April through August, hours are Monday through Saturday from 10am to 6pm (in July and August, also on Sunday from noon to 4pm).

EXPLORING THE TOWN

The 18th-century **St. Michael's Church,** on St. Michael's Street, was the original parish church of Dumfries. Its foundation is ancient—the site was sacred before the advent of Christianity, and a Christian church has stood here for more than 1,300 years. The earliest written records date from 1165 to 1214. The church and the churchyard are interesting to visit because of all their connections with Scottish history, continuing through World War II. You can still see the Burns family pew inside.

In St. Michael's Churchyard, a burial place for at least 900 years, stands the neo-Grecian **Burns Mausoleum.** Built of local sandstone and dripping with literary and patriotic nostalgia, the dome-capped mausoleum is one of the most important pilgrimage sites for Burns fans. The poet is buried here along with his wife, Jean Armour, and five of their children. Burns died in 1796, but his remains weren't moved to the tomb until 1815.

The **Mid Steeple**✸, on High Street, was built in 1707 as municipal buildings, a courthouse, and a prison. The old Scots "ell" measure of 37 inches (almost 1 meter) is carved on the front, and a table of distances includes the mileage to Huntingdon, England, which in the 18th century was the destination for Scottish cattle driven south for the London markets. Today it's used mostly as municipal archives, and all of its interior is for government office functions.

At Whitesands, the street paralleling the Nith's edge, **four bridges** span the river. The earliest was built by Devorgilla Balliol, widow of John Balliol. Their son, John, was made Scotland's "vassal king" by Edward I of England, the "Hammer of the Scots," who established himself as Scotland's overlord. The bridge (originally with nine arches but now with only six) is still in constant use as a footbridge.

The town's best shopping is along the High Street, which is lined with turn-of-the-20th-century facades, and nearby Queensberry Street. **Alternatives,** 73 Queensberry St. (© **01387/257-467**), is an attractive New Age shop stocking herbal remedies, artful wind chimes, and gift items, especially jewelry inspired by Celtic designs. You'll find men's and women's kilts in dozens of tartan patterns, as well as sweaters, overcoats, hats, and socks, always at realistic prices, at the **Edinburgh Woolen Mill,** 8 Church Place (© **01387/267-351**).

Burns House   In 1796, Scotland's national poet died in this unpretentious, terraced stone house off St. Michael's Street. Although he occupied the house during only the last 3 years of his life, it contains personal relics and mementos as well as much of the original furniture used by Burns during his creative years.

Burns St. ℭ **01387/255-297**. Free admission. Apr–Sept Mon–Sat 10am–5pm, Sun 2–5pm; Oct–Mar Tues–Sat 10am–1pm and 2–5pm.

Robert Burns Centre You'll find this converted 18th-century water mill on the banks of the River Nith. Facilities include an exhibit on the poet, a restaurant (see the Wishart's listing under "Dining," below), and a theater showing films about Burns and the town of Dumfries.

Mill Rd. ℭ **01387/264-808**. Exhibition free; theater £1.50 ($2.25) adults, 75p ($1.10) children, seniors, and students. Apr–Sept Mon–Sat 10am–8pm, Sun 2–5pm; Oct–Mar Tues–Sat 10am–1pm and 2–5pm. From Whitesands, cross the river at Devorgilla Bridge.

Dumfries Museum Southwestern Scotland's largest museum occupies a converted 18th-century windmill atop Corbelly Hill. Visit it only if you have extra time and an interest in the region's early geology, history, and archaeology. Some exhibits suggest the site's role as an astronomical observatory in 1836; note the telescope used to observe Halley's Comet in July 1836. The camera obscura provides panoramic views of the town and surrounding countryside.

Church St. ℭ **01387/253-374**. Museum free; camera obscura £1.50 ($2.25) adults, 75p ($1.10) children and seniors. Museum, Apr–Sept Mon–Sat 10am–5pm, Sun 2–5pm; Oct–Mar Tues–Sat 10am–1pm and 2–5pm. Camera obscura, Apr–Sept Mon–Sat 10am–5pm, Sun 2–5pm. Cross the river at St. Michael's Bridge Rd. and turn right onto Church St.

Old Bridge House Associated with the Burns House (see above), this building dates from 1660, when it replaced a structure that had been on the site since 1431. It has been restored and furnished in a style typical of the period between 1850 and 1900, with tons of worthy Victoriana. Devorgilla Bridge itself was constructed in the 16th century.

Mill Rd., at the far end of Devorgilla Bridge. ℭ **01387/256-904**. Free admission. Apr–Sept Mon–Sat 10am–5pm, Sun 2–5pm. From Whitesands, cross the river at Devorgilla Bridge.

FARTHER AFIELD

From Dumfries, you can set out hiking, biking, or driving in all directions. If you're looking for natural beauty, leave by A75 and drive 7½ miles (12km), turning right at the signpost for Shawhead. Once here, turn right again and follow the signs to **Glenkiln,** 10 miles (16km) from Dumfries. In this remote but scenic spot stands a wild landscape so perfect that Henry Moore decided to place his celebrated *King and Queen* sculpture here.

To explore the area on two wheels, go to the **Nithsdale Cycle Centre,** 46 Broon's Rd. (ℭ **01387/254-870**). Rental rates are £10 ($15) daily or £30 to £50 ($45 to $75) weekly, plus a 25% deposit. It's open Monday through Saturday from 10am to 5pm.

Sweetheart Abbey The village of New Abbey is dominated by Sweetheart Abbey's red-sandstone ruins. The walls are mostly extant, even though the roof is missing. Devorgilla Balliol founded the abbey in 1273. With the death of her husband, John Balliol the Elder, she became one of Europe's richest women—most of Galloway, as well as estates and castles in England and Normandy, belonged to her. Devorgilla founded Balliol College, Oxford, in her husband's memory. She kept his embalmed heart in a silver-and-ivory casket by her side for 21 years until her death in 1289 at age 80, when she and the casket were buried in front of the abbey altar. The abbey gained the name of "Dulce Cor," Latin for *sweet heart,* a term that has become a part of the English language.

On A710, New Abbey. © **01387/770-244** (regional office of Historic Scotland). Admission £1.50 ($2.25) adults, £1.10 ($1.65) seniors, 50p (75¢) children under 16. Apr–Sept daily 9:30am–6:30pm; Oct–Mar Mon–Wed and Sat 9:30am–4:30pm, Thurs 9:30am–1pm, Sun 2–4:30pm. Drive 7 miles (11km) southwest from Dumfries on A710 (follow the signs saying SOLWAY FIRTH HERITAGE).

Drumlanrig Castle   This pink castle, built between 1679 and 1689 in a parkland ringed by wild hills, is the seat of the dukes of Buccleuch and Queensberry and contains some outstanding paintings, including a famous Rembrandt, a Leonardo da Vinci, and a Holbein, plus relics related to Bonnie Prince Charlie. There's a playground with amusements for kids and a working crafts center in the old stable yard; the gardens are gradually being restored to their 1720 magnificence. Meals are served in the old kitchen, hung with gleaming copper.

Thornhill, 3 miles (5km) north of Thornhill off A76 and 16 miles (26km) southwest of A74 at Elvanfoot. © **01848/330-248** or 01848/331-555. Admission £6 ($9) adults, £4 ($6) seniors, £2 ($3) children, £14 ($21) per family. May–Aug Mon–Sat 11am–4pm, Sun noon–4pm. Closed Sept–Apr.

Ellisland Farm *Finds*   From 1788 to 1791, Robert Burns made his last attempt at farming at Ellisland Farm; it was here that he wrote "Tam o' Shanter." After his marriage to Jean Armour, Burns leased the farm from Patrick Miller under the stipulation that he'd assist in erecting the building that's the centerpiece of the homestead. It's still a working farm for sheep and cattle, with many aspects devoted to a museum and shrine honoring Burns and his literary statements. On a circular quarter-mile (about 400-m) trail ("the south trail") adjacent to the banks of the Nith, you can retrace the footsteps of Burns, who walked along it frequently during breaks from his writing.

6 miles (10km) north of Dumfries via A76 (follow the signs to Kilmarnock). © **01387/740-426.** Admission £1.50 ($2.25) adults, 75p ($1.10) children and seniors. Apr–Sept Mon–Fri 10am–5pm, Sun 2–5pm; Oct–Mar Tues–Sat 10am–4pm.

ACCOMMODATIONS

Cairndale Hotel & Leisure Club *⋆*   This four-story stone-fronted building from around 1900 houses the finest hotel in Dumfries, easily outdistancing the Station and all other competition. The Cairndale features handsome public rooms and carefully modernized guest rooms, each containing a bathroom with combination tub/shower. Executive rooms and suites have queen-size beds, minibars, and whirlpool baths.

132–136 English St., Dumfries, Galloway DG1 2DF. © **01387/254-111.** Fax 01387/250-555. www. cairndalehotel.co.uk. 91 units. £105–£125 ($157.50–$187.50) double; from £145 ($217.50) suite. Rates include breakfast. AE, DC, MC, V. Free parking. **Amenities:** Restaurant; bar; gym; spa; solarium; room service; babysitting; laundry/dry cleaning. *In room:* TV, coffeemaker, hair dryer.

The Station Hotel   This is among the most traditional lodgings in Dumfries, a few steps from the gingerbread-fringed train station. It was built in 1896 of hewn sandstone, in a design of heavy timbers, polished paneling, and soaring ceilings. The modernized but still somewhat dowdy guest rooms contain comfortable beds and shower-only bathrooms.

49 Lovers Walk, Dumfries, Galloway DG1 1LT. © **01387/254-316.** Fax 01387/250-388. www.stationhotel. co.uk. 32 units. £80–£90 ($120-$135) double. Rates include breakfast. AE, DC, MC, V. Free parking. **Amenities:** Restaurant; bar; golf can be arranged room service; babysitting. *In room:* TV, coffeemaker, hair dryer.

Trigony House Hotel   This pink-sandstone hotel was built around 1895 as the home of a local family. Its name (*trigony*) derives from the shape of the acreage, which is almost like a perfect isosceles triangle. Today, it contains a handful of comfortable but unpretentious high-ceilinged guest rooms, each opening onto countryside views. Your hosts, Robin and Thelma Pollack, will tell you all about the building's occupant during the 1930s: Frances Shakerley lived to be 107 within the walls of this house and thus became famous as the oldest woman in Scotland.

The hotel operates a busy pub and a dinner-only restaurant. Drop into the pub for affordable platters of simple food at lunch or dinner. Meals may include paté of smoked trout, haggis with whisky-flavored cream sauce, and strips of beef with whisky-and-oatmeal sauce.

On the Dumfries–Ayr trunk road, Thornhill, Dumfries, Galloway DG3 5EZ. © 01848/331-211. Fax 01848/331-303. www.trigonyhotel.co.uk. 8 units. £75–£80 ($112.50-$120) double. Rates include breakfast. MC, V. From Dumfries, drive 13 miles (21km) north along A76, following the signs to Thornhill. Trigony House is 1 mile (1.6km) south of Thornhill.

DINING

Bruno's ITALIAN   It may seem ironic to recommend an Italian restaurant in the heart of Robert Burns territory, but Bruno's serves some of the best food in town. It's unassuming, but that's part of the charm. The chef's repertoire is familiar—first-rate minestrone, homemade pizza and pasta, veal with ham, and spicy chicken—but everything is done with a certain flair.

3 Balmoral Rd. © 01387/255-757. Reservations required Fri–Sat. Main courses £5.95–£14.95 ($8.95–$22.45); fixed-price 3-course dinner £17.95 ($26.95); supper pasta menu £8.50 ($12.75). MC, V. Wed–Mon 5:30–10pm.

Globe Inn ℛ SCOTTISH   This is the traditional favorite. It was Burns's favorite haunt, in business since 1610, and he used an old Scottish expression, *howff* (meaning a small cozy room), to describe his local pub. He was definitely a regular: He had a child with the barmaid, Anna Park. You reach the pub down a narrow flagstone passage off High Street, opposite the Marks & Spencer department store. You can go for a meal (perhaps kipper paté, haggis, or Globe steak pie) or just to have a drink and play a game of dominoes. A little museum is devoted to Burns, and on window panes upstairs you can see verses he scratched with a diamond. Taps include Belhaven, Tennet's Lager, Galloway Ale, and Black Throne Cider.

56 High St. © 01387/252-335. Main courses £4.20–£5.20 ($6.30–$7.80). No credit cards. Mon–Thurs 10am–11pm; Fri–Sat 10am–midnight; Sun noon–11pm. Food served Mon–Sat 10–11:30am and noon–3pm.

Wishart's ℛ *Finds* SCOTTISH   This is the most unusual restaurant in Dumfries. It's in a renovated grain mill, which you reach by taking a lovely 10-minute stroll across the Nith from the commercial heart of town. Built around 1780 by prominent engineer Thomas Sneaton, the mill also shelters a small movie theater and the Robert Burns Centre (see above). The dining room's bare wood floors complement the forest-green painted brick walls, which display a riveting series of modern paintings (some for sale).

The offerings are prepared from Scottish ingredients and change with the seasons; they may include imaginative choices like sashimi of sea bass with wasabi, ginger, and garlic; a confit of wild salmon from the Nith, served with ratatouille, olive oil, and basil; and braised Highland beef with burgundy sauce, wild mushrooms, and parsley purée. Dessert may be strawberry soup with chantilly cream sauce.

In the Robert Burns Centre, Mill Rd. © 01387/259-679. Reservations recommended. Main courses £6.95–£14.95 ($10.45–$22.45). MC, V. Tues–Sat 7–9:30pm.

DUMFRIES AFTER DARK

The town's most famous pub is the previously recommended **Globe Inn,** 56 High St. (© **01387/252-335**), where Robert Burns tipped many a dram. An equally historic pub loaded with local color is **The Hole in the Wall,** 156 High St. (© **01387/252-770**), where live music is usually provided by an accordionist. If you want to go dancing, head for either of the town's two discos, **Chancers Nightclub,** 25 Munches St. (© **01387/263-170**), or **The Junction,** 36 High St. (© **01387/267-262**). The crowd and music at these two clubs change often, depending on the theme for the night, so call ahead for details.

8 Castle Douglas

16 miles (26km) SW of Dumfries, 98 miles (158km) SW of Edinburgh, 49 miles (79km) SE of Ayr

An old cattle- and sheep-market town, Castle Douglas, at the northern tip of Carlingwark Loch, is near such attractions as Threave Castle, Cardoness Castle, Kirkcudbright, and Sweetheart Abbey, and just southeast of the Galloway Forest Park. On one of the islets in the loch is an ancient lake dwelling known as a *crannog.*

ESSENTIALS

GETTING THERE   The nearest **rail station** is in Dumfries (see above); from there, you can take a bus to Castle Douglas. Call © **0345/484-950** for rail information. The **Great Western Bus Co.** runs buses from Dumfries to Castle Douglas every hour throughout the day and early evening; travel time is about 30 minutes and costs £1.80 ($2.70) one-way. Call © **0990/808-080** for bus information. If you're **driving** from Dumfries, head southwest along A75.

VISITOR INFORMATION   The **tourist office** is at the Markethill Car Park (© **01556/502-611**). April through October, it's open Monday through Friday from 10am to 6pm and Saturday from 10am to 5pm (in July and August, also Sunday from 10am to 5pm).

SEEING THE SIGHTS

Unique in Scotland, **Orchardton Tower,** 5½ miles (9km) southeast of Castle Douglas off A711, is an example of a round tower house (they were usually built in Ireland). It was constructed around 1450 by John Cairns, and later was purchased by a member of the Maxwell family. The adventures of one family member, Sir Robert Maxwell of Orchardton, a fervent Jacobite captured in the Battle of Culloden, figured in Sir Walter Scott's novel *Guy Mannering.* If you ask the custodian who lives at the cottage next door, he'll let you see inside for free.

The **Mote of Urr,** 5 miles (8km) northeast of Castle Douglas off B794, is a circular mound enclosed by a deep trench. This is an example of the motte-and-bailey type of defense popular in Norman days.

Threave Castle ⊛   Threave Castle is the ruined 14th-century stronghold of the Black Douglases. The seven-story tower was built between 1639 and 1690 by Archibald the Grim, Lord of Galloway. In 1455, Threave was the last Douglas stronghold to surrender to James II, who employed some of the most advanced armaments of his day (including a cannon similar to Mons Meg, the massive cannon now displayed in Edinburgh Castle) in its subjection. Over the doorway projects the gallows knob from which the Douglases hanged their enemies. In 1640, the castle was captured by the Covenanters (the rebellious group of Scots who questioned the king's right to make laws) and dismantled.

The site is owned by a public group known as Historic Scotland. To reach it, you must walk half a mile (0.8km) through farmlands and then take a small boat across the Dee. When you get to the river, ring a bell signaling the custodian to come and ferry you across. The last sailing is at 6pm. For information, contact Historic Scotland, Longmore House, Salisbury Place, Edinburgh (© **01316/ 688-800**).

1½ miles (2.5km) west of Castle Douglas on an islet in the River Dee. Admission (including ferry ride) £2 ($3) adults, £1.50 ($2.25) seniors, 75p ($1.10) children under 16. Apr–Sept Mon–Sat 9:30am–6:30pm, Sun 2–6:30pm. Closed Oct–Mar.

Threave Garden 🎀 A mile (1.6km) southeast of Threave Castle, these gardens are built around Threave House, a Scottish baronial mansion constructed during the Victorian era. It's run by the National Trust for Scotland, which uses the complex as a school for gardening and a wildfowl refuge. The garden is at its best in April, when the daffodils bloom, and in June, when rhododendrons and the rock garden are in flower. On site are a visitor center and restaurant.

Off A75 half a mile (1km) west of Castle Douglas. © **01556/502-575**. Admission £4.50 ($6.75) adults, £3.50 ($5.25) children and seniors. Garden, daily 9:30am–5:30pm; visitor center, Apr–Oct daily 9:30am–5:30pm.

EXPLORING THE COUNTRYSIDE

Castle Douglas's location near the northern edge of the estuary of Solway Firth offers panoramic views across the water stretching as far as England's Lake District. To best appreciate the beauty of the region, head to the nearby tiny village of **Auchencairn** (pop. 200), 6 miles (10km) south. (If you don't have a rental car, you can take one of about five daily buses from Carlingwark Street in Castle Douglas, for a fare of around 90p/$1.35 one-way). At the Balcary Bay Hotel (the only hotel in town), you'll find the start of a loop trail leading along the heather-clad, wind-whipped clifftops above the Solway Firth. Views extend out over Balcary Point and Rasscarel Bay. The walk is clearly marked with brown-and-white signs; allow about 2 hours.

If you want to explore the area by bike, rent one at **Ace Cycles,** Church Street in Castle Douglas (© **01556/504-542**), open Monday through Saturday from 9am to 12:30pm and 1:30 to 5pm. Rates are £8 to £10 ($12 to $15) per day; a £50 ($75) deposit is required.

ACCOMMODATIONS

Douglas Arms Hotel A 17th-century coaching inn, this old favorite is modernized behind its rather stark two-story facade. The public rooms are bright and cheerful, giving off a toasty feeling on a cold night. The guest rooms were recently refurbished and include shower-only bathrooms.

King St., Castle Douglas, Galloway DG7 1DB. © **01556/502-231**. Fax 01556/504-000. www. douglasarmshotel.co.uk. 24 units. £68.50 ($102.75) double. Rates include breakfast. AE, MC, V. **Amenities:** Restaurant, pub. *In room:* TV, coffeemaker.

King's Arms Hotel This inn provides reasonably priced accommodations ranging from single rooms to a family room; nine come with private, shower-only bathrooms. The helpful staff will direct you to various activities in the area, including a nine-hole golf course a 45-minute drive away. The sun patio is a great place for tea or coffee. The restaurant's cuisine is British with a Scottish emphasis; the range is extensive, featuring local produce, Solway salmon, and Galloway beef.

St. Andrew's St., Castle Douglas, Galloway DG7 1EL. ℭ **01556/502-626.** Fax 01556/502-097. www. galloway-golf.co.uk. 10 units, 9 with private bathroom. £56 ($84) double with bathroom. Rates include breakfast. MC, V. Free parking. **Amenities:** Restaurant, 3 bars. *In room:* Coffeemaker, hair dryer, no phone.

Longacre Manor   This dignified building on about 1½ (0.6 hectare) acres of forest and garden was constructed in 1927 as the home of a local grain trader. Under the gracious ownership of Elma and Charles Ball, it now offers plushly and conservatively furnished guest rooms, some with four-poster beds and all with shower-only bathrooms. The lounge is cozy, and a three-course dinner can be prepared and served in the dining room.

Ernespie Rd., Castle Douglas, Galloway DG7 1LE. ℭ **01556/503-576.** Fax 01556/503-886. www.about scotland.co.uk/south/longacre.html. 4 units. £60–£90 ($90–$135) double. Rates include breakfast. MC, V. From the center of Castle Douglas, drive half a mile (1km) north, following the signs to Dumfries. **Amenities:** Dining room. *In room:* TV, coffeemaker, hair dryer.

The Urr Valley Hotel ⟨★ *Finds*   Reached by a long drive, this country hotel in the scenic Urr Valley is set in the midst of 14 acres (5.7 hectares) of lush woodlands and gardens, a mile (1.6km) east of the center of Castle Douglas. You're welcomed into a real Scottish macho atmosphere of stag heads and antique rods and reels, along with paneled walls and fireplaces with log fires. Most of the guest rooms are spacious; two have been set aside for nonsmokers. You can have a drink or enjoy a pub meal in the lounge and bar. The main restaurant serves both French and Scottish cuisine, with an emphasis on local produce and fresh seafood such as Solway salmon.

Ernespie Rd., Castle Douglas, Galloway DG7 3JG. ℭ **01556/502-188.** Fax 01556/504-055. www.castle douglas.net/urrvalley. 19 units. £55–£70 ($82.50–$105) double; £65–£80 ($97.50–$120) family room. Rates include breakfast. AE, MC, V. Free parking. Take A75 toward Castle Douglas. **Amenities:** Restaurant, bar. *In room:* TV, coffeemaker, hair dryer.

DINING

Plumed Horse Restaurant SCOTTISH/INTERNATIONAL   Opened in July 1998, this restaurant combines high-quality cuisine with a relaxed, village atmosphere; it's set the rest of the local competition on its ear. The linen tablecloths, crystal, silver, and Villeroy & Boch tableware lend the Plumed Horse an air of elegance. Chef Tony Borthwick changes the menu regularly, but you might find roast Barbary duck breast, crisp filet of salmon, scallop ravioli, and roast monkfish among the choices. The restaurant has an extensive wine and champagne list.

Main St., Crossmichael (3 miles/5km from Castle Douglas). ℭ **01556/670-333.** Reservations required. Main courses £15.95–£18.95 ($23.95–$28.45). Fixed-price menus £12.95–£18.95 ($19.45–$28.45). MC, V. Tues–Fri and Sun 12:30–1:30pm; Tues–Sun 7–9:30pm. Take A713 toward Ayr.

9 Kirkcudbright: An Artists' Colony ⟨★

108 miles (174km) SW of Edinburgh, 28 miles (45km) SW of Dumfries, 103 miles (166km) S of Glasgow, 50 miles (80.5km) E of Stranraer, 10 miles (16km) SW of Castle Douglas

The ancient burgh of Kirkcudbright (Kir-*coo*-bree) is at the head of Kirkcudbright Bay on the Dee estuary. Many of this intriguing old town's color-washed houses belong to artists; a lively group of weavers, potters, and painters lives and works in the 18th-century streets and lanes. What makes Kirkcudbright so enchanting isn't really its sights (although it boasts several) but its artistic life and bohemian flavor. Various festivities take place in July and August; expect to find anything from marching bagpipe bands to exhibitions of Scottish country dancing to torchlight processions. And activities range from raft races to nearby walks, from a floodlit tattoo in front of MacLellan's Castle to a puppet festival.

ESSENTIALS

GETTING THERE   Kirkcudbright is on the same **bus** route that serves Castle Douglas from Dumfries, with departures during the day about once per hour. The 40-minute ride from Dumfries costs about £1.75 ($2.65) one-way. For bus information, call ℭ **0990/808-080** or the local tourist office. If you're **driving** from Castle Douglas, continue along A75 southwest until you come to the junction with A711, which takes you into Kirkcudbright.

VISITOR INFORMATION   The **tourist office** is at Harbour Square (ℭ **01557/330-494**). May through October, it's open Monday through Saturday from 10am to 3pm and Sunday from 1 to 4pm; it's closed November through April.

SEEING THE SIGHTS

In the old town **graveyard** are memorials to Covenanters and to Billy Marshall, the tinker (Gypsy) king who died in 1792 at age 120, reportedly having fathered four children after age 100.

MacLellan's Castle   Dominating the center of town is this castellated castle built in 1582 for the town's provost, Sir Thomas MacLellan. It has been a ruin since 1752, but it's an impressive ruin and worth a visit. A large staircase goes from the cellars on the ground floor to the Banqueting Hall, where a massive fireplace comes with what was called a "lairds lug" (spy hole). From almost anywhere in town, the jagged fangs of the castle loom overhead.

Off High St. ℭ **01557/331-856**. Admission £1.80 ($2.70) adults, £1.30 ($1.95) seniors, 75p ($1.10) children. Apr–Sept Mon–Sat 9:30am–6:30pm, Sun 2–6pm. Closed Oct–Mar.

Tolbooth Art Centre   The Tolbooth (1629) has functioned as a prison, town hall, and courthouse. In front of it is a 1610 Mercat Cross, while inside is a memorial to John Paul Jones (1747–92), the gardener's son from Kirkbean who became a slave trader, a privateer, and eventually the father of the American navy. In 1993, Queen Elizabeth inaugurated the building as a gallery displaying paintings by famous local artists. You'll find works by Jessie M. King, Lena Alexander, Robert Sivell, and S. J. Peploe.

High St. ℭ **01557/331-556**. Admission £1.50 ($2.25) adults, 75p ($1.10) seniors, students, and children. Combined ticket with the Stewartry Museum (see below) £2.50 ($3.75) adults, £1.25 ($1.90) seniors, students, and children. Apr–June and Aug–Oct Mon–Sat 11am–5pm, Sun 2–5pm; July Mon–Sat 10am–6pm, Sun 2–5pm; Nov–Mar Mon–Sat 11am–4pm.

Broughton House   Regular exhibits are displayed at this 18th-century mansion that once belonged to artist Edward Atkinson Hornel (1864–1933). His portrait by Bessie McNicol is displayed in the former dining room. Although largely forgotten today, Hornel was a famous artist in his day, known for his scenes depicting life in his native Galloway. With his bold and colorful style, he became one of the major figures of the Glasgow School of Art. Broughton contains a large reference library with a Burns collection, along with pictures by Hornel and other artists. One of the most appealing aspects of this place is Hornel's small but charming Japanese-style garden, whose plantings sometimes appeared in his paintings.

12 High St. ℭ **01557/330-437**. Admission £3.50 ($5.25) adults, £2.50 ($3.75) seniors and children, £9.50 ($14.25) per family. Apr–June and Sept–Oct daily 1–5:30pm; July–Aug daily 11am–5:30pm. Closed Nov–Mar.

Stewartry Museum   Built by the Victorians in 1892 as a showcase for the region's distinctive culture, this museum contains an unusual collection of antiquities, tools, and artworks depicting the history, culture, and sociology of this part of Galloway.

St. Mary St. ☎ 01557/331-643. Admission £1.50 ($2.25) adults, 75p ($1.10) seniors and students, free for children under 16. May–Sept Mon–Sat 11am–5pm (July–Aug also Sun 2–5pm); Oct–Apr Mon–Sat 11am–4pm.

ACCOMMODATIONS

Selkirk Arms Hotel ✦   This is a beloved old favorite and the finest inn in the area, built in the 1770s in a stone-fronted Georgian design with a slate roof. It was here that Robert Burns stayed when he composed the celebrated "Selkirk Grace." The guest rooms have standard furniture and garden views, plus bathrooms with a combination tub/shower. The restaurant/bistro offers a wide range of fresh local produce; bar lunches and suppers are also available. The lounge bar features an array of malt whiskies that would warm Burns's heart.

Old High St., Kirkcudbright, Galloway DG6 4JG. ☎ 01557/330-402. Fax 01557/331-639. www.selkirkarmshotel.co.uk. 16 units. £90 ($135) double. Rates include breakfast. AE, DC, MC, V. Free parking. **Amenities:** Restaurant, bar. *In room:* TV, coffeemaker, hair dryer.

DINING

Auld Alliance Restaurant   SCOTTISH/FRENCH   One of the most appealing restaurants in the region is this family-owned and -operated place in an interconnected pair of 1880s buildings constructed with stones from the ruins of Kirkcudbright Castle. The cooks are almost obsessed with the freshness of the fish they serve, and salmon (likely to have been caught several hours before preparation in the Kirkcudbright estuary and its tributary, the Dee) has all its legendary flavor. A house specialty is queenies (queen-size scallops from deeper waters than the great scallop).

5 Castle St. ☎ 01557/330-569. Reservations recommended. Main courses £9.50–£15 ($14.25–$22.50). MC, V. Apr–Oct Sun noon–2pm, Mon–Sat 6:30–9:30pm. Closed Halloween–Easter.

10 Gatehouse-of-Fleet

113 miles (182km) SW of Edinburgh, 33 miles (53km) SW of Dumfries, 42 miles (68km) E of Stranraer, 9 miles (14.5km) W of Kirkcudbright, 108 miles (174km) SW of Glasgow

On the Water of Fleet, the sleepy former cotton town of Gatehouse-of-Fleet is really a backwoods kind of place, so don't expect major attractions. But the Scots themselves like to come here—they cherish its setting among dark brooding hills and conifers. Lonely stretches of countryside lie nearby, ideal for walks and picnics in nearly all directions.

Gatehouse-of-Fleet was Kippletringan in Sir Walter Scott's *Guy Mannering*. Burns composed "Scots Wha' Hae wi' Wallace Bled" on the moors nearby and wrote it down in the Murray Arms Hotel here. The town's name probably dates from 1642, when the English government opened the first military road through Galloway to assist the passage of troops to Ireland. In 1661, Richard Murray of Cally was authorized by Parliament to widen the bridge and erect beside it an inn to serve as a tollhouse, with the innkeeper responsible for the maintenance of a 12-mile (19km) stretch of road. This is believed to have been the original house on the "gait" (road) that later became known as the "gait house of Fleet," and by 1790 it was being written in its present form and spelling. This ancient "gait house" is now part of the Murray Arms Hotel, used as a coffee room, and is the oldest building still in existence in the town.

ESSENTIALS

GETTING THERE   Four **buses** a day arrive in Gatehouse-of-Fleet from both Dumfries and Stranraer. Each route takes 60 to 70 minutes due to frequent stops along the way. The one-way fare from both Dumfries and Stranraer is around £2.80 ($4.20). For information, call © **0990/808-080.** If you're **driving** from Castle Douglas, continue west along A75.

VISITOR INFORMATION   The **tourist office** operates from the Car Park at the southern end of High Street (© **01557/814-212**). In April, May, June, September, and October, it's open daily from 10am to 5pm (to 6pm in July and August).

EXPLORING THE AREA

Mill on the Fleet   Most people pass through town en route to Cardoness Castle, but a worthy stop would be this heritage center installed in a former cotton mill. Skip the earphone-guided tour about the milling industry and concentrate instead on enjoying a light lunch, certainly a spot of tea, and some home-baked items in the tearoom. Look also for the shop selling gifts and local crafts.

High St. © 01557/814-099. Free admission. Easter–Oct daily 10am–5:30pm.

Tower of the McCullochs (Cardoness Castle)   Built in the 15th century on a rocky plateau above the Water of Fleet (River Fleet) and evocative of medieval Scotland at its spookiest, the McCulloch family's semi-ruined castle has a sinister murder hole positioned in the ceiling of its entrance passage. Through this trap door, boiling pitch was poured down onto attackers. The castle may be roofless, but you can still see the 15th-century tower house and even the four floors that rise above a turf mound. The original staircase is intact, as are the vaulted basement and some fireplaces and stone benches.

One member of the family, Sir Godfrey McCulloch, was the last person in Scotland to be executed by the "Maiden," the Scots version of the guillotine, at Edinburgh in 1697. The other family members didn't fare well either: To celebrate the birth of a new heir, they went skating on a nearby loch, but the ice wasn't firm yet, and all of them went to a watery grave.

Half a mile (1km) west of Gatehouse-of-Fleet, on Rte. 75. © 0131/668-8800. Admission £2 ($3) adults, £1.50 ($2.25) seniors, 75p ($1.10) children under 16. Apr–Sept daily 9:30am–6:30pm; Oct–Mar Sat 9:30am–4:30pm, Sun 2–4:30pm. From the town center, follow the signs to Creetown.

ACCOMMODATIONS & DINING

Cally Palace   The Cally Palace is a 1763 mansion on 150 acres (60.8 hectares) of gardens, loch, and wooded parkland. Especially popular with more mature travelers, it's an oasis of peace, a place to enjoy a few days' rest rather than a fleeting overnight. The public lounges are overscale, with some fine period pieces. The guest rooms come in widely varying styles and sizes; some are in a modern annex, others in the historic main building. Some have balconies opening onto the grounds, and each comes with a private, shower-only bathroom. From August to May, a dinner dance is held on Saturdays. Every night you can order a four-course table d'hôte dinner.

Along Hwy. A75, Gatehouse-of-Fleet, Galloway DG7 2DL. © 01557/814-341. Fax 01557/814-522. www. callypalace.co.uk. 56 units. £116 ($174) double; £138 ($207) suite. Rates include breakfast. Ask about golf packages. AE, MC, V. Free parking. Take A75 south for 1½ miles (2.5km). **Amenities:** Restaurant; bar; pool; on-site golf course; tennis court; sauna; table tennis; croquet. *In room:* TV, coffeemaker, hair dryer.

Murray Arms   The Murray Arms is a long white building that functioned as a posting inn in 1760. Its coffeehouse (which sometimes converts into a small-scale art gallery) is even older, dating back to 1642. This is where Burns wrote down his stirring song "Scots Wha' Hae wi' Wallace Bled," an occasion still commemorated by the Burns Room with its Leitch pictures. The inn has been considerably updated now that it's back in the Cally family—and that's as it should be, since it was James Murray of Cally who made it into a coaching inn so long ago. The guest rooms overlook the garden or the main street; each comes with a shower-only bathroom. Some rooms are equipped for travelers with disabilities. The attractive restaurant opens onto the garden; specialties include Galloway beef and fresh Solway Firth salmon.

Ann St., Gatehouse-of-Fleet, Galloway DG7 2HY. © **01557/814-207.** Fax 01557/814-370. www.murray arms.com. 13 units. £84 ($126) double. Rates include breakfast. AE, DC, MC, V. Free parking. **Amenities:** Restaurant, 2 bars; nearby golf and horseback riding; tennis courts; room service; babysitting. *In room:* TV, coffeemaker, hair dryer.

11 Stranraer

132 miles (212.5km) SW of Edinburgh, 75 miles (121km) W of Dumfries

The largest town in the area, Stranraer is the terminus of the 35-mile (56km) ferry crossing from Larne, Northern Ireland. An early chapel, built by a member of the Adair family near the 16th-century Castle of St. John, gave the settlement its original name of Chapel, later changed to Chapel of Stranrawer and then shortened to Stranraer. The name is supposed to have referred to the row ("raw") of original houses on the "strand," now largely buried beneath the streets. The Castle of St. John became the town jail and in the late 17th century held Covenanters during the campaigns of religious persecution. The rebellious Covenanters opposed the king's authority to make laws, feeling that should be the task of Parliament.

Frankly, if you're not going on to Ireland, you could skip Stranraer without any great loss to your enjoyment of Scotland. However, the beauty of Castle Kennedy Gardens is worth the trek, and you'll find lovely places to go for a walk or enjoy a picnic as you explore the countryside.

ESSENTIALS
GETTING THERE   Monday through Saturday, four **trains** per day run from Glasgow to Stranraer, with seven trains on Sunday. The one-way fare is £15 ($22.50); trip time is 2¾ to 3 hours. Call © **08457/484-950** for rail information.

There are about four **buses** a day into Stranraer from Dumfries, each requiring 2½ hours of transit time and a one-way fare of about £5 ($7.50). There are about 10 buses a day from Glasgow, taking 3¾ hours and costing £7 ($10.50) one-way. Call © **0990/808-080** for bus schedules.

If you're **driving** from Dumfries, continue west along A75.

Sealink Ferries travel between Stranraer and Belfast in Northern Ireland. Seven ferries per day depart Monday through Saturday, with five on Sunday. Trip time is 99 minutes. The one-way fare for travelers without cars is £22 ($33) per adult and £12 ($18) per child. A driver with a car pays £135 ($202.50) each way, and a driver with a car and up to four passengers pays £165 ($247.50). Weather conditions can interfere with ferry departures; call © **01776/702-262** for updates.

ALPS   ASPEN

AT&T Direct® Service

The easy way to call home from anywhere.

Global
connection
with the AT&T
Network

AT&T
direct
service

For the easy way to call home, take the attached wallet guide.

VISITOR INFORMATION   The **tourist office** is at Burns House, Harbour Street (© **01776/702-595**). It's open November through April, Monday through Saturday from 11am to 4pm; May and June, Monday through Saturday from 10am to 5pm and Sunday from 11am to 3pm; and July through October, Monday through Saturday from 9:30am to 5pm and Sunday from 10am to 4pm.

EXPLORING THE AREA

Our favorite drive in the area is the 50-mile (80.5km) excursion around the **Mull of Galloway,** reached via Stranraer by taking A77 south. Land of wild gorse and whin, this is rugged Galloway country (*wild gorse* is a low, thick, and prickly shrub, and *whin* is any hard, dark-colored rock). Along the way you'll pass sandy beaches (far too cold for those of us from milder climes), rugged cliffs, occasional sheltered bays, and sleepy villages and tiny fishing ports. Life here isn't as extreme as it first appears because the Gulf Stream nearby has a warming effect. On a clear day, you'll often have a good view of the Irish coastline.

Despite its small size, the town has a great number of shops. Most are clustered along Charlotte, George, and Castle streets. **Rogers Sports,** 26–30 Charlotte St. (© **01776/703-996**), can provide all kinds of gear for fair and foul weather and any equipment you might need for hiking the moors or hitting the links. The **China Shop (Jean Ralstons),** 34 Charlotte St. (© **01776/702-697**), carries most of the grand names of British porcelain and crystal, as well as cunning figurines of the animals that trek across the nearby hills. For women, two choice clothing shops are **Whispers,** 92 George St. (© **01776/706-591**), and **Nowadays,** 35 George St. (© **01776/703-938**).

Known throughout the region for its evocative landscapes by local artists is the **Waterloo Gallery,** Prince's Street (© **01776/702-888**). A short walk from the village of Ardwell, 7 miles (11km) south of Stranraer, at a crossroads known as Clachenmore, the **Clachenmore Art Gallery** (© **01776/860-200**) incorporates a coffee shop, a gift shop, and a winning collection of sculptures and paintings by British and Scottish artists.

Castle Kennedy Gardens   The main attraction here is the ruins of Castle Kennedy, a medieval monument whose glory days ended in 1716, when it was sacked and burned during a border raid by forces of James IV. The ruins are near the White Loch (named because of its clear waters) and the Black Loch (named because of its peat-impregnated dark waters). Surrounding the ruins are gardens containing one of the finest *pinetums* (pine groves) in Scotland. In early spring, you can wander among blossoming rhododendrons, azaleas, and magnolias. The estate's main building is Lochinch Castle, built in the neo-feudal baronial style in 1864 and today the home of Lord Stair (his mother is a cousin of Queen Elizabeth II). You can't go inside Lochinch Castle, except to visit the tearoom.

2 miles (3km) east of Stranraer on A75. © 01776/702-024. Admission £3 ($4.50) adults, £2 ($3) seniors, £1 ($1.50) children, £8 ($12) per family. Gardens Easter–Sept daily 10am–5pm (castle not open to the public).

ACCOMMODATIONS

Corsewall Lighthouse Hotel ⍟ *Finds*   This is a unique hotel for the area. In 1994, the solid stone walls, barns, and outbuildings of a lighthouse keeper's home were transformed into an upscale inn and restaurant set beside the 1815 lighthouse. Its light still beams at night, warning approaching ships entering the mouth of Loch Ryan. The setting is panoramic, and the place is full of 19th-century charm. Each uniquely decorated bedroom is spacious and elegant, with amenities such as individually controlled central heating and a shower-only bathroom. Some of the most scenic coastline in the Borders is within and near the 20-acre (8.1-hectare) grounds, with views that on a clear day can stretch all the way to the coast of Ireland. A wide variety of sea life, seals, birds, and deer can be spotted here. Dinners utilize many local ingredients (produce, beef, lamb, salmon, trout, and venison) prepared with skill and finesse. The pub is open to the public, and passersby are welcome to drop in for drinks and meals.

Kirkcolm, Stranraer, Galloway DG9 0QG. (C) 01776/853-220. Fax 01776/854-231. www.nimline.com/hotels/corsewall. 9 units. £65 ($97.50) per person double; £130 ($195) per person suite. Rates include dinner and breakfast. AE, MC, V. From Stranraer, take A77 for 12 miles (19km) north, following the signs to Kirkcolm and Corsewall Point. **Amenities:** Restaurant, bar; room service; babysitting; outdoor activities. *In room:* TV, coffeemaker, hair dryer.

Kildrochet House 👉   The stone walls of this atmospheric 1720 building, the dower house for the mother of the lord of the manor, were designed by William Adam, the father of star architect Robert Adam. The guest rooms evoke those in a private home and are outfitted with dignified furniture and neat little shower-only bathrooms. Each has a view over 3½ acres (1.4 hectares) of gardens and fields. Congenial owners Liz and Peter Witworth will prepare an evening meal, served in the family dining room, for any guest who gives advance notice.

Stranraer, Galloway DG9 9BB. (C) and fax **01776/820-216.** www.kildrochet.co.uk. 3 units. £54 ($81) double. Rates include breakfast. MC, V. Drive 3½ miles (6km) south of Stranraer, following A716. **Amenities:** Dining room (for guests only); lounge with TV. *In room:* Coffeemaker, no phone.

North West Castle Hotel 👉👉   This is Stranraer's largest and best hotel, its oldest part built in 1820 by Capt. Sir John Ross, R.N., the Arctic explorer. The original building has been expanded with a modern flat-roofed addition. The rooms in the older building have more atmosphere and space, but all are comfortably appointed and contain well-maintained bathrooms, most with combination tub/shower. The lounges are cozy, while the dining room is impressive. Fresh local ingredients are used in the restaurant, where Continental fare with Scottish overtones is served. The bars in the hotel's cellar are well stocked, but we prefer the Ross Lounge, with its views of the harbor. There's dancing to a live band most Saturday nights in winter.

Royal Crescent, Stranraer, Galloway DG9 8EH. (C) 01776/704-413. Fax 01776/702-646. www.northwest castle.co.uk. 73 units. £79.50 ($119.25) double; £95.50 ($143.25) suite; £109 ($163.50) penthouse. Rates include breakfast. AE, MC, V. Free parking. Walk 3 min. north from the ferryboat terminal. **Amenities:** Restaurant, 2 bars; pool; sauna; solarium; curling rink (Oct–Apr); game room. *In room:* TV, coffeemaker, hair dryer.

DINING

L'Apéritif Restaurant ITALIAN/INTERNATIONAL   Here you'll find some of the best and most reasonably priced food at the port. One of the two lounges contains a pub popular with locals. Homemade soups, fresh salads, pastas, and hot dishes are offered at lunch for around £6 ($9). In the evening, you have a choice of Continental meals or pizza upstairs.

London Rd., directly east of town. (C) **01776/702-991.** Reservations recommended. Main courses £7–£20 ($10.50–$30); fixed-price 3-course dinner (5:30–7pm) £10 ($15); pizzas £5.50–£7 ($8.25–$10.50). AE, MC, V. Mon–Sat noon–2pm and 5:30–9pm.

STRANRAER AFTER DARK

The town has a few good pubs where you can while away a foggy evening. Small and hospitable but not particularly historic is the **Bridge Pub,** Bridge Street

(© **01776/704-839**). **The Grapes,** 46 Bridge St. (© **01776/703-386**), has a vintage 1940s and 1950s decor and has been virtually untouched since it was modernized shortly after World War II. Also worth your tippling and attention is the pub on the ground floor of the **Royal Hotel,** 20–24 Hanover St. (© **01776/702-426**), where Thursday through Saturday nights you can enjoy live rock. If you're looking to dance, head for the town's best disco, **The Venue,** Hanover Street (no phone), open Thursday through Saturday.

12 Portpatrick: Where the Southern Upland Way Begins

141 miles (227km) SW of Edinburgh, 8 miles (13km) SW of Stranraer, 97 miles (156km) SW of Glasgow, 80 miles (129km) W of Dumfries

Until 1849, steamers sailed the 21 miles (34km) from Donaghdee in Northern Ireland to Portpatrick, which became a "Gretna Green" for the Irish who wanted to marry quickly. Couples would land on Saturday, have the banns called on Sunday, and marry on Monday. When the harbor silted up, Portpatrick was replaced by Stranraer (see above) as a port.

Today, you go to Portpatrick not because of its wealth of sights, although the Logan Botanic Gardens is worth the detour from Stranraer. You go instead because it's a major refueling stop for those driving along the Mull of Galloway. Portpatrick captures the flavor of an almost forgotten Scottish fishing port as few other towns do. It's a land of cliffs and rugged seascapes, with a lighthouse here and there and even a bird reserve.

Hikers come because Portpatrick is the beginning of one of the greatest long-distance footpaths in Scotland, the **Southern Upland Way** (see "The Best Hikes," in chapter 1). Starting here, the 212-mile (341-km) jaunt goes all the way to the Cockburnspath on the eastern coast of Scotland. Along the way, this path traverses the Galloway Forest Park and other scenic attractions of southern Scotland. Of course, very few will have the time or stamina to take the entire hike. But you can enjoy one of the least challenging stretches, going all the way from Portpatrick to Castle Kennedy (see above), some 7½ miles (12km).

ESSENTIALS

GETTING THERE   Go to Stranraer (see "Stranraer," above) by **train,** then take a bus to Portpatrick, 5 minutes away. For train information, call © **0345/ 484-950.** Bus no. 64 from Stranraer makes frequent runs throughout the day. The 5-minute ride costs around 95p ($1.40) one-way. For bus information, call © **0990/808-080.** If you're **driving** from Stranraer, take A77 southwest.

VISITOR INFORMATION   The nearest **tourist office** is in Stranraer (see above).

EXPLORING THE AREA

Commanding a clifftop 1½ miles (2.5km) south of the town center are the ruins of **Dunskey Castle,** a grim keep built in 1510. It's a dramatic site—the original stone walls and the chimney stacks, each rising abruptly from the top of the cliff, are all that remain. To walk or drive here from the town center, follow the clearly marked signs.

Some 10 miles (16km) south of Portpatrick is the little hamlet of Port Logan. In the vicinity is **Logan House** (not open to the public), the seat of the McDougall family, which claimed they could trace their ancestry so far back they were as old as the sun itself. This family laid out the gardens at Logan.

Fourteen miles (22.5km) south of Stranraer off B7065, the **Logan Botanic Garden** (© **01776/860-231**), an annex of the Royal Botanic Garden in Edinburgh, contains a wide range of plants from the world's temperate regions. Cordylines, palms, tree ferns, and flowering shrubs grow well in the mild climate of southwestern Scotland. March through October, the garden is open daily from 9:30am to 6pm. Admission is £3 ($4.50) for adults, £2.50 ($3.75) for seniors, £1 ($1.50) for children, and £7 ($10.50) for families. At the entrance is a pleasant refreshment room.

Portpatrick has become something of a magnet for individual artisans who produce charming (and sometimes eccentric) handcrafts. You'll find examples of handcrafted plant pots, slip-cast and glazed figurines, Spanish recycled glass, and Indian coffee tables at the port's largest gift shop, **Lighthouse Pottery,** South Pier (© **01776/810-284**). The **Green Gillie Crafts Shop,** High Street (no phone), specializes in woolen jerseys and mittens, throw rugs, and calfskins. At the **Copper Wheel,** High Street (call the local garage at © **01776/810-543** and ask for Ron Farquer), a highly skilled artisan grinds heraldic or freeform designs into wine glasses, beer mugs, and other objects. You can bring your own object or buy one from him. Anglers appreciate his renderings of trout or salmon on a line.

ACCOMMODATIONS

The **Crown Hotel** (see "Dining," below) also rents rooms.

Fernhill Hotel   This gray-stone 1872 building stands above the village, looking down at the harbor a 5-minute walk from the first tee of the clifftop Dunskey Golf Course (which is scenic but not challenging). Renovated in 1990, the guest rooms are decorated with flair. Most desirable are the six executive rooms opening onto the sea; three have private balconies. Each unit comes with a small, shower-only bathroom. The cocktail bar and the Victorian conservatory have a panoramic view over the town and sea. The excellent cuisine, using Scottish produce whenever available, is one of the reasons for staying here. The house specialty is fresh lobster.

Heugh Rd., Portpatrick, Galloway DG9 8TD. © **01776/810-220.** Fax 01776/810-596. www.mcmillanhotels. com. 23 units. £90–£104 ($135–$156) double. Rates include breakfast. AE, MC, V. Free parking. On the approach to Portpatrick, turn right at the War Memorial. **Amenities:** Restaurant, bar; limited room service and laundry service. *In room:* TV, coffeemaker, hair dryer.

Knockinaam Lodge ★★★   Built in 1869, Knockinaam Lodge is a three-story Victorian hunting lodge, surrounded on three sides by towering cliffs. It's a country house of charm and grace in a picturesque coastal setting, boasting some of the finest cuisine served in the south of Scotland. Since it's west of town, it is far more tranquil than any other hotel in the area. You get a real feel for Scottish manorial living here, especially as you read your paper in the morning room overlooking the sea. The bedrooms are tastefully decorated and filled with thoughtful little extras, along with modernized bathrooms with combination tub/showers. This award-winning establishment also boasts luxurious lawns that lead down to a pristine, private beach. It was here on these 30 acres (12.2 hectares) of private woodland that Sir Winston Churchill met General Eisenhower and their chiefs of staff during the dark days of World War II.

Portpatrick, Galloway DG9 9AD. © **01776/810-471.** Fax 01776/810-435. www.prideofbritainhotels.com. 10 units. £240–£330 ($360–$495) double. Rates include breakfast and dinner. AE, DC, MC, V. Free parking. From A77 or A75, follow signs to Portpatrick. It's 2 miles west of Lochans; watch for hotel sign on right. **Amenities:** Restaurant, bar; dry cleaning. *In room:* TV, hair dryer.

DINING

The **Knockinaam Lodge** serves the best food in the area (see "Accommodations," above).

Crown Hotel SEAFOOD/INTERNATIONAL   One of the region's most popular restaurants occupies the ground floor of a century-old stone-sided hotel. You might enjoy a drink in the pub before heading into the dining room, which opens onto a wide-angled view of the ocean. Meat is available, but the biggest draw is seafood: scampi, monkfish, scallops in wine sauce, mullet, cod, and plaice, salmon, or sole filets.

The Crown maintains 12 simple rooms upstairs, each with bathroom, TV, hair dryer, coffeemaker, and phone. Doubles rent for £76 ($114), which includes a hearty Scottish breakfast.

North Crescent, Portpatrick, Galloway DG9 8FX. © **01776/810-261.** Fax 01776/810-551. Reservations recommended. Main courses £10.65–£14.45 ($16–$21.70); fixed-price 3-course menu £14.95 ($22.45). MC, V. Daily noon–2:30pm and 6–10pm.

6

Glasgow & the Strathclyde Region

Glasgow ✦✦✦ is only 40 miles (64.5km) west of Edinburgh, but there's an amazing contrast between the two cities. Scotland's economic powerhouse and its largest city (Britain's third-largest), up-and-coming Glasgow is now the country's cultural capital and home to half the population. It has long been famous for ironworks and steelworks; the local shipbuilding industry produced the *Queen Mary,* the *Queen Elizabeth,* and other fabled ocean liners.

Once polluted by industry and plagued with some of the worst slums in Europe, Glasgow has been transformed. Urban development and the decision to locate the Scottish Exhibition and Conference Centre here have brought great changes: Industrial grime is being sandblasted away, overcrowding has been reduced, and more open space and less traffic congestion mean cleaner air. Glasgow also boasts a vibrant and even edgy arts scene; it's become one of the cultural capitals of Europe.

The splendor of the city has reemerged. John Betjeman and other critics have hailed Glasgow as "the greatest surviving example of a Victorian city." The planners of the 19th century thought on a grand scale when they designed the terraces and villas west and south of the center.

Glasgow's origins are ancient, making Edinburgh, for all its wealth of history, seem comparatively young. The village that grew up beside a fjord 20 miles (32km) from the mouth of the River Clyde as a medieval ecclesiastical center began its commercial prosperity in the 17th century. As it grew, the city engulfed the smaller medieval towns of Ardrie, Renfrew, Rutherglen, and Paisley.

Glasgow is part of Strathclyde, a powerful and populous district whose origins go back to the Middle Ages. Irish chroniclers wrote of the kingdom of Stratha Cluatha some 1,500 years ago, and Strathclyde was known to the Romans, who called its people Damnonii. The old capital, Dumbarton, on its high rock, provided a natural fortress in the days when locals had to defend themselves against enemy tribes.

The fortunes of Strathclyde changed dramatically in the 18th century, when the Clyde estuary became the gateway to the New World. Glasgow merchants grew rich on tobacco and then on cotton. It was Britain's fastest-growing region during the Industrial Revolution, and Glasgow was known as the Second City of the Empire. Until 1996, Strathclyde functioned as a government entity that included Glasgow, but it's now broken down into several new divisions: the City of Glasgow; Inverclyde, which includes the important industrial center of Greenock; and several others.

Glasgow is a good gateway for exploring the heart of Burns country, Culzean Castle, and the resorts along the Ayrshire coast, an hour away by

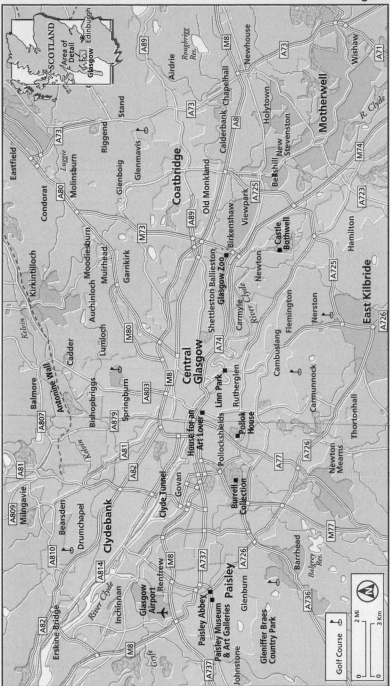

SCOTLAND

Area of
Detail

Edinburgh

Glasgow

A89
Roughrigg Res.
A89
Airdrie
M8
Newhouse
A73
Wishaw
A71

Stand
Riggend
Glenmavis
Glenboig
Coatbridge
Calderbank Chapelhall
Holytown
A8
New Stevenston
Motherwell
M74
R. Clyde

Eastfield
A73
Luggie
Molinsburn
Condorat
A80
Muirhead
Moodiesburn
Auchinloch
Garnkirk
A73
Old Monkland
A89
Viewpark
Birkenshaw
Birkenshaw
A725
Bellshill
Newton
Hamilton
A723

Kirkintilloch
Kelvin
Cadder
Lumloch
M80
A879
Springburn
A803
M8
Shettleston Ballieston
Glasgow Zoo
Castle Bothwell
Carmyle
River Clyde
Flemington
Nerston
A725
East Kilbride
A726

Balmore
Antonine Wall
Bishopbriggs
A807
A81
Govan
Clyde Tunnel
Central Glasgow
A74
Linn Park
Rutherglen
Pollokshields
Pollok House
Cambuslang
Carmunnock
A726
Thorntonhall

A809
Milngavie
A81
Kelvin
Bearsden
Drumchapel
Clydebank
A82
House for an Art Lover
Burrell Collection
A77
A726
Newton Mearns
M77

Erskine Bridge
A82
A810
A814
Inchinnan
River Clyde
Glasgow Airport
Renfrew
M8
A737
Paisley
A726
Barrhead
Balgray Res.
M77
A736

M8
A737
Johnstone
Paisley Abbey
Paisley Museum & Art Galleries
Gleniffer Braes Country Park
Glenburn
Glenburn
A736

Gryfe

Golf Course

2 Mi
3 Km

frequent train service (see "Side Trips from Glasgow: The Best of the Strathclyde Region," later in this chapter). From Glasgow, you can also tour Loch Lomond, Loch Katrine, and the Trossachs (see chapter 8, "Fife & the Central Highlands," for more information). After a day or so in Glasgow, you can head to Burns country for perhaps another night. Also on Glasgow's doorstep is the scenic estuary of the Firth of Clyde, which you can cruise on a paddle steamer. The Firth of Clyde, with its long sea lochs—Gareloch, Loch Long, Loch Goil, and Holy Loch—is one of the most scenic waterways in the world.

1 Essentials

ARRIVING

BY PLANE The **Glasgow Airport** is at Abbotsinch (© 0141/887-1111), 10 miles (16km) west of the city via M8. You can use the Glasgow CityLink bus service to get to the city center. From bus stop no. 2, take bus no. 900 or 901 to the Buchanan Street Bus Station in the center of town. The ride takes about 20 minutes and costs £3.30 ($4.95). A taxi to the city center costs about £15 ($22.50). You can reach Edinburgh by taking a bus from Glasgow Airport to Queens Station and then changing to a bus for Edinburgh. The entire journey, including the change, takes about 2 hours and costs £6.80 ($10.20) one-way or £10 ($15) round-trip.

Monday through Friday, **British Airways** (© 0181/897-4000 in London) runs almost hourly shuttle service from London's Heathrow Airport to Glasgow. The first flight departs London at 7:15am and the last at 8:15pm; service is reduced on weekends.

From mid-May to October, **American Airlines** (© 800/433-7300) offers a daily nonstop flight to Glasgow from Chicago; the rest of the year, you'll make at least one transfer. **Northwest Airlines** (© 800/225-2525) operates nonstop flights between Boston and Glasgow daily in summer, somewhat less frequently in winter.

KLM UK (© 0990/074-074) flies from Stansted and London City airports to Glasgow daily. **British Midland** (© 0345/554-554) flies from Heathrow to Glasgow. **Aer Lingus** (© 800/223-6537, or 01/844-4711 in Ireland) flies daily from Dublin to Glasgow. **Ryan Air** (© 0541/569-569 in England) flies several times a day from Dublin to Glasgow.

BY TRAIN The **Queen Street Station** serves the north and east of Scotland, with trains arriving from Edinburgh every 30 minutes during the day; the one-way trip between the two cities costs £7.30 ($10.95) and takes 50 minutes. You'll also be able to travel to such Highland destinations as Inverness and Fort William from here.

The **Central Station** serves southern Scotland, England, and Wales, with trains arriving from London's Euston and King's Cross Stations (© 0345/484-950 in London for schedules) frequently throughout the day (trip time is about 5½ hours). Try to avoid Sunday travel, as the frequency of trains is considerably reduced and the duration of the trip lengthened to at least 7 hours because of more stopovers en route.

For **National Rail Enquiries,** call © 0345/484-950. For sleeper reservations by credit card, contact Virgin West Coast at © 0345/991-995.

BY BUS The **Buchanan Street Bus Station** (© 0141/332-7133) is 2 blocks north of the Queen Street Station on North Hanover Street. **National Express**

(© **0990/808-080**) runs frequent daily coaches from London's Victoria Coach Station to Buchanan. Buses from London to Glasgow take 7½ to 8½ hours, depending on the number of stops. **Scottish CityLink** also has frequent bus service to and from Edinburgh, with a one-way ticket costing £3 to £5 ($4.50 to $7.50).

BY CAR   Glasgow is 40 miles (64.5km) west of Edinburgh, 221 miles (356km) north of Manchester, and 388 miles (625km) north of London. From England in the south, Glasgow is reached by M74, a continuation of M8 that goes right into the city, making an S curve. Call your hotel and find out what exit you should take. M8, another express motorway, links Glasgow and Edinburgh.

Other major routes into the city are A77 northeast from Prestwick and Ayr and A8 from the west (this becomes M8 around the port of Glasgow). A82 comes in from the northwest (the Highlands) on the north bank of the Clyde, and A80 also goes into the city. (This route is the southwestern section of M80 and M9 from Stirling.)

VISITOR INFORMATION

The **Greater Glasgow and Clyde Valley Tourist Board,** 11 George Sq. (© **0141/204-4400;** Underground: Buchanan St.), is the country's most helpful office. It's open October to May, Monday through Saturday from 9am to 6pm; June, Monday through Saturday from 9am to 7pm and Sunday from 10am to 6pm; July and August, Monday through Saturday from 9am to 8pm and Sunday from 10am to 6pm; and September, Monday through Saturday from 9am to 7pm and Sunday from 10am to 6pm.

CITY LAYOUT

The monumental heart of Glasgow—the Victorian City and the Merchant City, along with the Central Station—lies on the north bank of the **River Clyde.** The ancient center has as its core the great Cathedral of St. Kentigern, a perfect example of pre-Reformation Gothic architecture that dates in part to the 12th century. Behind it is the Necropolis, burial ground of many Victorians. Across the square is 1471 Provands Lordship, the city's oldest house. Down **High Street** you'll find the Tolbooth Steeple (1626) at Glasgow Cross, and nearer the River Clyde is **Glasgow Green,** Britain's first public park (1662).

Tips Finding an Address

Glasgow was built in various sections and districts over the years, and massive sections have been torn down—some for slum clearance, others to make way for new highways. Following a consistent street plan can be tough, as squares or terraces can suddenly interrupt a route you're tracing.

House numbers can run in odds or evens and clockwise or counterclockwise, and sometimes Glaswegians don't even use numbers at all. So don't be surprised to see something like "Blackfriars Street," without a number, given as an address. Get a detailed map of Glasgow before setting out. Always find the nearest cross street, and then look for your location from there. If it's a hotel or restaurant, the sign for the establishment is likely to be more prominent than the number anyway.

From Ingram Street, South Frederick Street will take you to **George Square,** with its many statues, including one dedicated to Sir Walter Scott. This is the center of modern Glasgow.

The **Merchant City,** a compact area of imposing buildings, is the location of the National Trust for Scotland's shop and visitor center at Hutcheson's Hall. The broad pedestrian thoroughfares of Buchanan, Argyle, and Sauchiehall streets are the heart of the shopping district.

Glasgow's **West End** is just a short taxi journey from the city center, easily accessible from any part of the city and close to M8 and the Clydeside Expressway. An extensive network of local bus routes serves the West End. The Glasgow Underground operates a circular service; by boarding at any station on the system, you can reach the four stations serving the district: Kelvinbridge, Hillhead (the most central), Kelvin Hall, and Partick. The West End is Britain's finest example of a great Victorian city, and the terraces of the Park Conservation Area rise to afford excellent views. Across Kelvingrove Park is the Art Gallery and Museum. Nearby, the tower of Glasgow University dominates Gilmorehill. Beyond is the Hunterian Art Gallery, home to a famous collection of Whistlers. Just a few strides away is Byres Road, a street of bars, shops, and restaurants. To the north is the Botanic Gardens.

A little more than 3 miles (5km) southwest of the city center is the **Pollok Country Park** and **Pollok Estate.** An extensive network of bus routes passes close by the area, which is also served by two suburban rail stations. An electric bus service is in operation from the Country Park gates on Pollokshaws Road to Pollok House and the Burrell Collection Gallery. The Burrell Collection is housed in the heavily wooded Pollok Country Park. This museum is Scotland's top tourist attraction and the focal point of any visit to the South Side. Nearby is the 18th-century Pollok House.

Extensive parklands and greenery characterize the city's southern environs. In addition to the Pollok Country Park and Estate, there's **Haggs Castle Golf Club,** home of the Glasgow Open, and **Bellahouston Park,** scene of the historic papal visit in 1983. En route to the Burrell Collection, you cross by the 148-acre **Queens Park,** honoring Mary Queen of Scots. Near **Maxwell Park** is the Haggs Castle Museum, housed in a 400-year-old building.

THE NEIGHBORHOODS IN BRIEF

See the "Glasgow Attractions" map on p. 180 to see the locations of the following neighborhoods.

Medieval Glasgow This is where St. Mungo arrived in A.D. 543 and built his little church in what's now the northeastern part of the city. At the top of High Street stands the Cathedral of St. Kentigern and one of Britain's largest Victorian cemeteries. You enter the Necropolis by crossing over the Bridge of Sighs. Old Glasgow's major terminus is the High Street Station, near the former site of the University of Glasgow. Glasgow Green, opening onto the River Clyde, has been a public park since 1662. Today, vastly restored medieval Glasgow is the best place for strolls.

Along the River Clyde It was once said: "The Clyde made Glasgow; Glasgow made the Clyde." Although the city is no longer so dependent on the river, you can still enjoy a stroll along the Clyde Walkway, which stretches from King Albert Bridge, at the western end of Glasgow Green, for 2 miles (3km) downstream to Stohcross, now the site of the Scottish Exhibition and Conference Centre. The river is crossed by several bridges, one named for Queen Victoria and another for her consort, Albert. This is one of the city's grandest walks; on these waters, Glasgow shipped its manufactured goods around the world. However, if time is limited, you may want to concentrate on the major museums and historic Glasgow instead.

The Merchant City Glasgow spread west of High Street in the 18th century, largely because of profits made from sugar, cotton, and tobacco in trade with the Americas. The Merchant City extends from Trongate and Argyle Street in the south to George Street in the north. Its major terminus is the Queen Street Station; its major shopping venue, Argyle Arcade. It's also the site of City Hall and Strathclyde University and boasts some of Britain's most elegant Georgian and Victorian buildings as well as Greek

Revival churches. Much of the area was once occupied by tobacco barons, but their buildings have been recycled for other uses.

Glasgow Center Continuing its western progression, the city center of Glasgow is now dominated by the Central Station on Hope Street. This is the major shopping district, including such venues as the Princes Square Shopping Mall. Also here are the Stock Exchange and the Anderston Bus Station (near the Central Station).

The West End Beyond Charing Cross in the west end are the University of Glasgow and several major galleries and museums, some of which are in Kelvingrove Park. The West End mixes culture, art, and parks, and is dominated by Glasgow University, with the university structures idyllically placed in various parks. The city itself has more green spaces per resident than any other in Europe; 40 acres (16.2 hectares) of the West End are taken up by the Botanic Garden.

2 Getting Around

The best way to explore Glasgow in on foot. The center is laid out on a grid system, which makes map reading relatively easy. However, many of the major attractions, such as the Burrell Collection, are in the surrounding environs, and for those you'll need to rely on public transportation.

Remember: Cars drive on the left, so when you cross streets make certain to look both ways.

BY BUS   Glasgow is serviced by **First Glasgow Bus Company.** The buses are in a variety of colors, the lighter ones (blue and yellow) tending to serve the Kelvin Central and Strathclyde rural areas, with the darker ones covering the urban zones. Service is frequent throughout the day, but greatly curtailed after 11pm. The major station is the **Buchanan Street Bus Station,** Killermont Street (© **0141/226-4826** for schedules), 2 blocks north of the Queen Station. Fares are £1.95 ($2.95), exact change required. A special round-trip bus ticket for £1.40 ($2.10) operates after 9:30am.

BY UNDERGROUND   The city's 15-stop subway is called the "Clockwork Orange" (for the vivid orange of the trains) by Glaswegians. Most Underground trains serve these stops every 5 minutes, with longer intervals between trains on Sunday and at night. The fare is 65p (95¢). Service is Monday through Saturday from 6:30am to 10pm and Sunday from 11am to 6pm.

The **Travel Centre** at St. Enoch Square (© **0141/226-4826**), 2 blocks from the Central Station, is open Monday through Saturday from 6:30am to 9:30pm and Sunday from 7am to 9:30pm. Here you can buy a £6 ($9) **Underground pass,** valid for a week's access to all the Tube lines of Glasgow, as well as access to all the trains serving routes between Central Station and the southern suburbs, or a £7.80 ($11.70) **day-tripper card,** covering one adult and one child for a day. For details, call © **0141/332-7133.**

BY TAXI   Taxis are the same excellent ones found in Edinburgh and London. You can hail them on the street or call **TOA Taxis** (© **0141/332-7070**). When a taxi is available on the street, a taxi sign on the roof is lit a bright yellow. Fares are displayed on a meter next to the driver. Most trips within the city cost £3.5 to £4 ($5.25 to $6). The meter starts at £1.60 ($2.40) and increases by 20p (30¢) every 200 feet (61m), with an extra 10p (15¢) assessed for each additional passenger after the first two. A 60p (90¢) surcharge is imposed from midnight to 6am. Tip at least 10% of the fare shown on the meter.

BY CAR   You're better off with public transportation, as driving around Glasgow is a tricky business, even for locals. It's a warren of one-way streets, and parking is expensive and difficult to find. Metered parking is available, but you'll need 20p (30¢) coins, entitling you to only 20 minutes. Watch out for zealous traffic wardens issuing tickets. Some zones are marked PERMIT HOLDERS ONLY—your vehicle will be towed if you have no permit. A yellow line along the curb indicates no parking. Parking lots open 24 hours a day are found at Anderston Cross and Cambridge, George, Mitchell, Oswald, and Waterloo streets.

If you want to rent a car to explore the countryside, it's best to arrange the rental before leaving home (see chapter 2, "Planning Your Trip to Scotland," for more information). If you want to rent a car locally, most companies will accept your American or Canadian driver's license. All the major rental agencies are represented at the airport. In addition, there's an **Avis** at 161 North St. (© **0141/ 221-2827;** Bus: 6 or 6A), a **Budget** at 101 Waterloo St. (© **0141/221-9241;** Bus: 38, 45, 48, or 57), and a **Europcar** at 38 Anderson Quay (© **0141/ 248-8788;** Bus: 38, 45, 48, or 57).

BY BICYCLE   Parts of Glasgow are fine for biking, or you might want to rent a bike and explore the surrounding countryside. For what the Scots call cycle hire, go to a well-recommended shop about a half mile (1km) west of the town center, just off Great Western Road: **Western End Cycles,** 19 Gibson St., in the Hillhead district (© **0141/339-1179;** Underground: Kelvin Bridge or Hillhead). The cost of £12 to £15 ($18 to $22.50) per day must be accompanied by a deposit of £50 ($75).

FAST FACTS: Glasgow

American Express   The office is at 115 Hope St. (© **0141/226-3077;** Bus: 38, 45, 48, or 57), open Monday through Friday from 8:30am to 5:30pm and Saturday from 9am to noon (June and July, Saturday to 4pm).

Business Hours   Most offices are open Monday through Friday from 9am to 5 or 5:30pm. Most banks are open Monday through Wednesday and Friday from 9:30am to 4pm, Thursday from 9:30am to 5:30pm, and Saturday from 10am to 7pm. Shops are generally open Monday through Saturday from 10am to 5:30 or 6pm. On Thursday, stores remain open until 7pm.

Currency Exchange The tourist office and the American Express office (see above) will exchange most major foreign currencies. City-center banks operate *bureaux de change,* and nearly all will cash traveler's checks if you have the proper ID. **Thomas Cook** has branches at the Glasgow Airport (© **0800/1300**) and at 15 Gordon St. (© **0141/201-7200**; Underground: Buchanan St.).

Dentists If you have an emergency, go to the Accident and Emergency Department of **Glasgow Dental Hospital & School NHS Trust,** 378 Sauchiehall St. (© **0141/211-9600**; Bus: 57). Its hours are Monday through Friday from 9:15am to 3:15pm and Sunday and holidays from 10:30am to noon.

Doctors The major hospital is the **Royal Infirmary,** 82–86 Castle St. (© **0141/211-4000**; Bus: 2 or 2A).

Embassies & Consulates See "Fast Facts: Scotland," in chapter 2.

Emergencies Call © **999** in an emergency to summon the police, an ambulance, or firefighters.

Hospitals See "Doctors," above.

Hotlines Women in crisis may want to call **Women's Aid** at © **0141/553-2022.** Gays and lesbians can call the **Strathclyde Gay and Lesbian Switchboard** (© **0141/332-8372**) daily from 7 to 10pm. The **Rape Crisis Centre** is at © **0141/331-1990.**

Internet Access The **Internet Café,** 569 Sauchiehall St. (© **0141/564-1052;** Underground: Buchanan St.; Bus: 57), charges £2.60 ($3.90) per 30 minutes. It's open Monday through Thursday from 9am to 11pm, Friday from 9am to 9pm, Saturday from 10am to 9pm, and Sunday from 10am to 11pm.

Laundry/Dry Cleaning Try the **Park Laundrette,** 14 Park Rd. (© **0141/337-1285;** Underground: Kelvin Bridge), open Monday through Friday from 8:30am to 7:30pm and Saturday and Sunday from 9am to 6:30pm.

Library The **Mitchell Library** is on North Street at Kent Road (© **0141/287-2999;** Bus: 57). One of the largest libraries in Europe, it's a massive 19th-century pile. Newspapers and books, as well as miles of microfilm, are available. It's open Monday through Thursday from 9am to 8pm and Friday and Saturday from 9am to 5pm.

Newspapers Published since 1783, the *Herald* is the major newspaper with national, international, and financial news, sports, and cultural listings; the *Evening Times* offers local news.

Pharmacies The best is **Boots,** 200 Sauchiehall St. (© **0141/332-1925;** Bus: 57), open Monday through Wednesday from 8:30am to 6pm, Thursday from 8:30am to 8pm, Friday and Saturday from 8:30am to 6pm, and Sunday from 11am to 5pm.

Police In a real emergency, call © **999.** For other inquiries, contact police headquarters at © **0141/532-2000.**

Post Office The main branch is at 47 St. Vincent's St. (© **0141/204-3689;** Underground: Buchanan St.; Bus: 6, 8, or 16). It's open Monday through Friday from 8:30am to 5:45pm and Saturday from 9am to 5:30pm.

Restrooms These can be found at rail stations, bus stations, air terminals, restaurants, hotels, pubs, and department stores. Glasgow also has a system of public toilets, often marked wc. Don't hesitate to use them, but they're likely to be closed late in the evening.

Safety Glasgow is the most dangerous city in Scotland, but it's relatively safe when compared to cities of its size in the United States. Muggings do occur, and often they're related to Glasgow's rather large drug problem. The famed razor gangs of Calton, Bridgeton, and the Gorbals are no longer around to earn the city a reputation for violence, but you still should keep alert.

Weather Call the Glasgow Weather Centre at ℭ **01891/248-7272.**

3 Accommodations

It's important to reserve your room well in advance (say, 2 months beforehand), especially in late July and August. Glasgow's rates are generally higher than those in Edinburgh, but many business hotels offer bargains on weekends. The airport and the downtown branches of Glasgow's tourist office offer an **Advance Reservations Service**—with 2 weeks' notice, you can book your hotel by calling ℭ **0141/221-0049.** The cost for this service is £3 ($4.50).

CENTRAL GLASGOW
VERY EXPENSIVE
Glasgow Hilton International ★★★ *(Kids)*   Glasgow's only government-rated five-star hotel occupies Scotland's tallest building (20 floors). Dignified and modern, it rises in the heart of the city's business district, near the northern end of Argyle Street and exit 18 (Charing Cross) of M8. The good-size guest rooms—plush and conservative, popular with both vacationers and business travelers—offer fine views as far as the Clyde dockyards. The executive floors enjoy the enhanced facilities of a semiprivate club. The youthful staff is alert and helpful.

1 William St., Glasgow G3 8HT. ℭ **800/445-8667** in the U.S. and Canada, or 0141/204-5555. Fax 0141/204-5004. www.hilton.com. 319 units. £104–£205 ($156–$307.50) double; £345–£580 ($517.50–$870) suite. Weekend discounts often available. AE, DC, MC, V. Parking £5 ($7.50). Bus: 62. **Amenities:** 2 restaurants (see Cameron's under "Dining," below), bar, lounge; pool; gym; Jacuzzi; sauna; boutiques; salon; room service; massage; babysitting, laundry/dry cleaning. *In room:* A/C, TV, minibar, coffeemaker, hair dryer.

The Millennium Hotel Glasgow ★   The 1810 Millennium (with a 1974 addition) is a landmark near the Queen Street Station, where trains depart for the north of Scotland. The high-ceilinged public rooms feature antiques and glistening marble panels. The worst rooms, called "Classics," are in the rear with no views; the train station noise can be intolerable. The best units, "Antiques," are at the front of the building facing St. George Square and have four-poster or elaborate sleigh beds.

The Millennium played a role in world history in 1941: Winston Churchill met in room 21 with FDR's envoy, Harry Hopkins. It was a pivotal meeting, in which Churchill secured Hopkins's support for the Lend-Lease Bill, a commitment that eventually helped usher the United States into World War II.

George Sq., Glasgow G2 IDS ℂ 0141/332-6711. Fax 0141/332-4264. www.millennium-hotels.com. 117 units. Mon–Thurs £125–£164 ($187.50–$246) double, Fri–Sun £99 ($148.50) double; £135–£186 ($202.50–$279) suite. Rates include breakfast Fri–Sun. AE, DC, MC, V. Parking £8 ($12). Underground: Buchanan St. **Amenities:** Restaurant, bar, lounge; gym; room service; babysitting; laundry. *In room:* A/C, TV w/ movies, dataport, coffeemaker, hair dryer, iron, safe.

EXPENSIVE

Glasgow Marriott ⚘ Amid a confusing set of access roads for the highways and commercial boulevards surrounding it, the 13-story Marriott challenges the Hilton as the top business hotel in town. Although we prefer the Hilton, the Marriott is cheaper, and its soaring profile at the Anderston exit of M8 adds a vivid accent to the skyline. The place is big, modern, and chain-hotel efficient. The medium-size guest rooms have everything you'd expect from a Marriott, such as king-size beds, combination tub/shower, and voice mail.

500 Argyle St., Glasgow G3 8RR. ℂ 800/228-9290 in the U.S. and Canada, or 0141/226-5577. Fax 0141/221-7676. www.marriotthotels.com. 300 units. £80–£179 ($120–$268.50) double; £200–£270 ($300–$405) suite. AE, DC, MC, V. Free parking. Underground: St. Enoch. **Amenities:** 4 restaurants, 2 bars; pool; squash court; gym; sauna; salon; room service, babysitting; laundry/dry cleaning. *In room:* A/C, TV, dataport, minibar, coffeemaker, hair dryer, safe.

Malmaison ⚘⚘ *Finds* This place beats out all competitors in having the best contemporary interior. The hip hotel opened in 1994 in a historically important building constructed in the 1830s as a Greek Orthodox church. In 1997, an annex with additional bedrooms was added, designed to preserve the architectural character of the church's exterior. Inside, few of the original details remain— the decor is sleek and ultramodern. Bedrooms vary in size from smallish to average, but are chic and appointed with extras like CD players, specially commissioned art, and top-of-the-line toiletries.

278 W. George St., Glasgow G2 4LL. ℂ 0141/572-1000. Fax 0141/572-1002. www.malmaison.com. 72 units. £110 ($165) double; from £150 ($225) suite. AE, DC, MC, V. Parking nearby £7 ($10.50). Bus: 11. **Amenities:** 2 restaurants (see Brasserie Malmaison under "Dining," below), bar; gym; room service; babysitting; laundry/ dry cleaning. *In room:* A/C, TV w/ movies, CD player, dataport, minibar, coffeemaker, hair dryer, safe.

Nairns ⚘ *Finds* Most of the Nairns fame comes from its stylish restaurant (see "Dining," later in this chapter), but its chic guest rooms are a charming hideaway. Behind an 18th-century brick facade are the Silver Room, graced with a four-poster stainless-steel bed and a bath by über-designer Philippe Starck; the Amber Room, filled with as many tones of honey-brown as possible; the Nantucket Room, a winter retreat filled with leather, nautical accessories, and wood paneling; and the Vermeer Room, whose decor was inspired by the works of the 17th-century Dutch painter.

13 Woodside Crescent, Glasgow G3 7UP. ℂ 0141/353-0707. Fax 0141/331-1684. www.nairns.co.uk. 4 units. £115–£178 ($172.50–$267) double. AE, DC, MC, V. Bus: 44. **Amenities:** Restaurant, lounge; room service; babysitting. *In room:* A/C, TV, minibar, coffeemaker, hair dryer.

Impressions

[Glasgow is] a place which I shall ever hold in contempt as being filled with a set of unmannerly, low-bred, narrow-minded wretches; the place itself, however, is really pretty, and were the present inhabitants taken out and drowned in the ocean, and others with generous souls put in their stead, it would be an honour to Scotland.

—David Boswell, in a letter to James Boswell (1767)

Glasgow Accommodations & Dining

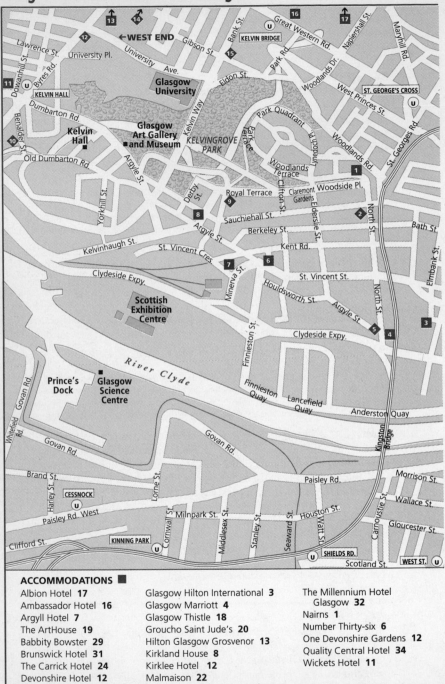

ACCOMMODATIONS ■

Albion Hotel **17**
Ambassador Hotel **16**
Argyll Hotel **7**
The ArtHouse **19**
Babbity Bowster **29**
Brunswick Hotel **31**
The Carrick Hotel **24**
Devonshire Hotel **12**

Glasgow Hilton International **3**
Glasgow Marriott **4**
Glasgow Thistle **18**
Groucho Saint Jude's **20**
Hilton Glasgow Grosvenor **13**
Kirkland House **8**
Kirklee Hotel **12**
Malmaison **22**

The Millennium Hotel
 Glasgow **32**
Nairns **1**
Number Thirty-six **6**
One Devonshire Gardens **12**
Quality Central Hotel **34**
Wickets Hotel **11**

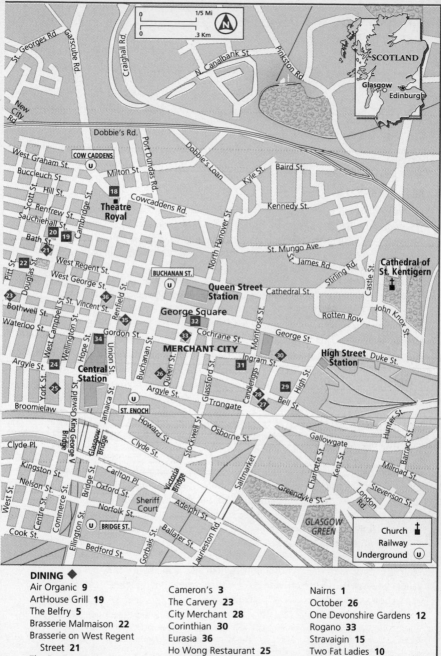

SCOTLAND

Glasgow
Edinburgh

DINING ◆

Air Organic **9**
ArtHouse Grill **19**
The Belfry **5**
Brasserie Malmaison **22**
Brasserie on West Regent
Street **21**
The Buttery **5**
Cafe Gandolfi **27**

Cameron's **3**
The Carvery **23**
City Merchant **28**
Corinthian **30**
Eurasia **36**
Ho Wong Restaurant **25**
La Parmigiana **14**
Mitchell's Charing Cross **2**

Nairns **1**
October **26**
One Devonshire Gardens **12**
Rogano **33**
Stravaigin **15**
Two Fat Ladies **10**
Ubiquitous Chip **12**
Yes **35**

MODERATE

The ArtHouse ⭐⭐ *(Finds* Acclaimed for its contemporary interior, this 1911 Edwardian building, 6 blocks northwest of Central Station, originally housed school board offices. Today, its conversion to a hotel is one of the most striking in Glasgow, with dramatic colors and textures blending in perfectly with the older structure. Commissioned art and period pieces evoke some of the original Edwardian splendor, although everything has been given a modern overlay with rich, bold tones. Sleek furniture and state-of-the-art bathrooms with a combination tub/shower are grace notes. The restaurant is one of the city's finest (see "Dining," later in this chapter).

129 Bath St., Glasgow G2 2SY. ℂ 0141/221-6789. Fax 0141/221-6789. info@arthousehotel.com. 65 units. £70–£140 ($105–$210) double. AE, DC, MC, V. Underground: Buchanan St. **Amenities:** Restaurant, bar; room service; laundry/dry cleaning. *In room:* TV, minibar, hair dryer.

Brunswick Hotel ⭐ *(Finds* In the Merchant City area, this new structure stands in dramatic contrast between two old warehouses, each 5 centuries old. A trendy minimalist design prevails, from the leather-walled restaurant to the bedrooms with their sleek look. The rooms are soothing and inviting with neutral tones, exceedingly comfortable mattresses, and tiny but adequate bathrooms (most with both tub and shower).

106–108 Brunswick St., Glasgow G1 ITF. ℂ **0141/552-0001**. Fax 0141/552-1551. www.scotland2000.com/brunswick. 22 units. £65–£95 ($97.50–$142.50) double. Rates include buffet breakfast. AE, DC, MC, V. Underground: Buchanan St. **Amenities:** Restaurant, bar; room service; laundry/dry cleaning. *In room:* A/C, TV, hair dryer.

Glasgow Thistle *(Kids* The lower floors of this recently refurbished hotel are imbued with a cheerful ambience. It boasts 18 function rooms—especially imposing is the grand ballroom, the largest of its kind in Scotland, seating 1,500. The Scottish-theme bedrooms are a decent size. Guests have free use of a gym a 5-minute walk away.

36 Cambridge St., Glasgow G2 3HN. ℂ **0141/332-3311**. Fax 0141/332-4050. 300 units. £95–£165 ($142.50–$247.50) double; from £225 ($337.50) suite. AE, DC, MC, V. Free parking. Underground: Cowcadden. **Amenities:** Restaurant, bar; access to nearby gym; room service; babysitting; laundry/dry cleaning. *In room:* A/C, TV, minibar, coffeemaker, hair dryer.

Groucho Saint Jude's ⭐⭐ Opened in 1999, Groucho Saint Jude's is hip, modern, and centrally located about 15 minutes from the airport. The two-story town house offers comfortable guest rooms and friendly service. All units have private bathrooms (some with showers, some with tubs) and warm, contemporary furnishings. The owner, a one-time member of the band Love & Money, attracts a young crowd of artists, musicians, writers, and celebs. The Groucho Club, which opened the hotel, remains the most sophisticated and sought-after club in London. But unlike London, which has a members-only policy, the Glasgow entry is open to all who reserve. Groucho Saint Jude's is named after the patron saint of sinners, which sets the tone.

190 Bath St., Glasgow, G2 4HG. ℂ **0141/352-8800**. Fax 0141/352-8801. www.grouchosaintjudes.com. 6 units. £95–£105 ($142.50–$157.50) double; £175 ($262.50) suite. Rates include continental breakfast. AE, MC, V. Metered parking. Underground: Cow Caddens. **Amenities:** Restaurant, bar; room service; laundry/dry cleaning. *In room:* TV, dataport, minibar, coffeemaker, hair dryer, iron.

Quality Central Hotel When it opened in 1883 by the rail station, the Central was the grandest Glasgow had seen, the landmark of the city's most famous street. Now restored to at least a glimmer of its former glory, the place may be too old-fashioned for some, but traditionalists like it. The baronial wooden

✐ Family-Friendly Hotels

Devonshire Hotel *(see p. 170)*   Although this elegant hotel is full of antiques, it's happy to cater to kids with toys, cots, and highchairs. There's an interconnecting bedroom that's perfect for families to book. Children are offered appropriate videos, and there are special facilities for heating food and sterilizing bottles. The restaurant is fully prepared to cook meals kids adore, like pizza or fish fingers.

Glasgow Hilton International *(see p. 164)*   Children arriving on the weekend are presented with fun packs, containing drawings, games, bubble bath, and comics. Kids will enjoy the pool. Cots and highchairs are available. Minsky's offers kids' meals, and room service is more than happy to provide the likes of sausages or chicken nuggets.

Glasgow Thistle *(see p. 168)*   This hotel offers spacious guest rooms suitable for tucking in children. Kids like the self-service carvery-style lunch, one of the best dining values in Glasgow.

staircase has been stripped and refinished, and sandblasting the facade revealed elaborate Victorian cornices and pilasters. The guest rooms, with an uninspired decor, are priced according to size and plumbing.

99 Gordon St., Glasgow G1 3SF. ✆ **0141/221-9680.** Fax 0141/226-3948. www.choicehotels.com. 222 units. £88–£125 ($132–$187.50) double, £135 ($202.50) suite. AE, DC, MC, V. Parking £8.50 ($12.75), or £1.80 ($2.70) overnight 5pm–10am. Underground: Central Station. **Amenities:** Restaurant, bar, coffee shop; pool; tennis courts; 2 gyms; Jacuzzi; sauna; room service; babysitting; laundry/dry cleaning. *In room:* TV, minibar, coffeemaker, hair dryer.

INEXPENSIVE

Babbity Bowster *(Value)*   In Merchant City, this small but delightful Robert Adam–designed hotel doubles as an art gallery. The guest rooms vary in size but are all attractive, with Victorian reproductions and white-lace bedding (some with shower only). The hotel attracts students and faculty from Strathclyde University and displays the work of Glaswegian artists (most are for sale). In summer, there's an outdoor barbecue area.

16–18 Blackfriars St., Glasgow G1 1PE. ✆ **0141/552-5055.** Fax 0141/552-7774. 6 units. £70 ($105) double. Rates include Scottish breakfast. AE, MC, V. Free parking. Underground: Buchanan St. **Amenities:** Restaurant, bar; room service. *In room:* TV, coffeemaker, no phone.

The Carrick Hotel *(Value)*   Two blocks west of the central rail depot, this contemporary seven-story hotel is surrounded by dreary commercial buildings, but is a viable budget option in the center of Glasgow. You check into a rather cramped area, but once upstairs, the rooms are more inviting—although they, too, are small. Location, location, location is what sells this property.

377 Argyle St. (opposite Cadogan Sq.), G2 8LL. ✆ **0141/248-2355.** Fax 0141/221-1014. 121 units. £62–£85 ($93–$127.50) double. AE, DC, MC, V. Underground: St. Enoch. **Amenities:** Restaurant, bar; room service; laundry/dry cleaning. *In room:* TV, hair dryer.

Kirkland House   On a quiet street about a 10-minute walk from the Glasgow Art Gallery and Museum, the university, and the Scottish Exhibition Centre, the Kirkland is an impeccably maintained 1832 Victorian crescent house. A mix of antiques and reproductions is used in the large guest rooms, each equipped with a shower bathroom. The owners are keen admirers of American swing music and display a collection of 78-rpm gramophone records, old photographs, and pictures.

42 St. Vincent Crescent, Glasgow G3 8NG. ℂ **0141/248-3458.** Fax 0141/221-5174. www.kirkland.gispnet. com. 5 units. £64–£72 ($96–$108) double. Rates include Scottish breakfast. No credit cards. Free parking. Underground: Exhibition Centre. *In room:* TV, coffeemaker, hair dryer (on request), no phone.

THE WEST END
VERY EXPENSIVE

Devonshire Hotel ⭐⭐⭐*(Kids)*   This is one of Glasgow's most charming small hotels, an imposing late-1800s Victorian terrace house with a blond-sandstone facade. Its mingling of perfect manners with a low-key attitude has attracted Michael Jackson, Whitney Houston, and other celebs. Rumors have been heard about a benign ghost on the top floor, but that doesn't bother the cheerfully efficient staff. Most of the plush guest rooms have antique furnishings and restored detailing and range from comfortably spacious to very large (some with shower only).

5 Devonshire Gardens, Glasgow G12 0UX. ℂ **0141/339-7878.** Fax 0141/339-3980. www.the-devonshire. co.uk. 14 units. £125–£215 ($187.50–$322.50) double; £220–£275 ($330–$412.50) suite. Children under 10 stay free in parents' room. AE, DC, MC, V. Underground: Hillhead. **Amenities:** Restaurant, bar; room service; laundry/dry cleaning. *In room:* TV, coffeemaker, hair dryer, iron.

One Devonshire Gardens ⭐⭐⭐   The Devonshire Hotel, above, is a gem and a charmer in every way. But this hotel tops even perfection, beating out the Hilton and all others as the most glamorous, most elegant, and most tranquil hotel in Scotland. It also serves a finer cuisine than any of the major Glasgow restaurants (see "Dining," later in this chapter). In the Hyndland district just west of the center, the house at no. 1 was built in 1880 and is now even more elegant than it was in its heyday. At the ring of the doorbell, a pair of Edwardian chambermaids with frilly aprons and dust bonnets appear to welcome you. Each of the eight guest rooms in this building is furnished in period style, with lots of luxurious accessories. The success of no. 1 led to the acquisition of nos. 2 and 3. The newer rooms have the same elegant touches and high price tags.

1–3 Devonshire Gardens, Glasgow G12 0UX. ℂ **0141/339-2001.** Fax 0141/337-1663. www.one-devonshire-gardens.com. 27 units. £125–£165 ($187.50–$247.50) double; from £275 ($412.50) suite. AE, DC, MC, V. Free parking. Underground: Hillhead. **Amenities:** Restaurant, bar; room service; laundry/dry cleaning. *In room:* TV, minibar, coffeemaker, hair dryer.

EXPENSIVE

Hilton Glasgow Grosvenor ⭐   The most interesting thing about this hotel is the way a team of award-winning engineers saved its early-20th-century neo-classical facade, using a revolutionary technique of impregnating the decaying sandstone with fiberglass and concrete. The Cypriot-owned Stakis company almost completely gutted the interior, reconstructing it in a casino-style sweep of crystal chandeliers and brassy accents. The hotel offers standard guest rooms (with combination tub/shower) that fill up mainly with business travelers during the week.

1–10 Grosvenor Terrace, Great Western Rd., Glasgow G12 0TA. ℂ **0141/339-8811.** Fax 0141/334-0710. www.hilton.com 96 units. Mon–Thurs £120 ($180) double, Fri–Sun £140 ($210) double; £190–£250 ($285–$375) suite. Rates include Scottish breakfast Fri–Sun. AE, DC, MC, V. Free parking. Underground: Hillhead. **Amenities:** Restaurant, bar, lounge; room service; babysitting; laundry/dry cleaning. *In room:* TV, minibar, coffeemaker, hair dryer, iron.

MODERATE

Wickets Hotel   Better known for its restaurant and bar than for its comfortable guest rooms, this hotel from the 1890s is an undiscovered West End gem, opposite one of the city's largest cricket grounds (the West of Scotland Cricket Club). The bedrooms are pleasantly spacious, each with a cheerful decor and a combination tub/shower. The restaurant is the glamour spot, offering moderately priced regional and Continental fare amid old photos of local cricket teams. Adjacent is an open-air beer garden, one of the few in Glasgow. Randall's wine bar sells wine by the glass in an Art Deco setting.

52–54 Fortrose St., Glasgow G11 5LP. © 0141/334-9334. Fax 0141/334-9334. www.wicketshotel.co.uk. 11 units. £69.95 ($104.95) double; £90–£105 ($135–$157.50) family room. Rates include Scottish breakfast. AE, DISC, MC, V. Free parking. Underground: Partick. **Amenities:** Restaurant, bar; room service; laundry/dry cleaning. *In room:* TV, coffeemaker, hair dryer, iron, safe.

INEXPENSIVE

Albion Hotel   This unpretentious hotel was formed by connecting two nearly identical beige-sandstone row houses in the heart of Glasgow's West End. It offers high-ceilinged guest rooms with modern furniture, some with both tub and shower. If your hotel needs are simple, you'll likely be happy here.

405–407 N. Woodside Rd., Glasgow G20 6NN. © 0141/339-8620. Fax 0141/334-8159. www.glasgow hotelsandapartments.co.uk/albion. 16 units. £54 ($81) double. Rates include breakfast. AE, DC, MC, V. Underground: Kelvin Bridge. **Amenities:** Lounge bar. *In room:* TV, dataport, coffeemaker, hair dryer, safe.

Ambassador Hotel ★ *Value*   Across from the Botanic Garden, this small hotel in an Edwardian town house (ca. 1900) is one of the better B&Bs in Glasgow. The good-size guest rooms are furnished with modern pieces, each with a combination tub/shower. The hotel is well situated for exploring the West End, with several galleries and many good local restaurants nearby.

7 Kelvin Dr., Glasgow G20 8QJ. © 0141/946-1018. Fax 0141/945-5377. www.glasgowhotelsandapartments. co.uk/ambassador. 16 units. £60 ($90) double. Rates include Scottish breakfast. AE, DC, MC, V. Free parking. Underground: Hillhead. **Amenities:** Lounge. *In room:* TV, dataport, coffeemaker, hair dryer, safe.

Argyll Hotel   This hotel is small but special, a Georgian building near Glasgow University, the Art Gallery and Museum, the Kelvin Hall International Sports Arena, and the Scottish Exhibition Centre. Although completely modernized, it shows a healthy respect for tradition. The guest rooms are comfortable, each with a combination tub/shower.

969–973 Sauchiehall St., Glasgow G3 7TQ. © 0141/337-3313. Fax 0141/337-3283. www.argyllhotelglasgow. co.uk. 38 units. £60–£70 ($90–$105) double. Rates include Scottish breakfast. AE, MC, V. Parking on nearby streets. Underground: Kelvin Hall. Bus: 9, 16, 42, 57, 62, or 64. **Amenities:** Restaurant, bar; room service; laundry/dry cleaning. *In room:* TV, hair dryer, coffeemaker.

Kirklee Hotel   This red-sandstone Edwardian terraced house is graced with a rose garden that has won several awards. Behind the ornate stained-glass door, you'll find average-size, high-ceilinged guest rooms, each with a combination shower/tub. Rosemary and Douglas Rogen will serve you breakfast in your room. The Kirklee is near the university, the Botanic Gardens, and the major art galleries.

11 Kensington Gate, Glasgow G12 9LG. © 0141/334-5555. Fax 0141/339-3828. www.olstravel.com/ hotel/kirklee. 9 units. £68 ($102) double. Rates include Scottish breakfast. AE, DC, MC, V. Parking on nearby streets. Underground: Hillhead. **Amenities:** Lounge. *In room:* TV, coffeemaker, hair dryer.

Number Thirty-Six   In the heart of the West End, this hotel occupies the two lower floors of a four-story sandstone building that was conceived as an apartment house in 1848. Hardworking entrepreneur John MacKay maintains the high-ceilinged pastel guest rooms in fine working order. Each is equipped with a tidy, shower-only bathroom.

36 St. Vincent Crescent, Glasgow G3 8NG. © 0141/248-2086. Fax 0141/221-1477. www.no36.co.uk. 6 units. £55 ($82.50) double. No credit cards. Bus: 42, 63, or 64. **Amenities:** Lounge; laundry. *In room:* A/C, TV, coffee-maker, hair dryer, no phone.

4 Dining

The days are long gone when a meal out in Glasgow meant mutton pie and chips. Some of the best Scottish food is found here (especially lamb from the Highlands, salmon, trout, Aberdeen Angus steaks, and exotic delights like moor grouse), and there's an ever-increasing number of ethnic restaurants. This still being Britain, however, you'll find the usual fish-and-chip joints, burger outlets, fried-chicken eateries, and endless pubs. Many restaurants close on Sunday, and most are shut by 2:30pm, reopening again for dinner around 6pm.

Note: For the locations of the restaurants below, see the "Glasgow Accommodations & Dining" map, on p. 166–167.

CENTRAL GLASGOW
VERY EXPENSIVE
Cameron's ☆☆ MODERN SCOTTISH   This is the most glamorous restaurant in Glasgow's best hotel, outfitted like a baronial hunting lodge in the wilds of the Highlands. The chef's conservative menu holds few surprises, but is a celebration of market-fresh ingredients deftly prepared. Small slip-ups sometimes mar the effect of a dish or two, but we have always come away pleased. Your best bet is to stay Scottish when ordering. Go with whisky-cured Isle of Arran salmon, confit of Highland duck, or Firth of Lorne sea scallops—and that's only the appetizers. For a main course, try rack of Scottish lamb with a crust of whisky-steeped oatmeal and Arran mustard.

In the Glasgow Hilton International, 1 William St. © 0141/204-5555. Reservations recommended. Main courses £22–£25 ($33–$37.50); table d'hôte menu £20–£26 ($30–$39) at lunch, £45 ($67.50) at dinner. AE, DC, MC, V. Mon–Fri noon–2:30pm and 7–10:15pm; Sat 7–10:15pm. Bus: 6A, 16, or 62.

Rogano ☆☆ SEAFOOD   Rogano boasts a perfectly preserved Art Deco interior from 1935, when Messrs. Rogers and Anderson combined their talents and names to create a restaurant that has hosted virtually every star of the British film industry. You can enjoy dinner amid lapis-lazuli clocks, etched mirrors, ceiling fans, semicircular banquettes, and potted palms. The menu always emphasizes seafood, such as halibut in champagne-and-oyster sauce and lobster grilled or Thermidor.

A less expensive menu is offered down in the **Cafe Rogano,** where main courses begin at £9.50 ($14.25).

11 Exchange Place. © 0141/248-4055. Reservations recommended. Main courses £19–£32 ($28.50–$48); fixed-price lunch £17.50 ($26.25). AE, DC, MC, V. Restaurant daily noon–2:30pm and 6:30–10:30pm (Sun noon–2:30pm and 6–10:30pm); cafe Mon–Thurs noon–11pm, Fri–Sat noon–midnight, Sun noon–11pm. Underground: Buchanan St.

EXPENSIVE
The Buttery ☆ SCOTTISH/FRENCH   This is the perfect hunter's restaurant, with oak panels and an air of baronial splendor. The anteroom bar used to be the pulpit of a church, and the waitresses wear high-necked costumes of which Queen Victoria would have approved. Menu items include smoked trout, rare roast beef, terrine of Scottish seafood, venison, and tuna steak with tarragon and tomato-butter sauce.

Adjacent is the **Oyster Bar,** outfitted in church-inspired Victoriana; its menu is shorter and a bit less expensive. **The Belfry,** which is less formal, is in the cellar (see below).

652 Argyle St. (📞 **0141/221-8188.** Reservations recommended. Restaurant main courses £14–£21 ($21–$31.50); table d'hôte lunch £17.50 ($26.25). Oyster Bar lunch main courses £14–£21 ($21–$31.50). AE, DC, MC, V. Mon–Fri noon–2:30pm; Mon–Sat 7–10:30pm. Underground: St. Enoch.

Eurasia ⊛ ASIAN FUSION/SCOTTISH   Ferrier Richardson enjoys a devoted following among serious Glasgow foodies. This stylish enclave is his latest venture. Here he marries the best of Scottish produce to the wealth of spices and herbs found in Asia. Start with the delectable vegetable and chili chicken spring rolls or the intriguing soup made with fresh tomatoes and flavored with jasmine and ginger. There is the expected array of teriyaki beef dishes, made with the best of Scottish beef, along with tempura fish and Scottish salmon with hot and sour vegetables, enhanced by a lime dressing. Ice cream doesn't get much better than the vanilla-seed flavor here, or try the Thai-inspired lemon-grass rice pudding.

150 St. Vincent St. (📞 **0141/204-1150.** Reservations required. Set lunches £14.95 ($22.45) for 2 courses, £17.95 ($26.95) for 3 courses; set dinner £26.95 ($40.45) for 2 courses, £33.50 ($50.25) for 3 courses. AE, DC, MC, V. Mon–Fri noon–2:30pm; Mon–Sat 7–11pm. Underground: St. Enoch.

Nairns ⊛ SCOTTISH/MEDITERRANEAN   This is one of Glasgow's hippest restaurants, thanks to Nick Nairn's cuisine and a style that blends cutting-edge London with traditional Glasgow. Guests dine in one of two monochromatic dining rooms in an 18th-century Georgian building. Menu items are likely to include fettuccine of shellfish with mint and coriander; carrot, honey, and ginger soup; and maize-fed chicken breast with leeks and prunes, served with a gratin dauphinois. Favorite desserts are classic lemon tart and Chivas whisky parfait with Earl Grey syrup.

In the Nairns Hotel, 13 Woodside Crescent. (📞 **0141/353-0707.** Reservations recommended. Fixed-price menu £14.50–£17.50 ($21.75–$26.25) lunch; £29 ($43.50) dinner. AE, DC, MC, V. Mon–Sat noon–2pm and 6–9:45pm.

Yes ⊛ MODERN EUROPEAN   Occupying a dignified building in one of Glasgow's most congested neighborhoods, Yes serves sophisticated cuisine in its cellar restaurant and simpler fare in its street-level cafe/bar. The cafe/bar's dishes bear a strong Mediterranean slant. Although the menu changes often, you'll

---

✏ Family-Friendly Restaurants

Brasserie Malmaison *(see p. 174)*   Dining here is like taking your kid to church—well, not really. The former Greek Orthodox church has given way to a Scottish and Continental cuisine. The chefs serve some of the city's best fries, salmon cakes, and grilled chicken dishes. Adjacent to the brasserie is a cafe with fresh salads, sandwiches, and pizzas.

Cafe Gandolfi *(see p. 176)*   Children always find something to order here, perhaps a soup-and-salad lunch. Of course, it has to be followed by one of the homemade ice creams, the best in the city.

Willow Tea Room *(see p. 176)*   Thousands of locals fondly remember coming here as children to enjoy delectable pastries and ice cream dishes—and it's still a big treat for any kid.

always find buffet-style antipasti as well as assorted pastas and seafood. The cellar room is more charming, with high windows and modern Scottish paintings. A pianist performs Wednesday through Saturday evenings. Expect dishes like gateau of haggis; vodka-cured salmon with caviar and baby baked potatoes with sour cream; or baked codfish with stuffed herb crust, smoked salmon strips, and vegetable sauce.

22 W. Nile St. © 0141/221-8044. Reservations recommended. Restaurant fixed-price lunches £14.95–£17.95 ($22.45–$26.95); fixed-price dinners £24.95 ($37.45). Cafe/bar lunch platters £3.50–£7.50 ($5.25–$11.25); fixed-price lunch £11.95 ($17.95); pre-theater fixed-price dinner £10.50–£12.95 ($15.75–$19.45). AE, DC, MC, V. Restaurant Mon–Fri noon–2:30pm and 7–11pm; cafe/bar Mon–Sat 10am–10:30pm (last order). Bus: 66.

MODERATE

ArtHouse Grill ⚸ _Finds_ CONTINENTAL   In one of Glasgow's most unusual hotels is this sophisticated, modern enclave. A rotisserie cooks succulent meats, there's a Guinness and oyster bar, and a Japanese teppanyaki grill serves as a stage for the theatrical experience of a meal here. Dig into the sage-flavored pork chop served with caramelized apples or the tender lamb shank braised to perfection and served with a mint-flavored couscous.

In the ArtHouse Hotel, 129 Bath St. © 0141/221-6789. Reservations required. Main courses £8.50–£20 ($12.75–$30). AE, DC, MC, V. Mon–Sat noon–3pm and 6–10pm. Underground: Buchanan St.

The Belfry ⚸ SCOTTISH/FRENCH   The pews, pulpits, and stained glass that adorn this place are from a church in northern England. It's the only pub in Glasgow where you can contemplate Christ in Majesty while you enjoy a pint of ale. The kitchen produces daily specials like steak pie with roast potatoes; roast rack of lamb with rosemary, thyme, and caramelized shallots; and the Belfry mussel bowl with shallots. The cook is well known for making clever use of fresh Scottish produce.

In the basement of the Buttery (see above), 652 Argyle St. © 0141/221-0630. Reservations recommended. Main courses £7.95–£10.50 ($11.95–$15.75). AE, DC, MC, V. Mon–Fri 12:30–2:30pm; Mon–Sat 5:30–10:30pm. Underground: St. Enoch.

Brasserie Malmaison _Kids_ SCOTTISH/CONTINENTAL   In a hip hotel converted from a Greek Orthodox church (see "Accommodations," above), this restaurant in the crypt, beneath the original vaults, serves imaginative food in a dark, masculine setting, with a large bar and wooden banquettes. Menu items arrive in generous portions and include French-style rumpsteak with garlic butter and pommes frites, salmon fish cakes with spinach, and grilled chicken with roasted red-pepper salsa.

In contrast, the greenhouse-inspired **Café Mal,** adjacent to the brasserie, has a menu of salads, sandwiches, pizzas, light platters, and drinks.

In the Malmaison Hotel, 278 W. George St. © 0141/572-1000. Reservations recommended for dinner Thurs–Sun. Brasserie main courses £8.95–£15 ($13.45–$22.50); Café Mal salads and platters £3.50–£7.95 ($5.25–$11.95). AE, DC, MC, V. Brasserie daily noon–2:30pm and 6–11pm; Café Mal daily noon–10:30pm. Bus: 11.

Brasserie on West Regent Street SCOTTISH/CONTINENTAL   This upscale brasserie, in a white-painted stone house, contains a pair of dining rooms that evoke an elegant supper club in gold, burgundies, and black, graced with live palm trees. The polite service from the white-aproned staff gives a nod to Rogano (see above), which is owned by the same investors. The fixed-price menus may include venison, Scottish oysters, Angus beef with pepper sauce, and various vegetarian dishes.

176 W. Regent St. © 0141/248-3801. Reservations not necessary. Table d'hôte menu £17.95 ($26.95). AE, DC, MC, V. Mon–Sat noon–11pm. Bus: Cowcadden St.

City Merchant SCOTTISH/INTERNATIONAL This cozy restaurant in the heart of the city offers friendly service and an extensive menu, and serves throughout the day. The cuisine is more reliable than stunning, but it delivers quite an array of well-prepared fresh food at a good price. Try the roast breast of duck, rack of lamb, or escalope of venison. Also tempting are the fast-seared scallops and classic smoked haddock. Some of the desserts evoke old-time Scotland, such as the clootie dumpling, made with flour, spices, and fried fruit and served with home-churned butter.

97–99 Candleriggs. ℭ **0141/553-1577.** Reservations recommended. Main courses £8.50–£23 ($12.75–$34.50); fixed-price lunch £10.50–£12.95 ($15.75–$19.45). AE, DC, MC, V. Mon–Sat noon–10:30pm; Sun 5–10pm. Underground: St. Enoch.

Ho Wong Restaurant ✿ CANTONESE Jimmy Ho and David Wong opened this remote outpost of their Hong Kong establishment 2 blocks from the Central Station. It's now one of the city's finest Chinese restaurants. There are at least eight duck dishes on the menu, along with four types of fresh lobster and some sizzling platters.

82 York St. ℭ **0141/221-3550.** Reservations required. Main courses £12–£18 ($18–$27); fixed-price 2-course lunch £8.50 ($12.75). AE, DC, MC, V. Mon–Sat noon–2pm and 5:30pm–midnight; Sun 6pm–midnight. Underground: Central Station.

Mitchell's Charing Cross MODERN SCOTTISH Named for its location near Glasgow's largest library (the Mitchell), this upscale bistro offers Scottish cuisine moderne in a large room lined with plants and paintings. Options may include red snapper, grouper, and salmon netted off the Hebridean coast; duck; and haggis with fresh tatties, neeps, and chive mayonnaise. Consider dropping in for a pint in the basement bar.

157 North St., Charing Cross. ℭ **0141/204-4312.** Reservations recommended. Main courses £6.25–£9.50 ($9.40–$14.25) lunch, £7.95–£12.50 ($11.95–$18.75) dinner; fixed-price pre-theater supper (5–7pm) £8.95–£10.95 ($13.45–$16.45). AE, DC, MC, V. Mon–Sat noon–2:30pm and 5–10pm. Bus: 23 or 57.

October ✿ INTERNATIONAL At the top of the Princes Square shopping district, this bar and restaurant offers a widely diverse cuisine. Of the several vegetarian dishes, one of the best is a type of potato sandwich filled with roasted vegetables. There's a wide array of choices—everything from club sandwiches to mussels with white wine to bites like potato wedges and nachos. For dessert, try the raspberry tart.

The Rooftop, Princes Sq., Buchanan St. ℭ **0141/221-0303.** Reservations recommended. Main courses £6.50–£10.50 ($9.75–$15.75). AE, MC, V. Mon–Thurs noon–8pm; Fri–Sun noon–5pm. Underground: St. Enoch.

Two Fat Ladies ✿ MODERN BRITISH/SEAFOOD This ranks high on the list of everybody's favorite restaurants, especially for irreverent diners who appreciate the unexpected. The "Two Fat Ladies" are its street number—a nickname for the number 88 in Scotland's church-sponsored bingo games (there's no connection to the "Two Fat Ladies" of TV Food Network fame). The custard-colored decor is minimalist and "post-punk." The restaurant packs in crowds for specialties like pan-fried squid salad with coriander-flavored yogurt sauce, grilled chicken salad with apple chutney, and charcoal-grilled king scallops with tomato-basil sauce. The best dessert is the Pavlova (a chewy meringue) with summer berries and Drambuie sauce.

88 Dumbarton Rd. ℭ **0141/339-1944.** Reservations recommended. Fixed-price pre-theater supper (6–7pm) £11.95–£15.95 ($17.95–$23.95); fixed-price dinner £22.95–£26.95 ($34.45–$40.45). MC, V. Tues–Sat 6–10pm. Bus: 16, 42, or 57.

Tea for Two

For tea, a light lunch, or a snack, try the famed **Willow Tea Room,** 217 Sauchiehall St. (© 0141/332-0521; Underground: Cowcaddens). When it opened in 1904, the Willow became a sensation because of its Charles Rennie Mackintosh design, and it has been restored to its original condition. It's considered fashionable to drop in for tea at any time of day. Reservations are recommended. Afternoon tea with pastry costs £7.75 ($11.65). It's open Monday through Saturday from 9:30am to 4:30pm and Sunday from noon to 4:15pm.

INEXPENSIVE

Cafe Gandolfi *Kids* SCOTTISH/FRENCH   Many students and young professionals will tell you this popular place in Merchant City is their favorite caff—you may sometimes have to wait for a table. A remake of a Victorian pub, it boasts rustic wooden floors, benches, and stools. If you don't fill up on soups and salads, try smoked venison with gratin dauphinois or smoked pheasant with an onion tartlet in winter. Vegetarians will find solace here.

64 Albion St. © 0141/552-6813. Reservations recommended on weekends. Main courses £8.50–£11.60 ($12.75–$17.40) MC, V. Mon–Sat 9am–11:30pm; Sun noon–11:30pm. Underground: St. Enoch/Cannon St.

The Carvery *Value* BRITISH   The price of a meal at the Carvery is low, considering what you get. In an ambience of brick-lined walls and pinpoint lighting, you can select from one of Glasgow's most amply stocked buffets, augmented by carved roasts and joints produced by uniformed chefs. This is hearty cooking of the type that has delighted Brits for years.

In the Forte Posthouse Hotel, Bothwell St. © 08704/009-032. Reservations required. Buffet £17.50 ($26.25). AE, DC, MC, V. Sun–Fri 6:30–10pm; Sat 5:30–10pm. Underground: Buchanan St.

Corinthian INTERNATIONAL   This restaurant in Lanarkshire House opened in 2000 with a 25-foot illuminated glass dome as its stunning centerpiece. Crystal chandeliers and rococo friezes make for a luxurious atmosphere. The menu is based on the freshest products available. You might feast on tender lamb brochettes from Highland sheep or an enticing grilled tuna. In the two bars, you can relax on Italian leather sofas while listening to music spun by the local DJ.

191 Ingram St. © 0141/552-1101. Reservations recommended. Main courses £6–£17 ($9–$25.50); fixed-price pre-theater dinner (daily 5:30–7pm) £9.75 ($14.65) for 2 courses, £12.50 ($18.75) for 3 courses. AE, MC, V. Mon–Sat noon–3am; Sun 12:30pm–1am. Underground: St. Enoch.

THE WEST END
EXPENSIVE

One Devonshire Gardens *Finds* SCOTTISH/FRENCH   Thanks to an intricate re-creation of the decor and service of the Edwardian Age, this hotel restaurant is one of Glasgow's most unusual venues. Drinks are served in the elegant drawing room, and you dine amid flowery Victorian-inspired striped wallpaper, with servers dressed in white shirts and black vests. Quality ingredients are handled with finesse. Perhaps you'll begin with curried-parsnip soup and follow with grilled sea bass or lemon sole.

In One Devonshire Gardens Hotel, 1 Devonshire Gardens. © 0141/339-2001. Reservations required. Fixed-price lunches £22.50–£27.50 ($33.75–$41.25); dinner main courses £16.50–£23 ($24.75–$34.50). AE, DC, MC, V. Sun–Fri noon–2pm; daily 7–10pm. Underground: Patrick.

Ubiquitous Chip ⚜ SCOTTISH This restaurant is inside the rough-textured stone walls of a former stable; its glass-covered courtyard boasts masses of climbing vines. Upstairs is a pub where simple platters are served with pints of lager and drams of whisky; these may include chicken, leek, and white-wine casserole or finnan haddies with bacon (but no fish-and-chips, as you might think from the name). The bistro-style restaurant might feature free-range chicken, shellfish with crispy seaweed snaps, or wild rabbit. Vegetarians are catered to at both places.

12 Ashton Lane, off Byres Rd. ℭ 0141/334-5007. Reservations recommended. Restaurant fixed-price lunch £18.95 ($28.45) for 2 courses, £23.95 ($35.95) for 3 courses; fixed-price dinner £27.95 ($41.95) for 2 courses, £33.95 ($50.95) for 3 courses. Bar meals £8 ($12) lunch; £10–£15 ($15–$22.50) dinner. AE, DC, MC, V. Restaurant Mon–Sat noon–2:30pm, daily 5:30–11pm; bar Mon–Sat 11am–midnight, Sun 12:30pm–midnight. Underground: Hillhead.

MODERATE
Air Organic ⚜ *Finds* ORGANIC FUSION Space-age Air Organic is designed like an airport lounge, with white walls and sky-blue tables. The menu, designed to look like a plane ticket, features both organic and non-organic foods. The Thai seafood broth with coconut, lime, and coriander is exceptional, as is the Thai pumpkin curry. The restaurant also specializes in Japanese cooking, offering a variety of bento boxes. We were especially taken with the char-siu roast pork with sticky mustard apples. For dessert, there's nothing better than the steamed banana and ginger pudding. The friendly service, wide range of choices, and unique design make this a place worth visiting.

36 Kelvingrove St. ℭ 0141/564-5200. Reservations recommended. Main courses £7–£16 ($10.50–$24); fixed-price 2-course dinner (daily 5–7pm) £12 ($18); bento boxes £10–£14 ($15–$21). AE, DC, MC, V. Sun–Thurs noon–10pm; Fri–Sat noon–11pm. Underground: Hillhead.

La Parmigiana *Value* ITALIAN This seems to be everyone's favorite trattoria, providing a cosmopolitan Continental atmosphere and a good change of pace from the typical Glasgow dining scene. Even Italians living in Glasgow swear by the food here. A long-established family dining room, it offers the usual array of pasta dishes, some especially delectable, like the lobster-stuffed ravioli in basil cream sauce. Try also the chargrilled scallops cooked quickly in olive oil and served with fresh lemon juice.

447 Great Western Rd. ℭ 0141/334-0686. Reservations required. Main courses £12.50–£16 ($18.75–$24); fixed-price lunch £9.50 ($14.25); fixed-price dinner £10.50–£12.50 ($15.75–$18.75). AE, DC, MC, V. Underground: Kelvinbridge.

Stravaigin ⚜⚜ GLOBAL We've never seen any restaurant like this in Glasgow. The chef and owner truly roams the globe for inspiration. Although some of his ideas might come from as far away as China or the Caribbean, he also knows how to use the finest of the regional bounty of Scotland. Expect concoctions such as Vietnamese-inspired marinated quail served on a candy smoked eggplant concasse. Rabbit is perfectly cooked and served with lentils from the Pyrenees, while mullet comes on a bed of Thai noodles with bits of mussels and mushrooms. Many locals finish with a selection of Scottish cheeses with quince jelly and bannocks.

26 Gibson St., Hillhead. ℭ 0141/334-2665. Reservations required. Fixed-price menus (lunch or dinner) £20–£26 ($30–$39). AE, DC, MC, V. Fri–Sat noon–2:30pm; Tues–Sun 5–11:30pm. Underground: Kelvinbridge.

5 Seeing the Sights

THE TOP ATTRACTIONS

The center of Glasgow is **George Square,** dominated by the **City Chambers**
Queen Victoria opened in 1888. Of the statues in the square, the most imposing is that of Sir Walter Scott, atop an 80-foot (24m) column. Naturally, you'll
find Victoria along with her beloved Albert, plus Robert Burns. The **Banqueting Hall,** lavishly decorated, is open to the public on most weekdays.

Burrell Collection ✦✦✦   This museum houses the mind-boggling treasures
left to Glasgow by Sir William Burrell, a wealthy shipowner who had a lifelong
passion for art. You can see a vast aggregation of furniture, textiles, ceramics,
stained glass, silver, art objects, and pictures (especially 19th-century French art)
in the dining room, hall, and drawing room reconstructed from Sir William's
home, Hutton Castle at Berwick-upon-Tweed. Ancient artifacts, Asian art, and
European decorative arts and paintings are featured. There is a restaurant on site,
and you can roam through the surrounding park, 3 miles (5km) south of
Glasgow Bridge.

Pollok Country Park, 2060 Pollokshaws Rd. ✆ 0141/287-2550. Free admission. Mon–Sat 10am–5pm;
Sun 11am–5pm. Closed Jan 1 and Dec 25. Bus: 45, 48, or 57.

Glasgow Art Gallery and Museum ✦✦✦   This is the finest municipal
gallery in Britain. It boasts a superb collection of Dutch and Italian old masters,
including Giorgione and Rembrandt; French 19th-century paintings by Millet,
Derain, and others; and Salvador Dalí's *Christ of St. John of the Cross.* Scottish
painting is well represented, from the 17th century to the present. One of the
major paintings here is Whistler's *Arrangement in Grey and Black no. 2: Portrait
of Thomas Carlyle,* the first Whistler to be hung in a British gallery. The artist took
great pride in his Scottish background. The museum also has an outstanding
collection of arms and armor, a large section devoted to natural history, and regularly changing displays from the decorative-art collections, plus furniture and
other items by Charles Rennie Mackintosh. Teas and light lunches are available
in the museum.

Kelvingrove. ✆ 0141/287-2699. Free admission. Mon–Sat 10am–5pm; Sun 11am–5pm. Underground:
Kelvin Hall.

Glasgow Science Centre ✦✦✦ *Kids*   This is Britain's most successful millennium project. On the banks of the River Clyde, it lies in the heart of the city,
opposite the Scottish Exhibition and Conference Centre, and is the focal point
of Glasgow's drive to become one of Europe's major high-tech locations. In three
landmark buildings, the center features the first titanium-clad structures in the
United Kingdom. Other features include innovative laboratories, multimedia
and science theaters, and interactive exhibits. Children will love the hands-on
activities: They can make their own soundtracks and animation, or star in their
own digital videos. At special shows and workshops, visitors see a glass smashed
by sound, "catch" shadows, experience a million volts of indoor lighting, and
build a lie detector. The IMAX Theatre, a first for Scotland, projects a picture
that's the size of a five-story tenement block onto the screen. The complex also
contains the only 360°-rotating tower in the world.

50 Pacific Quay. ✆ 0141/420-5010. www.gsc.org.uk. Admission £7 ($10.50) adults, £4.50 ($6.75) students
and seniors, £2.50 ($3.75) children under 7, £12 ($18) per family. IMAX tickets £5 ($7.50) adults, £3.50
($5.25) students and children, £12 ($18) per family. Daily 9am–5pm. Tube: from Buchan Street Station to
Cessnock; from there a 10-min. walk.

Hunterian Art Gallery ⭐⭐ This gallery owns the artistic estate of James McNeill Whistler, with some 60 of his paintings bestowed by his sister-in-law. It also boasts a Charles Rennie Mackintosh collection, including the architect's home (with his own furniture) on three levels, decorated in the original style. The main gallery exhibits 17th- and 18th-century paintings (Rembrandt to Rubens) and 19th- and 20th-century Scottish works. Temporary exhibits, selected from Scotland's largest collection of prints, are presented in the print gallery, which also houses a permanent display of print-making techniques.

University of Glasgow, Hillhead St. ℂ 0141/330-5431. Free admission. Mon–Sat 9:30am–5pm (Mackintosh House closed 12:30–1:30pm). Underground: Hillhead.

Hunterian Museum Opened in 1807, this is Glasgow's oldest museum, in the main Glasgow University buildings 2 miles (3km) west of the heart of the city. It's named after William Hunter, its early benefactor, who donated his private collections to get the museum going. The collection is wide-ranging, from dinosaur fossils to coins to relics of the Roman occupation and plunder by the Vikings. The story of Captain Cook's voyages is pieced together in ethnographic material from the South Seas. The museum has a bookstall and an 18th-century-style coffeehouse.

University of Glasgow, Gilmorehill Building. ℂ 0141/330-4221, ext. 4221. Free admission. Mon–Sat 9:30am–5pm; Sun 11am–5pm. Closed public holidays. Underground: Hillhead.

The Lighthouse (Scotland's Centre for Architecture, Design and the City) The Lighthouse, which opened in July 1999, is based in Charles Rennie Mackintosh's first public commission, which housed the *Glasgow Herald* from 1895. Unoccupied for 15 years, the building is now the site of a seven-story, state-of-the-art exhibition center with a unique blue neon-tracked escalator that leads to four galleries, lecture facilities, education suites, and a cafe.

The **Mackintosh Interpretation Centre** is the first facility to provide an overview of Mackintosh's art, design, and architecture. The impressive glass timeline wall illustrates his achievements. There are also interactive stations with models, drawings, and computer and video displays. Visitors can ride the lift up to the Mackintosh Tower and see a panorama of the city. The education program offers tours, lectures, films, and workshops for people of all ages. The Wee People's City is an interactive play area for children under 9. The IT Hotspot features Macintosh computers with printing facilities, video conferencing, and a large selection of software for research, training, and hands-on activities.

11 Mitchell Lane. ℂ 0141/221-6362. Free admission to the Lighthouse. Admission to Mackintosh Interpretation Center £2.50 ($3.75) adults, £2 ($3) seniors, £1 ($1.50) children. Mon, Wed, Fri–Sat 10:30am–5pm; Thurs 10:30am–8pm; Sun noon–5pm. Underground: Buchanan Station.

Museum of Transport ⭐⭐ This museum contains a fascinating collection of all forms of transportation and related technology. Displays include a simulated 1938 Glasgow street with period shopfronts, appropriate vehicles, and a reconstruction of one of the Glasgow Underground stations. The superb and varied ship models in the Clyde Room reflect the significance of Glasgow and the River Clyde as one of the world's foremost areas of shipbuilding and engineering.

1 Bunhouse Rd., Kelvin Hall. ℂ 0141/287-2720. Free admission. Mon–Thurs and Sat 10am–5pm; Sun and Fri 11am–5pm. Closed Jan 1 and Dec 25. Underground: Kelvin Hall.

People's Palace The People's Palace—built as a cultural center for the East End between 1895 and 1897—provides a visual record of the rise of Glasgow from its 1175–78 founding. Personal relics of Mary Queen of Scots represent

Glasgow Attractions

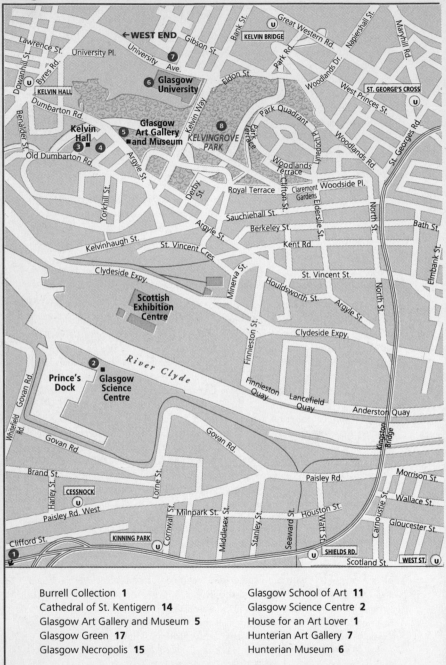

Burrell Collection **1**
Cathedral of St. Kentigern **14**
Glasgow Art Gallery and Museum **5**
Glasgow Green **17**
Glasgow Necropolis **15**

Glasgow School of Art **11**
Glasgow Science Centre **2**
House for an Art Lover **1**
Hunterian Art Gallery **7**
Hunterian Museum **6**

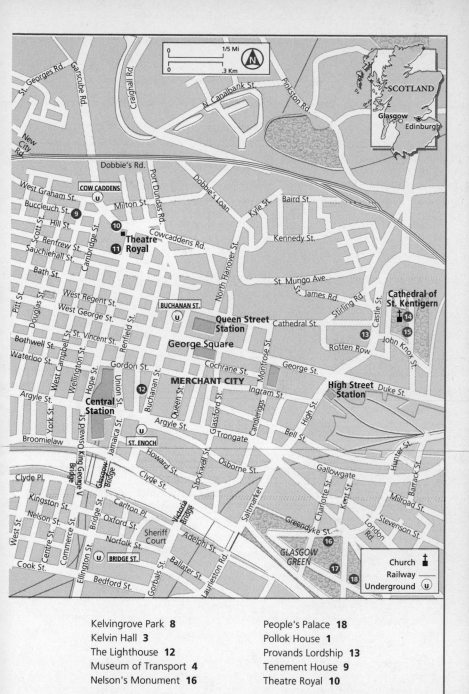

Kelvingrove Park **8** People's Palace **18**
Kelvin Hall **3** Pollok House **1**
The Lighthouse **12** Provands Lordship **13**
Museum of Transport **4** Tenement House **9**
Nelson's Monument **16** Theatre Royal **10**

A Man Ahead of His Time: Charles Rennie Mackintosh

Although legendary today, tragic genius Charles Rennie Mackintosh (1868–1928) was largely forgotten in Scotland at the time of his death. This brilliant architect, designer, and decorator is a perfect example of the old saw that the prophet is accorded little honor in his own country. His approach, poised between Art Nouveau and Bauhaus, influenced everyone from Frank Lloyd Wright in Chicago to Josef Hoffmann in Vienna. Mackintosh's ideas, however, were too revolutionary in Glasgow's Victorian age, with its pompous eclecticism and overstuffed fussiness.

Born on June 7, 1868, Mackintosh began his career in 1889 as a draftsman for the architectural firm of Honeyman & Keppie. By the 1880s, Glasgow had become the British Empire's second city, and hundreds of new homes, public buildings, rail stations, and factories were needed. The situation seemed the perfect opportunity for a rising young architect. In 1896, Mackintosh's design for a new headquarters of the Glasgow School of Art won a prestigious competition. (Actually, he won because his design was the cheapest to build.) He had drunk deeply from the creative cauldron of artistic development that swept Europe during the final days of the Belle Epoque, and his theories insisted not that decoration should be constructed but that construction should be decorated. The forms of nature, especially plants, were used in his interiors, which had a simplicity and harmony that were utterly new. Instant applause came from the Vienna secessionists and the Arts and Crafts movement in such faraway places as England and America, but Glasgow wasn't so pleased. Today, Mackintosh's design for the headquarters of the **Glasgow School of Art,** 167 Renfrew St. (© **0141/ 0353-4526**), near Charing Cross, is recognized as one of the city's greatest architectural treasures.

Alas, Mackintosh was neither tactful nor diplomatic, and he developed a reputation as a meticulous planner of rigid ideas who refused to compromise with builders or their crews. Later failures to win either commissions or architectural awards led to local ridicule of his avantgarde ideas, a break with his partners, and an eventual move out of Glasgow. He declared Glasgow a Philistine city. Recent research has shown he was actually exiled from his native Scotland in 1914 because of his Austrian/German artistic connections. In London, he continued to have difficulties, and his career there never got off the ground. By 1923, Mackintosh and his wife, English architect Margaret MacDonald, gave up the struggle and moved to the south of France. There he devoted himself to watercolor paintings of botanical specimens and landscapes. The Mackintoshes returned to London in 1927, where the architect died a year later.

Most of the acclaim that made Mackintosh the most famous designer ever to emerge from Scotland came from Europe, England, and the United States. In 1902, Hermann Muthesius, a leading German architect and critic, wrote, "In any enumeration of the creative geniuses of modern architecture, Charles Rennie Mackintosh must be counted among the first."

her reign. The bulk of the collections are from Victorian Glasgow, including posters, programs, and props from the music-hall era. Paintings of the city by John Knox and others, portraits of Glaswegians (even St. Mungo), and items relating to trades and industries (such as the Glasgow potteries and stained-glass studios, trade unions, and newspapers) are also featured. There's a tearoom in the Winter Gardens.

The palace is located in **Glasgow Green,** the city's oldest public park. In the park, seek out Nelson's Monument, the first of its kind in Britain, and the Saracen Fountain, opposite the palace.

Glasgow Green. ⓒ 0141/554-0223. Free admission. Mon–Sat 10am–5pm; Sun 11am–5pm. Closed Jan 1 and Dec 25. Bus: 14, 14A, 18, 18A, 18B, 20, or 62.

Pollok House   The ancestral home of the Maxwells, Pollok House was built around 1750, with additions from 1890 to 1908 designed by Robert Rowand Anderson. The house and its 360 acres (145.8 hectares) of parkland were given to the city of Glasgow in 1966. It contains one of the finest collections of Spanish paintings in Britain, with works by El Greco, Goya, and Murillo, among others.

Pollok Country Park, 2060 Pollokshaws Rd. ⓒ **0141/616-6410.** Free admission. Apr–Oct daily 10am–5pm; Nov–Mar daily 11am–4pm. Bus: 57 or 57A.

Tenement House   An 1892 building on Garnethill, not far from the shops of Sauchiehall Street, this house has been called a "Glasgow flat that time passed by." Until her death, Agnes Toward was an inveterate hoarder of domestic trivia. For 54 years she lived in this flat and stuffed it with the artifacts of her era, everything from a porcelain jawbox sink to such household aids as Monkey Brand soap. The property is now in the care of the National Trust for Scotland as a virtual museum of a vanished era.

145 Buccleuch St. ⓒ 0141/333-0183. Admission £3.50 ($5.25) adults, £2.50 ($3.75) seniors, students, and children. Mar–Oct daily 2–5pm. Underground: Cowcaddens.

ADDITIONAL ATTRACTIONS

Cathedral of St. Kentigern 𝖆𝖆𝖆   Also known as St. Mungo's, this cathedral was consecrated in 1136, burned down in 1192, and rebuilt soon after; the Laigh Kirk (lower church), whose vaulted crypt is said to be the finest in Europe, remains to this day. Visit the tomb of St. Mungo in the crypt, where a light always burns. The edifice is mainland Scotland's only complete medieval cathedral from the 12th and 13th centuries. It was once a place of pilgrimage, but 16th-century zeal purged it of all monuments of idolatry.

Highlights of the interior include the 1400s nave, with a stone screen (unique in Scotland) showing the seven deadly sins. Both the choir and the lower church are in the mid-1200s First Pointed style. The church, though a bit austere, is filled with intricate details left by long-ago craftspeople—note the tinctured bosses of the ambulatory vaulting in the back of the main altar. The lower church, reached via a set of steps north of the pulpit, is where Gothic reigns supreme, with an array of pointed arches and piers. Seek out, in particular, the Chapel of the Virgin, with its intricate net vaulting and bosses carved with fine detailing. The Blacader Aisle projecting from the south transept was the latest addition to the church, a two-story extension, of which only the lower part was completed in the late Gothic style.

For the best view of the cathedral, cross the Bridge of Sighs into the **Glasgow Necropolis** (ⓒ **0141/287-3961;** Bus: 2 or 27), the graveyard containing almost every type of architecture in the world. Built on a rocky hill and dominated by a statue of John Knox, this fascinating graveyard was opened in 1832. Typical of the mixing of all groups in this tolerant cosmopolitan city, the first person to be buried here was a Jew, Joseph Levi.

Cathedral St. © 0141/552-6891. Free admission. Apr–Sept Mon–Sat 9:30am–6pm, Sun 2–5pm; Oct–Mar Mon–Sat 9:30am–4pm, Sun 2–4pm. Sun mass at 11am and 6:30pm. Underground: Queen St. Station.

House for an Art Lover   This house, which opened in 1996, is based on an unrealized and incomplete 1901 competition entry of Charles Rennie Mackintosh. The impressive building, with its elegant interiors, was brought to life by contemporary artists and craftspeople. The tour begins in the main hall and leads through the dining room, with its lovely gesso panels, and on to the music room, which shows Mackintosh designs at their most inspirational. Also here are an art cafe, design shop, and striking parkland setting adjacent to Victorian walled gardens.

Bellahouston Park, Dumbreck Rd. © 0141/353-4770. Admission £3.50 ($5.25). Daily 10am–4pm. Underground: Ibrox. Bus: 9A, 39, 54, 59, or 36.

Provands Lordship   Built by Bishop Andrew Muirhead as a residence for churchmen, this is Glasgow's oldest house (1471) and the only pre-Reformation building of interest other than the cathedral. Over the years, it has been used as a pastry shop, a soda factory, the abode of Glasgow's city hangman, and a junk shop. The museum houses 17th- and 18th-century furniture, tapestries, and pictures.

Castle St., across from the Cathedral of St. Kentigern. © 0141/552-8819. Free admission. Mon and Wed–Sat 10am–5pm; Sun 11am–5pm. Underground: Queen St. Station.

ATTRACTIONS IN NEARBY PAISLEY

Paisley, 7 miles (11km) west of Glasgow, became a famous name in the weaving trade during the Industrial Revolution. The Paisley shawl was born here. Actually, the inspiration for the pattern came from India, but no matter—it's forever associated with this industrial town.

Paisley Abbey ✿✿   One of the great attractions of Strathclyde, this church grew out of a Cluniac abbey founded in 1163. It was nearly demolished in 1307

ℰ Frommer's Favorite Glasgow Experiences

Touring the Burrell Collection.   The pièce de résistance of Glasgow (some say of Scotland), this gallery is the city's major attraction. See what good taste and an unlimited budget can acquire in a lifetime.

Following Walkways & Cycle Paths.   Greater Glasgow has an array of trails and bike paths cutting through areas of historic interest and scenic beauty, including the Paisley/Irvine Cycle and Walkway, 17 miles (27km) of unused railway line converted to a trail.

Riding the World's Last Seagoing Paddle Steamer.   From spring to early fall, the *Waverley* (© 0141/221-8152) makes day trips to scenic spots on the Firth of Clyde, past docks that once supplied more than half the tonnage of oceangoing ships.

Shopping Paddy's Market.   This daily market by the railway arches on Shipbank Lane gives you the real flavor of the almost-vanished Glaswegian style of street vending.

on orders of Edward I of England, but was subsequently reconstructed. In the mid–16th century, a tower fell in, causing great damage to the transept and choir. New work began around the turn of the 20th century, and by 1928 Paisley Abbey was restored, including a superb stone-vaulted roof. A chapel is dedicated to the monk, St. Mirin, who founded the town. You can also see an 11-foot-high (3.3m) Celtic cross from the 10th century.

Abbey Close. ℂ 0141/889-7654. Free admission. Mon–Sat 10am–3:30pm; Sun mass year-round at 11am and 12:15pm, also at 6:30pm Sept–June. Take the Paisley train from Glasgow's Central Station.

Paisley Museum and Art Galleries   This museum is visited mainly for its famous collection of more than 700 Paisley shawls. The teardrop pattern dominated the world of fashion for some 70-odd years, and today the shawls are extremely valuable as collectors' items. Other exhibits relate to the history of Strathclyde.

High St. ℂ 0141/889-3151. Free admission. Tues–Sat 10am–5pm; Sun 2–5pm; public holidays 9am–5pm. Take the Paisley train from Glasgow's Central Station.

GARDENS & PARKS

Glasgow's 40-acre **Botanic Garden,** Great Western Road (ℂ **0141/334-2422;** Underground: Hillhead), is an extensive collection of tropical plants and herb gardens. It's acclaimed especially for its spectacular orchids and begonias. Open daily from 7am to dusk; admission is free.

Linn Park, on Clarkston Road (Bus: 24 or 36), is 212 acres (85.9 hectares) of pine and woodland, with many scenic walks along the river, plus an old snuff mill, pony rides, and a children's zoo. Open daily from 8am to dusk.

Gleniffer Braes Country Park, Glenfield Road, Paisley (ℂ **0141/ 884-3794**), covers 1,300 acres (526.5 hectares) of woodland and moorland and has picnic areas and an adventure playground. Open daily from dawn to dusk.

ORGANIZED TOURS

The *Waverley* is the world's last seagoing paddle steamer, and from late June to late August (depending on weather conditions), it offers 1-day trips from Anderston Quay to historic and scenic places beyond the Firth of Clyde. You're allowed to bring your own sandwiches for a picnic aboard, or you can enjoy lunch in the Waverley Restaurant. Boat tours cost £9 to £27 ($13.50 to $40.50). Contact **Waverley Excursions,** Waverley Terminal, Anderston Quay, Broomielaw (ℂ **0141/221-8152**).

There's also regular ferry service run by **Caledonian MacBrayne** (ℂ **01475/ 650-100**), in Gourock on the banks of the Clyde. The ferry stands close to the station in Gourock, connected to Glasgow Central Station by trains that leave every hour and take 30 to 45 minutes. The ferry service, which can take cars, runs every hour (less frequently in winter) to the attractive seaside resort of Dunoon at the mouth of the Clyde. The journey takes about 20 minutes. The round-trip costs £4.50 ($6.75) for adults and £2.25 ($3.40) for seniors and children.

The best Glasgow tours are run by **Scotguide Tours,** operated from the Strathclyde Passenger Centre at George Square, opposite the City Chambers (ℂ **0141/204-0444;** Underground: Buchanan St.). From March 27 to October 11, departures are every half hour between 9:30am and 4pm. The price is £7 ($10.50) for adults, £5.50 ($8.25) for students and seniors, and £2.50 ($3.75) for children under 7.

6 Special Events

The **Glasgow International Jazz Festival** opens in the last days of June and usually runs through the first week of July. This festival has attracted some big names in the past, including the late Miles Davis and also Dizzy Gillespie. Tickets are available from the Ticket Centre, Candleriggs (© **0141/287-5511**), but some free events are always announced.

On June 10, the **Bearsden** and **Milngavie Highland Games** are held at Burnbray in the small town of Milngavie (pronounced Mill-guy), 6 miles (10km) from Glasgow. The games include tug-of-war, wrestling, caber tossing, piping, and Highland dancing, and offer a fun day out of the city. Call Cameron Wallace at © **0141/942-5177** for details.

The **Glasgow Fair** (held during most of the month of July) is likely to have carnivals, tea dances, European circuses, Victorian rides, and even a country-and-western stampede. For information, call © **0141/287-2000**.

7 Sports & Outdoor Pursuits

BIKING   The tourist office provides maps with detailed bike paths. Rentals are available from **West End Cycles,** 16–18 Chancellor St. (© **0141/357-1344;** Underground: Kelvin Hall), charging £13 ($19.50) per day and requiring a deposit of £50 ($75) or two pieces of ID.

GOLF   Several courses are near Glasgow, but there's a limited number actually in the city itself. Two nine-hole courses are **Alexander Park,** Alexandra Parade (© **0141/556-1294**), and **Knightswood,** Lincoln Avenue (© **0141/959-6358**). Neither offers caddy service or rentals of clubs and carts. Both Alexander, a 2,281-yard (2,076m), par-31 course, and Knightswood, a 2,793-yard (2,542m), par-34 course, charge greens fees of £3.50 ($5.25) per round. Open daily from 8am to 5pm in winter; daily from 7am to 7pm in summer.

SPORTS COMPLEXES   The **Kelvin Hall International Sports Arena** is on Argyle Street (© **0141/357-2525;** Underground: Kelvin Hall), near the River Kelvin. It offers volleyball and basketball courts, as well as an indoor track. Daily from 9am to 10:30pm, you can use the weight room for £2.60 ($3.90) or the fully equipped gym for £3.85 ($5.80). This is also the country's major venue for national and international sports competitions; check with the tourist office for any events scheduled for the time of your visit.

The outdoor **Crownpoint Sports Complex,** 183 Crownpoint Rd. (© **0141/ 554-8274;** Bus 62 or 64), also hosts national and international tournaments. It has two artificial-turf parks, an athletics park, and a track. Nonmembers can use the complex Monday through Friday from 3 to 9:30pm and Saturday and Sunday from 10am to 5pm. Use of the track costs £1.90 ($2.85); the weight room costs £2.60 ($3.90).

Scotstoun Leisure Centre, James Drive, Scotstoun (© **0141/959-4000;** Bus: 9, 44, 62, or 64), is about 2 miles (3km) from the center of Glasgow. It's open Monday through Wednesday and Friday from 9am to 10pm, Thursday from 10am to 10pm, and Saturday and Sunday from 9am to 6pm. There's an obligatory induction of £6.20 ($9.30) for anyone wanting to use the gym; entry thereafter is £3.85 ($5.80).

WATERSPORTS & ICE-SKATING   The **Lagoon Leisure Centre,** Mill Street, Paisley (© **0141/889-4000**), offers indoor facilities including a freeform pool with a wave machine, fountains, and flume. You'll also find sauna suites with sunbeds, Jacuzzis, and a Finnish steam room. The ice rink boasts an international ice pad with six curling lanes and is home to the Paisley Pirates hockey team. There are also bar and catering facilities.

The center is open for swimming Monday through Friday from 10am to 10pm and Saturday and Sunday from 9:30am to 5pm. Monday from 9 to 10pm, it's adults only, and Wednesday from 9 to 10pm, it's women only. The sauna facilities are open Monday through Friday from 10am to 10pm, Saturday from 9am to 10pm, and Sunday from 9:30am to 5pm. Most days are segregated by gender, so call beforehand to check. Ice-skating is available Monday through Friday from 9:30am to noon and Monday, Wednesday, and Thursday from 1:30 to 4pm; Tuesday from 12:30 to 3pm and 7:30 to 9:30pm; Friday from 2:45 to 5pm and 7:30 to 10pm; and Saturday and Sunday from 10:45am to 12:45pm and 2:30 to 4:30pm. Admission to the rink is £2.35 to £3 ($3.55 to $4.50) for adults and £1.80 to £2.30 ($2.70 to $3.45) for children. You can go swimming for £2.50 ($3.75) for adults and £1.30 ($1.95) for children. A combined ticket for the pool and skating rink goes for £4.50 ($6.75) for adults and £3.30 ($4.95) for children. Use of the sauna is £3.20 to £4.60 ($4.80 to $6.90). There are frequent trains throughout the day from Glasgow Central Station to Paisley.

8 Shopping

One of the main hunting grounds is the 3-block-long, pedestrian-only **Sauchiehall Street,** Glasgow's fashion center, where you may find good bargains, particularly in woolen goods. **Argyle Street,** which runs by the Central Station, is another major shopping artery.

All dedicated world shoppers know of **Buchanan Street,** a premier pedestrian thoroughfare. This is the location of the famed Fraser's Department Store (see below). From Buchanan Street, you can also enter **Princes Square,** an excellent complex with many specialty stores, restaurants, and cafes.

In the heart of Glasgow is the city's latest and most innovative shopping complex, the **St. Enoch Shopping Centre** (Underground: St. Enoch; Bus: 16, 41, or 44), whose merchandise is less expensive, but a lot less posh, than what you'd find at Princes Square. You can shop under the biggest glass roof in Europe. The center is to the east of Central Station on St. Enoch Square.

The **Argyll Arcade** is at 30 Buchanan St. (Underground: Buchanan St.). Even if the year of its construction (1827) wasn't set in mosaic tiles above the entrance, you'd still know this is an old collection of shops beneath a curved glass ceiling. The arcade contains what's possibly the largest single concentration of retail **jewelers,** both antique and modern, in Europe. It's considered lucky to purchase a wedding ring here.

Dedicated fashion mavens should take a trip to the **Italian Shopping Centre** (Underground: Buchanan St.), a small complex in The Courtyard, off Ingram Street, where you'll find pieces by Versace, Prada, Gucci, and Armani.

The latest contribution to mall shopping has come in the form of the **Buchanan Galleries** (Underground: Buchanan St.), which connects Sauchiehall, Buchanan, and Argyll streets and was completed in 1999. This plush development includes an enormous **John Lewis department store** and the biggest **Habitat** in Europe—a nirvana for anyone wanting reasonably priced contemporary furniture or accessories.

The Barras, held Saturday and Sunday from 9am to 5pm, takes place about a quarter of a mile (about 0.5km) east of Glasgow Cross. This century-old market has some 800 traders selling their wares in stalls and shops. Not only can you

---

Tips **Bring That Passport!**

Take along your passport when you go shopping in case you make a purchase that entitles you to a **VAT (value-added tax)** refund. For details, see "Getting Your VAT Refund" under "Fast Facts: Scotland," in chapter 2.

---

browse for that special treasure but also become a part of Glasgow life and be amused by the buskers. **Paddy's Market,** by the rail arches on Shipbank Lane, operates daily if you'd like to see an old-fashioned slice of Glaswegian street vending.

General shopping hours are Monday through Saturday from 9am to 5:30 or 6pm, depending on the merchant. On Thursdays, many shops stay open to 8pm.

ANTIQUES

Victorian Village   This warren of tiny shops stands in a slightly claustrophobic cluster. Much of the merchandise isn't particularly noteworthy, but there are many exceptional pieces if you're willing to hunt. Several of the owners stock reasonably priced 19th-century articles; others sell old jewelry and clothing, and a helter-skelter of artifacts. 93 W. Regent St. (C) 0141/332-0808. Bus: 23, 38, 45, 48, or 57.

ART

Compass Gallery   This gallery offers refreshingly affordable pieces; you could find something special for as little as £40 ($60), depending on the exhibition. The curators tend to concentrate on local artists, often university students. 178 W. Regent St. (C) 0141/221-6370. Bus: 11, 18, 28, 42, 44, or 57.

Cyril Gerber Fine Art   One of Glasgow's most respected galleries veers away from the avant-garde, specializing in British paintings, sculptures, and ceramics crafted between 1880 and today, along with Scottish landscapes and cityscapes. Objects begin at around £200 ($300). 148 W. Regent St. (C) 0141/221-3095. Bus: 23, 38, 45, 48, or 57.

BOOKS

John Smith & Son   This is a thoroughly Scottish bookshop, part of Scotland's cultural history. It has the best collection of specialized guides to Scotland and maps to the country. 57 St. Vincent St. (C) 0141/552-3377. Bus: 6, 8, 9A, or 16.

DEPARTMENT STORES

Fraser's Department Store   Fraser's is Glasgow's version of Harrods. A soaring Victorian-era glass arcade rises four stories, and inside you'll find everything from clothing to crystal to handmade local artifacts of all kinds. Buchanan St. (C) 0141/221-3880. Underground: Buchanan St.

GIFTS & DESIGN

Catherine Shaw   This somewhat cramped gift shop carries cups, mugs, postcards, and gift items based on the designs of Charles Rennie Mackintosh. There are also some highly evocative Celtic mugs called *quaichs* (welcoming cups or whisky measures, depending on who you talk to) and tankards in both pewter and silver. It's a great place for easy-to-pack and somewhat offbeat gifts. Look for another branch at 32 Argyll Arcade ((C) **0141/221-9038**); entrances to the arcade are on both Argyll and Buchanan streets. 24 Gordon St. (C) **0141/204-4762**. Underground: Buchanan St.

Mackintosh Shop   This tiny shop prides itself on its stock of books, cards, stationery, coffee and beer mugs, glassware, and sterling-and-enamel jewelry created from the original designs of Charles Rennie Mackintosh.

Although the shop doesn't sell furniture, the staff will refer you to a craftsman whose work they approve of: **Bruce Hamilton, Furnituremaker,** 4 Woodcroft Ave., Broomhill (✆ **01505/322-550;** Bus: 6, 16, or 44), has been involved in the restoration of many Rennie Mackintosh interiors and has produced a worthy group of chairs, sideboards, and wardrobes authentic to Mackintosh's designs. Expect to pay around £250 ($375), not including upholstery fabric, for a copy of the designer's best-known chair (the Mackintosh-Ingram chair). In the foyer of the Glasgow School of Art, 167 Renfrew St. ✆ 0141/353-4526. Underground: Buchanan St. or Cowcaddens.

National Trust for Scotland Shop   Drop in here for maps, calendars, postcards, pictures, dish towels, bath accessories, and kitchenware. Some of the crockery is in Mackintosh-design styles. The neoclassical building, constructed as a charity and hospice in 1806, is on the site of a larger hospice built in 1641. Hutcheson's Hall, 158 Ingram St. ✆ 0141/552-8391. Underground: Buchanan St.

KILTS & TARTANS

Hector Russell   Founded in 1881, Hector Russell is the country's oldest kiltmaker. This elegant store might be the most prestigious in Scotland. The welcome of the experienced sales staff is genuinely warm-hearted. Crystal and gift items are sold on street level, but the real heart and soul of the place is on the lower level, where you'll find impeccably crafted and reasonably priced tweed jackets, tartan-patterned accessories, waistcoats, and sweaters of top-quality wool for men and women. Men's, women's, and children's hand-stitched kilts are available. 110 Buchanan St. ✆ 0141/221-0217. Underground: Central Station.

MUSIC

Virgin Retail Music   The staff here is both knowledgeable and charming, eager to pass on their love of Scottish music. This outlet offers the biggest and best selections of CDs and tapes in the city, with special strengths and insights in both traditional and contemporary Scottish music. Unit 4, Lewis Building, Argyll St. ✆ 0141/221-0103. Underground: St. Enoch.

PORCELAIN & CRYSTAL

Stockwell Bazaar   This is Glasgow's largest purveyor of porcelain, its four floors bulging with Royal Doulton, Wedgwood, Noritake, and Royal Worcester, plus crystal stemware by many manufacturers. Anything you buy can be insured and shipped to any address. 67–77 Glassford St. ✆ 0141/552-5781. Underground: St. Enoch.

9 Glasgow After Dark

Glasgow, not Edinburgh, is the cultural center of Scotland, and the city is alive with performances. Before you leave home, check *Time Out* (www.timeout. co.uk) for the latest round-up of who's playing in the clubs and concert halls. After you've arrived, pick up a copy of the free monthlies *Culture City* or *What's On* at the tourist office or your hotel. In addition, at most newsstands you can get a free copy of *The List,* published every other week. It details arts and other events for Edinburgh as well as Glasgow.

You can buy tickets to most cultural events at the **Ticket Centre,** City Hall, Candleriggs (✆ **0141/227-5511** or 0141/305-7500; Underground: St. Enoch). The box office sells tickets to at least a dozen theaters in the city. You can buy tickets in person Monday through Saturday from 9:30am to 6:30pm and Sunday from noon to 5pm. Phone reservations are accepted Monday through Saturday from 9am to 9pm and Sunday from noon to 5pm.

THE PERFORMING ARTS

OPERA & CLASSICAL MUSIC   The **Theatre Royal,** Hope Street and Cowcaddens Road (© 0141/332-9000; Underground: Cowcaddens; Bus: 23, 48, or 57), is the home of the **Scottish Opera** as well as of the **Scottish Ballet.** The theater also hosts visiting companies from around the world. Called "the most beautiful opera theatre in the kingdom" by the *Daily Telegraph,* it offers splendid Victorian Italian Renaissance plasterwork, glittering chandeliers, and 1,547 comfortable seats, plus spacious bars and buffets on all four levels. Ballet tickets run £5.50 to £35 ($8.25 to $52.50) and opera tickets £5.50 to £47 ($8.25 to $70.50). On performance days, the box office is open Monday through Saturday from 10am to 7:30pm; otherwise, hours are Monday through Saturday from 10am to 6pm.

In winter, the **Royal Scottish National Orchestra** offers Saturday concerts at the **Glasgow Royal Concert Hall,** 2 Sauchiehall St. (© 0141/332-6633; Underground: Buchanan St.). The **BBC Scottish Symphony Orchestra** presents Friday concerts at the **BBC Broadcasting House,** Queen Margaret Drive (Underground: St. Enoch), or at **City Halls,** Albion Street (Underground: St. Enoch). In summer, the Scottish National Orchestra has a short Promenade season (dates and venues are announced in the papers). Tickets to all concerts are available at the **Ticket Centre** (see above) and cost £8 to £25 ($12 to $37.50).

THEATER   Although hardly competition for London's, Glasgow's theater scene is certainly the equal of Edinburgh's. Young Scottish playwrights often make their debuts here, and you're likely to see anything from Steinbeck's *The Grapes of Wrath* to Wilde's *Salome* to *Romeo and Juliet* done in Edwardian dress.

The prime symbol of Glasgow's verve remains the **Citizens Theatre,** Gorbals and Ballater streets (© 0141/429-0022; Bus: 12 or 66), founded after World War II by James Bridie, a famous Glaswegian whose plays are still produced on occasion here. It's home to a repertory company, with tickets going for £5 to £15 ($7.50 to $22.50). The box office hours are Monday through Saturday from 9:30am to 6:30pm. The company is usually closed from June to the first week in August.

The **Glasgow Arts Centre,** 12 Washington St. (© 0141/221-4526; Bus: 2, 4, or 21), always seems to be doing something interesting, including children's productions and other theatrical performances. It's open Monday through Friday from 9:30am to 5pm and 6:30 to 10pm; in summer, it's closed in the evening. Performances are free. The **King's Theatre,** 297 Bath St. (© 0141/248-5153; Bus: 57), offers a wide range of productions, including straight plays, musicals, and comedies. In winter, it's noted for its pantomime presentations. Tickets are £6 to £26 ($9 to $39); the box office is open Monday through Saturday from 10am to 6pm.

The **Mitchell Theatre,** 6 Granville St. (© 0141/287-5511; Bus: 57), has earned a reputation for small-scale entertainment, ranging from dark drama to dance, as well as conferences and seminars. A small modern theater, it adjoins the well-known Mitchell Library. The box office is open on performance days from 4pm until the show. Ticket prices vary. The **Pavilion Theatre,** 121 Renfield St. (© 0141/332-1846; Bus: 21, 23, or 38), specializes in modern versions of vaudeville. The Pavilion sells its own tickets for £8 to £16 ($12 to $24);

they're not available at City Centre. The box office is open Monday through Saturday from 10am to 8pm.

The **Tron Theatre,** 63 Trongate (℗ **0141/552-4267;** Underground: St. Enoch), occupies one of the three oldest buildings in Glasgow, the former Tron Church. The church, with its famous Adam dome and checkered history, has been transformed into a small theater presenting the best of contemporary drama, dance, and music. The Tron also has a beautifully restored Victorian cafe and bar serving traditional home-cooked meals, including vegetarian dishes and a fine selection of beer and wine. The box office is open Monday through Saturday from 10am to 6pm, until 9pm by phone. Tickets are £3 to £8 ($4.50 to $12) for adults and £3 to £4 ($4.50 to $6) for children.

THE CLUB & MUSIC SCENE

Barrowland This hall seats 2,000 and is open only on nights shows are booked. July and August are the quiet months, as most shows are geared toward a student audience. The cover runs highest when the hall hosts popular bands like White Zombie or the Breeders. Gallowgate. ℗ 0141/552-4601. Underground: St. Enoch. Bus: 61 or 62. Cover £8–£20 ($12–$30).

Fury Murry's Most of the crowd here is made up of students looking for a good, sometimes rowdy, time listening to disco that's upbeat but not ultratrendy. It's in a cellar, a 2-minute walk from the very central St. Enoch Shopping Centre. There's a busy bar, a dance floor, and ample opportunities to meet the best and brightest in Scotland's university system. Jeans and T-shirts are the right garb. Open Thursday through Sunday from 10:30pm to 3:30am. Thursday and Friday features live bands; other nights are strictly for dancing. 96 Maxwell St. ℗ 0802/538-550. Underground: St. Enoch. Cover £2–£6 ($3–$9).

The Garage A big student crowd tests the limits of the 800-person capacity here on weekends. Downstairs, surrounded by rough stone walls, you feel like you're in a castle with a Britpop and indie soundtrack. Most regulars, however, gravitate to the huge main dance floor. Open daily from 11pm to 3am. 490 Sauchiehall St. ℗ 0141/332-1120. Underground: Buchanan St. Cover £5–£10 ($7.50–$15).

Grand Ole Opry In a sprawling building 1½ miles (2.5km) south of Glasgow's center, this is the largest club in Europe devoted to country-western music. A chuck wagon eatery serves affordable steaks and other such fare. Open Friday through Sunday and occasionally Thursday from 6:30pm to 12:30am. 2–4 Govan Rd., Paisley Toll Rd. ℗ 0141/429-5396. Bus: 23 or 23A. Cover £3–£10 ($4.50–$15).

King Tut's Wah-Wah Hut This sweaty, crowded rock bar is a good place to check out the Glasgow music and arts crowd, as well as local bands and the occasional international act. Successful Scottish acts My Bloody Valentine and Teenage Fan Club got their start here. Open Monday through Saturday from noon to midnight and Sunday from 6pm to midnight. 272 St. Vincent St. ℗ 0141/ 221-5279. Bus: 6, 8, 9, or 16. Cover £4–£10 ($6–$15).

Nice 'n' Sleazy This club books live acts Thursday through Sunday. The cover is quite reasonable, but can get pricey for bands like the Cranberries or Helmet. Holding some 200 patrons, it provides a rare opportunity to catch internationally popular bands in an intimate setting. Upstairs Sunday and Monday nights, DJs spin an eclectic mix of music for dancing, but most people come for the bands. Open daily from 11:30am to 11:45pm. 421 Sauchiehall St. ℗ 0141/ 333-9637. Bus: 23 or 48. Cover usually £3.50 ($5.25); higher if a big name is playing.

Renfrew Ferry   This old car ferry that once provided service on the River Clyde now hosts a Friday-night *ceilidh* (hoe-down) with traditional Scottish music and dancing. Other musical acts are booked infrequently during the year. 2 Clyde Place. ℂ **0169/826-5511.** Bus: 21, 23 38 45, 48, or 57. Cover £5.50 ($8.25).

The 13th Note   This club books mainly rock bands on Tuesday, Wednesday, and Thursday nights, and country and western on Monday. Friday, Saturday, and Sunday are dedicated to ambient and alternative music. It's a comfortably funky candlelit club open daily from noon to midnight. 50–60 Glassford St. ℂ **0141/553-1638.** Bus: 21, 23, or 38. No cover.

Victoria's Nightclub   Victoria's prides itself on being the only club in Scotland with cabaret performances. The club is on two floors of high-tech design in the heart of town, with a first-floor dance area and a second-floor cabaret bar and restaurant where singers, comedians, and other artistes amuse and titillate on Wednesday, Friday, and Saturday nights. Dress is smart casual. The dance club is open Wednesday through Sunday from 10:30pm to 3am; the cabaret is open Wednesday, Friday, and Saturday from 7:30pm to 3am. 98 Sauchiehall St. ℂ **0141/332-1444.** Underground: Buchanan St. Cover £8 ($12) for dance club only; £15.95 ($23.95) for dance club, cabaret, and buffet dinner.

PUBS & BARS

Bon Accord   This amiably battered pub is a longtime favorite. There's an array of hand-pumps—a dozen devoted to real British ales, the rest to beers and stouts from the Czech Republic, Belgium, Germany, Ireland, and Holland. Malt whiskies and affordable bar snacks are also available. Open Monday through Saturday until midnight, Sunday until 11pm. 153 North St. ℂ **0141/248-4427.** Bus: 6, 8, or 16.

Cask and Still   Here you can taste from a selection of more than 350 single malts, at a variety of strengths and maturities. Many prefer the malt whisky that has been aged in a sherry cask. There's good bar food at lunch. Open Monday through Thursday until 11pm, Friday and Saturday until midnight. 154 Hope St. ℂ **0141/333-0980.** Bus: 21, 23, or 38.

Corn Exchange   Opposite the Central Station, this place really was the Corn Exchange in the mid–19th century, but now is one of Glasgow's most popular pubs. Amid dark paneling and high ceilings, you can enjoy a pint of lager until 11pm Sunday through Wednesday, midnight Thursday through Saturday. Affordable pub grub is served daily from noon to 9pm. 88 Gordon St. ℂ **0141/ 248-5380.** Bus: 21, 23, or 38.

L'Attaché   This traditional pub is outfitted with stone floors and rows of decorative barrels. At the self-service food counter, you can order cheap steak pie, lasagna, and salads; at the bar, you can sample an impressive array of single malts. There's a disco on Friday and Saturday nights and live jazz on Saturday afternoons. Open Monday through Thursday until 11pm, Friday and Saturday until midnight, and Sunday from 5 to 11 pm. 27 Waterloo St. ℂ **0141/221-3210.** Bus: 21, 23, or 48.

GAY BARS & CLUBS

There's no strongly visible lesbian bar or nightclub scene in Glasgow. Many lesbians choose to frequent those that cater mainly to males.

Bennet's   A short walk from the Central Station and George Square, Bennet's is one of the major gay-lesbian clubs in town. On certain nights (especially

Tues), it's the most fun gay disco in Scotland. The crowd includes men and women from 17 to 60, and the music plays on and on, interrupted only by the occasional drag show. Performers are usually imported from London or the States; shows last about 30 minutes and begin after 1am Wednesday and Saturday. Open Wednesday through Sunday from 11pm to 3:30am. 90 Glassford St. ℂ 0141/552-5761. Underground: St. Enoch. Cover £2–£6 ($3–$9).

C. D. Frost   Named after the British actress, currently married to actor Jude Law, C. D. Frost is a busy bar catering primarily to a trendy young mixed crowd. It's minimalist chic, with low lighting. Drag acts are occasionally featured, but it's better known for the Wednesday-night quiz. Karaoke on Thursday and Sunday offers you the chance to murder a few old faves. Open daily until midnight. 8–10 W. George St. ℂ 0141/332-8005. Underground: Buchanan St.

Court Bar   This small, cozy pub is a popular meeting place for a gay-lesbian crowd to come together for drinks and talk. The pub gets decidedly more male after 7pm and is a good starting point for an evening on the town. Open daily from 10:30am to midnight. 69 Hutcheson St. ℂ 0141/552-2463. Underground: Buchanan St.

Waterloo Bar   The friendly bartenders here are a good source of info about what's happening in the gay scene. Attracting a slightly older crowd, Waterloo gets most packed during happy hour (from 9pm to midnight), when you can make your drink a double for just £2.50 ($3.75). Open daily until midnight. 306 Argyle St., near the Central Station. ℂ 0141/221-7359. Underground: Buchanan St.

10 Side Trips from Glasgow: The Best of the Strathclyde Region

Just as Sir Walter Scott dominates the Borders, the presence of Robert Burns is felt in the Strathclyde region around Ayr. A string of famous seaside resorts stretches from Girvan to Largs. Some of Britain's greatest golf courses, including Turnberry, are here. Glasgow makes a good gateway to Burns country, as it has excellent bus and rail connections to Ayr, which is your best bet for exploring the area. If you're driving, take A77 southwest from Glasgow to Ayr.

AYR: A POPULAR WEST COAST RESORT

The royal burgh of Ayr is the most popular resort on Scotland's west coast. Facing the Isle of Arran and the Firth of Clyde, it's 81 miles (130km) southwest of Edinburgh, and 35 miles (56km) southwest of Glasgow. A busy market town, it offers 2½ miles (4km) of beach (alas, spoiled by pollution), steamer cruises, fishing, and golf, and is a manufacturing center for fabrics and carpets. Ayr also boasts the top racecourse in Scotland.

Trains from Glasgow's Central Station (ℂ 0345/484-950) will whisk you to Ayr in 50 minutes; the fare is £4.95 ($7.45). Stagecoach Express (ℂ 01292/613-500) buses from Glasgow arrive in Ayr in 1½ hours, costing £4.70 ($7.05) one-way.

The **tourist office** is at Burns House, Burns Statue Square (ℂ 01292/288-688). It's open from Easter to August, Monday through Saturday from 9:15am to 6pm (July and August, also Sunday from 10am to 5pm); and September to Easter, Monday through Saturday from 9:15am to 5pm.

SEEING THE SIGHTS

Ayr is full of Burns associations. The 13th-century **Auld Brig o' Ayr,** the poet's "poor narrow footpath of a street where two wheelbarrows tremble when they meet" was renovated in 1910.

On Blackfriar's Walk on the banks of the River Ayr, the **Auld Kirk of Ayr** dates from 1653 to 1655, when it replaced the 12th-century Church of St. John, which had been seized by Cromwell and dismantled. Its greatest curiosity is a grim series of "mort safes" dating from 1655—they were used to cover freshly filled graves to discourage body-snatchers. Robert Burns was baptized in the kirk. The church is open Monday through Saturday from 8:30am to 7pm and Sunday from noon to 7pm.

The **Wallace Tower,** on High Street, rises some 112 feet (34m). Constructed in 1828, it has a statue of William Wallace (remember *Braveheart?*) by local sculptor James Thom. Tradition holds that Wallace was imprisoned here and made a daring escape.

Another architectural curiosity is **Loudoun Hall** (© 01292/616-183), Boat Vennal, at the junction of Hope and High streets, off Cross Street, in the heart of town. A wealthy merchant had this town house constructed in the late 1400s, and it's one of the oldest examples of burgh architecture left in the country. From mid-July to the end of August, it's open Monday through Saturday from 11am to 6pm.

About 1½ miles (2.5km) south of Ayr off the road to the Burns Cottage at Alloway (see below), the **Maclaurin Gallery and Rozelle House,** on Monument Road in Rozelle Park (© 01292/443-708), are installed in what were once stables and servants' quarters. A Henry Moore bronze sculpture and a major collection of contemporary art are on display. A nature trail winds through the woodland. It's open Monday through Saturday from 10am to 5pm (April October, also Sunday from 2 to 5pm). Admission is free.

The **Ayr Racecourse** (© 01292/264-179), about 1½ miles (2.5km) north of the town center, is open year-round. Races are usually held Friday, Saturday, and Monday, generally at 2:15pm. Peak racing season is May to October, with jumping events held in November, January, and April.

There are three nearby golf courses; the best is the municipal **Belle Isle Golf Course** (© 01292/441-258).

ACCOMMODATIONS

Fairfield House ⋇ On the seafront near Low Green, this 1912 Edwardian town house has been restored to its original elegance and converted into Ayr's

---

Backpacking the West Highland Way

One of Scotland's most legendary long-distance footpaths is the **West Highland Way** (see "The Best Hikes," in chapter 1), set aside by the government in 1967 to preserve its beauty. It begins north of Glasgow in the town of Milngavie and winds its way for 95 miles (153km) north along Loch Lomond with its bonnie, bonnie banks. The trail continues through Glencoe, site of a famous passage, and goes on to Fort William and eventually to Ben Nevis, Scotland's highest mountain. The most dramatic part of this walk is from the Bridge of Orchy to Glencoe.

Trains run frequently throughout the day from the Queen's Street railway station in central Glasgow to Milngavie, starting point of the walk. The 15-minute trip costs £2 ($3) one-way. For information and a map of this footpath, contact the **Scottish Tourist Board,** 23 Ravelston Terrace, Edinburgh EH4 3EU (© 0131/332-243; Underground: Buchanan St.).

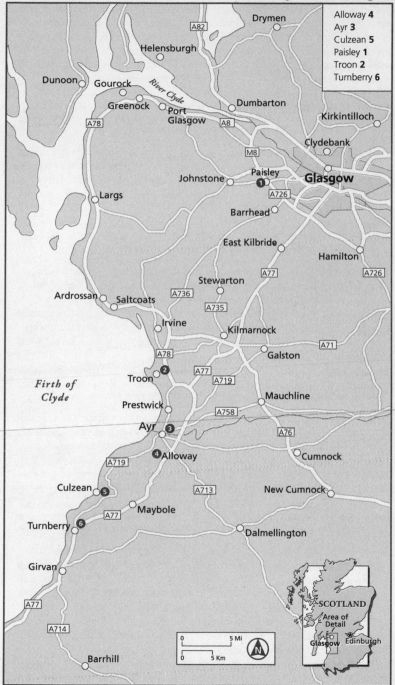

Side Trips from Glasgow

Alloway **4**
Ayr **3**
Culzean **5**
Paisley **1**
Troon **2**
Turnberry **6**

Drymen

A82

Helensburgh

Dunoon

Gourock

Greenock

Port Glasgow

River Clyde

Dumbarton

A8

Kirkintilloch

Clydebank

M8

A78

Johnstone

Paisley **1**

Glasgow

A726

Largs

Barrhead

East Kilbride

Hamilton

A726

A77

Stewarton

A736

A735

Ardrossan

Saltcoats

Irvine

Kilmarnock

Galston

A71

A78

Troon **2**

A77

A719

Firth of Clyde

Prestwick

Mauchline

Ayr **3**

A758

A76

4 Alloway

Cumnock

A719

Culzean **5**

A713

New Cumnock

Turnberry **6**

A77

Maybole

Dalmellington

Girvan

A77

A714

Barrhill

0   5 Mi
0   5 Km

N

SCOTLAND

Area of Detail

Glasgow

Edinburgh

195

best hotel. The staff is especially attentive and will help you arrange tee times at nearby golf courses. Lady Henrietta Spencer-Churchill, noted designer of classic British interiors, decorated the rooms in a country-house style. The guest rooms are large and luxurious, many done in chintz; most of the bathrooms have bidets and combination tub/showers. The food at Fairfield has been called an oasis in a culinary desert.

12 Fairfield Rd., Ayr, Ayrshire KA7 2AR. © **01292/267-461.** Fax 01292/261456. www.fairfieldhotel.co.uk. 43 units. £130 ($195) double; £160 ($240) suite. Rates include Scottish breakfast. AE, DC, MC, V. Free parking. **Amenities:** Restaurant, bar; leisure club with pool, gym, spa, sauna, steam room, and solarium; room service; laundry/dry cleaning. *In room:* TV, coffeemaker, hair dryer.

Jarvis International   This hotel is a few hundred yards from Ayr's seashore and 500 yards (455m) from the rail station. It offers large, refurbished guest rooms; many with views and all with neat, shower-only bathrooms. Bart's Bar and Grill is a lively place to meet and eat, with a selection of freshly roasted joints on the captain's table.

Dalblair Rd., Ayr, Ayrshire KA7 1UG. © **01292/269-331.** Fax 01292/610-722. www.jarvis.co.uk. 118 units. £105 ($157.50) double; £140 ($210) suite. AE, DC, MC, V. Free parking. **Amenities:** Restaurant, bar; nearby golf courses; leisure club; room service; laundry/dry cleaning. *In room:* TV, coffeemaker, hair dryer.

Pickwick Hotel   It may seem odd to have a hotel commemorating a character in a Charles Dickens novel in a town noted for its memories of Rabbie Burns, but this late-Victorian hotel, directly east of the Esplanade, does just that. Each routine guest room is of a decent size and bears a Dickensian title; all contain shower bathrooms. In the paneled Pickwick Club, you can soak up the Dickensian atmosphere and enjoy the simple but fresh food. High tea is served from 5 to 7pm.

19 Racecourse Rd., Ayr, Ayrshire KA7 2TD. © **01292/260-111.** Fax 01292/285-348. www.pickwickhotel. co.uk. 15 units. £70 ($105) double. Rates include Scottish breakfast. AE, MC, V. Free parking. **Amenities:** Restaurant, bar; room service; laundry/dry cleaning. *In room:* TV, coffeemaker, hair dryer.

Quality Station Hotel   The Station, an Ayr landmark since 1888, is still going strong. Connected to the town's rail station, it sits behind a red-sandstone exterior, and although it isn't the most modern hotel in town, many visitors consider its high ceilings, elaborate detailing, and old-world charm more than enough reason to check in. Many of the guest rooms are quite spacious but routinely furnished. All come with small shower-only bathrooms.

Burns Statue Sq., Ayr, Ayrshire KA7 3AT. © **01292/263-268.** Fax 01292/262-293. www.choicehotelseurope. com. 74 units. £83 ($124.50) double; £98 ($147) suite. AE, DC, MC, V. Free parking. **Amenities:** Restaurant, bar; health club with gym; Jacuzzi; sauna; room service; laundry service. *In room:* TV, coffeemaker, hair dryer.

Savoy Park Hotel ⚘   For more than 30 years, the Henderson family has welcomed guests to their classic country hotel, which was designed in the Victorian and Scottish baronial style. The atmosphere is traditional, with paneled walls and ornate ceilings, but modern conveniences have been discreetly added. The pricier bedrooms are larger and more charming. All units include shower-only bathrooms. Evoking a Highland hunting lodge, the Oak Room serves time-tested dishes such as baked lemon sole. The Savoy Park is a short drive from 30 first-rate golf courses, and fishing is also possible nearby.

16 Racecourse Rd., Ayr, Ayrshire KA7 2UT. © **01292/266-112.** Fax 01292/611-488. www.savoypark.com. 15 units. £75–£95 ($112.50–$142.50) double. Rates include breakfast. AE, MC, V. Free parking. Follow A70 for 2 miles (3km), go through Parkhouse St., turn left into Beresford Terrace, and make first right onto Bellvue Rd. **Amenities:** Restaurant, bar. *In room:* TV, coffeemaker, hair dryer, iron.

DINING

Fouter's Bistro MODERN SCOTTISH   In the historic heart of Ayr, this restaurant occupies the cellar of an 18th-century bank, retaining the original sandstone floor and a vaulted ceiling covered in terra-cotta tiles. The restaurant's name derives from Scottish argot: *foutering about* is a charming way of saying "bumbling about" (although this place is anything but bumbling). The seamless service focuses on modern Scottish cuisine with a nod to Thailand. You can sample the likes of venison with rowanberry sauce, local Gresshingham duck with black-cherry sauce, and seafood served with saffron cream sauce. In spring, one of the most delicious items is the organically reared lamb from the neighboring Carrick Hills.

2A Academy St. ℂ 01292/261-391. Reservations recommended. Main courses £5–£6 ($7.50–$9) at lunch, £9–£14.50 ($13.50–$21.75) at dinner; fixed-price lobster lunch (in season only) £14.50 ($21.75). AE, DC, MC, V. Tues–Sat noon–2pm and 6:30–10:30pm.

Tudor Restaurant SCOTTISH/INTERNATIONAL   This busy family-oriented restaurant is imbued with a real Tudor look with dark half-timbering. Most popular here are the fixed-price lunch and the high tea served from 3:15pm to closing. The food includes such rib-sticking specialties as a version of chicken Maryland (breaded and fried breast of chicken with bacon, tomatoes, peaches, and pineapple fritters).

8 Beresford Terrace, on Burns Statue Sq. ℂ 01292/261-404. Main courses from £5 ($7.50); fixed-price meal £4.90 ($7.35) for 2 courses, £5.50 ($8.25) for 3 courses; high tea £5–£8.50 ($7.50-$12.75). MC, V. Mon–Sat 9am–8pm; Sun noon–8pm.

AYR AFTER DARK

The famous **Rabbie's Bar,** Burns Statue Square (ℂ **01292/262-112**), mixes Scottish poetry with electronic music. The stone walls are highlighted with the pithy verses of Robert Burns, who used to drop in for a pint of ale and conversation. A portrait of Rabbie is painted directly onto the wall. However, don't come here expecting poetry readings in a quiet corner. The crowd, while not particularly literary, is talkative and fun and enjoys live music several nights a week. There's a busy bar, crowded banquettes and copper-topped tables, and a large TV showing videos. It's open Monday through Saturday from 11am to 12:30am and Sunday from noon to midnight.

ALLOWAY ⚘: BIRTHPLACE OF RABBIE BURNS

Some 2 miles (3km) south of Ayr, Alloway is where Scotland's national poet was born on January 25, 1759, in the gardener's cottage—the "auld clay biggin"—that his father, William Burns, built in 1757.

SEEING THE SIGHTS

Auld Brig Over the Ayr, mentioned in *Tam o' Shanter,* still spans the river, and **Alloway Auld Kirk,** also mentioned in the poem, stands roofless and haunted not far away. The poet's father is buried in the graveyard of the kirk.

Burns Cottage and Museum ⚘   The cottage still contains some of its original furniture, including the bed in which the poet was born. Chairs displayed here were said to have been used by Tam o' Shanter and Souter Johnnie. Beside the poet's cottage is a museum.

Alloway. ℂ 01292/441-215. Admission £2.80 ($4.20) adults, £1.40 ($2.10) children and seniors, £8 ($12) per family. Apr–Oct daily 9am–6pm; Nov–Mar Mon–Sat 10am–4pm, Sun noon–4pm. Drive 2 miles (3km) south of Ayr on B7024.

Ⓒ Robert Burns: National Poet & Penniless Genius

And, wow! Tam saw an unco sight!
Warlocks and witches in a dance:
Nae Cotillion, brent new frae France,
But hornpipes, jigs, strathspeys, and reels,
Put life and mettle in their heels.

—Robert Burns, *Tam o' Shanter*

Scotland's national poet, Robert Burns (1759–96), or Rabbie, carried the Scottish vernacular to its highest point in his satiric, earthly, and bawdy romantic poems and songs. Born in Alloway in Ayrshire on a wind-tossed night, Burns was the son of an impoverished gardener who encouraged him to read and seek an education. Burns became an unsuccessful farmer and later a taxman, but the world knows him as the "heaven-taught ploughman," author of the narrative masterpiece *Tam o' Shanter* and the humanitarian *A Man's a Man for A' That.*

Rabbie was a great womanizer ("Once heartily in love, never out of it") who fathered at least 15 children, 9 of whom were legitimate. In his short time on earth, he wrote about 370 poems and songs, only to die at age 37, wracked with rheumatic fever and harassed by his debtors for the sum of £5 ($7.50). His pregnant wife, Jean, had to beg a shilling from the poet's brother to feed her children on the day of his funeral.

Every year on his birthday, January 25, the poet is honored all over the world—from Edinburgh to San Francisco, from Bombay to Tokyo—at male-dominated Bachelors' Clubs like the one founded by Burns and his friends. Even Shakespeare doesn't get this kind of attention. At these Burns suppers, guests who are entitled get to wear kilts; non-Scottish admirers of the poet dress formally. After a dram of whisky is drunk as a welcome, the first course, or *Het Hail*, is carried in; it's invariably cock-a-leekie soup, made with chicken and leeks. Next comes *Caller Fish Frae Loch and Sea*, usually fresh salmon. But for the main course, there can be no deviation in the menu: It must be the Great Chieftan o' the Puddin' Race, the dreaded haggis. The chef comes in bearing the haggis on a large platter, preceded by a kilted piper playing "Scotland the Brave." Of course, everyone drinks a whisky to the health of the haggis—after all, a small nip is known as *uisge beatha* ("water of life").

The chairman of the club—again, after a quaff of whisky—takes out a Scottish dirk and recites Burns's "Address to a Haggis" before plunging the blade into the beast. Out gushes the meat, entrails, or whatever the chef decided to stuff into the sheep's stomach. This seasoned mix of minced meat, oatmeal, and onions is enjoyed by all the "bachelors."

The sad truth is that although haggis is consumed at all birthday celebrations for Burns, the poor poet missed out on it himself. He considered haggis "one of the most delicious meals on earth" but could rarely afford it, settling instead for *tatties* (mashed potatoes) or *neeps* (turnips).

Burns Monument and Gardens   About half a mile (1km) from the Burns Cottage, this monument is a Grecian-style building erected in 1823, containing relics, books, and manuscripts associated with Robert Burns. The gardens overlooking the River Doon contain shrubs; some were brought back from the Himalayas and are relatively rare. Everything is small-scale but choice.

Alloway. ℂ 01292/441-215. Admission 50p (75¢). Apr–Oct daily 9am–6pm; Nov–Mar Mon–Sat 10am–4pm, Sun noon–4pm. Drive 2 miles (3km) south of Ayr on B7024.

Tam o' Shanter Experience   Here, adjacent to the gardens of the Burns Monument, you can watch a film on Burns's life, his friends, and his poetry. There's a well-stocked gift shop plus a tearoom. The Russians are particularly fond of Burns and his poetry, and many visit annually to pore over his original manuscripts; the museum has been presented with a translation of the poem *Tam o' Shanter* by Russian enthusiasts.

Murdoch's Lane. ℂ 01292/443-700. Admission £1.40 ($2.10) adults, 70p ($1.05) children and seniors. Daily 9am–6pm. Drive 2 miles (3km) south of Ayr on B7024.

ACCOMMODATIONS & DINING

Belleisle House Hotel (Kids)   Beside A719, this imposing 1755 country house stands in a public park noted for its two golf courses. It has a stone exterior and interior paneling with ornate carvings depicting some scenes from Burns's *Tam o' Shanter*, with blazing fireplaces adding to the ambience. The guest rooms range from midsize to spacious; each has traditional furnishings and a small, shower-only bathroom. The place extends a special welcome to children and has a play area set aside for them. The Scottish cooking is excellent.

Belleisle Park, Doonfoot Rd., Alloway, Ayr, Ayrshire KA7 4DU. ℂ 01292/442-331. Fax 01292/445-325. 14 units. £75 ($112.50) double; £80 ($120) bridal suite. Rates include Scottish breakfast. AE, MC, V. Free parking. Drive 2 miles (3km) south of Ayr on A719. **Amenities:** 2 restaurants, 2 bars; nearby golf; room service; laundry/ dry cleaning. *In room:* TV, coffeemaker, hair dryer.

Brig o' Doon Hotel (Finds)   One of Scotland's most famous footbridges, the Brig o' Doon, is a few steps from this new-style hotel, on the river's east bank. With 2 acres (0.8 hectares) of gardens (so lovely that they often host weddings), this is the choice place to stay. Everything from the plumbing—mainly with both tub and shower—to the stylish guest rooms is state of the art. Reserve early, especially in summer.

Alloway, Ayr, Ayrshire KA7 4PQ. ℂ 01292/442-466. Fax 01292/441-999. www.costley-hotels.co.uk. 5 units. £100 ($150) double. Rates include Scottish breakfast. AE, MC, V. Free parking. Drive 2 miles (3km) south of Alloway on B7024. **Amenities:** Restaurant, bar; laundry service. *In room:* TV, coffeemaker, hair dryer.

CULZEAN

Twelve miles (19km) south-southwest of Ayr and 4 miles (6.5km) west of Maybole on A719 is Culzean Castle. Maidens Bus (no. 60) from the Sandgate Bus Station in Ayr runs to Calzean six times per day; a round-trip ticket is £4.20 ($6.30) for adults and £2 ($3) for children.

Culzean Castle (Finds Finds)   Built by famous Scottish architect Robert Adam in the late 18th century, this clifftop creation is a fine example of his castellated style, with a view to the south of Alisa Craig, a 1,100-foot-high (334m) rounded rock 10 miles (16km) offshore, a nesting ground and sanctuary for seabirds. Culzean (pronounced Cul-*lane*) replaced an earlier Scots tower house as the family seat of the powerful Kennedy clan. In 1945, the castle and grounds were given to the National Trust for Scotland. It's well worth a visit and is of special interest to Americans because of General Eisenhower's connection—in 1946, the National

Guest Flat was given to the general for his lifetime in gratitude for his services as supreme commander of Allied Forces in World War II. An exhibit of Eisenhower memorabilia, including his North African campaign desk, is sponsored by Scottish Heritage U.S.A., Inc. Culzean stands near the famous golf courses of Turnberry and Troon, a fact that particularly pleased the golf-loving Eisenhower. The tour also includes the celebrated round drawing room, delicately painted ceilings, and outstanding Adam oval staircase.

Overlooking the Firth of Clyde. ℭ 01655/884-455. Admission (including entrance to the Country Park below) £8 ($12) adults, £6 ($9) seniors and children, £20 ($30) per family. Apr–Oct daily 10am–5:30pm (last entrance half hour before closing). Closed Nov–Mar.

Culzean Country Park ℛ   Part of the land surrounding the castle includes what in 1969 became the first country park in Scotland. The 565-acre (228.8-hectare) grounds contain a walled garden, an aviary, a swan pond, a camellia house, an orangery, an adventure playground, and a newly restored 19th-century pagoda, as well as a deer park, miles of woodland paths, and beaches. It has gained an international reputation for its visitor center (Adam's home farm) and related visitor and educational services.

On the land surrounding Culzean Castle. ℭ 01655/884-400. Included in admission to Culzean Castle (see above). Daily 9am to dusk.

TURNBERRY: WORLD-CLASS GOLF ℛ

On the Firth of Clyde, the little town of Turnberry, south of the castle, was part of the Culzean Estate. It began to flourish early in the 20th century, when the Glasgow and South Western Railway developed rail service, golfing facilities, and a first-class hotel.

From the two original 13-hole golf courses, the complex has grown into the two 18-hole courses, Ailsa and Arran, known worldwide as the **Turnberry Hotel Golf Courses** (ℭ 01655/331-000). The Ailsa, one of the most exacting courses yet devised, has been the scene of numerous championship tournaments and PGA events. Come here for the prestige, but prepare yourself for the kind of weather a lobster fisherman in Maine might find daunting. (Its par is 70, its SSS, 72, and its yardage, 6,976/6,348m.) Newer, and usually shunted into the role of also-ran, is the Arran Course. Guests of the hotel get priority on the Ailsa course. The greens fee of £95 ($142.50) for guests, or £120 ($180) Monday through Friday and £150 ($225) Saturday and Sunday for nonguests, includes 18 holes on each course. Clubs rent for £35 ($52.50); caddy service costs £25 ($37.50), plus tip.

A short drive east of Turnberry takes you to **Souter Johnnie's Cottage,** Main Road, in Kirkoswald (ℭ 01655/760-603), 4 miles (6.5km) west of Maybole on A77. This was the 18th-century home of the village cobbler, John Davidson (Souter Johnnie), who, with his friend Douglas Graham of Shanter Farm, was immortalized by Burns in *Tam o' Shanter*. The cottage contains Burnsiana and contemporary cobbler's tools, and in the churchyard are the graves of Tam o' Shanter and Souter Johnnie. From Good Friday to September, the cottage is open daily from 11:30am to 5pm; in October, hours are Saturday and Sunday from 11:30am to 5pm. Off-season admittance is sometimes available by appointment. Admission is £3 ($4.50) for adults and £1.40 ($2.10) for seniors, students, and children.

A final sight is **Carleton Castle,** along A77 some 14 miles (22.5km) south of Culzean Castle and 3 miles (5km) south, following the coast, from the little seaside town of Girvan. In its heyday it was a watchtower, built to guard the coastline against invaders. A famous ballad grew out of a legend surrounding the castle: It was said to be the headquarters of a baron who married eight times. When this Bluebeard got tired of a wife, he pushed her over the cliff and found himself another. However, he proved no match for his eighth wife, May Cullean. "The Ballad of May Colvin" relates how she's supposed to have tricked and out-lived him.

ACCOMMODATIONS

Malin Court Hotel   On one of the most scenic strips of the Ayrshire coast, this well-run hotel fronts the Firth of Clyde and the Turnberry golf courses. It is not a great country house, but rather a serviceable, welcoming retreat offering a blend of informality and comfort. Bedrooms, mostly medium in size, have combination tub/showers. The staff can arrange hunting, fishing, riding, sailing, and golf.

Turnberry, Ayrshire KA26 9PB. © 01655/331-457. Fax 01655/331-072. www.malincourt.co.uk. 18 units. £105–£124 ($157.50–$186) double. Rates include breakfast. AE, DC, MC, V. Free parking. Take A74 to Ayr exit, then A719 to Turnberry and Maidens. **Amenities:** Restaurant (see "Dining," below), bar; health spa; gym; sauna; room service; laundry/dry cleaning. *In room:* TV, hair dryer, coffeemaker, iron.

Turnberry Hotel, Golf Courses, and Spa 🏵🏵🏵   The 1908 Turnberry, 50 miles (80.5km) south of Glasgow on A77, is a remarkable and opulent Edwardian property. From afar, you can see the hotel's white facade, red-tile roof, and dozens of gables. The public rooms contain Waterford crystal chandeliers, Ionic columns, molded ceilings, and oak paneling. Each guest room is furnished in unique early-1900s style and has a marble-sheathed bathroom with a combination tub/shower. The rooms, which vary in size, open onto views of the lawns, forests, and (in some cases) Scottish coastline.

Maidens Rd., Turnberry, Ayrshire KA26 9LT. © 01655/331-000. Fax 01655/331-706. www.westin.com. 221 units. £264–£340 ($396–$510) double; £395–£445 ($592.50–$667.50) suite. Rates include Scottish breakfast. AE, DC, DISC, MC, V. Free parking. **Amenities:** 3 restaurants, bar, lounge; tennis court; squash courts; gym; Turkish bath; room service; massage; babysitting; laundry/dry cleaning. *In room:* TV, dataport, minibar, coffeemaker, hair dryer, safe.

DINING

Cotters Restaurant SCOTTISH   Exemplary service, a scenic location, and the finest local ingredients make a winning combination. The modern, tasteful decor creates a casual, relaxed atmosphere. The lunch menu offers everything from melon slices to deep-fried haddock in beer batter. For dinner, you might start with melon and peaches glazed with an orange sabayon, or salmon and asparagus terrine with chive butter. For a main course, try the baked Ayrshire lamb and chicken mousseline wrapped in phyllo pastry. The tempting desserts include a chocolate and hazelnut tart, warm bread and plum pudding awash in a sea of vanilla sauce, and a fine selection of cheeses.

In the Malin Court Hotel, Turnberry. © 01655/331-457. Reservations recommended. Fixed-price menus £16–£20 ($24–$30); main courses £5–£12 ($7.50–$18). AE, DC, MC, V. Daily 12:30–2pm and 7:30–9pm.

TROON & THE ROYAL TROON GOLF CLUB 🏵

The resort town of Troon, 7 miles (11km) north of Ayr, 31 miles (50km) south-west of Glasgow, and 77 miles (124km) southwest of Edinburgh, looks out across the Firth of Clyde to the Isle of Arran. It's a 20th-century town, its earlier history having gone unrecorded. Troon takes its name from the curiously shaped promontory jutting out into the Clyde estuary. The promontory was called Trwyn, the Cymric word for "nose," and later this became Trone and then Troon.

Troon offers several golf links, including the **Royal Troon Golf Club,** Craigend Road ((C) **01292/311-555**). This is a 7,097-yard (6,458m) course (one of the longest in Scotland) with an SSS of 74 and a par of 71. Dignified Georgian and Victorian buildings and the faraway Isle of Arran are visible from the fairways, which seem deliberately designed to steer your golf balls into the sea or the dozens of sand traps flanking your shot. The Old Course is the more famous, reserved for men. Nonmembers may play only on certain days. A newer addition, the 6,289-yard (5,723m), par-71 Portland, is open to both men and women and is by some estimates even more challenging than the Old Course. The British Open has been played here off and on since 1923. The greens fee— £125 ($187.50) for a day—includes a buffet lunch and two 18-hole sets. For one round of play, a trolley rents for £4 ($6) and a caddy £25 ($37.50); club rental is £20 ($30) per round or £35 ($52.50) per day.

In summer, visitors find plenty of room on Troon's 2 miles (3km) of sandy beaches stretching along both sides of its harbor; the shallow waters make it a safe haven. From here you can take steamer trips to Arran and the Kyles of Bute.

Trains from Glasgow's Central Station arrive several times daily, a 40-minute trip. Call (C) **0345/484-950** for information. Trains also connect Ayr with Troon, a 10-minute ride. Buses and trains from Glasgow cost £4.50 ($6.75) each way. From Ayr, you can reach Troon and other parts of the area by bus; call (C) **0990/808-080** for details.

ACCOMMODATIONS

You also might want to consider **Highgrove House** (see "Dining," below).

Lochgreen House Hotel &&   Adjacent to the fairways of the Royal Troon Golf Course, one of Scotland's loveliest country-house hotels is set on 30 lush acres of forest and landscaped gardens. The property opens onto views of the Firth of Clyde and Ailsa Craig. The interior evokes a more elegant bygone time, with detailed cornices, antique furnishings, and elegant oak and cherry paneling. Guests meet and mingle in two luxurious sitting rooms with log fires, or take long walks on the well-landscaped grounds. The spacious bedrooms are well equipped with the finest mattresses and combination tub/showers.

Monktonhill Rd., Southwood, Troon, Ayrshire KA10 7EN. (C) 01292/313-343. Fax 011292/317-661. www.costley-hotels.co.uk. 15 units. £160 ($240) double. Rates include breakfast. AE, MC, V. Free parking. Take B749 to Troon. **Amenities:** Restaurant (see "Dining," below), lounge; tennis courts; room service; babysitting laundry/dry cleaning. *In room:* TV, hair dryer, coffeemaker.

Piersland House Hotel   This hotel was built more than a century ago by Sir Alexander Walker of the Johnnie Walker whisky family. The importation of 17,000 tons of topsoil transformed its marshy surface into a lush 4-acre (1.6-hectare) garden. The moderately sized guest rooms have traditional country-house styling and such amenities as combination tub/showers.

15 Craigend Rd., Troon, Ayrshire KA10 6HD. (C) 01292/314-747. Fax 01292/315-613. 28 units. £119–£135 ($178.50–$202.50) double; £135–£165 ($202.50–$247.50) cottage suite. Rates include Scottish breakfast. AE, DC, MC, V. Free parking. Drive 3 minutes south of the town center on B749. **Amenities:** Restaurant, bar, lounge; croquet; room service; babysitting; laundry/dry cleaning. *In room:* TV, hair dryer, coffeemaker.

DINING

The dining room at the **Piersland House Hotel** (see "Accommodations," above) is also recommended.

Fairways Restaurant   SCOTTISH/INTERNATIONAL   This landmark 1890s hotel stands on the Ayrshire coast overlooking the Royal Troon Golf

Course. The restaurant can satisfy your hunger pangs with some degree of style. Traditional Scottish and French dishes include pillows of smoked Scottish salmon, followed by turbot with langoustines or shrimp.

In the Marine Highland Hotel, 8 Crosbie Rd. © **01292/314-444.** Reservations required. Main courses £8.95–£13.95 ($13.45–$20.95) at lunch; fixed-price table d'hôte 4-course dinner £22.50 ($33.75). AE, DC, MC, V. Daily noon–2pm and 7–9:30pm.

Highgrove House TRADITIONAL SCOTTISH   This charming white-painted, red-roofed brick building is isolated on a hillside known for its scenic view over the sea and the Isle of Arran. The bustling restaurant moves big crowds in and out quickly. Menu items include several varieties of steamed salmon and Scottish venison with rowanberry sauce.

Upstairs are nine simple but comfortable guest rooms with TVs, phones, and hair dryers; breakfast included, they rent for £95 ($142.50).

Old Loan's Rd., Troon, Ayrshire KA10 7HL. © **01292/312-511.** Reservations recommended. Main courses £6–£12 ($9–$18) lunch; £11–£15 ($16.50–$22.50) dinner. AE, MC, V. Daily noon–2:30pm and 6–9:30pm. Drive 2 miles (3km) north of Troon on A78.

Lochgreen House Hotel Restaurant ℛ SCOTTISH/FRENCH   This is one of the region's most agreeable culinary stopovers, where you'll be tempted by the finest seafood, game, and Scottish beef. The elegant dining room, with its views of woodland and garden, somehow makes the food taste even better. The service is just as flawless. For a main course, sample the poached halibut on a mussel and fennel stew with saffron potatoes and chives. The wine list roams the world for inspiration, and the desserts often feature the fresh fruit of the season.

Monktonhill Rd., Southwood. © **01292/313-343.** Reservations required. Fixed-price 3-course lunch £21.50 ($32.25); fixed-price 4-course dinner £30 ($45). AE, MC, V. Daily noon–2pm and 7–9pm. Take B749 to Troon.

7

Argyll & the Southern Hebrides

The old county of Argyll (in Gaelic, *Earraghaidheal*, "coastland of the Gael") on and off the coast of western Scotland is a rewarding journey. Summers along the coast are usually cool and damp and winters relatively mild but wet, with little snow.

The major center of Gaelic culture for the district is **Oban** ("small bay"), a great port for the Western Isles. It's also the gateway to Mull, largest of the Inner Hebrides; to the Isle of Iona, the cradle of Scottish Christianity; and to Staffa, where Fingal's Cave inspired Mendelssohn to write the *Hebrides Overture*. (For these islands, see chapter 11, "The Hebridean Islands.") A number of colorful destinations are near the port town of Oban, including **Port Appin** and **Inveraray,** where you can soak up the atmosphere of this region in a more rural setting.

There are several island destinations off the Argyll coast meriting your time. The long **peninsula of Kintyre** separates the islands of the Firth of Clyde, including **Arran,** from the islands of the Inner Hebrides, notably **Mull, Islay,** and **Jura.** (For information on Mull, see chapter 11.)

From the Isle of Islay to the Mull of Kintyre, the climate is mild. The land is rich and lush, especially on Arran. The peat deposits on Islay lend flavor to the making of such fine malt whiskies as Lagavulin, Bruichladdick, and Laproaig. There's a diversity of scenic beauty: hills and glens, fast-rushing streams, and little roads that eventually lead to coastal villages displaying B&B signs in summer. The unspoiled and remote island of Jura is easily reached from Islay.

And the best news for last: These islands, as well as the Kintyre peninsula, are among the best travel bargains in the British Isles.

1 The Isle of Arran: Scotland in Miniature ★/★

Brodick: 74 miles (119km) W of Edinburgh, 29 miles (47km) W of Glasgow

At the mouth of the Firth of Clyde, the Isle of Arran is often described as "Scotland in miniature" because of its wild and varied scenery—the glens, moors, lochs, sandy bays, and rocky coasts that have made the country famous. Once you're on Arran, buses will take you to various villages, each with its own character. A coast road, 60 miles (97km) long, runs around the length of the island.

Arran boasts some splendid mountain scenery, notably the conical peak of **Goatfell** in the north (called the "mountain of the winds"), reaching a height of 2,866 feet (869m). Arran is also filled with beautiful glens, especially **Glen Sannox,** in the northeast, and **Glen Rosa,** north of Brodick. Students of geology flock to Arran to study igneous rocks of the Tertiary period. Cairns and standing stones at Tormore intrigue archaeologists as well. The island is only 25 miles (40km) long and 10 miles (16km) wide and can be seen in a single day.

Achamore House Gardens **15**	Castle Stalker **1**	Inveraray Castle **9**
Auchindran Township Open Air Museum **10**	Crarae Glen Gardens **12**	Islay Woolen Mill **13**
	Dunollie Castle **4**	Kildalton Crosses **14**
Brodick Castle **16**	Dunstaffnage Castle **5**	Kilchurn Castle **8**
Castle Lachlan **11**	Falls of Cruachan **7**	McCaig's Tower **3**
	Gylen Castle **2**	Pass of Brander **6**

ESSENTIALS

GETTING THERE   High-speed electric **trains** operate from Glasgow Central direct to Ardrossan Harbour, taking 1 hour and costing £4.50 ($6.75) one-way. For details, call ℂ **08457/484-950.** (If you're **driving** from Glasgow, head southwest along A737 until you reach Ardrossan.) At Ardrossan, you must make a 30-minute ferry crossing to Arran, arriving in Brodick, Arran's main town, on its east coast.

In summer, a small **ferry** runs between Lochranza (north of Arran) across to Claonaig in Argyll, providing a gateway to the Highlands and a visit to Kintyre. There are six boats daily; the fare is £37.20 to £46.40 ($55.80 to $69.60) for a vehicle, plus £8.50 ($12.75) per passenger for a return journey. For information, check with **Caledonian MacBrayne** (ℂ **0990/650-000**) at the ferry terminal in Gourock.

VISITOR INFORMATION The **tourist office** is at The Pier, Brodick (© **01770/302-140;** www.ayrshire-arran.com). It's open June through August, Monday through Saturday from 9am to 7:30pm and Sunday from 10am to 5pm; September through May, Monday through Saturday from 9am to 5pm.

EXPLORING THE ISLAND

After the ferry docks at Brodick, you may want to head for Arran's major sights, **Brodick Castle** and the **Isle of Arran Heritage Museum** (see below).

The best way to discover the island's beauty is to stroll around. Right beyond the Isle of Arran Heritage Museum, at the point where String Road divides the island, you can follow the signs to a beautiful spot called **Glen Rosa.** You might want to pack a picnic lunch before setting out. Another great walk is to the village of **Corriegills,** which is signposted along A841 south of Brodick and treats strollers to fine views of Brodick Bay.

The most intriguing walks on the island are signposted, but if you're really serious about hiking, stop by the tourist office and pick up *Seventy Walks in Arran* for £2.50 ($3.75) or *My Walks in Arran* for £2.25 ($3.40). While at the office, ask about any guided walks the Forestry Commission may be conducting. They're scheduled frequently in summer and range from 2 to 5 hours, costing £3 to £6 ($4.50 to $9).

If you'd prefer to do your exploring on two wheels, stop by **Mr. Bilsland,** The Gift Shop, Brodick (© **01770/302-272**). You'll pay a deposit of £10 to £20 ($15 to $30); rental rates are £7.50 to £9 ($11.25 to $13.50) daily or £27 to £35 ($40.50 to $52.50) weekly. Open daily from 9am to 6pm. **Brodick Cycles,** Brodick (© **01770/302-460**), requires a deposit of £5 to £25 ($7.50 to $37.50). Daily rentals range from £5 to £9.50 ($7.50 to $14.25), up to £20 to £35 ($30 to $52.50) for a full week. Open Monday through Saturday from 9am to 6pm and Sunday from 10am to 6pm.

South from Brodick is the village/resort of **Lamlash,** opening onto Lamlash Bay. From here, a ferry takes you over to Holy Island with its 1,000-foot (303m) peak. A disciple of St. Columba founded a church on this island. In the north, **Lochranza** is a village with unique appeal. It opens onto a bay of pebbles and sand, and in the background lie the ruins of a castle that reputedly was the hunting seat of Robert the Bruce.

Brodick Castle 𝄐𝄐   The historic home of the dukes of Hamilton, this red-sandstone castle dates from the 13th century and contains superb silver, antiques, portraits, and objets d'art. Some castle or other has stood on this site since about the 5th century, when the Dalriad Irish, a Celtic tribe, came here and founded their kingdom. The castle is now the property of the National Trust for Scotland and boasts award-winning gardens. Laid out in the 1920s by the duchess of Montrose, they're filled with shrubs, trees, perennials, and herbs from Tasmania, New Zealand, Chile, the Himalayas, and northern Britain. Especially noteworthy are the rhododendrons, which are one of the focal points of the Country Park bordering the more formal gardens.

1½ miles (2.5km) north of the Brodick pierhead. © **01770/302-202.** Admission to both castle and gardens £6 ($9) adults, £4 ($6) seniors and students, free for those under 19. Castle Apr–Oct daily 11am–4:30pm (to 5pm July–Aug); gardens and Country Park daily 11am to sunset. Bus: Any labeled "Brodick Castle."

Isle of Arran Heritage Museum   A compound of antique structures once used as outbuildings for the nearby castle, this museum provides the best overview of life on Arran from prehistoric times to the present. The most prominent of the buildings is a stone-sided cottage filled with 19th-century memorabilia,

Castle Sween
Keillmore
Lagg
Kilmory
Achahoish
Eilean Mor
Point of Knap
Sliabh Gaoil
Barmore Island
A83
KNAPDALE
Tarbert
E. Loch Tarbert
W. Tarbert
Portavadie
Glecknabae
Kildavanan
Kilberry Head
Kilberry
Ardpatrick
Kennacraig
Whitehouse
Skipness Castle
Ardlamont Point
Straad
Inchmarnock
Ardpatrick Point
W. Loch Tarbert
Claonaig
Skipness Point
Ardscalpsie Point
Ferry to Colonsay & Islay
PORT MÒR
Clachan
Sound of Bute
GIGHA ISLAND
Tarbert
Ballochroy
Crossaig
Lochranza
A841
Ardminish
A83
Catacol
Mid Sannox
Craro Island
Leim
Sound of Gigha
Pirnmill
Sannox Bay
Corrie
Gigalum Island
Tayinloan
Grogport
Goatfell
Cara Island
Killean
Brodick Castle
Muasdale
Carradale
Dougarie
Brodick Bay
Glenacardoch Point
Arnicle
Dippen
Saddell Abbey
Carradale Point
Heritage Museum
Glen Rosa
Glen Iorsa
Brodick
Glenbarr
Carradale Bay
ISLE OF ARRAN
Margnaheglish
Holy Island
Bellochantuy
Saddell
Lamlash
Drumadoon Point
Skeroblingarry
Blackwaterfoot
Kingcross Point
Kilchenzie
Peninver
Brown Head
Whiting Bay
Machrihanish
A83
Campbeltown
A841
Dippin Head
Drumlemble
Campbeltown Loch
Stewarton
Davaar Island
Lagg
Kildonan
Knocknaha
Kilmory
Rubha Dùin Bhàin
Conie Glen
Feochaig
Johnston's Point
Bennan Head
Sound of Pladda
Pladda
B842
South Carrine
Macharioch
Mull of Kintyre
Dunaverty Rock
Southend
Sheep Island
Sanda Sound
Sanda Island
Ferry to Ballycastle, Northern Ireland

0   5 Mi
0   10 Km

Airport ✈
Castle ♜
Golf ⛳
Lighthouse ※
Ferry Route - - -

SCOTLAND
Area of Detail
Edinburgh

costumes, and artifacts, including a working kitchen. Also on site are a blacksmith's shop and forge, geological artifacts, and an archive room housing historic records associated with Arran. Access to the archive room is reserved for scholars pursuing academic research.

Rosaburn, 1½ miles (2.5km) north of the Brodick ferry piers. ℂ 01770/302-636. Admission £2 ($3). Apr–Oct Mon–Sat 10am–5pm, Sun 11am–4pm. Bus: Any labeled "Brodick Castle."

SHOPPING
Divided into three businesses, the **Duchess Court Shops,** Home Farm, Brodick (ℂ **01770/302-831**), is made up of the Home Farm Kitchen, selling locally produced chutneys, jams, and marmalades; the Nature Shop, dealing in books, jewelry, wood carvings, T-shirts, and other assorted goods; and Something Special, featuring natural grooming products.

Six miles (10km) north of Brodick in Corrie, **Corriecraft & Antiques,** Hotel Square (ℂ **01770/810-661**), sells small Arran antiques and pottery. In Lamlash, **Patterson Arran Ltd.,** The Old Mill (ℂ **01770/600-606**), offers chutneys, mustards, preserves, and other locally produced condiments.

The **Old Byre Showroom,** Auchencar Farm (ℂ **01770/840-227**), 5 miles (8km) north of Blackwaterfoot along the coastal road in Machrie, sells sheepskin, leather, and tweeds, but its biggest draw is the large selection of locally produced wool sweaters.

ACCOMMODATIONS
IN BRODICK
Auchrannie Country House Hotel ℛℛ Acclaimed as the island's finest hotel and restaurant, this Victorian mansion (once the home of the dowager duchess of Hamilton) stands in pristine glory on 6 acres (2.4 hectares) of landscaped gardens and woods, about a mile (1.6km) from the Brodick ferry terminal. Guest rooms in the new wing are the most comfortable, but all units are furnished with taste, using select fabrics and decorative accessories. All of the well-maintained bathrooms contain combination tub/showers.

You can enjoy drinks in the cocktail bar or sun lounge before heading for the Garden Restaurant, which offers fixed-price dinners—pricey, but the finest on Arran (nonguests should reserve ahead). Brambles Bistro offers a wide range of snacks and tasty food throughout the day and evening.

Auchrannie Rd., Brodick, Isle of Arran KA27 8BZ. ℂ 01770/302-234. Fax 01770/302-812. www.auchrannie. co.uk. 28 units. £112–£144 ($168–$216) double with breakfast; £152–£172 ($228–$258) double with half-board. AE, MC, V. **Amenities:** 2 restaurants; bar; indoor pool; Turkish bath; turbo spa; sauna; solarium; room service; babysitting; laundry. *In room:* TV, minibar, coffeemaker, hair dryer.

Kilmichael Country House Hotel ℛℛ It was voted Country House Hotel of the Year in a "Taste of Scotland" contest in 1998, and if anything, it's better than ever. The island's most scenically located house, it's said to be the oldest on Arran, perhaps once a stamping ground for Robert the Bruce. A combination of the tasteful new and the antique is used throughout. The guest rooms are beautiful, as are the bathrooms, with luxury toiletries and combination tub/showers. The aura of gentility is reflected in the log fires and fresh flowers from the garden. The staff members are helpful and welcoming, and the food is noteworthy. International dishes are featured, and an attention to detail goes into the expensive fixed-price menus.

Brodick, Isle of Arran KA27 8BZ. ℂ 01770/302-234. Fax 01770/302-068. www.kilmichael.com. 9 units. £120 ($180) double; £150 ($225) suite. Rates include Scottish breakfast. **Amenities:** Restaurant; bar; lounge; room service; laundry. *In room:* TV, coffeemaker, hair dryer.

IN LAMLASH

Glenisle Hotel *Finds*   Across the road from the waterfront, with a view across the bay to the Holy Isle, Glenisle could be one of the oldest buildings in the village, but no one knows its age or even the century of its construction. The reception lounge, waterview dining room, and lounge where drinks are available are cheerfully decorated. Each relatively simple but comfortable guest room has flowered curtains, tasteful decor, and a small but tidy bathroom with tub and shower.

Shore Rd., Lamlash, Isle of Arran KA27 8LS. (C) **01770/600-559**. Fax 01770/600-966. 13 units. £40 ($60) per person with Scottish breakfast; £104 ($156) double with half-board. MC, V. Take the Whiting bus from Brodick. **Amenities:** Restaurant, bar; room service; laundry. *In room:* TV, coffeemaker, hair dryer.

IN WHITING BAY

Grange House Hotel *Kids*   Opening onto views across the Firth of Clyde, this country-house hotel is operated by Janet and Clive Hughes, who take a personal interest in their guests. A gabled stone house standing on landscaped grounds, the Grange offers tastefully furnished, traditional guest rooms. Some units can be arranged to accommodate a family, and one room is suitable for travelers with disabilities. Eight rooms open onto views of the Holy Isle and the Ayrshire coast. Some of the bathrooms are equipped with a tub, others with a shower only. The hosts no longer serve an evening meal, but are happy to make dinner reservations for you in the village.

Whiting Bay, Isle of Arran KA27 8QH. (C) and fax **01770/700-263**. 9 units, 7 with private bathroom. £52–£65 ($78–$97.50) double without bathroom; £56–£70 ($84–$105) double with bathroom. Rates include Scottish breakfast. MC, V. **Amenities:** Bar lounge; small fitness center; room service. *In room:* TV, coffeemaker, no phone.

Royal Hotel   This granite house, located in the center of the village beside the coastal road, was one of the first hotels ever built on Arran, going back to 1895. True to its original function as a temperance hotel, it serves no alcohol, but guests can bring bottles of their own wine or beer into the dining room, which serves moderately priced dinners nightly at one sitting. Some of the bedrooms enjoy a vista over the bay and its tidal flats. One unit contains a four-poster bed and lots of chintz, while another has a small sitting room. Each comes with a neat little shower-only bathroom.

Whiting Bay, Isle of Arran KA27 8PZ. (C) and fax **01770/700-286**. 6 units. £50 ($75) double or suite. Rates include Scottish breakfast. No credit cards. Closed Nov–Mar. Take the Whiting bus from Brodick. *In room:* TV, coffeemaker, hair dryer.

IN KILDONAN

Kildonan Hotel   Built as an inn in 1760, with a section added in 1928, this family-run hotel rises a few steps from the island's best beach. It's in Scottish farmhouse style, with a slate roof, white-painted stone walls, and ample views of seabirds and gray seals basking on the rocks of Pladda Island opposite. The staff can arrange diversions like putting, boating, fishing, table tennis, water-skiing, and scuba diving. The rooms range from small to midsize and are traditionally furnished; a few come with tub or shower.

The spacious dining room features moderately priced dinners; less formal lunches and dinners are served in the bar. A specialty is crab or lobster salad made from shellfish caught by one of the owner's sons. You'll likely see a crowd of locals by the pub's dartboard and billiards tables.

Kildonan, Isle of Arran, KA27 8SE. (C) **01770/820-207**. Fax 01770/820-320. 22 units, 6 with private bathroom. £48 ($72) double without bathroom; £56 ($84) double with bathroom. Rates include Scottish breakfast. No credit cards. **Amenities:** Restaurant, bar; room service. *In room:* No phone.

Seeing the Argyll on Horseback

There's no better way to experience the majestic beauty of the moors, highlands, and headlands in the Argyll area than on horseback. To arrange an outing, contact the **Ardfern Riding Centre**, Croabh Haven, Loch Gilphead, Argyll ℂ **01852/500-632**). A 1-hour ride costs £15 ($22.50), a 2-hour ride £25 ($37.50), and a 4-hour ride (with lunch) £37 ($55.50). In addition to maintaining around 16 horses and a working cattle-and-sheep farm between Oban and Loch Gilphead, the center has a cottage that groups of up to eight equestrians can rent for £200 to £295 ($300 to $442.50) per week. The center is open all year, but the best times to go are from May to early June and from September to October.

Kinloch Hotel   This hotel, composed of two cream-colored Victorian buildings, appears deceptively small from the road. It's actually the largest building in the village of Blackwaterfoot, with a contemporary wing jutting out along the coast. The midsize guest rooms are modestly comfortable and conservative. Most of the double rooms have sea views, but the singles tend to look out over the back gardens.

Blackwaterfoot, Isle of Arran KA27 8ET. ℂ **01770/860-444**. Fax 01770/860-447. www.kinloch-arran.com. 51 units. £64 ($96) per person with half-board (Scottish breakfast and dinner); £115 ($172.50) suite. AE, DC, MC, V. Take the Blackwaterfoot bus from Brokick. **Amenities:** Restaurant; bar; indoor pool; sauna; room service; babysitting; laundry. *In room:* TV, coffeemaker, hair dryer.

DINING
IN BRODICK

The hotels reviewed above also have fine restaurants.

Creelers Seafood Restaurant SCOTTISH   This choice lies in a minicompound of shops and bistros created from a 1920s-era farm associated with Brodick Castle. The most appealing of the places here is Creelers, a family-run operation specializing in some of the freshest seafood in Scotland, much of it pulled in from local fishing boats that day. The enterprise includes a "smokery" where salmon, scallops, and duck breast are carefully smoked and served almost immediately. You won't go wrong ordering any of the versions of smoked salmon, presented with capers and horseradish or with mushroom-studded risotto. Especially appealing are the seared Arran scallops with monkfish and pesto.

The Home Farm, about 1 mile (1.5km) north of the center of Brodick. ℂ **01770/302-810**. Reservations recommended. Fixed-price lunch £9.50–£10.50 ($14.25–$15.75); main courses £8–£14 ($12–$21) lunch; £12–£20 ($18–$30) dinner. MC, V. Tues–Sun noon–2:30pm and 6:30–10pm.

IN LAMLASH

Carraig Mhor ℛ CONTINENTAL   Carraig Mhor, in a modernized pebbledash (a mortar containing a mixture of pebbles) 1700s cottage in the village center overlooking the water, serves imaginative and beautifully presented dinners. The chef makes extensive use of local products, especially seafood and game. All bread and ice creams, among other offerings, are made on the premises. The menu changes seasonally, and there are separate dining rooms for smokers and nonsmokers.

Lamlash. ℂ **01770/600-453**. Reservations recommended. Fixed-price menus £18 ($27) for 2 courses, £22.50 ($33.75) for 3 courses. MC, V. Mon–Sat 7–9pm. Closed 2 weeks in Jan and first 2 weeks in Feb. Take the Whiting bus from Brodick.

ARRAN AFTER DARK

The **Brodick Bar,** in the center but without a street address (② **01770/ 302-169**), is an old wooden pub open Monday through Saturday from 11am to midnight. Drop in for some real Scottish ale and a bar meal of local seafood (meals are served Monday through Saturday from noon to 2:30pm and 5:30 to 10pm). Featuring wood-and-leather chairs and walls hung with old photographs and riding gear, **Duncan's Bar,** also in the center but with no street address (② **01770/302-531**), keeps the same hours and serves real cask ales and lagers. Meals, available daily from noon to 2pm and 5:30 to 8pm, always include a roast and seafood items.

2 The Kintyre Peninsula

The longest peninsula in Scotland, Kintyre stretches more than 60 miles (97km), with scenery galore, sleepy villages, and miles of sandy beaches. It's one of the country's most unspoiled areas, owing perhaps to its isolation. Kintyre was ancient Dalriada, the first kingdom of the Scots.

If you drive all the way to the tip of Kintyre, you'll be only 12 miles (19km) from Ireland. Kintyre is joined to the mainland of Scotland by a narrow neck of land near the old port of Tarbert. The largest town on the peninsula is the port of Campbeltown, on the southeastern coast.

ESSENTIALS

GETTING THERE   Loganair (② **0141/889-1111** in Glasgow) makes two 45-minute flights a day from the Glasgow Airport to Campbeltown, the chief town of Kintyre.

From Glasgow, you can take buses to the peninsula. The trip takes 4 hours and costs £10.50 ($15.75) one-way. Inquire at **Scottish CityLink,** Buchanan Street Bus Station, Glasgow (② **0990/505-050**).

Kintyre is virtually an island unto itself, and the most efficient way to travel is by car. From Glasgow, take A82 up to the Loch Lomond side and cut across to Arrochar and go over the "Rest and Be Thankful" route to Inveraray (A83). Then cut down along Loch Fyne to Lochgilphead and continue on A83 south to Tarbert, which can be your gateway to Kintyre. You can take A83 along the western coast or cut east at the junction of B8001 and follow it across the peninsula to B842, which you can take south to Carradale. If your target is Campbeltown, you can reach it by either the western shore (much faster and a better road) or the eastern shore.

TARBERT

A sheltered harbor protects the fishing port and yachting center of Tarbert, on a narrow neck of land at the northern tip of the Kintyre. It's between West Loch Tarbert and the head of herring-filled Loch Fyne and has been called the "world's prettiest fishing port."

Tarbert means "drawboat" in Norse and referred to a place where Vikings dragged their boats across land on rollers from one sea to another. In 1093, King Malcolm of Scotland and King Magnus Barelegs of Norway agreed the Western Isles were to belong to Norway and the mainland to Scotland. An island was defined as anything a Viking ship could sail around, so Magnus proclaimed Kintyre an island by having his dragon ship dragged across the mile (1.5km) of dry land from West Loch Tarbert on the Atlantic to East Loch Tarbert on Loch Fyne. After the Vikings gave way, Kintyre came under the control of the Mac-Donald lordship of the Isles.

SEEING THE SIGHTS

The castle at Tarbert dates from the 13th century and was later extended by Robert the Bruce. The castle ruins, **Bruce Castle,** are on a hillock above the village on the south side of the bay. The oldest part still standing is a keep from the 13th century.

One of the major attractions of the peninsula is the remains of **Skipness Castle and Chapel,** at Skipness along B8001, 10 miles (16km) south of Tarbert, opening onto Loch Fyne. The hamlet was once a Norse village. The ruins of the ancient chapel and 13th-century castle look out onto the Sounds of Kilbrannan and Bute. In its heyday, it could control shipping along Loch Fyne. A five-story tower remains.

Before striking out to visit the peninsula, consider stopping at the **Tairbeart Heritage Centre** (© **01880/820-190**), immediately south of the village. Through various artifacts and exhibits, it traces life on the peninsula that's now largely vanished. Admission is £3 ($4.50); open daily from 10am to 5pm.

ACCOMMODATIONS

Stonefield Castle Hotel 🏨🏨   The best hotel in the area occupies a commanding position on 66 acres (26.7 hectares) of wooded grounds and luxurious gardens 2 miles (3km) outside Tarbert. The Stonefield, with turrets and a steeply pitched roof, was built in the 19th century by the Campbells. The well-appointed guest rooms come in a variety of sizes, each with a combination tub/shower. The gardens are one of the world's best repositories for more than 20 species of tree-size Himalayan rhododendrons, which in April are a riot of color. The kitchen staff does its own baking, and meals feature produce from the hotel's garden.

Tarbert PA29 6YJ. © **01880/820-836.** Fax 01880/820-929. 33 units. Double £134–£148 ($201–$222) Double £154–£164 ($231–$246) Sun–Thurs, £184 ($276) Fri–Sat; suite £200 ($300) daily. Rates include half-board. AE, MC, V. **Amenities:** Restaurant, bar; outdoor pool; small gym; sauna; room service. *In room:* TV, coffeemaker, hair dryer.

West Loch Hotel   This 18th-century inn stands in a rural setting beside A83, a mile (1.6km) southwest of town in low-lying flatlands midway between the forest and the loch. The inn was originally built as a staging post for coaches and for farmers driving their cattle to market. It contains two bars and a handful of open fireplaces and wood-burning stoves. The small guest rooms are modestly furnished but comfortable, often with views of the estuary. Each has a small bathroom with either tub or shower. The pub and restaurant specialize in local seafood and game.

Tarbert PA29 6YF. © **01880/820-283.** Fax 01880/820-930. 7 units. £58 ($87) double. Rates include Scottish breakfast. MC, V. **Amenities:** Restaurant, 2 bars; limited room service. *In room:* TV, coffeemaker, hair dryer, no phone.

DINING

Anchorage Restaurant 🏨 *Finds* SCOTTISH/SEAFOOD   The Anchorage remains unpretentious despite its many culinary awards. Housed in a stone harborfront building that was once a customs house, it offers a daily menu of such perfectly crafted seafood dishes as king scallops sautéed with lemon-lime butter and brochette of monkfish with saffron rice. A selection of European wines is available to accompany your fish.

Harbour St., Quayside. © **01880/820-881.** Reservations recommended. Main courses £10–£16 ($15–$24). MC, V. Daily 7–10pm. Closed Jan.

CARRADALE 🎏

On the lusher eastern coast of Kintyre, 14 miles (22.5km) north of Campbeltown, Carradale is a small town opening onto the shores of Kilbrannan Sound. People come here to walk and relax; they can also go pony trekking, windsurfing, or picnicking in several scenic spots. **Carradale Beach** is equipped with facilities for watersports, and you can swim if you don't mind the chilly waters. The fishing fleet is anchored in the harbor, and herring boats set out from here each night.

Those interested in historic sites can seek out the ruins of **Saddell Abbey** along B842, 9 miles (14.5km) northwest of Campbeltown. This Cistercian abbey was built in the 12th century by one of the lords of the Isles. The walls of the original building remain, and there are several sculptured grave slabs.

Wallis Hunter Designs, The Steading (📞 **01583/431-683**), sells handcrafted gold and silver jewelry inspired by Celtic patterns and the designs of Charles Rennie Mackintosh. Hours are Monday through Friday from 8:30am to 5pm and Saturday from 9am to 1pm.

ACCOMMODATIONS & DINING

Carradale Hotel   Built around 1800, the Carradale was the first hotel to open on the eastern side of the peninsula. Set in a garden in the center of this hamlet opposite the War Memorial, it offers a comfortable high-ceilinged dining room, a lounge bar serving pub meals, and small, pleasantly furnished guest rooms. Fresh local produce, often from the hotel's garden, is used in the kitchen. Affordable bar meals are available at lunch and dinner; more expensive fixed-price dinners are served in the restaurant.

Carradale PA28 6RY. 📞 and fax **01583/431-223.** www.carradalehotel.com. 16 units, 12 with private bathroom. £51.50 ($77.25) per person double. Rates include breakfast. MC, V. **Amenities:** Restaurant, bar; mountain bikes; sauna; room service; laundry service. *In room:* TV, coffeemaker, hair dryer, no phone.

CAMPBELTOWN

Campbeltown is a fishing port and resort at the southern tip of the Kintyre Peninsula, 176 miles (283km) northwest of Edinburgh and 135 miles (217km) northwest of Glasgow. Popularly known as the "wee toon," Campbeltown has long been linked with fishing and has a shingle beach. For one of the greatest walks on the peninsula, see Davaar Island, below.

The **tourist office** is at MacKinnon House, The Pier (📞 **01586/552-056;** www.visitscottishheritage.org). It's open from late June to mid-September, Monday through Saturday from 9am to 6:30pm and Sunday from 11am to 5pm; mid-September to late October, Monday through Friday from 10am to 5pm and Sunday from 10am to 4pm; late October to March, Monday through Friday from 10am to 4pm; April, Monday through Saturday from 10am to 5pm; and May to late June, Monday through Saturday from 10am to 5pm and Sunday from noon to 5pm.

EXPLORING THE AREA

On the quayside in the heart of town is the 14th-century **Campbeltown Cross.** This Celtic cross is the finest piece of carving from the Middle Ages left in Kintyre.

One of the area's most famous golf courses, the **Machrilhansih Golf Club,** lies nearby (📞 **01586/810-213**). It's a 6,228-yard (5,667m), par-70 course. Monday through Friday and Sunday, the greens fees are £30 ($45) per round or £50 ($75) per day; on Saturday, the fees are £40 ($60) per round or £60 ($90) per day. No club rentals are available; trolleys cost £4 ($6.60).

Oystercatcher Crafts & Gallery, 10 Hall St. (© **01586/553-070**), sells Campbeltown pottery, wood carvings, and paintings by local artists. If you'd like to take a scenic drive and go shopping at the same time, head for **Ronachan Silks,** Ronachan Farmhouse at Clachan (© **01880/740-242**), 25 miles (40km) north of Campbeltown on Route 83. In this unusual location, you can buy fashionable clothing and accessories, including kimonos, caftans, women's scarves, men's ties, and cushions. Call ahead to confirm opening times.

ACCOMMODATIONS & DINING

Argyll Arms Hotel   The Duke of Argyll no longer calls this his home, although he still maintains a suite on the second floor even though he sold the imposing stone building to be converted into a hotel. The public rooms still possess an aura of Victorian opulence, but the guest rooms are modernized and fairly modest. The rooms come in a variety of sizes, each traditionally furnished and outfitted with a small bathroom with a combination tub/shower. The restaurant specializes in moderately priced fish fresh from the quay.

Main St., Campbeltown PA28 6AB. © **01586/553-431.** Fax 01586/553-594. www.members.aol.com/argyllarms/ArgyllArms.html. 25 units. £60 ($90) double. Rates include Scottish breakfast. AE, DC, MC, V. **Amenities:** Restaurant, 2 bars; laundry. *In room:* TV, coffeemaker, hair dryer, iron.

Craigard House   This 1882 inn is in a neck-and-neck race with Argyll Arms as the best place to stay in the area. The dignified, monastic-looking pile with a bell tower is perched on the northern edge of the loch, about a half mile (1km) from the town center. The guest rooms come with contemporary-looking furniture and some vestiges of the original plasterwork, while the public areas are more traditional and Victorian. Each unit comes with a small bathroom, some with tub, some with shower only.

The restaurant's weekly menu may include savory fish crepes, pan-fried duck breast with brandy and pepper-cream sauce, and chicken cacciatore.

Low Askomil, Campbeltown PA28 6EP. © **01586/554-242.** Fax 01586/551-137. 11 units. www.craigard-house.co.uk. £55–£100 ($82.50–$150) double. Rates include breakfast. MC, V. **Amenities:** Restaurant, bar; limited room service; laundry. *In room:* TV, coffeemaker.

CAMPBELTOWN AFTER DARK

Pubs, not surprisingly, are the nightlife here, including two that host live music. They're in the center of the village, next door to each other. The **Feathers Cross Street** (© **01586/554-604**), with stone walls, wooden floors, and hanging lamps, hosts free bands playing a range of musical styles on Thursday nights. Open daily from 11am to 12:30am. The **Commercial Cross Street** (© **01586/553-703**) has a variety of live music on Fridays and alternate Saturdays. A specialty here is real ale. Open Monday through Saturday from 11am to 1am and Sunday from 12:30pm to 1am. You'll find a quieter evening at the **Burnside**

Moments Escape to the Isle That Time Forgot

Davaar Island, in Campbeltown Loch, is accessible at low tide by those willing to cross the Dhorlin, a half-mile (1km) run of shingle-paved causeway; boat trips are also possible (ask at the tourist office). Once on the island, you can visit a **crucifixion cave painting,** the work of local Archibald MacKinnon, painted in 1887. It takes about 1½ hours to walk around this tidal island, with its natural rock gardens.

Finds **A Journey to Blood Rock**

Dunaverty Rock is a jagged hill marking the extreme southern tip of the Kintyre Peninsula. Located 9 miles (14.5km) south of Cambeltown and called "Blood Rock" by the locals, it was once the site of a MacDonald stronghold known as Dunaverty Castle, although nothing remains of it today. In 1647, it was the scene of a great massacre, in which some 300 citizens lost their lives. You can reach it by a local bus (marked SOUTH END) traveling from Campbeltown south about six times a day. Nearby, you'll find a series of isolated, unsupervised beaches and the 18-hole **Dunaverty Golf Course** (© 01586/830-677).

Bar, Burnside Street (© **01586/552-306**), open daily from 11am to 1am. Conversation and local single malts are the preferred distractions here.

SOUTHEND & THE MULL OF KINTYRE

Some 10 miles (16km) south of Campbeltown, the village of Southend stands across from the Mull of Kintyre, and Monday through Saturday three buses a day run here from Campbeltown. It has sandy beaches, a golf course, and views across the sea to the Island of Sanda and to Ireland. Legend has it that footprints on a rock near the ruin of an old chapel mark the spot where St. Columba first set foot on Scottish soil. Other historians suggest the footprints mark the spot where ancient kings were crowned.

About 11 miles (18km) from Campbeltown is the Mull of Kintyre. From Southend, you can take a narrow road until you reach the "gap," from which you can walk down to the lighthouse, a distance of 1½ miles (2.5km) before you reach the final point. Expect westerly gales as you go along. This is one of the wildest and most remote parts of the peninsula, and it's this desolation that appeals to visitors. The Mull of Kintyre is only 13 miles (21km) from Ireland. When local resident Paul McCartney made it the subject of a song, hundreds of fans flocked to the area.

3 The Isle of Gigha & Scotland's Finest Gardens

3 miles (5km) W of Kintyre's western coast

One of the southern Hebrides lying 3 miles (5km) off the Kintyre Peninsula's west coast, the 6-mile-long (10km) Isle of Gigha is often called sacred and legendary. Little changed over the centuries, it boasts Scotland's Garden of Eden.

ESSENTIALS

GETTING THERE   Take a **ferry** to Gigha from Tayinloan, halfway up the west coast of Kintyre. Sailings are daily and take about 20 minutes, depositing you at **Ardminish,** the main hamlet on Gigha. The round-trip fare is £17.90 ($26.85) for an auto plus £4.75 ($7.15) per passenger. For ferry schedules, call © **01880/730-253** in Kennacraig.

VISITOR INFORMATION   There's no local tourist office, so ask at Campbeltown on the Kintyre Peninsula (see "The Kintyre Peninsula," above).

GETTING AROUND   Because most likely you'll arrive without a car and there's no local bus service, you can either walk or call **Oliver's Taxi** at © **01583/505-251.**

SEEING THE SIGHTS

Gigha is visited mainly by those wanting to explore its famous gardens, Scotland's finest. Be prepared to spend your entire day walking. The **Achamore House Gardens** 𝒜𝒜𝒜, a mile (1.6km) from the ferry dock at Ardminish, overflow with roses, hydrangeas, camellias, rhododendrons, and azaleas. On a 50-acre (20.3-hectare) site, they were the creation of the late Sir James Horlick, one of the world's great gardeners. The house isn't open to the public, but the gardens are open year-round, daily from dawn to dusk. Admission is £2 ($3). For information about the gardens, call the Gigha Hotel (see below).

The island has a rich Viking past (the Vikings stored their loot here after plundering the west coast of Scotland), and cairns and ruins still remain. **Creag Bhan,** the highest hill, rises more than 330 feet (100m). From the top you can look out onto the islands of Islay and Jura as well as Kintyre; on a clear day, you can also see Ireland. The **Ogham Stone** is one of only two standing stones in the Hebrides that bears an Ogham inscription, a form of script used in the Scottish kingdom of Dalriada. High on a ridge overlooking the village of Ardminish are the ruins of the **Church of Kilchattan,** dating back to the 13th century.

ACCOMMODATIONS & DINING

Gigha Hotel 𝒜   Standing in a lonely, windswept location, this hotel lies a 5-minute walk from the island's ferry landing. Built in the 1700s as a farmhouse, it contains Gigha's only pub, one of its two restaurants, and its only accommodations except for some cottages. Each small but cozy room contains a shower-only bathroom. Rather expensive fixed-price dinners are served daily to both guests and nonguests; bar lunches are more affordable.

Ardminish, Isle of Gigha PA41 7AD. 𝒞 and fax **01583/505-254.** Fax 015835/052-44. www.isle-of-gigha. co.uk. 13 units, 11 with private bathroom. £120 ($180) double with shared facilities; £130 ($195) with private bathroom. Rates include half-board. MC, V. **Amenities:** Restaurant, bar; limited room service; laundry service. *In room:* TV, coffeemaker, hair dryer.

4 The Isle of Islay: Queen of the Hebrides 𝒜𝒜

16 miles (26km) W of the Kintyre Peninsula, ¾ mile (1km) SW of Jura

Islay (pronounced *eye*-lay) is the southernmost island of the Inner Hebrides, separated only by a narrow sound from Jura. At its maximum, Islay is only 20 miles (32km) wide and 25 miles (40km) long. Called the "Queen of the Hebrides," it's a peaceful and unspoiled island of moors, salmon-filled lochs, sandy bays, and wild rocky cliffs.

ESSENTIALS

GETTING THERE   Caledonian MacBrayne **ferries** (𝒞 **01475/650-100**) provide daily service to Islay. You leave West Tarbert on the Kintyre Peninsula, arriving in Port Askaig on Islay in about 2 hours. There's also service to Port Ellen. For information, call or check with Caledonian MacBrayne at the ferry terminal in Gourock.

VISITOR INFORMATION   The tourist office is at **Bowmore,** The Square (𝒞 **01496/810-254**). It's open May through September, Monday through Saturday from 9:30am to 5pm and Sunday from 2 to 5pm; and October through April, Monday through Friday from noon to 4pm.

EXPLORING THE ISLAND

Near **Port Charlotte** are the graves of the U.S. seamen and army troops who lost their lives in 1918 when their carriers, the *Tuscania* and the *Otranto,* were torpedoed off the shores of Islay. There's a memorial tower on the **Mull of Oa,** 8 miles (13km) from Port Ellen. For the greatest **walk** on the island, go along Mull of Oa Road heading toward the signposted solar-powered Carraig Fhada lighthouse, some 1½ miles (2.5km) away. The Oa peninsula was once the haunt of illicit whisky distillers and smugglers; the area is filled with sheer cliffs riddled with caves.

The island's capital is **Bowmore,** on the coast across from Port Askaig. Here you can see a fascinating Round Church (no corners for the devil to hide in). But the most important town is **Port Ellen** on the south coast, a holiday and golfing resort and Islay's principal port. The 18-hole **Machrie golf course** (© **01496/302-310**) is 3 miles (5km) from Port Ellen.

You can see the ancient seat of the lords of the Isles, the ruins of two castles, and several Celtic crosses. The ancient **Kildalton Crosses** are in the Kildalton churchyard, about 7½ miles (12km) northeast of Port Ellen—they're two of the finest Celtic crosses in Scotland. The ruins of the 14th-century fortress, **Dunyvaig Castle,** are just south of Kildalton.

In the southwestern part of Islay in Port Charlotte, the **Museum of Islay Life** (© **01496/850-358**) has a wide collection of island artifacts. The museum is open from Easter to October, Monday through Saturday from 10am to 4pm. Admission is £2.30 ($3.45) for adults, £2.30 ($3.45) for seniors, and £1 ($1.50) for children. The Portnahaven bus from Bowmore stops here.

Loch Gruinart cuts into the northern part of Islay, 7 miles (11km) northeast of Port Charlotte and 8 miles (13km) north of Bowmore. As the winter home for wild geese, it has attracted bird-watchers for decades. In 1984, the 3,000 acres (1,215 hectares) of moors and farmland around the loch were turned into the **Loch Gruinart Nature Reserve.**

This is another place for great walks. Beaches rise out of the falling tides, but they're too cold and rocky for serious swimming. This is a lonely and bleak coastline, but because of that it has a certain kind of beauty, especially as you make your way north along its eastern shoreline. On a clear day, you can see the Hebridean islands of Oronsay and Colonsay in the distance.

TOURING THE DISTILLERIES

The island is noted for its distilleries, which still produce single-malt Highland whiskies by the antiquated pot-still method. Of these, **Laphroaig Distillery,** less than a mile (1.5km) along the road from Ardbeg to Port Ellen (© **01496/302-418**), offers guided tours Monday through Friday, twice daily. Admission is free and includes a sample dram; call for an appointment. **Lagavoulin,** Port Ellen (© **01496/302-400**), offers tours Monday through Friday, three times a day. The admission of £3 ($4.50) includes a sample and a £3 ($4.50) voucher off the price of a bottle of whisky. The gift shop is open Monday through Friday from 8:30am to noon and 1 to 4:30pm.

Bowmore Distillery, School Street, Bowmore (© **01496/810-441**), conducts tours Monday through Friday, twice a day, with additional Saturday and weekday tour times in summer. The admission is £2 ($3), which includes samples and a voucher worth £2 ($3). Purchases can be made without taking the tour by stopping at the gift shop, open Monday through Friday from 9am to 4:30pm and Saturday from 10am to 12:30pm.

Port Askaig is home to two distilleries, **Bunnahabhain** (© **01496/840-646**), which offers free tours by appointment and runs a gift shop open Monday through Friday from 9am to 4pm, and **Coal Ila** (© **01496/840-207**), which has tours from Easter to September, Monday through Friday. Admission is £3 ($4.50). Its gift shop is open for visitors at the end of each tour.

SHOPPING

The **Islay Woolen Mill,** Bridgend (© **01496/810-563**), has been making a wide range of country tweeds and accessories for more than a century. It made all the tweeds used in Mel Gibson's *Braveheart.* The mill shop, open Monday through Saturday from 10am to 5pm, sells items made with the *Braveheart* tweeds as well as tasteful Shetland wool ties, mufflers, Jacob mufflers and ties, flat caps, travel rugs, and scarves.

Another good place to find souvenirs is **Port Ellen Pottery,** Port Ellen (© **01496/302-345**), which sells brightly colored goblets, jugs, mugs, and other functional wares daily from 10am to 5pm. Note that the shop is very small and doesn't handle shipping on larger purchases.

ACCOMMODATIONS

Bridgend Hotel *✿*   Victorian spires cap the slate-covered roofs, while roses creep up the walls of this hotel that's part of a complex including a roadside barn and one of the most beautiful gardens on Islay. This is one of the oldest hotels on the island, with somber charm and country pleasures. Guests enjoy drinks beside the open fireplaces in the Victorian cocktail lounge and the rustic pub, where locals gather at the end of the day. Many nonguests opt for a moderately priced dinner in the high-ceilinged dining room. The midsize bedrooms are comfortably and conservatively furnished, each with a small bathroom with either a tub or a shower.

Bridgend, Isle of Islay PA44 7PJ. © 01496/810-212. Fax 01496/810-960. 10 units. £44 ($66) per person; £60 ($90) per person with dinner. Rates include Scottish breakfast. MC, V. **Amenities:** Restaurant, 2 bars; room service; laundry. *In room:* TV, coffeemaker, hair dryer.

Lochside Hotel   Behind a lackluster facade, this welcoming hotel opens onto panoramic views over Loch Indaal. The guest rooms are comfortable and well maintained; each has a small, shower-only bathroom. The bar boasts one of the largest selections of Islay malt whiskies in the world, some 200 in all, and is a favorite hangout for locals. The restaurant specializes in moderately priced seafood but offers vegetarian options as well.

19 Shore St., Bowmore, Isle of Islay PA43 7LB. © 01496/810-244. Fax 01496/810-390. www.lochsidehotel. co.uk. 8 units. £69–£83 ($103.50–$124.50) double. Rates include breakfast. MC, V. Take ferry from Kennacraig, then the A846 to the village center. **Amenities:** Restaurant and bar; limited room service. *In room:* TV, coffeemaker.

Port Askaig Hotel   On the Sound of Islay overlooking the pier, this inn dates from the 18th century but was built on the site of an even older inn. It offers island hospitality and Scottish fare and is a favorite of anglers; the bar is popular with local fisherfolk. The guest rooms are a bit small, but each is furnished in a comfortable though not stylish way, with a little bathroom, some with shower only.

Hwy. A846 at the ferry crossing to Jura, Port Askaig, Isle of Islay PA46 7RD. © 01496/840-245. Fax 01496/ 840-295. www.portaskaig.co.uk. 8 units. £76 ($114) double. Rates include Scottish breakfast. V. **Amenities:** Restaurant, 2 bars; limited room service. *In room:* TV, coffeemaker, hair dryer, no phone.

Port Charlotte Hotel   This 1829 hotel—actually a trio of cottages joined together—stands next to the small sandy beaches of Port Charlotte with views over Loch Indaal. After being refurbished, it immediately won a four-crown rating from the Scottish Tourist Board. The guest rooms are beautiful, most decorated with antiques. Each has a small bathroom, some with both tub and shower. Public spaces include a large conservatory, a comfortable lounge, and a bar.

The restaurant is the best place to dine in the area. Typical dishes are sirloin of Islay steak, freshly caught Islay lobster, and grilled filet of Scottish turbot. For starters, try the Loch Fyne smoked salmon.

Main St., Port Charlotte, Isle of Islay PA48 7TU. ℭ **01496/850-360.** Fax 01496/850-361. 10 units. £90 ($135) double. Rates include Scottish breakfast. MC, V. **Amenities:** Restaurant, bar; limited room service; laundry. *In room:* TV, dataport, hair dryer, iron.

DINING

Other dining options include the restaurants at the hotels listed above.

The Croft Kitchen BRITISH   On the main highway running through town, this is a low-slung, homey, and utterly unpretentious place with a friendly staff. Holding no more than 40 customers at a time, it serves wine, beer, and whisky distilled on Islay, along with generous portions of down-home food. You'll find lots of fresh fish and shellfish, roasted Islay venison with rowanberry jelly, and steamed mussels with garlic mayonnaise.

Port Charlotte, Isle of Islay. ℭ **01496/850-230.** Sandwiches £1.70–£2.50 ($2.55–$3.75); main courses £8–£10 ($12–$15) lunch, £9–£14 ($13.50–$21) dinner. MC, V. Daily 10am–8:30pm (last order). Closed mid-Oct to mid-Mar.

ISLAY AFTER DARK

After work, distillery employees gather at the **Harbour Inn,** Main Street in Bowmore (ℭ **01496/810-330**), an old pub with stone walls, a fireplace, and wooden floors and furnishings. It's open Monday through Saturday from 11am to 1am and Sunday from noon to 1am. Local seafood is served at lunch and dinner. In summer, reservations are recommended.

5 The Isle of Jura: Deer Island ⭐

¾ mile (1km) E of Islay

Jura is the fourth largest of the Inner Hebrides, 27 miles (43km) long and varying from 2 to 8 miles (3 to 13km) in breadth. It takes its name from the Norse *jura*, meaning "deer island." The red deer on Jura—at 4 feet high (1.2m), the largest wild animals roaming Scotland—outnumber the people by about 20 to 1. The hearty islanders number only about 250, and most of them live along the east coast. Jura is relatively unknown, and its mountains, soaring cliffs, snug coves, and moors make it an inviting place.

George Orwell lived on Jura in the bitter postwar winters of 1946 and 1947. Although sick, he was working on his masterpiece *1984,* which was published in 1949. He almost lost his life when he and his adopted son ventured too close to the whirlpool in the Gulf of Corryvreckan. They were saved by local fishermen and he went on to finish his masterwork, only to die in London of tuberculosis in 1950.

ESSENTIALS

GETTING THERE   From Kennacraig (West Loch, Tarbert) you can go to Port Askaig on Islay (see above) taking one of the **Caledonian MacBrayne ferries** (ℭ **01880/730-253**). The cost is £53 ($79.50) for a car and £9.70 ($14.55) per passenger each way (4-day return tickets are more economical). From Port

Askaig, you can take a second ferry to Feolin on Jura; call **Western Ferries** (℡ **01496/840-681**). Car spaces must be booked in advance. The cost for a vehicle is £6.60 ($9.90), plus 90p ($1.35) for a passenger one-way.

VISITOR INFORMATION The Isle of Islay (see "The Isle of Islay: Queen of the Hebrides," above) has the nearest tourist information office.

EXPLORING THE ISLAND

Because most of the island is accessible only by foot, wear sturdy walking shoes and bring raingear. The best place for walks is the **Jura House Garden and Grounds,** at the southern tip. These grounds were laid out by the Victorians to take advantage of the natural beauty of the region, and you can experience the gardens' sheltered walks and panoramic views daily between 9am and 5pm. Admission is £2.50 ($3.75). From June to August, it's also the best place on the island to have tea, but only on Saturday and Sunday. Call ℡ **01496/820-315** for details.

The capital, **Craighouse,** is hardly more than a hamlet. From Islay, you can take a 5-minute ferry ride to Jura from Port Askaig, docking at the Feolin Ferry berth. The island's landscape is dominated by the **Paps of Jura** that reach a peak of 2,571 feet (780m) at Beinn-an-Oir. An arm of the sea, **Loch Tarbert** nearly divides the island, cutting into it for nearly 6 miles (10km).

The square tower of **Claig Castle,** now in ruins, was the stronghold of the MacDonalds until they were subdued by the Campbells in the 17th century. The **Jura Distillery,** at Craighouse (℡ **01496/820-240**), is closed in July and August but can be toured any other month for free. A sample is given at the end of the tour, which must be arranged by calling ahead.

The managers of the island's only hotel conduct special tours by Land Rover to such curiosities as the **Corryvreckan whirlpool,** notorious to west coast sailors. Inquire at the hotel; the cost is about £12 ($18).

ACCOMMODATIONS & DINING

Jura Hotel ✿ *Finds* The island's only hotel is a sprawling gray-walled building near the center of the hamlet. (Craighouse lies east of Feolin along the coast.) Sections date from the 1600s, but what you see today was built in 1956. The midsize guest rooms are of high quality; most have small bathrooms with tub/shower combinations. In this remote outpost, you'll be sure to get a tranquil night's sleep. Affordable meals are served daily at lunch and dinner; the dining room's specialty is Jura-bred venison.

Craighouse, Isle of Jura PA60 7XU. ℡ **01496/820-243.** Fax 01496/820249. 18 units, 12 with private bathroom. £70 ($105) double without bathroom; £80 ($120) double with bathroom; £100 ($150) suite. Rates include Scottish breakfast. AE, DC, MC, V. Closed 2 weeks in Dec–Jan. **Amenities:** Restaurant, 2 bars, lounge; limited room service. *In room:* Coffeemaker, no phone.

6 Inveraray ✿✿

99 miles (159km) NW of Edinburgh, 57 miles (92km) NW of Glasgow, 38 miles (61km) SE of Oban

The small resort and royal burgh of Inveraray occupies a splendid setting on the upper shores of Loch Fyne. It's particularly attractive when you approach from the east on A83. Across a little inlet, you can see the town lying peacefully on a bit of land fronting on the loch.

ESSENTIALS

GETTING THERE The nearest **rail station** is at Dumbarton, 45 miles (72km) southeast, where you can make bus connections to Inveraray. For rail schedules, call ℡ **08457/484-950.**

The National Express operates **buses** out of Glasgow, heading for Dumbarton, before continuing to Inveraray. Transit time is about 2 hours. Monday through Saturday, four buses make this run (only two on Sunday). The fare is £6 ($9) one-way, £10 ($15) round-trip. For bus schedules, call © 0990/808-080.

If you're **driving** from Oban, head east along A85 until you reach the junction with A819, at which point you continue south.

VISITOR INFORMATION   The **tourist office** is on Front Street (© 01499/ 302-063). It's open from June to mid-September, daily from 9am to 6pm; mid-September to October, April, and May, Monday through Saturday from 9am to 5pm and Sunday from noon to 5pm; and November to March, daily from noon to 4pm.

SEEING THE SIGHTS

At one end of the main street of the town is a **Celtic burial cross** from Iona. The parish church is divided by a wall that enables mass to be held simultaneously in Gaelic and English.

Because so many of its attractions and those in its environs involve walking, hope for a sunny day. A local beauty spot is the **Ardkinglas Woodland Garden** (© 01499/600-263), 4 miles (6.5km) east of Inveraray at the head of Loch Fyne. People drive from all over Britain to see Scotland's greatest collection of conifers and its masses of rhododendrons bursting into bloom in June. Admission is £2 ($3); it's open daily from 9am to 5pm.

If you have a car, you can explore this scenic part of Scotland from Cairndow. Head east along A83 until you reach the junction with A815, at which point proceed south along the western shore of Loch Fyne until you come to the famous inn at Creggans (see below), directly north of **Strachur.** Five miles (8km) south from the Creggans Inn along the loch will take you to the old **Castle Lachlan** at Strathiachian, the 13th-century castle of the MacLachlan clan. Now in romantic ruins, it was besieged by the English in 1745. The MacLachlans were fervent Jacobites and played a major role in the uprising.

Auchindran Township Open Air Museum   Auchindran is an original West Highland common tenancy township, a unique survivor of the long-gone townships once common in the Highlands. More than 20 structures remain, most of them restored to illustrate the lifestyle of Highlanders in bygone days. The visitor center features displays, a shop, and other facilities.

About 5 miles (8km) south of Inveraray on A83, just outside the hamlet of Furnace. © 01499/500-235. Admission £3.80 ($5.70) adults, £3 ($4.50) seniors, £1.80 ($2.70) children, £9.50 ($14.25) per family. Apr–Sept daily 10am–5pm.

Crarae Glen Gardens ⚘   Lying along Loch Fyne, these are among Scotland's most beautiful gardens, some 50 acres (20.3 hectares) of rich plantings along with waterfalls and panoramic vistas of the loch. You can enjoy the beauty while hiking one of the many paths.

8 miles (13km) southwest of Inveraray along A83, near the hamlet of Minard. © 0154/688-6614. Admission £2.50 ($3.75) adults, £1.50 ($2.25) children, £7 ($10.50) per family. (Oct–Mar payment is by the honor system—drop your money in the box at the entrance.) Daily 10am–5pm.

Inveraray Castle ⚘⚘   The hereditary seat of the dukes of Argyll, Inveraray Castle has been headquarters of the Clan Campbell since the early 15th century. The gray-green stone castle is among the earliest examples of Gothic Revival in Britain and offers a fine collection of pictures and 18th-century French furniture, old porcelain, and an Armoury Hall, which alone contains 1,300 pieces.

⌒ Hiking in Argyll Forest Park

Argyll Forest Park, in the southern Highlands, stretches almost to Loch Fyne and is made up of Benmore, Ardgartan, and Glenbranter. The park covers an area of 60,000 acres (24,3000 hectares), contains some of Scotland's most panoramic scenery, and takes in a wide variety of habitats, from lush forests and waterside to bleaker grassy moorlands and mountains. The Clyde sea lochs cut deep into the forested areas, somewhat in the way fjord "fingers" cut into the Norwegian coast; in the northern part are the Arrochar Alps (so called), where Ben Arthur reaches a height of 2,891 feet (877m).

The park attracts those interested in natural history and wildlife as well as rock climbers, hikers, and hill walkers. There are many recreational activities and dozens of forest walks for trail blazers with all degrees of skill. Trails leading through forests to the loftier peaks are strenuous and meant for skilled hikers; others are easier, including paths from the Younger Botanic Garden by Loch Eck leading to Puck's Glen.

There's abundant wildlife in the sea lochs: shark, sea otters, gray seals, sea scorpions, crabs, shrimp, sea lemons, sea anemones, and sea slugs, among other inhabitants. Boats and canoes are available for rent. One of the park's biggest thrills is exploring the underwater caves of Loch Long.

In the early spring and summer, the park trails are at their most beautiful—woodland birds create choruses of song, and the forest is filled with violets, wood anemones, primroses, and bluebells. Sometimes the wildflowers are so thick they're like carpets. In the rainy climate of the southern Highlands, ferns and mosses also grow in abundance.

To reach the park, take A83 to B828 heading for Loch Goll or follow A815 to Loch Eck and Loch Long. Both Arrochar and Tarbet, stops on the Glasgow–Fort William rail line, are on the periphery of the park's northeast frontier.

The best place for lodging is **Dunoon,** to the south on the Cowal Peninsula, an easy gateway to the park. Dunoon has been a holiday resort since 1790, created for the "merchant princes" of Glasgow. Recreational facilities abound, including an indoor pool, tennis courts, and an 18-hole golf course. To pick up information about the park and a trail map, go to the **Dunoon Tourist Center,** 7 Alexandra Parade (℡ **01369/ 703-785).** It's open April to late June, September, and October, Monday through Friday from 9am to 5:30pm and Saturday and Sunday from 10am to 5pm; late June to August, Monday through Saturday from 9am to 6pm and Sunday from 10am to 5pm; November to March, Monday through Thursday from 9am to 5:30pm and Friday from 9am to 5pm.

On the grounds is a **Combined Operations Museum,** the only one of its kind in the United Kingdom. It displays the role No. 1 Combined Training Centre played at Inveraray in World War II. On exhibit are scale models, newspaper reports, campaign maps, photographs, wartime posters and cartoons, training scenes, and other mementos. A shop sells souvenirs and a tearoom serves home-made cakes and scones.

³/₄ mile (1km) northeast of Inveraray on Loch Fyne. Ⓒ **01499/302-203**. Admission £5.30 ($7.95) adults, £4.50 ($6.75) seniors, £3.50 ($5.25) children, £14 ($21) per family. Apr–June and Sept to mid-Oct Mon–Thurs 10am–1pm and 2–5:45pm, Sun 1–5:45pm; July–Aug Mon–Sat 10am–5:45pm, Sun 1–5:45pm.

ACCOMMODATIONS & DINING

Argyll Hotel   This 1755 inn boasts views of Loch Fyne and Loch Shira. The comfortable, midsize guest rooms feature decors ranging from flowered chintz to modern, no-nonsense functionality. All units come with small, shower-only bathrooms. On site are a public bar, a guests-only cocktail lounge, and a digni-fied restaurant serving five-course dinners.

Front St., Inveraray PA32 8XB. Ⓒ **01499/302-466**. Fax 01499/302-389. www.the-argyll-hotel.co.uk. 24 units. £62–£74 ($93–$111) double. Rates include Scottish breakfast. MC, V. **Amenities:** Restaurant, bar; room service; laundry service. *In room:* TV, coffeemaker, hair dryer.

Creggans Inn ℱ   This inn commemorates the spot where Mary Queen of Scots is said to have disembarked from her ship in 1563 on her way through the Highlands. Painted white and flanked by gardens, the inn rises across A815 from the sea and is owned by Sir Charles MacLean and his mother, Lady MacLean, author of several best-selling cookbooks, most of which are for sale here. The guest rooms are elegant and understated, all traditionally furnished and well maintained. Each is equipped with a private bathroom with combination tub/shower. Guests may use the upstairs sitting room and the garden-style lounge. The restaurant has a charcoal grill that produces succulent versions of Aberdeen Angus steaks and lamb kebabs, but you can also enjoy fresh seafood and venison. Reservations are a must. The bar features pub lunches beside an open fire.

Strachur PA27 8BX. Ⓒ **01369/860-279**. Fax 01369/860-637. www.creggans-inn.co.uk. 20 units. £110–£160 ($165–$240) double; £160–£200 ($240–$300) suite. Rates include Scottish breakfast. AE, DC, MC, V. **Amenities:** Restaurant, bar; room service; laundry service. *In room:* TV, coffeemaker, hair dryer.

George Hotel ℱ   One of the most charming hotels in town lies behind a facade built around 1775. Part of the charm derives from the old-fashioned bar, where the Guinness simply seems to taste better than in less evocative settings. The public areas are marked with flagstone floors, beamed ceilings, and blazing fireplaces. The guest rooms are cozy, done in an old-fashioned Scottish style. Some have king-size beds (unusual for Scotland) and claw-foot tubs. The restau-rant is among the most popular in town with locals, serving moderately priced lunches and dinners daily. Your choices include steaks prepared with pepper or mushroom sauce, grilled halibut, and grilled Loch Fyne salmon with white wine, prawns, and scallops.

Main St. E, Inveraray PA32 8TT. Ⓒ **01499/302-111**. Fax 01499/302-098. www.thegeorgehotel.co.uk. 12 units. £50–£65 ($75–$97.50) double. Rates include breakfast. MC, V. **Amenities:** Restaurant, bar. *In room:* TV, coffeemaker, hair dryer (on request).

7 Loch Awe: Scotland's Longest Loch ℱℱ

99 miles (159km) NW of Edinburgh, 24 miles (39km) E of Oban, 68 miles (109km) NW of Glasgow

Only a mile (1.6km) wide in most places and 22 miles (35.5km) long, Loch Awe is the longest loch in Scotland and acted as a natural freshwater moat protecting the Campbells of Inveraray from their enemies to the north. Along its banks are many reminders of its fortified past. The Forestry Commission has vast forests and signposted trails in this area, and a modern road makes it possible to travel around Loch Awe easily, so more than ever it's a popular center for angling and walking.

ESSENTIALS

GETTING THERE   The nearest **train station** is in Oban, where you'd have to take a connecting bus. **Scottish CityLink,** 1 Queens Park Place in Oban (© **01631/562-856** for schedules), has service to Glasgow with stopovers at Loch Awe. If you're **driving** from Oban, head east along A85.

VISITOR INFORMATION   Consult the tourist office in Oban (see "Oban: Gateway to Mull & the Inner Hebrides," below).

EXPLORING THE AREA

To the east of the top of Loch Awe, **Dalmally** is small, but because of its strategic position it has witnessed a lot of Scottish history. Its 18th-century church is built in an octagonal shape.

The ruins of **Kilchurn Castle** are at the northern tip of Loch Awe, west of Dalmally, and across from the south bank village of Loch Awe. A stronghold of the Campbells of Glen Orchy in 1440, it's a spectacular ruin with much of the original structure still intact. The ruins have been completely reinforced and balconied so you can now explore when the weather permits. Access is from an unmarked graveled lot. You may need boots if the weather is bad.

More convenient is to take any of about five boats a day (from March to November) departing from the piers in the village of Loch Awe. The ferries are maintained by the **Loch Awe Steam Packet Company,** Loch Awe Piers (© **01838/200-440**). Transit across the loch (a 10-minute ride) costs £6 ($9) and includes entrance to the ruins of Kilchurn. This steamship company and the **Hotel Ardanaiseig** (see below) are the only sources of information about the castle, which doesn't maintain an on-site staff.

Once you reach the castle, don't expect a guided tour, as the site is likely to be abandoned except for a patrol of goats and sheep. You can wander at will through the ruins following a self-guided tour marked by signs.

Among other reminders of the days when the Campbells of Inveraray held supreme power in the Loch Awe region, there's a ruined **castle** at Fincharn, at the southern end of the loch, and another on the island of Fraoch Eilean. The Isle of Inishail has an ancient **chapel and burial ground.** The bulk of **Ben Cruachan,** rising to 3,689 feet (1,119m), dominates Loch Awe at its northern end and attracts climbers and hikers. On the Ben is the world's second-largest hydroelectric power station, which pumps water from Loch Awe to a reservoir high up on the mountain.

Below the mountain are the **Falls of Cruachan** and the wild **Pass of Brander,** where Robert the Bruce routed the Clan MacDougall in 1308. The Pass of Brander was the scene of many a fierce battle in bygone times. Through it the waters of the Awe flow on their way to Loch Etive. This winding sea loch is 19 miles (30.5km) long, stretching from Dun Dunstaffnage Bay at Oban to Glen Etive, reaching into the Moor of Rannoch at the foot of the 3,000-foot (910m) **Buachaille Etive** (the Shepherd of Etive), into which Glencoe also reaches.

ACCOMMODATIONS & DINING

Hotel Ardanaiseig 🏰🏰   This gray-stone manorial seat was built in 1834 by a Campbell patriarch, who also planted some of the rarest trees in Britain. Today, clusters of fruit trees stand in a walled garden, and the rhododendrons and azaleas are a joy in May and June. The hotel has formal sitting rooms graced with big chintzy chairs and fresh flowers. Upstairs, the bedrooms are uniquely and traditionally furnished. The price of a room depends on its size, ranging from a small unit to a master bedroom with a loch view. Some bathrooms come with a shower only.

Kilchrenan by Taynuilt PA35 1HE. ② **800/548-7790** in the U.S., 800/463-7595 in Canada, or 01866/833-333. Fax 01866/833-222. www.ardanaiseig-hotel.com. 16 units. £198–£258 ($297–$387) double. AE, DC, MC, V. Closed Jan to mid-Feb. Drive 21 miles (34km) south of Oban by following the signs to Taynuilt, then turning onto B845 toward Kilchrenan. Turn left at the Kilchrenan Pub and continue 3.9 miles (6km), following signs into Ardanaiseig. No children under 8 accepted. **Amenities:** Restaurant; tennis court; small exercise room. *In room:* TV, coffeemaker, hair dryer.

8 Oban: Gateway to Mull & the Inner Hebrides ⊀

85 miles (137km) NW of Glasgow, 50 miles (80.5km) SW of Fort William

One of Scotland's leading coastal resorts, the bustling port of Oban is in a sheltered bay almost landlocked by the island of Kerrera. A busy fishing port in the 18th century, Oban is now heavily dependent on tourism. Since it lacks major attractions of its own, it's often used as a major refueling stop for those exploring the greater west coast of Scotland.

ESSENTIALS

GETTING THERE From Glasgow, the West Highland **trains** run directly to Oban, with departures from Glasgow's Queen Street Station (call ② **08457/ 484-950** for 24-hour information). Three trains per day (only two on Sun) make the 3-hour run to Oban; a one-way fare costs £15 ($22.50).

Frequent **buses** depart from Buchanan Station in Glasgow, taking about the same time as the train, although a one-way fare is only £10 ($17). Call **Scottish CityLink** at ② **01631/332-7133** in Glasgow or ② **01631/562-856** in Oban.

If you're **driving** from Glasgow, head northwest along A82 until reaching Tyndrum, then go west along A85 until you come to Oban.

VISITOR INFORMATION The **tourist office** is on Argyll Square (② **01631/ 563-122**). It's open from April to mid-June and mid-September to October, Monday through Friday from 10am to 5:30pm and Saturday and Sunday from noon to 4pm; mid-June to mid-September, Monday through Saturday from 9am to 6:30pm and Sunday from 10am to 5pm; and November to March, Monday through Saturday from 9:30am to 5pm and Sunday from noon to 4pm.

SPECIAL EVENTS The **Oban Highland Games** are held in August, with massed pipe bands marching through the streets. The **Oban Pipe Band** regularly parades on the main street throughout summer.

EXPLORING THE AREA

To appreciate the coastal scenery of Oban to its fullest, consider renting a bike from **Oban Cycles**, 9 Craigard Rd. (② **01631/562-444**).

From **Pulpit Hill** in Oban, there's a fine view across the Firth of Lorn and the Sound of Mull. Overlooking the town is an unfinished replica of the Colosseum of Rome, **McCaig's Tower**, built by a banker, John Stuart McCaig, from 1897 to 1900. Its walls are 2 feet (61cm) thick and 37 to 40 feet (11 to 12m) high. The courtyard within is landscaped, and the tower is floodlit at night. Outsiders have been heard to refer to the tower as "McCaig's Folly," but Obanites are proud of the structure and deplore this term.

Near the little granite **Cathedral of the Isles,** 1 mile (1.6km) north of the end of the bay, is the ruin of the 13th-century **Dunollie Castle,** seat of the lords of Lorn, who once owned a third of Scotland.

On the island of Kerrera stands **Gylen Castle,** home of the MacDougalls, dating back to 1587.

You can visit **Dunstaffnage Castle** ☆ (© **01631/562-465**), 3½ miles (5.5km) north, believed to have been the royal seat of the Dalriadic monarchy in the 8th century. It was probably the site of the Scots court until Kenneth MacAlpin's unification of Scotland and the transfer of the seat of government to Scone in the 10th century. The present castle was built about 1263. The castle is open daily: April through October from 9am to 6:30pm (to 8pm July and August), and November through March from 9:30am to 4:30pm. Admission is £2 ($3) for adults, £1.40 ($2.10) for seniors, and 80p ($1.20) for children. You can take a bus from the Oban rail station to Dunbeg, but it's still a 1½-mile (2.5km) walk to the castle.

SHOPPING

Cathness Glass Oban, Railway Pier (© **01631/563-386**), is the best place for shopping, though you'll find plenty of gift and souvenir shops around town. At this center, locally produced glass items range from functional dinner- and glassware to purely artistic curios. This firm has one of the most prestigious reputations in Scotland.

Many of the craft items produced in local crofts and private homes eventually end up at gift shops in Oban, where they're proudly displayed as among the finest of their kind in the West Country. One of the best outlets is **McCaig's Warehouse,** Argyll Square (© **01631/566-335**), where the tartan patterns of virtually every clan in Scotland are for sale, either by the meter or in the form of kilts, jackets, traditional Highland garb, or a more modern interpretation of traditional fashions.

Celtic-patterned jewelry, made from gold, silver, or platinum and sometimes studded with semiprecious gems, is featured at **The Gem Box,** Esplanade (© **01631/562-180**).

If all other shopping options fail, consider the gift items at the **Oban Tourist Information Office,** Argyll Square (© **01631/563-122**). These range from tartans and jewelry to woodwork and glassware.

If you absolutely, positively must have a kilt, a cape, or a full outfit based on your favorite Highland regiment, head for one of the town's two best tailors: **Hector Russell, Kiltmaker,** Argyll Square (© **01631/570-240**), and **Geoffrey Tailors,** Argyll Square (© **01631/570-557**).

ACCOMMODATIONS

You may also want to check out the rooms offered at the **Balmoral Hotel** or the **Knipoch Hotel Restaurant** (see "Dining," below).

EXPENSIVE

Manor House ☆   This is your best bet for an overnight in Oban. On the outskirts of town, opening onto panoramic views of Oban Bay, this 1780 stone house was once owned by the duke of Argyll. Many antiques grace the public rooms. The guest rooms are filled with tasteful reproductions; all have private bathrooms, some with both tub and shower.

The restaurant is reason enough for a visit even if you're not a guest. You'll dine at a candlelit table dressed in elegant linen. The menu emphasizes seafood, but there are vegetarian dishes as well.

Gallanach Rd., Oban PA34 4LS. © 01631/562-087. Fax 01631/563-053. www.manorhouseoban.com. 11 units. £140–£160 ($210–$240) double. Rates include half-board. AE, MC, V. From the south side of Oban, follow the signs for the car ferry but continue past the ferry entrance for about half a mile (1km). No children under 12 accepted. **Amenities:** Restaurant, 2 bars; room service; laundry. *In room:* TV, coffeemaker, hair dryer.

MODERATE

Alexandra   On the promenade a mile (1.6km) from the train station, the late-1860s stone Alexandra boasts gables and turreted towers and a Regency front veranda. From its public room, you can look out onto Oban Bay, and two sun lounges overlook the seafront. The midsize guest rooms are modestly furnished but pleasing, with combination tub/showers. The restaurant, serving good food, opens onto dramatic sea views.

Corran Esplanade, Oban PA34 5AA. © 01631/562-381. Fax 01631/564-497. 79 units. £78.50–£135.50 ($117.75–$203.25). Rates include Scottish breakfast. AE, MC, V. **Amenities:** Restaurant, bar; indoor pool; small gym; steam room; room service; laundry. *In room:* TV, coffeemaker, hair dryer.

Caledonian Hotel   This choice, a favorite of coach tours, makes good on its promise of giving you a "taste of the Highlands." A fine example of Scottish 19th-century architecture, it occupies a landmark position, with a view opening onto the harbor and Oban Bay. This convenient location puts you close to the rail, bus, and ferry terminals from which you can book passage to the Isles. The guest rooms have up-to-date amenities and small bathrooms with combination tub/showers. The front rooms are the most desirable. Good, reasonably priced Scottish fare is served in the dining room.

Station Sq., Oban PA34 5RT. © 01631/563-133. Fax 01631/562-998. 70 units. £95–£125 ($142.50–$187.50) double. Rates include Scottish breakfast. AE, DC, MC, V. **Amenities:** Restaurant, bar; room service; laundry. *In room:* TV, coffeemaker, hair dryer.

Columba Hotel   This is one of the most impressive Victorian buildings in Oban, built in 1870 by the same McCaig who constructed the hilltop extravaganza known as McCaig's Tower. The location is among the best in town, and the dining room offers views of the port. The small guest rooms are unremarkable but well maintained, each with a small bathroom (some with shower only). The restaurant offers a mix of seafood and local produce. Live folk music is sometimes presented in the informal Harbour Inn Bar.

The Esplanade, North Pier, Oban PA34 5QD. © 01631/562-183. Fax 01631/564-683. 50 units. £79–£105 ($118.50–$157.50) double. Rates include breakfast. AE, MC, V. Free parking. The Scottish Midland Bus Company's Ganavan bus passes by. **Amenities:** Restaurant, bar; limited room service. *In room:* TV, coffeemaker, hair dryer.

Dungallan House Hotel ⚘   One of the more upscale inns around Oban is this home built around 1870 for the Campbells. It was used as a hospital during World War I and as a naval office during World War II, but today is the artfully furnished domain of George and Janice Stewart. The guest rooms have been refurbished, each with quality furnishings (some bathrooms contain showers only). Breakfasts are served in grand style in the formal dining room; dinners can be arranged, and although seating priority is granted to guests, nonguests can try calling ahead. Five acres (2 hectares) of forest and gardens surround the house, and views stretch out over the Bay of Oban.

Gallanach Rd., Oban PA34 4PD. © 01631/563-799. Fax 01631/566-711. www.dungallanhotel-oban.co.uk. 13 units, 11 with private bathroom. £78 ($117) double without bathroom; £109 ($163.50) double with bathroom. MC, V. Closed Nov–Mar. From Oban's center, drive half a mile (1km), following the signs to Gallanach. *In room:* TV, no phone.

INEXPENSIVE

Foxholes Country Hotel ⚘ *(Finds)* Far from a foxhole, this is actually a spacious country house set in a tranquil glen to the south of Oban, ideal for those seeking seclusion. The cozy, tasteful bedrooms are furnished traditionally; all open onto panoramic views of the countryside and the hotel's gardens. The bathrooms are in excellent condition, some with a combination tub/shower. The restaurant features moderately priced Scottish meals.

Cologin, Lerags, Oban. PA34 4SE. ⓒ 0161/564-982. www.hoteloban.com. 7 units. £58–£65 ($87–$97.50) double. Rates include full Scottish breakfast. MC, V. Closed Dec–Mar. Free parking. Take A816 3 miles south of Oban. **Amenities:** Restaurant, bar. *In room:* TV, coffeemaker, hair dryer, no phone.

Glenburnie One of Oban's genuinely grand houses is on the seafront esplanade. Built in 1897 as the surgical hospital and home of a prominent doctor, it's now a guesthouse operated by Graeme and Allyson Strachan, who have outfitted the rooms with comfy furniture, much of it antique. Bathrooms are small but tidy, most with combination tub/showers.

The Esplanade (a 5-minute walk west of the town center), Oban PA34 5AQ. ⓒ and fax **01631/562-089.** 14 units. £54–£74 ($81–$111) double. MC, V. Closed Nov–Mar. *In room:* TV, coffeemaker, no phone.

Lancaster Along the seafront on the crescent of the bay, the Lancaster is distinguished by its attractive pseudo-Tudor facade. Its public rooms command views of the islands of Lismore and Kerrera and even the more distant peaks of Mull. The guest rooms are modestly furnished in a somewhat 1960s style, some with complete bathrooms with tub/shower combinations. This is one of the only two hotels in Oban featuring a heated indoor pool. Its fully licensed dining room offers moderately priced dinners.

Corran Esplanade, Oban PA34 5AD. ⓒ and fax **01631/562-587.** 27 units, 24 with private bathroom; £60–£65 ($90–$97.50) double with bathroom. Rates include Scottish breakfast. MC, V. **Amenities:** Restaurant, bar lounge; indoor pool; Jacuzzi; sauna; solarium; room service. *In room:* TV, coffeemaker, hair dryer, no phone.

DINING
EXPENSIVE

Knipoch Hotel Restaurant ⚘⚘ SCOTTISH Oban offers a truly fine restaurant 6 miles (10km) south of town on the shores of Loch Feochan. This whitewashed Georgian house (the oldest part dates from 1592) contains three dining rooms and features a daily changing menu of five delectable courses. Salmon and halibut are smoked on the premises, and the menu relies heavily on Scottish produce. Try the cock-a-leekie soup, followed by Sound of Luing scallops. The wine cellar is excellent, especially its Bordeaux.

The hotel also rents 16 well-furnished rooms, charging £76 to £149 ($114 to $223.50) for a double, Scottish breakfast included.

Hwy. A816, Kilninver, Knipoch, by Oban PA34 4QT. ⓒ **01852/316-251.** Fax 01852/316249. www.knipoch hotel.co.uk. Reservations required. Table d'hôte dinner £29.50 ($44.25) for 3 courses, £39.50 ($59.25) for 5 courses. AE, DC, MC, V. Daily 7:30–9pm. Closed mid-Dec to mid-Feb. Drive 6 miles (10km) south of Oban on A816.

The Manor House ⚘ SCOTTISH Located in the 1780 house built by the Duke of Argyll, this formal but not stuffy restaurant overlooks Oban Bay and is one of the finest dining choices along the coast. Many visitors to the Highlands opt for venison, and here it comes with accompaniments such as black pudding, caramelized root vegetables, and rowanberry glaze. You might also try delicious fresh scallops wrapped in smoked bacon. The waitstaff will recite some selections for vegetarians. For something truly Scottish, finish with a dessert of marinated brambles with whisky custard.

In the Manor House Hotel, Gallanach Rd. ℭ 01631/562-087. Reservations recommended. Main courses £19 ($28.50); fixed-price 5-course meal £27.50 ($41.25). AE, MC, V. Tues 6:45–9pm; Wed–Sat noon–2pm and 6:45–9pm.

MODERATE

Balmoral Hotel BRITISH   At the top of a granite staircase whose corkscrew shape is an architectural marvel, this is one of the most popular restaurants in town. Filled with 19th-century charm, it contains Windsor chairs and repro- duction Georgian tables. Specialties include sliced chateaubriand with mush- rooms, smoked Tobermory trout, haggis with cream and whisky, venison casserole, and roast pheasant. Less expensive platters are served in the bar. The hotel stands on the eastern extension of the town's main commercial street (George Street), a 4-minute walk from the center.

The hotel rents 12 well-furnished rooms for £50 to £66 ($75 to $99) for a double, Scottish breakfast included.

Craigard Rd., Oban PA34 5AQ. ℭ 01631/562-731. Reservations recommended in midsummer. Main courses £6.50–£16.50 ($9.75–$24.75); bar meals £2.75–£7.50 ($4.15–$11.25). AE, DC, MC, V. May to mid-Oct daily noon–2pm and 6–10pm; Mar–Apr and mid-Oct to Dec daily noon–2pm and 6–8pm.

The Gathering BRITISH   Opened in 1882, this imposing building, ringed with verandas, is no longer a private hunting and social club. Today, its ground floor functions as an Irish pub (open Monday through Saturday from 11am to 1am and Sunday from noon to 11pm) and its wood-sheathed upper floor as a well-managed restaurant. Dishes are straightforward but tasty. Menu items include lots of local produce, fish, and game dishes, like pheasant, lobster, and lamb. Especially noteworthy are the Highland venison filets with port jelly sauce, loin of saddle of venison with herb-and-port sauce, and local crayfish lightly grilled in garlic butter.

Breadalbane St. ℭ 01631/565-421. Reservations recommended. Bar platters £4.95–£12.95 ($7.45–$19.45); fixed-price dinners in restaurant £10.95–£16.95 ($16.45–$25.45). AE, MC, V. June–Sept daily noon–2pm; year-round daily 5–10pm.

McTavish's Kitchen SCOTTISH   Like its cousin in Fort William, this place is dedicated to preserving the local cuisine. Downstairs is a self-service restaurant offering breakfast, lunch, dinner, and tea with shortbread and scones. Upstairs is the Lairds Bar, and on the ground floor is McTavish's Bar, where bar meals are available all day. The licensed second-floor restaurant has a more ambitious Scottish and Continental menu with higher prices. Offerings include haggis, Loch Fyne kippers (oak-smoked herring), prime Scottish steaks, smoked salmon, venison, and local mussels.

34 George St. ℭ 01631/563-064. Main courses £7–£14 ($10.50–$21); budget 2-course lunch £4.95 ($7.45); fixed-price 3-course dinners £8.95–£16.95 ($13.45–$25.45). MC, V. Self-service restaurant daily 9am–9pm; licensed restaurant daily noon–2pm and 6–10:30pm.

OBAN AFTER DARK

From mid-May to the end of September, entertainment is provided at Mac- Tavish's Kitchen (see above), with Scottish music and Highland dancing by local artists nightly from 8:30 to 10:30pm. The cover is £3.50 ($5.25) for adults and £1.75 ($2.65) for children. Reduced admission for diners is £1.75 ($2.65) for adults and £1 ($1.50) for children.

You can while away the evening with the locals at the **Oban Inn,** Stafford Street and the Esplanade (© **01631/562-484**), a popular pub with exposed beams and a flag-covered ceiling. Open daily from 11am to 1am.

SIDE TRIPS FROM OBAN
THE INNER & OUTER HEBRIDES

Oban is the gateway to **Mull,** largest of the Inner Hebrides, and to the island of **Iona.** See chapter 11 for information about these destinations.

The ferries to the offshore islands run only twice a day until summer; then there are cruises to Iona from early June to late September. For details about ferry services to Mull, Iona, and the Outer Hebrides, get in touch with **Caledonian MacBrayne** (© **0990/650-000** in Oban). It sails to 23 islands, with fares ranging from £40 ($60) per car and £6.30 ($9.45) per adult passenger for travel to Mull up to £139 ($208.50) per car plus £32 ($48) per adult passenger for travel to Barra. Book in advance, particularly in summer, as the ferries often sell out.

PORT APPIN

Some 24 miles (39km) north of Oban lies a scenic lochside district, including Lismore Island. Port Appin is a small village with stone cottages. On an islet near Port Appin, a famous landmark, **Castle Stalker,** was the ancient seat of the Stewarts of Appin, built in the 15th century by Duncan Stewart, son of the first chief of Appin. Dugald, the ninth chief, was forced to sell the estate in 1765, and the castle slowly fell into ruin. It was recently restored and is once again inhabited but no longer open to visitors. In *Monty Python and the Holy Grail,* this was depicted as "Castle Aaaaaaaaaaa." It lies at Portnacroish (where it's signposted), 10 miles (16km) down A828.

Accommodations & Dining

Airds Hotel 🐟🐟   The Airds is a former ferry inn dating from 1700 (now a Relais & Châteaux member) in one of the most panoramic spots in the district, midway between Oban and Fort William. It overlooks Loch Linnhe and Lismore Island and is an ideal center for touring the area. You can take forest walks, go pony trekking or fishing, or arrange for boat trips to see the seals and visit Lismore. The resident proprietors are the Allen family, who welcome you to their handsomely furnished rooms and tranquil setting.

But it's the fine Scottish cuisine that makes the Airds so outstanding. Daily menus are likely to include cream of red pepper and fennel soup; breast of wood pigeon with foie gras, truffles, chanterelles, and Madeira sauce; or wild salmon filet on a bed of honeyed eggplant with asparagus and hollandaise sauce.

Port Appin PA38 4DF. © 01631/730-236. Fax 01631/730-535. www.airds-hotel.com. 16 units. £98–£136 ($147–$204) double; £149 ($223.50) per person suite. Rates include Scottish breakfast and dinner. MC, V. **Amenities:** Restaurant, bar; room service; babysitting; laundry service; watersports. *In room:* TV, hair dryer.

Pierhouse   Although the restaurant associated with this hotel was established by two generations of the McLeod family in 1988, its guest rooms are among the newest in Argyll. In 1993, a two-story wing was added, featuring many rooms with views over the water. All units, ranging from small to midsize, are comfortably furnished and well maintained. The complex lies in the hamlet's center, adjacent to the pier where ferryboats depart every 2 hours for Lismore Island.

The restaurant was built as a fisherman's cottage more than 200 years ago. Its location at the edge of the pier allows much of its seafood to remain alive in underwater cages until just before cooking. Venison dishes are available as well.

Port Appin PA38 4DF. ⓒ **01631/730-302.** Fax 01631/730-400. 12 units. £60–£90 ($90–$135) double. Rates include Scottish breakfast. MC, V. **Amenities:** Restaurant, bar. *In room:* TV, coffeemaker, hair dryer.

8

Fife & the Central Highlands

North of the Firth of Forth from Edinburgh, the County of Fife still likes to call itself a kingdom. Even today, its name suggests the romantic episodes and pageantry during the reign of the early Stuart kings, and some 14 of Scotland's 66 royal burghs lay in this shire. You can visit many of the former royal palaces and castles, either restored or in colorful ruins.

Legendary **Loch Lomond** is the largest and most beautiful of the Scottish lakes. At Balloch in the south, it's a Lowland landscape of gentle hills and islands. But as it moves north, the loch narrows and takes on a stark, dramatic Highland character, with moody cloud formations and rugged steep hillsides.

The **Trossachs** is the collective name given to that wild Highland area east and northeast of Loch Lomond. Here and along Loch Lomond you find Scotland's finest scenery in moor, mountain, and loch. The area has been famed in history and romance ever since Sir Walter Scott's vivid descriptive passages in "The Lady of the Lake" and *Rob Roy.*

Many sections of the area lie on the doorsteps of Glasgow and Edinburgh; either city can be your gateway to the central Highlands. You can easily reach Dunfermline and St. Andrews by rail from Edinburgh. (St. Andrews also has good bus connections with Edinburgh.) By car, the main motorway is M9, the express highway that starts on the western outskirts of Edinburgh and is linked to M80 from Glasgow. M9 passes close to Stirling. M90, reached by crossing the Forth Road Bridge, will take you north into the Fife region. Stirling is the region's major rail center, with stops at such places as Dunblane, and much of Loch Lomond has rail connections. The towns and some villages have bus service, but you'll probably find the connections too limited or infrequent. For bus connections, Stirling is the central point.

However, your best bet for discovering the hidden villages and scenic lochside roads of the Trossachs or the fishing villages of East Neuk is by renting a car and driving at your own pace.

1 Dunfermline ✶ & Its Great Abbey

14 miles (22.5km) NW of Edinburgh, 39 miles (63km) NE of Glasgow, 52 miles (84km) SW of Dundee

The ancient town of Dunfermline was once the capital of Scotland and is easily reached by the Forth Road Bridge, opened by Elizabeth II in 1964. Scots called their former capital the "auld grey town," and it looms large in their history books. The city is still known for its Dunfermline Abbey and former royal palace (now largely gone). When Scotland reunited with England in 1603, the royal court departed to London, leaving Dunfermline to wither with only its memories. In time, however, the town revived as the center of Scottish linen making, specializing in damask. But by World War I, the market had largely disappeared.

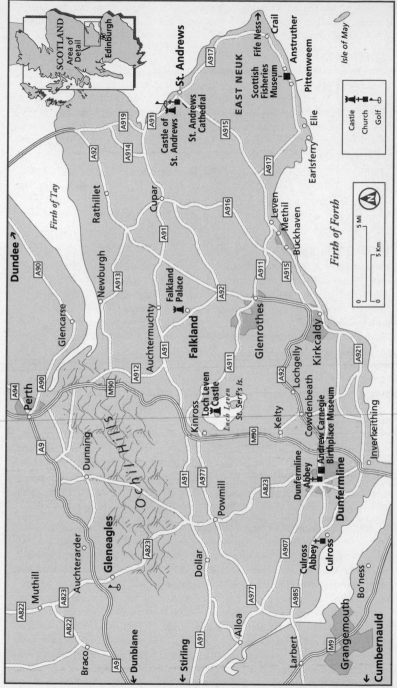

Some of the most interesting sights in Fife are within easy reach of Dunfermline, including one of Scotland's most beautiful villages, Culross. Dunfermline also makes the best base for exploring Loch Leven and Loch Leven Castle.

ESSENTIALS

GETTING THERE   Dunfermline is a stop along the main **rail** route from London via Edinburgh to Dundee, which means it has frequent connections to the Scottish capital. For schedules and fares, call ℂ **08457/484-950.** From its station at St. Andrews Square in Edinburgh, **Scottish CityLink** (ℂ **0990/505-050)** operates frequent bus service to Dunfermline. If you're **driving** from Edinburgh, take A90 west, cross the Forth Road Bridge, and follow the signs north to the center of Dunfermline.

VISITOR INFORMATION   A **tourist booth** is at 13–15 Maygate (ℂ **01383/720-999).** It's open from April to July and September to October, Monday through Saturday from 10am to 5pm; August, Monday through Saturday from 10am to 6pm and Sunday from 11:30am to 3:30pm; and November to March, Monday through Saturday from 10am to 5pm.

SEEING THE SIGHTS

Dunfermline Abbey and Palace ℛ   The abbey is on the site of two earlier structures, a Celtic church and an 11th-century house of worship dedicated to the Holy Trinity, under the auspices of Queen Margaret (later St. Margaret). Culdee Church, from the 5th and 6th centuries, was rebuilt in 1072. Traces of both buildings are visible beneath gratings in the floor of the old nave. In 1150, the church was replaced with a large abbey, the nave of which remains, an example of Norman architecture. Later, St. Margaret's shrine, the northwest baptismal porch, the spire on the northwest tower, and the flying buttresses were added. While Dunfermline was the capital of Scotland, 22 royal personages were buried in the abbey. However, the only visible memorial or burial places known are those of Queen Margaret and King Robert the Bruce, whose tomb lies beneath the pulpit.

The once-royal palace of Dunfermline stands adjacent to the abbey. The palace witnessed the birth of Charles I and James I. The last king to reside here was Charles II, in 1651. Today, only the southwest wall remains of this once-gargantuan edifice.

St. Margaret's St. ℂ 01383/739-026. Admission £2 ($3) adults, £1.50 ($2.25) seniors, 75p ($1.10) children. Apr–Sept daily 9:30am–6pm; Oct–Mar Mon–Wed and Sat 9:30am–4pm, Thurs 9:30am–noon, Sun 2–4pm.

Andrew Carnegie Birthplace Museum   In 1835, American industrialist and philanthropist Andrew Carnegie was born at a site about 200 yards (182m) down the hill from the abbey. The museum comprises the 18th-century weaver's cottage in which he was born and a memorial hall provided by his wife. Displays tell the story of the weaver's son who emigrated to the United States to become one of the richest men in the world. From the fortune he made in steel, Carnegie gave away more than £244 million ($366 million) before his death in 1919. Dunfermline received the first of the 2,811 free libraries he provided throughout Britain and the States and also received public baths and Pittencrieff Park and Glen, rich in history and natural charm. A statue in the park honors Carnegie, who once worked as a bobbin boy in a cotton factory.

At corner of Moodie St. and Priory Lane. ℂ 01383/724-302. Admission £2 ($3) adults, £1 ($1.50) seniors, free for children under 16. Apr–Oct Mon–Sat 11am–5pm, Sun 2–5pm. Closed Nov–Mar.

ACCOMMODATIONS

Davaar House Hotel and Restaurant   This large Georgian-style house, in a residential neighborhood a 5-minute walk west of the town center, was built late in the 19th century and boasts distinctive architectural features like a sweeping oak staircase, elaborate moldings, and marble mantelpieces. The largest guest rooms, with the loftiest ceilings, are one floor above street level; slightly less grand rooms are two floors above street level. Each is uniquely decorated in traditional Scottish style. Some of the bathrooms contain a shower only.

The restaurant here is recommended; it's open for dinner Monday through Saturday. Look for moderate prices and home-style cooking from a talented team, with dishes like Scottish salmon with mustard-dill sauce and supreme of chicken and broccoli in phyllo pastry and white-wine sauce.

126 Grieve St., Dunfermllne, Fife KY12 8DW. ⓒ 01383/721-886. Fax 01383/623-633. www.tasteofscotland. co.uk/davaar_house_hotel.html. 10 units. £75.80 ($113.70) double. Rate includes breakfast. MC, V. **Amenities:** Restaurant; limited room service; laundry. *In room:* TV, coffeemaker, hair dryer, iron.

Keavil House Hotel ⋒   This tranquil country hotel, only a 30-minute drive from Edinburgh, is set on 12 acres of forested land and gardens and offers lots of leisure facilities. The guest rooms are generous in size and well appointed, each with a midsize bathroom (some with tubs). Master bedrooms contain four-poster beds. The hotel offers fine, formal dining in its Conservatory Restaurant (see "Dining," below) and less formal food in its Armoury Alehouse & Grill.

Main St., Crossford, Dunfermline, Fife KY12 8QW. ⓒ 01383/736-258. Fax 01383/621-600. www. keavilhouse.co.uk. 47 units. £95–£115 ($142.50–$172.50) double; £125 ($187.50) family suite. AE, DC, MC, V. Free parking. Closed Dec 31–Jan 1. Take A994, 2 miles west of Dunfermline; the hotel is off the main street at the west end of village. **Amenities:** Restaurant, bar; finest leisure/health club in the area with pool, gym, Jacuzzi, sauna, and steam room; room service; babysitting; laundry. *In room:* TV, coffeemaker, hair dryer.

King Malcolm Thistle Hotel   The best in-town choice for either a meal or a bed is this stylish, modern, pastel-colored hotel on a roundabout a mile south of Dunfermline on A823. Named after the medieval king of Fife (and later of Scotland), Malcolm Canmore, it was built in 1972 but has been thoroughly revamped. Each well-furnished though rather standardized guest room comes with a combination tub/shower. Richmond's, a glass-sided bar and restaurant, offers Scottish and Continental cuisine at dinner daily.

Queensferry Rd., Dunfermline, Fife KY11 5DS. ⓒ 01383/722-611. Fax 01383/730-865. kingmalcolmhotel@ hotmail.com. 48 units. £124–£145 ($186–$217.50) double. Children under 14 stay free ln parents' room. AE, DC, MC, V. Bus: D3 or D4. **Amenities:** Restaurant, bar; limited room service; laundry/dry cleaning. *In room:* TV, coffeemaker, hair dryer.

DINING

Conservatory Restaurant MODERN SCOTTISH   Here you'll enjoy views of extensive gardens and some of the best of local produce, used deftly to create true "Taste of Scotland" specialties—and that means the best of Scottish beef, locally caught game, and fish from local rivers. Old-time recipes are given a modern twist; the imaginative dishes are served with flair and originality, appealing to both traditionalists and those with more adventurous tastes. Try the scallops on sugar snap peas with lobster sabayon, for example, or a real local specialty, a chanterelle and "tattie" scone pocket with a malt vinegar demi-glace. You can follow with dessert of caramelized heather honey and apple parfait. There's an extensive and well-chosen wine list.

If you want less formal dining, the hotel also offers the **Armoury Alehouse & Grill,** with a selection of local beef, fish, and game.

In the Keavil House Hotel, Main St., Crossford. ℰ **01383/736-258.** Reservations recommended. Main courses £10–£18 ($15–$27); fixed-price 3-course menu £24.10 ($36.15). AE, DC, MC, V. Daily noon–2pm and 7–9pm. Closed Dec 31–Jan 1.

New Victoria SCOTTISH   To reach Dunfermline's oldest restaurant, established in 1923, you must walk up 2 flights of stairs off High Street, in a pedestrian zone in the center overlooking the abbey. The cozy dining room serves generous portions of good old-fashioned cooking based on healthy ingredients. You might begin with a robust soup, then follow with steak-and-kidney pie, grilled fish, roast beef, or any of an array of grilled Aberdeen Angus steaks. It's also a good choice if you're in the neighborhood seeking a high tea.

2 Bruce St. ℰ **01383/724-175.** Main courses £3.95–£14.95 ($5.95–$22.45); Scottish high tea £5.45–£12.45 ($8.20–$18.70). MC, V. Mon–Thurs 11am–8pm; Fri–Sat 11am–9pm; Sun noon–7pm.

SIDE TRIPS FROM DUNFERMLINE: CULROSS & LOCH LEVEN

The old royal burgh of **Culross** 🌟🌟🌟, 6 miles (10km) west of Dunfermline, has been renovated by the Scottish National Trust and is one of the country's most beautiful. As you walk its cobblestone streets, admiring the whitewashed houses with their crow-stepped gables and red pantiled roofs, you'll feel as if you're taking a stroll back into the 17th century.

Set in tranquil walled gardens in the village center, **Culross Palace** 🌟🌟 (ℰ **01383/880-359**) was built between 1597 and 1611 for prosperous merchant George Bruce. It contains a most beautiful series of paintings on its wooden walls and ceilings portraying moral scenes with passages in Latin and Scottish, illustrating principles like "Honor your parents" and "The spoken word cannot be retracted." National Trust restoration from 1991 to 1994 involved replacing all the wooden paneling that had rotted with Russian pine, taking care to match the salvaged panels. During the restoration, archaeologists uncovered the remains of a foundation of a long-forgotten building on the east end of the courtyard and the original doorway; there are plans to restore it for use as the public entrance. From Easter to September, the palace is open daily from 12:30 to 4:40pm; in October, only the town house and study are open, Saturday and Sunday from 12:30 to 4:30pm; from November to Easter, visits are by appointment only. Admission is £5 ($7.50) for adults, £4 ($6) for seniors and students, free for those under 19, and £14 ($21) per family.

The other important attraction is 6 miles (10km) southwest of Dumferline (take A994, following the signs to Culross): **Culross Abbey,** a Cistercian monastery whose founding father was Malcolm, earl of Fife, in 1217. Parts of the nave are still intact, and the choir serves as the Culross parish church. There's also a central tower. From Easter Saturday to the last Saturday in August, the abbey is open daily from 9am to 7pm; at other times, you can visit by prior arrangement with the Church of Scotland (ℰ **01383/880-231**).

Loch Leven 🌟, 12 miles (19km) north of Dunfermline and 10 miles (16km) south of Falkland via A911, contains seven islands. On **St. Serf's,** the largest of the islands, are the ruins of the Priory of Loch Leven, built on the site of one of the oldest Culdee establishments in Scotland. If you're interested in seeing the ruins, contact the Kinross tourist office at ℰ **01577/863-680** and you'll be put in touch with one of the fishermen who make boat trips to the island.

In **Kinross,** 25 miles (40km) north of Edinburgh, you can take the ferry over to Castle Island to see the ruins of **Loch Leven Castle** (ℰ **07836/313-769**).

"Those never got luck who came to Loch Leven," and this saying sums up the history of this Douglas fortress dating from the late 14th century. Among its ill-fated prisoners, none was more notable than Mary Queen of Scots; inside its forbidding walls, she signed her abdication on July 24, 1567, but she escaped from Loch Leven on May 2, 1568. Thomas Percy, seventh earl of Northumberland, supported her cause and "lodged" in the castle for 3 years until he was handed over to the English, who beheaded him at York. Today, you can see a 14th-century tower house and a 16th-century curtain wall, all that remains of a castle that loomed large in Scottish history. The castle is open from April to September, daily from 9:30am to 6:30pm; and October to March, Monday through Saturday from 9:30am to 4:30pm and Sunday from 2 to 4:30pm. Admission is £3.30 ($4.95) for adults, £2.50 ($3.75) for seniors, and £1.20 ($1.80) for children. The admission includes the cost of a round-trip ferry from Kinross to Castle Island.

ACCOMMODATIONS & DINING

Dunclutha Guest House   A 3-minute walk northeast of the town center is this dignified stone house, which was built around 1890 for the priest at the adjacent Episcopal church. Today, it's the domain of Mrs. Pam McDonald, who infuses lots of personalized hominess into her hotel. The guest rooms are clean, well maintained, and (in most cases) sunny, thanks to big windows with garden views. Breakfast is the only meal served.

16 Victoria Rd., Leven, Fife KY8 4EX. © **01333/425-515.** Fax 01333/422-311. www.duncluthaguesthouse. com. 5 units. £50 ($75) double. Rate includes breakfast. AE, MC, V. **Amenities:** Lounge with games and piano; laundry facilities. *In room:* TV, coffeemaker, hair dryer (on request), no phone.

Nivingston Country House *(Finds)*   Nivingston, a converted stone farmhouse with parts dating from 1725, is on 12 acres (4.9 hectares) of gardens and offers modernized guest rooms with small, shower-only bathrooms. The hotel also serves some of the finest food around, using fresh local products like Scottish lamb and beef. Typical dishes range from rainbow trout sautéed with almonds, capers, and prawns to Scottish sirloin steak "Hare and Hounds," with red-wine and Dijon-mustard sauce, glazed with brown sugar. You make your dessert selection from a trolley of luscious treats wheeled to your table.

Hwy. 9097, Cleish Hills by B996, Cleish, Perthshire and Kinross KY13 7LS. © **01577/850-216.** Fax 01577/ 850-238. www.smoothhound.co.uk/hotels/nivingst.html. 17 units. £105 ($157.50) double; £140 ($210) suite. Rates include Scottish breakfast. Children under 13 stay free in parents' room. AE, MC, V. Closed Jan 1–14. Drive south of Kinross on B9097; it's 2 miles (3km) from exit 5 of M90. **Amenities:** Restaurant, bar; limited room service; laundry service. *In room:* TV, coffeemaker, hair dryer.

2 East Neuk's Scenic Fishing Villages *(★★)*

Within half an hour's drive south of St. Andrews, on the eastward-facing peninsula incorporating St. Andrews and Anstruther, is the district of East Neuk, dotted with some of eastern Scotland's most scenic and unspoiled fishing villages. You can't reach these villages by rail; the nearest stations are Ladybank, Cupar, and Leuchars, on the main London-Edinburgh-Dundee-Aberdeen line serving northeast Fife. Buses from St. Andrews connect the villages, but you'll really want to have your own car here.

If the weather's right, you can cycle among the villages along some of the most delightful back roads in Fife. Rent a bike at **East Neuk Outdoors,** Cellardyke Park in Anstruther (© **01333/311-929**). This same outfitter can also fix you up for a canoe trip.

PITTENWEEM

If you're at Pittenweem Monday through Saturday morning, try to get caught up in the action at the **fish auction** held under a large shed. The actual time depends on the tides. Afterward, go for a walk through the village and admire the sturdy stone homes, some of which have been preserved by Scotland's National Trust.

The *weem* in the name of the town means "cave," a reference to **St. Fillan's Cave** (© 01333/311-495), at Cove Wynd in the vicinity of the harbor. This cave is said to contain the shrine of St. Fillan, a hermit who lived in the 6th century. Hours are Tuesday through Saturday from 9:30am to 5pm and Sunday from noon to 5pm; admission is £1 ($1.50).

The best way to reach **Anstruther** (see below) is to hike the 1½ miles (2.5km) over to it, because the road isn't paved. If the day is clear, this is one of the loveliest walks in eastern Scotland. From Pittenweem, follow a signpost directing you to Anstruther; you'll cross Scottish meadows and can say hello to a few lambs. You can also take the walk in reverse, as most visitors do. In Anstruther, the path begins at the bottom of West Braes, a small cul-de-sac off the main road in the village.

ACCOMMODATIONS

The Pittenweem Harbour Guest House   Set directly on the harborfront, this charming stone building was erected around 1910 as a private home. The guest rooms contain pinewood furniture and comfortable twin beds, each a cozy, no-frills refuge from the chilly winds and crashing seas. All units have small, shower-only bathrooms. Since it's run by a local company and not by a family, Harbour is a bit more businesslike than a conventional B&B; in fact, it feels like a fishing lodge—the staff will direct you to local entrepreneurs who can take you out for a half day's fishing or point out spots on the nearby piers and boardwalks where a rod and reel might attract fish.

14 Mid Shore, Pittenweem, Fife KY10 2NL. © 01333/311-273. Fax 01333/310-014. www.pittenweem.com/index.htm. 4 units. £50 ($75) double. Rates include breakfast. Discounts of £4 ($6) per person Nov–Mar. AE, DC, MC, V. *In room:* TV, coffeemaker, hair dryer, no phone.

ANSTRUTHER

Once an important herring-fishing port, Anstruther is now a summer resort, 46 miles (74km) northeast of Edinburgh, 34 miles (55km) east of Dunfermline, 4 miles (6.5km) southwest of Crail, and 23 miles (37km) south of Dundee. The **tourist office** is on High Street (© 01333/311-073); it's open April through September, Monday through Saturday from 10am to 5pm and Sunday from noon to 5pm. (Tuesday through Thursday, it closes from 1 to 2pm.)

You'll enjoy taking a brisk stroll along the beaches here; it's too chilly for swimming, but it's invigorating and scenic nonetheless. The best nearby is **Billow Ness Beach,** a 10-minute walk east of the center.

The **Scottish Fisheries Museum,** St. Ayles, Harbourhead (© 01333/310-628; bus: 95), is down by the harbor. It was expanded in 1999 to include a neighboring building that was an 18th-century tavern, along with several recreations of restored fishing boats. Here you can follow the fisherfolk through every aspect of their industry—from the days of sail to modern times. Associated with the museum but afloat in the harbor is an old herring drifter, *The Reaper,* which you can board to look around. The museum is open from April to October, Monday through Saturday from 10am to 5:30pm and Sunday from

11am to 5pm; and November to March, Monday through Saturday from 10am to 4:30pm and Sunday from 2 to 4:30pm. Admission is £3.50 ($5.25) for adults, £2.50 ($3.75) for seniors and children, and £10 ($15) per family.

From the museum, you can walk to the tiny hamlet of **Cellardyke,** adjoining Anstruther. You'll see many charming stone houses and an ancient harbor, where in the year Victoria took the throne (1837), 140 vessels used to put out to sea. You can rent a bike from **East Neuk Outdoors,** Cellardyke Park (℗ **01333/ 311-929**), where rental rates are £10 ($15) per day and £35 ($52.50) per week, plus a deposit. It's open daily from 9am to 5pm.

The **Isle of May,** a nature reserve in the Firth of Forth, is accessible by boat from Anstruther. It's a bird observatory and a field station and contains the ruins of a 12th-century chapel as well as an early-19th-century lighthouse. **Jon and Lyn Raeper** (℗ **01333/310-103**) maintain a 100-passenger boat departing for the island from the Lifeboat Station in Anstruther Harbour every day between May and September, weather permitting. The 5-hour trip, door to door, costs £13 ($19.50) for adults, £11 ($16.50) for seniors and students, and £6 ($9) for children 3 to 14. Between May and July, expect to see hundreds, even thousands, of puffins, who mate on the Isle of May at that time.

ACCOMMODATIONS

Craw's Nest Hotel   This black-and-white step-gabled Scottish manse is a popular hotel, with views over the Firth of Forth and May Island. Many extensions were added under the direction of the owner, Mrs. Edward Clarke, and her son-in-law, Ian Birrell. The midsize guest rooms are handsomely appointed, each with a combination tub/shower. The public areas, including a lounge bar as well as a bustling public bar, are simply decorated and cozy. In the dining room, the food is good and the wine reasonably priced.

Bankwell Rd., Anstruther, Fife KY10 3DA. ℗ **01333/310-691.** Fax 01333/312-216. Crawnest@compuserve. com 50 units. £82 ($123) double. Rates include Scottish breakfast. AE, DC, MC, V. Bus: 95. **Amenities:** Restaurant, bar; limited room service; laundry/dry cleaning. *In room:* TV, coffeemaker, hair dryer.

Smuggler's Inn   This warmly inviting inn evokes memories of smuggling days, with low ceilings, uneven floors, and winding stairs. An inn has stood on this spot since 1300, and in Queen Anne's day it was a well-known tavern. The guest rooms are comfortably furnished; some bathrooms contain a shower only. The restaurant serves moderately priced regional cuisine at dinner nightly. Affordable bar lunches are also available.

High St., East Anstruther, Fife KY10 3DQ. ℗ **01333/310-506.** Fax 01333/312-706. 9 units. £59 ($88.50) double. Rates include Scottish breakfast. MC, V. Bus: 95. **Amenities:** Restaurant, 2 bars; room service; laundry. *In room:* TV, coffeemaker, hair dryer.

DINING

The Cellar SEAFOOD   Within the solid stone walls of a cellar that dates from 1875 (but possibly from the 16th century), this seafood restaurant is the best in town. It's lit by candlelight and, in winter, by twin fireplaces at opposite ends of the room. The menu offers fresh fish hauled in from nearby waters and prepared with light sauces. Examples are grilled halibut suprême dredged in bread crumbs and citrus juices and served with hollandaise sauce; lobster, monkfish, and scallops roasted with herb-and-garlic butter and served on sweet pepper risotto; and a limited array of meat dishes.

24 East Green, Anstruther. ℗ **01333/310-378.** Reservations recommended. Fixed-price menus £28.50–£32.50 ($42.75–$48.75). AE, DC, MC, V. Wed–Sat 12:30–1:30pm; Tues–Sat 7–9:30pm. Bus: 95.

Haven SCOTTISH　This unpretentious harborfront place (two connected 300-year-old fishermen's cottages) serves simple and wholesome food: pan-fried breaded prawns, halibut filets, Angus steaks, local crabmeat salad, and home-made soups and stews. The upper floor contains one of the town's most popular bars, where the same menu is served. The street level, more formal and sedate, is the site of high teas and evening meals.

1 Shore Rd., Cellardyke, Anstruther. © **01333/310-574.** Reservations recommended. Fixed-price 5-course menu £19.95 ($29.95); bar supper menu £7.85–£12.90 ($11.80–$19.35); high tea £6.95–£8.50 ($10.45–$12.75). MC, V. Sun–Thurs 11am–9pm; Fri–Sat 11am–10pm (depending on business, the street-level restaurant, but not the upstairs bar, might close several hours earlier during midwinter). Bus: 95; a James Anderson & Co. bus runs every hour from St. Andrews, 8 miles (13km) south, to the door of the restaurant.

ANSTRUTHER AFTER DARK

Dreel Tavern, 16 High St. (© **01333/310-727**), was a 16th-century coaching inn and is now a wood-and-stone pub where locals gather to unwind in the evening. Caledonian 80 Shilling and Orkney Dark Island are available on hand pump, along with two guest beers that change weekly. It's open Monday through Saturday from 11am to 11pm and Sunday from noon to 11pm.

ELIE 🅐

With its step-gabled houses and little harbor, Elie, 11 miles (18km) south of Anstruther, is many visitors' favorite village along the coast. Only a 25-minute car ride from Edinburgh, Elie and its close neighbor, Earlsferry, overlook a crescent of gold-sand beach, with more swimming possibilities to be found among sheltered coves. The name Elie is believed to be derived from the *ailie* (island) of Ardross, which now forms part of the harbor and is joined to the mainland by a road. A large stone building, a former granary, at the harbor is a reminder of the days when Elie was a busy trading port. Of all the villages of East Neuk, this one seems best suited for walks and hikes in all directions.

Earlsferry, to the west, got its name from an ancient ferry crossing, which Macduff, the thane of Fife, is supposed to have used in his escape from Macbeth.

East of the harbor stands a stone structure known as the **Lady's Tower,** used by Lady Janet Anstruther, a noted 18th-century beauty, as a bathing cabana. Another member of the Anstruther family, Sir John, added the interesting **bell tower** to the parish church that stands in the center of the village.

Beyond the lighthouse, on a point of land to the east of the harbor, lies **Ruby Bay,** so named because you can find garnets here. Farther along the coast is **Fossil Bay,** where you can find a variety of fossils.

ACCOMMODATIONS

The Elms *(Value* 　Run by Mr. and Mrs. Terras, this 1880 building is on the wide main street behind a conservative stone facade, with a crescent-shaped rose garden in front. The comfortably furnished but small guest rooms contain good beds, washbasins, and showers. Home cooking is a specialty of the place, and dishes include Scottish lamb, Pittenweem haddock, haggis, and Arbroath kippers. A simple dinner is available to nonguests. In the walled flower garden behind the house is a large conservatory for guests' use.

14 Park Place, Elie, Fife KY9 1DH. © and fax **01333/330-404.** 7 units. £50 ($75) double. Rates include Scottish breakfast. MC, V. *In room:* TV, hair dryer, coffeemaker, no phone.

Rockview Guest House *(Kids* 　Next to the Ship Inn (see below), the Rockview overlooks fine sandy beaches around Elie Bay. The family-run guesthouse can accommodate about 12 people. The small rooms are nicely furnished, each with a good bed and shower-only bathroom. Maintenance is of a high level, and the welcome is warm. A twin-bedded room has a bunk bed for younger children to share with their parents. Of course, food and drink are available at the Ship Inn.

The Toft, Elie, Fife KY9 IDT. ℂ **01333/330-246.** Fax 01333/330-864. shipinnelie@aol.com. 6 units. May–Oct £50 ($75) double. Rates include breakfast. MC, V. *In room:* TV, no phone.

DINING

Ship Inn ⚓ SCOTTISH   Even if you're not stopping over in Elie, we suggest you drop in at the Ship (from the center, follow the signs marked HARBOUR) and enjoy a pint of lager or real ale or a whisky from the large selection. The building occupied by this pub dates from 1778, and a bar has been in business here since 1830. In summer, you can sit outdoors and look over the water; in colder months, a fireplace burns brightly. On weekends in July and August, a barbecue operates outside. The set menu with daily specials features such items as steak pie, Angus beefsteaks, lasagna, and an abundance of fresh seafood.

The Toft. ℂ **01333/330-246.** Main courses £6.70–£17 ($10.05–$25.50). MC, V. Oct–Mar Mon–Sat noon–2pm and 6–7pm (to 9:30pm Fri–Sat), Sun noon–2:30pm; Apr–Sept Mon–Sat noon–2:30pm and 6–9:30pm, Sun 12:30–3pm and 6–9pm.

CRAIL ⚓⚓

The pearl of the East Neuk of Fife, Crail is 50 miles (80.5km) northeast of Edinburgh, 23 miles (37km) south of Dundee, and 9 miles (14.5km) south of St. Andrews. It's an artists' colony, and many painters live in cottages around the little harbor. Natural bathing facilities are at Roome Bay, and many beaches are nearby. The **Balcomie Golf Course** is one of the oldest in the world and is still in good condition.

The old town grew up along the harbor, and you can still see a lot of fishing cottages clustered here. Crab and lobster boats still set out hoping for a big catch. **Upper Crail** overlooks the harbor and also merits exploration. The **tollbooth** dates from 1598 and is crowned by a belfry. **Marketgate** is lined with trees and flanked by small two- and three-floor houses. Follow the walkway to **Castle Walk,** which offers the most panoramic view of Crail.

To understand the villages of East Neuk better, call at the **Crail Museum & Heritage Centre,** 62 Marketgate (ℂ **01333/450-869**), which contains artifacts related to fishing and the former trading links of these tiny villages. Admission is free. The center is open June to September, Monday through Saturday from 10am to 1pm and 2 to 5pm and Sunday from 2 to 5pm; and April to May, Saturday and Sunday from 2 to 5pm.

ACCOMMODATIONS & DINING

Croma Hotel   This guesthouse, a block off High Street near the harbor, offers small rooms, very simply furnished but comfortable. Bathrooms contain either a tub or a shower. One notable feature is the fully licensed Chart Room bar, open from 5pm to midnight, where you can drop in for drinks.

33–35 Nethergate, Crail, Fife KY10 3TU. ℂ **01333/450-239.** www.cromahotel.co.uk. 6 units, 4 with private bathroom. £42 ($63) double without bathroom; £50 ($75) double with bathroom. Rates include Scottish breakfast. MC, V. Closed Dec–Jan. **Amenities:** Bar; laundry. *In room:* TV, coffeemaker, hair dryer.

Denburn House   Near the town center, in a historic neighborhood known as Marketgate, this guesthouse occupies a 200-year-old, stone-sided building that retains many of its interior architectural features, including the paneling in the lounge and an elaborate staircase. In 1998, most of the interior was tastefully renovated; all guest rooms were redecorated in a conservative but very pleasing style, each with a shower-only bathroom. The rear garden offers a scattering of lawn furniture and access to the great Scottish outdoors. Everything is very low-key and unpretentious.

1 Marketgate, Crail, Fife KY10 3TQ. ℂ 01333/450-253. www.smoothhound.co.uk/hotels/denburnh.html. 6 units. £36–£55 ($54–$82.50) double. Rates include breakfast. DC, MC, V. **Amenities:** Lounge in summer. *In room:* TV, coffeemaker, hair dryer, no phone.

3 St. Andrews: The Birthplace of Golf ★★

14 miles (22.5km) SE of Dundee, 51 (82km) miles NE of Edinburgh

The medieval royal burgh of St. Andrews was once filled with monasteries and ancient houses that didn't survive the pillages of Henry VIII; regrettably, only a few ruins rising in ghostly dignity remain. Most of the town as you'll see it today was built of local stone during the 18th, 19th, and early 20th centuries. This historic sea town in northeast Fife is also known as the seat where the rules of golf in Britain and the world are codified and arbitrated. Golf was played for the first time in the 1400s, probably on the site of St. Andrews's Old Course, and was enjoyed by Mary Queen of Scots here in 1567. Golfers consider this town to be hallowed ground.

ESSENTIALS

GETTING THERE   About 15 BritRail **trains** per day stop 8 miles (13km) away at the town of Leuchars (rhymes with "euchres") on the London-Edinburgh-Dundee-Aberdeen run to the northeast. Trip time from Edinburgh to Leuchars is about an hour; a one-way fare is £8.10 ($12.15). For information, call ℂ 08457/484-950.

Once at Leuchars, you can take a **bus** the rest of the way to St. Andrews. Bus no. 95 departs about every 30 minutes. Fife Scottish bus no. X24 travels from Glasgow to Glenrothes daily, and from there, bus no. X59 runs to St. Andrews. Buses operate daily between 7am and midnight; the trip takes between 2½ and 3 hours. Buses arrive at the St. Andrews Bus Station, Station Road, just off City Road (ℂ 01334/474-238 for schedules).

If you're **driving** from Edinburgh, head northwest along A90 and cross the Forth Road Bridge north. Take A921 to the junction with A915 and continue northeast until you reach St. Andrews.

VISITOR INFORMATION   The **tourist office** is at 70 Market St. (ℂ 01334/472-021; www.standrews.com). It's open January to March, November, and December, Monday through Saturday from 9:30am to 5pm; April, Monday through Saturday from 9:30am to 5pm and Sunday from 11am to 5pm; May, June, September, and October, Monday through Saturday from 9:30am to 6pm and Sunday from 11am to 5pm; and July and August, Monday through Saturday from 9:30am to 7pm and Sunday from 10am to 6pm.

HITTING THE LINKS

All six of the St. Andrews courses are fully owned by the municipality and open to the public on a more-or-less democratic basis—ballots are polled a day in advance. This balloting system might be circumvented for players who reserve with the appropriate starters several days or weeks in advance. To play the hallowed Old Course, you must present a current handicap certificate and/or letter of introduction from a bona-fide golf club.

The misty and verdant golf courses are the very symbol of St. Andrews: the famous 6,566-yard (5,975m), par-72 **Old Course;** the 6,604-yard (6,010m), par-72 **New Course** (opened in 1896); the 6,805-yard (6,192.5m), par-71 **Jubilee Course** (opened in 1897 in honor of Queen Victoria); the 6,112-yard (5,562m), par-70 **Eden** (opened in 1914); the **Balgove** (a nine-hole course for children's golf training, opened in 1972); and the 5,094-yard (4,635.5m), par-67 **Strathtyrum** (the newest and most far-flung, an eight-hole course opened in 1993). Encircled by all of them is the world's most prestigious golf club, the **Royal and Ancient Golf Club** (© **01334/472-112**), founded in St. Andrews in 1754—it remains more or less rigidly closed as a private-membership men's club. The Royal and Ancient traditionally opens its doors to the public only on St. Andrews Day to view its legendary trophy room. This usually, but not always, falls around November 30.

The **Old Course,** Pilmour Cottage (© **01334/466-666**), is the world's most legendary temple of golf, one whose difficulty is shaped by nature and the long-ago paths of grazing sheep. Over the centuries, stately buildings have been erected near its start and finish. Aristocrats from virtually everywhere have lent their names and reputations to enhance its glamour, and its nuances have been debated, usually in reverent tones, by golfers in bars and on fairways through-out the world. This fabled par-72 course hosted the 2000 British Open, when golf fans from around the world watched in awe as Tiger Woods became the youngest golfer in history to complete a grand slam (and only the fifth golfer to ever perform the feat). Greens fees are £80 to £85 ($120 to $127.50), a caddy costs £28 ($42) plus tip, and clubs rent for £20 to £30 ($30 to $45) per round. There are no electric carts allowed; seniors and people with medical conditions can rent a trolley on afternoons only between May and September for £5 ($7.50).

Facilities for golfers in St. Andrews are legion. Beside the 18th hole of the Old Course, within premises owned and operated by the Rusacks Hotel, are links rooms with lockers, showers, and changing facilities, as well as a dining room and a bar. Virtually every hotel in town maintains some kind of facility to assist golfers.

For more details on golfing in St. Andrews (plus tips on golf associations and golf tours), see "Teeing Off: Golfing in Scotland," in chapter 3, "The Active Vacation Planner."

SEEING THE SIGHTS

Founded in 1411, the **University of St. Andrews** is the oldest in Scotland and the third oldest in Britain and has been called the Oxbridge of Scotland. At term time, you can see packs of students in their characteristic red gowns. The uni-versity grounds stretch west of the St. Andrews Castle between North Street and the Scores.

The university's most interesting buildings are the tower and church of St. Salvator's College and the courtyard of St. Mary's College, from 1538. An ancient thorn tree, said to have been planted by Mary Queen of Scots, stands near the college's chapel. St. Leonard's College church is also from medieval days. In 1645, the Scottish Parliament met in what was once the University Library and is now a students' reading room. A modern University Library, con-taining many rare ancient volumes, was opened in 1976.

Holy Trinity Church   Called the Town Kirk, this restored medieval church once stood on the grounds of the now-ruined cathedral (see below). The church was moved to its present site in 1410, considerably altered after the Reformation of 1560, and restored in the early 20th century. You'll find much fine stained glass and carvings inside.

Opposite St. Mary's College, off South St. ℂ 01334/474-494. Free admission, but call in advance to make sure someone is in attendance. Daily 10am–noon and 2–4pm.

St. Andrews Cathedral and Priory ℛ Near the Celtic settlement of

St. Mary of the Rock, by the sea at the east end of town, is the semi-ruin of St. Andrews Cathedral and Priory. It was founded in 1160 and begun in the Romanesque style; however, the cathedral's construction suffered many setbacks. By the time of its consecration in 1318 in the presence of King Robert the Bruce, it had a Gothic overlay. At the time the largest church in Scotland, the cathedral established St. Andrews as the ecclesiastical capital of the country, but today the ruins can only suggest its former beauty and importance. There's a collection of early Christian and medieval monuments, as well as artifacts discovered on the cathedral site.

Off Pends Rd. ℂ 01334/472-563. Admission £2 ($3) adults, £1.50 ($2.25) seniors, 75p ($1.10) children 5–15. Apr–Sept daily 9:30am–5pm; Oct–Mar Mon–Sat 9:30am–4pm, Sun 2–4pm.

Castle of St. Andrews ℛ This ruined 13th-century castle eerily poised at

the edge of the sea boasts a bottle dungeon and secret passages. Founded in the early part of the 13th century, it was reconstructed several times and was once a bishop's palace and later a prison for reformers. The bottle dungeon is carved 24 feet (7m) down into the rock, and both prisoners and food were dropped through it. There's said to be no nastier dungeon in all Scotland.

Much of the eeriness here concerns the 1546 arrest of religious reformer George Wishart and the show trial that followed. Convicted by a group of Catholic prelates spearheaded by Cardinal Beaton, Wishart was burned at the stake, reputedly while Beaton and his entourage watched from an upper-floor window. Vowing revenge, a group of reformers waited 3 months before gaining access to the castle while disguised as stonemasons. They overpowered the guards (some they killed, some they threw into the castle's moat) and murdered Beaton—and, rather bizarrely, preserved his corpse in salt so they could eventually give it a proper burial. The reformers retained control of the castle for several months, until the Catholic forces of the earl of Arran laid siege. As part of their efforts, the attackers almost completed a tunnel (they called it "a mine"), dug virtually through rock, beneath the castle walls. The (Protestant) defenders, in response, dug a tunnel ("a countermine") of their own, which intersected the first tunnel at a higher elevation, allowing the defenders to drop rocks, boiling oil, or whatever else on the attackers' heads. The resulting underground battle took on epic proportions during the virtually implacable year-long siege. As part of the tour, you can stumble down the narrow countermine to the place where besieged and besiegers met in this clash.

The Scores, 300 yd. (273m) northwest of the cathedral. ℂ 01334/477-196. Admission £2.80 ($4.20) adults, £2 ($3) seniors, £1 ($1.50) children. Combined tickets (Castle and Cathedral) £4 ($6) adults, £3 ($4.50) seniors, £1.20 ($1.80) children. Apr–Sept daily 9:30am–6:30pm; Oct–Mar daily 9:30am–4:30pm.

Secret Bunker ℛ Scotland's best-kept secret for 40 years of cold war, this

amazing labyrinth, built 100 feet (30m) below ground and encased in 15 feet (4.5m) of reinforced concrete, is where central government and military commanders would have run the country from if the United Kingdom had been attacked and nuclear war broken out. Built (in great secrecy) in 1951 to withstand aerial attack, it has a guardhouse entrance designed to look like a traditional Scottish farmhouse. You can visit the BBC studio where emergency broadcasts to Scotland would have been made and the switchboard room set up to handle 2,800 outside lines. The bunker could allow 300 people to live, work, and sleep in safety while coordinating war efforts, like aboveground retaliation. It also contains two cinemas showing authentic cold war films, an audiovisual theater, a cafe, and a gift shop.

You can wander at will through the underground labyrinth, but 30-minute guided tours depart daily at 11am, 1pm, and 3pm. For some amazing reason, the chapel here has been the site of several local weddings since decommissioning in 1993.

Underground Nuclear Command Centre, Crown Buildings (near St. Andrews), Fife. © 01333/310-301. Admission £6.70 ($10.05) adults, £5 ($7.50) seniors, £3.45 ($5.20) children 5–16. £17 ($25.50) per family. Apr–Oct daily 10am–5pm. From St. Andrews, follow the signs to Anstruther, driving 7½ miles (12km) south. At that point, signs show the way to the bunker.

SHOPPING

Specializing in Scottish art, **St. Andrews Fine Arts,** 84A Market St. (© 01334/ 474-080), also sells prints, drawings, and watercolors. All paintings were produced within the national boundaries of Scotland sometime between 1800 and the present. **Graeme Renton,** 72 South St. (© 01334/476-334), is one of Scotland's leading dealers of Oriental carpets, whether you're seeking antique rugs or reasonably priced reproductions. Rugs come in many sizes, prices, and styles. At **St. Andrews Pottery Shop,** 4 Church Sq. (© 01334/477-744), an array of decorative stoneware, ceramics, and enameled jewelry—most of it produced locally—is for sale. **Bonkers,** 80 Market St. (© 01334/473-919), is a typical tourist shop, hawking T-shirts, regional pottery, and other souvenirs, along with cards and stationery.

ACCOMMODATIONS
EXPENSIVE

Peat Inn ⨝⨝   About 7 miles from St. Andrews, in the village of Cupar, the Peat was built in 1760 and is currently an inn and post office. It offers beautifully furnished guest rooms and spacious suites, accompanied by David Wilson's exceptional cuisine in the restaurant. Some bathrooms have tubs as well as showers.

The restaurant uses almost all local ingredients—even the pigeons come from a St. Andrews farm. (They're prepared in a pastry case with wild mushrooms or in Armagnac-and-juniper sauce.) For a main course, try the roast monkfish and lobster with asparagus and wild mushrooms. The dessert specialty is a trio of caramel-flavored sweets, including crème caramel, caramel-flavored ice cream, and a caramelized apple pastry, all drizzled with caramel sauce. Lunch and dinner are served Tuesday through Saturday; prices are high.

Cupar, Fife KY15 5LH. © 01334/840-206. Fax 01334/840-530. www.peatinn.co.uk. 8 units. £150 ($225) suite for 2. Rates include Scottish breakfast. AE, MC, V. From St. Andrews, drive 7 miles (11km) southwest along A915, then branch onto B940. **Amenities:** Restaurant, bar; limited room service; dry cleaning; bike rental. *In room:* TV, coffeemaker, iron.

Rufflets Country House ⨝   The garden-and-golf crowd loves this cozy 1924 country house in a 10-acre (4.1-hectare) garden. Each good-size guest room is furnished in a homelike way (often in Queen Anne style), some with canopied or four-poster beds and all with combination tub/showers. The most modern rooms are in the new wing, but traditionalists request space in the handsome main building. Reserve well in advance, as Rufflets is very popular with British vacationers.

Even if you aren't staying here, you may want to reserve a table at the garden-style Rufflets Hotel Restaurant, overlooking the award-winning garden. Excellent fresh ingredients are used in the Continental and Scottish dishes.

Strathkinness Low Rd., St. Andrews, Fife KY16 9TX. ℂ **01334/472-594.** Fax 01334/478-703. www.rufflets. co.uk. 22 units. £190–£240 ($285–$360) double. Rates include Scottish breakfast. AE, DC, MC, V. Take B939 for 1½ miles (2.5km) from St. Andrews. **Amenities:** Restaurant, bar; room service; babysitting; laundry/ dry cleaning. *In room:* TV, coffeemaker, hair dryer.

Rusacks   A grand Victorian pile built in 1887 by Josef Rusack, a German from Silesia who recognized St. Andrews's potential as a golf capital, Rusacks sits at the edge of the famous 18th hole of Pilmour Links of the Old Course. The hotel's stone walls are capped with neoclassical gables and slate roofs. Inside, chintz picks up the tones from the bouquets of flowers sent in fresh twice a week. Between the panels and Ionic columns of the public rooms, racks of lend-able books re-create the atmosphere of a private country-house library. Upstairs, the spacious guest rooms contain some carved antiques and all modern conveniences, but nothing to equal the St. Andrews Old Course Hotel (see below). Each unit comes with a beautifully maintained private bathroom with combination tub/shower.

The basement Golf Club has golf-related photos, trompe-l'oeil racks of books, Chesterfield sofas, and vested waiters. Light meals and snacks are served here. The Old Course restaurant, overlooking the 18th hole, offers daily specials along with local game, meat, and fish, accompanied by a wine list from a well-stocked cellar.

Pilmour Links, St. Andrews, Fife KY16 9JQ. ℂ **800/225-5843** in the U.S., or 01334/474-321. Fax 01334/ 477-896. www.heritage-hotels.com. 68 units. £110–£189 ($165–$283.50) double; from £240 ($360) suite. AE, DC, MC, V. **Amenities:** 2 restaurants, bar; small exercise room; room service; babysitting; laundry. *In room:* TV, coffeemaker, hair dryer.

St. Andrews Golf Hotel ℱ   A combination of greenery, sea mists, and tradition makes this late-Victorian property extremely popular with golfers, despite the fact that many of them confuse it at first glance with the larger and more prestigious St. Andrews Old Course Hotel (see below). About 200 yards (182m) from the first tee-off of the famous golf course, it was built as a private home and later expanded and transformed into a hotel run by Brian and Maureen Hughes. The comfortable but unstylish guest rooms have combination tub/showers. The units in the front get the view but also the noise. Bar lunches are served Monday through Saturday, and table d'hôte dinners are presented nightly in an oak-paneled restaurant with a fireplace.

40 The Scores, St. Andrews, Fife KY16 9AS. ℂ **01334/472-611.** Fax 01334/472-188. www.standrews-golf. co.uk. 22 units. £150–£175 ($225–$262.50) double; £195–£205 ($292.50–$307.50) suite. Rates include Scottish breakfast. AE, DC, MC, V. **Amenities:** Restaurant, 2 bars; room service; laundry/dry cleaning. *In room:* TV, coffeemaker, hair dryer.

St. Andrews Old Course Hotel ℱℱℱ   Many dedicated golfers choose the St. Andrews Old Course Hotel, close to A91 on the outskirts of town, where it overlooks the 17th fairway, the Road Hole of the Old Course. (Don't let the name mislead you: The hotel isn't related to the links of the same name, and guests here find access to the course just as difficult as it is elsewhere.) Fortified by finnan haddie and porridge, a real old-fashioned Scottish breakfast, you can face that diabolical stretch of greenery where the Scots have been whacking away since the early 15th century. Some £16 million ($24 million) has been spent to transform the place into a world-class hotel (with price tags to match), and the facade was altered to keep it in line with St. Andrews's more traditional buildings; its balconies afford top-view seats at all golf tournaments. The guest rooms and suites have been remodeled and refurbished, offering traditional wooden furniture and state-of-the-art marble bathrooms.

Well-prepared and high-priced international cuisine is served in the Road Hole Grill. In summer, light meals and afternoon tea are offered in a casual dining room known as Sands.

Old Station Rd., St. Andrews, Fife KY16 9SP. © 01334/474-371. Fax 01334/477-668. www.oldcoursehotel.co.uk. 137 units. £270–£350 ($405–$525) double; from £345–£395 ($517.50–$592.50) suite. Rates include Scottish breakfast. Children under 12 stay free in parents' room. AE, DC, MC, V. **Amenities:** Restaurant, bar; pro shop; pool; spa; Jacuzzi; steam rooms; beauty/therapy salons; 24-hour room service; massage room; babysitting; laundry. *In room:* TV, minibar, coffeemaker, hair dryer.

MODERATE

Inn at Lathones *&* Once a coaching inn, this 200-year-old manor has been thoughtfully restored and provides a reasonable alternative for golfers who can't afford the grand hotels. All of its midsize guest rooms are nicely furnished, with individually controlled heating and combination tub/showers. Two units have log-burning stoves and Jacuzzis. The public rooms reflect Scottish tradition, with open fires and beamed ceilings. The restaurant is under the guidance of chef Marc Guiburt, who has created a French-inspired Continental cuisine using fresh Scottish produce.

By Largoward, St. Andrews, Fife KY9 1JE. © 01334/840-494. Fax 01334/840-694. www.theinn.co.uk. 14 units. £100–£140 ($150–$210) double. Rates include Scottish breakfast. MC, V. Take A915 for 5 miles (8km) southwest of the center of St. Andrews. **Amenities:** 2 restaurants, bar; limited tour desk; room service; laundry. *In room:* TV, coffeemaker, hair dryer.

Russell Hotel Once a 19th-century private home, the Russell enjoys an ideal location overlooking St. Andrews Bay, a 2-minute walk from the Old Course's first tee. It's well run by Gordon and Fiona de Vries and offers fully equipped though standard guest rooms (some with tub-only bathrooms). The cozy Victorian pub serves drinks and bar suppers to a loyal local crowd, while the rather unremarkable restaurant offers moderately priced fixed-price dinners nightly.

26 The Scores, St. Andrews, Fife KY16 9AS. © 01334/473-447. Fax 01334/478-279. www.russellhotelstandrews.co.uk. 10 units. £76–£100 ($114–$150) double. Rates include Scottish breakfast. AE, MC, V. Closed Dec 24–Jan 12. **Amenities:** Restaurant, bar; room service; laundry. *In room:* TV, coffeemaker, hair dryer.

INEXPENSIVE

Ashleigh House Hotel This B&B near the town center was built in 1883 as a fever hospital to quarantine patients afflicted with scarlet fever, diphtheria, and other plagues of the day. After World War I, it was transformed into an orphanage; in the late 1980s, it was finally converted to a B&B. The trio of thick-walled stone cottages are connected by means of covered passageways. On site is a bar with a wide assortment of single malts and a rough-and-ready kind of charm. The guest rooms are outfitted with good beds and flowered upholstery (some with tub- or shower-only bathrooms).

37 St. Mary St., St. Andrews, Fife KY16 8AZ. © 01334/475-429. Fax 01334/474383. 10 units, 9 with private bathroom. £40–£60 ($60–$90) double without bathroom; £70–£95 ($105–$142.50) double with bathroom. Rates include breakfast. MC, V. **Amenities:** Bar; sauna; solarium. *In room:* TV, coffeemaker, hair dryer.

Bell Craig Guest House Occupying a century-old–stone-fronted house, this B&B is in a historic neighborhood, a 3-minute walk from the Old Course. This guesthouse has had long practice at housing the parents of students at the nearby university. Sheila Black, the hardworking owner, runs the place with decency and pride and makes a point to spruce up each room in a different style at regular intervals. (Our favorite is the room done in tartan.) Each unit is high-ceilinged, cozy, completely unpretentious, and well scrubbed.

8 Murray Park, St. Andrews, Fife KY16 9AW. ⓒ **01334/472-962.** www.bellcraig.co.uk. 6 units. £45–£57 ($67.50–$85.50) double. Rates include breakfast. MC, V. *In room:* TV, coffeemaker, hair dryer, no phone.

DINING

Grange Inn SCOTTISH/SEAFOOD   An old-fashioned hospitality prevails in this country cottage with its garden, offering a good choice of dishes made from fresh produce. Local beef and lamb always appear on the menu, as do fish and shellfish from the fishing villages of East Neuk. Fruits and herbs come from Cupar. Typical of the offerings are beef filet with port sauce complemented by wild mushrooms, or chicken suprême stuffed with julienne of vegetables and coated with almonds. A classic opener and an old favorite is a stew of mussels and onions.

Grange Rd., at Grange (on B959). ⓒ **01334/472-670.** Reservations recommended. Fixed-price menus £21.95–£27 ($32.95–$40.50). DC, MC, V. Daily 12:30–2pm and 7–8:45pm. Drive about 1½ miles (2.5km) from St. Andrews on B959.

Ostlers Close ⭐ BRITISH/INTERNATIONAL   Sophisticated and intensely concerned with the quality of its cuisine, this charming restaurant occupies a 17th-century building that functioned in the early 20th century as a temperance hotel. Today, in the heart of the hamlet of Cupar, it contains a kitchen in what used to be the hotel's stables, with a severely elegant set of dining rooms in the hotel's former public areas. Menu items are based on seasonal Scottish produce and are likely to include roasted saddle of roe venison with wild-mushroom sauce; pan-fried scallops with fresh asparagus and butter sauce; a fresh medley of seafood with champagne-flavored butter sauce; and filet of Scottish lamb stuffed with skirlie, an old-fashioned but flavorful combination of bacon-flavored oat-meal and herbs. Whenever it's available, opt for the confit of duckling with salted pork and lentils.

25 Bonnygate, in the nearby town of Cupar, 7 miles (11km) from St. Andrews. ⓒ **01334/655-574.** Reservations recommended. Main courses £9.50–£13.98 ($14.25–$20.95) lunch; £14–£22 ($21–$33) dinner. AE, MC, V. Tues–Fri 12:15–2pm; Tues–Sat 7–9:30pm. Closed 2 weeks mid-May. From St. Andrews, go along A91 for 7 miles (11km) to the southwest until you reach the village of Cupar.

ST. ANDREWS AFTER DARK

The cultural center of St. Andrews is the **Byre Theatre,** Abbey Street (ⓒ **01334/ 476-288**), which features drama ranging from Shakespeare to musical comedies. Recently rebuilt from the foundation up, it reopened in July 2001. Tickets cost £10 ($15) for adults and £6 ($9) for children. Pick up the weekly *What's On in Fife* from the local tourist office to find out what's featured.

Victoria, 1A St. Mary's Place (ⓒ **01334/476-964**), is the place to catch a live band in St. Andrews. This student-filled pub features folk, rock, and blues acts on Thursday and Saturday, as well as karaoke every Friday. There's no live music during the summer. John Smiths, Beamish Stout, McEwans Lager, 78 Shilling, and 80 Shilling are available on tap. Open daily from 10am to 1am.

A pub since 1904, the **Central Bar,** at the corner of Market and College streets (ⓒ **01334/478-296**), is an antiquated room with a jukebox, and it may become rowdy during a football or tennis match. The best brews here are Old Peculiar, Theakstons XB, and McEwans Lager. Open daily from 11:30am to 1am.

Chariots, in the Scores Hotel (*(C)* **01334/472-451**), attracts mainly a local crowd, ranging from 30 to 60 years old, who gather in the evening for conversation over a few pints. Despite a strong regional tradition of beer brewing, two outsiders, Guinness and Millers, are featured on tap. Open daily from noon to midnight.

4 Falkland: One of Scotland's Loveliest Villages

21 miles (34km) N of Edinburgh

The royal burgh of Falkland, containing cobblestone streets and crooked houses, lies at the northern base of the hill of East Lomond. Its notable sight is Falkland Palace and Gardens, now owned by the National Trust of Scotland and forever associated with memories of Mary Queen of Scots. In your rush to visit the royal palace, try not to forget to walk around Falkland itself. It's one of the loveliest villages in Scotland.

ESSENTIALS

GETTING THERE   From Edinburgh, take the **train** to Markinch, the closest rail link to Falkland; the trip takes 30 minutes. Call *(C)* **08457/484-950** for schedules. From Markinch, **bus** no. 36 connects with arriving trains and runs to Falkland in 15 minutes.

If you're **driving,** take A90 northwest of Edinburgh across the Forth Road Bridge, then continue northeast along A921, which leads into A92. At the junction with A912, head northwest to Falkland.

VISITOR INFORMATION   The nearest **tourist office** is at 19 Shytes Causeway, Kirkcaldy (*(C)* **01592/267-775**), 13 miles (21km) south of Falkland. It's open Monday through Saturday from 10am to 5pm (to 5:30pm in August).

SEEING THE PALACE

Falkland Palace and Gardens *(R)*   Since the 14th century, Falkland has been connected with Scottish kings and queens. Originally a castle stood on the site of today's palace, but it was replaced in the 16th century. Falkland then became a favorite seat of the Scottish court. James V died here, and Mary Queen of Scots used to come to Falkland for hunting and hawking. It was also here that Francis Stuart, fifth earl of Bothwell, tried to seize his young cousin, James VI, son of Mary Queen of Scots. The gardens have been laid out according to the original royal plans. Falkland also boasts the oldest royal tennis court in the United Kingdom.

High St. *(C)* 01337/857-397. Admission to palace and gardens £5 ($7.50) adults; £4 ($6) seniors, students, and children; £14 ($21) per family. Admission to garden only £2.50 ($3.75) adults; £1.70 ($2.55) seniors, students, and children; £7 ($10.50) per family. Apr–Oct Mon–Sat 11am–5:30pm, Sun 1:30–5:30pm. Closed Nov–Mar.

ACCOMMODATIONS

Covenanter Hotel   This has been a popular inn since the early 18th century. The hotel, located on a small square opposite the church and palace, is built of local stone, with high chimneys, wooden shutters, and a Georgian entry. The guest rooms range from small to midsize, each traditionally furnished and modestly modernized. For before-dinner drinks, try the Covenanter Cocktail Bar; the old-style dining room serves moderately priced lunch and dinner daily. There's also a moderately priced bistro serving selections like beef-and-ale pie, grilled trout, various steaks, and vegetarian dishes.

The Square, Falkland, Fife KY15 7BU. *(C)* 01337/857-224. Fax 01337/857-163. www.covenanterhotel.com. 7 units. £48 ($72) double or apt. Rates Include Scottish breakfast. AE, DC, MC, V. **Amenities:** 2 restaurants; bar; laundry service. *In room:* TV, coffeemaker, hair dryer, iron.

DINING

Kind Kyttock's Kitchen SCOTTISH   Situated near the palace, this restaurant is also an art gallery that displays local crafts and paintings. A specialty is homemade oat cakes with cheese; the salads are good as well. The bread is also homemade, very fresh tasting. For a tea, we suggest pancakes with fruit and fresh cream. Even better, however, are the tarts with fresh cream. A cup of scotch broth, served with a slice of whole-meal bread, is a favorite.

Cross Wynd. ℂ 01337/857-477. Main courses £3.50–£5.25 ($5.25–$7.90). AE, MC, V. Tues–Sun 10:30am–5:30pm. Closed Dec 24–Jan 5.

5 Stirling ⟨★⟨★

37 miles (59.5km) NW of Edinburgh, 28 miles (45km) NE of Glasgow

Stirling is dominated by its impressive castle, perched on a 250-foot (76m) basalt rock formed by the Rivers Forth and Clyde and the relatively small parcel of land between them. The ancient town of Stirling, on the main east–west route across Scotland, grew up around the castle. It lies in the heart of an area so turbulent in Scottish history it was called the "cockpit of Scotland." (Here "cockpit" refers to the pit where male chickens would be forced to engage in cockfights.) One memorable battle fought here was the Battle of Bannockburn in 1314, when Robert I (the Bruce) defeated the army of Edward II of England and gained Scotland its independence. Another was the Battle of Stirling Bridge in 1297 (see "The True Story of *Braveheart*," below).

Ever since the release of Mel Gibson's *Braveheart*, world attention has focused on the Scottish national hero William Wallace, a freedom fighter who became known as the "hammer and scourge" of the English. However, *Braveheart* was filmed mostly in Ireland, and the Battle of Stirling Bridge in the movie was played out on a plain with not a bridge in sight.

Stirling is the central crossroads of Scotland, giving easy access by rail and road to all its major towns and cities. If you use it as a base, you'll be only a short distance from many attractions, including Loch Lomond, the Trossachs, and the Highlands.

ESSENTIALS

GETTING THERE   Frequent **trains** run between Glasgow and Stirling (a 45-minute trip) and between Edinburgh and Stirling (a 60-minute trip). A 1-day round-trip ticket from Edinburgh costs £5.50 to £8.80 ($8.25 to $13.20); from Glasgow, £6.20 to £7.70 ($9.30 to $11.55). For schedules, call **National Express Enquiries** (ℂ 08457/484-950).

Frequent **buses** run to Stirling from Glasgow (a 45-minute trip). A 1-day round-trip ticket from Glasgow costs £4.20 ($6.30). Check with **Scottish CityLink** (ℂ 0990/505-050) for details.

If you're **driving** from Glasgow, head northeast along A80 to M80, at which point continue north. From Edinburgh, head northwest along M9.

VISITOR INFORMATION   The **tourist office** is at 41 Dumbarton Rd. (ℂ 01786/475-019). It's open from April to mid-May, Monday through Saturday from 9am to 5pm; mid-May to June, Monday through Saturday from 9am to 6pm and Sunday from 10am to 4pm; July and August, Monday through Saturday from 9am to 7pm and Sunday from 10am to 5pm; September, Monday through Saturday from 9am to 6pm and Sunday from 10am to 5pm; October, Monday through Saturday from 9:30am to 5pm; and November to March, Monday through Friday from 10am to 5pm and Saturday from 10am to 4pm.

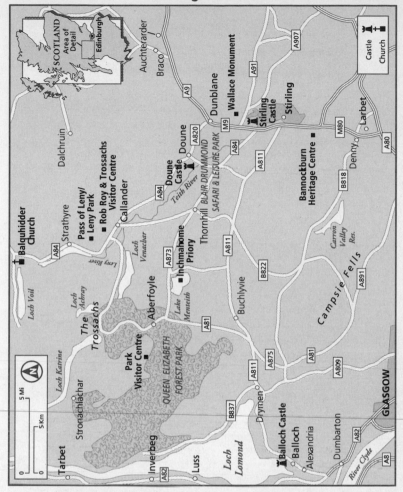

SEEING THE SIGHTS

To get a real feel for Stirling, stroll the **Back Walk,** beginning near Rob Roy's statue, near the Guildhall in the town center. Following this trail along the outside of the town's once-fortified walls, you'll have good views, see an old watchtower (and a place where prisoners were hanged), and eventually reach Stirling Castle.

Stirling Castle ★★ There are traces of a 7th-century royal habitation of the Stirling area, and on the right bank of the Forth, Stirling Castle dates from the Middle Ages, when its location on a dividing line between the Lowlands and the Highlands made it the key to the Highlands. The castle became an important seat of two kings, James IV and James V, both of whom added to it, the latter following classic Renaissance style, then relatively unknown in Britain. Mary Queen of Scots lived here as an infant monarch for the first 4 years of her life. After its final defeat in 1746, Bonnie Prince Charlie's army stopped here. Later,

The True Story of *Braveheart*

Sir Robert the Bruce at Bannockburn
Beat the English in every wheel and turn,
And made them fly in great dismay
From off the field without delay . . .
                    —William McGonagall, "The Battle of Bannockburn"

Robert the Bruce (1274–1329) was the first of three kings of Scotland named Robert. Although neither Mel Gibson nor Liam Neeson selected this daring man as the subject for a movie, they might well have done so, for Robert the Bruce led a life filled with all the excitement and thrills of a 1930s Errol Flynn adventure flick.

In 1292, Edward I of England gave the Scottish crown to John de Balliol, known as the "vassal king," demanding Scotland pay homage to the English throne. But instead, the Scots formed what was to become known as the Auld Alliance with France in October 1295. Edward viewed this as a declaration of war, and the "Hammer of Scotland" stormed into Scotland, devastating the countryside and capturing and taking home the Stone of Destiny from Scone (the coronation stone of Scottish kings).

William Wallace (1274–1305) defeated the English at the 1297 Battle of Stirling Bridge and was made "Guardian of the Realm." Edward, in turn, defeated Wallace at the Battle of Falkirk the following year. Outlawed for his activities, Wallace hid for 7 years until his capture, at which time he was paraded through the streets of London and hanged and drawn and quartered, with his entrails burned before his eyes as he died. This horrific English method of execution reputedly was devised by Edward especially for Wallace.

Robert the Bruce replaced Wallace as "Guardian of Scotland." In March 1306, Bruce had himself crowned king of Scotland. Edward rushed north and defeated Bruce's forces at Methven and Dalry. Like Wallace, Bruce became an outlaw, forced into hiding, probably on the island of Rathlin off the Irish coast. There he was said to have learned patience, courage, and hope by watching a spider persevere in spinning a web, swinging from one rafter to another on a fragile thread.

In 1307, he returned to Scotland, where he captured Perth in 1313 and Edinburgh in 1314. At Bannockburn, also in 1314, he defeated the forces of Edward's son, Edward II. The pope excommunicated Bruce, and his sovereignty was not recognized by the royal houses of Europe.

Upon Edward III's coronation in 1327, the Scots launched a raid into England. The following year, Edward was almost captured when he led a retaliatory army into Scotland. But in 1328 a peace treaty was signed, acknowledging Scotland's independence. David, Bruce's 4-year-old son, was "married" to Joan, Edward III's 7-year-old sister. The Bruce ruled Scotland wisely until his death at Cardross Castle on the Clyde.

the castle became an army barracks and headquarters of the Argyll and Sutherland Highlanders, one of Britain's most celebrated regiments. An audiovisual
presentation explains what you're about to see.

In the castle is the **Museum of the Argyll and Sutherland Highlanders**
(℃ **01786/475-165**), presenting an excellent exhibit of colors, pipe banners,
and regimental silver, along with medals (some of which go back to the Battle
of Waterloo) won by Scottish soldiers for valor. Run by Britain's Ministry of
Defense, it functions as a showcase for a military unit, some of whose members
were, at press time, in Kosovo and Bosnia as part of the U.N. peacekeeping force.

Upper Castle Hill. ℃ **01786/450-000**. Admission to castle £6 ($9) adults, £4.50 ($6.75) seniors, £1.50
($2.25) children; free admission to museum. Castle Apr–Sept daily 9:30am–6pm, Oct–Mar daily
9:30am–5pm; museum year-round Mon–Sat 10am–5:45pm, Sun 11am–4:45pm.

Church of the Holy Rude ℛ   From the early 15th century, the Church of the
Holy Rude is said to be the only church in the country still in use that has witnessed a coronation. It was 1567 when the 13-month-old James VI was crowned
here, Mary Queen of Scots' son who was to become James I of England. John
Knox preached the sermon. Constructed with the simplest of building tools
more than 600 years ago and built as a reminder of the cross (*rude*) on which
Christ was supposedly crucified, the church is memorable for its rough but
evocative stonework and its elaborate 19th-century stained glass—particularly
on the south side of the choir. Recent restorations have been done in the most
tasteful and unobtrusive of styles.

St. John St. ℃ **01786/475-275**. Free admission. May–Sept daily 10am–5pm. Closed Oct–Apr.

EXPLORING NEARBY BANNOCKBURN

You can take an interesting detour to Bannockburn, a name that looms large in
Scottish history. It was there that Robert the Bruce, his army of 6,000 outnumbered three to one, defeated the forces of Edward II in 1314. Before nightfall on
that day, Robert the Bruce had won back the throne of Scotland. The battlefield,
which makes for a peaceful walk today, lies off M80, 2 miles (3km) south of
Stirling.

At the **Bannockburn Heritage Centre,** Glasgow Road (℃ **01786/812-664**),
an audiovisual presentation tells the story of these events, while *The Kingdom of
the Scots* exhibit traces the history of Scotland from William Wallace to the
Union of Crowns. The queen herself came here in 1964 to unveil an equestrian
statue of Bruce. The site is open all year, while the Heritage Centre and shop are
open April through October, daily from 10am to 5:30pm, and in March,
November, and December, daily from 10:30am to 4pm. The last audiovisual
showing is at 5:30pm. Admission is £2.50 ($3.75) for adults, £1.70 ($2.55) for
seniors and children, and £7 ($10.50) per family.

From the **Borestone,** where Robert the Bruce commanded his forces at the
start of his battle for Stirling, you can see Stirling Castle and the Forth Valley.
He planted his standards (flags) as inspiration for his troops, and today a flag-
pole capped with the standards of Scotland still flies proudly from atop this low
hill. It's located off M80/M9 at Junction 9.

SHOPPING

Stirling's town center has some interesting shopping. One good hunting ground
is the **Thistle Centre** indoor shopping plaza, home of about 65 shops at the
junction of Port Street and Murray Place.

The book dealer **McCutcheon's,** 51 Baker St. (© **01786/461-771**), specializes in antiquarian volumes and carries a startlingly vast range of books.

The best woolen goods are at **R. R. Henderson,** 6–8 Friar St. (© **01786/473-681**), a Highland outfitter selling not only sweaters and scarves but also made-to-order kilts and tartans.

Some of the best shopping is not in Stirling itself but in the outlying area. Take A9 to Larbert and at the roundabout follow A18 west until you see the sign for **Barbara Davidson's Pottery Studio,** Muirhall Farm, Larbert (© **01324/554-430**), 9 miles (14.5km) south of Stirling. At this 18th-century farmstead, one of Scotland's best-known potters operates her studio and workshop. A large selection of functional wares is exhibited and sold here.

East of Stirling, three towns form the **Mill Trail Country:** Alva, Alloa, and Tillicoultry. Many quality textile mills have factory outlets here, offering bargain prices on cotton, woolens, and even cashmere goods. The best selection of sweaters is available at **Inverallen Handknitters Ltd.,** Alva Industrial Estate, Alva (© **01259/762-292**). The hand-knitted traditional sweaters here are particularly appealing. A good selection of clothing for children and infants supplements the selections for men and women at **Glen Alva Ltd.,** Hallpark, Whine Road, Alloa (© **01259/723-024**). If you're inspired to knit your own creation, head to **Patons & Baldwins,** Kilcraigo Mill, Alloa (© **01325/394-394**), which manufactures quality yarns.

For directions, hours, and other information, contact the **Mill Trail Visitor Centre,** West Stirling Street, Alva (© **01259/769-696**), 9 miles (14.5km) east of the center of Stirling. It's open January through June and October through December, daily from 10am to 5pm; July through September, daily from 9am to 5pm.

ACCOMMODATIONS
EXPENSIVE

Stirling Highland Hotel ℛ   Stirling's newest hotel has also become its most important. The stylish Highland was installed in what was once the Old High School, a Victorian building to which everyone in town has an emotional link. The historic atmosphere was treated with respect, and many of the architectural features were kept intact. Florals, tartans, and solid wood furnishings dominate both the public rooms and the guest rooms; the fairly routine guest rooms are in a three-story annex. Each unit comes with a shower; a few are equipped with tubs as well. From its position close to Stirling Castle, the hotel enjoys views of the town and surrounding region. Rather high-priced Scottish cuisine is featured in Scholars Restaurant, while Rizzio's Restaurant serves Italian fare.

Spittal St., Stirling, Stirlingshire FK8 1DU. © **01786/272-727.** Fax 01786/272-829. www.paramount-hotels. co.uk. 96 units. £136–£150 ($204–$225) double; £170–£190 ($255–$285) suite. AE, DC, MC, V. **Amenities:** 2 restaurants; indoor pool; squash courts; gym; Jacuzzi; snooker room; solarium; steam room; room service; babysitting; laundry. *In room:* TV, coffeemaker, hair dryer.

MODERATE

Golden Lion Hotel   About a block downhill from Holyrood Church, the Golden Lion dates from 1786, when it was a coaching inn; but, its sandstone shell was greatly enlarged with the addition of modern wings in 1962. It's now one of the oldest and largest hotels in town and has recently improved and modernized most of its guest rooms. The rooms are simple and easy on the eye, with combination tub/showers.

8–10 King St., Stirling, Stirlingshire FK8 2ND. © 01786/475-351. Fax 01786/472-755. www.miltonhotels. com. 67 units. £87–£96 ($130.50–$144) double. Rates include Scottish breakfast. AE, DC, MC, V. **Amenities:** Restaurant, bar; room service; laundry/dry cleaning. *In room:* TV, coffeemaker, hair dryer.

Park Lodge Hotel ✿ This stylish hotel occupies a 19th-century Italianate mansion, across from a city park in a residential neighborhood. Built of stone blocks and slates, it has a Doric portico, Tudor-style chimney pots, a Georgian-era core from 1825, and century-old climbing roses and wisteria. Anne and Georges Marquetty house guests in 10 upstairs rooms and suggest they dine at their elegant restaurant, The Heritage (see below). Each bedroom contains antique furnishings (room 6 has a four-poster bed) as well as combination tub/shower. You might enjoy tea in the walled garden, with its widely spaced iron benches and terra-cotta statues. On the other side of tall casement windows is a pair of French-inspired salons.

32 Park Terrace, Stirling, Stirlingshire FK8 2JS. © 01786/474-862. Fax 01786/449-748. www.parklodge.net. 10 units. £87–£96 ($130.50–$144) double. Rates include Scottish breakfast. MC, V. Bus: 51 or 52. **Amenities:** Restaurant, bar; room service; laundry. *In room:* TV, coffeemaker, hair dryer.

Terraces Hotel (Value) Built originally as a fine Georgian house of sandstone, this hotel stands on a raised terrace in a quiet residential neighborhood and is now one of the best values in town. Each midsize guest room is furnished in a country-house motif of flowered curtains and solidly traditional furniture (some bathrooms contain showers only). The half-paneled cocktail bar and velvet-upholstered restaurant are popular settings for local parties and wedding receptions. Melville's Restaurant offers a moderately priced Scottish and Continental menu.

4 Melville Terrace, Stirling, Stirlingshire FK8 2ND. © 01786/472-268. Fax 01786/450-314. www. terraceshotel.co.uk. 18 units. £90 ($135) double. Rates include Scottish breakfast. AE, DC, MC, V. **Amenities:** Restaurant, bar; pool; room service; laundry. *In room:* TV, dataport, coffeemaker, hair dryer.

INEXPENSIVE

Allan's Guest House (Kids) Private and personal, this rambling 1840s stone house is the domain of Mrs. Allan, who rents two of her five bedrooms to paying guests. The cozy rooms are painted and decorated in shades of pale pink. This place welcomes families with small children.

15 Albert Place (a 10-minute walk north of the town center), Stirling FK8 2RE. © 01786/475-175. 2 units, none with private bathroom. £42 ($63) double. Rates include breakfast. No credit cards. Closed Nov–Feb. *In room:* Coffeemaker, no phone.

West Plean House ✿ (Value) This working farm is a delight. It not only has a lovely walled garden but also makes a great base for taking walks into the surrounding woodland. The helpful, welcoming hosts offer extremely good value. Their guest rooms are spacious and well furnished, with an eye to comfort and conveniences; each is equipped with a shower-only bathroom. The home-cooked breakfast makes the place a winner.

Denny Rd., 3½ miles (6km) from Stirling on A872, Stirling FK7 8HA. © and fax 01786/480-550. westplean@virgin.net. 3 units. £48–£52 ($72–$78) double. Rates include breakfast. No credit cards. Closed Jan–Feb. *In room:* TV, coffeemaker, no phone.

DINING

The Heritage ✿ FRENCH/SCOTTISH Culinary sophistication and beautiful decor rank this as one of the best restaurants in the district. It's in the stylish Park Lodge Hotel (see above), on a quiet residential street near the center of town, a 5-minute walk east of the rail station. You can enjoy a drink in the gentleman's parlor, with somber walls and enviable antiques, before descending to the low-ceilinged basement. Amid a French-inspired decor, you'll taste some of the best cuisine in Stirling, prepared with finesse by Georges Marquetty. In his youth, he worked as an executive chef in Paris and later spent 12 years in Cincinnati (where he was voted one of the leading chefs of America). His specialties include scallops, scampi, and prawns in Pernod sauce; filet of wild venison with port and black-currant sauce; scallops with smoked ham in lemon sauce; and foie gras with truffles.

At the Park Lodge Hotel, 32 Park Terrace, Stirling. ℭ **01786/473-660.** Fax 01786/449-748. Reservations recommended. Main courses £6–£12 ($9–$18); fixed-price 2-course lunch £12 ($18); fixed-price 3-course dinner £18.50 ($27.75). MC, V. Daily noon–2pm and 6:30–9:30pm. Closed Sun in winter.

Riverway Restaurant SCOTTISH   This fully licensed restaurant enjoys a local reputation for good food at moderate prices. It has panoramic views of Stirling Castle, the Wallace Monument, and the Ochil Hills. The Riverway offers well-prepared food like honeyed lamb cutlets, deep-fried haddock, and grilled sirloin steaks. At lunch, you can order a real Scottish menu, including haggis, neeps, and tatties. The high-tea menu has such rib-sticking fare as fried liver, bacon, and onions. Wine of the house is sold by the glass or the bottle.

Kildean, ½ mile (1km) from the center of Stirling, just off M8 beside Junction 10. ℭ **01786/475-734.** Main courses £5.70–£11.50 ($8.55–$17.25); high tea £6.95–£12.50 ($10.45–$18.75). MC, V. Daily 10am–noon (coffee and scones), noon–3pm, and 3–6:30pm (high tea). Closed Mon in summer; closed Sun morning–Mon Nov–Easter.

STIRLING AFTER DARK

On the campus of Stirling University, the **Macrobert Arts Centre** (ℭ **01786/ 461-081**) offers plays, music, films, and art exhibits. The 497-seat main theater often presents dramas and concerts, while the 140-seat studio theater is used mainly for films. Cinema tickets cost £3.50 ($5.25) for adults and £2.50 ($3.75) for seniors and children, while theater tickets generally run £7 to £10 ($10.50 to $15). Admission to most concerts is £10 to £13 ($15 to $19.50). Call for current listings.

All That Jazz, 9 Upper Craigs (ℭ **01786/451-130**), is a lively bar popular with students. Music is usually provided via the stereo, but bands also appear infrequently. The bar serves a good range of single malts and pints of Kronenberg, Beamish Red, and McEwans. The adjoining restaurant serves a mix of Cajun and traditional Scottish fare, including the dreaded haggis, between 5 and 10pm nightly. The same menu is available throughout the day in the bar, which is open nightly until midnight or 1am.

O'Neill's, 11 Maxwell Place (ℭ **01786/459-901**), is a traditional Irish pub popular with Scottish students. Irish and Scottish folk bands play here. To find out who's on, check the flyers posted in the pub. There's never a cover. Daily from 11am to 1am.

Barnton Bar/Bistro, 3 Barnton St. (ℭ **01786/461-698**), is an Art Nouveau–style bar with marble-topped tables and high ceilings edged with ornate cornices. It's the center of gay life in Stirling but draws a mixed crowd of students, professionals, and old-timers as well. The Wednesday Quiz Night, where drinkers compete in general-knowledge trivia, is quite popular. There's no cover.

6 Dunblane & Its Grand Cathedral

7 miles (11km) N of Stirling, 42 miles (68km) NW of Edinburgh, 29 miles (47km) SW of Perth, 33 miles (53km) NE of Glasgow

A small cathedral city on the banks of the Allan Water, Dunblane takes its name from the Celtic church of St. Blane, which once stood on the site now occupied by the fine 13th-century Gothic cathedral. The cathedral is the main reason to visit; if that doesn't interest you, you'll find more romantic and lovelier places from which to explore the nearby Trossachs and Loch Lomond (say, Callander or Aberfoyle).

ESSENTIALS

GETTING THERE   **Trains** run between Glasgow and Dunblane with a stopover at Stirling; a one-way fare costs £4.70 ($7.05). Rail connections are also possible through Edinburgh via Stirling for £6.40 ($9.60) one-way. For 24-hour information, call ℂ **08457/484-950.**

Buses travel from the Goosecroft Bus Station in Stirling to Dunblane, costing £1.65 ($2.50) each way. Call ℂ **01786/446-474** in Stirling for schedules, or contact **First Edinburgh Busline** at ℂ **01324/613-777.**

If you're **driving** from Stirling, continue north along M9 to Dunblane.

VISITOR INFORMATION   A year-round **tourist office** is on Stirling Road (ℂ **01786/824-428**). It's open in July and August, Monday through Saturday from 10am to 6pm and Sunday from noon to 5pm; and May, June, and the first 3 weeks of September, Monday through Saturday from 10am to 5pm.

SEEING THE SIGHTS

After you visit the cathedral, you can wander and discover the streets around it. They're narrow and twisting and flanked by mellow old town houses, many from the 18th century.

Dunblane Cathedral 𝓡𝓡   An excellent example of 13th-century Gothic ecclesiastic architecture, this cathedral was spared the ravages of attackers who destroyed other Scottish worship centers. Altered in the 15th century and restored several times in the 19th and 20th centuries, it may have suffered most from neglect subsequent to the Reformation. A Jesse Tree window is in the west end of the building; of interest are the stalls, the misericords, the pulpit with carved figures of early ecclesiastical figures, and the wooden barrel-vaulted roof with colorful armorials. A Celtic stone from about A.D. 900 is in the north aisle.

Cathedral Close. ℂ **01786/823-388.** Free admission. Apr–Sept Mon–Sat 9:30am–6:30pm, Sun noon–6:30pm; Oct–Mar Mon–Sat 9:30am–4:30pm, Sun 2–4:30pm.

Cathedral Museum   In the 1624 Dean's House, the Cathedral Museum contains articles and papers displaying the story of Dunblane and its ancient cathedral; you can also visit an enclosed garden with a very old (restored) well. A 1687 structure on the grounds contains the library of Bishop Robert Leighton, an outstanding 17th-century churchman; if you're a serious scholar, you'll find a great deal of material on the effects of the troubled times in Scotland, most from before the Industrial Revolution. It's open the same hours as the Cathedral Museum.

On Cathedral Square in the Dean's House. ℂ **01786/823-440.** Free admission. May–Sept Mon–Sat 10:30am–1pm and 2–4:30pm.

ACCOMMODATIONS

Cromlix House _ℛℛℛ_ This manor house, built in 1880 as the seat of a family that has owned the surrounding 3,000 acres (1,215 hectares) for the past 500 years, is now the area's most elegant hotel. The owners still live on the estate and derive part of their income from organizing hunting and fishing expeditions in the surrounding moors and forests and on the River Allan. Croquet mallets, wellies, and fishing rods in the entrance evoke the atmosphere. Fishing in three private lakes, hunting, and tennis are all available, and you can enjoy walks through the surrounding forests and farmland. The manor has an elegant drawing room with big bow windows, and antiques are scattered about both the public and guest rooms. Bouquets of fresh flowers and open fires in cool weather add to the overall comfort. Most of the guest rooms (including eight suites with sitting rooms) have Queen Anne furnishings as well as combination tub/showers.

Kinbuck, Dunblane FK15 9JT. ℂ 01786/822-125. Fax 01786/825-450. www.cromlixhouse.com. 14 units. £205–£235 ($307.50–$352.50) double; £235–£325 ($352.50–$487.50) suite. AE, DC, MC, V. Closed Jan. Take A9 to B8033; the hotel is 3¹/₄ miles (5km) north of Dunblane just beyond the village of Kinbuck. **Amenities:** Restaurant, bar; tennis court; tour desk; room service; laundry. _In room:_ TV, coffeemaker, hair dryer.

Kippenross _ℛ_ _(Finds_ This country manor boasts a richer and more unusual history than many of the region's B&Bs. It was built in 1750 according to the Palladian-neoclassical lines of William Adam, father of Britain's most celebrated neoclassical architect, Robert Adam. Surrounded by 200 acres of parks, lawns, and gardens and artfully landscaped with exotic plantings, it's a perfect example of Scottish country-house living, supervised by the Stirling-Aird family. Two of the guest rooms overlook the sprawling front lawns; the other overlooks the forests at the back. Each unit comes with a tub or shower. Guests are welcomed into the family's drawing room and to formal breakfasts in the dining room; Susan Stirling-Aird prepares elegant dinners for those who reserve in advance. You're invited to bring your own liquor or wine, because the place doesn't have a liquor license. Susan's husband, Patrick, is a devoted ornithologist and bird-watcher.

Dunblane FK15 0LQ. ℂ 01786/824-048. Fax 01786/823-124. www.aboutscotland.com/stirling/kippenross. html. 3 units. £65 ($97.50) double. MC, V. From Stirling, drive 5 miles (8km) north, taking A9 toward Perth, then exiting onto B8033 and following the signs to Dunblane. **Amenities:** Dining room. _In room:_ No phone.

7 Doune _(★_ & Its Medieval Castle

41 miles (66km) NW of Edinburgh, 35 miles (56km) N of Glasgow, 8 miles (13km) NW of Stirling, 5 miles (8km) W of Dunblane

The small market town of Doune is a good center for exploring the Trossachs. The Rivers Teith and Ardoch flow through Doune. The town is visited today by those wanting to see one of the best-preserved medieval castles in Scotland as well as those who like to stop by the Blair Drummond Safari and Leisure Park. Accommodations and food can be found in nearby Dunblane or Stirling.

ESSENTIALS

GETTING THERE Stirling (see "Stirling," earlier in this chapter) is the closest **rail** link to Doune. **Buses** from the Stirling bus station on Goosecroft run throughout the day to Doune. Call ℂ **0990/808-080** for information. If you're **driving** from Dunblane (see "Dunblane & Its Grand Cathedral," above), continue west along A820.

VISITOR INFORMATION The nearest **tourist office** is at Dunblane (see section 6, "Dunblane & Its Grand Cathedral," above).

SEEING THE SIGHTS

Doune Castle ✿   This castle, once a royal palace, stands on the banks of the River Teith. Now owned by the earl of Moray, it was restored in 1883, making it one of the best preserved of Scotland's medieval castles. A keep-gatehouse rises about four floors to a height of almost 100 feet (30m), and to its right is a complex of structures containing the former great halls of the castle. Curtain walls with walks envelop three sides of a large patio. Note the outside staircase rising to the second floor of the lord's grand hall.

Hwy. A820, 4 miles (6.5km) west of Dunblane. ℂ 01786/841-742. Admission £2.50 ($3.75) adults, £1.90 ($2.85) seniors, £1 ($1.50) children. Apr–Sept daily 9:30am–6pm; Oct–Mar Mon–Wed 9:30am–4pm, Thurs 9:30am–noon, Sat 10am–4pm, Sun 2–4pm.

Blair Drummond Safari and Leisure Park   South of Doune is the Blair Drummond Safari and Leisure Park. You meet the typical cast of animal-safari characters here, but the park also offers a jungle cruise, a giant Astroglide, and an amusement arcade, as well as a pet farm and a performing sea lion show. You can have refreshments at the Watering Hole Bar or in the Ranch Kitchen (ℂ **01786/841-430**), or use one of the picnic areas.

Blair Drummond. ℂ **01786/841-456.** Admission £8.50 ($12.75) adults, £4.50 ($6.75) seniors and children 3–14. Easter to early Oct daily 10am–5:30pm. Take exit 10 off M9 onto A84 near Stirling.

8 Callander ✶ & a Trio of Lochs

16 miles (26km) NW of Stirling, 43 miles (69km) N of Glasgow, 52 miles (84km) NW of Edinburgh, 42 miles (68km) W of Perth

In Gaelic, the Trossachs means the "bristled country," an allusion to its luxuriant vegetation. The thickly wooded valley contains three lochs: Venachar, Achray, and Katrine. In summer, the steamer on Loch Katrine offers a fine view of the splendid scenery.

For many, the small town of Callander makes the best base for exploring the Trossachs and Loch Katrine, Loch Achray, and Loch Venachar. (The town of Aberfoyle, discussed later in this chapter, is another excellent choice.) For years, motorists—and before them, passengers traveling by bumpy coach—stopped here to rest up on the once-difficult journey between Edinburgh and Oban.

Callander stands at the entrance to the Pass of Leny in the shadow of the Callander Crags. The Rivers Teith and Leny meet to the west of the town.

ESSENTIALS

GETTING THERE   Stirling (see "Stirling," earlier in this chapter) is the nearest **rail** link. Once at Stirling, continue to Callander on a First Edinburgh bus from the Stirling station on Goosecroft Road. Contact the bus station at ℂ **01786/446-474** or **First Edinburgh Buses** at ℂ **01324/613-777.** A one-way fare is £2.90 ($4.35). If you're **driving** from Stirling, head north along M9, cutting northwest at the junction of A84 to Callander, bypassing Doune.

VISITOR INFORMATION   The **Rob Roy & Trossachs Visitor Centre** is at Ancaster Square (ℂ **01877/330-342**). It distributes a map pinpointing all the sights. It's open in January and February, Saturday and Sunday from 11am to 4:30pm; March through May and October through December, daily from 10am to 5pm; June, daily from 9:30am to 6pm; July and August, daily from 9am to 9pm; and September, daily from 10am to 6pm. The second floor is home to a permanent Rob Roy exhibit, complete with a video presentation about his life and times. Entrance is £2.90 ($4.35) for adults, £2.05 ($3.10) for seniors and students, and £1.25 ($1.90) for children.

EXPLORING THE AREA

In the scenic Leny Hills to the west of Callander beyond the Pass of Leny lie **Leny Park** and **Leny Falls.** At one time all the lands in Leny Park were part of the Leny estate, home of the Buchanan clan for more than 1,000 years. In the wild Leny Glen, a naturalist's paradise, you can see deer grazing. Leny Falls is an impressive sight, near the confluence of the River Leny and the River Teith. The remains of an abandoned railway make for a wonderful footpath or cycling path for exploring this scenic area. Rent a bike at **Wheels/Trossachs Backpackers,** on Invertrossachs Road, Callander (© **01877/331-100;** www.Scottish-hostel. co.uk), which charges £10 ($15) for a full day, £6 ($9) for a half day, and £35 ($52.50) for a week. It also provides bikers with sleeping rooms for £12.50 ($18.75) per night, conducts organized walks, and can arrange canoe trips. Open daily from 10am to 6pm.

Four miles (6.5km) beyond the Pass of Leny lies **Loch Lubnaig** ("crooked lake"), divided into two reaches by a rock and considered fine fishing waters. Nearby is **Little Leny,** the ancestral burial ground of the Buchanans.

You'll find more falls at **Bracklinn,** 1½ miles (2.5km) northeast of Callander. In a gorge above the town, Bracklinn is one of the most scenic of the local beauty spots.

One of the most interesting sites around Callander is **Balquhidder Church** ⚘, 13 miles (21km) northwest off A84. This is the burial place of Rob Roy MacGregor. The church also has the St. Angus Stone from the 8th century, a 17th-century bell, and some Gaelic Bibles.

A good selection of woolens can be found at **Callander Woollen Mill,** 12–18 Main St. (© **01877/330-273**)—everything from scarves, skirts, and jackets to kilts, trousers, and knitwear. Another outlet for woolen goods, tartans, and woven rugs is the **Trossachs Woollen Mill** (© **01877/330-178**), 1 mile (1.6km) north of Callander on A84 in the hamlet of Kilmahog.

The town has an excellent golf course, the wooded and scenic **Callendar Golf Course,** Aveland Road (© **01877/330-090**). At this 5,125-yard (4,664m) par-66 course, greens fees are £9 to £18 ($13.50 to $27) per round or £26 ($39) per day on weekdays, and £13 to £26 ($19.50 to $39) per round or £31 ($46.50) per day on Saturdays and Sundays. The trolley charge is included in club rental, which runs from £10 to £15 ($15 to $22.50) for 18 holes. No caddy service is available. The hilly fairways offer fine views, and the tricky moorland layout demands accurate tee shots.

ACCOMMODATIONS

Rooms are also available at **Dalgair Hotel** (see "Dining," below).

Arden House ⚘   This stone-sided Victorian B&B is instantly recognizable to several generations of British TV viewers because of its 1970s role as the setting for a BBC series, *Dr. Finlay's Casebook.* (Its plot involved two bachelor doctors and their interactions with their attractive housekeeper and the fictional town of Tannochbrae, which was modeled after Callander.) Built in 1870 as a vacation home for Lady Willoughby and still maintained by two attractive bachelors, William Jackson and Ian Mitchell, it offers a soothing rest amid an acre of gardens at the base of a rocky outcropping known as the Callendar Crags. The (0.41 hectare) well-known Bracklinn Falls are within a 5-minute walk. The public areas boast Victorian antiques, while the high-ceilinged guest rooms are tasteful and comfortable. (The most appealing is the plush Tannochbrae Suite.) Each unit comes with a shower; only the suite's bathroom has a tub. No smoking is permitted.

Bracklinn Rd., Callander FK17 8EQ. © **01877/330-235.** Fax 01877/330-235. www.smoothhound.co.uk/hotels/arden. 6 units. £55 ($82.50) double; £65 ($97.50) suite. Rates include breakfast. MC, V. From Callander, walk 5 minutes north, following the signs to Bracklinn Falls. No children under 14 accepted. *In room:* TV, coffeemaker, hair dryer, no phone.

Highland House Hotel   Owned and managed by Robert and Lorna Leckie, who took over in 1998, this Georgian stone building stands on a quiet, tree-lined street a few yards from the Teith and a short walk from the visitor center. All of the guest rooms are charming. Scottish-style meals are served nightly in the dining room or in simpler versions at the bar. Game casserole, with choice pieces of game in a rich red wine and port gravy, is a house specialty. The lounge offers 20 to 25 brands of malt whiskies, some relatively obscure.

S. Church St. (just off A84, near Ancaster Sq.), Callander FK17 8BN. © **01877/330-269.** Fax 01877/339-004. www.highlandhousehotel.co.uk. 9 units. £40–£50 ($60–$75) double. Rates include Scottish breakfast. MC, V. **Amenities:** Dining room, lounge; limited room service. *In room:* TV, coffeemaker.

Roman Camp Country House Hotel ✻✻✻   This is the leading hotel in town. Once a 17th-century hunting lodge with pink walls and small gray-roofed towers, it was built on the site of a Roman camp. Today you head up a 200-yard (182m) driveway, with shaggy Highland cattle and sheep grazing on either side; in summer, flower beds are in bloom. Inside the gracious country house, some of the guest rooms are furnished with bedhead crowns, gilt-framed mirrors, and stenciled furnishings, while others are contemporary with blond-wood pieces. One unit has been adapted for travelers with disabilities; most have shower-only bathrooms. The dining room was converted in the 1930s from the old kitchen. The ceiling design is based on Scottish painted ceilings of the 16th and 17th centuries. The library, with its ornate plasterwork and richly grained paneling, is an elegant holdover from yesteryear.

Main St., Callander FK17 8BG. © **01877/330-003.** Fax 01877/331-533. www.roman-camp-hotel.co.uk. 17 units. £110–£165 ($165–$247.50) double; from £190 ($285) suite. Rates include Scottish breakfast. AE, DC, MC, V. As you approach Callander on A84, the entrance to the hotel is signposted between 2 pink cottages on Callander's Main St. **Amenities:** Restaurant, bar; limited room service. *In room:* TV, coffeemaker, hair dryer.

⟮Finds A Side Trip to Loch Voil

This was an area known to Rob Roy MacGregor, who died in 1734 but lives on in legend as the Robin Hood of Scotland and in the Liam Neeson film. If you visit Rob Roy's grave at Balquhidder, you may find this remote part of Scotland so enchanting you'll want to continue to drive west and explore the **Braes o' Balquhidder** and the banks of **Loch Voil,** where you can enjoy some of the loveliest countryside walks in the Trossachs. You can go through the churchyard where the Scottish hero is buried up to Kirkton Glen, continuing along through grasslands to a little lake. This signposted footpath leads to the next valley, called Glen Dochart, before it links up once again with A84, on which Callander lies.

DINING

Dalgair Hotel SCOTTISH   This place is best known for its food and wine cellar. The bar, lined in gray bricks, boasts rustic accessories and flickering candles. Australian, German, and Austrian wines, sold by the glass, give the place the aura of a wine bar, while the food ranges from Dover or lemon sole to steaks and game casseroles. More formal meals are served after dark in the restaurant, where menu items might include sliced pork on cucumber noodles with oregano and ginger sauce, chicken filet in champagne-butter sauce, and preparations of salmon and Angus steaks.

The hotel's eight rooms contain hair dryers, TVs, and combination tub/showers. Rates are £50 to £72 ($75 to $108) double, including breakfast.

113–115 Main St., Callander. ℂ **01877/330-283.** Fax 01877/331-114. www.dalgair-house-hotel.co.uk. Reservations recommended in restaurant, not necessary in bar. Table d'hôte 3-course menu £17.50 ($26.25); main courses £10.50–£16 ($15.75–$24) in restaurant, £5–£11.95 ($7.50–$17.95) in bar. AE, DC, MC, V. Restaurant daily 6:30–9pm; bar food service daily 11am–9pm.

Lade Inn INTERNATIONAL/SCOTTISH   This is a local favorite. Surrounded by fields and within earshot of the Leny River, the Lade was built as a teahouse, and then converted after World War II to a pub and restaurant. It attracts residents from the surrounding farmlands as well as visitors from afar to enjoy the Highland scenery (which includes Ben Ledi, one of the region's most prominent peaks) and sample the wide range of cask-conditioned ales and cider. If you're hungry, owners Angela and Paul Roebuck prepare meals of such Scottish standards as rack of lamb, pigeon, venison, steaks, salmon, and trout.

Trossachs Rd. at Kilmahog, Callander. ℂ **01877/330-152.** Main courses £6.85–£14.95 ($10.30–$22.45). MC, V. Mon–Sat noon–2:30pm and 5:30–9pm; Sun 12:30–9pm. Lies 1 mile (1.6km) north of Callander on A84.

CALLANDER AFTER DARK

The **Brigend Hotel Pub,** Bridgend (ℂ **01877/330-130**), is an old watering hole that has been done up in matching dusky red wood paneling and carpeting. Tennant brews are available on tap. Friday and Saturday bring karaoke, while Sunday nights feature live Scottish music. Open daily from 11am to 1am. Another old-fashioned bar that's a local favorite is the **Crown Hotel Pub,** 13 Main St. (ℂ **01877/330-040**); it sometimes features live folk music. Otherwise it's a mellow old place for a pint of lager. Open Sunday through Thursday from 11am to 11pm, Friday and Saturday from 11am to 1am.

9 Aberfoyle: Gateway to the Trossachs ⟨★

56 miles (90km) NW of Edinburgh, 27 miles (43.5km) N of Glasgow

Looking like an alpine village in the heart of Rob Roy country, the small resort of Aberfoyle, near Loch Ard, is the gateway to the Trossachs, one of the most beautiful and bucolic regions of Scotland. As one poet wrote: "So wondrous and wild, the whole might seem the scenery of a fair dream."

This was the land of Rob Roy (1671–1734), the outlaw and leader of the MacGregors. Sir Walter Scott recounted the outlaw's exploits in *Rob Roy,* first published in 1818. Scott's romantic poem "The Lady of the Lake" greatly increased tourism to the area, eventually attracting Queen Victoria, who was enchanted by its beauty. Wordsworth and Coleridge were eventually lured here away from England's Lake District. Wordsworth was so inspired, he wrote "To a Highland Girl."

ESSENTIALS

GETTING THERE It's tough to get here by public transportation; you'll really need to drive. From Stirling, take A84 west until you reach the junction of A873 and continue west to Aberfoyle.

VISITOR INFORMATION The **Trossachs Discovery Centre** is on Main Street (✆ **01877/382-352**). It's open April through June, daily from 10am to 5pm; July and August, daily from 9:30am to 7pm; September and October, daily from 9:30am to 5pm; and November through March, Monday through Friday from 10am to 5pm and Saturday from 10am to 4pm.

EXPLORING THE AREA

About 4 miles (6.5km) east of Aberfoyle on A81, **Inchmahome Priory** stands on an island in Lake Menteith. From the Port of Menteith, you can take a ferry to the island if the weather's right. The fare is £3.50 ($5.25) for adults, £2.30 ($3.45) for seniors and students, and £1.30 ($1.95) for children. Once here, you'll find the ruins of a 13th-century Augustinian house where Mary Queen of Scots was sent as a baby in 1547. For information, call ✆ **01877/385-294.**

A nature lover's delight, the **Queen Elizabeth Forest Park** ⚜ lies between the eastern shore of Loch Lomond and the Trossachs. Some 45,000 acres (18,225 hectares) of moor, woodland, and mountain have been set aside as a preserve for walking and exploring. From mid-March to mid-September, it's open daily from 10am to 6pm. Admission is free. From the lodge, you'll enjoy views of Ben Lomond, the Menteith Hills, and the Campsie Fells. For walking maps and information, stop at the **Queen Elizabeth Park Visitor Centre** (✆ **01877/ 382-258**), in the David Marshall Lodge, off A821, 1 mile (1.6km) north of Aberfoyle.

Another great walk in the area is the **Highland Boundary Fault Walk,** which goes along the Highland boundary fault edge. Here you can see the most panoramic views of the Highlands to the north and the Lowlands to the south. It begins 6 miles (10km) south of the Trossachs on A821. Detailed information is provided by the Forestry Commission in Abeyfoyle (✆ **01877/382-383**).

North of Aberfoyle, **Dukes Pass** (A821) climbs through Achray Forest past the Queen Elizabeth Forest Park Visitor Centre (see above), where you can stop for snacks and a panoramic view of the Forth Valley. Information on numerous walks, cycling routes, the Achray scenic forest drive, picnic sites, parking areas, and many other activities is available at the center. The road runs to the Trossachs between Lochs Achray and Katrine.

Loch Katrine ⚜⚜, where Rob Roy MacGregor was born, owes its fame to Sir Walter Scott's poem "The Lady of the Lake." The loch is the principal reservoir of the city of Glasgow. A small steamer, the **SS *Sir Walter Scott,*** plies the waters of the loch, which has submerged the romantic poet's Silver Strand. Sailings are twice a day from Easter to late October, between Trossachs Pier and Stronachlachar, at a round-trip fare of about £5.80 ($8.70) for adults and £3.60 ($5.40) for children and seniors, or £15.60 ($23.40) per family. Prices vary depending on time of day. (Morning sailings are more expensive.) Complete information on sailing schedules is available from the **Strathclyde Water Department,** Lower Clyde Division, 419 Balmore Rd., Glasgow, Lanarkshire G22 6NU (✆ **0141/355-5333**). Light refreshments are available at Trossachs Pier.

If you'd like to explore the countryside on two wheels, head for **Trossachs' Cycle Hire,** Trossachs Holiday Park, Aberfoyle (✆ **01877/382-614**). The rental rates are £13 ($19.50) per day and £35 ($52.50) per week. Open March through October, daily from 8:30am to 6pm.

Shoppers will want to check out the **Scottish Wool Centre,** Main Street (© **01877/382-850**), which sells a big selection of knitwear and woolens from surrounding mills, including jackets, hats, rugs, sweaters, and cashmere items. It also houses an amphitheater that holds a textile display area, along with live specimens of different breeds of Scottish sheep (but no clones yet). Spinning and weaving demonstrations are presented, and baby lambs fill a children's petting zoo. Admission to the shop is free, but the exhibition costs £3 ($4.50) for adults or £6 ($9) per family. The whole complex is open daily from 10am to 6pm, with exhibitions taking place at 11am, noon, 2pm, and 3pm.

ACCOMMODATIONS

Covenanters Inn Hotel   This hotel is set on 6 acres (2.4 hectares) of land overlooking the waters of the River Forth. It was a private home in the early 1800s, but was enlarged in the 1960s and 1980s and transformed into this inn. Its guest rooms are dignified and comfortable, in Scottish country-house style. Some of the bathrooms contain showers only. The hotel's name comes from the famous convention held here in 1949, when a group of Scots church and political leaders issued a then-famous Second Covenant promoting the separation of Scotland from England. On Christmas Eve of 1952, the hotel again became famous (or notorious) after the theft from Westminster Abbey of the Stone of Scone. Following appeals from Buckingham Palace, the Stone was recovered after having spent a night here, it's claimed. (A controversy continues as to the authenticity of the recovered artifact.)

Conjecture and speculation about the event still go on, sometimes heatedly, in the bar. The bar serves drinks from a wide selection of single-malt whiskies, as well as affordable meals. The more formal restaurant offers moderately priced dinners.

Duchray Rd. (about ½ mile/1km southwest of Aberfoyle), Aberfoyle FK8 3XD. © **01877/382-347.** Fax 01877/382-785. covenantersin@aberfoyle.co.uk. 50 units. £96–£118 ($144–$177) double. Rates include half-board. AE, DC, MC, V. **Amenities:** Restaurant, bar; limited room service. In room: TV, coffeemaker, hair dryer.

Creag-Ard House   One of the most stately houses in the region is this stone-sided Victorian villa whose steep rooflines and stone-ringed bay windows give it an appealingly quirky, even Gothic-looking allure. Built in 1885 on 3 acres (1.2 hectares) of forested parkland with spectacular stands of azaleas and rhododendrons (blooming in May), it offers cozy, well-upholstered rooms with attractive furniture, lots of sun, and combination tub/shower bathrooms. If advance notice is given, dinners can be prepared for guests.

Milton, Aberfoyle FK8 3TQ. © **01877/382-297.** 6 units. £60–£75 ($90–$112.50) double. Rates include breakfast. MC, V. From Aberfoyle, drive 1 mile (1.6km) west, following B829 toward Kinlochard. **Amenities:** Bar; limited room service. In room: TV, coffeemaker, no phone.

Loch Achray Hotel   This sprawling, white-sided hotel is a short walk from Loch Achray on an isolated 45-acre (18.2-hectare) estate between Callander and Aberfoyle. Although parts of its foundation date from Jacobean times, the bulk of what you'll see today was built around the early 1900s as a resort for people interested in the flora and fauna of the Highlands. From the hotel, you can step directly into the Achray Forest, part of the vast Queen Elizabeth National Park. The midsize guest rooms are simple and contemporary, each with views over the forest. All units contain bathrooms with showers; some come with bathtubs as well. The dining room serves moderately priced dinners nightly. The bar features live traditional music every night, including a full-scale ceilidh every Thursday. The hotel is usually heavily booked with tour groups.

9 miles (14.5km) east of Callander on A821, The Trossachs FK17 3HZ. ℂ **01877/376-229.** Fax 01877/ 376-278. 83 units. £60–£84 ($90–$126) double. Rates include Scottish breakfast. AE, MC, V. Closed 2 weeks in Jan. **Amenities:** Restaurant, bar; room service; laundry. *In room:* TV, coffeemaker, no phone.

DINING

Braeval Restaurant ℛ SCOTTISH   Overlooking a golf course, this restaurant is housed in a former stone mill, and owners Andrew and Pauline Carter have kept an antique waterwheel to remind diners of the building's former function. The chefs here display inventiveness and solid technique. We especially like how the kitchen takes full advantage of the region's riches, including game in season. The repertoire embraces both traditional and modern British dishes on a changing fixed-price menu. You might begin with game terrine with pear chutney; for main dishes, sample such delights as seared bass bream with salad Niçoise, a lasagna of chicken livers flavored with lemon and thyme, or filet of salmon with mussel-and-basil butter sauce.

Callander Rd. (A81). ℂ **01877/382-711.** Reservations required. Main courses £8–£12 ($12–$18); Sat night fixed-price menu £22–£30 ($33–$45). MC, V. Tues–Sun 10am–5pm; Sat 7:30–9pm by reservation only. Closed 1 week in Feb, 1 week in June, and 2 weeks in Oct. Drive 1 mile (1.6km) east of Aberfoyle on A81 (Callander Rd.).

10 On the Bonnie, Bonnie Banks of Loch Lomond ℛℛℛ

The largest of Scotland's lochs, Loch Lomond was the center of the ancient district of Lennox, in the possession of the branch of the Stewart (Stuart) family to which Lord Darnley (second husband of Mary Queen of Scots) belonged. The ruins of Lennox Castle are on Inchmurrin, one of the 30 islands of the loch; Inchmurrin has ecclesiastical ruins and is noted for its yew trees, planted by King Robert the Bruce to ensure a suitable supply of wood for the bows of his archers. The loch is fed by at least 10 rivers from west, east, and north and is about 24 miles (39km) long; it stretches 5 miles (8km) at its widest point. On the eastern side is Ben Lomond, which rises to a height of 3,192 feet (968m).

The song "Loch Lomond" is supposed to have been composed by one of Bonnie Prince Charlie's captured followers on the eve of his execution in Carlisle Jail. The "low road" of the song is the path through the underworld that his spirit will follow to his native land after death, more quickly than his friends can travel to Scotland by the ordinary high road.

The easiest way to see the famous loch is not by car but by one of the local ships owned by **Sweeney's Cruisers Ltd.,** and based at Sweeney's Shipyard, 26 Balloch Rd., Balloch (ℂ **01389/752-376**). Cruises on various boats last about an hour and sail from Balloch toward a wooded island, Inchmurrin, year-round home to five families, several vacation chalets, and a summer-only nudist colony. The ship doesn't dock at the island, however. In summer, departures are every hour between 10:30am and 7:30pm. (Departures in other months are based on demand.) The cost is £5.20 ($7.80) per person round-trip.

Of course, you can also see the loch on foot. One of the great marked footpaths of Scotland, the **West Highland Way** ℛℛ goes along the complete eastern sector of the lovely loch. The footpath actually begins at Milngavie outside Glasgow. Serious backpackers often do the entire 95-mile (153km) trail, but you can tackle just sections of it for marvelous day hikes that will allow you to enjoy the scenery along Loch Lomond.

BALLOCH

At the southern end of Loch Lomond, Balloch is the most touristy of the towns and villages around the lake. It grew up on the River Leven, where the water leaves Loch Lomond and flows south to the Clyde. Today, Balloch is visited chiefly by those wanting to take boat trips on Loch Lomond; these sail in season from Balloch Pier.

The 200-acre (81-hectare) **Balloch Castle Country Park** is on the bonnie banks of Loch Lomond, three quarters of a mile (1.2km) north of Balloch Station. The present **Balloch Castle** (℗ **01389/722-600**), replacing one that dated from 1238, was constructed in 1808 for John Buchanan of Ardoch in the castle-Gothic style. Its visitor center explains the history of the property. The site has a walled garden, and the trees and shrubs, especially the rhododendrons and azaleas, reach the zenith of their beauty in late May and early June. You can also visit a Fairy Glen. The park is open all year, daily from 8am to dusk, with no admission charged. From Easter to the end of October, the visitor center is open daily between 10am and 6pm.

Dumbarton District's Countryside Ranger Service is based at Balloch Castle and conducts **guided walks** at various locations around Loch Lomond throughout the summer.

ACCOMMODATIONS & DINING

Ardoch House ℛ   This impeccably maintained 1830s white farmhouse is now a welcoming hotel after extensive renovations by owner and architect David Morgan. Set amid 130 acres (52.7 hectares) of rolling countryside, with spectacular views over the foothills of the Highlands, it provides one of the most charming small-scale accommodations in the region. The guest rooms have large windows, pleasant carpeting and upholsteries, and a sense of intelligent design that gracefully marries newfangled techniques with the building's original core. All bathrooms come with showers, and some have tubs as well. Guests are invited into the drawing room, where Lintie Morgan, David's wife, gracefully evokes the region's history and dispenses tips on whatever might interest you. Breakfast is the only meal served, but the Morgans will direct you to any of several pubs and restaurants nearby. No smoking is permitted.

Gartocharn, near Balloch G83 8ND. ℗ **01389/830-279.** Fax 01389/930-623. 3 units. £72 ($108) double. Rates include breakfast. MC, V. Closed Nov–Apr. From Balloch, drive along A811 toward Stirling and Gartocharn. Just before Gartocharn, turn left at the 30mph traffic sign. *In room:* TV.

Balloch Hotel   Called Balloch's grande dame hotel, this was the first hotel to be built in the town. In 1860, it welcomed the Empress Eugénie, wife of Napoleon III, when she toured Scotland. (She slept in the Inchmoan Room.) It stands beside the river in the center of the village, offering basic, functionally furnished rooms (some with shower only).

Balloch Rd., Balloch G83 8LQ. ℗ **01389/752-579.** Fax 01389/755-604. 14 units. £63 ($94.50) double. Rates include Scottish breakfast. AE, DC, MC, V. Closed Jan 1 and Dec 25. **Amenities:** Restaurant, bar; limited room service. *In room:* TV, coffeemaker, hair dryer.

DeVere Cameron House ℛℛℛ   Twenty minutes from the Glasgow airport and surrounded by 108 acres (43.7 hectares) of lush woodland, this ancestral home of novelist Tobias Smollet is a luxurious resort combining elegance, leisure, and adventure. Decorated in soft, warm colors, the good-size rooms are comfortable and handsomely furnished. The five suites boast sitting rooms with panoramic views. All rooms are equipped with modern bathrooms with combination tub/showers.

The resort has three on-site restaurants, all of which require reservations. The Georgian Room, the most formal (jacket and tie required), offers extremely pricey gourmet meals prepared by an award-winning chef. The menu changes regularly, but the quality of the food doesn't.

Alexandria, Loch Lomond, G83 8QZ. ℂ 01389/755-565. Fax 01389/759-522. www.cameronhouse.co.uk. 96 units. £235–£265 ($352.50–$397.50) double; £475 ($712.50) suite. Rates include full Scottish breakfast and membership to the Leisure Club. Children under 17 stay free in parents' room. AE, DC, MC, V. Take M8 to A82 to Loch Lomand; follow signs to hotel. **Amenities:** 3 restaurants, 3 bars; 9-hole golf course; lagoon pool surrounded by palm trees; tennis courts; squash courts; facilities for windsurfing, water-skiing, and sailing; archery lessons; croquet; Leisure Club; walled garden; children's adventure playground; gym; steam room; room service; massages; babysitting; laundry service. In addition, the hotel's *Celtic Warrior* takes guests on cruises of Loch Lomond, and several boats in a 225-slip marina can be rented for fishing. *In room:* TV, mini-bar (on request), coffeemaker, hair dryer.

LUSS

The village of Luss, 9 miles (14.5km) north of Ballock on A82 on the western side of Loch Lomond, is the traditional home of the Colquhouns. Among its stone cottages, on the water's edge, is a branch of the Highland Arts Studios of Seil. Cruises on the loch and boat rentals may be arranged at a nearby jetty.

If your travels in Scotland inspire you to put on a kilt and blow your own set of bagpipes, stop by **Thistle Bagpipe Works** (ℂ 01436/860-250), in the center of Luss. Here, not only can you order custom-made bagpipes but you can also purchase a clan kilt to go with the instrument. Your neighbors back home will be thrilled.

ACCOMMODATIONS

The Lodge on Loch Lomond Hotel   Surrounded by mountain, loch, and woodland, you can live in Scottish country-house style and take in panoramic views of legendary Loch Lomond. The hotel, in fact, was designed to take in the views. But that's not the only reason to stay here. This lodging, much improved in recent years, offers tasteful bedrooms with combination tub/showers and numerous comforts. The executive rooms are set up for wheelchair access, and each contains a two-person sauna. The hotel will also arrange local activities, including salmon fishing and private charter cruises along with horseback riding. The fine restaurant is an excellent reason to stay here, or at least to drop in for an evening (see "Dining," below).

Luss, Argyll G83 8PA. ℂ 01436/860-201. Fax 01436/860-203. www.loch-lomond.co.uk. 29 units. £135–£175 ($202.50–$262.50); £180 ($270) suite. Rates include full Scottish breakfast. AE, MC, V. Free parking. Take A82 from Glasgow. **Amenities:** Restaurant, bar; room service; laundry. *In room:* TV, coffeemaker, hair dryer.

DINING

The Lodge on Loch Lomond Restaurant ℱ SCOTTISH   Using only the finest and freshest local ingredients, this restaurant serves individually prepared meals that are the best in the area. The accommodating staff makes this a relaxed, comfortable place. Although the menu changes, main courses might include pan-fried venison loin with haggis skirlie, or speared tiger prawns with chili and garlic nut-brown butter. There is a wide selection of Aberdeen Angus beef priced according to weight, and lobster is served in a multitude of ways. For something really Scottish, try roast pheasant with bacon-braised barley and a whisky cream sauce. Those who want a lighter meal can opt for a burger, fish-and-chips, pasta, or pizza. The quality of the food is excellent, matched by panoramic views of the loch.

In the Lodge at Loch Lomond Hotel, Luss. ℂ 01436/860-201. Reservations recommended. Main courses £8.95–£19.50 ($13.45–$29.25). AE, MC, V. Daily noon–2:30pm and 6–9:30pm.

TARBET

On the western shores of Loch Lomond, Tarbet isn't to be confused with the larger center of Tarbert, headquarters of the Loch Fyne herring industry. Loch Lomond's Tarbet is merely a village and summer-holiday base with limited accommodations. In the distance, you can see the majesty of Ben Lomond. Boats can be launched from the pier, and Tarbet is one of the stops of the steamship *Countess Fiona*.

ACCOMMODATIONS & DINING

Tarbet Hotel   The Tarbet stands where a simple inn existed more than 400 years ago, at the junction of A82 and A83. A coaching inn was built on the foundation in 1760, and a baronial facade and mock-fortification crenellations were added during the Victorian era. The midsize guest rooms are functional, well furnished, and comfortable, each with a bathroom with combination tub/shower. A cozy cocktail lounge looks past a row of very old yew trees onto the lake. Open to guests only, the dining room serves good meals utilizing local produce. The bistro-style snack bar, the Baguetterie, serves sandwiches Thursday through Sunday from 10am to 4pm.

Tarbet, Arrochar G83 7DE. (℃) **01301/702-228.** Fax 01301/702-673. 80 units. £200 ($300) double. Rates are all-inclusive. MC, V. Closed Jan. **Amenities:** Restaurant, bar. *In room:* TV, coffeemaker, no phone.

9

Aberdeen & the Tayside & Grampian Regions

The two historic regions of Tayside and Grampian offer a vast array of sightseeing, even though they're relatively small. Tayside, for example, is about 85 miles (137km) east to west and 60 miles (97km) south to north. The regions share the North Sea coast between the Firth of Tay in the south and the Firth of Moray farther north, and the so-called Highland Line separating the Lowlands in the south from the Highlands in the north crosses both. The Grampians, Scotland's highest mountain range, are to the west of this line.

Carved out of the old counties of Perth and Angus, **Tayside** is named for its major river, the 119-mile-long (192km) Tay. The region is easy to explore, and its waters offer some of Europe's best salmon and trout fishing. Tayside abounds with heather-clad Highland hills, long blue lochs under forested banks, and miles of walking trails. Perth and Dundee are among Scotland's largest cities. Tayside provided the backdrop for many novels by Sir Walter Scott, including *The Fair Maid of Perth, Waverley,* and *The Abbot.* And its golf courses are world famous, ranging from the trio of 18-hole courses at Gleneagles to the open championships links at Carnoustie.

Grampian boasts Aberdeen, Scotland's third-largest city, and Braemar, site of the most famous of the Highland Gatherings. The queen herself comes here for holidays, to stay at Balmoral Castle, her private residence, a tradition dating back to the days of Queen Victoria and her consort, Prince Albert. As you journey on the scenic roads of Scotland's northeast, you'll pass moorland and peaty lochs, wood glens and rushing rivers, granite-stone villages and ancient castles, and fishing harbors as well as North Sea beach resorts.

1 Perth ★: Gateway to the Highlands & Scone Palace

44 miles (71km) N of Edinburgh, 22 miles (35km) SW of Dundee, 64 miles (103km) NE of Glasgow

From its majestic position on the Tay, the ancient city of Perth was the capital of Scotland until the mid–15th century. Here the Highlands meet the Lowlands. Perth makes a good stop if you're heading north to the Highlands. Perth itself has only a few historic buildings, but it does offer some good shopping. The main attraction, Scone Place, lies on the outskirts, and the surrounding countryside is wonderful for strolling and hiking.

ESSENTIALS
GETTING THERE   ScotRail (© 08457/484-950) provides service between Edinburgh and Perth (trip time: 90 min.), with continuing service to Dundee. The cost is £9.40 ($14.10) from Edinburgh.

Edinburgh and Perth are connected by frequent **Scottish CityLink** (© **0990/ 505-050**) buses (trip time: 1½ hr.). The fare is £5 ($7.50).

If you're **driving** from Edinburgh, take A90 northwest and go across the Forth Road Bridge, continuing north along M90 (trip time: 1½ hr.).

VISITOR INFORMATION The **tourist office** is at Lower City Mills, West Mill Street (© **01738/450-600**), and is open April to June, daily from 9am to 6pm; July to September, daily from 9am to 7pm; October, daily from 9am to 6pm; and November to March, Monday through Saturday from 10am to 5pm.

SPECIAL EVENTS In May, the 10-day **Perth Festival of the Arts** attracts international orchestras and chamber music societies. There are some dance recitals as well, and a recent trend is a celebration of some aspects of pop culture. Concerts are held in churches, auditoriums, even Scone Palace.

SEEING THE SIGHTS

For the best view of this scenic part of Scotland, take Bowerswell Road a mile (1.6km) to the east of Perth center to visit **Kinnouill Hill,** rising 792 feet (240m). After an easy climb, you can get a bird's-eye view of the geological Highland Line dividing the Highlands from the Lowlands. A marked nature trail beginning at the Braes Road car park leads, after a 25-minute walk, to the panoramic view from the top. Here you can see a folly, the **Kinnouill Watch Tower,** and its counterpart, a mile (1.6km) to the east, **Binn Hill.** Both structures are imitations of castles along the Rhine.

Balhousie Castle In the 16th century, this was the home of the earls of Kinnoull, but today it houses the Black Watch Regimental Museum, with hundreds of weapons, medals, and documents of the Black Watch Regiment from the 18th century on. It's filled with curiosities like the back door of Spandau Prison in Berlin, which was rescued from destruction after Rudolf Hess died and the prison was torn down. The regiment was recruited in 1739 by Gen. George Wade to help the government pacify rebellious Highlanders and became famous all over the United Kingdom for its black tartans in contrast to the red of government troops.

After visiting the castle, you can explore **North Inch,** a 100-acre (40.5-hectare) parkland extending north along the west bank of the Tay. This is the best place for a long walk in the Perth area. The grounds are given over mainly to sports facilities, particularly the domed Bells Sports Centre. North Inch, as depicted in Scott's *The Fair Maid of Perth,* was the site of the great 1396 Clan Combat between 30 champions from the clans Kay and Chattan, attended by Robert III and his queen.

Hay St., right beyond Rose Terrace on the west side of North Inch. © 0131/310-8530. Free admission. May–Sept Mon–Sat 10am–4:30pm; Oct–Apr Mon–Fri 10am–3:30pm.

Branklyn Garden This once-private garden now belongs to the National Trust for Scotland. It has a superb collection of rhododendrons, alpines, and herbaceous and peat-garden plants from all over the world.

116 Dundee Rd. (A85), Branklyn. © 01738/625-535. Admission £3.50 ($5.25) adults; £1 ($1.50) children, students, and seniors; £6.40 ($9.60) per family. Mar–Oct daily 9:30am–sunset. Closed Nov–Feb.

Kirk of St. John the Baptist This is the main sightseeing attraction of "the fair city." It's believed that the original foundation is from Pictish times. The present choir dates from 1440 and the nave from 1490. In 1559, John Knox preached his famous sermon attacking idolatry, which caused a turbulent wave

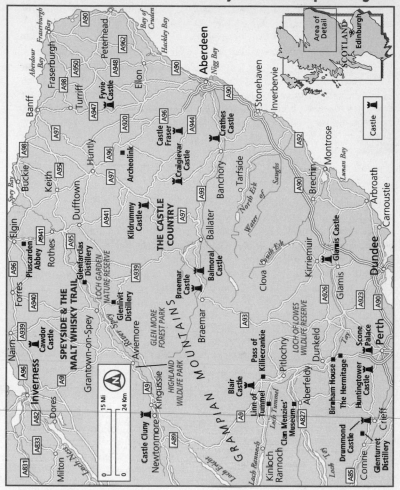

of iconoclasm to sweep across the land. In its wake, religious artifacts, stained glass, and organs were destroyed all over Scotland.

31 St. John Place. ℂ 01738/638-482. Free admission. June–Sept Mon–Fri 10am–4pm, Sun 12:30–2pm.

Perth Art Gallery and Museum   This museum displays paintings illustrating the town's history along with archaeological artifacts. The growth of the whisky industry and its major role in the area's economy is particularly emphasized. You'll find everything from grandfather clocks to Georgian silver to even an effigy of a 65-pound (29kg) salmon caught by some proud fisherman back in 1922. The most notable artworks are large Scottish landscapes by John Millais (1829–96). Horatio McCulloch (1805–67) was known as a specialist of Highland scenes, and his *Loch Katrine* (1866) is one of his finest works.

George St., at the intersection of Tay St. and Perth Bridge. ℂ 01738/632-488. Free admission. Mon–Sat 10am–5pm.

Round House and Fergusson Gallery   If you're interested in Scottish art, head for the Fergusson Gallery, which displays some 6,000 works of Scottish artist J. D. Fergusson (1874–1961). Fergusson is acclaimed as one of the best watercolorists in the country, and his Scottish scenes are widely produced on postcards and calendars. In the paintings *Princess Street Gardens* and *The White Dress,* you can view the muted colors of his early portraits and landscapes. Later, as he was more inspired by Fauvism, his work became more vibrant and luminous, as evoked by *Cassis from the West* and *Sails at Royan.* His female nudes, however, always generate the most excitement, especially *Danu Mother of the Gods, The Parasol,* and *Bathers in Green.* The Red Dress (1950) is very evocative of Glasgow scenes.

Marshall Place. (ⓒ 01738/441-944. Free admission. Mon–Sat 10am–5pm.

SHOPPING

Cairncross Ltd., 18 St. John's St. (ⓒ **01738/624-367**), sells jewelry, both custom-made and from other manufacturers. The specialty is Scottish freshwater pearls. **Timothy Hardie,** 25 St. John's St. (ⓒ **01738/633-127**), deals in antique jewelry and has a large selection of Victorian pieces. It also sells antique silver tea services. **Whispers of the Past,** 15 George St. (ⓒ **01738/635-472**), offers an odd mix of items: jewelry, both new and antique, ranging from costume baubles to quality gold and silver pieces; china; pine furniture; and some linens.

C & C Proudfoot, Unit 104, 104 South St. (ⓒ **01738/632-483**), is an eclectic shop whose merchandise includes leather jackets, hand-knitted Arran sweaters, Barbour waxed-cotton jackets, sheepskin jackets and rugs, and wool rugs, as well as a range of handbags, briefcases, scarves, and gloves.

Watson of Perth, 163–167 High St. (ⓒ **01738/639-861**), has been in business since 1900. It specializes in bone china produced by Royal Doulton, Wedgwood, and others; it also offers cut crystal from Edinburgh, Stuart, and Waterford.

Caithness Glass, Inveralmond Industrial Estate, on A9 (ⓒ **01738/637-373**), is a glass factory on the edge of Perth. Follow A9, going through the roundabout marked A9 NORTH to Inverness; the factory is in the industrial complex a short way past the roundabout. Its outlet sells paperweights, vases, and bowls, balanced with a range of Royal Doulton items. While here, you can watch the glassblowers at work.

Perthshire Shop, Lower City Mills, Mill Street (ⓒ **01738/627-958**), sells jams, mustards, and oatmeal along with items produced in the neighboring mills. There are wooden bowls, *spirtles* (wooden stirrers often used in making porridge), and Perthshire tartan scarves and ties, along with a large selection of cookbooks.

HITTING THE LINKS NEARBY

North of Perth is one of Scotland's acclaimed golf links, the 18-hole **Blairgowrie,** Golf Course Road, Rosemont, Blairgowrie (ⓒ **01250/872-622**), which includes 6,229 yards (5,668m) of playing area with a par of 72. This is a challenging course, with a rolling, wild layout of pine, birch, and fir; you might even spot a deer or two grazing on the course. The greens fees are £40 to £55 ($60 to $82.50) for one round, £70 ($105) for the day, with even higher rates on weekends. There's a pro shop where you can rent clubs and trolleys; caddy service is £20 ($30), plus tip.

ACCOMMODATIONS

Auld Manse Guest House   Across the River Tay from the rest of Perth, this guesthouse lies in a quiet residential neighborhood. The stone-sided house was built in 1887 as the manse (rector's home) for a Presbyterian church that was demolished to make room for an apartment complex in the 1950s. Don't be fooled by the modest proportions you see from the front, as the building sprawls back from the road. The rather frilly guest rooms come complete with ruffles and pink flourishes, along with small, shower-only bathrooms. If advance notice is given, dinners can be prepared. No smoking is permitted.

Pitcullen Crescent, Perth PH2 7HT. ⓒ **01738/629-187.** Fax 01738/629-187. www.s-h-systems.co.uk/hotels/ auldman.html. 5 units. £40 ($60) double. Rates include breakfast. MC, V. Bus: 7. *In room:* TV, coffeemaker, hair dryer, no phone.

Dupplin Castle ⚜⚜   This dignified stucco-sheathed mansion with sandstone mullions was built in 1968 by well-known architect Schomber Scott. With 30 acres (12.2 hectares) of grounds and spectacular gardens (some specimens are 250 years old), the site is one of the most beautiful near Perth. The large guest rooms are decorated in good taste, with antique furniture. Many units overlook the valley of the River Earn, and all come with bathrooms with combination tub/showers. Guests can relax and watch TV in the lounge. You can enjoy a pricey dinner in casually elegant country-house style if you reserve 24 hours in advance.

Near Aberdalgie, Perth PH2 0PY. ⓒ **01738/623-224.** Fax 01738/444-140. www.dupplin.co.uk. 7 units. £110–£130 ($165–$195) double. Rates include Scottish breakfast. MC, V. From Perth, follow the main highway (M90) to Glasgow, turning left onto B9112 toward Aberdalgie and Forteviot. **Amenities:** Dining room; clay shooting. *In room:* Coffeemaker, hair dryer.

Hunting Tower ⚜   This late-Victorian country house with a mock Tudor facade is set on 3½ acres (1.4 hectares) of well-manicured gardens. Taste and concern went into both the public rooms and the distinguished guest rooms, which range from rather large to compact. Seven have spa bathrooms, and the others come with regular combination tub/showers. The cottage suites are in a renovated bungalow; each has twin beds and a sitting room. The fine Scottish and Continental cuisine is reason enough to stay here. The elegant main restaurant serves nightly table d'hôte dinners.

Crieff Rd. (3½ miles/5.5km west of Perth on A85), Perth PH1 3JT. ⓒ **01738/583-771.** Fax 01738/583-777. www.huntingtowerhotel.co.uk. 34 units. £89.50 ($134.25) double; from £99.50 ($149.25) cottage suite. Rates include Scottish breakfast. AE, DC, MC, V. **Amenities:** Restaurant, bar; room service; laundry service. *In room:* TV, minibar, coffeemaker, hair dryer.

Kinfauns Castle ⚜⚜⚜   When James Smith, the Scot who ran all of Asia's Hiltons, was told in the 1990s to ship out from his base in Hong Kong, he returned home with some of the Hilton's best furnishings. He installed them in this venerable late-Victorian castle, making for an unusual decorative wedding of Scotland and the Far East. Guests here stay in the lap of luxury on 26 acres (10.5 hectares) of forested lands and gardens close to the Highlands. The grandeur of the entrance hall sets the tone, holding the six tartans of the families who have inhabited the castle. The gallery continues the baronial theme, with a ceiling decorated with gold-leaf rosettes and an ornately carved fireplace. The luxurious bedrooms are individually decorated in great style, with modern amenities such as marble bathrooms with phones. Many units have real log fireplaces. Of special interest is the Lady Gray lounge, which is unchanged since the castle was built 2 centuries ago; it contains the original marble fireplace and William Morris machine-printed wallpaper from 1910. The Library Restaurant (see below) serves the finest food in the area.

Kinfauns (3 miles/5km east of Perth on A90), Perth PH2 7JZ. © **01738/620-777.** Fax 01738/620-778. www.kinfaunscastle.co.uk. 16 units. £180 ($270) double; £260 ($390) junior suite; £300 ($450) suite. Rates include Scottish breakfast. AE, MC, V. Closed 3 weeks in Jan. **Amenities:** Restaurant, bar; nearby golf and other outdoor activities; concierge; room service; laundry service. *In room:* TV, coffeemaker, hair dryer.

Parklands Hotel & Restaurant ✿   This hotel near the rail station opened in 1991 and immediately became the most fashionable lodging within Perth itself. Allen Deeson set out to create a country-house hotel in the middle of the city, and succeeded admirably. The beautifully decorated guest rooms, filled with wood paneling and cornices, overlook the South Inch Park. All are spacious and well appointed, each with a bathroom with combination tub/shower. Breakfast begins with such classic Scottish dishes as Loch Fyne kippers, deviled kidneys, smoked kedgeree, and scrambled eggs with smoked salmon. For dinner, you can enjoy sautéed chicken livers with ginger dressing and marinated oysters in citrus juices flavored with dill and garlic.

2 St. Leonard's Bank, Perth PH2 8EB. © **01738/622-451.** Fax 01738/622-046. centuryhousehotel@ compuserve.com. 14 units. £89–£105 ($133.50–$157.50) double. Rates include breakfast. AE, DC, MC, V. **Amenities:** Restaurant, bar; room service; laundry/dry cleaning. *In room:* TV, coffeemaker, hair dryer.

DINING

Keracher's Restaurant and Oyster Bar ✿   SCOTTISH/SEAFOOD   For five generations, the Kerachers have been serving some of the finest seafood in Perth. Chef Andrew Keracher carries on the family tradition by using the freshest ingredients, which are cooked to order. Food is prepared with imagination and panache, but also with a healthy respect for the natural tastes and textures of the produce. Among the main courses on the extensive menu are filet of Scottish salmon glazed with honey-mustard and served with a leek and vermouth cream sauce. For dessert, try the steamed ginger pudding with vanilla ice cream and lime Anglais. The Oyster Bar has a retail counter where you can grab a quick, tasty range of Keracher products.

168 South St. (45 min. from Edinburgh on the A90). © **01738/449-777.** Reservations recommended. Main courses £7.50–£15.90 ($11.25–$23.85). MC, V. Tues–Sat noon–2pm and 6–10pm. Closed first 2 weeks in Jan.

Let's Eat ✿   BRITISH/INTERNATIONAL   The most visually striking, and most appealing, restaurant in Perth occupies an 1822 theater and intersperses its tables amid soaring white columns. There's a particularly cozy lounge, site of a log-burning stove and comfy sofas, where you might want a drink before your meal. Menu items, which change frequently, are among the most thoughtful and sophisticated in town. They might include a gratin of goat cheese studded with roasted peppers and served with rocket salad, new potatoes, and chutney; grilled brochettes of monkfish with king prawns, rice, and salad; handmade black puddings served with "smash" (mashed potatoes), applesauce, and onion gravy; and risotto studded with wild mushrooms. Be careful not to confuse this restaurant with its less grand, less expensive sibling, Let's Eat Again (see below).

77–79 Kinnoul St. © **01738/643-377.** Reservations recommended. Main courses £6.50–£11 ($9.75–$16.50) lunch; £8–£15 ($12–$22.50) dinner. AE, MC, V. Tues–Sat noon–2pm and 6:30–9:45pm.

Let's Eat Again BRITISH/INTERNATIONAL   Set within a bright yellow 19th-century private home with lime green trim, this upbeat bistro caters to the young at heart with well-prepared but relatively inexpensive versions of

Mediterranean and international cuisine—like what you expect in a trendy eatery in London. Your meal might consist of charcoal-grilled Mediterranean vegetables with mozzarella; smoked haddock and chive-laced risotto; smoked local venison with spicy pears; salmon and codfish cakes with lemon-flavored butter sauce; or Thai-style chicken curry with noodles. The more upscale Let's Eat, described above, is under the same management.

33 George St. ☎ **1738/633-771**. Reservations recommended. Main courses £7–£12 ($10.50–$18). AE, MC, V. Tues–Sat noon–2pm and 6–9:30pm.

The Library Restaurant 😒😒 SCOTTISH If you'd like to dine in a grand castle with equally grand food and service, head here. Using the costliest of Scottish ingredients, all deftly handled, chef Jeremy Brazelle has established a reputation for excellence. The best of venison, Angus beef, and salmon are offered along with one of the finest wine lists in the area. A sample meal might include pumpkin-and-leek soup followed by filet of halibut with buttered noodles, stir-fried vegetables, and chili and soy dressing. You might also try roast rump of black-faced lamb with fresh vegetables cooked in the Provençal style with virgin olive oil and garlic.

In Kinfauns Castle (see "Accommodations," above). ☎ **01738/620-777**. Reservations required. Jacket and tie required for men. Fixed-price 3-course lunch £18.50–£20.50 ($27.75–$30.75); fixed-price dinner £32 ($48) for 3 courses, £35 ($52.50) for 5 courses. AE, MC, V. Daily noon–1:30pm and 7–8:30pm. Closed 3 weeks in Jan.

Littlejohn's INTERNATIONAL On one of Perth's busiest commercial streets, behind a century-old facade, this restaurant consists of one large dining room with old-fashioned wood paneling, antique signs, and lots of Scottish charm. Despite the conservative nature of the setting, the food offerings are eclectic and include pizzas, pastas, tortillas, burgers, steaks, and an occasional lobster dish.

24 St. John's St. ☎ **01738/639-888**. Main courses £3.95–£12.85 ($5.95–$19.30). AE, DC, MC, V. Daily 10am–11pm.

PERTH AFTER DARK

The Victorian **Perth Repertory Theatre**, 185 High St. (☎ **01738/621-031**), hosts performances of plays and musicals between mid-September and May. From the end of May to early June, it's also a venue for some of the events of the Perth Festival of the Arts. The box office is open Monday through Saturday from 10am to 7:30pm. Tickets cost £6 to £14 ($9 to $21).

Perth City Hall, King Edward Street (☎ **01738/475-200**), is a year-round venue for musical performances and dances; many local organizations (including the Freemasons, the Royal Geographical Society, churches, and various amateur societies) book events here year after year. Entertainment is usually along the lines of a classical concert or a Highland ball.

A SIDE TRIP TO SCONE

Old Scone, 3km (2 miles) from Perth on the River Tay, was the ancient capital of the Picts. The early Scottish monarchs were enthroned on a lump of sandstone called the "Stone of Destiny." In 1296, Edward I, the "Hammer of the Scots," moved the stone to Westminster Abbey, and for hundreds of years it rested under the chair on which British monarchs were crowned. The Scots have always bitterly resented this theft, and at last it has been returned to Scotland, to find a permanent home in Edinburgh Castle, where it can be viewed by the public.

The seat of the earls of Mansfield and birthplace of David Douglas (of fir-tree fame), **Scone Palace** 𝆺𝅥 (© **01738/552-300**) was largely rebuilt in 1802, incorporating the old palace of 1580. Inside is an impressive collection of French furniture, china, ivories, and 16th-century needlework, including bed hangings executed by Mary Queen of Scots. A fine collection of rare conifers is found on the grounds in the Pinetum. To reach the palace, head northeast of Perth on A93. The site is open from Good Friday to mid-October, daily from 9:30am to 4:45pm. Admission to the house and grounds is £5.90 ($8.85) for adults, £5.10 ($7.65) for seniors, £3.40 ($5.10) for children 16 and under. Admission to the grounds only is £2.90 ($4.35) for adults and £1.70 ($2.55) for children.

ACCOMMODATIONS & DINING

The Murrayshall 𝆺𝅥𝆺𝅥 This elegant country-house hotel, set on 300 acres (121.5 hectares) of parkland, was completely refurbished in 1987 and reopened as one of the showpieces of Perthshire. Its challenging golf courses make it a favorite of golfers. Bedrooms come in a wide range of traditional styles and sizes. The suites and executive rooms have the best amenities and views. The standard rooms are also comfortable, but lack the character of the others. Some bathrooms contain showers only. On a windy night in Scotland, there is no better place to be than the well-stocked bar with its log fire.

New Scone, Perthshire PH2 7PH. © 01738/551-171. Fax 01738/552-595. 27 units. £130–£140 ($195–$210) double; from £160 ($240) suite; £160 ($240) lodge. Rates include Scottish breakfast. AE, DC, MC, V. Take A94 for 1½ miles (2.5km) east of New Scone. **Amenities:** 2 restaurants, 2 bars; 2 golf courses; tennis courts; gym; room service; babysitting; laundry/dry cleaning. *In room:* TV, hair dryer.

2 Gleneagles: Hitting the Links

56 miles NE of the Glasgow Airport, 50 miles NW of the Edinburgh Airport

Gleneagles provides a good but pricey base from which to explore central Scotland. This famous golf center and sports complex is on a moor between Strath Earn and Strath Allan. The center gets its name from the Gaelic *Gleann-an-Eaglias,* meaning "glen of the church." St. Mungo's Chapel, higher up the glen, has monuments of the Haldane family.

Gleneagles has several 18-hole golf courses connected with the hotel: the **King's Course,** the longest one, and the **Queen's Course,** next in length, are among the best in Scotland, and the sports complex is one of the best equipped in Europe.

ESSENTIALS

GETTING THERE The town is on A9, about halfway between Perth and Stirling, a short distance from the village of Auchterarder. The **train** from Perth costs £3.90 ($5.85) and takes 15 minutes; from Edinburgh, it costs £8.40 ($12.60) and takes 1 hour and 40 minutes. For information, call © **08457/ 484-950.** The only **bus** service departs from Glasgow. The trip takes slightly more than an hour and costs £6 ($9). For information, call © **0870/608-2608.**

VISITOR INFORMATION The **tourist center** is at 90 High St., Auchterarder (© **01764/663-450**), about 1½ miles (2.5km) east of Gleneagles. It's open November to March, Monday through Friday from 9:30am to 5pm and Saturday from 11am to 3pm; April to June, Monday through Saturday from 9:30am to 5:30pm and Sunday from 11am to 4pm; July and August, Monday through Saturday from 9am to 7pm and Sunday from 11am to 6pm; and September and October, Monday through Saturday from 9:30am to 5:30pm and Sunday from 11am to 4pm.

ACCOMMODATIONS & DINING

Auchterarder House ★★★ A fine example of 1830s architecture and construction in the Scots Jacobean style, this mansion has been completely restored and the interior refurbished to a high standard of luxury, with a mix of Victorian and modern decor. The house has elegant public areas and comfortable guest rooms, cared for by a well-mannered staff whose aim is to please.

1 mile (1.6km) from Gleneagles (off B8062 between Auchterarder and Crieff), Auchterarder PH3 1DZ. ℂ 01764/663-646. Fax 01764/662-939. www.auchterarderhouse.com. 15 units. £170–£295 ($255–$442.50) double. Rates include Scottish breakfast. AE, DC, DISC, MC, V. Free parking. **Amenities:** Restaurant; croquet lawn; room service; babysitting; laundry/dry cleaning. *In room:* TV, hair dryer.

Gleneagles Hotel ★★★ Britain's greatest golf hotel stands on its own 830-acre (336.2-hectare) estate. When it was built in isolated grandeur in 1924, it was Scotland's only five-star hotel. It is still a true resort and has tried to keep up with the times by offering spa treatments. Public rooms are classical, with pilasters and pillars. The guest rooms vary greatly in size; the best and most spacious choices are in the 60 to 90 block series. The less desirable rooms are called courtyard units, a bit small and equipped with shower-only bathrooms. As for cuisine, the golfers rarely complain, but no one dines here to collect recipes.

Auchterarder PH3 1NF. ℂ 01764/662-231. Fax 01764/662-134. www.gleneagles.com. 211 units. £255–£410 ($382.50–$615) double; £575–£680 ($862.50–$1,020) suite. Rates include Scottish breakfast. AE, DC, MC, V. Free parking. Take A9 for 1½ miles (2.5km) southwest of Auchterarder. **Amenities:** 3 restaurants, 2 bars; pool; spa; hunting excursions; room service; babysitting; laundry/dry cleaning. *In room:* TV, minibar, coffeemaker, hair dryer, iron, safe.

3 Crieff ★ & Drummond Castle Gardens ★

18 miles (29km) W of Perth, 60 miles (97km) NW of Edinburgh, 50 miles (80.5km) NE of Glasgow

At the edge of the Perthshire Highlands, with good fishing and golf, Crieff makes a pleasant stop. This small burgh was the seat of the court of the earls of Strathearn until 1747. Visitors come to see two major attractions: the Glenturret Distillery, the oldest in Scotland, and Drummond Castle Gardens, one of the most formal gardens in Europe.

ESSENTIALS

GETTING THERE There's no direct rail service. The nearest **train stations** are 9 miles (14.5km) away at Gleneagles and 18 miles (29km) away at Perth. Call ℂ 08457/484-950 for schedules. From Perth, you'll find regular connecting **bus** service hourly during the day. For information, call **Stagecoach** (ℂ 01738/629-339). The bus service from Gleneagles is too poor to recommend, though you can hire a taxi for £20 to £30 ($30 to $45).

VISITOR INFORMATION The **tourist office** is in the Town Hall on High Street (ℂ 01764/652-578). It's open November to March, Monday through Friday from 9:30am to 5pm and Saturday from 10am to 2pm; April to June, Monday through Saturday from 9:30am to 5:30pm and Sunday from 11am to 4pm; July and August, Monday through Saturday from 9am to 7pm and Sunday from 11am to 6pm, and September and October, Monday through Saturday from 9:30am to 5:30pm and Sunday from 11am to 4pm.

EXPLORING THE AREA

If you're in the mood for hiking, follow the signposts in town to **Knock Hill,** which towers over Crieff. You'll be rewarded with some of the most dramatic views of the Highlands. For a scenic drive, head out to **Smaa Glen,** a narrow

V-shaped valley north of Crieff. Hills rise on either side to 2,000 feet (607m). Here you'll encounter some of the loveliest moorland countryside in the Highlands as well as **Ossian's Stone,** marking the grave of Ossian, the 3rd-century bard. Leave Crieff by A85, and then branch left to take A822. The glen is signposted.

At the factory outlet for **Stuart Crystal,** Muthill Road (© **01764/654-004**), a cutter demonstrates his craft on certain days, and there's also a falconry display outside when the weather permits. (Call ahead to check on both.) During demonstrations, one-of-a-kind patterns are cut, and these pieces, available for sale, are very popular as souvenirs. The shop also sells crystal by Wedgwood and Waterford, as well as a line of handcrafted Ortak jewelry, Dunoon glazed stoneware mugs, and Heritage bronze figurines. You can relax and admire your purchases in the cafe.

The **Crieff Visitor Centre,** on A822 directly south of Crieff (© **01764/654-014**), not only dispenses information but also is the site of a paperweight manufacturer, a small pottery factory, and an inexpensive restaurant. During the week, you can see paperweights being made. Open daily in summer from 9am to 6pm, daily in winter from 10am to 4pm.

Drummond Castle Gardens ☆   The gardens of Drummond Castle, first laid out in the early 17th century by John Drummond, second earl of Perth, are among the finest formal gardens in Europe. There's a panoramic view from the upper terrace, overlooking an example of an early Victorian parterre in the form of St. Andrew's Cross. The multifaceted sundial by John Mylne, master mason to Charles I, has been the centerpiece since 1630.

Grimsthorpe, Crieff. © **01764/681-257.** Admission £3.50 ($5.25) adults, £2.50 ($3.75) seniors, £1.50 ($2.25) children. May–Oct daily 2–6pm; Easter weekend 2–6pm. Closed Nov–Apr. Take A822 for 3 miles (5km) south of Crieff.

Glenturret Distillery Ltd.   Scotland's oldest distillery, Glenturret was established in 1775 on the banks of the River Turret. Visitors can see the milling of malt, mashing, fermentation, distillation, and cask filling, followed by a free "wee dram" dispensed at the end of the tour. Guided tours take about 25 minutes and leave at frequent intervals. A 20-minute video, *The Water of Life,* is presented adjacent to a small museum devoted to the implements of the whisky trade.

Hwy. A85, Glenturret. © **01764/656-565.** Guided tours £3.50 ($5.25) adults, £3 ($4.50) seniors, £2.30 ($3.45) children 12–17, £9 ($13.50) per family. Mar–Dec Mon–Sat 9:30am–6pm, Sun noon–6pm; Feb Mon–Fri 11:30am–4:30pm, Sun noon–4pm. Closed Jan and Dec 25–26. Take A85 toward Comrie; ³/₄ mile (1.2km) from Crieff, turn right at the crossroads.

ACCOMMODATIONS

Murraypark Hotel   Built by a sea captain in the 19th century, this stone-fronted house is in a residential neighborhood about a 10-minute walk from Crieff's center and close to a golf course. Bedrooms vary in size and shape, but most open onto views. The older wing's decor is traditional Victorian. Although rooms in the newer wing (1993) are more comfortable, they are hardly as evocative. The neatly maintained bathrooms contain combination tub/showers.

Connaught Terrace, Crieff PH7 3DJ. © **01764/653-731.** Fax 01764/655-311. www.murraypark.com. 19 units. £70 ($105) double or suite. Rates include Scottish breakfast. AE, MC, V. Free parking. **Amenities:** Dining room, bar; room service; babysitting. *In room:* TV, coffeemaker, hair dryer.

DINING

The Bank MODERN SCOTTISH   This dignified red-sandstone building was constructed in 1901 as a branch of the British Linen Bank, now part of the Bank of Scotland. Today, it contains one of the most appealing restaurants in town, thanks to the superb cuisine, a hardworking staff, and a decor of mostly original paneling, an ornate plaster ceiling, and a huge arched window. Menu items may include wild mushroom risotto with truffle oil and cheddar cheese from the Isle of Mull; prime rib of Scottish beef with potatoes and red-wine sauce; and charcoal-grilled salmon with crayfish, asparagus, and shellfish-studded saffron sauce.

32 High St. © 01764/656-575. Reservations recommended. Main courses £8–£12 ($12–$18). AE, MC, V. Daily noon–2:30pm; Tues–Sat 7–10pm (Aug, also Sun 7–10pm).

4 Aberfeldy ⍟

76 miles (122km) NW of Edinburgh, 73 miles (117.5km) NE of Glasgow, 15 miles (24km) SW of Pitlochry, 32 miles (51.5km) NW of Perth

The Birks o' Aberfeldy are among the beauty spots made famous by Robert Burns. (His poem refers to the silver birches in the town.) Once a Pictish center, Aberfeldy makes a fine base for touring Perthshire's glens and lochs. Loch Tay is 6 miles (10km) west, Glen Lyon 15 miles (24km) west, and Kinloch Rannoch 18 miles (29km) northwest. Of the trio, Glen Lyon is one of central Scotland's most beautiful glens and reason enough to go to sleepy Aberfeldy in the first place. The bridge spanning the Tay was built in 1733 by Gen. George Wade. For a lovely walk, stroll just south of the town center to encounter the thundering Falls of Moness.

ESSENTIALS

GETTING THERE   There's no direct rail service into Aberfeldy. You can take a **train** to either Perth or Pitlochry, and then continue the rest of the way by bus. Call © 08457/484-950 for schedules. The private bus line **Stagecoach** (© 01738/629-339) handles connections to Aberfeldy and serves the smaller towns and villages in the area. If you're **driving** from Crieff, take A822 on a winding road north to Aberfeldy. The drive from Perth takes 30 to 45 minutes.

VISITOR INFORMATION   The **tourist office** is at the Square (© 01887/ 820-276). Hours are July and August, daily from 9:30am to 5pm; April to June and September to October, daily from 9am to 5:30pm; and October to March, Monday through Saturday from 9am to 5:30pm.

EXPLORING THE AREA

On the opposite bank of the Tay, west of the center, is the **Clan Menzies' Museum** (© 01887/820-982), a formerly fortified tower and house from the 1500s now devoted to regional exhibits. From April to mid-October, it's open Monday through Saturday from 10:30am to 5pm and Sunday from 2 to 5pm. Admission is £3.50 ($5.25) for adults, £3 ($4.50) for seniors, and £2 ($3) for children.

If you'd like to go boating on Loch Tay, head for the **Loch Tay Boating Centre,** Carlin and Brett, Pier Road at Kenmore (© 01887/830-291), which rents canoes and cabin cruisers from April to October.

Aberfeldy Golf Club (© 01887/820-535), is an 18-hole, par-68 flatland course on the banks of the River Tay. The river comes into play on several holes, and if you're not careful, you'll be making trips back to the pro shop for more balls. Greens fees are £15 ($22.50) for 18 holes (£20/$30 on weekends), and fees for pull carts are £2 ($3) per round. April to October, the club is open daily from 8am to 11pm. During other months, call ahead.

Aberfeldy is a good base for exploring **Glen Lyon** *☆*, one of the most beautiful glens in the central part of the country, with forests, prehistoric sites, and a raging river. It's Scotland's longest glen and the best place for long country walks. Follow A827 to Fearnan, then head north to Fortingall (signposted). A curiosity in the glen is the **Fortingall yew,** which you can see in the churchyard close to the Fortingall Hotel. The tree may be 3,000 years old, and it looks its age. An old Scottish legend claims Pontius Pilate was born next to this weather-beaten old tree; his father, or so the story goes, was once a Roman legionnaire in Scotland.

The town's shops offer good buys in tweeds and tartans, plus other items of Highland dress. The **Highland Gift Shop,** Bridgend (*☎* **01887/820-257**), sells only products of Scotland, from Ortak silver jewelry, hand-knit sweaters, and crystal to shortbread, sweets, and anything that can be made of tartan, including soft children's toys. **P & J Haggart,** 32 Dunkeld St. (*☎* **01887/820-306**), is a manufacturer of tweeds that turns out an array of men's and women's clothing. Much of what you'll find is outdoor wear.

ACCOMMODATIONS & DINING

Farleyer House Hotel *☆*   A tranquil oasis, this hotel is full of character and stands on 70 acres (28.4 hectares) of grounds in the Tay Valley. Although restored and altered over the years, the building dates back to the 1500s. The public areas are immaculate and beautifully furnished. The guest rooms are well maintained and comfortable, with tub-and-shower bathrooms. The staff entertains guests as if they were in a private home.

Hwy. B846, Aberfeldy PH15 2JE. *☎* **01887/820-332.** Fax 01887/829-430. www.taste-of-scotland. com/farleyer_house_hotel.html. 19 units. £120–£140 ($180–$210) double; £120–£150 ($180–$225) family suite. Rates include breakfast. AE, DC, MC, V. Take B846 for 2 miles (3km) west of Aberfeldy. **Amenities:** 2 restaurants, 2 bars; room service; babysitting; laundry/dry cleaning. *In room:* TV, coffeemaker.

Guinach House   This hotel's restaurant is one of the most sophisticated in the region, and to overnight here without experiencing it would be unfortunate indeed. The setting is a stone-sided house built around 1900 by a sea captain who wanted to retire as far inland as possible: The oak tree visible from the windows of many rooms has been pinpointed by surveyors as the geographic heart of Scotland, equidistant from each of the outer boundaries. Surrounded by 3 acres (1.2 hectares) of gardens, the Guinach offers nicely decorated high-ceilinged guest rooms, each with a tidy, shower-only bathroom.

On the night of our last meal here, two memorable specialties were the parcels of smoked salmon stuffed with smoked-salmon mousse on a bed of continental lettuce leaves, served with lime–olive oil dressing, and the pheasant breast with wild mushroom and stuffed game in puff pastry.

The Birks, Aberfeldy PH15 2ET. *☎* **01887/820-251.** Fax 01887/829-607. 7 units. £91 ($136.50) double with breakfast; £136 ($204) double with breakfast and dinner. MC, V. **Amenities:** Restaurant, bar; nearby golf course. *In room:* TV, coffeemaker, hair dryer, iron.

5 Dunkeld *☆*

58 miles (93km) N of Edinburgh, 14 miles (22.5km) N of Perth, 98 miles (158km) SW of Aberdeen

Dunkeld lies in a thickly wooded valley of the Tay at the edge of the Perthshire Highlands. Once a major ecclesiastical center, it's one of the seats of ancient Scottish history and was an important center of the Celtic church. The town is a definite stop for those doing the cathedral tour, as it's the site of one of Scotland's most famous cathedrals, now a substantial ruin. But there's much more to Dunkeld than that. It's an attractively restored town that invites exploration on foot. Don't miss taking a leisurely stroll to admire the beautiful 17th-century houses on Cathedral Street.

ESSENTIALS

GETTING THERE **Trains** from Perth arrive every 2 hours and cost £5 ($7.50). Travel time is 1½ hours. Call © **08457/484-950** for schedules. Pitlochry-bound **buses** leaving from Perth make a stopover in Dunkeld, letting you off at the Dunkeld Car Park, which is at the train station. Trip time is 50 minutes; the cost is £3.10 ($4.65). Contact **Stagecoach** at © **01738/629-339** for schedules. If you're **driving,** from Aberfeldy take A827 east until you reach the junction of A9 heading south to Dunkeld.

VISITOR INFORMATION A **tourist office** is at The Cross (© **01350/727-688**). It's open April to June, Monday through Saturday from 9:30am to 5:30pm and Sunday from 11am to 4pm; July 1 to September 8, Monday through Saturday from 9am to 7:30pm and Sunday from 11am to 7pm; September 9 to October 27, Monday through Saturday from 9:30am to 5:30pm and Sunday from 11am to 4pm; and October 28 to December, Monday through Saturday from 9:30am to 1:30pm (closed January to March).

EXPLORING THE AREA

The National Trust for Scotland has restored many of the old houses and shops around the marketplace and cathedral that had fallen into decay. The trust owns 20 houses on **High Street** 𝒜 and **Cathedral Street** 𝒜 as well. Many of them were constructed in the late 17th century after the rebuilding of the town following the Battle of Dunkeld. The Trust runs the **Ell Shop,** The Cross (© **01350/727-460**), open from Easter weekend to December 24, Monday through Saturday from 10am to 5:30pm.

Shakespeare fans may want to seek out the oak and sycamore in front of the destroyed **Birnam House,** a mile (1.6km) south. This was believed to be a remnant of the **Birnam Wood.** (In Shakespeare's "Scottish play," you may recall, Macbeth could be defeated only when Birnam Wood came to Dunsinane.)

The surrounding countryside is beautiful, and you can take great walks and day hikes that stretch out on both sides of the River Tay going from Dunkeld to Birnam. In all, there are 36 miles (58km) of paths that have been joined to create a network of circular routes. Pick up maps and detailed descriptions from the tourist office and set out on a day's adventure, armed with the makings of a picnic, of course.

The **Hermitage,** off A9 about 2 miles (3km) west of Dunkeld, was called a folly when it was built in 1758. Today, it makes for one of the most scenic woodland walks in the area. It was built above the wooded gorge of the River Braan and restored in 1984. There's no staff here; it's always accessible and free.

Our favorite spot in the area is the **Loch of Lowes Wildlife Reserve** (© **01350/727-337**), 2 miles (3km) from the center of town, along A923 heading northeast. It can be accessed from the south shore, where there's an observation lookout and a visitor center. Filled with rich flora and fauna, the 245-acre (99.2-hectare) reserve takes in the freshwater lake that's home to rare ospreys. Although common in the United States, these large brown-and-white sea-eagles are on the endangered-species list in Britain, and bird-watchers from all over the country come here to observe them.

The 18-hole golf course at **Dunkeld & Birnam** (© **01350/727-524**) is touted as the best in the area, with sweeping views of the surrounding environs. Greens fees are £18 ($27) for 18 holes Monday through Friday, £21 ($31.50) for 18 holes Saturday and Sunday. Pull carts are available for £2 ($3) per round. Hours are daily from 9am to 1pm. From October to March, greens fees are reduced to £9 to £10 ($13.50 to $15). There's no official dress code, although if the starter feels you are not dressed "appropriately," you will be asked to "smarten up" the next time you play the course.

Dunkeld Cathedral   Founded in A.D. 815 along the River Tay, this was converted from a church to a cathedral in 1127 by David I. It was built, damaged, and rebuilt in stages between 1452 and 1575. Its greatest destruction occurred in 1560, when the Reformers, who viewed it as a citadel of idolatry, burned the roof. Traces of the 12th-century structure clearly remain today. The choir of the ruined cathedral was renovated in the early part of the 17th century to serve as a parish church. Note the unusual windows at the triforium level. The late Gothic tower was finished in 1501. Surprisingly, it contains an elegant effigy and tomb of the so-called Wolf of Badenoch, known as the slayer of cathedrals and churches in Scotland.

Cathedral St. © **01350/727-688**. Free admission. Apr–Sept Mon–Sat 9:30am–6:30pm, Sun 2–6:30pm; Oct–Mar Sun 9:30am–4pm.

ACCOMMODATIONS & DINING

Atholl Arms Hotel   At the foot of the Telford Bridge, the Atholl Arms is the traditional choice. It was built in the early 1800s by the duke of Atholl as a coaching inn. Today, it has the aura of a respectable country home, plus comfortable midsize guest rooms, each with a small, shower-only bathroom. The pub, with a crackling log fireplace, is popular with locals and serves simple lunches. More elaborate dinners are served in the restaurant.

Bridgehead, Dunkeld PH8 0AQ. © and fax **01350/727-219**. www.s-h-systems.co.uk/a05486.html. 14 units. £60–£65 ($90–$97.50) double. AE, MC, V. **Amenities:** Restaurant, bar; room service; laundry service. In room: TV, coffeemaker, hair dryer.

Birnam House Hotel   This mock-medieval building was erected in 1863 in the baronial style as a vacation home for a wealthy industrialist. In the 1980s and 1990s, many modernizations were made, stripping the interior of at least some of its ornate detail. What you'll find today is a cozy set of high-ceilinged guest rooms, each uniquely decorated; most of the bathrooms contain combination tub/showers. A bar serves affordable lunches, while formal dinners are served nightly in the restaurant. A 5-minute walk away is the last tree remaining from Birnam Wood, so feared by Macbeth.

Perta Rd., Birnam, Dunkeld PH8 0BQ. © **01350/727-462**. Fax 01350/728-979. www.s-h-systems.co.uk/ hotels/birnamho.html. 30 units. £64–£76 ($96–$114) double. Rates include breakfast. AE, DC, MC, V. From Dunkeld, drive south across the Dunkeld Bridge; you'll then see Perta Rd. and the hotel. **Amenities:** Restaurant, bar; limited room service. In room: TV, coffeemaker, hair dryer (on request).

Hilton Dunkeld House ✦✦   This Hilton, offering the quiet dignity of a Scottish country house, is ranked as one of the leading leisure and sports hotels in the area. On the banks of the Tay, the surrounding grounds—280 acres (113.4 hectares) in all—make for a parklike setting. The house is beautifully kept, and rooms come in a wide range of sizes, styles, and furnishings. In 1999, a new nine-room wing was added. You can fish for salmon and trout right on the grounds.

Dunkeld PH8 0HX. © **01350/727-771.** Fax 01350/728-924. www.hilton.com. 97 units. £149 ($223.50) double; £199–£219 ($298.50–$328.50) suite. Rates include Scottish breakfast. AE, DC, MC, V. **Amenities:** Restaurant, 2 bars; pool; tennis courts; fishing; health club; room service; babysitting; laundry/dry cleaning. *In room:* TV, minibar, coffeemaker, hair dryer.

Kinnaird ⭐⭐⭐   On a 9,000-acre (3,645-hectare) private estate, this is a small hotel of great charm and comfort. Built in 1770 as a hunting lodge, the house has been restored to its previous grandeur. All the beautifully furnished rooms have king-size beds, full private bathrooms, and views. Some overlook the valley of the River Tay; others open onto gardens and woodlands. There are eight cottages on the estate, two of which sleep eight and the others four.

Kinnaird Estate, Kinnaird, Dunkeld PH8 0LB. © **01796/482-440.** Fax 01796/482-289. www.kinnairdestate. com. 9 units and 8 cottages. £275–£345 ($412.50–$517.50) double; £440 ($660) suite; £375–£1,000 ($562.50–$1,500) cottage. Rates include dinner and Scottish breakfast. MC, V. Free parking. No children under 12 accepted in the hotel. **Amenities:** Restaurant, bar; tennis courts; fishing and hunting excursions; room service; babysitting; laundry/dry cleaning. *In room:* TV, hair dryer.

6 Pitlochry ⭐: A Taste of the Whisky Trail

71 miles (114km) NW of Edinburgh, 27 miles (43.5km) NW of Perth, 15 miles (24km) N of Dunkeld

A popular resort, Pitlochry is a good base for touring the Valley of the Tummel. Ever since Queen Victoria declared it one of the finest resorts in Europe, it has drawn the hordes. It's also home to the renowned **Pitlochry Festival Theatre,** Scotland's theater in the hills.

Pitlochry doesn't exist just to entertain visitors, although it would appear that way in summer—it also produces scotch whisky. And it's a good overnight stop between Edinburgh and Inverness, 85 miles (137km) north. You can spend a very busy day in town, visiting its famous distilleries, seeing its dam and fish ladder, and budgeting some time for the beauty spots in the environs, especially Loch Rannoch and the Pass of Killiecrankie, both ideal for walks. At Blair Atholl stands one of the most highly visited and intriguing castles in the country, Blair Castle.

ESSENTIALS

GETTING THERE   Five **trains** (© **08457/484-950**) per day arrive from Edinburgh, and an additional three from Glasgow (trip time from each: 2 hours). A one-way fare is £19 ($28.50) from either city. **Buses** arrive hourly from Perth. The one-way fare is £3 ($4.50). Contact **Stagecoach** (© **01738/629-339**) for schedules. If you're **driving** from Perth, continue northwest along A9.

VISITOR INFORMATION   The **tourist office** is at 22 Atholl Rd. (© **01796/472-215**). From June to September, it's open daily from 9am to 8pm; May and October, hours are daily from 9am to 6pm; and November to April, hours are Monday through Friday from 9am to 5pm and Saturday from 10am to 3pm.

EXPLORING THE AREA

Pitlochry Dam was created because a power station was needed, but in effect the engineers created a new loch. The famous **salmon ladder** was built to help the struggling salmon upstream. An underwater portion of the ladder has been enclosed in glass to give fascinated sightseers a look. An exhibition (© **01796/ 473-152**) is open from Easter to the last Sunday in October, daily from 10am to 5:30pm; it costs £2 ($3) for adults, £1.20 ($1.80) for seniors, and £1 ($1.50) for children.

There are terrific scenic hikes along the **Linn of Tummel,** with several sign-posted trails going along the river and into the forest directly to the north of the center. Just north of here you come to the stunning **Pass of Killiecrankie** *&*. If you're driving, follow A9 north. The national trust has established the **Killiecrankie Visitor Centre** (© **01796/473-233**) here, open April to October daily from 10am to 5:30pm. You can learn about a famous battle that occurred here during the 1689 Jacobite rebellion. John Graham of Cleverhouse (1649–89) rallied the mainly Highlander Jacobite army to meet government troops. Graham was killed, and the cause of Scottish independence soon fizzled.

B8019 leads to **Loch Rannoch,** almost 10 miles (16km) long and three quarters of a mile (1.2km) wide. For many, this is one of the most beautiful lakes in the Highlands. The setting so impressed Robert Louis Stevenson, he wrote about it in *Kidnapped* (1886): "Much of it was red with heather, much of the rest broken up with bogs and hags and peaty pools." To see this desolate but awesomely beautiful spot, follow B8019 to the Linn of Tummel north of Pitlochry, venturing onto B846 at the Bridge of Tummel.

Shoppers will want to check out **McNaughtons,** Station Road (© **01796/ 472-722**), which offers a full range of Highland wear, including tweeds, tartans, and the inevitable kilts. There's also a fabric center, where a variety of Scottish fabrics can be purchased by the meter.

Bell's Blair Atholl Distillery   In 2000, Bell's celebrated 203 years as a popular whisky distillery. Visitors can take a distillery tour; the fee charged to adults is redeemable as a voucher off the price of any single-malt purchased in the visitor center.

Perth Rd., 1½ miles (2.5km) south of town. © **01796/482-003.** Admission £3 ($4.50) adults. Tours given Mar–Oct Mon–Sat 9:30am–4pm, Sun noon–5pm; Nov–Feb Mon–Fri 10am–4pm, by arrangement.

Blair Castle *&*   The major excursion from Pitlochry is to this castle north of the Pass of Killiecrankie. Home of the dukes of Atholl, it's one of the great historic castles of Scotland. Over the years, it has seen many alterations and was finally turned into the Georgian mansion you see today, although it dates from 1269. Allow about 2 hours to see the palace's antiques, 18th-century interiors, and paintings, along with an outstanding arms, armor, and porcelain collection. In the Stewart room, note the portrait of Mary Queen of Scots and her son, James VI. The Picture Staircase is a stunning achievement. On the second floor, you can visit a small Georgian drawing room, the Blue Bedroom once occupied by Victorian beauty Louisa Moncrieffe, and the Tapestry Room with a superb collection of Flemish tapestries. After viewing the castle, you can stroll through the Victorian walled garden and take a long walk in the parklands.

Blair Atholl. © **01796/481-207.** Admission £6.25 ($9.40) adults, £5.25 ($7.90) seniors, £4 ($6) children. Apr to late Oct daily 10am–6pm. Closed Nov–Mar. From the town center, follow A9 to Blair Atholl, where you'll see signs.

Edradour Distillery   Take A924 east toward Braemar to find this distillery, Scotland's smallest, 2 miles (3km) outside of town. The visitor center offers distillery tours throughout the day, and the gift shop sells Edradour single malts, as well as various blends that contain the whisky.

On A924, Pitlochry. © **01796/472-095.** Free admission. Mar–Oct Mon–Sat 9:30am–5pm, Sun noon–5pm; Nov–Feb Mon–Sat 10am–4pm.

ACCOMMODATIONS

East Haugh House (see "Dining," below) also rents rooms.

Balrobin This traditional Scottish country house opens onto views of the Perthshire Hills and the Tummel Valley. Originally a 19th-century cottage used for fishing and shooting holidays, it's now a government-rated two-star hotel with average-size guest rooms furnished in simple provincial style (with shower-only bathrooms). Added to the "auld hoose" were a west and east wing in keeping with the stone construction. Affordable dinners are served nightly, and there's a guests-only bar and country lounge. No smoking is permitted.

Higher Oakfield, Pitlochry PH16 5HT. (C) **01796/472-901.** Fax 01796/474-200. www.balrobin.co.uk. 16 units. £50–£70 ($75–$105) double. Rates include Scottish breakfast. MC, V. Closed Nov. **Amenities:** Restaurant, bar. *In room:* TV, coffeemaker, hair dryer, no phone.

Green Park Hotel The Green Park is about half a mile (1km) from the center, at the northwest end of Pitlochry. Against a backdrop of woodland, the white-painted mansion with its carved eaves enjoys a scenic position; its lawn reaches to the shores of Loch Faskally. Ask for one of the half dozen or so rooms in the garden wing, all of which enjoy a loch view. Some units contain showers only. Guests can order drinks in a lounge overlooking the water (where there's no smoking). Popular during festival season, the dining room serves dinner nightly, with many traditional Scottish dishes.

Clunie Bridge Rd., Pitlochry PH16 5JY. (C) **01796/473-248.** Fax 01796/473-520. www.thegreenpark.co.uk. 39 units. £66–£128 ($99–$192) double. Rates include half-board. MC, V. **Amenities:** Restaurant, bar. *In room:* TV, coffeemaker, hair dryer.

Hotel Acarsaid This graceful but solid-looking stone house dates from 1880, when it was the home of the countess of Kilbride. Greatly expanded, the hotel contains cozy guest rooms, with contemporary furnishings and immaculately kept, shower-only bathrooms. The bar serves snacks at lunch (for guests only), while the more elaborate restaurant offers fixed-price dinners. Menu items focus on fresh ingredients, most of them Scottish.

8 Atholl Rd., Pitlochry PH16 5BX. (C) **01796/472-389.** Fax 01796/473-952. www.acarsaidhotel.com. 19 units. £50–£72 ($75–$108) double. Rates include breakfast. MC, V. **Amenities:** Restaurant, bar; access to nearby health club; laundry service. *In room:* TV, coffeemaker, hair dryer.

Killiecrankie Hotel 🦌 This typically Scottish country house, built in 1840, is surrounded by 4 acres (1.6 hectares) of lawns and woodlands. The guest rooms are individually decorated in subtle tones. Most of the bathrooms contain combination shower/tubs. The walls are a foot thick, so light sleepers can rest in peace. The restaurant serves expensive dinners that feature fresh produce and seasonal meat, fish, and game. The bar is open to guests only.

A924, Killiecrankie PH16 5LG. (C) **01796/473-220.** Fax 01796/472-451. www.killiecrankiehotel.co.uk. 10 units. £120–£178 ($180–$267) double. MC, V. Free parking. Signposted from A9 north of Pitlochry. **Amenities:** Restaurant, bar; room service. *In room:* TV, coffeemaker, hair dryer.

Knockendarroch House 🦌 *Finds* Built in 1880, this award-winning Victorian mansion opens onto panoramic views of the Tummel Valley. The bedrooms, which vary in size and style, are attractively decorated in cool colors; each contains a bathroom with a combination tub/shower. The cozy attic units have balconies overlooking the rooftops of Pitlochry. Guests are offered a free glass of sherry before dinner, which might be wild venison chops in red wine and juniper berry jus, or mushroom and nut roast on the chiffonade of cabbage in rich tomato and sherry sauce. The food is of the finest quality, and prices are more moderate than might be expected. Reservations are required. Overall, the warmth of the staff and the evocative atmosphere of the mansion make it a place worth visiting.

Higher Oakfield, Pitlochry PH16 5HT. ⑦ **01796/473-473.** Fax 01796/474-068. www.knockendarroch.co.uk. 12 units. £118 ($177) double. Rates include breakfast and dinner. AE, MC, V. Closed Nov–Mar. Turn off A9 going north at PITLOCHRY sign. After rail bridge, take 1st right, then 2nd left. **Amenities:** Restaurant, bar; room service; laundry service. *In room:* TV, coffeemaker, hair dryer.

Pine Trees Hotel ℛ   This country house was built in 1892 on 14 acres (5.7 hectares), only a 15-minute walk from the town center and 5 minutes from the golf course, home of the Highland Open Championships. The family-run Pine Trees has spacious public rooms, an atmosphere of warmth, and a reputation for good food and wine. The guest rooms are in either the main house or a 1970s annex designed to blend into the period of the central structure. All bathrooms have combination tub/showers. Bar lunches and full lunch and dinner menus are offered, with fresh and smoked salmon always featured. Trout and salmon fishing can usually be arranged.

Strathview Terrace, Pitlochry PH16 5QR. ⑦ **01796/472-121.** Fax 01796/472-460. www.pinetreeshotel.co.uk. 20 units. £68–£140 ($102–$210) double. Rates include Scottish breakfast. MC, V. Turn right up Larchwood Rd., below the golf course on the north side of Pitlochry. **Amenities:** Restaurant, bar; dry cleaning. *In room:* TV, coffeemaker, hair dryer.

DINING

East Haugh House MODERN BRITISH   Although it contains 13 comfortable guest rooms, East Haugh House is best known for its well-prepared cuisine. In a Teutonic-looking granite house commissioned in the 1600s by the duke of Atholl for one of his tenant farmers, it offers a menu that relies exclusively on fresh Scottish ingredients. Meals in the cozy bar may include mixed grills, steaks, and haggis. The cuisine in the elegant restaurant is more adventurous, featuring such dishes as zucchini flowers stuffed with wild-mushroom duxelle, terrine of local pigeon with orange salad and *mange tout* (a kind of bean), and many variations of salmon.

The spacious guest rooms will make you think you're staying in a country mansion. Including a Scottish breakfast, doubles run £59 to £110 ($88.50 to $165).

Old Perth Rd., East Haugh, Pitlochry PH16 5JS. ⑦ **01796/473-121.** Fax 01796/472-473. www. easthaugh.co.uk. Reservations recommended. Table d'hôte dinner £27.95 ($41.95); bar platters £1.75–£16 ($2.65–$24). MC, V. Restaurant daily 7–9pm; bar daily noon–2:30pm and 6–9pm. Drive 1 mile (1.6km) south of Pitlochry on A9 toward Inverness; it's across the road from the Tummell River.

PITLOCHRY AFTER DARK

The town is famous for its **Pitlochry Festival Theatre** (⑦ **01796/484-626**). Founded in 1951, it draws people from all over the world to its repertory of plays, concerts, and varying art exhibits, presented from April 30 to October 9. The theater complex opened in 1981 on the banks of the River Tummel near the dam and fish ladder, with a parking area; a restaurant serving coffee, lunch, and dinner; and other facilities for visitors. Tickets for plays and concerts are £14 to £18 ($21 to $27).

For the area's best pub, head to the peaceful grounds of the **Killiecrankie Hotel,** signposted from A9 north of Pitlochry (⑦ **01796/473-220**). It serves 20 malt whiskies as well as reasonably priced great food. Upholstered chairs, wildlife paintings, and plants and flowers make for an inviting atmosphere.

7 Dundee & Glamis Castle

63 miles (101.5km) N of Edinburgh, 67 miles (108km) SW of Aberdeen, 22 miles (35.5km) NE of Perth, 83 miles (134km) NE of Glasgow

The old seaport of Dundee, the fourth-largest city in Scotland, is now an industrial city on the north shore of the Firth of Tay. When steamers took over the whaling industry from sailing vessels, Dundee took the lead as home port for the ships from the 1860s until World War I. Long known for its jute and flax operations, Dundee is linked with the production of rich Dundee fruitcakes and Dundee marmalades and jams.

Spanning the Firth of Tay is the **Tay Railway Bridge,** opened in 1888. Constructed over the tidal estuary, the bridge is 2 miles (3km) long, one of the longest in Europe. There's also a road bridge 1¼ miles (2km) long, with four traffic lanes and a walkway in the center.

Dundee has only minor attractions itself, but it's a base for exploring Glamis Castle (one of the most famous in Scotland) and the little town of Kirriemuir, which Sir James M. Barrie, author of *Peter Pan,* disguised in fiction as the Thrums. Dundee also makes a good base for those who want to play at one of Scotland's most famous golf courses, Carnoustie.

ESSENTIALS

GETTING THERE ScotRail offers frequent train service between Perth, Dundee, and Aberdeen. A one-way fare from Perth is £4.60 ($6.90); from Aberdeen, £17.40 ($26.10). Phone ℘ **08457/484-950** for schedules. **Scottish CityLink** (℘ **0990/505-050**) buses offer frequent service from Edinburgh and Glasgow. If you're **driving,** the fastest way to reach Dundee is to cut south back to Perth along A9 and link up with A972 going east.

VISITOR INFORMATION The **tourist office** is at 21 Castle St. (℘ **01382/ 527-527.** Hours are April to September, Monday through Saturday from 9am to 6pm and Sunday from 10am to 4pm; and October to March, Monday through Saturday from 9am to 5pm.

EXPLORING THE AREA

For a panoramic view of Dundee, the Tay Bridge across to Fife, and the mountains to the north, go to **Dundee Law,** a 572-foot (173.5m) hill a mile (1.6km) north of the city. The hill is an ancient volcanic plug.

Caird Park (℘ **01382/453-606**) is an 18-hole, par-72 course that presents most golfers with an average challenge. It's quite flat, but there are more than a few bunkers to navigate. A restaurant and bar are on the premises. Greens fees are £15 ($22.50) for 18 holes, or £25 ($37.50) for a day ticket. No carts of any sort are allowed. Open April to October, daily from 7am to 8pm.

Broughty Castle This 15th-century estuary fort is 4 miles (6.5km) east of the city center at Broughty Ferry, a fishing village that was the terminus for ferries crossing the Firth of Tay until the bridges were built. Besieged by the English in the 16th century and attacked by Cromwell's army under General Monk in the 17th, it was restored in 1861 as part of Britain's coastal defenses. The museum has displays on local history, arms and armor, seashore life, and Dundee's whaling story. The observation area at the top of the castle provides fine views of the Tay estuary and northeast Fife.

Castle Green, Broughty Ferry, ℘ 01382/436-916. Free admission. July–Sept Mon 11am–5pm, Tues–Thurs 10am–1pm and 2–5pm, Sun 2–5pm; Oct–June Mon 11am–5pm, Tues–Thurs 10am–1pm and 2–5pm. Bus: 75 or 76.

HMS *Unicorn* ☞ This 46-gun ship of war commissioned in 1824 by the Royal Navy, now the oldest British-built ship afloat, has been restored. You can explore all four decks: the quarter-deck with its 32-pound (14.5kg) carronades, the gundeck with its battery of 18-pound (8kg) cannons and captain's quarters, the berth deck with its officers' cabins and crew's hammocks, and the orlop deck and hold. Various displays portraying life in the sailing navy and the history of the *Unicorn* make this a rewarding visit.

Victoria Dock. ℂ **01382/200-900.** Admission £3.50 ($5.25) adults, £2.50 ($3.75) seniors and children, £7.50–£9.50 ($11.25–$14.25) per family. Easter–Oct daily 10am–5pm; Nov–Easter Wed–Sun 10am–4pm. Bus: 6, 23, or 78.

RRS *Discovery* ☞ This weather-beaten vessel was used by Capt. Robert Scott on polar explorations. An exhibit details Scott's first two expeditions to the Antarctic, and onboard displays re-create the rugged life on the ship.

Discovery Quay, Discovery Point. ℂ **01382/201-245.** Admission £5.95 ($8.95) adults, £4.45 ($6.70) seniors, £3.85 ($5.80) children. Combination ticket for *Discovery* and Verdart Works (see below) £10–£15 ($15–$22.50) adults, £7.75 ($11.65) seniors, £7 ($10.50) children. Apr–Oct Mon–Sat 10am–5pm, Sun 11am–5pm; Nov–Mar Mon–Sat 10am–4pm, Sun 11am–4pm.

Verdant Works This refurbished ex-mill, known as the Jute House, is dedicated to the history of an industry that sustained Dundee throughout most of the 19th and 20th centuries. The first floor shows how raw jute from Bangladesh was processed and includes a display on a weaver's loom. On the second floor is a section on the socio-historical aspect of the city and how the different social classes lived in 19th-century Dundee. In the courtyard are 18th- and 19th-century street games, such as stilts and whips and tops.

West Henderson's Wind. ℂ **01382/225-282.** Admission £5.95 ($8.95) adults, £4.45 ($6.70) seniors, £3.85 ($5.80) children. Apr–Oct Mon–Sat 10am–5pm, Sun 11am–5pm; Nov–Mar Mon–Sat 10am–4pm, Sun 11am–4pm.

ACCOMMODATIONS

Craigtay Hotel Although this hotel was constructed around the core of an 18th-century farm building, few if any hints of its age are visible. In the 1960s, it was Dundee's first disco, before a local entrepreneur transformed it into a tearoom. Much enlarged and modernized, it's now a small hotel with functional guest rooms and small, shower-only bathrooms. The pub and restaurant serve moderately priced dinners nightly.

101 Broughty Ferry Rd, Tayside, Dundee DD4 6JE. ℂ **01382/451-142.** Fax 01382/452-940. www. craigtay.co.uk. 18 units. £51–£70 ($76.50–$105) double. AE, MC, V. From Dundee, drive 1 mile (1.6km) east of town, following signs to Broughty Ferry. **Amenities:** Restaurant, bar. *In room:* TV, coffeemaker, hair dryer (on request), iron.

Hilton Dundee ☞ This chain hotel helps to rejuvenate the once-seedy waterfront of Dundee. Built in a severe modern style, the five-story block contains well-furnished guest rooms, some of which overlook the Firth, the river, or the Tay Bridge. The rooms contain bright floral upholstery and draperies, blond wood furnishings, and small bathrooms with combination tub/showers.

Earl Grey Place, Dundee DD1 4DE. ℂ **01382/229-271.** Fax 01382/200-072. www.hilton.com. 129 units. £120–£140 ($180–$210) double; from £220 ($330) suite. AE, DC, MC, V. Free parking. Bus: 1A, 1B, or 20. **Amenities:** Restaurant; pool; spa; room service; babysitting; laundry/dry cleaning. *In room:* TV, coffeemaker, hair dryer, safe.

Invercarse Hotel In landscaped gardens overlooking the River Tay, this hotel offers well-maintained guest rooms, in a variety of sizes, that open onto views across the Tay to the hills of the Kingdom of Fife. Many prefer it for its fresh air, tranquil location, and Victorian country-house aura.

371 Perth Rd. (3 miles/5km west of town center), Dundee DD2 1PG. ℂ 01382/669-231. Fax 01382/644-112. 44 units. £90 ($135) double; £100 ($150) suite. Rates include Scottish breakfast. AE, DC, MC, V. Free parking. **Amenities:** Restaurant, bar; room service; laundry/dry cleaning. *In room:* TV, coffeemaker, hair dryer.

DINING

Other dining options include the restaurants in the hotels listed above.

Jahangir Tandoori INDIAN   Built around an indoor fish pond in a dining room draped with the soft folds of an embroidered tent, this is the best Indian restaurant in Dundee and one of the most exotic in the region. Meals are prepared with fresh ingredients and cover recipes from both north and south India. The food is sometimes slow-cooked in clay pots and is seasoned to the degree of spiciness you prefer. Both meat and vegetarian dishes are available.

1 Sessions St., at the corner of Hawk Hill. ℂ 01382/202-022. Reservations recommended. Main courses £6.50–£15 ($9.75–$22.50). AE, MC, V. Daily 5pm–midnight.

DUNDEE AFTER DARK

The **Dundee Rep Theatre,** Tay Square (ℂ **01382/223-530**), is likely to stage any and everything from *Peter Pan* to an opera, from plays to Scottish ballet or even flamenco. You can purchase tickets Monday through Saturday from 10am to 7:30pm (to 6pm on performance days). Tickets generally cost £5 to £15 ($7.50 to $22.50). On site is the **Het Theatercafe** (ℂ **01382/206-699**), open Monday from noon to 7:30pm, Tuesday through Thursday from noon to 9pm, Friday from noon to 10:30pm, and Saturday from noon to 10:30pm. Main courses are £6 to £10 ($9 to $15).

A SIDE TRIP TO GLAMIS CASTLE

The little village of Glamis (pronounced without the *i*) grew up around its famous castle. After Balmoral, visitors to Scotland most want to see Glamis Castle for its architecture and its link with the crown.

Glamis Castle 🎔🎔   For 6 centuries, this castle has been connected to members of the British royal family: Queen Elizabeth, the Queen Mother, was brought up here, and Princess Margaret was born here, making her the first royal princess born in Scotland in 3 centuries. The present owner, the queen's great-nephew, is the 18th earl of Strathmore and Kinghorne and the direct descendant of the first earl. The castle contains Duncan's Hall, where the Victorians claimed Macbeth murdered King Duncan. (In the play, the murder takes place at Macbeth's castle near Inverness.) In fact, Shakespeare was erroneous as well—he had Macbeth named Thane of Glamis, but Glamis wasn't made a thanedom until years after the play takes place.

The present Glamis Castle dates from the early 15th century, but there are records of a hunting lodge having been here in the 11th century. Glamis Castle has been in the possession of the Lyon family since 1372, when it was given to Sir John Lyon by Robert II. Four years later, Sir John married the king's daughter, Princess Joanna. The castle was altered in the 17th century and restored and enlarged in the 18th and 19th centuries. It contains some fine plaster ceilings, furniture, and paintings. You'll also want to stroll its gardens.

A self-service restaurant has been installed in the old kitchens, with a chalkboard featuring daily specials and excellent home-cooked and baked dishes.

Glamis. ℂ 01307/840-393. Admission to castle and gardens £6 ($9) adults, £3 ($4.50) children, £16.50 ($24.75) per family. Admission to grounds only £3 ($4.50) adults, £1.50 ($2.25) children. End of Mar to end

In Search of Peter Pan

The little town of **Kirriemuir** is reached by heading north of Glamis Castle for 4 miles (6.5km) or by traveling 16 miles (26km) north of Dundee via A929 and A928. Thousands of visitors per year come here to pay their respects to Sir James M. Barrie (1860–1937), author of *Peter Pan.*

The little town of red-sandstone houses and narrow crooked streets, in the heart of Scotland's raspberry country, saw the birth of Barrie in 1860. His father was employed as a hand-loom weaver of linen. **Barrie's birthplace** still stands at 9 Brechin Rd. (© 01575/572-646), now a property of the National Trust for Scotland. The small house contains manuscripts and mementos of the writer. From May to September, the house is open Monday through Saturday from 11am to 5pm and Sunday from 1:30 to 5pm; October, hours are Saturday from 11am to 5pm and Sunday from 1:30 to 5pm. Admission is £3.50 ($5.25) for adults, £2.50 ($3.75) for seniors, students, and children.

Barrie first became known for his sometimes-cynical tales of Kirriemuir, disguised as Thrums, in such works as *Auld Licht Idylls* (1888) and *A Window in Thrums* (1889). Barrie then turned to the theater and in time became known for bringing supernatural and sentimental ideas to the stage. It's said that talking to a group of children while walking his dog gave him the idea for the stories about Peter Pan, which were first presented to the public in 1904. It wasn't until 1957 that *When Wendy Grew Up: An Afterthought* was published.

He went on to write more dramas, including *Alice Sit-by-the-Fire* (1905), *What Every Woman Knows* (1908), *The Will* (1913), and *Mary Rose* (1920), the latter a very popular play in its day. But who remembers these works today except a Barrie scholar? On the other hand, Peter Pan has become a legendary figure, known by almost every child in the Western world through films, plays, musicals, and the original book.

Although he spent most of his working life in London, Barrie is buried in Kirriemuir Cemetery. To reach **Barrie's grave**, turn left off Brechin Road and follow the cemetery road upward. The path is clearly marked, taking you to the grave pavilion. A camera obscura in the **Barrie Pavilion** on Kirriemuir Hill gives views over Strathmore to Dundee and north to the Highlands.

of Oct, daily 10:30am–5:30pm. Buses from Dundee to Glamis run Mon–Sat; the 35-minute ride costs £3.70 ($5.55) one-way. *Note:* Buses don't stop in front of the castle, which lies 1 mile (1.6km) from the bus stop.

ACCOMMODATIONS

Castleton House 🛱 *Finds* This Victorian hotel is run with love and care by its owners, Anthony and Sheila Lilly. In cool weather, you're greeted by welcoming coal fires in the lounge; the youthful staff is the most considerate we've encountered in the area. Rooms of various sizes are furnished with reproductions of antiques. Each has a small bathroom (some with shower only).

Eassie by Glamis, Forfar, Tayside DD8 1SJ. ℂ 01307/840-340. Fax 01307/840-506. www.castletonglamis.
co.uk. 6 units. £110 ($165) double. Children under 11 stay free in parents' room. Rates include Scottish
breakfast. MC, V. Drive 3 miles (5km) west of Glamis on A94. **Amenities:** 2 restaurants, bar; room service;
babysitting; laundry/dry cleaning. *In room:* TV, coffeemaker, hair dryer.

DINING

Strathomore Arms CONTINENTAL/SCOTTISH   Try this place near the
castle for one of the best lunches in the area. You might begin with the freshly
made soup of the day or the fresh prawns. Regularly featured dishes could
include steak pie or venison. For something a little more exotic, go for the
Indian chicken breast marinated in yogurt and spices; vegetarians can order
phyllo parcels stuffed with asparagus and cauliflower.

The Square, Glamis. ℂ 01307/840-248. Reservations recommended. Main courses £5.50–£15
($8.25–$22.50). AE, MC, V. Daily noon–2pm and 6:30–9pm.

8 Carnoustie

12 miles E of Dundee, 59 miles SW of Aberdeen, 68 miles NE of Edinburgh

Carnoustie is the home of the famous **Carnoustie Golf Links,** Links Parade
(ℂ **01241/853-789;** fax 01241/852-720). Incorporated in 1880, much of the
town of Carnoustie was built because of the stream of golfers who came here to
play. Records as early as 1560 refer to *gowff* being played on the surrounding
fields, and by the reign of Queen Victoria, the course had developed into a factory for training golf instructors and champions who spread word of the game
throughout the Empire. Skilled golfers call the course stimulating; neophytes
refer to it as treacherous. In 1999, the British Open was held here. This 6,941-
yard (6,316m), par-72 championship course requires the use of a caddy, costing
£30 ($45) for 18 holes. Electric golf carts aren't allowed, but you can rent a
trolley for £3 ($4.50) per round. Greens fees are £75 ($112.50), and club rental,
available at **Simpson's Golf Shop,** 6 Links Parade (ℂ **01241/854-477**), or **David
Low's,** 7 Links Ave. (ℂ **01241/853-439**), costs £10 to £15 ($15 to $22.50).

Carnoustie is also home to the **Burnside Course** and the **Buddon Links
Course,** opened in the 1970s.

To reach Carnoustie from Dundee, go east 10 miles (16km) along A92 or
take the coastal road, A930, which is signposted.

ACCOMMODATIONS

Carnoustie Links Hotel   Sheila and Joe McClory run this government-rated
three-star hotel overlooking the 18th green of the Carnoustie Golf Links. The
tasteful bedrooms are individually decorated, and four are large enough for families. Many open onto panoramic views of the Links, the Tay Estuary, and the
countryside. All units come with small bathrooms (most with shower only).
Golfers meet at the lounge and pub, Hogan's Alley, with its extensive collection
of golf memorabilia. The restaurant is known for its wholesome food.

Links Parade, Carnoustie DD7 7JF. ℂ 01241/853-273. Fax 01241/853-319. www.links-hotel.com. 7 units.
£70–£110 ($105–$165) double. Rates include breakfast. MC, V. Free parking. Off A92, adjoining the golf
course. **Amenities:** Restaurant, bar; tour desk; car-rental desk; laundry/dry cleaning. *In room:* TV, coffeemaker,
hair dryer.

DINING

11 Park Avenue ☞ SCOTTISH   A few steps from High Street, this restaurant is the most prestigious in town. Menu items are made with the freshest
ingredients. Depending on the season, the chef might tempt you with Scottish

mussels in white-wine sauce or lamb filet with fresh basil and tomato-flavored port-wine sauce. For dessert, nothing is better than the caramelized lemon tart or the selection of Scottish cheeses.

11 Park Ave. ℂ 01241/853-336. Reservations recommended. Main courses £11–£16.95 ($16.50-$25.45). AE, DC, MC, V. Apr–Sept Tues–Sat noon–2pm and 7–10pm; Oct–Dec and Feb–Mar Tues–Sat 7–10pm. Closed Jan.

9 Aberdeen ⋆⋆: The Granite City

130 miles (209km) NE of Edinburgh, 67 miles (108km) N of Dundee

Bordered by fine sandy beaches (delightful if you're a polar bear), Scotland's third city, Aberdeen, is often called the "Granite City" because its buildings are constructed largely of pink or gray granite, hewn from the Rubislaw quarries. The harbor is one of the country's largest fishing ports, filled with kipper and deep-sea trawlers, and Aberdeen lies on the banks of the salmon- and trout-filled Don and Dee rivers. Spanning the Don is the **Brig o' Balgownie,** a steep Gothic arch begun in 1285.

Although it hardly compares with Glasgow and Edinburgh, Aberdeen is the center of a vibrant university; it boasts a few marvelous museums and galleries; and it's known for great nightlife and shopping, the best in the northeast. Old Aberdeen is the seat of one of Scotland's major cathedrals, St. Machars. It's also a good base for exploring the greatest castles of Grampian and the towns and villages along the splendid salmon river, Deeside.

ESSENTIALS

GETTING THERE   Aberdeen is served by a number of airlines, including British Airways, British Midland, EasyJet, and KLM. For information, phone the **Aberdeen Airport** (ℂ **01224/722-331**), 7 miles (11km) from the heart of town. Bus service to town costs £1.45 ($2.20) one-way; taxis cost about £10 ($15).

Aberdeen has direct **rail** links to the major cities of Britain. The following prices are for tickets bought on the day of departure, excluding Friday, when prices are higher. Nineteen trains per normal weekday arrive from Edinburgh; a regular one-way ticket costs £19.80 ($29.70). Trip time is about 3½ hours. Some 19 trains per day arrive from Glasgow, costing £28 ($42) one-way or £44.30 ($66.45) round-trip. Some 12 trains per day arrive from London, with a one-way fare of £66.90 ($100.35) and a round-trip fare of only £90.50 ($135.75). SuperSaver fares, available by avoiding travel on Friday and Saturday, make the price difference between one-way and round-trip fares negligible. Another way of saving £10 ($15) on fares is by reserving through the booking agency Apex. For fares in Scotland, call ℂ **0845/755-0033** with at least 48 hours' notice. For fares from London, call ℂ **0845/722-5225** with a minimum of 1 week's notice. For schedules, call ℂ **08457/484-950.**

Several **bus** companies have express routes serving Aberdeen, and many offer special round-trip fares to passengers avoiding travel on Friday or Saturday. Frequent buses arrive from both Glasgow, costing £20 to £24.50 ($30 to $36.75) round-trip, and from Edinburgh, costing £18 to £23 ($27 to $34.50) round-trip. There are also frequent arrivals from Inverness; round-trip fare is £9.50 to £11.20 ($14.25 to $16.80). For bus schedules in Aberdeen, call ℂ **01224/212-266.**

If you're **driving** from the south, go via Edinburgh over the Forth and Tay Road Bridges and take the coastal road. From the north and west, approach the area from the much improved A9, which links Perth, Inverness, and Wick.

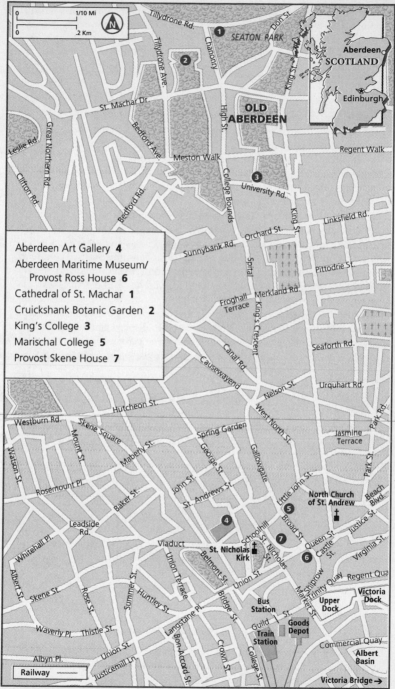

Aberdeen

0   1/10 Mi
0   .2 Km

N

Tillydrone Rd.

SEATON PARK

Don St.

St. Machar Dr.

Tillydrone Ave.

Chanonry

OLD ABERDEEN

High St.

King's Way

St. Nuns

SCOTLAND

Aberdeen

Edinburgh

Regent Walk

Meston Walk

Bedford Ave.

College Bounds

University Rd.

Leslie Rd.

Great Northern Rd.

Clifton Rd.

Bedford Rd.

Linksfield Rd.

Orchard St.

King St.

Sunnybank Rd.

Pittodrie St.

Spital

Merkland Rd.

King's Crescent

Froghall Terrace

Seaforth Rd.

Canal Rd.

Causewayend

Nelson St.

Urquhart Rd.

Park Rd.

Hutcheon St.

West North St.

Jasmine Terrace

Westburn Rd.

Skene Square

Mount St.

Spring Garden

Maberly St.

George St.

Watson St.

Rosemount Pl.

Baker St.

John St.

St. Andrews St.

Little John St.

Gallowgate

North Church of St. Andrew

Beach Blvd.

Leadside Rd.

Whitehall Pl.

Viaduct

St. Nicholas Kirk

Schoolhill

Broad St.

St. Nicholas

Queen St.

Castle St.

Justice St.

Virginia St.

Park St.

Albert St.

Skene St.

Rose St.

Summer St.

Huntley St.

Union Terrace

Belmont St.

Bridge St.

Union St.

Market St.

Shiprow

Trinity Quay

Regent Quay

Upper Dock

Victoria Dock

Waverly Pl.

Thistle St.

Langstane Pl.

Bon-Accord St.

Bus Station

Guild St.

Goods Depot

Albyn Pl.

Justicemill Ln.

Union St.

Crown St.

College St.

Train Station

Commercial Quay

Albert Basin

Railway ———

Victoria Bridge →

Aberdeen Art Gallery **4**

Aberdeen Maritime Museum/
Provost Ross House **6**

Cathedral of St. Machar **1**

Cruickshank Botanic Garden **2**

King's College **3**

Marischal College **5**

Provost Skene House **7**

VISITOR INFORMATION The **Aberdeen Tourist Information Centre** is in St. Nicholas House, Broad Street (© **01224/632-727**). July and August, it's open Monday through Friday from 9am to 7pm, Saturday from 9am to 5pm, and Sunday from 10am to 4pm; April to June and September, hours are Monday through Friday from 9am to 5pm and Saturday from 10am to 2pm; October to March, it's open Monday through Friday from 9am to 5pm and Saturday from 10am to 2pm.

SEEING THE SIGHTS

In old Aberdeen is **Aberdeen University**, a fusion of two colleges. Reached along University Road, **King's College** (© **01224/272-137;** Bus: 6, 20) is Great Britain's oldest school of medicine. The college is known for its chapel (ca. A.D. 1500) with pre-Reformation carved woodwork, the finest of its kind in Scotland; it's open daily from 9am to 4:30pm and charges no admission. On Broad Street is **Marischal College** (© **01224/273-131**), founded in 1593 by Earl Marischal—it's the world's second-biggest granite structure (El Escorial outside Madrid is much larger). While King's College was Catholic, Marischal was Protestant. The main structure is no longer in use, but on site is the free Marischal Museum, with exhibits on the university and the Scottish culture of the northeast; open Monday through Saturday from 10am to 5pm and Sunday from 2 to 5pm. In 1860, the colleges joined together to form the nucleus of the University of Aberdeen.

Also at the University of Aberdeen, the **Cruickshank Botanic Garden,** St. Machar Drive (© **01224/272-704;** Bus: 6, 20), displays alpines, shrubs, and many herbaceous plants, along with rock and water gardens. It's open Monday through Friday from 9am to 5pm; in summer, it's also open Saturday and Sunday from 2 to 5pm. Admission is free.

The **Cathedral of St. Machar,** Chanonry (© **01224/485-988** in the morning, or 01224/317-424 in the afternoon; Bus: 1, 2, 3, 4, 5, 6, 7, or 26), was founded in 1131, but the present structure dates from the 15th century. Its splendid heraldic ceiling contains three rows of shields. Be sure to note the pre-Reformation woodwork and the magnificent modern stained-glass windows by Douglas Strachan. The cathedral is open daily from 9am to 5pm.

Alpine Bikes, 66–70 Holburn St. (© **01224/211-455**), will rent you a bike for £12 ($18) daily or £24 ($36) for weekends, with weekly rates at £60 ($90). It's open Sunday from 11am to 5pm, Monday through Wednesday and Friday and Saturday from 9am to 6pm, and Thursday from 9am to 8pm.

Aberdeen Art Gallery ✿ Built in 1884 in a neoclassical design by A. Marshall MacKenzie, this building houses one of the most important art collections in Great Britain. It contains 18th-century portraits by Raeburn, Hogarth, Ramsay, and Reynolds and acclaimed 20th-century works by Paul Nash, Ben Nicholson, and Francis Bacon. The exhibits also include excellent pieces by Monet, Pissarro, Sisley, and Bonnard as well as a collection of Scottish domestic silver. Special exhibits and events are frequently offered.

Schoolhill. © 01224/523-700. Free admission. Mon–Sat 10am–5pm; Sun 2–5pm. Bus: 20.

Aberdeen Maritime Museum Using a unique collection of ship models, paintings, artifacts, computer interaction, and exhibits, this museum tells the story of the city's long and fascinating relationship with the sea. A major display on the offshore oil industry features a model of the Murchison oil platform. The complex is on four floors, incorporating the 1593 Provost Ross House linked by a modern glass structure to the granite Trinity Church. Windows open onto panoramic views of the harbor.

Shiprow. ℭ 01224/337-700. Free admission. Mon–Sat 10am–5pm; Sun noon–3pm. Bus: 20.

Provost Skene House This attraction is named for a rich merchant who was Lord Provost of Aberdeen from 1676 to 1685. Off Broad Street, it's a museum with period rooms and artifacts of domestic life. Provost Skene's kitchen has been converted into a cafe.

5 Guestrow, off Broad St. ℭ 01224/641-086. Free admission. Mon–Fri 10am–5pm, Sat 10am–4pm, Sun 1–3pm. Bus: 20.

Dunnottar Castle The well-preserved ruins of Dunnottar are on a rocky promontory towering 160 feet (48.5m) above the surging sea, and the best way to get here is by a dramatic 30-minute walk from Stonehaven along the cliffs. The ruins include a great square tower and a chapel built in 1392. William Wallace stormed it in 1297, but failed to take it. In 1991, it was the setting for Zeffirelli's film of *Hamlet*, starring Mel Gibson.

2 miles (3km) south of Stonehaven off A92. ℭ 01569/762-173. Admission £3.50 ($5.25) adults, £2 ($3) seniors and students, £1 ($1.50) children. Easter–Oct Mon–Sat 9am–6pm, Sun 2–5pm; Nov–Easter Mon–Fri 9am–3:30pm. From Aberdeen, you can take Bluebird Northern bus no. 101 to Stonehaven, costing £4.40 ($6.60) round-trip, and then walk for 5 min. Trains run about every half hour from Aberdeen to Stonehaven, costing £4–£5.30 ($6–$7.95) round-trip. The trip takes 30 min.

SHOPPING

Visitors will want to focus on the specialty shops on **Chapel** and **Thistle streets** and the well-known chains on **George** and **Union streets**.

Of interest to collectors, **Colin Wood,** 25 Rose St. (ℭ 01224/643-019), stocks furniture, wall clocks, and grandfather clocks from the 17th to the early 20th centuries. Its specialty, however, is maps from the Elizabethan through the Victorian eras. The shop also sells 17th- to early-20th-century prints of northern Scotland. The eclectic mix of bric-a-brac antiques at **Elizabeth Watts Studio,** 69 Thistle St. (ℭ 01224/647-232), includes glass, brass, antique jewelry, china, silver, and a few small furniture pieces. The shop is best known for its china and glass restoration studio.

You'll find a multitude of gifts at **Nova,** 20 Chapel St. (ℭ 01224/641-270), which stocks china, silver jewelry, rugs, clothing, toys, cards, and gift paper.

To trace your Scottish ancestry, go to the **Aberdeen Family History Shop,** 164 King St. (ℭ 01224/646-323), where membership to the Aberdeen and North East Family History Society costs $12. Once you join, you can go through a vast range of publications kept on hand to help members trace their family histories.

Other interesting shops are **Grandad's Attic,** 12 Marischal St. (ℭ 01224/213-699), selling antiques and collectibles, specializing in Art Deco ceramics and pine furniture; **Just Scottish,** 4 Upperkirkgate (ℭ 01224/621-755), retailers of quality items—all made in Scotland, including ceramics, knitwear, textiles, silver, and jewelry; and **Alex Scott & Co.,** 43 Schoolhill (ℭ 01224/643-924), the town's finest kiltmakers.

HITTING THE LINKS

Aberdeen has a good range of golf courses in and around the city, with several other notable courses within an easy drive. As always, reservations are essential at any course. If the two below don't suit you, ask the tourist office for details on other options.

Among the top courses is **Balgownie, the Royal Aberdeen Golf Club** (℗ **01224/702-221**), created in 1780 in classic links style. Its uneven layout, sea breezes, and grassy sand dunes add to the challenge of this 6,204-yard (5,646m), par-70 course. Greens fees are £60 to £70 ($90 to $105) per round, or £85 ($127.50) per day, but only Monday through Friday.

Seven miles (11km) west of Aberdeen, the par-69 **West Hills Golf Course,** West Hill Heights, West Hill Skene (℗ and fax **01224/740-159**), features 5,921 yards (5,388m) of playing area. Greens fees are £14 ($21) for nonguests and £7 ($10.50) for guests Monday through Friday, or £20 ($30) for nonguests and £10 ($15) for guests Saturday and Sunday.

ACCOMMODATIONS

Because of increasing numbers of tourists and business travelers to the Granite City, Europe's offshore oil capital, hotels are likely to be heavily booked any time of year. If you haven't reserved ahead, stop by the **Aberdeen Tourist Information Centre,** St. Nicholas House on Broad Street (℗ **01224/632-727**), where the staff can usually find just the right lodging for you—whether a family-run B&B, guesthouse, or hotel. A £2.50 ($3.75) service fee is charged.

Rooms are also available at **Ferryhill House** (see "Dining," below).

EXPENSIVE

Caledonian Thistle Hotel 𝒦 The Caledonian Thistle occupies a grand stone-fronted Victorian in the center of Aberdeen. Recent restorations have added a veneer of Georgian gloss to one of the most elegant series of public rooms in town. The tasteful guest rooms are at the top of a 19th-century stairwell, with Corinthian columns and a freestanding atrium. They vary a good deal in size, but all contain double-glazed windows and combination tub/showers.

10–14 Union Terrace (off Union St.), Aberdeen AB10 1WE. ℗ **01224/640-233.** Fax 01224/641-627. www. thistlehotels.com. 77 units. £97–£117 ($145.50–$175.50) double; from £185 ($277.50) suite. Children under 12 stay free in parents' room. AE, DC, MC, V. Free parking. Bus: 16 or 17. **Amenities:** 2 restaurants (see Elrond's Cafe Bar, below), bar; room service; laundry/dry cleaning. In room: TV, coffeemaker, hair dryer.

Hilton Aberdeen Treetop 𝒦 A 10-minute drive west of the center of Aberdeen off A93, this comfortable hotel built in the 1960s and renovated in 1991 offers a sweeping white facade of traditional design. The windows of its contemporary guest rooms look over landscaped grounds; some units have balconies with lake views, half are set aside for nonsmokers, and all have well-maintained bathrooms with combination tub/showers.

161 Springfield Rd., Aberdeen AB15 7AQ. ℗ **01224/313-377.** Fax 01224/312-028. www.hilton.com. 112 units. £90–£135 ($135–$202.50) double; £145–£155 ($217.50–$232.50) suite. AE, DC, MC, V. Free parking. Bus: 11. **Amenities:** Restaurant, bar; room service; babysitting; laundry/dry cleaning. In room: TV, minibar, coffeemaker, hair dryer, iron.

Marcliffe at Pitfodels 𝒦𝒦𝒦 On the city's western edge less than half an hour from the airport, this deluxe three-story manor house was constructed around a courtyard and stands on 6 acres (2.4 hectares) of landscaped grounds. Oriental rugs, stone floors, tartan sofas, and a scattering of antiques set the tone in the public rooms. The spacious guest rooms are furnished with Chippendale and reproduction pieces, plus a host of extras like fresh milk in the minibar. Each tiled bathroom comes with a combination tub/shower.

At breakfast, you can sample Aberdeen *rowies*, a local specialty that's like a flattened croissant. The conservatory restaurant offers regional dishes, while the Invery Room is favored by businesspeople entertaining out-of-town guests. In the library lounge, you can choose from more than 130 scotches, 500 wines, and 70 cognacs.

N. Deeside Rd., Aberdeen AB1 9YA. © 01224/861-000. Fax 01224/868-860. www.marcliffe.com. 42 units. £165–£185 ($247.50–$277.50) double. AE, DC, MC, V. Free parking. Drive about a mile (1.6km) off A90 at the Aberdeen ring road, A93. **Amenities:** 2 restaurants, bar; room service; laundry/dry cleaning. *In room:* TV, minibar, coffeemaker, hair dryer, iron.

Simpsons ℛ   This popular hotel, which opened in 1998, is comprised of two traditional granite town houses. Rooms are decorated with furniture from Spain and painted in rich, bold colors that create a Mediterranean ambience. Bathrooms come with combination tub/showers. The bar offers a range of moderately priced Scottish and international dishes, including fresh crab ravioli and saddle of lamb Wellington.

59 Queens Rd., Aberdeen AB15 4YP. © 01224/327-777. Fax 01224/327-700. www.simpsonshotel.co.uk. 37 units. Sun–Thurs £120–£135 ($180–$202.50) double; Fri–Sat £80–£90 ($120–$135) double. Rates include breakfast. AE, MC, V. Follow signs for A96 North and turn right at Queens Rd. roundabout. **Amenities:** Restaurant, bar; spa; sauna; room service; babysitting; laundry/dry cleaning. *In room:* A/C, TV, minibar, coffeemaker, hair dryer, iron.

MODERATE

Craiglynn Hotel   This hotel was created from a granite-block Victorian built in 1901 as a home for a successful fish merchant. The high-ceilinged bedrooms are monochromatic, with traditional furniture and small bathrooms with combination tub/showers. If advance notice is given, a moderately priced dinner can be prepared, featuring dishes like fricasee of lamb and a house version of sticky toffee pudding with Drambuie-flavored ice cream. No smoking is permitted.

36 Fonthill Rd., Aberdeen AB11 6UJ. © 01224/584-050. Fax 01224/212-225. www.craiglynn.co.uk. 9 units, 7 with private bathroom. £60–£78 ($90–$117) double with bathroom. Rates include breakfast. AE, MC, V. Bus: 17. *In room:* TV.

Jays Guest House (Value   This is one of the nicest guesthouses in Aberdeen, located near the university and the Offshore Survival Centre. Everything runs smoothly, and the newly renovated guest rooms are bright and airy, each with combination tub/shower.

422 King St., Aberdeen AB24 3BR. © and fax 01224/638-295. www.jaysguesthouse.co.uk. 10 units. £56–£80 ($84–$120) double. Rates include Scottish breakfast. MC, V. Free parking. Bus: 1, 2, 3, 4, or 7. *In room:* TV, coffeemaker, no phone.

Mannofield Hotel   Built of silver granite around 1880, this hotel is a Victorian fantasy of step gables, turrets, spires, bay windows, and a sweeping mahogany-and-teakwood staircase. Owners Bruce and Dorothy Cryle offer a warm Scottish welcome. The guest rooms, refurbished in 1998 with paisley curtains and quilts, are equipped with well-maintained, shower-only bathrooms.

447 Great Western Rd., Aberdeen AB10 6NL. © 01224/315-888. Fax 01224/208-971. www.tartan-collection.co.uk. 9 units. £69 ($103.50) double; £79 ($118.50) family room. Rates include Scottish breakfast. AE, DC, MC, V. Free parking. Bus: 18, 24. **Amenities:** Restaurant, lounge; room service; babysitting; laundry/dry cleaning. *In room:* TV, coffeemaker, hair dryer.

CASTLE & COUNTRY-HOUSE LIVING NEARBY

Ardoe House Hotel ℛ (Finds   This turreted baronial 1878 house sits in the midst of lush gardens and manicured grounds, offering panoramic views of the River Dee. Though it's close to Aberdeen, it's a world apart. Its old-fashioned interior, with wood paneling, carved fireplaces, and stained-glass windows, reflects the best in traditional Victorian style. The mansion was recently expanded, but even so, each room is individually decorated and well appointed with many extras, including immaculate bathrooms with combination tub/showers. In the formal dining room, you can order a blend of traditional and modern Scottish cuisine, using fresh local ingredients that are prepared with French flair.

S. Deeside Rd. (3 miles/5km south of Aberdeen on B9077), Blairs, Aberdeen AB12 5YP. ℂ 01224/867-355. Fax 01224/861-283. www.olstravel.com/hotel/ardoe. 114 units. £104–£150 ($156–$225) double. MC, V. **Amenities:** Restaurant, bar; pool; health club; beauty spa; steam room; sauna; room service; laundry/dry cleaning. *In room:* TV, dataport, coffeemaker, hair dryer, iron.

Kildrummy Castle Hotel ☆☆   This 19th-century gray-stone mansion, on acres of landscaped gardens, overlooks the ruined castle of Kildrummy. Its guest rooms vary in size; most come with combination tub/shower. The public rooms have oak-paneled walls and ceilings, mullioned windows, and window seats. The drawing room and bar opens onto a flagstone terrace. Traditional Scottish food, including Cullen skink (smoked haddock soup) and filet of sole stuffed with smoked Scottish salmon, is served in the dining room.

Kildrummy by Alford AB33 8RA. ℂ 019755/71288. Fax 019755/71345. www.kildrummycastlehotel.co.uk. 16 units. £145–£170 ($217.50–$255) double. Rates include Scottish breakfast. AE, MC, V. Closed Jan. From Aberdeen, take A944 and follow signs to Alford; then take A97, following signs to Kildrummy. **Amenities:** Restaurant, bar; room service; babysitting; laundry service. *In room:* TV, coffeemaker, hair dryer.

Pittodrie House Hotel ☆☆   Dating from 1490, the castle here was burned down and then rebuilt in 1675 as a family home—and that in turn became a country-house hotel when Royal Deeside became prominent through Queen Victoria's adoption of Balmoral as her holiday retreat. The guest rooms are divided between those in the old house (with good views and antique furniture) and the smaller rooms in the recent extension (decorated in keeping with the style of the house but with less atmosphere). Most of the bathrooms have combination tub/showers. The public rooms boast antiques, oil paintings, and open fires. The elegant restaurant serves venison, grouse, partridge, pheasant, and fresh fish.

Chapel of Garioch, Pitcaple AB5 5HS. ℂ 01467/681-444. Fax 01467/681-648. www.macdonaldhotels.co.uk. 27 units. £140 ($210) double. Rates include Scottish breakfast. AE, DC, MC, V. From Aberdeen, take A96, following signs to Inverness; remain on A96, bypassing Inverurie, then follow signs to Chapel of Garioch. **Amenities:** Restaurant, bar; room service; laundry service. *In room:* TV, coffeemaker, hair dryer.

Thainstone House Hotel & Country Club ☆☆☆   One of northeast Scotland's most elegant country hotels, set on 40 acres (16.2 hectares), the four-star Thainstone House is a Palladian-style mansion whose adornments give it the air of a country club. It can serve as both a retreat and a center for exploring this historic part of Scotland, including the Malt Whisky Trail. Guests enter the mansion, which was designed by Archibald Simpson (the famed architect of many of Aberdeen's public buildings), through a grand portal up an elegant stairway. The high ceilings, columns, neoclassical plaster reliefs, and cornices evoke Simpson's trip to Italy. A new section of the house skillfully blends the old with the new. The elegantly furnished guest rooms vary in size; each contains both tub and shower. The chef turns out a Continental and Scottish menu with a light, inventive touch.

Inverurie AB51 5NT. ℂ 01467/621-643. Fax 01467/625-084. www.macdonaldhotels.co.uk. 48 units. £84–£112 ($126–$168) double; £180 ($270) suite. Rates include Scottish breakfast. AE, DC, MC, V. From Aberdeen, take A96, following signs to Inverness; just before Inverurie, turn left and follow signs to the hotel. **Amenities:** Restaurant, bar; pool; gym; Jacuzzi; steam room; room service; babysitting; laundry service. *In room:* TV, coffeemaker, hair dryer.

DINING

Elrond's Cafe Bar INTERNATIONAL   White marble floors, a long oak-capped bar, candlelight, and a garden-inspired decor create the ambience here. No one will mind if you show up for just a drink, a pot of tea, a midday salad or snack, or a full-blown feast. Specialties are burgers, steaks, pastas, fresh fish, chicken Kiev, and vegetarian dishes. This isn't the world's greatest food, but it's popular nevertheless.

In the Caledonian Thistle Hotel, 10–14 Union Terrace. ✆ 01224/640-233. Main courses £5.95–£12.50 ($8.95–$18.75); pot of tea with pastry £2 ($3). AE, DC, MC, V. Mon–Sat 10am–midnight; Sun 10am–11pm. Bus: 16 or 17.

Ferryhill House INTERNATIONAL   In its own park and garden on the city's southern outskirts, Ferryhill House was built 250 years ago by the region's most successful brick maker and quarry master. It has Georgian detailing, but recent refurbishment has removed many of the original panels. There's a fireplace for chilly afternoons and a beer garden for midsummer. The restaurant boasts one of the region's largest collections of single-malt whiskies—more than 140 brands. Food items include steak or vegetable tempura, chicken fajita, fried haddock filet, pastas, and chili.

Ferryhill House also rents nine standard guest rooms, each with TV, phone, and hair dryer. Doubles, including breakfast, are £79 ($118.50) Sunday through Thursday, £50 ($75) Friday and Saturday.

Bon Accord St., Aberdeen AB11 6UA. ✆. 01224/590-867. Fax 01224/586-947. Reservations recommended Sat–Sun. Main courses £6–£12 ($9–$18). AE, DC, MC, V. Free parking. Bus: 16.

Howies Restaurant ✦ SCOTTISH/INTERNATIONAL   This is the latest—and even better—reincarnation of the locally famous Gerard's, which stood here for many years. Modern Scottish cookery with international influences is presented exceedingly well. The medallions of Aberdeen Angus filet are always reliable, as are the fresh fish and chicken dishes, each prepared with a certain flair. The bar stocks a wide range of single malts and ports in addition to some wines unavailable elsewhere in the region.

50 Chapel St. ✆ 01224/639-500. Reservations recommended. Fixed-price lunch £5.50–£9.50 ($8.25–$14.25); fixed-price dinner £11–£17 ($16.50–$25.50). AE, DC, MC, V. Daily noon–2:30pm and 6–10:30pm.

Martha's Vineyard Bistro/The Courtyard Restaurant SCOTTISH/ CONTINENTAL   One of the most appealing restaurant complexes in Aberdeen occupies two floors of what was built around 1900 as an extension of the local hospital. Today, a robust and rustic-looking bistro (Martha's Vineyard) is on the street level, with a more formal restaurant (The Courtyard) upstairs. The bistro menu ranges from smoked salmon and asparagus salad to gigot of lamb with a compote of leeks in mustard sauce. Upstairs, you'll find dishes like local brie wrapped in smoked salmon or rosemary-flavored loin of Highland venison with wild mushrooms.

Alford Lane. ✆ 01224/213-795. Reservations recommended in the Courtyard, not necessary in Martha's Vineyard. Main courses £6–£10 ($9–$15) in bistro; £10–£16 ($15–$24) in restaurant. AE, DC, MC, V. Mon–Sat noon–2:15pm; Tues–Sat 6:30–9:45pm. Bus: 1, 2, 3, or 4.

Silver Darling ✦✦ FRENCH/SEAFOOD   Silver Darling (a local nickname for herring) is a definite asset to the dining scene in Aberdeen. Occupying a former Customs House at the mouth of the harbor, it spins a culinary fantasy around the freshest catch of the day. You might begin with a savory fish soup, almost Mediterranean in flavor, then go on to one of the barbecued fish dishes.

Pocra Quay, Footdee. ℂ **01224/576-229.** Reservations recommended. Main courses £13.90–£22 ($20.85–$33); 2-course fixed-price lunch £19.90 ($29.85); 3-course fixed-price lunch £24 ($36). AE, DC, MC, V. Mon–Fri noon–2pm and 7–9:30pm; Sat 7–9:30pm. Closed Dec 23–Jan 8. Bus: 14 or 15.

ABERDEEN AFTER DARK

Tickets to events at most venues are available by calling the **Aberdeen Box Office** (ℂ **01224/641-122**), open Monday through Saturday from 9am to 6:30pm.

THE PERFORMING ARTS The **Aberdeen Arts Centre,** King Street (ℂ **01224/635-208**), has a 350-seat theater that hosts everything from poetry readings to plays and concerts. Ticket prices and performance times vary; call for information. Also on the premises is a 60-seat video projection theater that screens world cinema offerings. A large gallery holds month-long exhibitions of visual art in many different media. A cafe/bar, offering light meals and drinks, is open during performance times.

Near Tarves, about 20 miles (32km) from Aberdeen, is **Haddo House** (ℂ **01651/851-440**), which hosts operas, ballets, and plays from Easter to October. An early-20th-century hall built of pitch pine, Haddo House is based on the Canadian town halls that Lord Aberdeen saw in his travels abroad. Follow B9005, 18 miles (29km) north to Tarves, then follow the National Trust and Haddo House signs 2 miles (3km) east. Ticket prices range from £6.50 to £13 ($9.75–$19.50). Admittance to the house is £5.50 ($8.25) for adults and £4.40 ($6.60) for seniors and children. The house is open daily from 1:30 to 5pm, the shop from 11am to 6pm, and the gardens from 9:30am to 4pm. A stylish cafe offers light meals, tea, and other beverages from Easter to October, daily from 11am to 6pm.

The 19th-century **Music Hall,** Union Street (ℂ **01224/641-122**), is an ornately gilded 1,282-seat theater that stages concerts by the Scottish National Orchestra, the Scottish Chamber Orchestra, visiting international orchestras, and pop bands. Tickets average £7.50 to £9.50 ($11.25 to $14.25). The **Aberdeen International Youth Festival** is held here in August and features youth orchestras, choirs, and dance and theater ensembles. Tickets range from £1.50 to £20 ($2.25 to $30). Contact the Music Hall or the Aberdeen Box Office for more information.

The only theater in the world built entirely of granite, the 1,445-seat **His Majesty's Theatre** (1906), Rosemount Viaduct (ℂ **01224/641-122**), stages operas, dance performances, dramas, classical concerts, musicals, and comedy shows year-round. Tickets range from £7 to £20 ($10.50 to $30).

The **Lemon Tree,** 5 W. North St. (ℂ **01224/642-230**), is a mixed venue. Its 150-seat theater stages dance recitals, theatrical productions, and stand-up comedy, with tickets generally between £4 and £15 ($6 and $22.50). Downstairs, the 500-seat cafe/theater hosts folk, rock, blues, jazz, and comedy acts.

DANCE CLUBS **DeNiro's,** 120 Union St. (ℂ **01224/640-641**), has dancing to house music on Friday and Saturday nights. The cover is £7 ($10.50), but may vary depending on the guest DJ.

The **Pelican,** in the Hotel Metro, 17 Market St. (ℂ **01224/583-275**), offers dancing Thursday through Saturday nights. The cover is £3 to £6 ($4.50 to $9). There's a live band every second Thursday.

Scotland's Castle Trail

Scotland's Castle Trail—taking visitors to fairy tale castles, imposing stately homes, magnificent ruins, and splendid gardens open to the public—has now been launched. The only signposted route of its kind in Scotland, it guides motorists around rural Aberdeenshire. The accompanying leaflet highlights 11 of the finest properties, from the ruins of the 13th-century Kildrummy Castle and the elegant five-towered Fyvie Castle to two grand examples of the work of the 18th-century architect William Adam—Duff House and Haddo House.

The leaflet also has details of other places that can be visited, including Balmoral Castle, a royal home since Queen Victoria's day; and Pitmedden Garden, where the centerpiece Great Garden was laid out in 1675. The leaflet, *Scotland's Castle Trail,* is available at local tourist offices or by calling ℂ **01224/632-727.** Information can also be found on the Aberdeen and Grampian Tourist Board Web site (**www.agtb.org**).

The ever-popular **Ministry,** 16 Dee St. (ℂ **01224/211-661**), is a sophisticated club with different theme nights. On Friday, guest DJs from England and America take over the sound system. Cover ranges from £2 to £12 ($3 to $18).

A PUB   The **Prince of Wales,** 7 St. Nicholas Lane (ℂ **01224/640-597**), in the heart of the shopping district, is the best place in the old city center to get a pint. Furnished with pews in screened booths, it boasts Aberdeen's longest bar counter. At lunch, it's bustling with regulars who devour chicken in cider sauce or Guinness pie.

SIDE TRIPS FROM ABERDEEN: ARCHEOLINK & CASTLE COUNTRY

Aberdeen is the center of "castle country"—40 inhabited castles lie within a 40-mile (64.5km) radius. We've described the best of them below, along with Archeolink, which explores the area's cultural changes over the centuries.

Archeolink ⓡ   Although there are more than 4,000 prehistoric sites around Aberdeenshire, this museum offers the most historically accurate, most imaginative, and most ecologically sensitive interpretation. Opened in 1997, it occupies 40 acres (16.2 hectares) whose centerpiece, Berryhill, contains a ruined Iron Age fortress. Lavish landscaping encourages visits by both able-bodied hill climbers and—thanks to a series of ramps—visitors with wheelchairs.

The museum is a celebration of the epic cultural changes that have swept over northeastern Scotland through the previous 70 centuries. The centerpiece is a massive turf-covered concrete dome resembling a small hill. Your tour begins with a 20-minute film showing views of the surrounding landscapes and the equivalent landscapes 7,000 years ago. Dioramas provide insight into the region's stone circles and dolmens, and there are gruesome re-creations of Iron Age battles and hunting scenes. Especially intriguing is a gallery devoted to myths and legends. One section of the site, Archeoquest, provides computer-generated personalized details on other prehistoric sites in Aberdeenshire, with directions and access information printed on takeaway maps.

Oyne, near Insch. ℂ **01464/851-500.** Admission £4 ($6) adults, £3.40 ($5.10) seniors and children 5–16, £12 ($18) per family. Apr–Oct daily 11am–5pm. From Aberdeen, drive 23 miles (37km) northwest along A96, following the signs to Inverness. Turn north onto B9002, going another 1½ miles (2.5km), following the signs.

Castle Fraser ⚑ One of the most impressive of the fortresslike castles of Mar, Castle Fraser stands on 25 acres (10.1 hectares) of parkland. The sixth laird, Michael Fraser, began the structure in 1575, and his son finished it in 1636. Visitors can see the spectacular Great Hall and wander around the grounds, which include·an 18th-century walled garden.

Sauchen, Inverurie. ℂ 01330/833-463. Admission £5 ($7.50) adults, £3.50 ($5.25) seniors, £1.30 ($1.95) children, free for children under 5. Easter weekend and Oct Sat–Sun 2–4:45pm; May–June daily 1:30–5pm; July–Aug daily 11am–4:45pm; Sept daily 1:30–5:30pm. Closed Nov–Apr. Head 3 miles (5km) south of Kemnay, 16 miles (26km) west of Aberdeen, off A944.

Fyvie Castle ⚑ The National Trust for Scotland opened this castle to the public in 1986. The oldest part, dating from the 13th century, has been called the grandest existing example of Scottish baronial architecture. There are five towers, named after the families who lived here over 5 centuries. Fyvie, which means "deer hill" in Gaelic, was built in a royal hunting forest. The interior, created by the first Lord Leith of Fyvie, reflects the opulence of the Edwardian era. His collections contain arms and armor, 16th-century tapestries, and important artworks by Raeburn, Gainsborough, and Romney.

Turriff, on the Aberdeen–Banff rd. ℂ 01651/891266. Admission £4.40 ($6.60) adults, £2.90 ($4.35) seniors and children. Apr–June and Sept daily 1:30–4:45pm; July–Aug daily 11am–4:45pm; Oct Sat–Sun 1:30–4:45pm. Closed Nov–Mar. Take A947 for 23 miles (37km) northwest of Aberdeen.

Kildrummy Castle ⚑ Once the ancient seat of the earls of Mar, this is the most extensive example of a 13th-century castle in Scotland. You can still see the four round towers, the hall, and the chapel from the original structure. The great gatehouse and other remains date from the 16th century.

Hwy. A97, Kildrummy. ℂ. 019755/71331. Admission £2 ($3) adults, £1.50 ($2.25) seniors, 75p ($1.10) children. Easter–Sept daily 9:30am–6:30pm; Oct–Nov daily 9:30am–4pm. Closed Dec–Easter. Take A97 for 35 miles (56km) west of Aberdeen; it's signposted off A97, 10 miles (16km) west of Alford.

10 Banchory: Gateway to Crathes & Craigievar Castles

118 miles (190km) NE of Edinburgh, 17 miles (27km) W of Aberdeen, 55 miles (88.5km) NE of Dundee

In lower Deeside, the pleasant resort of Banchory is rich in woodland and river scenery. Most visitors come to see two of the most popular castles in the Grampian region: Crathes and Craigievar. Once here, they often find themselves enjoying the riverside town itself, the largest community along Deeside.

If you have the time, take the South Deeside Road branching to the left and following the signs to Cairn o' Mount along B974. This leads to the village of Fettercairn. Nearby is the **Bridge of Feugh** (known as Brig o' Feuch), the local beauty spot spanning the water of Feugh. It makes a great walk, especially in the fall, when you can marvel at the brilliant colors of the trees. A narrow gorge opens onto panoramic views of waterfalls.

ESSENTIALS

GETTING THERE The nearest **rail** service goes to Aberdeen (ℂ 08457/ 484-950 for schedules). From there, a Bluebird **bus** runs between the bus station on Guild Street in Aberdeen and Braemar, going via Banchory. For information, call ℂ 01224/212-266 in Aberdeen. If you're **driving** from Aberdeen, head west along A93; or from Braemar, head east along A93.

VISITOR INFORMATION The **tourist office** is on Bridge Street (ℂ 01330/ 822-000). It's open April through October, daily during peak months.

SEEING THE SIGHTS

Craigievar Castle ⭐ Structurally unchanged since its completion in 1626, Craigievar Castle is an exceptional tower house where Scottish baronial architecture reached its pinnacle of achievement. The descendants of the castle builder, William Forbes, had continuously lived there until it came under the care of the National Trust for Scotland in 1963. The family collection of furnishings is complete.

Some 4 miles (6.4km) south of the castle, on a small road leading off A980, near Lumphanan, is **Macbeth's Cairn,** where the historical Macbeth is supposed to have fought his last battle. Built of timber in a rounded format known by historians as "motte and bailey," it's now nothing more than a steep-sided rounded hillock marked with a sign and a flag.

Hwy. A980, 6 miles (10km) south of Alford. ⓒ **013398/83635.** Admission £6 ($9) adults, £4 ($6) seniors and children. Castle May–Sept daily 1:30–4:45pm. Grounds year-round daily 9:30am–sunset. Head west on A96 to Alford, then south on A980.

Crathes Castle and Gardens ⭐⭐ This castle, 2 miles (3km) east of Banchory, has royal historical associations from 1323, when the lands of Leys were granted to the Burnett family by King Robert the Bruce. The castle's features include remarkable late-16th-century painted ceilings and a garden that's a composite of eight separate gardens, giving a display all year. The great yew hedges date from 1702. The grounds are ideal for nature study, and there are five trails, including a long-distance layout with ranger service. The complex includes a licensed restaurant, a visitor center, a souvenir shop, a plant sales area, a wayfaring course, and picnic areas.

Banchory. ⓒ **01330/844-525.** Admission £7 ($10.50) adults, £5 ($7.50) children and seniors, £19 ($28.50) per family. Grounds, adventure area, and park daily 9:30am–sunset; visitor center, shop, and restaurant Good Friday–Oct daily 10:30am–5:30pm; castle Good Friday–Oct daily 11am–4:45pm. From Banchory, take A93, following the signs to Aberdeen.

ACCOMMODATIONS

Banchory Lodge ⭐ On the banks of the Dee, where the Dee joins the Water of the Feugh, is this 18th-century country house with much Georgian charm. Some of the guest rooms overlook the river; others are in a deluxe annex added in 1994. They range in size from adequate to quite small. All come with tidy bathrooms, most with combination tub/shower. In the dining room, the furnishings and decor are in period style, and specialties include fresh Dee salmon and Aberdeen Angus roast beef. You can fish from the lawn or in one of the hotel's boats by arrangement.

Dee St., Banchory AB31 5HS. ⓒ **01330/822-625.** Fax 01330/825-019. www.banchorylodge.co.uk. 22 units. £130–£150 ($195–$225) double. Rates include half-board. AE, DC, MC, V. **Amenities:** Restaurant, bar, 2 lounges; bike rental; room service; laundry service. *In room:* TV, coffeemaker, hair dryer.

The Burnett Arms Despite frequent renovations, this place still feels like a mid-19th-century coaching inn, with its white-painted facade and black trim. Most of the guest rooms have high ceilings and more space than you'd expect. The best and most dramatic is the Bridal Suite, which is technically not a suite but a large room with a sprawling half-tester bed. All units contain small, shower-only bathrooms. Affordable lunches and dinners are available in the busy bar; high tea is also popular here.

25 High St., Banchory AB31 5TD. ⓒ **01330/824-944.** Fax 01330/825-553. www.burnettarms.co.uk. 16 units. £78 ($117) double. AE, DC, MC, V. **Amenities:** Restaurant, 2 bars; room service. *In room:* TV, dataport, coffeemaker, hair dryer.

Raemoir House Raemoir House stands on 3,500 acres (1,417.5 hectares) of grounds and offers both shooting and fishing. The old-fashioned hotel has a ballroom, fine tapestries, and log fires burning in the colder months. The guest rooms are handsomely decorated; some superior units have paneled walls hung with tapestries. The bathrooms are interesting—some contain old-world Edwardian tubs and others state-of-the-art spa baths. What's so lovely about Scotland is its curious mix: in this case, an 18th-century manor house with its own helipad. The adjoining 16th-century Ha House was once used by Mary Queen of Scots. Fixed-price lunches and dinners are served in an attractive Georgian dining room (see "Dining," below).

Hwy. A980, Banchory AB31 4ED. ① **01330/824-884.** Fax 01330/822-171. www.raemoir.com. 24 units. £80–£90 ($120–$135) double; from £125 ($187.50) suite. Rates include Scottish breakfast. AE, DC, MC, V. Free parking. Turn off A93 at the eastern end of Banchory onto A980 (Raemoir Rd.); the hotel entrance is at the junction 2 miles (3km) down the road. **Amenities:** Restaurant, bar; room service; babysitting; dry cleaning. *In room:* TV, coffeemaker, hair dryer.

Tor-Na-Coille *Finds* Tor-Na-Coille is an 1873 country-house hotel—really a Victorian ivy-clad mansion—standing on 8 acres (3.2 hectares) of wooded grounds. The public rooms are suitably comfortable, and the whisky always tastes good in the modern bar. If you're on your way to see Balmoral or to attend the Highland Gathering at Braemar, you can relax here and enjoy the gracious hospitality. The hotel is interesting architecturally, and the room assigned to you may have a lot of character. Most of the bathrooms have combination tub/showers. Light lunches in the bar may include smoked venison sausage blended with rum and red wine. Dinner is rather expensive, and is accompanied by a pianist on the weekends.

Inchmarlo Rd., Banchory AB31 4AB. ① **01330/822-242.** Fax 01330/824-012. 23 units. £110 ($165) double. Rates include Scottish breakfast. Children under 12 stay free in parents' room. AE, MC, V. Closed Dec 25–27. Free parking. **Amenities:** Restaurant, bar; croquet; 2 squash courts; concierge; room service; babysitting; laundry service. *In room:* TV, coffeemaker, hair dryer.

DINING

Milton Restaurant SCOTTISH/INTERNATIONAL This restaurant is in a complex of galleries and gift shops occupying converted farm buildings east of Banchory in the village of Crathes. Inside, in an artfully rustic setting that includes lots of exposed stone, elaborate iron railings, and potted plants, you'll find a cozy, hip, and friendly environment, where the kitchen is right on top of the latest culinary trends in Glasgow and London. Creative compilations of the mostly Scottish ingredients include fried calamari with sun-dried tomatoes and olive butter; your choice of either a bagel or a bun with rib-eye steak and Stilton cheese; and an excellent version of Thai-style chicken with Asian greens.

North Deeside Rd., Crathes. ① **01330/844-566.** Reservations recommended. Main courses £13–£15 ($19.50–$22.50) lunch; £5–£12 ($7.50–$18) dinner. MC, V. Tues–Sat 10am–10pm, Sun 10:30am–9pm. From Banchory, drive 2 miles (3km) east, following the signs to Aberdeen and Crathes.

Raemoir House Restaurant MODERN SCOTTISH On a visit to Scotland, you need to have at least one meal in a Scottish baronial setting. At this previously recommended hotel, you can dine in a Georgian room with views of the garden and distant hills. The ingredients are always first rate and the preparation imaginative. For a "taste of Scotland," opt for the roast saddle of venison with quail mousseline. Lighter and less elaborate dishes are also available.

In the Raemoir House Hotel, Hwy. A980. ① **01330/824-884.** Reservations recommended. Fixed-price 2-course dinner £24 ($36); 3-course dinner £29.50 ($44.25). AE, MC, V. Daily noon–2pm and 7–9pm.

11 Ballater & Balmoral Castle ⟨★

111 miles (179km) N of Edinburgh, 41 miles (66km) W of Aberdeen, 67 miles (108km) NE of Perth, 70 miles (113km) SE of Inverness

On the Dee River, with the Grampian Mountains in the background, Ballater is a resort center, but most visitors come here with only one goal in mind—to walk the grounds of Balmoral Castle, the far northern home of the Windsors. The town still centers on its Station Square, where the royal family used to be photographed as they arrived to spend holidays. (The railway is now closed.) From Ballater, you can drive west to view the scenery of Glen Muick and Lochnagar, where you'll see herds of deer. Incidentally, the drive between Ballater and Braemar (see "Braemar," below) is very scenic.

ESSENTIALS

GETTING THERE   The nearest **rail** service gets you to Aberdeen (℡ 08457/ 484-950 for schedules). From there, regular **buses** run daily from Aberdeen west to Ballater (a 1¾-hour trip). The bus station in Aberdeen is on Guild Street (℡ 01224/212-266), beside the train station. From Braemar, bus no. 201 runs to Ballater, a 30-minute trip. The one-way fare is £3 ($4.50). If you're **driving** from Aberdeen, head west along A93. From Braemar, go east along A93.

VISITOR INFORMATION   The **tourist office** is at Station Square (℡ 01339/ 755-306). Hours are July and August, daily from 10am to 1pm and 2pm to 6pm; and September, October, May, and June, Monday through Saturday from 10am to 1pm and 2 to 5pm and Sunday from 1 to 5pm. Closed November through April.

SEEING THE SIGHTS

Countrywear, 15 and 35 Bridge St. (℡ 01339/755-453), offers country clothing, guns, fishing tackle, and other outdoor-related items. At no. 35, a range of women's clothing, including handknits, woolens, and tartans, is sold. **Goodbrand Knitwear,** 1 Braemar Rd. (℡ 01339/755-947), sells Scottish machine-made knitwear, with a few hand-knit pieces thrown in. Clothing for children, men, and women is available in Shetland wool, lamb's wool, and cashmere.

McEwan Gallery, on A939, 1 mile (1.6km) west of Ballater (℡ 01339/ 755-429), has been selling Scottish paintings, from 17th-century works to contemporary pieces, for a quarter of a century. It also has a large selection of antiquarian books.

Dee Valley Confectioners, Station Square (℡ 01339/755-499), manufactures all its own sweets. Among the delectables are hard boilings (hard sugar candies), macaroon bars, toffee, and shortbread.

Balmoral Castle ⟨★   "This dear paradise" is how Queen Victoria described Balmoral Castle, rebuilt in the Scottish baronial style by her beloved Albert. And Balmoral was the setting for the story of Victoria and her faithful servant, John Brown, as shown in the film *Mrs. Brown.* Today, Balmoral is still a private residence of the British sovereign. Albert, Victoria's prince consort, leased the property in 1848 and bought it in 1852. As the original castle of the Farquharsons proved too small, the present edifice was built, completed in 1855. Its principal feature is a 100-foot (30m) tower. Of the actual castle, only the ballroom is open to the public; it houses an exhibit of pictures, porcelain, and works of art. On the grounds are many memorials to the royal family, along with gardens, country walks, souvenir shops, a refreshment room, and pony trekking for £20 ($30) for a 2-hour ride (available to adults and children over 12 from 10am to noon or 2 to 4pm).

7 miles (11km) west off A93, Balmoral, Ballater. ① 01339/742-334. Admission £4.50 ($6.75) adults, £3.50 ($5.25) seniors, £1 ($1.50) children 5–16. Mid-Apr to July daily 10am–5pm. Braemar bus from Aberdeen to Crathie bus station; Balmoral Castle is signposted from there (¼-mile/0.5km walk).

ACCOMMODATIONS

You can also stay at the **Green Inn** (see "Dining," below).

Balgonie Country House 𝒦 *Finds*   In the heart of Royal Deeside, to the west of town, this Edwardian country house is set amid 4 acres (1.6 hectares) of gardens, overlooking the Ballater Golf Course and providing panoramic views of Glen Muick. It offers a peaceful haven of beautifully furnished rooms (some with shower only) and fine Scottish food (see "Dining," below). The owners can advise on golfing, salmon fishing, and hiking in the area.

Braemar Place, Ballater AB35 5NQ. ① 01339/755-482. www.royaldeesidehotels.com. 9 units. £120 ($180) double. Rates include breakfast. AE, MC, V. Closed Jan. Free parking. Signposted off A93, Ballater-Perth, on the western outskirts. **Amenities:** Restaurant, bar; nearby golf. *In room:* TV, hair dryer.

Darroch Learg Hotel 𝒦   Built in 1888 as an elegant country home, this pink-granite hotel stands in 5 acres (2 hectares) of lush woodlands opening onto views of the Dee Valley toward the Grampian Mountains. Constructed at the peak of the golden age of Victorian Royal Deeside, the hotel is imbued with a relaxing charm. The individually decorated bedrooms are divided between the main house and Oakhall, a baronial mansion on the same grounds. Some units have four-poster beds and private terraces; some are equipped for guests with disabilities; and all have well-maintained bathrooms with showers. The hotel's main attraction is its Conservatory Restaurant, which is open to nonguests (see "Dining" below). The chef will accommodate special diets by arrangement.

Darroch Learg, Braemar Rd. (on A93 at the west end of Ballater), Ballater AB35 5UX. ① 01339/755-443. Fax 01339/755-252. www.scotlandsheritagehotels.co.uk. 18 units. £126–£156 ($189–$234) double in main house; £80 ($120) double in Oakhall. Rates include breakfast. AE, DC, MC, V. Closed Christmas and last 3 weeks in Jan. Free parking. **Amenities:** Restaurant, bar; room service; laundry service. *In room:* TV, coffeemaker, hair dryer.

Deeside Hotel   This well-managed guesthouse occupies an 1890 pink-granite house surrounded by an acre (0.41 hectare) of late-Victorian garden, a 3-minute walk west of the town center. The small guest rooms are simple, with white walls, wood furniture, and shower-only bathrooms. Upscale dinners are prepared nightly. Recent offerings included grilled oatmeal-dredged herring with Dijon mustard sauce and venison filet with hawthorn jelly.

45 Braemar Rd., Ballater AB35 5RQ. ① 01339/755-420. Fax 01339/755-357. www.deesidehotel.co.uk. 9 units. £46–£53 ($69–$79.50) double. Rates include breakfast. MC, V. Closed Jan. **Amenities:** Restaurant, bar. *In room:* TV, coffeemaker, no phone.

Hilton Craigendarroch Hotel 𝒦   This hotel, built in the Scottish baronial style, is set amid old trees on a 28-acre (11.3-hectare) estate. Modern comforts have been added, but a 19th-century aura remains. The luxurious public areas include a study with oak paneling, a log fire, and book-lined shelves. The fair-size guest rooms, opening onto views of Ballater and the River Dee, are furnished uniquely (with shower-only bathrooms).

Braemar Rd., Ballater AB35 5XA. ① 01339/755-858. Fax 01339/755-447. www.hilton.com. 45 units. £169 ($253.50) double; £244 ($366) suite. Rates include Scottish breakfast. Half-board £15 ($22.50) extra per person. AE, DC, MC, V. **Amenities:** 2 restaurants (see the Oaks Restaurant, below); bar; tennis courts; salon; 24-hour room service; babysitting; laundry/dry cleaning. *In room:* TV, fridge; hair dryer.

Monaltrie Hotel *(Kids* This hotel, built in 1835 of Aberdeen granite, was the first in the region and accommodated the clients of a now-defunct spa. Today the place bustles with a clientele who come for the live music played in its pub and for the savory food (including Thai cuisine) served in its restaurants. Each of the fair-size guest rooms has an unobtrusive monochromatic decor and neatly maintained, shower-only bathroom. The hotel is a 3-minute walk east of the center of town.

5 Bridge Sq., Ballater AB35 5QJ. © **01339/755-417.** Fax 01339/755-180. www.monaltriehotel. freeserve.co.uk. 24 units. £60–£70 ($90–$105) double. Rates include Scottish breakfast. AE, DC, MC, V. Free parking. **Amenities:** 2 restaurants, bar; children's play area. *In room:* TV, coffeemaker, hair dryer.

DINING

Balgonie Country House Restaurant SCOTTISH/FRENCH For Scottish salmon, local game, or Aberdeen Angus beef, this restaurant is among the finest in the Royal Deeside. John and Priscilla Finnie welcome hotel guests and nonguests to their dining room, where the kitchen makes a major effort to secure some of the finest Scottish products. The menu changes daily, but you're likely to find tender filet of beef flambéed in cognac and topped with black peppercorn sauce, or loin of lamb with a red currant jus. While enjoying views of the Glenmuick Hills, you can delight in any number of French-inspired dishes, such as halibut with asparagus and a tomato confit.

In the Balgonie Country House (see "Accommodations," above), Braemar Place. © **01339/755-482.** Reservations recommended. Fixed-price 4-course menu £30 ($45). AE, MC, V. Daily 12:30–2pm and 7–9pm. Closed Jan.

The Conservatory Restaurant *⋟* SCOTTISH Head here for innovative, imaginative cuisine. This award-winning dining room affords views over the River Dee. The chef uses only the freshest ingredients, like lamb, venison, and Aberdeen Angus beef. Seafood options include filet of halibut with basil and olive oil crust combined with fried squid and avocado salsa.

In the Darroch Learg Hotel (see "Accommodations," above), Darroch Learg, Braemar Rd. © **01339/755-443.** Reservations required. Fixed-price 3-course menu £35 ($52.50). AE, DC, MC, V. Daily 12:30–2pm and 7–9pm. Closed Christmas and last 3 weeks in Jan.

Green Inn SCOTTISH This former temperance hotel is now one of the finest dining rooms in town, especially for traditional Scottish dishes. The chef places emphasis on local produce, including homegrown vegetables when available. In season, loin of venison is served with a bramble sauce, and you can always count on fresh salmon and the best of Angus beef.

Three simply furnished double rooms, with shower-only bathroom, TV, and half-board, go for £55 ($82.50) per person.

9 Victoria Rd. © and fax **01339/755-701.** Reservations required. Fixed-price menu £25 ($37.50) for 2 courses; £29.50 ($44.25) for 3 courses. AE, DC, MC, V. Mar–Oct daily 7–9pm; Nov–Feb Tues–Sat 7–9pm.

La Mangia Toia ITALIAN In a converted early-18th-century stable beside the River Dee in the heart of Ballater, this is one of the most architecturally unusual restaurants in the region. Amid a deliberately rustic decor that includes artfully positioned bales of hay, lots of horsey accessories, and a high wooden ceiling, you can order from a widely varied menu that includes a savory array of barbecue dishes. Examples are chicken, salmon, pastas, meal-size salads, baguette sandwiches, steaks, and fresh fish, usually prepared as simply as possible as a means of allowing the basic freshness and flavor to come through. Everybody's favorite dessert seems to be sticky toffee pudding.

Bridge Sq. © **01339/755-999.** Main courses £3.50–£8 ($5.25–$12) lunch; £7–£13 ($10.50–$19.50) dinner. MC, V. Mon–Fri 5–10pm; Sat–Sun noon–10pm.

Oaks Restaurant *𝒞* BRITISH   The most glamorous restaurant in the region, the Oaks is in a century-old mansion that was originally built by the marmalade kings of Britain, the Keiller family. This is the most upscale of the restaurants in a resort complex that includes hotel rooms, time-share villas, and access to a nearby golf course. To start, try the venison and duck terrine flavored with orange and brandy and served with a warm black conch vinaigrette. Main courses include roast rack of lamb, breast of Grampian chicken, and loin of venison.

In the Hilton Craigendarroch Hotel, Braemar Rd. *𝒞* **01339/755-858.** Reservations strongly recommended. Fixed-price 4-course dinner £29 ($43.50). AE, DC, MC, V. Daily 7–10:30pm.

BALLATER AFTER DARK

The **Coach House Hotel Pub,** 1 Netherley Place (*𝒞* **01339/755-462**), is an old pub that has been refurbished as a contemporary bar. Every other Sunday, there's karaoke, but the real draw is the conversation and the on-tap selections. **Monaltrie Hotel Pub,** 5 Bridge Sq. (*𝒞* **01339/755-417**), and its host hotel have been around for 200 years. On Friday, there's a band, usually country-western, and a cover.

12 Braemar

85 miles (137km) N of Edinburgh, 58 miles (93km) W of Aberdeen, 51 miles (82km) N of Perth

In the heart of some of Grampian's most beautiful scenery, Braemar is known for its romantic castle. It's also a good center for exploring the area that includes Balmoral Castle (see above) and is home to the most famous of the Highland Gatherings. The village is set against a massive backdrop of hills, covered with heather in summer, where Clunie Water joins the River Dee. The massive **Cairn Toul** towers over Braemar, reaching a height of 4,241 feet (1,286.5m).

ESSENTIALS

GETTING THERE   The nearest **rail** service runs to Aberdeen (*𝒞* **08457/ 484-950** for schedules). From there, six daily **buses** run west to Braemar (trip time: 2 hr.). One-way fare is £6 ($9). The bus station in Aberdeen is on Guild Street (*𝒞* **01224/212-266**), beside the train station. If you're **driving** from Dundee, return west toward Perth, then head north along A93, following the signs into Braemar. The 70-mile (113km) drive takes 70 to 90 minutes.

VISITOR INFORMATION   The **tourist office** is in The Mews, Mar Road (*𝒞* **01339/742-208**). It's open in June, daily from 10am to 6pm; July and August, daily from 9am to 7pm; and September, daily from 10am to 1pm and 2 to 6pm. Off-season hours are Monday through Saturday from 10am to 1pm and 2 to 5pm, Sunday from noon to 5pm.

SPECIAL EVENTS   The spectacular **Royal Highland Gathering** takes place in late August or early September in the Princess Royal and Duke of Fife Memorial Park. The queen herself often attends the gathering. These ancient games are thought to have been originated by King Malcolm Canmore, a chieftain who ruled much of Scotland at the time of the Norman conquest of England. For details, call the tourist office (see above). Braemar is overrun with visitors at this time, so book your hotel room by April if you want to stay anywhere within a 20-mile (32km) radius.

EXPLORING THE AREA

You might be able to spot members of the royal family at **Crathie Church,** 9 miles (14.5km) east of Braemar on A93 (*𝒞* **01339/742-208**). They attend

Sunday services here when they're in residence at Balmoral. Services are at 11:30am; otherwise, the church is open to view April to October, Monday through Saturday from 9:30am to 5:30pm and Sunday from 2 to 5:30pm.

Nature lovers may want to drive to the **Linn of Dee,** 6 miles (10km) west of Braemar, a narrow chasm on the River Dee that's the best place for scenic walks. Other beautiful spots for day hikes include **Glen Muick, Loch Muick,** and **Lochnagar.** The unmanned **Glenmuick Wildlife Trust Visitor Centre,** reached by a minor road, is located in Glen Muick, off the South Deeside road. You can pick up leaflets here, but for more information, contact the Memorial Ranger Service at © 01339/755-059. An access road joins B976 at a point 16 miles (26km) east of Braemar. The tourist office (see above) will give you a map pinpointing these idyllic places.

Braemar Golf Course (© 01339/741-618) is the highest course in the country. The green of the second hole, the trickiest on the course, is 1,250 feet (380m) above sea level. Greens fees are as follows: Monday through Friday, £15 ($22.50) for 18 holes and £18 ($27) for a day; Saturday and Sunday, £15 ($22.50) for 18 holes and £23 ($34.50) for a day. Pull carts can be rented for £2 ($3) per day; clubs go for £5 ($7.50) per day. The course is open April to October daily. (Call in advance, as hours can vary.)

Shoppers might check out **Capercaille,** 3 Invercauld Rd. (© 01339/741-249), which has quality crafts, mostly of Scottish manufacture. Pottery, carved wood, jewelry, and handmade toys are representative of the items found here. At **Lamont Sporran,** 8 Invercauld Rd. (© 01339/741-404), you can find complete Highland outfits, including *sporran* (the small leather or fur pouch used in place of pockets when wearing a kilt), kilts, belts, jackets, stockings, and brogues. **McLeans of Braemar,** 10–12 Invercauld Rd. (© 01339/741-629), carries regional products from knickknacks to clothing. Among the items are stag-horn and cow-horn crafts, jewelry, china, Scottish woolens, tartans, and men's and women's country clothing.

Braemar Castle 𝒜   This romantic 17th-century castle is a fully furnished private residence with architectural grace, scenic charm, and historical interest. The castle has barrel-vaulted ceilings and an underground prison and is known for its remarkable star-shaped defensive curtain wall.

On the Aberdeen–Ballater–Perth Rd. (A93). © 01339/741-219. Admission £3 ($4.50) adults, £2.50 ($3.75) seniors and students, £1 ($1.50) children 5–15. Mon after Easter–Oct, Sat–Thurs 10am–6pm. Closed Nov–Easter. Take A93 for ½ mile (0.8km) northeast of Braemar.

ACCOMMODATIONS & DINING

Braemar Lodge Hotel   This hotel, popular with skiers who frequent the nearby Glenshee slopes, is set on 2 acres (0.81 hectares) of grounds at the head of Glen Clunie. It's near the cottage where Robert Louis Stevenson wrote *Treasure Island.* On cool evenings, guests are greeted with log fires. Bedrooms are bright and airy. They vary in shape and size, but each contains a well-maintained bathroom with tub/shower. Two units are large enough for families. Also on the grounds are three recently built log cabins with all the modern conveniences; each can sleep up to six.

6 Glenshee Rd., Braemar AB35 5YQ. © and fax 01339/741-627. 7 units. £70 ($105) double; £200–£500 ($300–$750) cabin. Rates include Scottish breakfast. MC, V. Free parking. Closed Nov. **Amenities:** Restaurant; laundry/dry cleaning. *In room:* TV, hair dryer, no phone.

Callater Lodge Hotel *(Finds)*   Full of rural charm, this granite house stands about a quarter of a mile (0.5km) south of the center of Braemar, off the side of the highway in a 1-acre (0.41-hectare) garden. Built around 1865, with a small-scale enlargement completed during the 1970s, it bristles with bay and dormer windows and offers a different decor in each of its cozy guest rooms. The owners will prepare picnics and offer advice on great scenic places to hike. Evening meals can be arranged.

9 Glenshee Rd., Braemar AB35 5YQ. ℂ **01339/741-275.** Fax 01339/741-345. www.hotel-braemar.co.uk. 7 units, 6 with private bathroom. £46–£50 ($69–$75) double without bathroom; £50–£56 ($75–$84) double with bathroom. MC, V. Closed Nov–Dec. Free parking. *In room:* TV, coffeemaker, hair dryer, no phone.

Invercauld Arms Thistle Hotel ⨍   This old granite building, part of which dates from the 18th century, is now the leading inn of Braemar. In cool weather, there's a roaring log fire on the hearth. Guest rooms are comfortably furnished but rather uninspired; they come in a wide range of sizes (some with shower only). The restaurant serves Scottish and international fare. From here you can go hill walking and see deer, golden eagles, and other wildlife. Fishing and skiing are other pursuits in the nearby area.

Braemar AB35 5YR. ℂ **01339/741-605.** Fax 01339/741-428. 68 units. £109 ($163.50) double. Rates include Scottish breakfast. AE, DC, MC, V. Free parking. Bus: 201. **Amenities:** Restaurant, bar; room service; baby-sitting; laundry/dry cleaning. *In room:* TV, coffeemaker, hair dryer.

BRAEMAR AFTER DARK

The **Fife Arms Pub,** in the Fife Arms Hotel, Mar Road (ℂ **01339/741-644**), has free live music, usually Scottish dance bands, on two weeknights, plus live rock on Saturday. Although the **Invercauld Arms Pub,** in the Invercauld Arms Thistle Hotel (ℂ **01339/741-605;** see above), has retained its wooden beamed ceiling, it has been modernized into a typical bar. It's a popular gathering spot for locals.

13 Speyside

The valley of the second-largest river in Scotland, the Spey, is north and south of Aviemore and a land of great natural beauty. A journey north through Speyside will take you toward the Malt Whisky Trail. The Spey is born in the Highlands above Loch Laggan, 40 miles (64.5km) south of Inverness, and runs between the towering Cairngorms on the east and the Monadhliath Mountains on the west. Little more than a creek at its inception, it gains in force, fed by the many "burns" draining water from the hills. It's one of Scotland's great rivers for salmon fishing, and its major center is Grantown-on-Spey.

NEWTONMORE

In Gaelic, "New Town on the Moor" is written *Bail ur ant Sleibh.* Founded in the early 1800s, it's now a village of some 1,000 people, many of whom still understand Gaelic. The Highland resort of Newtonmore is a good center for the Grampian and Monadhliath mountains and offers excellent fishing, golfing, pony trekking, and hill walking. It could easily become your base for touring this scenic area, as it is 46 miles (74km) from Fort William on the west coast, 46 miles (74km) from Inverness to the north, and 38 miles (61km) from Pitlochry to the southeast. It's also 113 miles (182km) northwest of Edinburgh.

For a dramatic walk, climb a track from the village past the Calder River to Loch Dubh and the massive **Carn Ban** (3,087 ft./936m), where eagles fly. **Castle Cluny,** ancient seat of the MacPherson chiefs, is 6 miles (10km) west of Newtonmore. There's no local tourist office, but if you're staying at one of the little inns or guesthouses in the area, the reception desk will hook you up with activities.

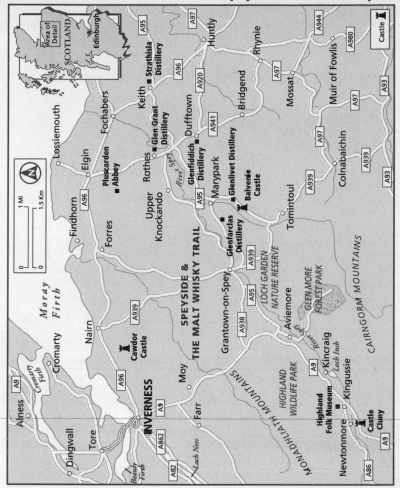

If you follow A86 southwest of Newtonmore, you'll come to the hamlet of Laggan near the junction with A889, which crosses the River Spey. From here you can follow an unclassified road (signposted) running west up the glen to **Garvamore.** This is an area of great scenic beauty. After 6 miles (10km), the road comes to **Garvamore Bridge,** at the south side of Corrieyairack Pass. Built in 1735, this dual-arched bridge was constructed so troops would be able to travel quickly to the Highlands to suppress any possible uprising. Return to A86 and continue west along the western shore of Loch Laggan. The route along this lake offers panoramic views of the Highlands, the kind of scenery Scotland is famous for.

ACCOMMODATIONS & DINING

Pines Hotel   Built in 1903, this somber-looking house sits on a hill overlooking the Spey Valley just west of the hamlet's center. Your hosts are Colin and Pamela Walker, who charge the bargain price of £25 ($37.50) for a double if it's taken by one person. All rooms have pleasant views of the countryside and come with small but neat shower-only bathrooms. The food is wholesome, straightforward Scottish cuisine. Pamela is an expert on desserts and is very generous about creating special treats for diabetics.

Station Rd., Newtonmore PH20 1AR. ℂ **01540/673-271.** 5 units. £47–£50 ($70.50–$75) double. Rates include Scottish breakfast. MC, V. Free parking. Closed Dec 28–Jan 15. *In room:* TV, coffeemaker, hair dryer, no phone.

KINGUSSIE

Your next stop along the Spey might be at the little summer resort and winter ski center of **Kingussie** (pronounced King-*you*-see). It's the so-called capital of Badenoch, a district known as the "drowned land" because the Spey can flood the valley when the snows of a severe winter melt in spring. It's a great center for hiking through beautiful scenery of glen and loch.

Kingussie practically adjoins Newtonmore (see above), for it lies directly southeast along A86. The location is 117 miles (188km) northwest of Edinburgh, 40 miles (64.5km) south of Inverness, and 12 miles (19km) southwest of Aviemore. Five trains per day arrive from Edinburgh, taking 2¾ hours and costing £28.70 ($43.05) one-way. Trains also arrive from Aberdeen at the rate of one per hour (with a change of trains at either Perth or Inverness). The trip takes 4 hours and costs £22.30 ($33.45) one-way.

EXPLORING THE AREA

Kingussie is in one of Scotland's most scenic areas, and you can set off hiking in many directions. Directly south, A9 passes through panoramic scenery set against a backdrop of moor, woodlands, and hills. The highway passes through **Glen Trim** to **Dalwhinnie,** going through the **Pass of Drumochter.** You can also take A86 west from Kingussie to **Glen Roy** and **Spean Bridge,** driving through lush glens set off by towering hills. The road dips and climbs beside beautiful **Loch Laggan.** At several points, you might want to get out of your car and go for long walks, past secret lochans and hidden glens. Perhaps you'll even stumble on Brigadoon.

If you'd like to go hiking, the tourist office will help you plan a trip into the **Monadhliath Mountains** ("gray moors" in Gaelic). They loom immediately northward over Kingussie, separating Speyside from the Great Glen. The **Cairngorm Mountains** are far better known, forming the southern flank of Speyside, but the Monadhliaths are equally as beautiful and far less crowded with other hikers in summer.

Insh Marshes, 2 miles (3km) from Kingussie along B970, after passing by the Ruthven Barracks (see below), is a nature reserve with some of the area's lushest scenery. Six types of wild orchids alone grow here. At two lookout points, high above the marshes, you'll have a good vantage point to spot various birds of prey and hundreds of waterfowl.

Highland Folk Museum ⚐ This was the first folk museum established in Scotland (1934) and remains one of the most important. Its collections are based on the Highlanders' life, and you'll see domestic, agricultural, and industrial items. Open-air exhibits include a *turf kailyard* (kitchen garden), a Lewis Island black house, and old vehicles and carts. Traditional events like spinning, music making, and handcraft fairs are held throughout summer.

Duke St. ℂ **01540/661-307.** Admission £5 ($7.50) adults, £3 ($4.50) children and seniors, £15 ($22.50) per family. Apr–Oct Mon–Fri 10:30am–4pm, Sat–Sun 1–4pm.

Ruthven Barracks   From a distance, this site evokes a ruined castle on a mound, but it's really the ruins of 18th-century barracks rising out of a hill in the flat River Spey valley floor. After the 1715 Jacobite rising, this was one of four infantry barracks constructed to maintain law and order in the area. But in 1746, Ruthven fell to a second Jacobite attack, when it was largely destroyed except for the ruins you see today. It was here Bonnie Prince Charlie gave his final order, "Let every man seek his own safety." This signaled the absolute end of the doomed cause.

½ mile (1km) south of Kingussie. ⓒ 0131/668-8600. Free admission. Daily 24 hr. From Kingussie, drive south along Ruthven Street to B970, then follow the signs to the barracks.

ACCOMMODATIONS & DINING

The Cross ⭐⭐⭐   A former tweed mill has been converted into this charming hotel and dining room, the finest in this part of Scotland. The simple but stylish bedrooms feature contemporary furnishings and modern bathrooms. The restaurant is among the most outstanding in the Highlands; of the 24 spaces at night, 18 are reserved for hotel guests. The dining room has an open beamed ceiling and French doors leading to a terrace over the water's edge, where alfresco meals are served. Full of experimental energy, the chef turns out such dishes as marinated and roasted quail on pickled vegetables, Atlantic cod with roasted red pepper sauce, and wild pigeon with grapes. A fixed-price five-course dinner costs £37.50 ($56.25) for those lucky enough to get a reservation.

Ardbroilach Rd., Kinguissie PH21 1TC. ⓒ 01540/661-166. Fax 01540/661-080. www.thecross.co.uk. 9 units. £115 ($172.50) per person. Rates include breakfast and dinner. MC, V. **Amenities:** Restaurant (closed Tues and Dec–Feb). In room: TV.

Homewood Lodge ⭐ (Kids   One of the best B&Bs in the area, this small Highland house in a garden and woodland setting offers large, simply furnished rooms, each with a shower-only bathroom. The sitting room has an open fireplace. Good traditional fare is served in the evening (reservations recommended). Summer barbecues are also offered, and children are welcome.

Newtonmore Rd., Kingussie PH21 1HD. ⓒ 01540/661-507. www.homewood-lodge-kingussie.co.uk. 4 units. £40 ($60) double. Rates include Scottish breakfast. No credit cards. Free parking. **Amenities:** Dining area; laundry/dry cleaning. In room: TV, coffeemaker, hair dryer, no phone.

Osprey Hotel   This 1895 Victorian structure, 300 yards (275m) from the rail station, is a convenient place to stay, with comfortable though plain bedrooms, all with shower-only bathrooms, electric blankets, and electric fires. The place is known for its fresh, homemade food. Prime Scottish meats are served; in summer, salmon and trout from local rivers are offered either fresh or peat-smoked.

Ruthven Rd. (at High St.), Kingussie PH21 1EN. ⓒ and fax 01540/661-510. www.ospreyhotel.co.uk. 8 units. £85–£98 ($127.50–$147) double. Rates include half-board. AE, DC, MC, V. Free parking. **Amenities:** Restaurant, bar; babysitting. In room: TV, coffeemaker, hair dryer, no phone.

KINCRAIG

Kincraig enjoys a scenic spot at the northern end of Loch Insh, overlooking the Spey Valley to the west and the Cairngorm Mountains to the east. From Kingussie, continue northeast along A9 (the route north to Aviemore) to reach Kincraig, 37 miles (59.5km) south of Inverness and 119 miles (191.5km) northwest of Edinburgh.

About a mile (1.6km) from Kincraig, 6 miles (10km) south of Aviemore, beside B9152, is the entrance to the **Highland Wildlife Park** ⭐ (ⓒ **01540/ 651-270**). Established in 1972 on 260 acres (105.3 hectares), it incorporates a valley ringed with mountains and terrain that includes peat bogs, birch and pine forests, and tundra. Some of the animals you'll see here are exceedingly rare outside the park—herds of European bison, who enjoy rolling around in the peat bogs; red deer; shaggy Highland cattle; wild horses; gray wolves; pine martens (a form of tree weasel); and bears. Among the protected birds are golden eagles and several species of grouse. Roads within the park are designed as drive-thrus allowing maximum exposure to the terrain, thanks to many winding turns. Sixty acres (24.3 hectares) of the park are reserved for trekkers, walkers, and hill climbers. Facilities include a visitor center with a lackluster gift shop, a cafe, and an exhibition center with ample parking and picnic sites available. The park opens daily at 10am. From April to October, the last entrance is at 4pm, except during July and August, when the last entrance is at 5pm. From November to March, the last entrance is at 2pm. All people and vehicles are expected to vacate the park within 2 hours of the day's last admission. Admission is £6.50 ($9.75) for adults, £5.40 ($8.10) for seniors, £4.35 ($6.55) for children, and £21.70 ($32.55) per family.

ACCOMMODATIONS & DINING

March House   This 1980 house almost looks like a contemporary Swedish chalet. Its focal points are an iron wood-burning stove, a pine-sheathed conservatory and library, and sweeping views over a dramatic mountain tableau. Each guest room's decor is based on a different floral theme, such as poppies; all units contain immaculate, shower-only bathrooms. Guests divert themselves with long walks in the surrounding forest.

Reserve in advance for dinner, which is a good value. Since the place is unlicensed, bring your own beer or wine. A recent meal here included crêpes with a creamy leek, ham, and mushroom filling, followed by grilled Scottish lamb with lemon-flavored cabbage and raspberry sauce.

Lagganlia, Feshiebridge, Kincraig PH21 1NG. ℂ 01540/651-388. www.kincraig.com/march/default.htm. 6 units. £44 ($66) double. MC, V. From Kincraig, follow B970 east to Feshiebridge. Cross the bridge and drive uphill until you see the red telephone box on the right. Turn right and continue driving for ½ mile (1km). Total distance from Kincraig is 2 miles (3km). **Amenities:** Restaurant. *In room:* Coffeemaker, hair dryer, no phone.

GRANTOWN-ON-SPEY

This vacation resort, with its gray-granite buildings, is 34 miles (55km) southeast of Inverness in a wooded valley with views of the Cairngorm Mountains. One of Scotland's many 18th-century planned towns, it was founded on a heather-covered moor in 1765 by Sir James Grant. It's now a key center for winter sports; fishermen are also attracted to the salmon fishing here. Using the town as your base, you can explore the valleys of the Don and Dee, the Cairngorms, and Culloden Moor, scene of the historic 1746 battle where Bonnie Prince Charlie was defeated.

The **tourist office** is on High Street (ℂ 01479/872773). Hours are April to October, Monday through Saturday from 9am to 7pm and Sunday from 10am to 5pm; and November to March, Monday through Friday from 9am to 5pm and Saturday from 10am to 5pm.

EXPLORING THE AREA

Grantown-on-Spey is the best center for touring the **Cairngorms** (*Am Monadh Ruadh,* or "red hills," in Gaelic), so called because of the pink granite on their plateaus. This mountain range is excellent for skiing in winter or cycling, golfing, and fishing during warmer months. The local tourist office (see above) can also offer advice about watersports on Loch Morlick and Lock Insh nearby.

The Cairngorm Mountains stretch for 50 miles (80.5km), a huge range that takes in 50 peaks, often rising more than 3,000 feet (910m). Much of the plateau of the Cairngorms is a stony desert carved out by the last Ice Age. The road up Glen More past Loch Morlick leads to a chairlift going all the way to the summit. The cost is £7 ($10.50); it's open daily from 9am to 4:30pm, often later in midsummer. For information, call © 01479/861-261. This is a very popular lift in the ski season, from December to April. The ranger service also operates a program of walks in the area, which can be arranged by calling the **Ranger Base** at © 01479/861-703. For information about rock and ice climbing, bike tours, and guided walks, call Ron Walker of **Talisman Activities** (© 01479/841-576).

Eight miles (13km) south of Grantown-on-Spey is the **Loch Garden Nature Reserve,** known for its breeding ospreys. This highly endangered species is zealously protected by the government. A viewing platform is provided, and you can visit daily in summer from 9am to 5pm; admission is free.

The Kist, 74 High St. (© 01479/873-043), offers regional souvenirs such as Orkney silverware, Border Fine Arts figurines, limited-edition paintings, jewelry, recycled glassware, and Edinburgh, Waterford, and Stuart crystal.

ACCOMMODATIONS

Garth Hotel   The elegant Garth stands on 4 acres (1.6 hectares) beside the town square. Guests enjoy the use of a spacious lounge, whose high ceilings, wood-burning stove, and vine-covered veranda make it an attractive place for morning coffee or afternoon tea. The handsomely furnished guest rooms have all the necessary amenities, including well-maintained bathrooms with shower units. Extensive meals with a French slant make use of fresh local produce.

The Square, Castle Rd., Grantown-on-Spey, Morayshire PH26 3HN. © 01479/872-836. Fax 01479/872-116. 17 units. £59–£69 ($88.50–$103.50) double. Rates include Scottish breakfast. MC, V. Free parking. **Amenities:** Restaurant, bar; room service; laundry/dry cleaning. *In room:* TV, coffeemaker, hair dryer.

Skye of Curr Hotel ⚘ *(Finds)*   A splendid country home set on 2½ acres (1 hectare) of private grounds and woods, this is a welcoming place for an extended stay. Built in 1902 as a Victorian hunting lodge for the Lipton tea family, the hotel overlooks the Cairgorm Mountains and retains many of its original Victorian features, including open fireplaces and wood paneling. Bedrooms are well appointed, with immaculate, shower-only bathrooms.

3 miles south of Grantown-on-Spey by A95 on A938, Dulnain Bridge, PH26 3PA. © 01479/851-345. Fax 01479/821-173. www.skyeofcurr.com. 9 units. £70 ($105) double with breakfast; £110 ($165) double with breakfast and dinner. MC, V. **Amenities:** Restaurant, 2 bars, lounge. *In room:* TV, hair dryer, coffeemaker, no phone.

Tulchan Lodge ⚘⚘   Built in 1906 to serve as the 23,000-acre (9,315-hectare) Tulchan estate's fishing and shooting lodge, this is a place for both outdoor-oriented visitors and travelers who want to experience a place designed with the elegance required by Edward VII, who came here for sports. The lodge has panoramic views of the Spey Valley, and each room is unique in size and furnishings. Most of the bathrooms contain combination tub/showers. Scottish and international dishes are served in the elegant dining rooms to guests only.

Advie, Grantown-on-Spey PH26 3PW. © 01807/510-200. Fax 01807/510-234. www.tulchan.com. 13 units. £350–£500 ($525–$750) double. Rates include full board. MC, V. Closed Feb–Mar. Drive 9 miles (14km) northeast of Grantown on B9102. **Amenities:** 2 dining rooms, lounge; tennis court; shooting; room service; babysitting; laundry/dry cleaning. *In room:* TV, hair dryer.

DINING

Craggan Mill BRITISH/ITALIAN   This licensed restaurant and lounge bar, a 10-minute walk south of the town center, is housed in a restored granite mill whose waterwheel is still visible. Your appetizer might be smoked trout in deference to Scotland, or ravioli inspired by sunny Italy. Move on to a main course of chicken cacciatore, followed by rum-raisin ice cream or peach Melba. You've probably had better versions of all the dishes, but what you get isn't bad and is reasonably priced. A good selection of Italian wines is offered.

Hwy. A95, ¾ mile (1.2km) south of Grantown-on-Spey. (**01479/872-288.** Reservations recommended. Main courses £3.95–£12.50 ($5.95–$18.75). MC, V. May–Sept daily noon–2pm and 6–10pm; Oct–Apr Tues–Sun 7–10pm. Closed first 2 weeks in Nov.

14 West Grampian ⁄★ & the Malt Whisky Trail ⁄★⁄★

Much of the West Grampian region is in the Moray district, on the southern shore of the Moray Firth, a great inlet cutting into the northeastern coast of Scotland and stretching in a triangular shape south from the coast to the wild heart of the Cairngorm Mountains near Aviemore. It's a land steeped in history, as its many castles, battle sites, and ancient monuments testify. It's also very sports oriented, attracting fishermen and golfers.

The major attraction is the 70-mile-long (113km) **Malt Whisky Trail,** running through the glens of Speyside. There are four main malt distilleries in the area, known for their production of *uisge beatha* ("water of life"): Glenlivet, Glenfiddich, Glenfarclas, and Strathisla. Allow about an hour each to visit them. Half the malt distilleries in the country lie along the River Spey and its tributaries, where peat smoke and Highland water are used to turn out single-malt (unblended) whisky.

GLENLIVET & GLENFARCLAS

To reach your first distillery on the Malt Whisky Trail, leave Grantown-on-Spey and head east along A95 until you come to the junction with B9008. Go south along this route and you can't miss it. The **Glenlivet Reception Centre** ((**01542/783-220**) is 10 miles (16km) north of the nearest town, Tomintoul. From mid-March to the end of October, it's open Monday through Saturday from 10am to 4pm and Sunday from 12:30 to 4pm; July and August, hours are Monday through Saturday from 10am to 6pm and Sunday from 12:30 to 6pm. The £2.50 ($3.75) admission for visitors over 18 includes a £2 ($3) voucher off the purchase of a bottle of whisky.

Back on A95, you can visit the **Glenfarclas Distillery,** at Ballindalloch ((**01807/500-245**), one of only two malt-whisky distilleries still independent of the giants. Founded in 1836, Glenfarclas is managed by the fifth generation of the Grant family. It's open Monday through Friday from 9am to 5pm (June to September, also open Saturday from 10am to 4pm and Sunday from 12:30 to 4:30pm). The £2.50 ($3.75) admission for visitors over 18 includes a £7 ($10.50) discount on any purchase of £10 ($15) or more.

ACCOMMODATIONS & DINING

Minmore House Hotel ⁄★   Standing on 5 acres (2 hectares) of grounds adjacent to the Glenlivet Distillery, this impressive country house was once the home of the distillery owners. The elegant drawing room opens onto views of the plush Ladder Hills. The guest rooms are well furnished and contain combination tub/showers. Drinks can be enjoyed in the oak-paneled lounge bar, which has an open log fire on chilly nights.

Glenlivet, Ballindalloch AB37 9DB. ℂ **01807/590-378.** Fax 01807/590-472. www.smoothhound.co.uk/ hotels/minmore.html. 10 units. £150–£160 ($225–$240) double. Rates include breakfast, afternoon tea, and 4-course dinner. MC, V. Closed mid-Oct to mid-Apr. **Amenities:** Dining room, bar; pool. *In room:* Coffeemaker, hair dryer.

DUFFTOWN

James Duff, the fourth earl of Fife, founded Dufftown in 1817. The four main streets of town converge at the battlemented **clock tower,** which is also the **tourist office** (ℂ **01340/820-501**). April to June, September, and October, the office is open Monday through Saturday from 10am to 1pm and 2 to 5:30pm and Sunday from 1 to 5pm; July and August hours are Monday through Saturday from 10am to 7pm and Sunday from 1 to 7pm.

A center of the whisky-distilling industry, Dufftown is surrounded by seven malt distilleries. The family-owned **Glenfiddich Distillery** is on A941, half a mile (1km) north (ℂ **01340/820-373**). It's open Monday through Friday from 9:30am to 4:30pm (Easter to mid-October, also Saturday from 9:30am to 4:30pm and Sunday from noon to 4:30pm). Guides in kilts show you around the plant and explain the process of distilling, and a film on the history of distilling is shown. The first whisky was produced on Christmas Day back in 1887.

Other sights include **Balvenie Castle,** along A941 (ℂ **01340/820-121**), the ruins of a moated 14th-century stronghold that lie on the south side of the Glenfiddich Distillery. During her northern campaign against the earl of Huntly, Mary Queen of Scots spent 2 nights here. April to September, it's open daily from 9:30am to 6:30pm. Admission is £1.50 ($2.25) for adults, £1 ($1.50) for seniors, and 50p (75¢) for children.

Mortlach Parish Church, in Dufftown, is one of the oldest places of Christian worship in the country. Its reputed to have been founded in A.D. 566 by St. Moluag. The present church was reconstructed in 1931 and incorporates portions of an older building.

DINING

Taste of Speyside ℛ SCOTTISH   True to its name, this restaurant in the town center, just off the main square, avidly promotes Speyside cuisine as well as the product of Speyside's 46 distilleries. A platter including a slice of smoked salmon, smoked venison, smoked trout, paté flavored with malt whisky, locally made cheese (cow or goat), salads, and homemade oat cakes is offered at noon and at night. Nourishing soup is made fresh daily and is served with homemade bread. There's also a choice of meat pies, including rabbit or venison with red wine and herbs. For dessert, try Scotch Mist, which contains fresh cream, malt whisky, and crumbled meringue.

10 Balvenie St. ℂ **01340/820-860.** Reservations recommended for dinner. Main courses £9.50–£12.50 ($14.25–$18.75); Speyside platter £10 ($15) lunch, £13 ($19.50) dinner. MC, V. Mon–Sat noon–9pm. Closed Nov–Feb.

KEITH

Keith, 11 miles (18km) northwest of Huntly, grew up because of its strategic location, where the main road and rail routes between Inverness and Aberdeen cross the River Isla. It has an ancient history, but owes its present look to the town planning of the late 18th and early 19th centuries.

The oldest continuously operating distillery in the Scottish Highlands, the **Strathisla Distillery,** Seafield Avenue in Keith (ℂ **01542/783-044**), was established in 1786 and operates as a proudly individualistic producer of single malts under the supervision of Chivas & Glenlivet (a division of Seagrams). It's open February to mid-March, Monday through Friday from 9:30am to 4pm; and mid-March to November, Monday through Saturday from 9:30am to 4pm and Sunday from 12:30 to 4pm. Admission is £4 ($6) for adults and free for children 8 to 18; children under 8 aren't admitted. The admission includes a £2 ($3) voucher redeemable in the distillery shop against a 25.4-fluid-ounce (70cl) bottle of whisky. Note that tours of this distillery are self-guided.

ACCOMMODATIONS & DINING

Grange House *ℛ* *Finds* On 8 acres (3.2 hectares) of untamed garden and fields, this lovely home is a former manse from 1815, with a Victorian wing added in 1898. It's outfitted in an inviting style with exceedingly comfortable beds, plus immaculate shower-only bathrooms. The drawing room offers a log fire, a piano, and plenty of books and magazines. The house is ideally located for the Speyside whisky trail, but is also convenient to outdoor activities such as bird-watching, fishing, horseback riding, and golf. Dinners can be arranged. No smoking is permitted.

Grange, Keith, Banffshire AB55 6RY. ℭ and fax **01542/870-206.** www.aboutscotland.com/banff/grangehouse.html. 2 units. £55 ($82.50) double. Rates include breakfast. No credit cards. From Keith, drive 3 miles (5km) east of town on A95, following the signs to Banff, into the hamlet of Grange. **Amenities:** Dining area; babysitting; laundry/dry cleaning. *In room:* Coffeemaker, hair dryer, no phone.

ROTHES

A Speyside town with five distilleries, Rothes is just to the south of the Glen of Rothes, 49 miles (79km) east of Inverness and 62 miles (100km) northwest of Aberdeen. Founded in 1766, the town is between Ben Aigan and Conerock Hill. A little settlement, the basis of the town today, grew up around **Rothes Castle,** ancient stronghold of the Leslie family, who lived here until 1622. Only a single massive wall of the castle remains.

The region's best distillery tours are offered by the **Glen Grant Distillery** (ℭ **01542/783-318**). Opened in 1840 by a hardworking and hard-drinking pair of brothers, James and John Grant, and now administered by the Chivas & Glenlivit Group (a division of Seagrams), it's half a mile (1km) north of Rothes, beside the Elgin-Perth (A941) highway. It's open April to October, Monday through Saturday from 10am to 4pm and Sunday from 12:30 to 4pm. Admission is £3 ($4.50) for adults and free for children 8 to 18; children under 8 aren't allowed. Visits include the opportunity to buy the brand's whisky at a discount. Although the Grant family's nearby mansion was demolished in the early 1990s, its gardens (from 1896) were revitalized and restored recently. The waterfall that functions as the centerpiece of the garden's upper region is worth a visit.

ELGIN *ℛ*

The center of local government in the Moray district and an ancient royal burgh, the cathedral city of Elgin is on the Lossie River, 38 miles (61km) east of Inverness and 68 miles (109.5km) northwest of Aberdeen. The city's medieval plan has been retained, with "wynds" and "pends" connecting the main artery with other streets. The castle, as was customary in medieval town layouts, stood at one end of the main thoroughfare, with the cathedral—now a magnificent ruin—at the other. Nothing remains of the castle, but the site is a great place for a scenic walk. Samuel Johnson and James Boswell came this way on their Highland tour and reported a "vile dinner" at the Red Lion Inn in 1773.

Lady Hill stands on High Street, opposite the post office. This is the hilltop location of what was once the royal castle of Elgin. **Birnie Kirk,** at Birnie, 3 miles (5km) south of Elgin and west of A941 to Rothes, was for a time the seat of a bishopric. It dates from about 1140, when it was constructed on the site of a much earlier church founded by St. Brendan. One of the few Norman churches in Scotland still in regular use, it's open daily from 10am to 4pm.

On King Street are the ruins of the **Elgin Cathedral** (© 01343/547-171), off North College Street near A96. It was founded in 1224 but destroyed in 1390 by the "wolf of Badenoch," the natural son of Robert II. After its destruction, the citizens of Elgin rebuilt their beloved cathedral and turned it into one of the most attractive and graceful buildings in Scotland. However, when the central tower collapsed in 1711, the cathedral was allowed to fall into decay. It's open April to September, daily from 9:30am to 6:30pm; and October to March, Monday through Wednesday and Saturday from 9:30am to 4:30pm, Thursday from 9:30am to 12:30pm, and Sunday from 2 to 4:30pm. Admission is £2.80 ($4.20) for adults, £2 ($3) for seniors, and £1 ($1.50) for children.

After exploring Elgin, you can drive 6 miles (10km) southwest to **Pluscarden Abbey,** off B9010. This is one of the most beautiful drives in the area, through the bucolic Black Burn Valley where a priory was founded in 1230 by Alexander II. After long centuries of decline, a new order of Benedictines arrived in 1974 and re-established monastic life. You can visit restored transepts, monastic buildings, and the church choir. The admission is free to this active religious community, which is open daily from 5am to 8:30pm.

If you're a fan of Scottish ruins, head for **Spynie Palace** (© 01343/546-358), reached along A941. The former 15th-century headquarters of the bishops of Moray was used until 1573, when it was allowed to fall into ruins—for safety reasons, you can view them only from the outside. This is another great place for country walks, and from the top of a tower are magnificent vistas over the Laigh of Moray. It's open April to September, daily from 9:30am to 6:30pm; and October to March, Saturday from 9:30am to 4pm and Sunday from 2 to 4:30pm. Admission is £2 ($3).

ACCOMMODATIONS

Mansion House Hotel (ⓡⓡ)   This elegantly appointed hotel, with the baronial proportions of the original design intact, is at the edge of the River Lossie, about a quarter of a mile (about .5km) from the center of Elgin. The guest rooms are standard; most have four-poster beds and all have combination tub/showers.

The Haugh, Elgin IV30 IAW. © 01343/548-811. Fax 01343/547-916. 23 units. £120–£150 ($180–$225) double. Rates include Scottish breakfast. AE, DC, MC, V. Follow A96 onto Alexandra Rd. to the turnoff onto Haugh Rd. **Amenities:** Restaurant, bar; leisure club with pool, gym; Jacuzzi; room service; babysitting; laundry service. In room: TV, coffeemaker, hair dryer.

DINING

Abbey Court Restaurant SCOTTISH/ITALIAN   Abbey Court, in the center of town behind the county building, is an excellent restaurant decorated with stone- and earth-colored quarry tile, along with an artificial pergola, a separate bistro corner, and a more formal dining area in the rear. The fresh pasta is homemade and fresh fish delivered daily. The cooking is straightforward and unpretentious.

15 Greyfriars St. © 01343/542-849. Reservations recommended. Main courses £7.95–£16.95 ($11.95–$25.45). AE, DC, MC, V. Mon–Sat noon–2pm; Mon–Thurs 6:30–9:30pm; Fri–Sat 6:30–10pm.

ELGIN AFTER DARK

Linked historically to the Stewart clan as far back as 1715, **Thunderton House Pub,** Thunderton Place (© **01343/554-921**), is an 11th-century building best known as the place where Bonnie Prince Charlie stayed in 1746 on his way to Culloden. Nowadays, the old pub is a gathering place for locals who amuse themselves with karaoke on Thursday and Sunday. A band is booked occasionally.

The traditional Irish pub **Flanagan's,** 4 Shepherd's Close (© **01343/ 549-737**), is a small, dark bar with brick walls and old floorboards; it draws a crowd for Irish and folk bands on weekends. **Cottarhouse,** Thornhill Road (© **01343/547-903**), is composed of two ancient cottages and has retained the original wood floors, stone fireplaces, and stone walls. Saturdays bring live traditional music.

FINDHORN

As you travel westward from Elgin to Forres, a turn to the right and then to the left will bring you to Findhorn, a tiny village that used to be a busy commercial fishing port and is today the home of the famous Findhorn Foundation. Findhorn lies at the end of B9011, and a local bus from Forres stops here. These days, the unique tidal bay at the mouth of the River Findhorn makes the village an ideal center for yacht racing, sailing, and windsurfing.

Just before Findhorn Village, you'll see the home of the **Findhorn Foundation,** The Park, Forres IV36 0TZ (© **01309/690-311**), an international educational community founded in 1962 and based on spiritual principles and organic farming. It owns and runs the **Findhorn Bay Caravan Park** (© **01309/ 690-203**) and the macrobiotically conscious **Phoenix Shop** (© **01309/ 690-110**), where you can buy health foods, books, and craft items. Tours of the complex are offered Wednesday through Monday morning at 10am and every afternoon, April to September, at 2pm. The complex is unpretentious and includes good numbers of aluminum-sided buildings and trailers—but the organization's theories of interdenominational spiritual healing have won it much more fame than its simple setting would suggest. If you're interested in living in the Findhorn community for a while, working and studying, write to the address above or call © **01309/673-655.**

ACCOMMODATIONS & DINING

Crown & Anchor Inn   The Crown & Anchor dates from 1739, when it was constructed to cater to travelers making the run between Edinburgh and Inverness. On the seafront near the pier, it serves bar snacks and meals daily, with a house specialty of fresh fish from both the sea and the local rivers. Locals drop in to enjoy the real ales and malt whiskies served in the bar. The small guest rooms are modestly furnished but clean, each with a small bathroom with shower.

Findhorn IV36 3YF. © **01309/690-243.** Fax 01309/690-201. 8 units. £50 ($75) double. Rates include Scottish breakfast. DC, MC, V. Free parking. **Amenities:** Restaurant; bar. *In room:* TV, no phone.

10

Inverness & the West Highlands

The romantic glens and rugged mountain landscapes of the West Highlands are timeless and pristine. You can see deer grazing only yards from the highway and stop by your own secluded loch to enjoy a picnic or to fish for trout and salmon. The shadow of Macbeth still stalks the land. (Locals will tell you this 11th-century king was much maligned by Shakespeare.) The area's most famous resident, however, is said to live in mysterious Loch Ness: First sighted by St. Columba in the 6th century, "Nessie" has cleverly evaded searchers ever since.

Centuries of invasions, rebellions, and clan feuds are distant memories now. The Highlands aren't as remote as they once were, when many Londoners seriously believed the men of the Highlands had tails.

Fort William is a major center for the West Highlands, surrounded by wildly beautiful **Lochaber,** the "land of bens, glens, and heroes." Dominating the area is **Ben Nevis,** Britain's highest mountain. This district is the western end of what is known as the **Glen Mor**—the Great Glen, geologically a fissure dividing the northwest of Scotland from the southeast and containing Loch Lochy, Loch Oich, and Loch Ness. The Caledonian Canal, opened in 1847, linked these lochs, the River Ness, and Moray Firth, providing sailing boats a safe alternative to the stormy route around the north of Scotland. Larger steamships made the canal out of date commercially, but fishing boats and pleasure steamers still use it. Good roads run the length of the Great Glen, partly following the line of Gen. George Wade's military road. The English general became famous for his road and bridge building in Scotland, which did much to open the Highlands to greater access from the south. From Fort William, you can take steamer trips to Staffa and Iona (see chapter 11, "The Hebridean Islands," for more information).

Aviemore and the villages and towns of the Spey Valley offer many activities for the visitor. In the Spey Valley you're at the doorway to the **Malt Whisky Trail** (see chapter 9, "Aberdeen & the Tayside & Grampian Regions," for more information). Aviemore is the winter-sports capital of Britain, and Aviemore Centre offers a multitude of outdoor pursuits: golfing, angling, skiing, and ice-skating.

Inverness and legendary **Loch Ness** are the most popular attractions of the West Highlands and overcrowded in summer, but they're surrounded by villages and towns that also make good centers, especially if you're driving. If you're dependent on public transportation, make Inverness your base, as it has good rail and bus connections to the rest of Scotland and also to England.

Finally, if you have the time to spare, you can extend your stay by visiting the loneliest part of Scotland, the far north. This section of the Highlands, **Sutherland** and **Caithness,** isn't for everyone. Crumbling watchtowers no longer stand guard over anything except the sheep-cropped wilderness. Moss-green glens give way to inland lochs and sea fords. Summer, of course, is the best time to view these deep-blue lochs, towering cliffs, and gentle glens. Many relics of Scotland's turbulent past dot the landscape, with castles left in ruins. Today, visitors come to get away from it all and enjoy outdoor activities in a wild, pristine setting. Potteries and craft centers have also sprung up, with artisans taking inspiration from their surroundings and putting it to work in silversmithing, stone polishing, glass-making, and most definitely weaving.

1 Around Loch Linnhe & Loch Leven

South of Fort William is one of the most historic sections of Scotland, a group of settlements around Loch Linnhe and Loch Leven (not the also-famous Loch Leven near Dunfermline). The best-known village is **Glencoe,** site of the famous 1692 massacre when the Campbells slaughtered the MacDonalds. Glencoe is the most dramatic glen in Scotland, austere in its beauty. Around both lochs are impressive landscapes and moorland, with flora and fauna unique to the West Highlands. Robert Louis Stevenson captured much of the essence of this moorland and wilderness in his novel *Kidnapped.*

The best all-around outfitter is **Alfresco Adventure,** Onich (② 01855/ 821-248). Nick and Angie Scott will rent motorboats, canoes, sailboats, fishing tackle, and more; they're a great source of advice for enjoying the great Highland outdoors. They also offer guided hill walks at £20 ($30) per person for half a day, plus guided canoe trips at £40 ($60) per person for a full day.

ONICH

On the shores of Loch Linnhe, the charming little village of Onich lies to the north of Ballachulish Bridge, 9 miles (14.5km) southwest of Fort William. It's a good center if you're taking the western route to Inverness or going to Skye and Fort William.

ACCOMMODATIONS & DINING

Allt-nan-Ros Hotel This inn lies across the highway from the edge of the loch and boasts dozens of elaborate gables and interesting architectural touches. Allt-nan-Ros was built around 1885 as a hunting lodge and weekend getaway for an industrialist. Today, this much-enlarged place with relatively recent additions offers comfortable guest rooms and a well-managed dining room open to the public. The rooms have dark mahogany furniture and floral-patterned upholsteries in an Edwardian country-house style, and most offer views of the loch or the stream running through the garden. Some bathrooms contain showers only.

Onich PH33 6RY. ② 0185/582-1210. Fax 0185/582-1462. www.allt-nan-ros.co.uk. 20 units. £90–£110 ($135–$165) double. Rates include breakfast. AE, DC, MC, V. From Fort William, drive 10 miles (16km) south along A82. **Amenities:** Restaurant; bar; room service; babysitting. *In room:* TV.

The Lodge on the Loch Hotel ⟨⟩ Between the edge of the loch and a semi-forested rocky ridge, this granite hotel dates from the 19th century. Only a handful of the high-ceilinged guest rooms are in the mansion's core; most are in a bulky-looking 1960s extension but are just as comfortable, with a mix of conservative and traditional furnishings. The most expensive units have plush extras

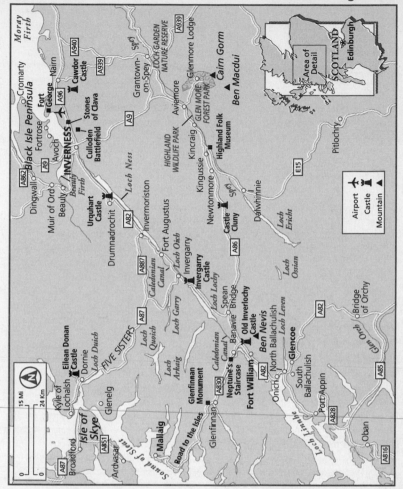

like CD players, bathrobes, and Jacuzzi baths. If the hotel is full, there are two other choices (under the same management) within a short drive.

The restaurant is one of the big draws, serving an expensive fixed-price dinner that features Scottish produce and many preparations of salmon, trout, and pheasant. There's also a cocktail bar with a log fire and a fine selection of whiskies.

Onich PH33 6RY. © **0185/582-1237.** Fax 0185/582-1238. www.freedomglen.co.uk. 19 units, 17 with private bathroom. £180–£200 ($270–$300) double. Rates include breakfast and dinner. MC, V. Closed Nov–Mar. From Fort William, drive 15 miles (24km) south of town, following A82 and the signs to Glasgow. **Amenities:** Restaurant, bar; pool; gym; steam room/sauna; massages. *In room:* TV, hair dryer, iron.

GLENCOE: SCENERY & SORROW 🏵🏵

Near the spot where Loch Leven joins Loch Linnhe, **Ballachulish Bridge** links the villages of North and South Ballachulish at the entrance to Glencoe. The bridge saves a long drive to the head of the loch if you're coming from the north, but the scenic drive to Kinlochleven lets you come on the celebrated wild

Glencoe from the east. Glencoe runs from Rannoch Moor to Loch Leven between majestic mountains, including 3,766-foot (1,142m) **Bidean nam Bian.** This is an area of massive splendor, with towering peaks and mysterious glens where you can well imagine the fierce battle among the kilted Highlanders to the skirl of the pipes and the beat of the drums.

Known as the "Glen of Weeping," Glencoe is the place where, on February 11, 1692, the Campbells massacred the MacDonalds—men, women, and children—who'd been their hosts for 12 days. Although mass killings weren't uncommon in those times, this one shocked even the Highlanders because it was a breach of hospitality. The **Monument to the Massacre of Glencoe,** at Carnoch, was erected by the chief of the MacDonald clan. After the incident, the crime of "murder under trust" was introduced into Scottish law as an aggravated form of murder that carried the same penalty as treason.

Glen Orchy, to the south, is well worth a visit for its wild river and photogenic mountain scenery. It was the birthplace of Gaelic bard Duncan Ban MacIntyre, whose masterpiece is the song "In Praise of Ben Doran."

This is great country for hiking and biking. In Glencoe village, go to the **Mountain Bike Hire,** at the Clachaig Inn (© **01855/811-252**), where you can not only rent a bike but also get advice about scenic routes that suit your ability. The cost is £8.50 ($12.75) per half day or £12.50 ($18.75) per day.

ACCOMMODATIONS & DINING

You can also base yourself in Fort William (see "Fort William: Gateway to Ben Nevis," below) and explore the Glencoe area on day trips.

Ballachulish House 🔒🔒 This charming country inn's lime-washed stone form dates back to the 1700s, though it was tastefully expanded in 1997. The owners spent enormous sums renovating the place, and since then have hosted the occasional celebrity. The guest rooms have flowered wallpaper and a mix of old and new furniture; each has a view of the loch or forest. The more luxurious units have bathrooms with both tub and shower. There's ample opportunity for long walks beside the loch. (Sometimes one of the owners' dogs will join you.) Dinner is a treat, making use of fresh ingredients and careful preparation.

Ballachulish PA39 4JX. © **01855/811266.** 56 units. £140–£200 ($210–$300) double. Rates include dinner and breakfast. MC, V. Closed Jan. Drive west of Ballachulish for 2½ miles (4km), following A82 until it intersects with A828. Follow the signs to Ballachulish House. **Amenities:** Restaurant, bar; billiard room. *In room:* TV.

Clachaig Inn   After the bleakness of Glencoe, the trees ringing this place make it seem like an oasis. It's the only hotel in the glen, on the site where the massacre took place. The Daynes family offers Highland hospitality, good food, and an excellent selection of British ales. They rent some contemporary chalets in the back garden, plus several small to midsize guest rooms in the main house. The furnishings are basic, each of the double rooms comes with a small, shower-only bathroom Live folk music brings the place alive on Saturday and Wednesday nights.

Glencoe, Ballachulish PA39 4HX. © **01855/811-252.** Fax 01855/811-679. www.clachaig.com. 20 units, 17 with private bathroom. £66–£90 ($99–$135) double with bathroom. Rates include Scottish breakfast. MC, V. The inn is reached by a gravel road off the main highway; watch for signs. **Amenities:** Restaurant, 3 bars; nearby health club. *In room:* TV.

King's House Hotel   The solid walls of this historic inn were built in the 1600s on a windswept plateau beside A82, 12 miles (19km) southeast of Glencoe village, at the strategic point where Glencoe joins the Glen Etive near a jagged mountain, Buachaille Etive Mor. Most of the modestly furnished guest rooms offer sweeping views; about half are equipped with small, tub-only bathrooms. Bedrooms rather lack amenities other than a phone. Simple meals are served in the bar; the dining room boasts a selection of fine wines and freshly prepared meals. The hotel is a 30-minute walk from a ski center with a chairlift.

Glencoe PA39 4HZ. ☎ **01855/851-259.** Fax 01855/851-216. 22 units, 12 with private bathroom. £48 ($72) double without bathroom; £54 ($81) double with bathroom. MC, V. Arrange with the hosts to be met at the Bridge of Orchy rail station. **Amenities:** Restaurant, bar; nearby ski center.

2 Fort William ⭐: Gateway to Ben Nevis ⭐⭐

133 miles (214km) NW of Edinburgh, 68 miles (109.5km) S of Inverness, 104 miles (167.5km) N of Glasgow

Fort William, on the shores of Loch Linnhe, is the best place for an overnight stop between here and Inverness in the northeast. It's a good base for exploring **Ben Nevis,** Scotland's highest mountain, and also for a day trip to Glencoe (see above).

Fort William stands on the site of a fort built by General Monk in 1655 to help crush any rebellion Highlanders might have been plotting. After several reconstructions, it was finally torn down in 1864 to make way for the railroad. During the notorious Highland Clearances, many starving and evicted people were shipped from here to the United States. Today, Fort William is a bustling town, thriving on the summer tourist trade and filled with shops, hotels, and cafes.

ESSENTIALS

GETTING THERE Fort William is a major stop on the West Highland rail line that begins at the Queen Street Station in Glasgow and ends at Mallaig on the west coast. Three **trains** a day run this route at a one-way cost of £21 ($31.50). For schedules, contact the tourist office (see below) or call ☎ **01463/239-026** in Inverness.

Four **buses** run from Glasgow to Fort William per day, taking 3 hours and costing £11.20 ($16.80) one-way. Call the Buchanan Bus Station at ☎ **0870/332-7133** in Glasgow for schedules.

If you're **driving** from Glasgow, head north along A82.

VISITOR INFORMATION The **tourist office** is at Cameron Centre, Cameron Square (☎ **01397/703-781**). It's open April and May, Monday through Saturday from 9am to 5pm and Sunday from 10am to 4pm; June to mid-July, Monday through Saturday from 9am to 6pm and Sunday from 10am to 5pm; mid-July to August, Monday through Saturday from 9am to 8:30pm and Sunday from 9am to 6pm; September and October, Monday through Saturday from 9am to 6pm and Sunday from 10am to 5pm; and November to March, Monday through Friday from 9am to 5pm and Saturday from 10am to 4pm.

EXPLORING THE AREA

You can reach the ruins of **Old Inverlochy Castle,** scene of a famous battle, by driving 2 miles (3km) north of Fort William on A82. Built in the 13th century, the ruined castle still has round corner towers and a walled courtyard. One of the towers was the keep, the other a water gate. The castle looms in the pages of Scottish history—in 1645, a small army of Scots defeated government forces here, although 1,500 men were lost.

Neptune's Staircase, 3 miles (5km) northwest of Fort William off A830 at Banavie, is a series of nine locks that were constructed at the same time as the Caledonian Canal, raising Telford's canal 64 feet (19.5m). This "staircase" is one of Scotland's most prominent engineering triumphs of the mid–19th century, when the eastern seacoast at Inverness was connected, via the canal, to the western seacoast at Fort William. This greatly shortened the distance required for goods moving from the North Sea to the Atlantic Ocean and bypassed the treacherous storms that often rage around Scotland's northern tier.

Because much of Fort William is relatively flat, consider biking. The best rentals are at **Off Beat Bikes,** 117 High St. (② **01397/704-008**), costing £8.50 to £10 ($12.75 to $15) for a half day, £12.50 to £15 ($18.75 to $22.50) for a full day. It's open Monday through Saturday from 9am to 5:30pm and Sunday from 9:30am to 5pm.

In the north end of town, the **Ben Nevis Woolen Mill,** Belford Road (② **01397/704-244**), is only a shop, not a functioning woolen mill, with a large

Climbing Britain's Tallest Mountain

In the Central Highlands, **Ben Nevis,** at 4,406 feet (1,336.5m), is the tallest mountain in Britain. Although it's not exactly ready to challenge the towering Alps, Ben Nevis can still give hikers a good workout. The pony track to the top is often filled with walkers tackling the difficult 8-hour jaunt. The unpredictable Scottish weather adds to the challenge, requiring you to dress in layers and bring along at least a waterproof jacket. The mean monthly temperature of Ben Nevis falls below freezing; snow has been reported at all times of year, even during the hottest months of July and August. Howling winds are frequent.

Hikers head up for the view, but it's not guaranteed due to weather conditions. On a clear day, you can see the Irish foothills some 120 miles (193km) away, the Hebridean Isle of Rhum 92 miles (148km) away, and the Glencoe peaks (Ben Lawers, Torridon, and the Cairngorms). If you don't want to climb, a cable car can take to a height of 2,300 feet (698m) for viewing.

The trail is much rougher but even more beautiful if approached from Glen Nevis, one of the country's most scenic glens. Clear rivers and cascading waterfalls add to the drama of the scenery; meadows and moors seem straight out of Austria.

Before going, discuss the climb with the staff at the tourist office in Fort William. They can give you advice as well as maps, and they'll pinpoint the best starting places. A signpost to the north of Nevis Bridge points to the path up Ben Nevis. Allow 8½ hours total for the under-10-mile (16km) trip. Take along a windbreaker, sturdy footwear, food, and water.

A word of warning: Sudden weather changes may pose a safety hazard. And that final 1,000 feet (303m) is really steep terrain, but having gone this far, few can resist the challenge. Some Brits call Ben Nevis the "top of the world." It really isn't—it just feels that way when you finally reach the peak.

selection of clothing and accessories: wools, tweeds, tartans, and some hand-knit Arran sweaters. An on-premises restaurant features regional fare.

Shoppers might also want to check out the **Granite House,** High Street (© **01397/703-651**). The owners call themselves "giftmongers" and carry a large selection of Scottish jewelry; watches; Royal Doulton and Lilliput Lane china; crystal by Edinburgh and Wedgwood; and more than 1,000 Irish and Scottish music CDs and an array of traditional instruments.

Scottish Crafts & Whisky Centre, 135–139 High St. (© **01397/704-406**), is another place with a good mix of the best of all things Scottish: regionally produced jewelry, rugs, clothing, rare whiskies, and handmade chocolates by Fergusons.

West Highland Museum   The collection in this museum sheds light on all aspects of local history, especially the 1745 Jacobite Rising; it also has sections on tartans and folk life.

Cameron Sq., in the center of town next to the tourist office. © 01397/702-169. Admission £2 ($3) adults, £1.50 ($2.25) seniors, 50p (75¢) children. June–Sept Mon–Sat 10am–5pm (July–Aug also Sun 2–5pm); Oct–May Mon–Sat 10am–4pm.

Glenfinnan Monument   At Glenfinnan at the head of Loch Shiel, this monument marks the spot where Bonnie Prince Charlie unfurled his proud red-and-white silk banner on August 19, 1745, in his ill-fated attempt to restore the Stuarts to the British throne. The figure of a kilted Highlander tops the monument. At the visitor center, you can learn of the prince's campaign from Glenfinnan to Derby that ended in his defeat at Culloden.

About 14 miles (22.5km) west of Fort William, on A830 toward Mallaig. © 01397/722-250 for visitor center. Admission to visitor center £1.50 ($2.25). Visitor center mid-May to Aug daily 9:30am–6pm; Sept to early May daily 10am–5pm.

ACCOMMODATIONS

There's no shortage of B&Bs in Fort William; the tourist office can supply you with a list if the selections below are full.

VERY EXPENSIVE

Inverlochy Castle 𝕲𝕲𝕲   Inverlochy Castle, against the scenic backdrop of Ben Nevis, hosted Queen Victoria in her day and remains the premier address in this entire part of Scotland. Back then, it was a newly built (1870) Scottish mansion; the monarch claimed in her diary, "I never saw a lovelier or more romantic spot." Now a Relais & Châteaux property, the Inverlochy has undergone a major refurbishment but has retained its charm. Luxurious appointments, antiques, artwork, and crystal, plus a profusion of flowers, create a mood of elegance and refinement. The prices certainly reflect this opulence.

The cuisine here is some of the finest in Scotland, with food cooked to order and served on silver platters. See "Dining," below, for details. Nonguests can dine here if there's room, but reservations are mandatory.

Torlundy, Fort William PH33 6SN. © 01397/702-177. Fax 01397/702-953. 17 units. £290–£380 ($435–$570) double; from £390–£480 ($585–$720) suite. Rates include Scottish breakfast. AE, MC, V. Closed early Jan to late Feb. Free valet parking. Take A82 for 3 miles (5km) northeast of town. **Amenities:** Restaurant, bar; tennis court; game fishing; room service; babysitting; laundry. *In room:* TV, hair dryer.

MODERATE

Alexandra   Across from the rail terminal, the Alexandra boasts the tall gables and formidable granite walls so common in this part of the Highlands. It has been completely modernized, offering pleasant and comfortably furnished guest rooms with shower-only bathrooms. The chef makes excellent use of fresh fish, and the wine cellar is amply endowed. Guests have free use of the facilities at the nearby Milton Hotel and Leisure Club.

The Parade, Fort William PH33 6AZ. Ⓒ **01397/702-241.** Fax 01397/705-554. www.miltonhotels.com. 97 units. £95–£115 ($142.50–$172.50) double. Rates include Scottish breakfast. AE, DC, MC, V. Free parking. **Amenities:** Restaurant, bar; access to nearby leisure club (with pool, gym, and more); room service; laundry. *In room:* TV, coffeemaker.

The Moorings Hotel   One of the most up-to-date hotels in the region, the Moorings was designed in a traditional style in the mid-1970s, with bay and dormer windows and a black-and-white facade. The interior is richly paneled in the Jacobean style. The guest rooms are attractive and modern, each with a shower-only bathroom. Bar lunches and suppers are offered in the Mariner Wine Bar, while more formal meals are served in the Moorings Restaurant, where an even greater selection of wine (more than 200 vintages) accompanies dishes like smoked venison, Scottish oysters, homemade terrines, and wild salmon in lemon-butter sauce.

Banavie, Fort William PH33 7LY. Ⓒ **01397/772-797.** Fax 01397/772-441. 29 units. £68–£96 ($102–$144) double. Rates include Scottish breakfast. AE, DC, MC, V. Drive 3 miles (5km) north of Fort William to the hamlet of Banavie, beside B8004. **Amenities:** Restaurant, bar. *In room:* TV, coffeemaker, hair dryer.

INEXPENSIVE

Croit Anna Hotel   Overlooking Loch Linnhe, the Croit Anna Hotel opens onto fine views of the Ardgour Hills. It's owned and managed by the same family who built it on a traditional Highland croft that has been in their possession for more than 250 years. All the midsize guest rooms have tidily kept but small shower-only bathrooms. Entertainment is provided on most evenings in season.

Druimarbin, Fort William PH33 6RR. Ⓒ **01397/702-268.** Fax 01397/704-099. 92 units, 80 with private bathroom. £36–£42 ($54–$63) double without bathroom; £65–£93 ($97.50–$139.50) double with bathroom. Rates include Scottish breakfast. MC, V. Closed Nov–Mar. Take A82 for 2½ miles (4km) south of town. **Amenities:** Dining room, lounge; laundry. *In room:* TV, coffeemaker, hair dryer, no phone.

Lime Tree Studio Gallery   This well-kept B&B is housed in what is reputed to be the oldest fully surviving building in Fort William. It was built in the early 1800s in the town center as the manse (pastor's residence) for the nearby Church of Scotland. Today, it offers pastel guest rooms (with small, shower-only bathrooms) and exhibition space for local painters, including respected artist David Wilson.

Achintore Rd., Fort William PH33 6RQ. Ⓒ **01397/701-806.** www.limetreestudio.co.uk. 5 units, 3 with private bathroom. £30–£32 ($45–$48) double without bathroom; £36–£45 ($54–$67.50) double with bathroom. AE, DC, MC, V. *In room:* TV, coffeemaker, hair dryer (on request), no phone.

Lochview Guest House *(Value*   South from the center of Fort William and about a 15-minute walk uphill is this guesthouse, designed around 1950. The guest rooms have been outfitted with comfortable furnishings by Denise and Alan Kirk, who maintain the acre (0.41 hectare) of lawn surrounding their building and protect the view sweeping down over the loch and the rest of the town. Each unit comes with a small, shower-only bathroom. Other guesthouses in town might be more historic—but for the price, Lochview represents good value, and the Kirk family is unfailingly generous. No smoking is permitted.

Heathercroft, Argyll Rd., Fort William PH33 6RE. Ⓒ and fax **01397/703-149.** www.lochview.co.uk. 8 units. £44–£54 ($66–$81) double. Rates include breakfast. MC, V. Closed Nov–Mar. *In room:* TV, no phone.

DINING

Crannog Seafood Restaurant SEAFOOD   Occupying a converted ticket office and bait store in a quayside setting overlooking Loche Linnhe, this restaurant serves seafood so fresh, locals claim "it fairly leaps at you." Much of the fish comes from the owners' own fishing vessels or from their smokehouse. Bouillabaisse is a specialty, as are Loch Linnhe prawns and langoustines. A vegetarian dish of the day is invariably featured.

Town Pier. © 01397/705-589. Reservations recommended. Main courses £9.95–£16.50 ($14.95–$24.75). MC, V. Daily noon–2:30pm and 6–9:30pm. Closed Jan 1–2 and Dec 25–26.

Inverlochy Castle 🌺🌺🌺 BRITISH   This is one of the grandest restaurants in Britain (as it should be, at these prices!). The cuisine here has been celebrated ever since Queen Victoria got a sudden attack of the munchies and stopped in "for a good tuck-in." The kitchen uses carefully selected local ingredients, including salmon from Spean, crayfish from Loch Linnhe, and produce from the hotel's own gardens. Partridge and grouse are offered in season, and roast filet of Aberdeen Angus beef is a classic. The chefs also do their own baking, and their specialty, an orange soufflé, may be the best we've ever tasted. Dinner is served in rooms decorated with period and elaborate furniture presented as gifts to Inverlochy Castle from the king of Norway. The formal service is the finest in the Highlands.

Torlundy, Fort William PH33 6SN. © 01397/702-177. Reservations required. Fixed-price lunch £29.50 ($44.25); fixed-price dinner £48 ($72). AE, MC, V. Daily 12:30–1:45pm and 7–9:15pm. Closed Jan–Feb.

FORT WILLIAM AFTER DARK

Ben Nevis Pub, 103–109 High St. (© **01397/702-295**), offers free entertainment by rock, blues, jazz, and folk bands on Thursday and Friday. **Grog & Gruel,** 66 High St. (© **01397/705-078**), serves up regional cask-conditioned ales. There's an occasional live band, ranging from rock and pop to folk and Scottish music.

McTavish's Kitchen, High Street (© **01397/702-406**), puts on a Scottish show just for tourists. It's fun but corny, featuring tartan-clad dancers, bagpipes, and other traditional instruments every night between May and September. You can see the show with or without dinner. A three-course "Taste of Scotland" meal costs £14.95 ($22.45). The cover for the show is £1.75 ($2.65) for adults and £1 ($1.50) for children if you're eating; the show alone is £3.50 ($5.25) for adults and £1.75 ($2.65) for children.

3 Mallaig ⍟: Gateway to the Isle of Skye & the Hebrides

179 miles (288km) NW of Edinburgh, 47 miles (76km) NW of Fort William, 96 miles (154.5km) NW of Oban

People visit the small fishing village of Mallaig mainly because it's the departure point for the Isle of Skye (see chapter 11). Most of the fun of Mallaig is getting here, as the road from Fort William is one of the more scenic in Scotland. Steamers call here for the Kyle of Lochalsh, the Isle of Skye, the Outer Hebrides, and the sea lochs of the northwest coast. At the tip of a peninsula, Mallaig is surrounded by moody lochs and hills.

ESSENTIALS

GETTING THERE   **Trains** from Fort William to Mallaig take you along one of the most panoramic routes in Scotland; the trip is a marvelous experience in and of itself. Four trains per day make the 1½- to 2-hour run; service drops to one train on Sundays in winter. A one-way ticket costs about £7.40 ($11.10). Call © 08457/550-033 for departure times.

Two **buses** per day run to Mallaig from Fort William (a 90-minute trip); a one-way ticket costs £4.80 to £5 ($7.20 to $7.50). Call **Sheil Buses** (© 01967/431-272) for departure times.

If you're **driving** from Fort William, take A830, the scenic road, west to Mallaig.

VISITOR INFORMATION   The **tourist office** (© 01687/462-170) is in the center of Mallaig, on Main Street; look for signs. April through June, September, and October, it's open Monday through Saturday from 10am to 6:30pm and Sunday from 10am to 4pm; July and August, hours are Monday through Saturday from 10am to 6:30pm and Sunday from 10am to 5pm; November through March, it's open Monday, Wednesday, and Friday from 10am to 2pm.

EXPLORING THE AREA

If you find yourself with time to spare while waiting for a ferry departure, you can visit **Mallaig Marine World,** at the Harbour (© 01687/462-292), which has the finest collection of sea creatures from the Sound of Sleat. It's open daily in June from 9am to 6pm and July through August from 9am to 7pm. Admission is £2.75 ($4.15).

If you have a lot more time, consider contacting **Bruce Watt Sea Cruises,** Western Isles Guest House © 01687/462-320). This outfitter conducts cruises up the Sound of Sleat, the body of water separating the Isle of Skye from the Scottish mainland. Passengers enjoy panoramic vistas of the lochs Hourn and Nevis. The cost ranges between £8 and £12 ($12 and $18).

If you have a car, you can take an unmarked road immediately south of Mallaig, going to the remote **Loch Morar,** at some 1,000 feet (303m) known as the deepest lake in the country. This remote part of the Highlands makes for a lovely walk.

ACCOMMODATIONS & DINING

Marine Hotel   This family-owned business is in the vicinity of the train station. All of the comfortably furnished but basic guest rooms contain firm beds and small, shower-only bathrooms. Guests gather in the cocktail bar or TV lounge after enjoying a home-cooked meal, usually locally caught seafood.

10 Station Rd, Mallaig PH41 4PY. © 01687/462-217. Fax 01687/462-821. www.road-to-the-isles.org.uk/marine-hotel.html. 19 units. £56–£64 ($84–$96) double. Rates include Scottish breakfast. Half-board £42–£45 ($63–$67.50) per person. MC, V. **Amenities:** Restaurant, bar, TV lounge. *In room:* TV, coffeemaker, hair dryer, no phone.

Springbank Guest House   On the eastern outskirts of town, across the coastal road from the harbor, this white-painted stone house dates from 1900. A newer wing is now the site of the comfortable guest lounge. Views from the somewhat spartan but well-scrubbed rooms encompass the coastline of Skye; some have a sloping garret-style ceiling. Each unit comes with a small, shower-only bathroom. Your hosts are members of the Smith family, who enjoy socializing at breakfast and will prepare a moderately priced dinner on request.

East Bay, Mallaig PH141 4QF. © and fax 01687/462-459. www.road-to-the-isles.org.uk/springbank.html. 7 units, none with private bathroom. £32–£36 ($48–$54) double. Rates include breakfast. MC, V. **Amenities:** Restaurant, guest lounge. *In room:* TV, coffeemaker, no phone.

4 Invergarry

25 miles (40km) NE of Fort William, 158 (254km) miles NW of Edinburgh

A Highland center for fishing and for exploring Glen Mor and Loch Ness, Invergarry is noted for its fine scenery. At Invergarry, the road through the western Highland glens and mountains begins, forming one part of the famous "Road to the Isles" that terminates at Kyle of Lochalsh. If you're rushed for time, you can easily skip this place. Most people stop off here to stay at the Glengarry Castle Hotel, which looks haunted and even has the ruins of a long-abandoned castle on its grounds.

ESSENTIALS

GETTING THERE   The nearest **rail service** runs to Fort William, where you'll have to take a connecting bus to get to Invergarry, a half-hour ride away. **Highland Omnibuses** offer this service. The tourist office in Fort William can provide schedules. If you're **driving** from Fort William, proceed north on the Inverness road (A82) to Invergarry.

VISITOR INFORMATION   The nearest **tourist office** is in Fort William (see "Fort William: Gateway to Ben Nevis," earlier in this chapter).

SEEING THE SIGHTS

From Invergarry, drive 3½ miles (5.5km) south, following A82 toward Fort William if you want to visit the 1812 monument **Well of the Heads** (*Tobar nan Ceann* in Gaelic). The only sign indicating the well's position is a grocery store (Well of the Seven Heads Grocery & Convenience Mart). At the store, a staff member will direct you down a short forest path to the well itself. The well was erected by MacDonnell of Glengarry to commemorate the decapitation of seven brothers who had murdered the two sons of a 17th-century chief of Clan Keppoch, a branch of the MacDonnells at Glengarry. An obelisk supports the bronzed heads of the seven victims. The legend of the well, alas, is more exciting than the actual site.

On the grounds of Glengarry Castle Hotel (see below), you can see the meager ruins of **Invergarry Castle**, the stronghold of the MacDonnells of Glengarry. A few grim walls remain. The site of the castle on Raven's Rock, overlooking Loch Oich in the Great Glen, was a strategic one in the days of clan feuds and Jacobite risings. Because the castle ruins aren't safe, you can view them only from outside. From Invergarry, drive 1½ miles (2.5km) south, following A82 toward Fort William, then turn off to follow the signs pointing to the hotel. The ruins lie beside the hotel's very long main driveway, surrounded by trees.

ACCOMMODATIONS & DINING

Glengarry Castle Hotel   This 1866–69 mansion, with gables and chimneys, is an impressive sight on the River Garry; on the extensive grounds are the ruins of Invergarry Castle (see above). Glengarry makes a pleasant base for fishing, tennis, walking, and rowing. The midsize to spacious guest rooms are comfortably old-fashioned, like something from the 1950s, and each comes with a small bathroom with tub. The dining room offers good, home-cooked, but rather basic meals. Nightly fixed-price dinners are rather high-priced. Affordable light lunches are served, but the special Sunday version is more elaborate and expensive.

Invergarry PH35 4HW. ☎ **01809/501-254.** Fax 01809/501-207. www.glengarry.net. 26 units. £90–£140 ($135–$210) double. Rates include Scottish breakfast. MC, V. From Invergarry, drive 1½ miles (2.5km) south, following A82 toward Fort William; turn off to follow signs pointing to the hotel. **Amenities:** Restaurant, 2 bars; tennis court. *In room:* TV, coffeemaker, hair dryer.

5 Aviemore ⊘★

129 miles (208km) N of Edinburgh, 29 miles (47km) SE of Inverness, 85 miles (137km) N of Perth

A bit tacky for our tastes, Aviemore, a year-round resort on the Spey, was opened in 1966 in the heart of the Highlands, at the foot of the historic rock of **Craigellachie.** The center of Aviemore itself, with ugly concrete structures, has little of the flavor of Scotland. But visitors flock here for its accessibility to some of the most beautiful scenery in the Highlands, especially the Cairngorm Mountains, known for its skiing in winter and hiking in summer.

ESSENTIALS

GETTING THERE   Aviemore, on the main Inverness–Edinburgh rail line, is the area's major transportation hub. Some 12 **trains** a day from Inverness (a 45-minute ride) pass through; the fare is £11 ($16.50) one-way. Twelve trains per day also arrive from Glasgow or Edinburgh. Trip time from each city is 3 hours, and a one-way ticket from either is £30 ($45). For rail schedules in Aviemore, call ⓒ **01479/810-221.**

Aviemore is on the main Inverness–Edinburgh **bus** line, with frequent service. The trip from Edinburgh takes about 3 hours (ⓒ **0990/808-080** in Edinburgh for schedules) and costs £4.90 ($7.35). Frequent buses throughout the day also arrive from Inverness, a 40-minute ride.

If you're **driving** from Edinburgh, after crossing the Forth Bridge Road, take M90 to Perth, then continue the rest of the way along A9 into Aviemore.

VISITOR INFORMATION   The **Highlands of Scotland Tourist Office** (Aviemore branch) is on Grampian Road (ⓒ **01479/810-363**). It's open from June to August, Monday through Friday from 9am to 7pm, Saturday from 9am to 6pm, and Sunday from 10am to 5pm; and September to May, Monday through Friday from 9am to 5pm and Saturday and Sunday from 10am to 5pm.

EXPLORING THE AREA

North of Aviemore, the **Strathspey Railway,** Dalfaber Road (ⓒ **01479/810-725**), is your best bet in Scotland to learn firsthand what it was like to ride the rails in the 19th century. The railway follows the valley of the River Spey between Boat of Garten and Aviemore, a distance of 5 miles (8km). The train is drawn by a coal-burning steam locomotive. The newest locomotive used was made nearly 4 decades ago, while the oldest is of 1899 vintage. The trip is meant to re-create the total experience of travel on a Scottish steam railway that once carried wealthy Victorians toward their hunting lodges in North Britain. The round-trip takes about an hour. The rail station at Boat of Garten, where you can board the train, has also been restored.

Round-trip passage costs £8 ($12) first-class or £5.60 ($8.40) third-class. Schedules change frequently, but from July to the end of August, trains make five round-trips daily. From May to June and September, they run daily, and from March to April and October they run Saturday, Sunday, Wednesday, and Thursday. There's no regular service in winter; however, special Christmas-season trips are made during which Santa Claus makes an appearance. To complete the experience, you can wine and dine aboard on Wednesdays in July and August, when a single-seating casual lunch is served; the cost for the fare and meal is £17.50 ($26.25). Reservations must be made for the meals. The dining car is a replica of a Pullman parlor car. For reservations and hours of departure, call ⓒ **01479/831-692.**

For the grandest view of the Cairngorm peaks, take the **Cairngorm Chairlift** (© **01479/861-261**), whose lowest section is 10 miles (16km) east of Aviemore. A round-trip passage on the longest chairlift in Scotland costs £6 ($9) for adults and £3.60 ($5.40) for children. In summer, the lift runs daily from 9am to 5pm (to 5:30pm July and Aug). In winter, hours are daily from 9am to 4pm; the uppermost reaches are closed during periods of high winds. The highest section is 4,084 feet (1,239m) above sea level. On a clear summer day, you can see Ben Nevis in the west, and the vista of Strathspey is spectacular, from Loch Morlich in the Rothiemurchus Forest to the Spey Valley.

Skiers are attracted to the area any time after October, when snow can be expected. You can rent ski equipment and clothing at the day lodge at the main Cairngorm parking area. Weather patterns can change quickly in the Cairngorm massif; call the above number for a report on the latest conditions. To reach the area, take A951, branching off from A9 at Aviemore, then head for the parking area at the day lodge.

If you'd like to explore the countryside on two wheels, **Speyside Sports,** Main Street (© **01479/810-656**), charges rates of £6 ($9) for a half day, £10 ($15) for a full day, and £35 ($52.50) for 6 days. **Bothy Bikes,** 81 Grampian Rd. (© **01479/810-111**), has rates of £10 ($15) for a half day and £14 ($21) for a full day.

The tourist office can give you hiking maps and offer advice, especially about weather conditions. One of the best trails is reached by following B9760 to the signposted **Glen More Forest Park,** in the vicinity of Loch Morlich.

ACCOMMODATIONS

Aviemore Highlands Hotel   This resort hotel caters to an outdoorsy clientele. It's a labyrinthine complex of wings, staircases, and long halls, which funnel into public rooms with big windows overlooking the countryside. In summer, doors open to reveal flagstone terraces ringed with viburnum and juniper. You can drink in the Illicit Still Bar, which has an antique whisky still and copper-top tables. The main restaurant is capped with a soaring ceiling, trussed with beams. The midsize guest rooms are well furnished, and some family rooms are also available. The bathrooms are tidily organized, some with shower only. You can use all the leisure and sports facilities at the Red McGregor.

Aviemore Mountain Resort, Aviemore PH22 1PJ. © **01479/810-771.** Fax 01479/811-473. www.aviehighlands. demon.co.uk. 103 units. £70–£100 ($105–$150) double. Rates include Scottish breakfast. AE, DC, MC, V. **Amenities:** Restaurant, bar; access to nearby leisure and sports facilities; room service; laundry. *In room:* TV, coffeemaker, hair dryer.

Corrour House Hotel ℛ *(Finds*   This isolated granite house is an oasis of personality in a sea of impersonal hotels. Built around 1880 on 4 acres (1.6 hectares) of forest and garden, it contains simple but comfortable rooms that are attractively decorated, each with a shower-only bathroom. Your hosts are the Catto family, who will prepare dinner if arranged in advance. Many of their dishes have a true "taste of Scotland" flavor, including Ballindalloch pheasant with a sauce made from red wine, oranges, red currants, and fresh herbs.

On B970, Inverdruie by Aviemore PH22 1QH. © **01479/810-220.** Fax 01479/811-500. www. corrourhousehotel.co.uk 8 units. £80 ($120) double. Rates include breakfast. AE, MC, V. Closed mid-Nov to Christmas. From Aviemore, drive ½ mile (1km) east, following the signs to Glenmore. **Amenities:** Dining room. *In room:* TV, coffeemaker.

Hilton Aviemore ℛ *(Kids*   This is the resort's best hotel because of its extensive sports and leisure facilities, spead across 65 acres (26.3 hectares) of tree-studded grounds. The midsize guest rooms are spacious and well appointed, with comfortable furnishings and average-size bathrooms, some with both tub and shower. You have a choice of two dining rooms, although the food is fairly standard. There's often evening entertainment, particularly on weekends. In winter, downhill and cross-country ski equipment and lessons are available. The sports and leisure hall's Fun House caters to children.

Rothiemurchus, Aviemore PH22 1QN. © **01479/810-661.** Fax 01479/811-309. www.hilton.com. 175 units. £120 ($180) double; £170 ($255) suite. Half-board rates available for a minimum 2-night stay. AE, DC, MC, V. **Amenities:** 2 restaurants; bar; 2 heated pools; Jacuzzi; sauna; steam bath; game room; salon; room service; babysitting; laundry. *In room:* TV, coffeemaker, hair dryer.

Lynwilg House ⟨⋆⟩   The Victorian solidity of this house is particularly noteworthy in Aviemore, considering the relative modernity of the other resort hotels. It was built by the duke of Richmond in the 1880s. Today, it retains 4 acres of its original park and gardens overlooking the mountains, with high-ceilinged (1.6 hectares) guest rooms containing comfortable furnishings and shower-only bathrooms. In front of the house is a croquet lawn, and at the bottom of the well-tended garden is a stream where guests like to relax.

Rte. A9, Aviemore PH22 1PZ. © **01479/811-685.** www.lynwilg.co.uk. 4 units. £60–£70 ($90–$105) double. Rates include breakfast. MC, V. Follow A9 for 1½ miles (2.5km) south of Aviemore's center, following the signs to Perth. **Amenities:** Dining room. *In room:* TV, coffeemaker, no phone.

DINING

The Bar/The Restaurant SCOTTISH   Although the golf course, health club, and leisure facilities of this country club are open only to members, visitors are welcome in the cozy bar and restaurant, which is outfitted in tartan carpets and heavy brocade curtains. In the bar, where live entertainment is featured nightly, the fare includes venison cutlets, sandwiches, steak pies, and a variety of malt whiskies. The restaurant serves seafood, such as skewered tiger prawns soaked with butter, as well as grilled Angus steaks, main-course salads, and a limited number of vegetarian dishes. Several nights per week, the restaurant hosts theme nights with entertainment.

In the Dalfaber Golf and Country Club, about 1 mile (1.6km) north of the center of Aviemore. © **01479/ 811-244.** Reservations required in restaurant. Golfer's menu (Thurs only) £6 ($9); Sun lunch £5.95 ($8.95); bar platters £4.75–£7.95 ($7.15–$11.95). MC, V. Restaurant Mon–Sat 7:30–9:30pm, Sun noon–9:30pm; bar daily 11am–11pm.

AVIEMORE AFTER DARK

Crofters, off Grampian Road at the Aviemore Mountain Resort (© **01479/ 810-771**), a 2-minute walk from the center of Aviemore, has dancing nightly from 10pm to 1am, with guest DJs bringing in their own music and setting the mood. No cover is charged.

6 Along Loch Ness ⟨⋆⟩⟨⋆⟩

Sir Peter Scott's *Nessitera rhombopteryx,* one of the world's great mysteries, continues to elude her pursuers. The Loch Ness monster, or "Nessie" as she's more familiarly known, has captured the imagination of the world, drawing thousands of visitors yearly to Loch Ness. Half a century ago, A82 was built alongside the banks of the loch's western shores, and since then many more sightings have been claimed.

All types of high-tech underwater contraptions have gone in after the Loch Ness monster, but no one can find her in spite of the photographs and film footage you might have seen in magazines or on TV. Dr. Robert Rines and his associates at the Academy of Applied Science in Massachusetts maintain an all-year watch with sonar-triggered cameras and strobe lights suspended from a raft in Urquhart Bay. However, some people in Inverness aren't keen on collaring the monster, and you can't blame them: An old prophecy predicts a violent end for Inverness if the monster is ever captured.

The loch is 24 miles (39km) long, 1 mile (1.6km) wide, and some 755 feet (229m) deep. If you'd like to stay along the loch and monster-watch instead of basing yourself at Inverness, we've listed some choices below. Even if the monster doesn't put in an appearance, you'll enjoy the scenery. In summer, you can take boat cruises across Loch Ness from both Fort Augustus and Inverness.

If you're driving, take A82 between Fort Augustus and Inverness running along Loch Ness. Buses from either Fort Augustus or Inverness also traverse A82, taking you to Drumnadrochit.

DRUMNADROCHIT

The bucolic village of Drumnadrochit is about a mile (1.6km) from Loch Ness at the entrance to Glen Urquhart. It's the nearest village to the part of the loch in which sightings of the monster have been reported most frequently.

Although most visitors arrive at Drumnadrochit to see the Loch Ness monster exhibit (see below), you can also take an offbeat adventure in the great outdoors at the **Highland Riding Centre,** Borlum Farm (✆ **01456/450-220**). This is an 850-acre (344.3-hectare) sheep farm on moorlands overlooking Loch Ness; follow A82 for about 14 miles (22.5km) west of Inverness and make a reservation in advance. One- to 2-hour tours depart almost daily, depending on demand, and cost £14 to £23 ($21 to $34.50).

Wilderness Cycles, The Cottage (✆ **01456/450-223**), will rent you a bike so you can go exploring on your own. Rentals are £7 ($10.50) per half day, £12 ($18) per day, and £50 ($75) per week. It's open daily from 9am to 6pm.

Official Loch Ness Monster Exhibition This is Drumnadrochit's big attraction, featuring a scale replica of Nessie. It opened in 1980 and has been packing 'em in ever since. Follow Nessie's story from A.D. 565 to the present in photographs, audio, and video, and then climb aboard the sonar research vessel *John Murray.* This is the most visited place in the Highlands of Scotland, with more than 200,000 visitors annually.

Drumnadrochit. (✆ **01456/450-573**. Admission £5.95 ($8.95) adults, £4.50 ($6.75) students, £3.50 ($5.25) seniors and children 7–16, £14.95 ($22.45) per family. Easter–May daily 9:30am–5pm; June and Sept daily 9:30am–6pm; July–Aug daily 9am–8pm; Oct daily 9:30am–5:30pm; Nov–Easter daily 10am–4pm.

Urquhart Castle This ruined castle, one of Scotland's largest, is on a promontory overlooking Loch Ness. The chief of Clan Grant owned the castle in 1509, and most of the extensive ruins date from that period. In 1692, the castle was blown up by the Grants to prevent it from becoming a Jacobite stronghold. Rising from crumbling walls, the jagged keep still remains. It's at Urquhart Castle that sightings of the Loch Ness monster are most often reported.

Loch Ness along A82. (✆ **01456/450-551**. Admission £3.80 ($5.70) adults, £2.80 ($4.20) seniors, £1.20 ($1.80) children. Apr–Sept daily 9:30am–6:30pm (to 8:30pm July–Aug); Oct–Mar daily 9:30am–3:45pm. Drive 1½ miles (2.5km) southeast of Drumnadrochit on A82.

ACCOMMODATIONS & DINING

Polmaily House Hotel ℛ   This is a snug haven in a sea of Loss Ness tourism and overcommercialization. The Edwardian inn, on an 18-acre (7.3-hectare)

Ⓘ Spotting Nessie

She's affectionately known as Nessie, but her more formal name is *Nessitera rhombopteryx*, and she has the unflattering appellation of the Loch Ness monster. Is she the beast that never was, or the world's most famous living animal? You decide. Real or imagined, she's Scotland's virtual mascot, and even if she doesn't exist, she's one of the major attractions of the country. Who can drive along the dark waters of Loch Ness without staring at the murky depths and expecting a head or a couple of humps to appear above the water's surface at any minute?

Nessie's lineage is ancient. An appearance in A.D. 565 was recorded by respected 7th-century biographer St. Adamnan, not known as a spinner of tall tales. The claim is that St. Columba was en route along Loch Ness to convert Brude, king of the Picts, to Christianity. The saint ordered a monk to swim across the loch and retrieve a boat. However, as he was in midswim, Nessie attacked. The monk's life was saved only when Columba confronted the sea beast with a sign of the cross and a shouted invocation.

Columba's calming effect on Nessie must have lasted over the centuries, because no attacks have been reported since. Of course, there was that accident in the 1500s when a chronicle reported that "a terrible beast issuing out of the water early one morning about midsummer knocked down trees and killed three men with its tail." Again, in 1961, 30 hotel guests reported seeing two humps that rose out of the water just before their craft exploded and sank. Bertram Mill has offered £20,000 ($30,000) to have the monster delivered alive to his circus.

Because Scotland is the land not only of Nessie but also whisky, it might be assumed that some of these sightings were hallucinations brought on by the consumption of far too many "wee drams." However, sightings have come from people of impeccable credentials who were stone sober. Nessie seems to like to show herself to monks, perhaps a tradition dating from St. Columba. Several monks at the Fort Augustus Abbey claim to have seen her. A monk who's an organist at Westminster Cathedral reported a sighting in 1973.

Belief in Nessie's existence is so strong that midget yellow submarines and all types of high-tech underwater contraptions have been used in an attempt to track her down. Many photographs exist—most of them faked—usually from the site of the ruins of Urquhart Castle on the loch's shore. Other photographs haven't been so easily explained.

If Nessie does exist, exactly who is she? A sole survivor from prehistoric times? A gigantic sea snake? It has even been suggested she's a cosmic wanderer through time. Chances are you won't see her on your visit, but you can see a fantasy replica of the sea beast at the Official Loch Ness Monster Exhibition at Drumnadrochit.

estate with mixed gardens and woodland, is believed to have been built in 1776 and now re-creates manorial country-house living. The spacious and elegant guest rooms contain tasteful antiques, high ceilings, leaded-glass windows, and flowered wallpaper. The restaurant attracts locals as well as hotel guests with dishes like Aberdeen beef and fresh salmon.

Drumnadrochit IV3 6XT. ℂ **01456/450-343.** Fax 01456/450-813. 14 units. www.polmaily.co.uk. £104–£136 ($156–$204) double. Rates include Scottish breakfast. MC, V. Drive 2 miles (3km) west of Drumnadrochit on A831. **Amenities:** Restaurant; heated indoor pool; tennis court; small gym; croquet lawn; sauna. In room: TV, coffeemaker.

FORT AUGUSTUS

Fort Augustus, 36 miles (58km) south of Inverness along A82 and 166 miles (267km) northwest of Edinburgh, stands at the head (the southernmost end) of Loch Ness. The town became fortified after the 1715 Jacobite rising. Gen. George Wade, of road- and bridge-building fame, headquartered here in 1724, and in 1729, the government constructed a fort along the banks of the loch, naming it Augustus after William Augustus, duke of Cumerland, son of George II. Jacobites seized the fort in 1745 and controlled it until the Scottish defeat at Culloden. Now gone, Wade's fort was turned into the Fort Augustus Abbey at the south end of Loch Ness. A Benedictine order was installed in 1867, and the monks today run a Catholic secondary school on the site.

Fort Augustus is mainly a refueling stop for those who want to stay on Loch Ness itself—perhaps in hopes of seeing the monster—instead of dropping anchor in a larger town like Fort William to the south or Inverness to the north. The only other reason to stop by is that it's the most panoramic place to see the locks of the Caledonian Canal in action.

Bisecting the actual village of Fort Augustus, the locks of the **Caledonian Canal** are a popular attraction when boats are passing through. Running across the loftiest sections of Scotland, the canal was constructed between 1803 and 1822. Almost in a straight line, it makes its way from Inverness in the north to Corpach in the vicinity of Fort William. The canal is 60 miles (97km) long: 22 man-made miles (35.5km), and the rest are natural lochs.

Caley Cruisers, Canal Road, Inverness (ℂ **01463/236-328;** fax 01463/714-879; www.caleycruisers.co.uk), maintains a fleet of 50 cruisers (with skippers) that groups of two to six people can rent from March to October—even if their marine experience is relatively limited. Rentals last for 1 week, long enough to negotiate the 60 miles (97km) of the Caledonian Canal in both directions between Inverness and Fort William. (There are about 15 locks en route; tolls are included in the rental fee). Depending on the craft's size and the season, a week's rental ranges from £377 to £1,468 ($565.50 to $2,202); the cost of fuel and taxes for a week is £60 to £80 ($90 to $120), plus another £40 ($60) for a reasonably priced insurance policy. Except for the waters of Loch Ness, which can be rough, the canal is calm enough and doesn't pose the dangers of cruising on the open sea.

ACCOMMODATIONS & DINING

Inchnacardoch Lodge   Inchnacardoch Lodge is a family-run hotel in a panoramic setting overlooking Loch Ness, half a mile (1km) north of the town center. Once a country residence of the Fraser clan's chief, Lord Lovat, the hotel offers comfortable guest rooms along with efficiently organized bathrooms, most with combination tub/showers. The common areas have recently been refurbished, but the traditional ambience remains. You can relax in the bar while watching the waters for the mysterious monster; a wee dram of malt too much and you may just find her. If you can tear yourself away from the view of the water, the hotel restaurant offers moderately priced main courses. No smoking is permitted.

Hwy. A82, Fort Augustus PH32 4BL. ℰ **01320/366-258.** Fax 10320/366-248. lochness97@aol.com. 15 units. £64–£76 ($96–$114) double. Rates include Scottish breakfast. AE, DC, MC, V. **Amenities:** Restaurant, bar, lounge. *In room:* TV, coffeemaker, hair dryer.

7 Inverness ⭐: Capital of the Highlands

156 miles (251km) NW of Edinburgh, 134 miles (216km) NW of Dundee, 134 miles (216km) W of Aberdeen

The capital of the Highlands, Inverness is a royal burgh and seaport at the north end of Great Glen on both sides of the Ness River. For such a historic town, the sights are rather meager, but Inverness makes a good base for touring. If your time is limited, confine your visits to Culloden Battlefield, Cawdor Castle of *Macbeth* fame (see section 8, "Nairn & Cawdor Castle," later in this chapter), and Black Isle (see section 9, "The Black Isle Peninsula," later in this chapter), the most enchanting and scenic peninsula in Scotland.

ESSENTIALS

GETTING THERE   Domestic flights from various parts of Britain arrive at the **Inverness Airport.** Flight time from London's Heathrow to the Inverness/ Dalcross Airport is 1¾ hours. Call ℰ **01463/232-471** in Inverness for flight information.

Some five to seven **trains** per day arrive from Glasglow and Edinburgh (on Sun, two or three trains). The train takes 3½ hours from either city; a one-way fare from either is £33 ($49.50). Trains pull into Station Square, off Academy Street in Inverness (ℰ **0345/484-950** for schedules).

Scottish CityLink coaches provide service for the area (ℰ **0990/505-050** for schedules). Frequent service through the day is possible from either Edinburgh or Glasglow (a 4-hour trip each way), at a one-way fare of £12.50 ($18.75) or £12 ($18), respectively. The bus station is at Farraline Park, off Academy Street (ℰ **01463/233-371**).

If you're **driving** from Edinburgh, take M9 north to Perth, then follow along the Great North Road (A9) until you reach Inverness.

VISITOR INFORMATION   The Inverness branch of the **Highlands of Scotland Tourist Board** is at Castle Wynd, off Bridge Street (ℰ **01463/ 234-353**). It's open from October to mid-April, Monday through Friday from 9am to 5pm and Saturday from 10am to 4pm; mid-April to May, Monday through Friday from 9am to 5pm, Saturday from 9:30am to 5pm, and Sunday from 9:30am to 4pm; June, Monday through Friday from 9am to 6pm, Saturday from 9am to 5pm, and Sunday from 9:30am to 5pm; July and August, Monday through Saturday from 9am to 6pm and Sunday from 9:30am to 5pm; and September, Monday through Saturday from 9am to 6pm and Sunday from 9:30am to 5pm.

SPECIAL EVENTS   During July's **Highland Games,** with their sporting competitions and festive balls, the season in Inverness reaches its social peak. For information and exact dates, consult the tourist office (see above).

SEEING THE SIGHTS

Inverness is one of the oldest inhabited sites in Scotland. On **Craig Phadrig** are the remains of a vitrified fort, believed to date from the 4th century B.C. One of the most important prehistoric monuments in the north, the **Stones of Clava**

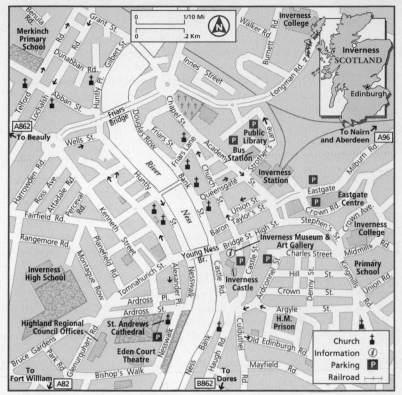

are about 6 miles (10km) east of Inverness on the road to Nairn. These cairns and standing stones are from the Bronze Age.

The old castle of Inverness stood to the east of the present street Castlehill, and the site still retains the name "Auld Castlehill." David I built the first stone castle in Inverness around 1141, and the **Clock Tower** is all that remains of a fort erected by Cromwell's army between 1652 and 1657. The rebellious Scots blew up the old castle in 1746 to keep it from falling to government troops, and the present **castle** was constructed by the Victorians in the 19th century. Today, this landmark houses the law courts of Inverness and local government offices.

The 16th-century **Abertarff House,** Church Street, is now the headquarters of An Comunn Gaidhealach, the Highland association that preserves the Gaelic language and culture. Opposite the town hall is the **Old Mercat Cross,** with its Stone of the Tubs, said to be the stone on which women rested their washtubs as they ascended from the river. Known as "Clachnacudainn," the lozenge-shaped stone was the spot where local early kings were crowned.

St. Andrew's Cathedral (1866–69), Ardross Street, is the northernmost diocese of the Scottish Episcopal church and a fine example of Victorian architecture, both imposing and richly decorated. Be sure to check out the icons given to Bishop Eden by the tsar of Russia. The cathedral is open daily from 8:30am to 6pm. For information, get in touch with the Provost, 15 Ardross St. (℃ **01463/233-535**).

Moments The Hill of the Fairies

West of the river rises the wooded hill of **Tomnahurich,** known as the "hill of the fairies." Now a cemetery, it's the best place to go for a country walk, with panoramic views. The boat-shaped hillock is immediately to the southwest of the center. In the Ness are wooded islands, linked to Inverness by suspension bridges, that have been turned into parks.

If you're interested in bus tours of the Highlands and cruises on Loch Ness, contact **Inverness Traction,** 6 Burnett Rd. (© **01463/239-292**). In summer, there are also cruises along the Caledonian Canal from Inverness into Loch Ness.

Shoppers might want to check out a family-owned shrine to Scottish kilt-making, **Duncan Chisholm & Sons,** 47–53 Castle St. (© **01463/234-599**). The tartans of at least 50 of Scotland's largest clans are available in the form of kilts and kilt jackets for men and women. A section is devoted to Scottish gifts and memorabilia. You can visit the on-premises workshop. The town's best jewelry store, with unique bangles and bracelets inspired by the decorative traditions of Celtic Scotland, is **D&H Norval,** 88 Church St. (© **01463/232-739**).

Golfers can head about 40 miles (64.5km) north to hit the links at the renowned **Royal Dornoch Golf Club** (see "Sutherland: The Gem of Scotland," later in this chapter for details). Closer at hand, the 5,451-yard (4,960m) **Torvean Golf Course,** Glen Q Road (© **01463/711-434**), offers an 18-hole, par-68 course with greens fees of £13.70 ($20.55) Monday through Thursday and £15.60 ($23.40) Friday through Sunday.

Inverness Museum and Art Gallery   This museum in the town center is a top attraction, its displays representing the social and natural history, archaeology, art, and culture of the Scottish Highlands, with special emphasis on the Inverness district. Don't miss the important collection of Highland silver and reconstructed silversmith's workshop, displays on the life of the clans, a reconstruction of a local taxidermist's workshop, and a reconstructed 1920s Inverness kitchen.

Castle Wynd, off Bridge St. © **01463/237-114.** Free admission. Mon–Sat 9am–5pm.

Culloden Battlefield ⚘   At Culloden Battlefield, Bonnie Prince Charlie and the Jacobite army were finally crushed on April 16, 1746. A path leads from the visitor center through the Field of the English, where 52 men of the duke of Cumberland's forces who died during the battle are said to be buried. Features of interest include the **Graves of the Clans,** communal burial places with simple stones bearing individual clan names; the great **memorial cairn,** erected in 1881; the **Well of the Dead;** and the huge **Cumberland Stone,** from which the victorious "Butcher" Cumberland is said to have reviewed the scene. The battle lasted only 40 minutes; the prince's army lost some 1,200 men out of 5,000, and the king's army 300 of 9,000. In the visitor center is an audiovisual presentation on the background and history of the famous battle. Also on the premises are a restaurant and bookshop.

Culloden Moor, 6 miles (10km) southeast of Inverness. © **01463/790-607** for visitor center. Admission to visitor center £3.50 ($5.25) adults, £2.50 ($3.75) seniors and children, £8.90 ($13.35) per family. Visitor center Feb–Mar and Nov–Dec daily 10am–4pm; Apr–Oct daily 9am–6pm.

Queen's Own Highlanders Regimental Museum at Fort George   Fort George was called the "most considerable fortress and best situated in Great

Britain" in 1748 by Lt. Col. James Wolfe, who went on to fame as Wolfe of Quebec. Built after the Battle of Culloden, the fort was occupied by the Hanoverian army of George II and is still an active army barracks. The rampart, almost a mile (1.6km) around, encloses some 42 acres (6.1 hectares). Dr. Samuel Johnson and James Boswell visited here in 1773 on their Highland trek. The fort contains the Queen's Own Highlanders Regimental Museum, with regimental exhibits from 1778 to today.

On Moray Firth by the village of Ardersier, 11 miles (18km) northeast of Inverness, 8 miles (13km) northwest of Cawdor along B9006. © **01463/224380.** Free admission. Apr–Sept daily 10am–6pm; Oct–Mar Mon–Fri 10am–4pm.

ACCOMMODATIONS
EXPENSIVE
Bunchrew House Hotel and Restaurant ☆ This fine Scottish mansion on the shores of Beauly Firth is the ancestral home of both the Fraser and the McKenzie clans. The house dates to 1621 and is set on 15 acres (6.1 hectares) of landscaped gardens. You'll get a glimpse of a bygone era while relaxing in the paneled drawing room with roaring log fires. The guest rooms are individually decorated; the Lovat Suite, for example, has a canopied four-poster bed. Some bathrooms contain showers only. Guests can dine in the candlelit restaurant on prime Scottish beef, fresh lobster and crayfish, local game, and fresh vegetables.

Bunchrew, Inverness, Inverness-shire IV3 8TA. © **01463/234-917.** Fax 01463/710-620. www.bunchrew-inverness.co.uk. 11 units. £140–£195 ($210–$292.50) suite for 2. Rates include Scottish breakfast. AE, MC, V. Drive 3 miles (5km) west of Inverness on A862. **Amenities:** Restaurant; free fishing on the estate; room service; babysitting; laundry. *In room:* TV, fridge, coffeemaker, hair dryer, iron.

Culloden House ☆☆ This is the most elegant country retreat in the area. Culloden House, a Georgian mansion with a much-photographed Adam facade, includes part of the Renaissance castle in which Bonnie Prince Charlie slept the night before Culloden, the last great battle on British soil. Superbly isolated, with extensive gardens and parkland, it's perfect for a relaxed Highland holiday. At the iron gates to the broad front lawn, a piper in full Highland garb often plays at sundown, the skirl of the bagpipe accompanied by the barking of house dogs. The prince of Wales and the crown prince of Japan have stayed here, perfectly at home among the exquisite furnishings and handsome plaster friezes. The cozy yet spacious guest rooms have sylvan views and a history-laden atmosphere.

Culloden, Inverness IV1 7BZ. © **01463/790-461.** Fax 01463/792-181. www.cullodenhouse.co.uk. 28 units. £190 ($285) double; £270 ($405) suite. Rates include Scottish breakfast. AE, DC, MC, V. Drive 3 miles (5km) east of Inverness on A96. **Amenities:** Restaurant; bar; tennis court; sauna; solarium; room service; laundry. *In room:* TV, coffeemaker, hair dryer.

Dunain Park Hotel ☆☆ The Dunain Park stands in 6 acres (2.4 hectares) of garden and woods between Loch Ness and Inverness. This 18th-century house is furnished with fine antiques, allowing it to retain its atmosphere of a private country house. Although Dunain Park has won its fame mainly as a restaurant (see "Dining," below), it does offer guest rooms with a host of thoughtful details and pretty furnishings. Each unit has a shower or tub bathroom.

Dunain Park, Inverness IV3 8JN. © **01463/230-512.** Fax 01463/224-532. www.Dunainparkhotel.co.uk. 13 units. £160–£208 ($240–$312) double or cottage; from £200 ($300) suite. Rates Include Scottish breakfast. AE, DC, MC, V. Drive 2 miles (3km) southwest of Inverness on A82. **Amenities:** Restaurant; bar; indoor heated pool; room service; babysitting; laundry. *In room:* TV, coffeemaker, hair dryer.

MODERATE

Glen Mhor Hotel   On the River Ness, this house of gables and bay windows is a hospitable family-run hotel. Many of the individually styled guest rooms have views of the river, castle, and cathedral; some are suitable for families. Some bathrooms contain showers only. In the Riverview Restaurant, you can enjoy such fine food as salmon caught right outside. The wine list is one of the best in the country.

9–12 Ness Bank, Inverness IV2 4SG. © **01463/234-308.** Fax 01463/713-170. www.glen-mhor.com. 45 units. £84–£102 ($126–$153) double; from £120 ($180) junior suite. Rates include Scottish breakfast. AE, DC, MC, V. **Amenities:** Restaurant, bistro bar; room service. *In room:* TV, dataport, coffeemaker, hair dryer.

Glenmoriston Town House Hotel ⚐ *Kids*   Set on the River Ness, a short walk from the town center, is this early-1900s stone-sided hotel. Rooms have been individually decorated and stylishly refurbished, with spacious private bathrooms with both tub and shower. Some accommodations have four-poster beds, and others are suitable for families. Guests enjoy temporary membership at a nearby squash and tennis club. Ristorante La Riviera (see "Dining," below) specializes in fine Italian cuisine.

20 Ness Bank, Inverness IV2 4SF. © **01463/223-777.** Fax 01463/712-378. www.glenmoriston.com. 15 units. £95–£135 ($142.50–$202.50) double. Rates include full Scottish breakfast. AE, MC, V. Free parking. **Amenities:** 2 restaurants, bar; access to nearby squash, tennis courts, gym, and sauna; room service; dry cleaning. *In room:* TV, fax, dataport, coffeemaker, hair dryer.

Inverness Marriott Hotel ⚐   Once a private mansion, this charming 18th-century country house sits on 4 acres (1.6 hectares) of woodland garden adjacent to an 18-hole golf course. The furnishings throughout are of high quality, and all guest rooms are attractively outfitted, each with tub or shower bathroom. The staff maintains the country-house atmosphere with an informal and hospitable style. The fish dishes at dinner are exceptional. Bar lunches and snack meals offer a wide choice, including Scottish fare. A notice in the lobby states that Robert Burns dined here in 1787 and the "Charles" who signed the guest register in 1982 was (you guessed it) the prince of Wales.

Culcabock Rd., Inverness IV2 3LP. © **01463/237-166.** Fax 01463/225-208. www.marriott.com. 82 units. £78–£98 ($117–$147) double; £148 ($222) suite. Rates include Scottish breakfast. Children under 14 stay free in parents' room. AE, DC, MC, V. Take Kingsmill Rd. 1 mile (1.6km) east of the center of Inverness. **Amenities:** Restaurant, bar; indoor pool; fitness room; spa; 3-hole minigolf course; room service; babysitting; laundry. *In room:* TV, coffeemaker, hair dryer.

The Royal Highland Hotel   It's like Inverness of yesterday at this somber gray-stone hotel, built in 1859 across from the train station to celebrate the arrival of rail lines connecting the Highlands, through Inverness, to the rest of Britain. Today, it's an antiques-strewn, slightly faded hotel, despite the gradual modernizations and the contemporary decor in half of the guest rooms (the other half is charmingly dowdy). Each unit has a shower or tub bathroom. The massive lobby contains the showiest staircase in Inverness. The dining room retains its elaborate high ceiling and a sense of the Victorian age. Seafood and shellfish are house specialties.

18 Academy St., Inverness IV1 1LG. © **01463/231-926.** Fax 01463/710-705. www.royalhighlandhotel.co.uk. 70 units. £99 ($148.50) double. Rates include breakfast. AE, DC, MC, V. **Amenities:** Restaurant, bar. *In room:* TV, coffeemaker, hair dryer.

INEXPENSIVE

Ballifeary House Hotel *Value*   This well-maintained 1876 Victorian stone villa, with a pleasant garden, is one of the area's better B&Bs. Mr. and Mrs. Luscombe, the owners, offer their guests individual attention. The rooms, although a bit small, are comfortably furnished, with shower-only bathrooms. This no-smoking hotel discourages families with small children.

10 Ballifeary Rd., Inverness IV3 5PJ. © **01463/235-572.** Fax 01463/717-583. www.ballifearyhousehotel. co.uk. 5 units. £70–£76 ($105–$114) double. Rates include Scottish breakfast. MC, V. Closed mid-Oct to Easter. *In room:* TV, coffeemaker, hair dryer, no phone.

Felstead Guest House ☆ *Finds* Right on the River Ness, this delightful discovery lies within walking distance of the heart of town. A Georgian structure of architectural interest, it was built in 1830 and has been extensively upgraded since then, though still retaining its original grace. The owners have decorated the rooms with taste and an eye toward comfort. The shower-only bathrooms are immaculately maintained. Thoughtful touches abound, such as freshly cut flowers and bubble baths. Scottish produce is featured at the morning breakfast.

18 Ness Bank. Inverness IV2 4SF. © and fax **01463/231634.** www.jafsoft.com/felstead/felstead.html. 8 units. £48–£68 ($72–$102) double. MC, V. *In room:* TV, no phone.

Ivybank Guest House *Value* This is one of the better B&Bs in town. Located off Castle Road about a 10-minute walk north of the town center, Ivybank was built in 1836 and retains its original fireplaces and an oak-paneled and beamed hall with a rosewood staircase. It features a walled garden and comfortably furnished guest rooms, each with hot and cold running water. Three units contain shower-only bathrooms. Mrs. Catherine Cameron is the gracious hostess, making guests feel at ease. Breakfast is the only meal served.

28 Old Edinburgh Rd., Inverness IV2 3HJ. © and fax **01463/232-796.** www.ivybankguesthouse.com. 5 units, 3 with private bathroom. £45–£50 ($67.50–$75) double without bathroom; £50–£55 ($75–$82.50) double with bathroom. Rates include Scottish breakfast. AE, DC, MC, V. Ample parking in the walled garden. *In room:* TV, coffeemaker, hair dryer, no phone.

Trafford Bank In a residential neighborhood about half a mile (1km) west of Invernesss center, this dignified sandstone house was built in 1873 as the manse for the Episcopal bishop. In 1994, when the bishop retired in a huff because of the ordination of women, the manse became available and was bought by Peter and Caroline McKenzie. Today, it's a B&B with five comfortable guest rooms (with shower-only bathrooms) and a social life revolving around copious Scottish breakfasts. The McKenzies work hard to make your stay pleasant; they provide complimentary pickup from the bus and train stations as well as the airport, fresh fruit and flowers in your room, and dinners if arranged in advance.

96 Fairfiled Rd., Invernesss IV3 5LL. © **0143/241-414.** 5 units. £70 ($105) double. Rates include breakfast. AE, MC, V. Bus: 19. From the town center, cross the Ness Bridge and turn right at the first traffic light. *In room:* TV, coffeemaker, hair dryer, no phone.

DINING

Café 1 INTERNATIONAL/SCOTTISH FUSION One of the most pleasant restaurants in town is in a century-old stone-fronted building on a street dotted with shops. Inside, you'll find varnished paneling, wooden tables, potted plants, and a soothing New Age atmosphere. Dine on generous portions of venison steak with bean spouts, beetroot, and red caramelized port jus; over-baked salmon on sweet potatoes with lime-cream sauce; and vegetarian tart studded with caramelized onions and zucchini. For dessert, try the dark-chocolate tart with white-chocolate shavings.

75 Castle St. © **01463/716-363.** Reservations recommended. Main courses £5–£6.50 ($7.50–$9.75) lunch; £7–£12.50 ($10.50–$18.75) dinner. MC, V, Mon–Sat noon–2pm and 6–9:30pm.

Dickens International Restaurant INTERNATIONAL   On a downtown street next to the oldest house in Inverness, Aberton House, this restaurant boasts a decor that has been revamped and updated with furnishings in the style created by Charlie Rennie Mackintosh (1868–1928), Scotland's most famous designer. A wide selection of European, Chinese, and international dishes is offered, including seafood and vegetarian options, Dickens's own steak, aromatic duck, and chateaubriand. The wide choice of side dishes ranges from fried rice to bean sprouts to cauliflower with cheese.

77–79 Church St. ℂ 01463/713-111. Reservations required on weekends. Main courses £8–£13.20 ($12–$19.80). AE, DC, MC, V. Daily noon–2pm and 5:30–11pm.

Dunain Park Restaurant ⚜ SCOTTISH   Ann Nicoll presides over the kitchen here, offering Scottish fare with French flair. A game terrine of chicken and guinea fowl is layered with venison and pigeon, meats are wrapped in bacon and served with a delicious onion confit, and Shetland salmon is baked in sea salt and served with a white port, lime, and ginger sauce. The restaurant also specializes in Aberdeen Angus steaks.

In the Dunain Park Hotel, Dunain Park. ℂ 01463/230-512. Reservations recommended. Main courses £15.95–£17.95 ($23.95–$26.95). AE, DC, MC, V. Daily 7–9pm.

Kong's Restaurant CHINESE/THAI   Spicy and reasonably priced food awaits you here; especially noteworthy is the large variety of appetizers, including some dishes from Vietnam. Try the Thai chicken wings or the Szechuan squid before moving on to a wide array of seafood and poultry dishes, along with a selection of pork and beef. The Thai green and red curry dishes are especially flavorful, and the chef's specialties include Peking roast duck and steamed sole flavored with ginger and spring onions. Vegetarians are well catered to here.

64–66 Academy St. ℂ 01463/237-755. Reservations recommended. Main courses £6.90–£8.65 ($10.35–$13); fixed-price menus £12.95–£21 ($19.45–$31.50). AE, MC, V. Mon–Sat noon–2pm; daily 5:30–11pm.

Ristorante La Riviera BRITISH/ITALIAN   Often hosting local family celebrations, this rather staid restaurant occupies the ground floor of an early-1900s stone-sided hotel on the riverbank near the center of Inverness. Meals here are part of an entire evening's entertainment, so plan on spending several leisurely hours. Menu items include involtini of smoked salmon stuffed with seafood mousseline, presented with saffron- and dill-flavored dressing; and Scottish beef filet with wild-mushroom polenta, shallots, and Parmesan crackling.

In the Glenmoriston Town House Hotel, 20 Ness Bank. ℂ 01463/223-777. Reservations recommended. Main courses £15–£16.90 ($22.50–$25.35); t2-course fixed-price menu £19.50 ($29.25); 3-course fixed-price menu £25.95 ($38.95). AE, DC, MC, V. Daily noon–2pm and 6:30–9:30pm.

Riva INTERNATIONAL   One of Inverness's newest restaurants occupies a site on the opposite *riva* (riverbank) from the rest of the town. Deliberately unpretentious, it has only 18 tables. At least a dozen kinds of pastas are offered as either starters or main courses. Entrees include tagliatelle with crumbly meatballs, monkfish in red-pepper sauce, and chicken with crispy Parma ham and risotto. Between mealtimes, the place functions as a simple cafe serving sandwiches.

4–6 Ness Walk. ℂ 01463/237-377. Reservations required. Main courses £5.95–£12 ($8.95–$18) in restaurant; sandwiches £3.95 ($5.95) in cafe. MC, V. Restaurant Mon–Sat noon–2pm and 6–9:30pm (last order), Sun 6–9:30pm; cafe Mon–Sat 10am–9:30pm, except during above-mentioned meal hours.

INVERNESS AFTER DARK

It may be the capital of the Highlands, but Inverness is a sprawling small town without much nightlife. You can spend an evening in the town's pubs sampling single-malt whiskies or beers on tap. Although they may not have the authentic charm of the isolated pubs in more rural areas, you'll still find a lot of Highlander flavor. Try the pub in the **Loch Ness House Hotel,** Glenurquhart Road (© **01463/231-248**), on the western periphery of town; **Gellions Pub,** 8–14 Bridge St. (© **01463/233-648**); and **Gunsmith's Pub,** 30 Union St. (© **01463/710-519**). For punk rock and heavy metal, head for either of the town's discos: **Blue,** Rose Street (© **01463/222-712**), or **Gs,** 9–21 Castle St. (© **01463/233-322**).

SIDE TRIPS FROM INVERNESS

MUIR OF ORD

This small town, 10 miles (16km) west of Inverness, makes a good touring center for a history-rich part of Scotland. If you stay at the hotel recommended below, you can take day trips around Black Isle, which boasts beautiful scenery (see section 9, "The Black Isle Peninsula," later in this chapter). Outdoorsy types are drawn here for fishing, golf, and shooting.

Accommodations & Dining

Dower House 🛠 *Finds*   This charming guesthouse is a perfect base for exploring the area. The rooms are decorated in the fine tradition of a Scottish country house, with flowers cut from the garden. Each comes with a good-size bathroom with combination tub/shower. A small three-bedroom cottage is perfect for families. Be sure to make reservations for the Dower House well in advance; the comfortable atmosphere is very much in demand.

Even if you don't stay here, you might want to call for a dinner reservation. After a cocktail in the lounge, you proceed to the dining room for a four-course meal of modern British cuisine utilizing produce grown on the grounds; expensive fixed-price menus are served nightly.

Highfleld, Muir of Ord IV6 7XN. © **01463/870-090**. Fax 01463/870-090. www.thedowerhouse.co.uk. 5 units. £110–£120 ($165–$180) double; £130–£150 ($195–$225) suite or cottage. MC, V. Rates include Scottish breakfast. Drive 1 mile (1.5km) north of A862. **Amenities:** Restaurant, bar; room service; babysitting. *In room:* TV, coffeemaker, hair dryer, iron.

BEAULY 🛠

The French monks who settled here in the 13th century named it literally "beautiful place"—and it still is. You'll see the **Highland Craftpoint** on your left as you come from Inverness. In summer, there's an interesting exhibit of Scottish handcrafts. Beauly is 12 miles (19km) west of Inverness on A862, and Inverness Traction, a local bus company, has hourly service from Inverness.

Dating from 1230, the **Beauly Priory** (© **01463/782-309**), now a roofless shell, is the only remaining one of three priories built for the Valliscaulian order, an austere body drawing its main components from the Cistercians and the Carthusians. Some notable windows and window arcading are still left among the ruins. Hugh Fraser of Lovat erected the Chapel of the Holy Cross on the nave's north side in the early 15th century. You can tour the priory at any time; if it's locked, ask for a key from the Priory Hotel across the way.

If you're interested in tweeds, don't miss **Campbells of Beauly,** Highland Tweed House (© **01463/782-239**), operated by the same family since 1858. An excellent selection of fine tweeds and tartans is offered, and you can have your material tailored. Blankets, travel rugs, tweed hats, and kilts are sold, as well as cashmere and lambswool sweaters. It's on the main street at the south end of the village square, next to the Royal Bank of Scotland.

Accommodations & Dining

Priory Hotel 🔔   The Priory Hotel is on the historic main square of town, a short walk from the ruins of the priory. The hotel has recently expanded into an adjacent building, adding four rooms to its well-furnished offerings. A frequently changing dinner menu features a variety of fish and local game as well as a good selection of steaks; bar meals are similar dishes served in smaller portions. In addition, high tea is served daily.

The Square, Beauly IV4 7BX. ℭ 01463/782-309. Fax 01463/782-531. www.priory-hotel.com. 36 units. £85 ($127.50) double. Rates include Scottish breakfast. AE, DC, MC, V. **Amenities:** Restaurant, bar; nearby golf course; room service; laundry/dry cleaning. *In room:* TV, dataport, coffeemaker, hair dryer, iron.

8 Nairn & Cawdor Castle 🔔

172 miles (277km) N of Edinburgh, 91 miles (146.5km) NW of Aberdeen, 16 miles (26km) E of Inverness

A favorite family seaside resort on the sheltered Moray Firth, Nairn (from the Gaelic for "Water of Alders") is a royal burgh at the mouth of the Nairn River. Its fishing harbor was constructed in 1820, and golf has been played here since 1672—as it still is today.

ESSENTIALS

GETTING THERE   Nairn can be reached by **train** from the south, with a change at either Aberdeen or Inverness. The service between Inverness and Nairn is frequent; this is the most popular route. For information, check with the Inverness train station at Station Square (ℭ **0345/484-950**). Inverness Traction runs daily **buses** from Inverness to Nairn. Call ℭ **0990/808-080** for schedules. If you're **driving** from Inverness, take A96 east to Nairn.

VISITOR INFORMATION   The **tourist office** is at 62 King St. (ℭ **01667/ 452-753**). It's open April to mid-May, Monday through Saturday from 10am to 5pm; mid-May to June, Monday through Saturday from 10am to 5pm and Sunday from 11am to 4pm; July and August, Monday through Saturday from 9am to 6pm and Sunday from 10am to 5pm; and September and October, Monday through Saturday from 10am to 5pm.

EXPLORING THE AREA

A large, normally uncrowded beach draws visitors in summer. Anglers also find the area a good spot. Nairn is great walking country, and the tourist office will give you a map and details about the various possibilities, including hikes along the banks of the River Nairn. The best walks are the five **Cawdor Castle Nature Trails.** They're signposted from Cawdor Castle of *Macbeth* fame, taking you along some of the loveliest and most varied forests and wooded areas in the Highlands.

   Brodie Country, on A96, 3 miles (5km) east of Nairn in Brodie (ℭ **01309/ 641-555**), is a family-owned shopping complex with a variety of merchandise. Of greatest interest are the regionally produced knitwear, gift items, and foodstuffs; the latter includes smoked meats, jams, and mustards. Also on the premises is a fully licensed restaurant serving Scottish cuisine daily from 9:30am to 5:30pm (to 7pm Thurs).

Nairn Antiques, St. Ninian Place (℗ 01667/453-303), carries a broad range of antiques as well as upscale crafts and reproductions. Particularly noteworthy are the collections of Scottish pottery, silver, and fine porcelains. This is the only shop in the northern country to stock Lalique crystal from France.

A Taste of Moray, on the Nairn-Inverness Road, 6 miles (10km) north of Nairn (℗ 01667/462-340), is all about the pleasures of preparing and consuming Scottish cuisine, with products ranging from quality cookware to Scottish condiments and smoked meats. The adjacent restaurant serves seafood dishes and steaks daily from 10am to 8pm.

The 18-hole **Nairn Dunbar Golf Club,** Loch Loy Road (℗ 01667/452-741), consists of 6,700 yards (6,097m) of playing area with a par of 72. Greens fees are £33 ($49.50) per round or £42 ($63) per day Monday through Friday, £40 ($60) per round or £53 ($79.50) per day Saturday and Sunday.

Cawdor Castle ⚔ To the south of Nairn, you'll encounter 600 years of Highland history at Cawdor Castle, the home of the thanes of Cawdor since the early 14th century. Although the castle was constructed 2 centuries after his time, it has nevertheless been romantically linked to Shakespeare's *Macbeth,* once the thane of Cawdor. The castle has all the architectural ingredients you'd associate with the Middle Ages: a drawbridge, an ancient tower, and fortified walls. Its severity is softened by the handsome gardens and rolling lawns. On the grounds are five nature trails through beautiful woodland, a nine-hole golf course, a putting green, a snack bar, a picnic area, shops, and a licensed restaurant serving hot meals, teas, and coffees all day.

Between Inverness and Nairn on B9090 off A96, Cawdor. ℗ 01667/404-615. Admission £6.10 ($9.15) adults, £5.10 ($7.65) seniors, £3.30 ($4.95) children 5–15. May to second Sun in Oct daily 10am–5pm.

ACCOMMODATIONS

The Boath House ⚔⚔ This Georgian mansion is set amid 20 acres (8.1 hectares) of lush greenery. Built in 1825, the house has been restored to its original elegance. Bedrooms are splendidly decorated with antiques and period furniture, along with amenities like combination tub/showers. In spite of its classic look, the atmosphere is relaxed and informal. There are two lounges and a library where you can enjoy a dram of whisky. An on-site salon is open to both guests and nonguests, offering everything from aromatherapy to galvanic slimming treatments. The salon uses only products with natural ingredients from pure plant and flower essences. The hotel is also home to an award-winning restaurant (see "Dining," below).

On A96, 2 miles east of Nairn, Auldearn, Nairn IV12 5TE. ℗ 01667/454-896. Fax 01667/455-469. www.boath-house.com. £110–£175 ($165–$262.50) double. Rates include breakfast. AE, DC, MC, V. Free parking. **Amenities:** Restaurant, 2 bars; spa treatments. *In room:* TV, coffeemaker, hair dryer.

Clifton House ⚔⚔ *(Finds* This intimate hotel reflects the dynamic personality of J. Gordon Macintyre, owner of the vine-covered, honey-sandstone Victorian mansion. His home for over 60 years, it stands on the seafront, 3 minutes from the beach and equidistant to both golf links. Mr. Macintyre has spent a great deal of time and care in decorating and refurbishing the house. Most of the furniture is antique; the collection of paintings, engravings, and drawings is unusual and extensive. Each guest room is pleasantly appointed, with complete shower-and-tub bathroom. Mr. Macintyre organizes a series of concerts, plays, and recitals to entertain his guests. The hotel is a licensed theater, and performances are presented September through March. The Clifton has the most extensive wine list in the north of Scotland and also serves the best food in Nairn.

1–3 Viewfield St., Nairn, Nairnshire IV12 4HW. ✆ 01667/453-119. Fax 01667/452-836. www.clifton-hotel. co.uk. 12 units. £110–£117 ($165–$175.50) double. Rates include Scottish breakfast. AE, DC, MC, V. Turn east of the town roundabout on A96. **Amenities:** Restaurant. *In room:* Coffeemaker, hair dryer, no phone.

Greenlawns Private Hotel *(Value)* This Victorian house within easy reach of the beaches and golf courses is a pleasant base for touring the Loch Ness region. The owners have completely refurbished the house while retaining its traditional charm. All of the good-size guest rooms come with shower-only bathrooms. No smoking is permitted.

13 Seafield St., Nairn IV12 4HG. ✆ 01667/452-738. Fax 01667/452-738. www.greenlawns.uk.com. 7 units. £40–£58 ($60–$87) double. Rates include Scottish breakfast. AE, MC, V. Turn down Albert St. from A96. **Amenities:** Dining room; babysitting. *In room:* TV, coffeemaker, no phone.

DINING

The Boath House Restaurant *(★★)* SCOTTISH/CONTINENTAL Located in a Georgian mansion, this restaurant has won numerous awards. Traditional Scottish fare is given a Continental twist to create a well-balanced menu that changes daily. The atmosphere is romantic with antique decor, and in the evening, the room is bathed in candlelight. Menu items might include seared filet of sea bass on a citrus couscous, tapenade, and a basil-infused oil, or roasted gray-legged partridge with a ragout of red cabbage and onion. There is also a good selection of wines.

In the Boath House, Auldearn. ✆ 01667/454-896. Reservations recommended. Fixed-price 5-course dinner £37.50 ($56.25); fixed-price lunch £27.50 ($41.25). AE, DC, MC, V. Daily noon–2pm and 7–9pm. Closed Mon–Tues to nonguests. On A96, 2 miles east of Nairn.

Cawdor Tavern SCOTTISH This atmospheric restaurant occupies what was built as a stone-sided carpenter shop for Cawdor Castle, fewer than 500 feet (152m) away. Many visitors opt for just a drink, choosing any of the single-malt whiskies that adorn the bar. Others come for the food, served in generous portions with a focus on local produce and regional fish and meats. Examples include duck in white-wine sauce, crabmeat-and-salmon cakes with chive-cream sauce, and an unusual preparation of chicken stuffed with haggis (nationalistically labeled "chicken Culloden").

The Lane, Cawdor. ✆ 01667/404-777. Reservations recommended for dinner. Main courses £4.95–£10.95 ($7.45–$16.45) lunch; £6.95–£15.95 ($10.45–$23.95) dinner; fixed-price menus £18.95–£25 ($28.45–$37.50). AE, MC, V. Daily noon–2:30pm and 5:30–9pm.

The Longhouse SCOTTISH Opened in 1997, the domain of the Rennie family is a cream-colored stone house in the center of town, named after the early-1900s building's long and narrow design. Cozy and candlelit, it seats only 33 diners at a time. The menu is less ambitious at lunch, when platters are likely to include lasagna, fried fish, and roasted pork with wine sauce. High tea is favored by locals inclined to retire early. At dinner, the cuisine shines. Its tradition is strongly Scottish—expect sauces laced with whisky and dishes like black pudding with whisky-mustard sauce; rack of lamb with wine-rosemary sauce and mint-infused poached pears; and mussels in white wine, onion, and dill sauce. Desserts usually include a slice of shortbread with fresh cream and fresh raspberries. The restaurant is licensed only for alcohol served with meals.

8 Harbour St. (℃ 01667/455-532. Reservations recommended. Main courses £3.50–£7.50 ($5.25–$11.25) lunch; £5.95–£18 ($8.95-$27) dinner; high tea £6.50 ($9.75). AE, MC, V. Daily lunch 10am–4:30pm; high tea 4–6:30pm; dinner 5–10pm. Closed Wed from Oct–Mar and 2 weeks in Oct.

NAIRN AFTER DARK

Locals gather to drink and talk at the **Claymore House Hotel Bar,** Seabank Road (℃ **01667/453-731**). During cold weather, an open fireplace takes the chill out of the air, as does the selection of malt whiskies. The **Millford Hotel Pub,** Mill Road (℃ **01667/453-941**), features free live music on Saturday, mainly middle-of-the-road country, pop, blues, or folk bands. Once a month, there's a country-western night with dancing.

Clifton House, 1–3 Viewfield St. (℃ **01667/453-119**), offers classical concerts by solo artists and small ensembles about once every 3 weeks between September and May. It also stages two plays a year, in November and February or March, with an admission of £9 to £14 ($13.50 to $21). An optional Scottish buffet dinner is available for an additional £20 ($30).

9 The Black Isle Peninsula ⟨★⟩

Cromarty: 23 miles (37km) NW of Inverness (via Kessock Bridge)

The Black Isle is one of Scotland's most enchanting peninsulas, a land rich in history, beauty, and mystery. Part of Ross and Cromarty County, it's northwest of Inverness, a 20-minute drive or bus ride away. A car tour would be about 37 miles (59.5km), but allow plenty of time for stops and country walks along the way.

There's much confusion about the name of the peninsula, because it's neither black nor an island. In summer, the land is green and fertile, with tropical plants flourishing. It has forests, fields of broom and whin, and scattered coastal villages. The peninsula has been inhabited for 7,000 years, as 60-odd prehistoric sites testify. Pictish kings, whose thrones passed down through the female line, once ruled this land. Then the Vikings held sway, and the evidence of many Gallows Hills testifies their justice was harsh.

ESSENTIALS

GETTING THERE   The nearest **rail service** goes to Inverness. From there, the Highland Bus and Coach Company serves the peninsula (nos. 26, 26A, and 126), making stops at North Kessock, Munlochy, Avoch, Fortrose, Rosemarkie, and Cromarty. **Buses** depart from Farraline Park in Inverness (℃ **01463/233-371** for schedules).

If you're **driving,** head to Fortrose as your first stop (see below), take A9 north from Inverness. (Follow the signs toward Wick.) Follow A9 for 4 miles (6.5km) until you see the Kessock Bridge. Go over the bridge and take the second road to the right, toward Munlocky. (Fortrose is 8 miles/13km from this turnoff.) Follow A832 through the village of Munlochy and at the junction take the road right, signposted Fortrose. Continue straight on through Avoch to Fortrose.

VISITOR INFORMATION   Ask at the **Inverness tourist office** (see "Inverness: Capital of the Highlands," earlier in this chapter) for details on Black Isle, because the peninsula is often included on a day tour from that city.

FORTROSE ⟨★⟩ & ROSEMARKIE

Fortrose is a good place to start. Along the way, you'll pass a celebrated wishing well, or **clootie well,** festooned with rags. Dedicated to St. Boniface, the well has a long tradition, dating back to pagan times. It's said that anyone removing a rag will inherit the misfortunes of the person who placed it there.

The ruins of **Fortrose Cathedral** stand in this sleepy village. Founded in the 13th century, the cathedral was dedicated to St. Peter and St. Boniface. You can still see fine detailing from the 14th century. If the stones scattered about don't seem to number enough to fill in the gaps, it's because Cromwell's men removed many of them to help build a fort in Inverness. There are no formal hours; you can wander through the ruins at any time.

Fortrose adjoins **Rosemarkie,** up the road. The site has been inhabited since the Bronze Age. A center of Pictish culture, the town saw the arrival of the first Christian missionaries. It's reported that St. Moluag founded a monastery here in the 6th century. Rosemarkie became a royal burgh in 1216. The twin hamlets share a golf course today, and they're the site of the Chanonry Sailing Club, whose annual regatta brings entries from all over Scotland. Right beyond Rosemarkie is the mysterious **Fairy Glen,** signposted at the end of the village. It's one of the loveliest places in the Black Isle for a long walk.

ACCOMMODATIONS & DINING

Royal Hotel   Built in 1865 as a coaching inn, the Royal overlooks the ancient monument of Fortrose Cathedral. The traditional Victorian house has recently undergone extensive renovations, mostly to upgrade the bedrooms. Proprietor Graham Law has left the common areas mostly untouched, preferring to retain the mix of modern and traditional decor. The hotel has two bars and a lounge where pub meals are served. The restaurant serves traditional Scottish fare made from locally produced ingredients.

At the corner of Union and High Sts., Fortrose IV10 8SU. (℗ 01381/620-236. 17 units, 11 with private bathroom. £44 ($66) double without bathroom; £60 ($90) double with bathroom. Rates include breakfast. MC, V. **Amenities:** Restaurant, 2 bars, lounge. In room: TV, coffeemaker, hair dryer, no phone.

CROMARTY

Cromarty stands at the tip of the peninsula, where the North and South Sutors guard the entrance to the Cromarty Firth, the second-deepest inland waterway estuary in Europe, always of strategic importance to the Royal Navy. Much of the Black Isle invites country walks, but in Cromarty you may want to stay in the village itself, exploring each street with its rows of terraced cottages seemingly hunched against the prevailing north winds. The town has been handsomely restored, and the old merchants' houses are superb examples of domestic architecture of the 18th century.

Once a flourishing port and a former royal burgh, the town gave the world a famous son: Hugh Miller. Born here in 1802, Miller was a stonemason as a young man, but in time he became a recognized expert in the field of geology, as well as a powerful man of letters in Scotland. **Hugh Miller's Cottage,** Church Street (℗ **01381/600-245**), contains many of his personal belongings and collections of geological specimens. The thatched cottage was built in 1698. From May to September, it's open Monday through Saturday from 11am to 1pm and 2 to 5pm and Sunday from 2 to 5pm. Admission is £2.50 ($3.75) for adults, £1.70 ($2.55) for students and seniors, and £7 ($10.50) per family.

ACCOMMODATIONS & DINING

Royal Hotel   The only hotel in town sits on an embankment near one of the deepest estuaries in Europe. Around 1940, the British navy combined a series of waterfront buildings into living quarters for sailors. Today, the hotel is a cozy enclave with wood-burning stoves and open fireplaces. The guest rooms are traditionally furnished. The dining room, which spills onto a glassed-in extension opening onto the harbor, features specialties like steaks and stroganoff. You can also enjoy a good bar menu, with a tempting list of burgers, crêpes, and salads.

Marine Terrace, Cromarty IV11 8YN. (℃ **01381/600-217.** Fax 01381/600-813 10 units. £59–£80 ($88.50–$120) double. Rates include Scottish breakfast. AE, DC, MC, V. Bus: 26, 26A, or 126 from Inverness. **Amenities:** Restaurant, 2 bars; tour desk; babysitting. *In room:* TV, coffeemaker, hair dryer, no phone.

10 Sutherland: The Gem of Scotland

Sutherland has more sheep than people (a 20-to-1 ratio). It's genuinely off the beaten track, but if you have time to travel this far, you'll find it perhaps the most beautiful county in Scotland. Adding to the haunting beauty are lochs and rivers, heather-covered moors and mountains—in all, 2,000 square miles (5,200sq km) of territory. It may not offer many "attractions," but it's a wonderful setting for outdoor pursuits like golf and fishing.

To the northwest of Inverness, Sutherland has three coastlines—on the north and west, the Atlantic, and on the east, the North Sea. Most villages have populations of only 100 or so hearty souls. Sutherland was the scene of the notorious 19th-century Highland Clearances, when many residents were driven out from their ancestral crofts. Many made their way to the New World. In many a deserted glen, you can still see traces of former crofting villages.

DORNOCH ✦

The ancient cathedral city of Dornoch, 63 miles (101.5km) northwest of Inverness and 219 miles (352.5km) northwest of Edinburgh, is Sutherland's major town and the area's most interesting stop. The major sightseeing attraction nearby is **Dornoch Cathedral** (see below). Dornoch is also known for its sandy beaches, but we find they're best left for polar bears if you want to go swimming. However, they do make for lovely walks.

A **tourist office** is at the Square (℃ **01862/810-400**). It's open year-round Monday through Friday, plus Saturday and Sunday during peak months.

From the Inverness bus station at Farraline Park, off Academy Street (call ℃ **01463/233-371** for schedules), three local companies run daily **buses** to Dornoch: Stagecoach, Caledonian Express, and Scottish CityLink. The trip takes between 60 and 90 minutes and costs £7.50 ($11.25) one-way.

EXPLORING THE AREA

The village of Dornoch has long been known for its golf club on the sheltered shores of Dornoch Firth, the northernmost first-class course in the world. The turf of the **Royal Dornoch Golf Club,** Golf Road (℃ **01862/810-219**), is considered sacred by aficionados. Golf was first played here by monks in 1614. A curious meander of the Gulf Stream as it bypasses northern Scotland keeps the climate balmier than you'd expect. The club itself was founded in 1877, and a royal charter was granted by Edward VII in 1906. Prince Andrew and the duchess of Sutherland are both members today. Its SSS is 73; its par is 70 for an 18-hole yardage of 6,185 (5,628m). Greens fees are from £45 to £70 ($67.50 to $105), with a 7-day ticket available costing £50 to £100 ($75 to $150). Golf club and trolley rentals are £20 to £30 ($30 to $45) and £3 ($4.50), respectively. Caddy service is available for £20 to £30 ($30 to $45) plus tip.

Dornoch Cathedral, Castle Street, was built in the 13th century and partially destroyed by fire in 1570. It has undergone many restorations, but you can still see its fine 13th-century stonework. The cathedral is famous for its modern stained-glass windows—three are in memory of Andrew Carnegie, the American steel king. The cathedral is open daily from 9am to dusk. The **Plaiden Ell,** found in the cathedral's cemetery where a marketplace used to be, was a medieval method for measuring cloth. (An *ell* was a unit of measure equaling about 38 inches/ 96.5cm.) The Ell is carved in stone in a flat shape similar to a tombstone's, but with two pieces of metal rising about 2 inches (5cm) above the level of the stone. The distance between those two pieces of metal is an ell. In one of the gardens is the 1722 **witch's stone** marking the spot where the last burning of a so-called witch took place in Scotland.

If the weather is fair, Dornoch is great for country strolls, as the town is flanked by miles of clean sand opening onto chilly waters. You can often see migrant birds on these beaches. At **Embo,** some 3 miles (5km) north of the beaches of Dornoch, you'll come across the remains of two funereal vaults believed to date from around 2000 B.C.

You can drive another 2 miles (3km) north of Embo to the shores of lovely **Loch Fleet,** where there's a meager ruin of **Skelbo Castle.** It's now on a lonely grassy mound, but in the 14th century Skelbo was a powerful fortification.

Shoppers should check out the **Dornoch Craft Centre,** Town Jail, Castle Street (© **01862/810-555**), in the center of town opposite the cathedral. You can wander through the selection of crafts, jewelry, and pottery, and then visit the Textile Hall and browse through the range of knitwear, tartans, mohair goods, and tweeds.

ACCOMMODATIONS & DINING

Carnegie Club at Skibo Castle ☆☆☆ Skibo Castle is as massive a baronial house as you're likely to find in Scotland, an Edwardian pile created from a unique combination of Scottish heritage and one of the most potent fortunes of the Industrial Revolution. Steel magnate Andrew Carnegie, who emigrated from Scotland's woolen mills to America in the mid–19th century, yearned for a return to the land of his birth after he acquired his fortune. After he bought the historic but dilapidated Skibo, 5 miles (8km) east of Dornoch, in 1898 (for the relatively reasonable price of £85,000/$144,500), Carnegie and his second wife, Louise, massively enlarged the place, pouring £2 million ($3.4 million) into its refurbishment. Here they welcomed a stream of distinguished visitors, including Edward VII, during the months they spent in Scotland in their final years.

In 1990, Peter de Savary, the force behind posh semiprivate clubs in London and Antigua, acquired the property and its 7,000 acres (2,835 hectares), installed an 18-hole golf course designed by Donald Steel, and created a resort that's a combination golf mecca and semiprivate club for the celebs, CEOs, and aristocrats who can afford the sky-high rates. Meals are served at a long table in the style of an Edwardian house party. Evenings of Scottish dance are featured every Saturday; other nights, there are dinner performances of Scottish flute, Celtic harp, or piano. Sports opportunities include trap and skeet shooting, falconry, trout and salmon fishing, and golf (on the resort's course or at the nearby Royal Dornoch Course).

Skibo Castle, Dornoch IV25 3RQ. © **01862/894-600.** Fax 01862/894-601. www.carnegie.co.uk. 46 units. £575 ($862.50) double members; £700–£800 ($1,050–$1,200) double nonmembers. Rates include meals, drinks, and sporting activities (including greens fees at the resort's golf course). Membership costs £3,000 ($4,500) per year per family. AE, DC, MC, V. The club will send a car to Dornoch or anywhere in Inverness to meet new arrivals. **Amenities:** Dining room (guests only); golf course. *In room:* TV, hair dryer.

Dornoch Castle Hotel   This unusual hotel, close to the Royal Dornoch Golf Course, occupies what was once the residence of the bishops of Caithness, built

The Far North

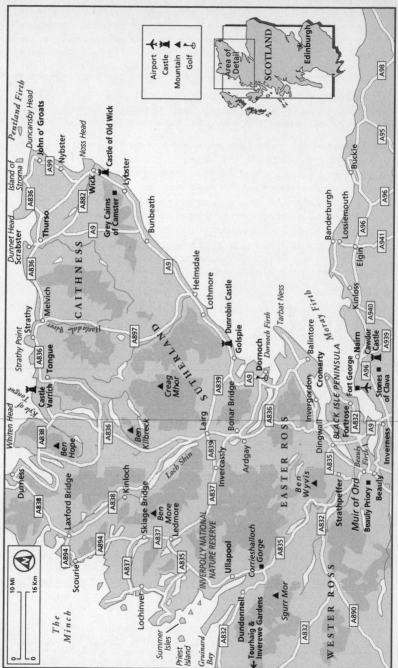

Airport
Castle
Mountain
Golf

SCOTLAND
Edinburgh

Area of Detail

A98
A95
A96
A941
A96
A940
A939
A832
A9
A890
A832

Pentland Firth
Duncansby Head
John o' Groats
Nybster
Noss Head
Island of Stroma
Castle of Old Wick
Wick
Lybster
A99
A882
Grey Cairns of Camster
Dunnet Head
Scrabster
Thurso
A836
A836
Bunbeath
A9
Helmsdale
Melvich
Lothmore
Strathy Point
Strathy
CAITHNESS
Dunrobin Castle
Golspie
A897
Tarbat Ness
Whiten Head
Tongue
Castle Varrich
SUTHERLAND
Creag Mhor
Dornoch Firth
Dornoch
A9
Moray Firth
Balintore
Cromarty
Nairn
Cawdor Castle
Stones of Clava
Kinloss
Lossiemouth
Banderburgh
Buckie
Elgin
Kyle of Tongue
Ben Hope
A838
A836
Ben Kilbreck
Lairg
A839
Bonar Bridge
Invercassly
A836
Invergordon
BLACK ISLE PENINSULA
Fort George
Fortrose
A832
Durness
Laxford Bridge
A838
Kinloch
Skiage Bridge
A836
A837
A839
Ardgay
EASTER ROSS
Ben Wyvis
Dingwall
A835
Inverness
A838
Ben More
Ledmore
Loch Shin
A837
INVERPOLLY NATIONAL NATURE RESERVE
Ullapool
A835
Strathpeffer
Muir of Ord
Beauly Priory
Beauly
Beauly Firth
A832
Scourie
A894
A894
A837
Corrieshalloch Gorge
Lochinver
Summer Isles
Priest Island
Gruinard Bay
Dundonnell
Sgurr Mor
Teurhaig & Inverewe Gardens
A832
WESTER ROSS
The Minch
10 Mi
16 Km
0
0

353

of stone in the center of town in the late 15th or early 16th century. Today, its winding stairs, labyrinthine corridors, and impenetrable cellars have been converted into a well-directed hotel and restaurant. The guest rooms are in the original building and an extension overlooking the garden; all tend to be dowdy, however. Most bathrooms contain combination tub/showers. Restaurant specialties include leg of Sutherland lamb with onion marmalade and Highland Estate venison with black currants. Reservations are suggested.

Castle St., Dornoch IV25 3SD. © **01862/810-216.** Fax 01862/810-981. 17 units. £76–£110 ($114–$165) double. Rates include Scottish breakfast. AE, MC, V. **Amenities:** Restaurant, bar; nearby golf courses. In room: TV.

Fourpenny Cottage This pleasant cottage, 1½ miles (2.5km) north of the famous Royal Dornoch course, is a favorite of golfers. To cater to them, the owners recently installed a warm-up green, where golfers can practice before heading onto the formal course. The guest rooms are divided among the main house, a reconstruction of an antique crofter's cottage, and a modern annex. Sheila Board and her family prepare hearty breakfasts and maintain the cozy rooms. The ambience is informal, akin to that in a private home.

Embo Rd., Dornoch IV25 3HR. © and fax **01862/810-727.** http://homepages.tesco.net/~fourpenny. 4 units. £32 ($48) per person. Rates include Scottish breakfast. No credit cards. Closed Dec–Mar. From Dornoch center, drive 3 miles (5km) south on the Embo-Golspie Rd. In room: TV, no phone.

GOLSPIE

This family resort town with a golf course sits on A9 and looks out across the water to the Dornoch Firth, with a crescent of sandy beach. Golspie, 228 miles (367km) northwest of Edinburgh and 72 miles (116km) northwest of Inverness, is visited chiefly because of its towering Dunrobin Castle.

Dunrobin Castle 🏰 Home of the earls and dukes of Sutherland, Dunrobin is the most northerly of the great houses of Scotland and also the biggest in the northern Highlands, dating in part from the early 13th century. Its formal gardens are laid out in the manner of Versailles. On the grounds is a museum containing many relics from the Sutherland family. Some of the castle's 180 rooms are open to the public—the ornately furnished dining room, a billiard room, and the room and gilded four-poster bed where Queen Victoria slept when she visited in 1872.

½ mile (1km) northeast of Golspie on A9. © **01408/633-177.** Admission £6 ($9) adults; £4.50 ($6.75) students, seniors, and children 5–16; £17 ($25.50) per family. Apr–May and Oct Mon–Sat 10:30am–4:30pm, Sun noon–4pm; June–Sept daily 10:30am–5:30pm. Last entrance 30 minutes before closing.

ACCOMMODATIONS & DINING

Golf Links Hotel The best place to stay in Golspie dates from the early 1900s, when it was built as the stone rectory for the local minister. Many of the guests are golfers drawn to the nearby Golspie, Royal Dornoch, and Brora courses. The rooms in the main building are well furnished, each with a midsize bathroom with tub and shower. Scottish and Continental cuisine are served in a dining room with a view of Ben Bhraggie.

Church St., Golspie KW10 6TT. © **01408/633-408.** Fax 01408/634-184. www.golflinkshotel.co.uk. 9 units. £55 ($82.50) double. Rates include Scottish breakfast. MC, V. **Amenities:** Restaurant, bar; nearby golf course; tour desk; laundry service. In room: TV, coffeemaker, hair dryer, iron, no phone.

TONGUE

Heading north along A836, you cross high moors and brooding peaks to Tongue, 257 miles (414km) northwest of Edinburgh and 101 miles (163km) northwest of Inverness. For the nature lover and hiker, there's a lot to see, from the mighty cliffs of **Clo Mor,** near Cape Wrath (known for its large colonies of puffins), to waterfalls like **Eas-Coul-Aulin** (the highest in Britain) and the **Falls of Shin,** where you can see salmon leap. Masses of land, like **Ben Loyal** (known as the queen of Scottish mountains), suddenly rise from a barren landscape. Any of the district's tourist offices, including the one in Dornoch, can provide a map of the local hills, valleys, and trails. The one closest to the above-mentioned trekking sites is the office on Main Street in Bettyhill (© **01641/521-342**), a coastal village about 15 miles (24km) from Tongue.

West of Tongue on a promontory stand the ruins of **Castle Varrich,** said to have been built by the Vikings. Possibly dating from the 14th century, this castle was the Mackay stronghold. This is a great place for a walk.

A rather dramatic walk from the center is to the **Kyle of Tongue,** crossed by a narrow causeway. Protected from the wild and raging sea nearby, this is a long, shallow inlet. At low tide, wearing a pair of boots, you can walk out to Rabbit Island, a little isle lying at the mouth of Kyle of Tongue. You'll pass towering cliffs, sandy bays, odd rock formations, and deserted rocky islets that time has seemingly forgotten.

ACCOMMODATIONS & DINING

Ben Loyal Hotel This is a good choice, with everything under the careful attention of Paul and Elaine Lewis. The guest rooms are a bit plain but comfortably furnished in traditional style, with shower-only bathrooms and electric blankets. Several superior rooms have four-poster beds and views over the castle ruins and loch. Home-cooked meals feature local beef and produce grown on the grounds. A fine wine list and an assortment of malt whiskies complement the cuisine. The Ben Loyal incorporates 19th-century stables, a former post office, a shop, and a village bakery.

Main St., Tongue IV27 4XE. © **01847/611-216.** Fax 01847/611-212. www.benloyal.co.uk. 11 units. £64–£66 ($96–$99) double. Rates include breakfast and dinner. MC, V. **Amenities:** Restaurant, bar; babysitting. *In room:* TV, coffeemaker.

Tongue Hotel *☞* Since Queen Victoria's day, the best place to stay in town has been the Tongue Hotel, a mile (1.6km) north of the village center beside the road leading to Durness. Built of gray stone in the baronial style in 1850, it began as a hunting lodge for the duke of Sutherland. The hotel opens onto the Kyle of Tongue and still possesses much of its original character. Both the public rooms and the guest rooms are decorated in Victorian style, with flowered curtains and well-upholstered furniture. Most of the bathrooms contain combination tub/showers.

The quality of the food is well known locally. A hearty, moderately priced dinner usually includes a choice of game or fresh fish caught in the region. Affordable bar meals are served in the popular pub, with an open fireplace and impressive collection of whiskies, and the more sedate cocktail lounge.

Tongue, Sutherland IV27 4XD. © **01847/611-206.** Fax 01847/611-345. www.scottish-selection.co.uk. 15 units. £70–£90 ($105–$135) double. Rates include Scottish breakfast. MC, V. **Amenities:** Restaurant, 2 bars; laundry service. *In room:* TV, coffeemaker, hair dryer.

11 Caithness: Unspoiled Country

It doesn't look like the Highlands at all, but Caithness is the northernmost county of mainland Scotland, where the ancient landscape is gentle and rolling. Within its 700 square miles (1,820sq km) you'll find signs of the Stone Age— the enigmatic Grey Cairns of Camster date from 4000 B.C. The county is filled with cairns, mysterious stone rows and circles, and standing stones. The Vikings once occupied this place with its rock stacks, old harbors, craggy cliffs, and quiet coves, and many place names are in Old Norse. It has churches from the Middle Ages, as well as towering castles on cliff tops. The Queen Mother's home, the Castle of Mey, dating from 1570, is between John o' Groats and Thurso.

Rich in bird and animal life, Caithness is unspoiled country. Fishing draws people to the area: Wild brown trout are found in some 100 lochs, along with salmon in the Thurso and Wick Rivers. Most people head for Caithness with John o' Groats as their final destination. John o' Groats is popularly called the extreme northern tip of the British mainland. Actually, Dunnet Head is farther north by a few miles.

Scrabster, a ferry harbor, is the main car-and-passenger service that operates all year to the Orkney Islands (see chapter 12, "The Orkney & Shetland Islands," for more information). There are day trips in summer.

WICK

The famous old herring port of Wick, on the eastern coastline of Caithness, 287 miles (462km) northwest of Edinburgh and 126 miles (203km) northwest of Inverness, is a popular stop for those heading north to explore what's often called the John o' Groats Peninsula. The town has some claim as a holiday resort as well: Robert Louis Stevenson spent part of his boyhood in Wick when his father worked here on an engineering project. Today, a sleepy nostalgia hangs over the town. There's daily bus and rail service from Inverness, from which train connections are possible via Edinburgh, Glasgow, or Stirling.

At **Caithness Glass,** Airport Industrial Estates (℘ **01955/602-286**), you can watch the glassblowing and tour the factory Monday through Friday from 9am to 5pm. The shop and restaurant are open Monday through Friday from 9am to 5pm and Saturday from 9am to 1pm (Saturday to 5pm from June to September). The **Wick Heritage Centre,** 20 Bank Row (℘ **01955/605-393**), has many exhibits pertaining to Wick's herring-fishing industry in days of yore. From May to October, it's open Monday through Saturday from 10am to 5pm; last entrance is at 3:45pm. Admission is £2 ($3) for adults and £50p (75¢) for children 5 to 16.

The most important sites in the area are the two megalithic **Grey Cairns of Camster,** 6 miles (10km) north of Lybster on the Watten Road off A9. The ruins of the **Castle of Old Wick** are also worth exploring, and they're always accessible. The location is off A9, 1½ miles (2.5km) south of Wick. Once known as Castle Olipant, the ruined structure dates back to the 14th century. You can still see three floors of the old castle rising on a rocky promontory.

ACCOMMODATIONS & DINING
Breadalbane House Hotel This 1891 building on the southern outskirts of town, a 5-minute walk from the center, was once the home of a furniture maker. It's now an unpretentious guesthouse with traditionally decorated rooms. You can dine in the restaurant or in the cozy bar. Food offerings vary from curries and steaks to a traditional roast dinner served on weekends.

20 Breadalbane Crescent, Wick KW1 5AQ. ℘ 01955/603-911. Fax 01955/603-911. 10 units, 8 with private bathroom. £55 ($82.50) double with bathroom. Rates include Scottish breakfast. AE, MC, V. **Amenities:** Restaurant, 2 bars; nearby health club; babysitting (by arrangement). *In room:* TV, coffeemaker, no phone.

Mackay's This recently refurbished hotel on the south shore of the River Wick is the home of the Lamont family, who has welcomed guests for more than 40 years. All bedrooms are tastefully decorated and provide well-maintained, shower-only bathrooms. In the heart of Wick, the hotel is a short walk to the Heritage Center and the swimming pool and leisure center. The restaurant, specializing in traditional Scottish fare, offers fixed-price five-course meals.

Union St. (opposite Caithness General Hospital), Wick KW1 5ED. © 01955/602-323. Fax 01955/605-930. www. mackayshotel.co.uk. £80 ($120) double; £90 ($135) family room. Rates include breakfast. AE, MC, V. Closed Jan 1–2. **Amenities:** Restaurant, 2 bars; access to nearby leisure center. *In room:* TV, coffeemaker, hair dryer.

JOHN O' GROATS

John o' Groats, 17 miles (27km) north of Wick, is the northern equivalent of Land's End at the tip of the Cornish peninsula in England. The southern tip of England is 878 miles (1,413.5km) south of John o' Groats. From here, there are views north to the Orkney Islands and the Pentland Firth.

John o' Groats was named after a Dutch ferryman, Jan de Groot. His tombstone can still be seen at Cabisbay Church. The town abounds in souvenir shops, some selling small Arctic cowrie shells once used as decoration by the first settlers in Caithness. You can take interesting walks along the coast to **Duncansby Head,** 2 miles (3km) east—one of the most dramatic coastlines in this part of Scotland. Many species of sea birds, especially puffins, live among the jagged cliffs. A road leads out to a lighthouse suspended on the cliffs; from here you get a panoramic view over Pentland Firth. These turbulent waters have been a nightmare to mariners, with some 400 wrecks reported in the past century and a half.

In summer, there's daily passenger-only ferry service to Orkney. Bus tours of the island are included. The Orkney Islands are just a 45-minute sail from John o' Groats across the Pentland Firth (see chapter 12).

ACCOMMODATIONS & DINING

Seaview Hotel The Seaview is a family-run hotel whose severe and streamlined sides rise abruptly from a flat, windswept landscape beside the town's only highway. Built in the 1950s, it's covered with a roughly textured white stucco that locals refer to as pebble dash. Each guest room is rather austere but comfortable, with a shower-only bathroom and electric blanket. Bar lunches and dinners draw an appreciative crowd to the pub. Main courses in the restaurant are moderately priced.

John o' Groats KW1 4YR. © and fax 01955/611-220. 9 units, 5 with private bathroom. £29–£32 ($43.50–$48) double without bathroom; £36–£40 ($54–$60) double with bathroom. Rates include Scottish breakfast. MC, V. **Amenities:** Restaurant, bar; nearby golf course. *In room:* TV, coffeemaker, no phone.

The Arts in John O' Groats

In an old converted country school, the **Lythe Arts Centre** (© 01955/ 641-270) stages year-round performances of innovative and experimental works by small touring companies, from drama and dance to jazz, folk, and new music. There's also a permanent collection of art related to northern Scotland, and July and August bring touring exhibits of contemporary art, photography, and some crafts. Exhibits are open daily from 10am to 6pm; admission is £1.50 ($2.25) for adults, £1 ($1.50) for seniors, and 50p (75¢) for students and children. Performances usually start at 8pm. Advance booking is necessary for all shows, so call ahead. Tickets cost £9 ($13.50) for adults, £6 ($9) for seniors, and £4 ($6) for students and children. Coffee, tea, and light snacks are available on performance evenings. The arts center is signposted, 4 miles (6.5km) off A99 between Wick and John o' Groats.

THURSO

Many visitors drive through the northern port of Thurso as they're heading for Scrabster, where ferries leave for the Orkney Islands (see chapter 12). The town, on the River Thurso, is of only mild interest, used mainly as a refueling stop for those who have made it this far north. It remains a big, bustling holiday resort with a still-active fishing fleet. In the center, many restored sandstone town houses date from the 1700s.

Once an important and major Viking stronghold, Thurso—meaning "river of the god Thor"—knew its greatest power and prestige in the 11th century, when it was ruled by Thorfinn, who had defeated King Duncan's nephew in 1040. In medieval times, Thurso became the major trading town between Scotland and the Norse countries.

To the west are the cliffs of Holborn Head and Dunnet Head, which boast a lighthouse. Many visitors walk out to the most northern point of mainland Britain for its panoramic views of the southern tier of the Orkneys. The town is 133 miles (214km) northwest of Inverness, 21 miles (34km) northwest of Wick, and 20 miles (32km) west of John o Groats.

If you'd like to explore by bike, head for the **Bike Shop,** 35 High St. (© **01847/896-124**), where rental rates are £10 ($15) daily or £50 ($75) weekly. The deposit is £25 ($37.50). Open Monday through Saturday from 10am to 5pm.

For information on Thurso, visit the summer-only **tourist office** at Riverside (© **01847/892-371**).

ACCOMMODATIONS & DINING

The New Weigh Inn & Lodges ✦   This is the most modern hotel in the far north of Scotland, overlooking the Pentland Firth with panoramic views that extend (on a clear day) to the Orkney Islands. It's on the outskirts of Thurso, at the junction of the A9 to Scrabster Harbour and the main artery leading to the western coast of the Highlands. Many travelers planning to take the morning car ferry to the Orkney Islands stay overnight here. The wide variety of accommodations includes doubles, twins, singles, and even family rooms. Some bathrooms contain showers only.

Burnside, Thurso. KW14 TUG. © **01847/893-722.** Fax 01847/892112. www.weighinn.co.uk/frmain.htm. 58 units. £58–£78 ($87–$117) double. MC, V. **Amenities:** Restaurant, bar. *In room:* TV, coffeemaker.

Park Hotel   With an almost Scandinavian style, this hotel offers comfortable, adequately furnished rooms with small, shower-only bathrooms; eight units can accommodate families. Guests receive a warm reception and friendly service. Both the lounge and restaurant offer reasonably priced meals accompanied by a fine selection of wines, beers, and malt whiskies. High tea is served as well.

Located on the right-hand side of the A9 on approach to the Thurso town center, Thurso KW14 8RE. © **01847/893-251.** Fax 01847/893-252. parkthurso@yahoo.co.uk. 11 units. £70 ($105) double. Rates include full Scottish breakfast. AE, DC, MC, V. Closed Jan 1–3. **Amenities:** Restaurant, bar, lounge; nearby golf and pool. *In room:* TV, coffeemaker, hair dryer.

ULLAPOOL ✦

Ullapool is an interesting village, the largest in Wester Ross, 59 miles (95km) northwest of Inverness and 238 miles (383km) north of Glasgow. It was built by the British Fishery Society in 1788 as a port for herring fishers and is still a busy harbor. The original town plan hasn't been changed, and many of the buildings look much as they did at the time of their construction. Ullapool has long been an embarkation point for travelers crossing the Minch, a section of the North Atlantic separating Scotland from the Outer Hebrides.

EXPLORING THE AREA

One of our favorite towns in this region of Scotland, Ullapool was founded on the lovely shores of the salt lake **Loch Broom.** The site of the ferry docks for the island of Lewis, Ullapool remains a bustling fishing station. It's also the best embarkation point for trips to the Summer Isles (see below).

One of the most dramatic and scenic views in the north of Scotland is possible from Ullapool, a 40-mile (64.5km) run north following the signposts to the village of Lochiner. Take A835 north from Ullapool, enjoying the views of Loch Broom as you go along. You'll pass the hamlet of Armair on Loch Kanaird, then come to the **Inverpolly National Nature Reserve** of some 27,000 acres (10,935 hectares), including lochs and lochans along with the peaks of Cul Mor at 2,786 feet (845m), Cul Beag at 2,523 feet (765m), and Stac Pollaidth at 2,010 feet (610m).

At **Knockan,** 15 miles (24km) north of Ullapool, a signposted nature trail along the cliff offers the most dramatic views in the area and is the best place to observe the regional flora, fauna, and geology.

At the Ledmore junction, take A837 to the left, passing along **Loch Awe,** with the mountain peaks of Canisp at 2,779 feet (843m) and Ben More Assynt at 3,230 feet (980m) forming a backdrop. You'll reach the lovely 6-mile-long (10km) **Loch Assynt.** The road along this lake-dotted landscape eventually carries you to **Lochiner,** a hamlet with fewer than 300 souls. It's known for its scenery, sandy coves, and crofting communities. For tourist information, call ✆ **01854/612-135.**

There are a number of day trips you can take from Ullapool, including a jaunt to the **Corrieshalloch Gorge,** 12 miles (19km) southeast, a nature reserve along A835 at Braemore. From this point, the Falls of Measach plunge 150 feet (45.5m) into a mile-long wooded gorge. A bridge over the chasm and a viewing platform offer a panoramic way to enjoy this spectacular scenery.

Another interesting excursion is to the **Inverewe Gardens** (✆ **01445/ 781-200**). An exotic mixture of plants from the South Pacific, the Himalayas, and South America allows the gardens to have color year-round. They can be reached along A832, 6 miles (10km) northeast of Gairloch. Open Monday through Saturday from 9:30am to 7pm and Sunday from noon to 7pm. Admission is £5 ($7.50) for adults, £4 ($6) for seniors and children, and £14 ($21) per family.

From either Ullapool or Achiltibuie, you can take excursions in season to the **Summer Isles** ⋆⋆, a beautiful group of almost uninhabited islands off the coast. They get their name because sheep are transported here in summer for grazing; the islands are a mecca for bird-watchers. Boat schedules vary, depending on weather conditions. Information is available from the **tourist office** on Argyle Street (✆ **01854/612-135**).

ACCOMMODATIONS

Altanaharrie Inn ⋆⋆⋆ (Finds) This is one of those places you feel you shouldn't tell anyone about, for fear they won't have room for you when you arrive. The Altanaharrie was once a 17th-century drover's inn on the banks of Loch Broom. There's no access by road, so you're brought over the loch by private launch. Once you've landed, you're greeted with a log fire in the lounge and a dram before dinner. The cooking is among the best in northwest Scotland, using locally caught seafood. Shellfish is kept in creels in the loch until ready for consumption. There's no choice on the five-course menu, but you're asked your preferences and allergies beforehand. The guest rooms are uncomplicated but exceedingly inviting, housed either in the main building or in small cottages on the grounds. There are no TVs, no room phones, nothing to distract. At night the generator is switched off, and candles and torches provide needed illumination. In the morning, it's a delight to find a breakfast that might include homemade jams, buttery croissants, and perhaps even venison sausages.

Loch Broom, Ullapool IV26 2SS. (℃) **01854/633-230.** 8 units. £165–£205 ($247.50–$307.50) per person. Rates include half-board. AE, MC, V. Closed Nov–Easter. Transportation is by private ferry. **Amenities:** Restaurant, lounge; room service. *In room:* Hair dryer, no phone.

Dromnan Guest House *(Value)* Mrs. MacDonald is your host at this 1970s stone guesthouse on the southern outskirts of town, a 10-minute walk from the center. The place is very well maintained, and the guest rooms are described by the kindly owner as being decorated in a combination of Marks & Spencer department-store goods and Shand-Kydd wallpapers and fabrics designed by the mother of the late Princess Diana. Each unit is equipped with a small bathroom with shower.

Garve Rd., Ullapool IV26 2SX. (℃) **01854/612-333.** Fax 01854/613-364. www.dromnan.co.uk. 7 units. £36–£48 ($54–$72) double. Rates include breakfast. DC, MC, V. **Amenities:** TV lounge; access to nearby leisure center (with pool, sauna, and tennis courts). *In room:* TV, coffeemaker, hair dryer, no phone.

Royal Hotel The Royal sits on a knoll on the Inverness side of town, overlooking the harborfront. Graced with curved walls and large sheets of glass, it was reconstructed in 1961 from an older building, with an added east wing. It offers well-furnished guest rooms, half with balconies opening onto views of Loch Broom. All are equipped with shower-only bathrooms. Live entertainment is offered in season. Scottish fare is served in the dining area; afterward, guests sit around a log fire in the well-appointed lounge.

Garve Rd., Ullapool IV26 2SY. (℃) **01854/612-181** or 01942/824-824 for reservations. Fax 01854/612-951. 50 units. £60–£70 ($90–$105) double. 2-night minimum stay. Rates include Scottish breakfast. MC, V. Closed Nov to early Mar. **Amenities:** Restaurant, bar. *In room:* TV, coffeemaker, hair dryer (on request).

DINING

Mariner's Restaurant SCOTTISH/INTERNATIONAL Within the simple confines of a somewhat battered building, this restaurant serves food that is both upscale and elegant. Its design (ca. 1970s) might remind you of a roadside motel, if not for the wild and verdant scenery around you. Lunches are rather deceptively promoted as bar snacks, even though they include full-fledged waitress service and elaborate versions of lobster, oak-roasted smoked salmon, and haggis with black pudding. Dinners are in the same price range as lunch, but are served in a separate dining room.

On the premises are 10 motel rooms, clean and unassuming but not particularly distinctive. Doubles go for £50 ($75) and come with TV and phone.

North Rd. (℃) **01854/612-161.** Reservations recommended. Main courses £8–£22 ($12–$33). DC, MC, V. Daily noon–2pm and 5:30–9:30pm.

11

The Hebridean Islands

Once the Hebridean islands were visited only by geologists, bird-watchers, and the occasional fisher or mountain climber. Today, the chain of islands just off the Scottish mainland that makes up the Inner Hebrides is becoming more and more accessible to the general visitor. But what about the Outer Hebrides? One of the lesser-known parts of western Europe, these are a splintered sweep of windswept islands stretching for some 130 miles (209km) from the Butt of Lewis in the north all the way to Barra Head in the south. With rugged cliffs, clean beaches, archaeological treasures, and tiny bays, the Outer Hebrides lure more and more visitors every year.

From Gourock, the ferry terminal near Glasgow, **Caledonian MacBrayne** (✆ **01475/650-100** for information, or 0990/650-000 for reservations) sails to 23 Scottish islands in the Firth of Clyde and the Western Isles, including Skye and Mull, as well as the Outer Hebrides. The company also offers inclusive tours ideal for visiting places well off the beaten track.

If you're driving from the mainland, you can take the "Road to the Isles," heading for the Kyle of Lochalsh if your destination is Skye. For Mull and Iona, Oban is your port. These islands are part of the Inner Hebrides and enjoy fairly good connections with the mainland. The more remote Outer Hebrides are linked by car ferries from mainland ports like Ullapool (✆ **01851/702-361** in Stornoway for schedules). The main islands to visit here are Lewis and Harris. Glasgow has air service to the airport at Stornoway on Lewis; call British Airways (✆ **0345/222-111** in Glasgow) for details.

EXPLORING THE INNER HEBRIDES If you travel to the Inner Hebrides, the chain of islands just off the west coast of the Scottish mainland, you'll be following in the footsteps of Samuel Johnson and his faithful Boswell. The **Isle of Skye** is the largest. **Mull** has wild scenery and golf courses, and just off its shores is the important **Iona,** the isle that played a major part not only in the spread of Christianity in Britain, but also in the preservation of the culture and learning of the ancient world when it was being forgotten all over Europe. Adventurous travelers will also seek out **Coll** and **Tyree** as well as the **Isle of Colonsay** and **Rhum (Rum), Eigg,** or the tiny island of **Raasay,** off Skye.

If your time is limited, we suggest you concentrate on Skye. It offers your best chance for getting the flavor of the Hebrides in a nutshell, all in a 2-day trip. The island's natural beauty ranges from the rugged Trotternish Peninsula to the jagged peaks of the Cuillin Hills. The Cuillins are called both Black Cuillins (the hills encircling the glacial trough of Loch Coruisk) and Red Cuillins (based on the pink granite found in the hills). A favorite of hill climbers, these often harsh mountains make for some of the grandest walks in Skye.

Our favorite drive in all the Hebrides is to the Trotternish Peninsula and northeast Skye, which you can easily tour in a day from Portree. This is only a 20-mile (32km) peninsula but is so fascinating you can easily spend a day enjoying it. The highlight of the drive is 8 miles (13km) north of Portree: the **Old Man of Storr,** a stone pinnacle standing 160 feet (48.5m) high. Once at the top, you'll be rewarded with great views of the island.

If you have time for one more Hebridean island, make it **Mull.** From Mull you can also spend an afternoon visiting the ancient ecclesiastical center off the coast at **Iona.** Spend the morning exploring parts of Mull, including a visit to Torosay Castle and Gardens. Have lunch on Mull, and then hop over to the little island of Iona.

EXPLORING THE OUTER HEBRIDES At first you may feel you've come to a lunar landscape where there's a sense of infinite time. The character of the Outer Hebrides is quite different from that of the Inner Hebrides. This string of islands, stretching for 130 miles (209km), is about 40 miles (64.5km) off the northwest coast of Scotland, and the main islands to visit are **Lewis** and **Harris** (parts of the same island despite the different names), **North Uist, Benbecula, South Uist,** and **Barra.** The archipelago also takes in some minor offshore islands. Gaelic is

spoken here; its gentle cadence is said to have been the language spoken in the Garden of Eden. Presbyterianism is still very strong (in one B&B, watching TV on Sunday is forbidden). Before you go, you might read Compton Mackenzie's novel *Whisky Galore.*

The islands knew 2 centuries of Viking invasions, but today are the retreat of many a disenchanted artist from the mainland. They come here, take over old crofter's cottages, and devote their days to such pursuits as pottery making and weaving. Birdwatchers flock here to see the habitats of the red-necked phalarope, corncrake, golden eagle, Arctic skua, and grayleg goose. Golfers come to play on these far-northern courses, including one at Stornoway (Lewis) and another at Askernish (South Uist). Anglers come to fish for salmon, brown trout, and sea trout.

You can see much of the dim past on these islands, including a version of Stonehenge. A good time to visit is June and July, when adults' and children's choirs compete for honors at festivals celebrating Gaelic music and poetry. Each of the main islands has accommodations, most small, family-run guesthouses and hotels. Many are crofter's cottages that take in B&B guests, mainly in summer. Advance reservations are important.

1 Kyle of Lochalsh: Gateway to the Isle of Skye

204 miles (329km) NW of Edinburgh, 82 (132km) miles SW of Inverness, 125 miles (201km) N of Oban

The popular Kyle of Lochalsh is the gateway to the island of Skye (now reached by toll bridge). You can drive the length of Skye in a day, returning to the mainland by night if you want.

ESSENTIALS
GETTING THERE Four **trains** per day (two on Sunday) arrive from Inverness, taking about 2½ hours and costing £51.50 ($77.25) each way. Call ℃ **08457/484-950** for schedules.

Both **Scottish CityLink** and **Skye-Ways** coaches arrive daily from Glasgow at the Kyle of Lochalsh (trip time: 5 hours), costing £16.30 (24.45) each way. Skye-Ways also operates three buses a day from Inverness (trip time: 2 hours), costing £12 ($18) one-way. Call ℃ **0990/808-080** for schedules.

The Hebrides

If you're **driving** from Fort William, head north along A82 to Invergarry, where you cut west onto A87 to the Kyle of Lochalsh.

VISITOR INFORMATION   The **tourist office** is at the Kyle of Lochalsh Car Park (© **01599/534-276;** www.highlandfreedom.com). It's open April to June, Monday through Saturday from 9am to 5:30pm; July and August, Monday through Saturday from 9am to 7pm and Sunday from 10am to 4pm; September and October, Monday through Friday from 9am to 5pm; and November to March, Monday through Friday from 9am to 5pm and Saturday from 10am to 4pm.

A NEARBY ATTRACTION

Eilean Donan Castle   This romantic castle was built in 1214 as a defense against the Danes. In ruins for 200 years, it was restored by Colonel MacRae of Clan MacRae in 1932 and is now a clan war memorial and museum, containing Jacobite relics, mostly with clan connections. A shop here sells kilts, woolens, and souvenirs.

Dornie. © **01599/555-202.** Admission £3.95 ($5.95) adults; £3.20 ($4.80) seniors, students, and children; £9.50 ($14.25) per family. Apr–Oct daily 10am–5:30pm; Mar and Nov daily 10am–4pm. Drive 8 miles (13km) east of the Kyle of Lochalsh on A87.

ACCOMMODATIONS

The lodgings here are limited, just barely adequate to meet the demand for rooms.

Kyle Hotel   This modernized stone hotel in the center of town, a 5-minute walk from the train station, is your best all-around bet in the moderate category. The midsize guest rooms are furnished in a functional style, with neatly kept bathrooms (some with shower only). The hotel serves reasonably priced dinners in the lounge nightly.

Main St., Kyle of Lochalsh IV40 8AB. © **01599/534-204.** Fax 01599/534-932. 31 units. £75–£90 ($112.50–$135) double. Rates include Scottish breakfast. AE, MC, V. **Amenities:** Restaurant, bar, lounge; room service; laundry. *In room:* TV, coffeemaker, hair dryer.

Lochalsh Hotel *&*   This landmark hotel is the most refined nesting ground in the area. It was built as a luxury oasis when the British Railway finally extended its tracks in this direction. The hotel's crafted small-paned windows with hardwood and brass fittings will remind you of those on an oceangoing yacht. The comfortable guest rooms have been stylishly overhauled; all of the state-of-the-art bathrooms contain combination tub/showers. Upscale dinners in the restaurant include the best Scottish cuisine and ingredients, accompanied by a panoramic view.

Ferry Rd., Kyle of Lochalsh IV40 8AF. © **01599/534-202.** Fax 01599/534-881. 38 units. £65–£95 ($97.50–$142.50) double. Rates include Scottish breakfast. AE,MC, V. **Amenities:** Restaurant, bar; laundry. *In room:* TV, coffeemaker, hair dryer.

DINING

The Seafood Restaurant *&* SEAFOOD   This blue-and-white clapboard building (1880) was originally a waiting room for rail passengers en route to other destinations, but now it's one of the most frequented restaurants in town. The menu items are flavorful but unfussy, prepared with attention to detail. The best examples are Lochalsh langoustines in herb-flavored butter sauce and local queen scallops in white-wine sauce.

In the Railway Station. © **01599/534-813.** Main courses £6–£10 ($9–$15) lunch; £8–£15 ($12–$22.50) dinner. MC, V. Mon–Fri 10am–3pm; daily 6–9pm. Closed Oct–Easter.

2 The Isle of Skye: Star of the Hebrides *(★(★

83 miles (134km) W of Inverness, 176 miles (283km) NW of Edinburgh, 146 miles (235km) NW of Glasgow

Off the northwest coast of Scotland, the mystical Isle of Skye, largest of the Inner Hebrides, is 48 miles (77km) long and varies between 3 and 25 miles (5km and 40km) wide. It's separated from the mainland by the Sound of Sleat (pronounced Slate). At Kyleakin, on the eastern end, the channel is only a quarter of a mile (about 0.5km) wide.

Dominating the land of summer seas, streams, woodland glens, mountain passes, cliffs, and waterfalls are the **Cuillin Hills** *(★★★*, a range of jagged black mountains that are a mecca for rock climbers. The Sleat Peninsula, the island's southernmost arm, is known as the "Garden of Skye." There are many stories as to the origin of the name *Skye*. Some believe it's from the Norse *ski*, meaning "cloud," and others say it's from the Gaelic word for "winged." There are Norse names on the island, however, as the Norsemen held sway for 4 centuries before 1263. Overlooking the Kyle is the ruined **Castle Moal**, once the home of a Norwegian princess.

On the island you can explore castle ruins, *duns* (hill forts), and *brochs* (prehistoric round stone towers). For the Scots, the island will forever evoke images of Flora MacDonald, who conducted the disguised Bonnie Prince Charlie to Skye after the Culloden defeat.

ESSENTIALS

GETTING THERE   From the Kyle of Lochalsh, drive west along the new toll bridge over the strait to Kyleakin; it costs £5.50 ($8.25) to cross one-way.

VISITOR INFORMATION   The **tourist office** is at Bayfield House in Portree (✆ **01478/612-137;** www.highlandfreedom.com). It's open April to June, Monday through Saturday from 9am to 5:30pm; July to mid-August, Monday through Saturday from 9am to 8pm and Sunday from 10am to 4pm; mid-August to October, Monday through Saturday from 9am to 5:30pm; and November to March, Monday through Friday from 9am to 5pm and Saturday from 10am to 4pm.

OUTDOOR PURSUITS AROUND THE ISLAND

BIKING   Gently undulating hills, coupled with the good roads and a relative lack of traffic, make the Isle of Skye appealing to cyclists. The island's premier rental outfits are **Island Cycles,** The Green, in the coastal city of Portree (✆ **01478/613-121**), and **Fairwinds Bicycle Hire,** Elgol Road, Broadford (✆ **01471/822-270**), farther inland, near the center of the island. Both charge £10 to £12 ($15 to $18) a day. Island Cycles is open Monday through Saturday from 9:30am to 5pm; Fairwinds is open daily from 9am to 6pm.

BOATING   The coast of Skye is the most ruggedly beautiful this side of the Norwegian fjords, and several entrepreneurs offer boat trips letting you drink in the scenery. Foremost is **Bella Jane Boat Trips,** The Harbourfront, Elgol (✆ **0800/731-3089** in Britain, or 01471/866-244). From the piers in the village of Elgol, you'll board a sturdy vessel that sails (if there's enough business) daily between Easter and October into the rock-ringed borders of Loch Coruisk, at the foot of the Cuillin Hills, which are rich in bird life. Most visitors opt for the standard return trip; you're carried to the base of the hills, deposited for 90 minutes of wandering, and then returned over water to Elgol. It lasts 3 hours and costs £13.50 ($20.25) per person. If you're hardy and really interested in hiking, you can extend this experience to a full day.

GOLF   Golfing on Skye means an almost total lack of supervision, weather that can rain out or dry out a game with almost no notice, and often a lack of players. Whether you find this charming depends on your expectations, but overall, the island's best course is the nine-hole **Isle of Skye Golf Club** (② **01478/ 650-414**), adjacent to the hamlet of Sconser, on the southeast coast. Maintained by the local municipality, it has a simple snack bar and bar, and an on-again–off-again employee who cuts the grass whenever necessary. Less desirable but still prized for its convenience to residents of the **Skeabost House Hotel** (see "Skeabost Bridge," later in this chapter) is the 9-hole course associated with the hotel. Nonguests can play if they phone ahead for a reservation. Greens fees at both courses are £14 ($21) for a full day's play.

HIKING   Any branch of Skye's tourist office will offer advice on the many hikes available through the heather and glens of the island. For a walking adventure advised only for the stout-hearted and the fit, consider extending a boat trip on the Bella Jane (see above) with an additional 14-mile (22.5km) overland hike from the Cuillin Hills back to more heavily populated regions of the island. To do this, take the boat trip (one-way only) from Elgol to the Cuillin Hills. From here, brown-and-white signs direct you across an undulating, rock-strewn landscape to the Sligachan Hotel (see below), the premier hotel for trekkers. You can overnight at the hotel or take a bus or taxi the remaining 7 miles (11km) back to Portree.

KYLEAKIN

The seaport community of Kyleakin is the site of the old ferry terminal where the boats from the Scottish mainland used to arrive before Skye became linked by a bridge. Many visitors still prefer to stay here rather than on more remote, less convenient parts of the island.

Kyleakin opens onto a small bay and is dominated by a ruin, **Castle Maol,** on a jagged knoll. For a lovely walk, go from the town center up to this ruin from the 12th century, when it was a fortified stronghold of the Mackinnon clan.

ACCOMMODATIONS & DINING

Dunringell Hotel 👍   Rhododendrons and azaleas on this hotel's 4½ acres (1.8 hectares) provide a riot of color from March to July. Built in 1912, many of the Dunringell's modestly furnished guest rooms open onto scenic views; some units have showers, others tub baths. There are lounges for both smokers and nonsmokers. For those who wish to participate, the proprietors, Mr. and Mrs. MacPherson, hold a short worship service in one of the lounges each evening. As the hotel is not licensed, no alcoholic beverages are permitted in the dining room or lounges.

Kyleakin, Isle of Skye IV41 8PR. ② 01599/534-180. Fax 01599/534-460. www.dunringell-hotel.co.uk. 18 units, 10 with private bathroom. £36–£46 ($54–$69) double without bathroom; £46–£66 ($69–$99) double with bathroom. Rates include Scottish breakfast. MC, V. **Amenities:** Dining room; babysitting. *In room:* TV, coffeemaker, hair dryer.

White Heather Hotel   These two connected buildings provide basic accommodations with up-to-date amenities. The small guest rooms are simple but well maintained (some with shower only). Moderately priced dinners are served nightly in the dining room. The lounge, licensed only to serve guests, has a pleasant view of the Castle Maol. The hotel is convenient to both the ferry dock and the bus terminals.

Kyleakln, Isle of Skye IV41 8PL. ℂ **01599/534-577**. Fax 01599/534-427. www.whiteheatherhotel.co.uk. 10 units. £44–£54 ($66–$81) double. Rates include Scottish breakfast. MC, V. Closed Oct–Feb. **Amenities:** Restaurant. *In room:* TV, coffeemaker, no phone.

SLIGACHAN

The village of Sligachan sits at the head of a sea loch in a setting of scenic beauty with views of the Cuillin Hills (pronounced *Coo*-lin). It's one of the best bases for exploring Skye because of its central location. Visitors enjoy sea-trout fishing, with an occasional salmon caught on the Sligachan River. It's also possible to rent a boat from the hotel below to explore the Storr Lochs, 15 miles (24km) from Sligachan, known for good brown-trout fishing from May to September.

ACCOMMODATIONS & DINING

Sligachan Hotel   This family-run hotel nestles at the foot of the Cuillins on the main road between Portree and Kyleakin and is an ideal center from which to explore Skye. It's one of Skye's oldest coaching inns, built sometime in the 19th century. The guest rooms are old and a bit outdated, but still reasonably comfortable, each with a tub and shower. And the food is good, consisting of freshly caught seafood and at least one vegetarian selection served at dinner nightly. The bar also serves simple meals in front of an open fireplace.

Sligachan, Isle of Skye IV47 8SW. ℂ **01478/650-204**. Fax 01478/650-207. www.sligachan.demon.co.uk. 22 units. £60–£80 ($90–$120) double. Rates include Scottish breakfast. MC, V. **Amenities:** Restaurant, bar; limited room service; laundry. *In room:* TV, coffeemaker, hair dryer, no phone.

Ⓒ Crafts on Skye

Edinbane Pottery, on A850, 8 miles (13km) east of Dunvegan (Ⓒ **01470/582-234**), celebrates its 30th anniversary in 2002. The three artists working in this studio produce wood-fired stoneware and salt-glazed pottery, and they can fill custom orders in a wide range of finishes.

Artist Tom Mackenzie's etchings, prints, aquatints, and greeting cards are all inspired by the scenery and day-to-day life of the island. You can find his work at **Skye Original Prints at Portree,** 1 Wentworth St. (Ⓒ **01478/612-544**).

Since 1974, Stewart John Wilson has been designing and producing silver and gold jewelry, ceramic tiles, cheese boards, platters, and clocks, all featuring intricate Celtic patterns. You can see his work at **Skye Silver,** in the Old School, on Glendale Road (B884), 7 miles (11km) west of Dunvegan (Ⓒ **01470/511-263**). The selection of tiles is especially vast.

Craft Encounters, in the Post Office building in Broadford (Ⓒ **01471/822-754**), showcases many of Skye's talented artists. You'll find pewter jewelry, stained-glass light catchers, salt-dough bric-a-brac, folk and landscape paintings, tartan ties, and handmade jumpers (sweaters). Celtic patterns show up on glassware, tableware, linens, and pieces of marquetry. The island's musical talent is represented in a selection of traditional Scottish music CDs.

Skye Batik, The Green (Ⓒ **01478/613-331**), is one of the best crafts shops in Scotland. It sells wall hangings and cotton, tweed, wool, and linen clothing handprinted with Celtic designs from the 6th to the 8th centuries.

In **Harlequin Knitwear,** next to the Duisdale Hotel on Sleat (Ⓒ **01471/833-321**), local knitter Chryssy Gibbs designs men's and women's machine-knit Shetland wool sweaters. Her work is bright and colorful.

For more knitwear, go to **Ragamuffin,** on the pier in Armadale (Ⓒ **01471/844-217**), featuring quality Scottish, Irish, and British handknits for the whole family as well as accessories like hats, gloves, and scarves.

PORTREE 🐾🐾

Skye's capital, Portree, is the port for steamers making trips around the island and linking Skye with the 15-mile-long (24km) island of Raasay. Sligachan, 9 miles (14.5km) south, and Glenbrittle, 7 miles (11km) farther southwest, are centers for climbing the Cuillin Hills.

ACCOMMODATIONS

Bosville Hotel   This well-established hotel stands in the center of Portree and commands panoramic views of the harbor and the Cuillin Hills. It's a bright, welcoming inn known equally for its cuisine (see the Chandlery Restaurant, below) and for its bedrooms. Accommodations are generally spacious and well decorated, with such amenities as combination tub/shower bathrooms.

Bosville Terrace, Portree, Isle of Skye IV51 9DG. © **01478/612-846.** Fax 01478/613-434. www.macleodhotels. co.uk/bosville. 15 units. £60–£90 ($90–$135) double. Rates include breakfast. AE, MC, V. **Amenities:** Restaurant, bar; room service; babysitting; laundry. *In room:* TV, coffeemaker, hair dryer.

Cuillin Hills Hotel ⟨℟⟩   This stone-sided manor was built in the 1820s as a hunting lodge for the MacDonald clan. Half a mile (almost 1km) north of Portree's center, the comfortable hotel appeals to hikers and bird-watchers. Views from the guest rooms encompass the unspoiled Cuillin Hills, Portree's harbor, or the sea. Each unit is outfitted with reproductions of old-fashioned furniture, flowered wallpaper, and a combination tub/shower. Rather expensive dinners are available to both guests and nonguests who phone in advance.

Portree, Isle of Skye IV51 9LU. © **01478/612-003.** Fax 01478/613-092. 29 units. £90–£140 ($135–$210) double. Rates include breakfast. AE, MC, V. **Amenities:** Restaurant, bar; room service; laundry. *In room:* TV, coffeemaker, hair dryer, iron.

Rosedale Hotel   In one of the more secluded parts of Portree, on the harbor 100 yards (91m) from the village square, the Rosedale opens directly onto the sea. It was created from a row of dwellings dating from the reign of William IV. The midsize guest rooms in this warm and welcoming place are decorated in modern style and have combination tub/showers. The dining room serves expensive Scottish fare with the requisite seafood.

Beaumont Crescent, Portree, Isle of Skye IV51 9DF. © **01478/613-131.** Fax 01478/612-531. www. rosedalehotelskye.co.uk. 23 units. £76–£98 ($114–$147) double. Rates include Scottish breakfast. MC, V. **Amenities:** Restaurant, coffee shop, bar, lounge; room service; laundry. *In room:* TV, coffeemaker; hair dryer.

Royal Hotel   The Royal stands on a hill facing the water and is said to have extended hospitality to Bonnie Prince Charlie during his 1746 flight. In less dramatic circumstances, you can book one of its comfortable, small-to-midsize guest rooms; the preferred ones open onto the sea, and all have combination tub/showers. Formal meals and bar snacks are offered.

Bank St., Portree, Isle of Skye IV51 9BU. © **01478/612-525.** Fax 01478/613-198. www.royal-hotel. demon.co.uk. 25 units. £70–£90 ($105–$135) double. Rates include Scottish breakfast. MC, V. **Amenities:** 2 restaurants, bar, lounge; small gym; room service; laundry. *In room:* TV, coffeemaker, hair dryer.

DINING
The Chandlery Restaurant SCOTTISH/SEAFOOD   This restaurant attracts visitors and locals alike. The highly skilled chef creates delicious, innovative dishes such as king scallops with green garlic butter and crispy bacon, medaillons of Aberdeen Angus, and a dessert of ripe pear poached in port and flavored with cinnamon, served with a tartlet of whisky, honey, and oatmeal ice cream.

In the Bosville Hotel, Bosville Terrace. © **01478/612-846.** Reservations recommended. Main courses £13.95–£21.50 ($20.95–$32.25). AE, MC, V. Daily 11am–10pm.

UIG ⟨℟⟩
The village of Uig is on Trotternish, the largest Skye peninsula. The ferry port for Harris and Uist in the Outer Hebrides, it's 15 miles (24km) north of Portree and 49 miles (79km) from the Kyle of Lochalsh. Many people like to anchor here because it's convenient for early departures. Uig is also one of the most beautiful places in Skye to spend the night, as it opens onto Uig Bay and is known for its sunrises and sunsets.

Now a virtual ruin and only of passing interest, **Monkstadt House,** 1½ miles (2.5km) north, is where Flora MacDonald brought Bonnie Prince Charlie after their escape from Benbecula. This famous Scottish heroine was buried in **Kilmuir churchyard,** 5 miles (8km) north.

While on the Trotternish peninsula, you can also visit the **Skye Museum of Island Life** (© 01470/552-206), at Kilmuir. The old way of island life is preserved here, along with artifacts based on farming on the crofts. Some interiors from the 18th and 19th centuries have been reconstructed. Admission is £1.75 ($2.65) for adults, £1.25 ($1.90) for seniors and students, and 75p ($1.10) for children. From Easter to October, the museum is open Monday through Saturday from 9:30am to 5:30pm.

ACCOMMODATIONS & DINING

Ferry Inn   This building was first a bank and later a post office, but today this hotel's main focus is its popular pub, serving affordable meals. There are a handful of cozy guest rooms upstairs, each comfortably furnished. You'll recognize this place in the town center by its roadside design of late-Victorian gables.

Uig, Isle of Skye IV51 9XP. © 01470/542-242. 6 units. £66–£80 ($99–$120) double. Rates include Scottish breakfast. MC, V. **Amenities:** 2 restaurants, 2 bars; exercise machines; room service; laundry. *In room:* TV, coffeemaker.

DUNVEGAN

The village of Dunvegan, northwest of Portree, grew up around Skye's principal sight: **Dunvegan Castle** ⚁ (© 01470/521-206), the seat of the chiefs of Clan MacLeod, who have lived here for 750 years. Standing on a rocky promontory and said to be Britain's oldest inhabited castle, it was once accessible only by boat, but now the moat is bridged and the castle open to the public. It holds many relics, like a "fairy flag" believed to have been given to the MacLeods by woodland spirits and reputed to have brought good luck in battle. The castle is open daily: March to October from 10am to 5:30pm and November to February from 11am to 4pm. Admission to the castle and gardens is £5.50 ($8.25) for adults, £5 ($7.50) for seniors, and £3 ($4.50) for children. Admission to the gardens only is £3.80 ($5.70) for adults and seniors and £2 ($3) for children.

ACCOMMODATIONS

Atholl House Hotel (Kids)   Opposite the post office and near Dunvegan Castle, this hotel rents well-furnished guest rooms with tub or shower bathrooms. Two units have four-poster beds along with the best views of the mountain moorland and Loch Dunvegan. The chef prepares quality cuisine using an abundance of locally caught seafood.

Dunvegan, Isle of Skye IV55 8WA. © 01470/521-219. Fax 01470/521-481. www.athollhotel.demon.co.uk. 8 units, 7 with private bathroom. £64–£80 ($96–$120) double; £80–£90 ($120–$135) double with four-poster bed; from £85 ($127.50) per person family room. Rates include Scottish breakfast. AE, MC, V. **Amenities:** Restaurant, bar; room service; laundry. *In room:* TV, coffeemaker, phone (in some).

DINING

Three Chimneys Restaurant ⚁⚁ SCOTTISH   The Three Chimneys, in a stone crofter's house, is the winner of multiple awards. An exceptionally good starter is the wild duck paté, with wafer-thin grilled potato scones. Specialties are fresh seafood and Highland game, with examples like roasted wild salmon with warm lime-and-peppercorn vinaigrette and a trio of Highland game (venison, wild hare, and pigeon) with a sauce of beet root and black currants. The dessert menu includes scrumptious treats like marmalade pudding and Drambuie custard. More than 100 vintages from the wine list are available to accompany your meal.

ⓒ The Young Pretender

He was called **Bonnie Prince Charlie**, and he blazed across the pages of British history in his gallant but ill-fated attempt to regain the British crown for the Catholic Jacobite dynasty. Born in 1720 in exile in Rome, Charles Edward Stuart had a direct claim to the throne of Britain but had lost the succession to the German Protestant House of Hanover.

On July 23, 1745, when the prince landed on the Isle of Eriskay from France, islanders advised the 25-year-old pretender to return home. Within 2 days, he crossed to the mainland at Loch nan Uamh in Arisaig to rally support, and on August 19, raised his royal standard at Glenfinnan. Many clans rallied to his call, and backed by 1,200 troops, he marched south, gathering an ever larger army as he went.

Amazingly, he took Edinburgh by stealth on September 17. And on September 21, the prince's army crushingly defeated the English at the Battle of Prestonpans. The prince proclaimed his father as James VIII, king of Scotland, with himself as regent. For a few weeks, he held court at the Palace of Holyroodhouse in Edinburgh.

On November 8, he directed his army south, crossing into England and capturing the town of Carlisle. His invading armies took Kendal, Penrith, Lancaster, and Preston. Even Manchester fell, as the Scots were joined by English Jacobites. By December, they were only 120 miles (193km) from London. There was panic in the streets of the English capital, and King George planned an escape to Hanover.

Charles wanted to press forward, but his military advisers warned him to turn back. Slowly they retreated to Scotland and settled down for the winter in Inverness. In the meantime, the duke of Cumberland's army was moving up to challenge the prince's forces. Charles decided to confront them on the desolate Moor of Culloden, an ill-fated choice. On the morning of April 16, 1746, backed by anti-Jacobite Scots, the English army crushed the Scottish forces and earned for its general the name of "Butcher Cumberland." The Battle of Culloden ended in notorious atrocities, including the burning alive of injured prisoners and the killing of women and children.

The prince began 5 long months of wandering across the Highlands and Islands. He had a £30,000 ($51,000) price tag on his head—unbelievable wealth in those days—but no one turned him in. Finally, in the words of the song, he went "over the sea to Skye" disguised as the servant girl of Flora MacDonald, the Highland heroine. On September 20, Bonnie Prince Charlie returned to France secretly on the vessel *L'Heureux*. There he drifted and drank, eventually ending in Rome, where he died, all but forgotten by the world. A piper played "Lochaber No More" outside the window of his death chamber.

His brother assumed the Jacobite mantle, and—believe it or not—there's still a claimant to the throne today. His name is Prince Michael Stuart. He lives in exile in Paris but stays abreast of events in Scotland and even has plans of what he'll do "when [he's] restored to the throne, as [he] inevitably will be."

Six luxurious suites are located a few steps away from the restaurant. The House Over-By boasts a panoramic view of the sea, and each suite is fully equipped with amenities such as a TV, VCR, CD player, phone, and hair dryer. The cost is £190 ($285) double, including breakfast. Both the restaurant and the suites have been given a five-star rating by the Scottish Tourist Board.

Hwy. B884, Colbost. ℂ **01470/511-258.** Fax 01470/511358. www.threechimneys.co.uk. Reservations required for dinner, recommended for lunch. Fixed-price menu £12.95 ($19.45) for 2 courses, £16–£18 ($24–$27) for 3 courses; fixed-price dinner £24 ($36) for 2 courses, £30 ($45) for 3 courses, £30–£40 ($45–$60) for 4 courses. MC, V. Mon–Sat 12:30–2:30pm (last order) and 6:30–9:30pm (last order). Drive 4 miles (6.5km) west of Dunvegan on B884.

SKEABOST BRIDGE

Eastward from Dunvegan, Skeabost Bridge has an island cemetery of great antiquity. The graves of four Crusaders are here.

ACCOMMODATIONS & DINING

Skeabost House Hotel 🦌   This is one of the most inviting country homes on Skye, 35 miles (56km) west of the Kyle of Lochalsh and 6 miles (10km) north of Portree. Built in 1870 as a private estate, it has been converted into a lochside hotel boasting dormers, chimneys, tower, and gables. The Skeabost owns 8 miles (13km) of the bank of the River Snizort, so it attracts many folks who come to fish. In addition, guests can play the hotel's par-3 golf course. The comfortable bedrooms come in a variety of shapes and sizes, each with combination tub/shower. The main dining room offers expensive table d'hôte menus focusing on seafood.

Skeabost Bridge, Isle of Skye IV51 9NP. ℂ **01470/532-202.** Fax 01470/532-454. www.sol.co.uk/s/skeabost. 26 units. £69–£115 ($103.50–$172.50) double. Rates include Scottish breakfast. MC, V. Closed Dec–Mar. **Amenities:** 2 restaurants, bar; golf course; room service; babysitting; laundry. *In room:* TV, coffeemaker, hair dryer.

SLEAT PENINSULA

A lot of Skye can look melancholy and forlorn, especially in misty weather. For a change of landscape head for the **Sleat Peninsula,** the southeastern section of the island. Because of the lushness of its vegetation (the shores are washed by the warmer waters of the Gulf Stream), it has long been known as the "Garden of Skye." As you drive along, you'll note the intense green of the landscape and the well-kept grounds of locals' homes.

A ruined stronghold of the MacDonalds, **Knock Castle** is off A851 some 12 miles (19km) south of Broadford. Another MacDonald stronghold, **Dunsgiath Castle** has some well-preserved ruins open to view. They're found at Tokavaig on an unclassified road (watch for a sign) at a point 20 miles (32km) south and southwest of Broadford. You can visit both these evocative ruins for free, day or night. Inquire at the number given below for the Armadale Castle Gardens & Museum of the Isle.

Armadale Castle Gardens & Museum of the Isles   You don't have to have MacDonald as your last name to enjoy a stop at Skye's award-winning Clan Donald Visitor Centre. From Broadford, travel along a winding seaside road to the ruins of Armadale Castle and the rebuilt baronial stables. A multimedia exhibit tells of the lost culture of the ancient Gaelic world under the MacDonalds as lords of the Isles. The countryside ranger service offers a full summer program of guided walks and talks to introduce you to several miles of trails and the history of the Highland estate. A licensed restaurant in the stables offers good local food, from tea to a full meal. The drive from the ferry at Kyleakin is about 30 minutes, and the center is along A851 (follow the signs) near the Armadale-Mallaig ferry.

Armadale. ℂ 01471/844-305. Admission £4 ($6) adults, £3 ($4.50) seniors and children 5–15, £12 ($18) per family. Apr–Oct daily 9:30am–5:30pm.

ACCOMMODATIONS & DINING

Ardvasar Hotel *(ᴋ (Kids* The oldest part of this 250-year-old coaching inn is a stone-trimmed pub in what was once a stable. In 1990, a major renovation added bathrooms with tub and shower to each of the guest rooms and a cottage-cozy decor that includes pastels and chintz. Virtually everyone in the area comes to the restaurant for a mug of lager and a taste of the fine cuisine. Menu items include starters like peppered mushrooms with hot brandy sauce, followed by smoked chicken with cranberry sauce, although seafood is the specialty.

Ardvasar, Isle of Skye IV45 8RS. ℂ 01471/844-223. Fax 01471/844-495. www.ardvasarhotel.com. 10 units. £80 ($120) double; from £105 ($157.50) family room. Rates include Scottish breakfast. MC, V. **Amenities:** Restaurant, bar; limited room service; laundry. *In room:* TV, coffeemaker, hair dryer.

Fiordhem *(ᴋ (Finds* Some kind of stone-sided house has stood in this spot for hundreds of years. The present version, a snug little retreat, is a rebuilt fisherman's cottage within 20 feet (about 6m) of the edge of Loch Eishort. In the sitting room are comfortable armchairs and an open fireplace. The small guest rooms boast panoramic views of the Cuillin Hills and the islands of Canna and Rhum. Each is equipped with a shower-only bathroom. The dining room is pleasantly furnished with antiques, and the welcome is warm and hearty. Fresh seafood, lamb, and venison are featured.

Ord, Sleat, Isle of Skye IV44 8RN. ℂ 01471/855-226. www.host.co.uk. 3 units. £42 ($63) per person. 3-night minimum stay. Rates include half-board. MC, V. Closed Oct–Easter. Take A852 south along the eastern coast of Skye, but cut west along an unclassified road toward Ord to the west coast of the island. **Amenities:** Dining room. *In room:* Coffeemaker, no phone.

Kinloch Lodge *(ᴋ* The white-stone walls of this manor are visible from across the scrub- and pine-covered hillsides bordering the property. Built in 1680 as a hunting lodge, it's now the elegant residence of Lord and Lady MacDonald. Portraits of the family's 18th-century forebears are a striking feature of the reception rooms, as are the open fireplaces and the scores of antiques. The guest rooms come in various shapes and sizes (some with shower only); from the windows of some, you can occasionally glimpse the sea. Every evening, you can enjoy drinks in the drawing room before dining on one of the upscale meals for which Lady MacDonald is famous. The author of 13 cookbooks, she applies her imaginative recipes to ingredients shot, trapped, netted, or grown on Skye.

Isleornsay, Sleat, Isle of Skye IV43 8QY. ℂ 01471/833-333. Fax 01471/833-277. www.kinloch-lodge.co.uk. 15 units. £106–£156 ($159–$234) double. Rates include Scottish breakfast. AE, MC, V. **Amenities:** Dining room, bar, lounge. *In room:* TV, coffeemaker.

3 Rhum (Rum)

9 miles (14.5km) SW of the Isle of Skye

The enticingly named island of Rhum is only about 8 miles (13km) wide and 8 miles long. There are those who'll tell you not to go: "If you like a barren desert where it rains all the time, you'll love Rhum," a skipper in Mallaig recently told us. It's stark, all right. And very wet. In fact, with more than 90 inches (229cm) of rainfall recorded annually, it's said to be the wettest island of the Inner Hebrides.

Since the mid-1950s, Rhum has been owned by the Edinburgh-based Nature Conservancy Council, an ecological conservation group. Attempts are being made to bring back the sea eagle, which inhabited the island in Queen Victoria's day. On this storm-tossed outpost in summer, mountain climbers meet challenging peaks and anglers come for good trout fishing. Bird-lovers seek out the Manx shearwaters that live on the island in great numbers. Red deer and ponies, along with the wildflowers of summer, add color to an otherwise bleak landscape.

ESSENTIALS

GETTING THERE   A passenger **ferry** from Mallaig, on the western coast of Scotland, leaves about four times a week. No cars are allowed on the island. For information, contact **Caledonian MacBrayne** (© **01687/462-403** in Mallaig).

Before You Go . . .

Before traveling to Rhum, you must contact **Denise Reed**, the reserve manager at the Scottish Natural Heritage Nature Reserve, by calling © **01687/462-026**. The office will assist you in organizing accommodations on the island.

Sailings are from May to September only, on Monday and Wednesday at 10:30am, Friday at 6am, and Saturday at 5am and 12:30pm. A round-trip is £12.35 ($18.55) for adults. **Arisaig Marine** (© **01687/450-224**) sails from Arisaig to Rhum on Tuesday, Thursday, Saturday, and Sunday at 11am. A round-trip ticket is £18 ($27) for adults, £7 ($10.50) for children 12 to 16, and £4 ($6) for those under 12.

Schedules can vary, so it's best to call for confirmations. It takes about 2 hours to reach Rhum from one of these ports.

ACCOMMODATIONS & DINING

Kinloch Castle ★★ *(Finds)*   You'll be astonished that in such a forbidding place, you can come across a hotel that has been called "Britain's most intact example of an Edwardian country house." On the seafront in the center of Rhum's biggest hamlet, Kinloch, this mansion was completed in 1901 for Sir George Boullough, a wealthy Lancashire textile magnate. The castle still contains a ballroom, a massive Adam-style fireplace, and monumental paintings and stuffed animals. The former servants' quarters are now a simple and functional hostel, while the more elegant private rooms are furnished with four-poster beds (these share spacious bathrooms with tubs). Because guests spend their days trekking around the island, all lunches are packed picnics at £4.50 ($6.75) per person. The restaurant serves breakfasts and hearty dinners at reasonable prices.

Kinloch, Isle of Rhum PH43 4RR. © and fax **01687/462-037**. 27 units, none with private bathroom; 52 hostel beds. Rooms £60 ($90) double; hostel £12 ($18) per person, in rooms with 2–5 beds. MC, V. **Amenities:** Restaurant. *In room:* No phone.

4 Eigg & Muck

Eigg: 4 miles (6.5km) SE of Rhum; Muck: 7 (11km) miles SW of Eigg

The tiny islands of Eigg and Muck lie in the Sea of the Hebrides, which separates the Inner from the Outer Hebrides. If you're doing the whirlwind tour of Europe, Eigg and Muck will hardly top your agenda. They appeal only to nature lovers seeking a variety of Hebridean scenery and a chance to look at life of long ago. If your time is limited and you can visit only one isle, make it Eigg, which has the most dramatic scenery.

ESSENTIALS

GETTING THERE   Before venturing to either Eigg or Muck, confirm the schedule of the ferry's return. Because service isn't every day, you may find yourself staying at least 2 nights on either island. **Caledonian MacBrayne** (© 01687/ 462-403 in Mallaig) sails from Mallaig to Eigg on Monday, Tuesday, and Thursday at 10:30am, Friday at 6am, and Saturday at 5am and 12:30pm. The round-trip ticket is £9.20 ($13.80) for adults and £4.30 ($6.45) for children. From Arisaig, **Arisaig Marine** (© 01687/450-224) sails to Muck on Monday, Wednesday, and Friday (but departure days and times can vary). Sailings to Eigg are Friday through Wednesday. Most departures are at either 11 or 11:30am (subject to change, based on weather conditions). The round-trip fare for either is £15 ($22.50).

VISITOR INFORMATION   For assistance in finding accommodations on Eigg or for general information, contact **Mrs. Mairi Kirk,** 7 Cleadane, Isle of Eigg (© 01687/482-416). Lodging rates range from £26 to £35 ($39 to $52.50) per person, double occupancy.

EIGG

Eigg, about 4½ miles by 3 miles (7km by 5km), is some 12 miles (19km) out in the Atlantic. The island is owned by the Isle of Eigg Heritage Trust, which consists of about 70 island residents and the Highland Council and Scottish Wildlife Trust. The farmers, shepherds, fishermen, and innkeepers who live here raised the $2.4 million to buy their island through a worldwide public appeal over the Internet.

The **Sgurr of Eigg,** a tall column of lava, is thought to be the biggest such pitchstone (volcanic rock) mass in the United Kingdom. Climbers on its north side try to attain its impressive height of 1,300 feet (394m). It's said that the last of the pterodactyls roosted here.

After your arrival at **Galmisdale,** the principal hamlet and pier, you can take an antique bus to Cleadale. Once there, walk across moors to **Camas Sgiotaig,** with its well-known beach of the Singing Sands. Since the island is crisscrossed with paths and tracks, and access isn't restricted, you can walk in any direction that captures your fancy.

Visitors come to Eigg for the remoteness and the sense of living in the 19th century. The island is known for its plant, animal, and bird life, including golden eagles and seals. In summer, you can sometimes see minke whales and porpoises in the offshore waters. The island's resident warden leads guided walks of Eigg once a week in summer; call © 01687/482-477 for details.

MUCK

Lying 7 miles (11km) southwest of Eigg, Muck has such an unappetizing name that visitors may turn away. However, the name of this 2½-square-mile (6.5sq km) island was originally a Gaelic word, *muic,* meaning "island of the sow." Naturalists come here to see everything from rare butterflies to otters. Large colonies of nesting seabirds can be viewed in May and June.

Muck is actually a farm. There are hardly more than 30 people, and all are concerned with the running of the farm. The entire island is owned by two brothers: the Laird of Muck, Lawrence MacEwan, and his younger brother, Ewen MacEwan. There are no vehicles on the island except for bicycles and tractors.

What's the real reason to come? To see and explore a tiny, fragile Hebridean community that has survived, sometimes at great odds. That it carries on, and that its locals still eke out a living from farmland and sea, is reason enough. The scenery and the solitude are wonderful, as are the cattle, sheep, hens, house cats, and ducks roaming with relative freedom. If you walk to the top of the highest hill, **Ben Airean,** at 451 feet (137m), you'll have a panoramic view of Muck and its neighbor islands of Rhum and Eigg.

ACCOMMODATIONS & DINING
Port Mhor House   This solidly weatherproof hotel was built by Ewen MacEwan from 1975 to 1980; most of its building materials were barged in from the mainland. The small guest rooms are functional and well maintained. Guests can get a drink in the sitting room, where a log fire blazes during cold weather. The kitchen uses produce from the island's farm for plain and wholesome fare well suited to the brisk climate. Vegetarian dishes are available on request.

Port Mhor (a few steps from the ferry landing), Isle of Muck PH42 4RP. ℂ and fax **01687/462-365.** 8 units, none with private bathroom. £70 ($105) double. Rates include half-board. No credit cards. Closed Sept 15–May 15. **Amenities:** Restaurant, lounge; babysitting; laundry. *In room:* No phone.

5 Coll & Tyree

90 miles (145km) NW of Glasgow, 48 miles (77km) W of Fort William

If you like your scenery stark and tranquil, try tiny Coll and Tyree. The outermost of the Inner Hebrides, they're exposed to the open Atlantic and said to have the highest sunshine records in Britain. On Tyree (also spelled Tiree), the shell-sand *machair* (sand dunes) increase the arable area, differentiating it from the other inner isles.

Trees are rare on either island, but that doesn't mean they're bleak. Both are rich in flora, with some 500 species, along with bird life. It's estimated that some 150 bird species are found here, including Arctic skuas and razorbills. Both common and gray seals have breeding colonies on the islands. Boat rentals and sea angling can be arranged. Many visitors bicycle around the islands, and there are a few cars for rent. Tyree has the least expensive method of transport: A mail bus serves most of the island.

GETTING TO THE ISLANDS
British Airways (ℂ **0345/222-111** in Glasgow) flies directly to Tyree from Glasgow, with about six 90-minute flights per week (none on Sun). A **car ferry** sails from Oban to Coll (a 3-hour trip, costing £19.35/$29.05 round-trip) and Tyree (an extra 45 minutes), but in very rare instances gales may force cancellation of the trip. If the gale is very strong, you might be stranded on an island for a while, waiting for the next departure. Details and bookings, essential for cars, are available from **Caledonian MacBrayne** (ℂ **0990/650-000**).

COLL
Lying in the seemingly timeless world of the Celtic west, the island of Coll, with a population of some 130 hearty souls, is rich in history. Distances from one place to another are small, since the island averages about 3 miles (5km) in breadth; at its longest point, it stretches for some 13 miles (21km).

Coll has a partially restored castle, **Breacachadh,** rising majestically from its southeastern side. A stronghold of the Macleans in the 15th century, it is now a private residence. On some occasions, it's open to the public. Immediately adjacent is the so-called **New Castle,** built for Hector Maclean in 1750. It provided shelter for Samuel Johnson and James Boswell when they were stranded on the island for 10 days because of storms at sea. The castle, still a private home, was altered considerably in the 19th century and embellished with pepper-pot turrets and parapets.

In the western part of the island at Totronald are two standing stones called **Na Sgeulachan** ("Teller of Tales"). The stones pre-date the Druids and are thought to have been the site of a temple. The highest point on Coll is **Ben Hogh** (340 feet/103m), which you can climb for a panoramic view.

On the road to Sorisdale, at **Killunaig,** stand the ruins of a church from the late Middle Ages and a burial ground. Going on to **Sorisdale,** you'll see the ruins of houses occupied by crofters earlier in this century. Hundreds of families once lived here. Some were chased away in the wake of the potato famine, and many were forced out in Land Clearance programs.

ACCOMMODATIONS & DINING

Isle of Coll Hotel   This hotel enjoys the dubious honor of being immediately rejected by Samuel Johnson and James Boswell as an inappropriate place to spend the night during their 18th-century tour of Scotland. (They eventually succeeded in securing lodgings with the laird of Coll.) Today, the small-to-midsize guest rooms are far more comfortable, with electric blankets, tub bathrooms, and simple but functional furniture. The dining room serves good but rather expensive dinners. The hotel contains the town's only pub, so you're likely to meet locals over a pint of ale and a platter of more affordable bar food. The hotel sits on a hilltop at the end of the Arinagour estuary, about a 10-minute walk north of town, beside B8071.

Arinagour, Isle of Coll PA78 6SZ. ℂ 01879/230-334. Fax 01879/230-317. 6 units, 3 with private bathroom. £50 ($75) double without bathroom; £60 ($90) double with bathroom. Rates include Scottish breakfast. MC, V. The hotel sits on a hilltop at the end of the Arinagour estuary, about a 10-min. walk north of town, beside B8071. **Amenities:** Restaurant, bar; sauna; children's play area. *In room:* TV, coffeemaker, hair dryer, no phone.

TYREE (TIREE)

A fertile island, one of the richest in the Hebrides, flat Tyree has a population of some 800 residents, mostly in farming communities, who enjoy its gentle landscape, sandy beaches, and rolling hills. As you travel about the island, you'll see many 1800s crofter's houses with thatched roofs. In 1886, the duke of Argyll caused a scandal when he sent in marines and police to clear the crofters off the land. Many were sent destitute to Canada.

Most of the population is centered around **Scarinish,** with its little stone harbor where lobster boats put in. Fishing isn't what it used to be; the appearance of fast and dangerous squalls and storms are said to scatter the fleet as far as the shores of North America.

Bird-watchers are drawn to the shores of **Loch Bhasapoll,** a favorite gathering place of wild geese and ducks, and to a cave on the coast at **Kenavara,** where many seabirds can be observed.

Ancient duns and forts are scattered around Tyree. The best of these is a broch at **Vaul Bay,** with walls more than 12 feet (3.5m) thick. At **Balephetrish,** on the northern rim of the island, stands a huge granite boulder. Locals call it the Ringing Stone, because when struck it gives off a metallic sound. In the western part of the island, at Kilkenneth, are the ruins of the **Chapel of St. Kenneth,** a comrade of St. Columba.

ACCOMMODATIONS & DINING

Tiree Lodge Hotel   This is the nerve center of the island. Built as a simple hunting lodge around 1790, it was greatly enlarged in the 1970s with a modern addition. A mile (1.6km) east of the island's only ferry landing, the hotel contains one of Tyree's two pubs and attracts a crowd of locals and visitors. The small guest rooms are well maintained and comfortable; most units contain a small, shower-only bathroom.

Kirkatol, Isle of Tyree PA77 6TW. © **01879/220-368.** Fax 01879/220-884. 11 units, 9 with private bathroom. £46 ($69) double without bathroom; £54 ($81) double with bathroom. Rates include Scottish breakfast. MC, V. **Amenities:** Restaurant, bar. *In room:* TV, coffeemaker, hair dryer (on request), no phone.

6 Mull ⒡

121 miles (195km) NW of Edinburgh, 90 miles (145km) NW of Glasgow

The third-largest island in the Hebrides, Mull is rich in legend and folklore, a land of ghosts, monsters, and the wee folk. The island is wild and mountainous, characterized by sea lochs and sandy bars. Mull was known to the classical Greeks, and its prehistoric past is recalled in forts, duns, and stone circles. Be sure to bring a raincoat: Mull is known as one of the wettest islands in the Hebrides, a fact that upset Dr. Johnson, who visited in 1773.

Many visitors consider Mull more beautiful than Skye, a controversy we don't choose to get involved in because we love them both. Mull has varied scenery with many waterfalls, and the wild countryside was the scene of many of David Balfour's adventures in *Kidnapped,* by Robert Louis Stevenson. Its highest peak is **Ben More,** at 3,169 feet (961m), but it also has many flat areas. The island's wildlife includes roe deer, golden eagles, polecats, seabirds, and feral goats. Mull is also a jumping-off point to visit Iona and Staffa (see section 7, "Iona & Staffa: An Abbey & a Musical Cave," later in this chapter).

Guarding the bay (you'll see it as you cross on the ferry) is **Duart Castle,** restored just before World War I. In the bay—somewhere—lies the *Florencia,* a Spanish galleon that went down laden with treasure. Many attempts have been made to find it and bring it up, but so far all have failed. To the southeast, near Salen, are the 14th-century ruins of **Aros Castle,** once a stronghold of the Mac-Donalds, lords of the Isles. On the far south coast at Lochbuie, **Moy Castle** has a water-filled dungeon.

At the end of the day, you might enjoy a dram from the **Tobermory Malt Whisky Distillery,** in Tobermory (© **01688/302-647**), which opened in 1823. Tours are given Monday through Friday from 10:30am to 4pm; the cost is £3 ($4.50) for adults, £1.50 ($2.25) for seniors, and free for children. Be sure to call in advance, as the distillery seems to shut down from time to time.

ESSENTIALS

GETTING THERE It's a 45-minute trip by **car ferry** from Oban to Craignure, on Mull. For departure times, contact **Caledonian MacBrayne** (© **0990/ 650-000**). From Oban, there are about five or six sailings per day at a round-trip cost of £6.20 ($9.30) for adults and £3.05 ($4.60) for children. The cost for a car is £42 ($63) for a 5-day return ticket.

⒯ips A Word on Driving

If you're driving along any of Mull's single-track roads, remember to take your time and let the sheep and cattle have the right of way. Also, a car coming downhill toward you has the right of way, so look for a spot to pull off.

(Moments Close Encounters with Nature

Several operators will take you out to see whales, dolphins, and seals. Two of the best are **Sea Life Surveys**, Beadoun, Breidwood, Tobermory (© **01688/400-223**), and a hardworking entrepreneur named **Mr. Liverty**, High Street (© **01688/302-048**), who maintains midsize boats for 6 to 12 passengers each. At each, you pay £15 ($22.50) for a half-day excursion that offers sweeping views of the Mull coast and active colonies of seals and sea birds.

Visitors can also experience the wildlife-rich natural habitat with **Island Encounters** (© **01680/300-441**). Guided by a local expert, you can spend the day on a safari, exploring the most remote and scenic areas of the island in a comfortable eight-seat vehicle. The cost for the day is £24.50 ($36.75) for adults and £19 ($28.50) for children under 15. Binoculars and lunch are included in the price, and pick-up can be arranged at all ferry terminals on Mull.

GETTING AROUND   Use **Bowmans Coaches Mull** (© **01680/812-313**) to go around the island. Coaches connect with the ferry at least three times per day and will take you to Fionnphort or Tobermory for £7.40 ($11.10) or £5.35 ($8.05) round-trip. Another option is to buy a ticket combining the cost of the ferry with a guided bus tour to Fionnphort and Iona. The tour begins when you board the 10am ferry and ends at about 5:40pm, back at Oban. The cost is £21 ($31.50) for adults and £12 ($18) for children.

VISITOR INFORMATION   The **tourist office** is on Main Street in Tobermory (© **01688/302-182**). From Easter to October, it's open Monday through Friday from 9am to 5pm (to 6pm in July and August).

SPECIAL EVENTS   In July, the **Mull Highland Games** feature traditional events such as bagpipes, caber tossing, and dancing. The **Tour of Mull Rally** is held in early October. Ask at the tourist office for exact dates.

OUTDOOR PURSUITS AROUND THE ISLAND

BIKING   Its combinations of heather-clad, rock-strewn moors and sylvan forests make Mull especially appropriate for cycling. To rent a bike, try **On Yer Bike**, The Pierhead, in Craignure (© **01680/812-487**), 22 miles (35.5km) from Tobermory. In Tobermory itself, consider **Brown's**, High Street (© **01688/302-020**). Both charge £13 to £15 ($19.50 to 22.50) per day and are open daily from 10am to around 7pm.

GOLF   Golf isn't exactly as grand out here as on the fabled courses elsewhere in Scotland. The best of the lot is the nine-hole **Western Isles Golf Course**, about a quarter of a mile (about 0.5km) north of Tobermory. You're not likely to even see another player or employee here most times of the year. The course's agent/administrator is **Brown's Hardware Store**, High Street, Tobermory (© **01688/302-020**), where you pay the greens fees of £13 ($19.50) per day and the rental fee for clubs of £5 ($7.50) per day. Twenty-two miles (35.5km) west of Tobermory is the isolated nine-hole **Craignure Golf Course**, with an honesty box into which you deposit the greens fees of £11 ($16.50) per day. For information about this course, contact its secretary, D. Howitt, at © **01680/812-487**.

HIKING   The island is wonderful for hiking. You'll probably drive off to a trailhead, park your car beside the road (most residents boast they haven't locked their car in decades), and then set off on foot in total isolation. The tourist office sells two books, each costing £2.95 ($4.45): *Walks in North Mull* and *Walks in South Mull.* They provide detailed options for specific routes with historic, ethnographical, scenic, or geological interest. Dress in layers, and wear some- thing waterproof.

CRAIGNURE

Even passengers who arrive with a car might want to take a 20-minute excursion on the **Mull Railway,** Old Pier Station, Craignure (© **01680/812-494**), the only passenger rail in the Hebrides. It was inaugurated in 1983, but its puffing engine and narrow-gauge tracks are thoroughly old-fashioned. The tracks begin at the Old Pier in Craignure, running 1½ miles (2.5km) to Torosay Castle and its famous gardens. The view is one of unspoiled mountains, glens, and seaside; you can sometimes see otters, eagles, and deer. The trains operate from Easter to mid-October; the most frequent service is from June to mid-September, when daily trips begin around 11am. One-way fares are £2.70 ($4.05) for adults, £1.70 ($2.55) for children, and £7 ($10.50) for families. For details, call the Mull & West Highland Railway Company at © **01680/300-389.**

A good way to see the sights of Mull is to book a ticket for "The Mull Expe- rience," a tour offered by **Caledonian MacBrayne.** For information, call **Torosay Castle** (© **01680/812-421**). The tour begins in Oban, where you board a ferry for Craignure. Once in Craignure, you catch the train to Torosay Castle, where you'll spend a few hours exploring. The next stop is the castle of Duart. You then return to Oban by ferry. The tour is offered from May to September at a cost of £17.50 ($26.25) for adults and £9.10 ($13.65) for children.

Torosay Castle and Gardens   This is the only privately occupied castle and garden in the western Highlands open daily to the public. The Victorian mansion was built in the mid–19th century by David Bryce, a famous Scottish architect. In his early years, Winston Churchill was a frequent visitor. One writer said a visit here is like returning to the Edwardian age of leisure, and so it is. To the surprise of visitors, the armchairs are labeled PLEASE SIT DOWN instead of PLEASE KEEP OFF. The portraits are by such famous artists as Sargent. You can wander through 12 acres (4.9 hectares) of Italian-style terraced gardens, enjoy- ing extensive views of the Appin coastline from Ben Nevis to Ben Cruachen.

1½ miles (2.5km) south of Craignure on A849. © 01680/812-421. Admission to castle and gardens £5 ($7.50) adults, £3.70 ($5.55) seniors and students, £2.20 ($3.30) children 6–16, £12 ($18) per family. Admission to gardens and tearoom only £3.50 ($5.25) adults, £2.75 ($4.15) seniors and students, £1.20 ($1.80) children. Easter to mid-Oct daily 10:30am–5:30pm.

Duart Castle ℛ   You can visit both Torosay Castle (see above) and Duart Castle on the same day. Located 3 miles (5km) west of Torosay, this castle dates from the 13th century and was the home of the fiery Maclean clan. A majestic structure, it was sacked in 1791 by the dukes of Argyll in retaliation for the Macleans' support of the Stuarts in 1715 and 1745. It was allowed to fall into ruins until Sir Fitzroy Maclean, the 26th chief of the clan and grandfather of the present occupant, began a restoration in 1911 at the age of 76. It had been his ambition since he was a boy to see his ancestral home restored (he lived until he was 102).

Off A849, on the eastern point of Mull. © 01680/812-309. Admission £3.80 ($5.70) adults, £3 ($4.50) seniors and students, £1.85 ($2.80) children 3–15, £9.20 ($13.80) per family. May to mid-Oct daily 10:30am–6pm.

⟮*Moments* A Stunning View

Even locals sometimes drive out of their way to catch the sunset over the **Gribun Rock,** a large peninsula midway along the island's western coast, whose centerpiece is the windy uplands of Ben More. The entire stretch of single-lane highway on the western flank of Ben More is a particularly spectacular highlight. To reach it from Tobermory or Craignure, follow the signs to the hamlet of Salen, then drive west to Gribun. En route, you'll pass through the hamlets of Knock, Balnahard, and Balevuin. From dozens of points along the way, views stretch over the clifftops, encompassing the setting sun (if your timing is right) as well as the isles of Staffa, Coll, and Tiree.

ACCOMMODATIONS & DINING

Isle of Mull   This inn stands near the ferry and the meeting point of the Sound of Mull and Loch Linnhe. From the picture windows of its public rooms, you'll have panoramic vistas of mountains and the island of Lismore. The small guest rooms are handsomely furnished and come with bathrooms offering combination tub/showers. The chef serves British and Continental food in the attractive dining room.

Craignure, Isle of Mull PA65 6BB. ⟮Ⓒ⟯ **01680/812-351.** Fax 01680/812-462. 87 units. £65–£95 ($97.50–$142.50). Rates include Scottish breakfast. MC, V. Closed mid-Oct to mid-Mar. **Amenities:** Restaurant, bar; limited room service. *In room:* TV, coffeemaker, hair dryer.

SALEN

Near Salen are the ruins of **Aros Castle,** once a stronghold of the lords of the Isles, the MacDonalds. It dates from the 14th century and was last occupied in the 17th century. Most of the former castle has been carted off, but the site is still visible 11 miles southeast of Tobermory.

ACCOMMODATIONS & DINING

Glenforsa Hotel   This 1968 Norwegian pine log construction, in secluded grounds by the Sound of Mull and the River Forsa 11 miles (18km) southeast of Tobermory, is known in late summer for its seafront and salmon. The guest rooms are well appointed. The bar serves an array of tempting food, with venison, trout, and salmon offered in season for guests and nonguests alike. The hotel has an adjacent grass airstrip, at which private and charter planes can land from dawn to dusk.

By Salen, Aros, Isle of Mull PA72 6JN. ⟮Ⓒ⟯ **01680/300-377.** Fax 01680/300-535. www.glenforsa.co.uk. 13 units, 12 with private bathroom. £60–£75 ($90–$112.50) double. Rates include Scottish breakfast. MC, V. **Amenities:** Restaurant, lounge, bar; limited room service. *In room:* Coffeemaker, no phone.

TOBERMORY

Mull Museum (Ⓒ **01688/302-208**) has exhibits relating to the island, displayed in an old bakery building on Main Street. From Easter to mid-October, it's open Monday through Friday from 10am to 4pm and Saturday from 10am to 1pm. Admission is £1 ($1.50) for adults and 20p (30¢) for children.

Isle of Mull Silver, Main Street (Ⓒ **01688/302-345**), stocks jewelry made by a number of Scottish designers. Among the unique items made on the premises are traditional Scottish silver *quaich* (drinking vessels) and christening spoons. **Mull Pottery,** Main Street (Ⓒ **01688/302-057**), features tableware, ovenware, and lamps in seashore, seagull, and turquoise patterns. **Tackle & Books,** Main Street (℗ **01688/302-336**), carries fishing gear, bait, and an impressive array of reading materials—especially works by local authors and anything in print about Mull.

The **Western Isle Golf Course** dates from the 1930s and is said to have possibly the best views of any golf course in the world.

ACCOMMODATIONS

Tobermory Hotel   On the upper end of the town's main street, this hotel offers a sense of privacy. The majority of the bedrooms have views of the fishing boats in the harbor just off the road; the others have views of the tree-dotted cliff that rises abruptly behind the hotel. The bathrooms are small but neat (some with shower only). The dining room serves dinner nightly.

53 Main St., Tobermory, Isle of Mull PA75 6NT. ℗ **01688/302-091.** Fax 01688/302-254. www. thetobermoryhotel.com. 16 units. £72–£92 ($108–$138) double. Rates include Scottish breakfast. MC, V. Parking available on nearby streets. **Amenities:** Restaurant, bar; limited room service; laundry. *In room:* TV, coffeemaker, no phone.

Western Isles Hotel   In a scenic location on a bluff above the harbor, the Western Isles is a large, gray-stone country inn. It was constructed by the Sandeman sherry company in the late 1880s as a hunting and fishing lodge for top-level staff and customers. The current owners welcome guests to homey rooms decorated in a mix of styles, with small bathrooms with combination tub/showers. The hotel has a conservatory bar as well as an upscale restaurant.

Tobermory, Isle of Mull PA75 6PR. ℗ **01688/302-012.** Fax 01688/302-297. www.mullhotel.com. 25 units. £77–£128 ($115.50–$192) double; £136 ($204) suite. Rates include Scottish breakfast. AE, MC, V. Closed Dec 18–28. **Amenities:** Restaurant, bar; limited room service. *In room:* TV, coffeemaker, hair dryer.

DINING

Gannet's Restaurant SCOTTISH   This place enjoys a quayside setting in one of the stone-fronted 200-year-old buildings along Main Street. It's one of the best independent restaurants here. You get fresh seafood, much of it caught locally, along with salads, juicy steaks, and some fine vegetable dishes, finished off by creamy desserts. During the day, you might stop in for sandwiches and fresh coffee.

25 Main St. ℗ **01688/302-203.** Main courses £6.80–£12.95 ($10.20–$19.45). MC, V. Easter–Oct daily 10am–9:30pm; Nov–Easter daily 10am–3:30pm.

TOBERMORY AFTER DARK

Macgochan's Pub, Ledag (℗ **01688/302-350**), is an old traditional pub that has free Scottish music most nights from 8pm to 1am. There's also a game room with a pool table. The **Mishnish Hotel,** Main Street (℗ **01688/302-009**), is a faux-traditional pub featuring Scottish music nightly. In pleasant weather, you can step into the beer garden for a breath of fresh air.

DERVAIG ⚘

The loveliest village on Mull, Dervaig (Little Grove) is an 8-mile (13km) drive west from Tobermory. The **Old Byre Heritage Centre** (℗ **01688/400-229**) houses one of the most charming museums you could hope to find. The main exhibit features 25 scale models, painstakingly made by a local historian, showing the history of Mull from the first settlers to the Highland Clearances. A fully licensed tearoom serves light meals. Admission is £3 ($4.50) for adults, £2 ($3) for seniors and students, and £1.50 ($2.25) for children 5 to 12. From Easter to

October, it's open daily from 10:30am to 6:30pm. Take the twice-daily bus from Tobermory.

Just outside Dervaig is the **Mull Little Theater,** founded in 1966, seating 43. According to the *Guinness Book of World Records,* this makes it the smallest professional theater in Great Britain. See "Dervaig After Dark," below, for details.

From Dervaig, you can cruise to the lonely **Treshnish Isles,** a sanctuary for seabirds and seals. From April to September, a local entrepreneur operates the *Turus Mara* (✆ **01688/400-242**), carrying up to 60 passengers on half-day visits at £14.50 ($21.75) or full-day visits at £29.50 ($44.25). The boat departs from the Ulva Ferry Piers, on the west side of Mull. The Treshnish Isles are murky, muddy, and boggy, so bring dry clothes, boots, and a sense of humor.

ACCOMMODATIONS

Druimard Hotel   In the northwest of the island, this restored Victorian country house opens to views of an idyllic glen and the River Bellart where it flows into Loch Cuin and out to sea. For old-fashioned Scottish comfort and a tranquil atmosphere, this is the place to be. The bedrooms are tastefully furnished and contain small, shower-only bathrooms. Your hosts are a font of information about Mull. They'll arrange cruises to remote isles, wildlife expeditions, and even whale-watching jaunts. Even if you don't stay here, consider a visit to their winning restaurant (see below).

Dervaig, Isle of Mull PA75 6QW. ✆ and fax **01688/400-345.** www.druimard.co.uk. 5 units. £124–£152 ($186–$228) double. Rates include breakfast and dinner. MC, V. Closed Nov–Mar. Follow signs to Mull Little Theatre. **Amenities:** Restaurant. *In room:* TV, coffeemaker, hair dryer.

Druimnacroish Hotel   This is like a haven of escape from modern life. The owners have recently refurbished and upgraded the place. TVs and phones are purposely not included in the rooms (although they're available if requested). There's one self-catering apartment available for weekly stays. The moderately priced meals feature simple modern Scottish cuisine, taking full advantage of fresh local produce.

Dervaig, Isle of Mull PA75 6QW. ✆ and fax **01688/400-274.** www.druimnacroish.co.uk. 6 units. £60–£72 ($90–$108) double; £225–£275 ($337.50–$412.50) self-catering apt for 1 week. Room rates include Scottish breakfast. AE, MC, V. **Amenities:** Restaurant, bar, lounge; limited room service. *In room:* Coffeemaker, no phone.

DINING

Druimard Hotel Restaurant ✿ SCOTTISH   This acclaimed restaurant offers a varied menu based on local produce and supplies, ranging from the freshest of fish to tender Scottish beef. The cuisine is skillfully prepared, often with unusual sauces. You might begin with a real Scottish creation: creamy smoked haddock soup. The potato pancake topped with spring onion crème fraîche and a basil oil dressing will win you over. Meat-eaters dig into the filet of Aberdeen Angus topped with local oysters and parsley pesto on a bed of celeriac, wild mushrooms, and baby spinach with caramelized shallots and red-wine sauce.

In the Druimard Hotel, Dervaig. ✆ **01688/400-345.** Reservations recommended. Fixed-price 5-course dinner £28.50 ($42.75). MC, V. Daily 6:30–8:30pm. Closed Nov–Mar.

DERVAIG AFTER DARK

Located 8½ miles (14km) west of Tobermory, the **Mull Little Theatre,** Tobermory-Dervaig Rd. (✆ **01688/400-377**), is indeed quite small, with an audience capacity of 43 people for the dramas staged inside a former byre (stable). The season runs from Easter to September, with visiting companies as well as the small-but-capable Mull Theater Company filling the bill. Adult tickets run £12 ($18); seniors; students, and children pay £6.50 ($9.75). Tickets should be reserved in advance. There's no seat allocation, so arrive early.

FIONNPHORT

At the western tip of the Ross of Mull, Fionnphort is a tiny port that sees a lot of traffic. This is where the road ends and regular ferry passage is available across the mile-long (1.5km) Sound of Iona to the Isle of Iona, one of the most visited attractions in Scotland. Less than 2 miles (3km) to the south is the tidal island of Erraid, where David Balfour had adventures in Stevenson's *Kidnapped.*

ACCOMMODATIONS

Achaban House *Kids*   Its almost indestructible walls (3 feet/1m thick in places) were built in 1820 of pink granite for the supervisor of the local quarry. Shortly after, the building was converted into the manse (pastor's residence) for the local church. Today, it sits beside the town's only highway, a 10-minute walk east of the ferry landing. All rooms have private bathrooms (some with shower only), though some are across the hall. One family room is available. Fixed-price dinners can be prepared on request and might include excellent poached local salmon wrapped in a sheath of herbs. No smoking is permitted.

Fionnphort, Isle of Mull PA66 6BL. ℂ **01681/700-205.** Fax 01681/700-649. www.achabanhouse.co.uk. 6 units. £44 ($66) double; £52–£64 ($78-$96) family room. Rates include Scottish breakfast. MC,V. **Amenities:** Dining room. *In room:* Coffeemaker, no phone.

DINING

Keel Row SCOTTISH   The undisputed leader in providing food and drink to passengers waiting for a ferry to Iona, this friendly place is in two connected buildings near the pier. Food is served in a cedar-sided building overlooking the waterfront, while drinks are offered in a 19th-century stone cottage whose blazing fireplace adds cheer to many a gray day. Meal options include spicy fried crab with coriander, onions, tomatoes, and spices served with turmeric rice and salad, or the national dish of haggis with neeps and tatties (turnips and mashed potatoes).

At the harborfront, at the end of A849. ℂ **01681/700-458.** Main courses £6.80–£12 ($10.20–$18); sandwiches and burgers £2.70–£4.50 ($4.05–$6.75). MC, V. Restaurant summer only, daily noon–3pm and 6–8:45pm; snacks and drinks year-round, daily noon–8pm; meals served in the bar during winter, daily 6–8pm, and drinks year-round, daily noon–8pm; meals served in the bar during winter, daily 6–8pm.

7 Iona ⟨★⟩ & Staffa ⟨★⟩: An Abbey & a Musical Cave

Iona: ⅛ mile (about 20m) W of Mull; Staffa: 6 miles (10km) NE of Iona

A remote, low-lying, and treeless green island with high cliffs and rolling meadows, Iona is off the southwestern coast of Mull across the Sound of Iona. It's only 1 mile by 3½ miles (1.5km by 5.5km). Staffa, with its famous musical cave, is a 75-acre (30.4-hectare) island in the Inner Hebrides, lying to the west of Mull.

IONA

Iona has been known as a place of spiritual power and pilgrimage for centuries and was the site of the first Christian settlement in Scotland, preserving the learning that was nearly lost in the Dark Ages.

The island was owned by the dukes of Argyll from 1695, but to pay £1 million ($1.5 million) in real-estate taxes, the 12th duke was forced to sell it to Sir Hugh Fraser, former owner of Harrods. He secured Iona's future and made it possible for money raised by the National Trust for Scotland to be turned over to the trustees of the restored abbey. The only village on Iona, **Baille Mor,** sits in the most sheltered spot, allowing some trees and garden plots to be cultivated. The best way to get around Iona is to walk. If that's not for you, you can take horse-drawn carriage tours given by **Island Carriages** (② **01681/704-230**).

Iona is accessible only by passenger ferry from the Island of Mull. (Cars must remain on Mull.) Service is informal but fairly frequent in summer. In the off-season, transport depends entirely on the weather. The round-trip fare is £4 ($6). Call **Caledonian MacBrayne** (② **01688/302-017** in Tobermory) for exact times.

Today, the island attracts nearly 1,000 visitors a week in high season. Most come to see the Benedictine **Iona Abbey** ⚮, part of which dates from the 13th century. People also come to visit relics of the settlement founded here by St. Columba in A.D. 563, from which Celtic Christianity spread through Scotland and beyond to Europe. The abbey has been restored by the Iona Community, which leads tours and runs a coffee shop daily from 10am to 4:30pm; a voluntary contribution of £2 ($3.00) is requested. The community also offers room and board to interested visitors, conducts workshops on Christianity, sponsors a youth camp, and each Wednesday leads a 7-mile (11km) hike to the island's holy and historic spots.

---

② Staying at Iona Abbey

Some people consider a visit to Iona the highlight of their trip to Scotland. Besides feeling impressed by the unusual historical and archaeological site, many gain a renewed interest in the power of religion. If that's what you're seeking, you can contact the **Iona Community** (② **01681/700-404**), an ecumenical religious group that maintains a communal lifestyle in the ancient abbey and offers full board and accommodation to visitors who want to share in the community's daily life. The only ordained members of the group are its two wardens, who are members of either the Presbyterian Church of Scotland or the Scottish Episcopal Church.

From March to October, the community leads a series of discussion seminars, each stretching from Saturday to Saturday. A recent example focused on the role of the Christian Church in the united Europe of the 21st century. The cost of a week's full board during one of these seminars is £195 ($292.50) per person. The abbey also opens to guests from late November to mid-December, although no seminars are offered then. The per-week price is the same as in summer. Guests are expected to contribute about 30 minutes per day to the execution of some kind of household chore. The daily schedule involves a wake-up call at 8am, communal breakfast at 8:20am, a morning religious service, and plenty of unscheduled time for conversation, study, and contemplation. Up to 44 guests can be accommodated at one time in bunk-bedded twin rooms without private bathrooms. In addition to the abbey, there's the Iona Community's center for reconciliation, the **MacLeod Centre,** built for youth, people with disabilities, and families. It accommodates up to 50 guests, during summer only. For further details, phone ② **01681/700-404.**

Despite the many visitors, the atmosphere on the island remains peaceful and spiritual. You can walk off among the sheep and cows that wander freely everywhere to the top of **Dun-I,** a small mountain, and contemplate the ocean and the landscape as though you were the only person on earth.

ACCOMMODATIONS & DINING

Most of the islanders live by crofting and fishing and supplement their income by taking in paying guests in season, usually charging very low or at least fair prices. You can, of course, check into the hotels below, but a stay in a private home may be an altogether rewarding adventure.

Argyll Hotel ♣ *(Finds* Housed in an 1868 Victorian, this hotel stands 200 yards (182m) from the ferry dock, overlooking the Sound of Iona and Mull. The small guest rooms are comfortably furnished, each with a combination tub/shower. The good home cooking includes very fresh fish and baking; vegetarian meals are available. The hotel is licensed to serve alcohol to guests.

Isle of Iona PA76 6SJ. ℂ 01681/700-334. Fax 01681/700-510. www.argyllhoteliona.co.uk. 15 units, 14 with private bathroom. £96–£121 ($144–$181.50) double with bathroom. Rates include Scottish breakfast. MC, V. Closed early Oct to Mar. **Amenities:** Restaurant, bar, lounge; limited room service. *In room:* Hair dryer, no phone.

St. Columba Hotel This hotel, built of clapboard and white stone, is just uphill from the village about a quarter of a mile (0.5km) from the jetty. Built as a manse for Presbyterian clergy in 1847, its guest rooms are rather monastic, but clean and reasonably comfortable for the price. Bathrooms are small with either a tub or a shower. Try to get a room overlooking the sea, and reserve well in advance in summer. A set dinner is served nightly at 7pm, with hearty and wholesome food. Vegetarian meals are available on request.

Isle of Iona PA76 6SL. ℂ 01681/700-304. Fax 01681/700-688. www.stcolumba-hotel.co.uk. 27 units. £112–£144 ($168–$216) double. Rates include half-board. MC, V. Closed Oct 17 to mid-Mar. **Amenities:** Restaurant, bar, lounge; limited room service. *In room:* Coffeemaker, hair dryer, no phone.

STAFFA

The attraction of the island of Staffa, 6 miles (10km) north of Iona, is **Fingal's Cave** ♣, a lure to visitors for more than 200 years and the inspiration for music, poetry, paintings, and prose. Its Gaelic name, *An Uamh Ehinn,* means "musical cave." It's the only such formation known in the world that has basalt columns; over the centuries, the sea has carved a huge cavern in the basalt, leaving massive hexagonal columns. The sound of the crashing waves and swirling waters (the music) caused Mendelssohn to write the *Fingal's Cave Overture.* Turner painted the cave on canvas, and Keats, Wordsworth, and Tennyson all praised it in their poetry.

Staffa has been uninhabited for more than 170 years, but you can still explore the cave, which is strictly protected by the National Trust from development. Entrance is free, requiring only payment for boat passage from Mull or Iona at £12.50 ($18.75) for adults and £5 ($7.50) for children. The boat runs twice daily from Iona and Mull between March and October. Rubber-soled shoes and warm clothing are recommended. Reservations are important; call **Mrs. Carol Kirkpatrick,** whose husband, David, operates the boat, at *Tigh-na-Traigh* (House by the Shore), Isle of Iona (ℂ **01681/700-358**).

8 Colonsay

15 miles (24km) S of the Isle of Mull

The most remote of the islands of Argyll, Colonsay shares some of the same characteristics as Iona, Tyree, and Coll. To the west, it faces nothing but the open Atlantic—only a lighthouse stands between Colonsay and Canada. The island encompasses 20 square miles (52sq km). It's more tranquil than Mull and Skye because it doesn't accommodate day-trippers.

A ferry, operated by **Caledonian MacBrayne** (© **0990/650-000** for schedules), sails between Oban and Colonsay three times a week. The 37-mile (59.5km) crossing takes 2½ hours.

You can explore all parts of the island along its one-lane roads. Many visitors prefer to rent a bike rather than drive. You can also rent sailing dinghies and rowboats and sail around the island, following in the grand tradition of the Vikings. Go to the **Isle of Colonsay Hotel** (see below), whose staff can rent you a bike (£5/$7.50 per day or £15/$22.50 per week) or put you in touch with local fishermen and entrepreneurs; the boat should cost around £15 ($22.50) per hour.

Wildlife abounds, including golden eagles, falcons, gray seals, otters, and wild goats with elegant horns and long shaggy hair. Prehistoric forts, stone circles, and single standing stones attest to the antiquity of Colonsay, which has been occupied since the Stone Age.

It's estimated there are some 500 species of flora on the island. The gardens of the 1722 **Colonsay House** (not open to the public) are filled with rare rhododendrons, magnolias, and eucalyptus, even palm trees; from April to October, you can visit Wednesday from noon to 5pm and Friday from 2 to 5pm for £3 ($4.50). There's also an 18-hole golf course.

The little island of **Oransay** was named for Oran, a disciple of St. Columba. It's joined at low tide by the Strand, and you can wade across the sands during a 2-hour period. The ancient monastic ruins here date from the 6th century.

ACCOMMODATIONS & DINING

Isle of Colonsay Hotel ® _Finds_   This is Great Britain's most isolated hotel and Colonsay's social center. Its 18th-century gables and chimneys rise above surrounding herb and vegetable gardens. The bedrooms are small and decidedly informal, with basic but comfortable furnishings. Guests who want to get close-up views of the island's abundant flora and fauna can ask to be dropped off by courtesy car to go on rambles. A meal in the tongue-and-groove-paneled dining room is an event for locals, who appreciate the ambience of the cocktail lounge and bar. The inn serves lunch and rather expensive fixed-price dinners daily, with selections like homemade soup, fresh mussels, and vegetables from the garden.

Isle of Colonsay PA61 7YP. © 01951/200-316. Fax 01951/200-353. www.colonsay.org.uk/hotel.html. 12 units, 9 with private bathroom. £69–£85 ($103.50–$127.50) per person double. Rates include half-board. MC, V. **Amenities:** Restaurant, bar; scooter rental. _In room:_ TV, coffeemaker, hair dryer, iron, no phone.

9 Lewis ®: Island of Heather

209 miles (336.5km) NW of Edinburgh, 213 miles (343km) NW of Glasgow

The most northerly of the Outer Hebrides and also the largest at 60 miles (100km) long and 18 to 28 miles (29 to 45km) across, Lewis is easily reached by ferry from Ullapool (see chapter 10, "Inverness & the West Highlands," for more information). The island was once known as Lews, or, more poetically, the "island of heather"—the sweetness of the lamb raised here is said to come from their heather diet. Lewis and Harris (see "Harris," below) form part of the same island, stretching for a total of 95 miles (153km). Filled with marshy peat bogs, Lewis's landscape is relatively treeless, thanks in part to Norse raider Magnus Barelegs. He and his Viking warriors burned most of the trees, leaving Lewis as bare as his shanks.

Even though the whole world has heard of Harris tweed, it might as well be called Lewis tweed, as Stornoway has taken over the industry. On the eastern side of the island and with a population of 5,000, **Stornoway** is the only real town in the Outer Hebrides; it's a landlocked harbor where you can see gray seals along with fishing boats. There are some 600 weavers on the island, and one of the attractions of this rather bleak port is visiting a mill shop or a weaver's cottage.

ESSENTIALS

GETTING THERE   An **airport,** which doubles as an RAF base, is 3½ miles (5.5km) from the center of Stornoway. Stornoway receives flights from Glasgow and Inverness Monday through Saturday, as well as frequent service from Benbecula. Phone **British Airways** (© **0345/222-111** in Glasgow) to make reservations.

Monday through Saturday, **Caledonian MacBrayne** (© **0990/650-000** at the ferry terminal in Gourock) operates two or three ferries from Ullapool to Stornoway. One-way passage costs £13 ($19.50). Cars can be transported as well. Trip time is 3½ hours.

VISITOR INFORMATION   The **Western Isles Tourist Board,** which has information about all the Outer Hebrides, is at 26 Cromwell St., Stornoway (© **01851/703-088**). It's open April to October, Monday, Tuesday, Thursday, and Saturday from 9am to 6pm and 8 to 9pm, and Wednesday and Friday from 9am to 8pm; and October to April, Monday through Friday from 9am to 5pm.

EXPLORING THE ISLAND

The major attraction is the Neolithic temple of Callanish, called the **Standing Stones of Callanish** ⟨₭₭⟩. Off A858, 16 miles (26km) west of Stornoway, this unique cruciform setting of megaliths is outranked in prehistoric archaeological splendor only by Stonehenge. From a circle of 13 stones, a road of 19 monoliths leads north. Branching off to the south, east, and west are rows of more stones. A tiny chambered tomb is inside the circle. You can wander among the ruins for free, day or night. The "visitor center" provides historical background and charges £1.75 ($2.65) if you want to see videos on the site. It's open Monday through Saturday from 10am to 6pm (9am to 6:30pm in July and August). Also here are a gift shop and cafe.

Just west of the harbor at Stornoway, you can visit the grounds of 1818 **Lews Castle** (which uses the old spelling). The castle itself is closed to the public, but you can wander through the garden, which is at its flowery best in May.

At Arnol, 15 miles (24km) northwest of Stornoway off A858, is the thatched **Lewis Black House** (© **01851/710-395**), constructed without mortar and preserved to show what a typical Hebridean dwelling looked like. It's called a "black house" because it was believed the smoke from the open peat fires was good for the thatched roof—the Leodhasach (as the islanders are called) built their houses with no chimneys so the smoke could pass through the thatch. From April to September, it's open Monday through Saturday from 9:30am to 6:30pm (to 4pm October through March). Admission is £2.80 ($4.20) for adults, £2 ($3) for seniors, and £1 ($1.50) for children.

Watersports in the Outer Hebrides

The seas and inlets around the Outer Hebrides are dotted with scenic coves and underwater shipwrecks. The best way to view some of the wreckage close up is through the diving tours offered by **Scalpay Diving Services,** 34 Out End, Isle of Scarpay (© **01859/540-328**), midway between Harris and Lewis (easily accessible from both by bridges).

If you prefer the quiet and calm paddling of a sea kayak, contact **Hebridean Explorations,** 19 West View Terrace, Stornoway, Isle of Lewis (© **01851/705-655**), which offers rentals, guided tours, and advice about how best to view the flora and fauna.

And if you'd rather just be a passenger, you might take a day cruise with **Sea Trek,** 16 Uigen, Miavaig, Isle of Lewis (© **01851/672-464**); **Island Cruising,** 1 Erista, Uig, Isle of Lewis (© **01851/672-381**); or **Strond Wildlife Charters,** 1 Strond, Isle of Harris (© **01859/520-204**). All specialize in full- and half-day cruises that focus on the wildlife, bird life, and ecology of the Hebridean archipelago, usually with special emphasis on the seal colonies that thrive offshore.

At 19 feet (6m) tall and 6 feet (2m) wide, the **Clach an Trushal** at Balanthrushal, Barvas, is the largest single monolith in northern Scotland. It's signposted beside the main highway leading north from Stornoway. Along A858, 20 miles (32km) northwest of Stornoway, stands **Dun Carloway Broch,** a 30-foot (9m) broch (round-sided stone tower) left over from the Iron Age. You can visit at any time for free.

At Dun Borranish, near the village of Ardroil, the famous **Lewis Chessmen** were dug up in 1831 outside Uig Sands. Made of walrus tusks and reputed to have been carved around A.D. 500, they now form an outstanding exhibit in the British Museum in London. If you're a chess player, you may want to purchase a reproduction set in Lewis.

At Ness, toward that northerly outpost, the Butt of Lewis, is **St. Moluag's Church,** a Scottish Episcopal church. You can attend an occasional service here. The chapel, known in Gaelic as *Teampull Mhor* ("big temple"), is from about the 12th century, founded by Olav the Black during the Norse occupation.

Borge Pottery, on A857 at Borve, 17 miles (27km) from Stornoway on the road to Ness (© **01851/850-345**), has been in business for more than 20 years, producing hand-thrown stoneware in pink, blue, red, green, black, and cream. Its name is spelled with a *g,* the Gaelic spelling of Borve.

The Isle of Lewis's contribution to the world of golf is the 18-hole **Golf Club,** Willow Glen Road, about a mile (1.5km) from Stornoway (© **01851/702-240**). It's a windswept, isolated course carved out of the moors. Greens fees are £20 ($30).

If you'd like to rent a bike, head for **Alex Dan's Cycle Centre,** 67 Kenneth St., Stornoway (© **01851/704-025**).

ACCOMMODATIONS

Cabarfeidh Hotel 🏨 *Finds*   About a mile (1.6km) north of Stornoway, midway between Laxdale and Newmarket, the Cabarfeidh is one of the best hotels on Lewis, designed as a contemporary arrangement of cubes. It was built by a Mackenzie, who named it after the battle cry of his fighting clan, "stag antlers," and the decor includes a collection of just that. The pleasant guest rooms have small, shower-only bathrooms. The dining room offers the best local produce, fresh fish and local beef and lamb. The convivial bar is shaped like a Viking longship.

Manor Park, Stornoway, Lewis, Outer Hebrides H51 2EU. ℂ 01851/702-604. Fax 01851/705-572. www. calahotels.com. 46 units. £92 ($138) double. Rates include Scottish breakfast. AE, DC, MC, V. **Amenities:** Restaurant, bar; room service; babysitting; laundry service. *In room:* TV, coffeemaker, hair dryer.

Seaforth Hotel   A 5-minute walk from the town center, the Seaforth is one of the most modern hotels in the Outer Hebrides. The guest rooms are well equipped, each with a small bathroom with shower. The public rooms have several full-size snooker tables; there's a bar as well as a basement nightclub open Friday and Saturday. The restaurant offers a reasonably priced three-course dinner menu. The fare is rather plain but hearty.

9 James St., Stornoway, Lewis, Outer Hebrides HS1 2QN. ℂ 01851/702-740. Fax 01851/703-900. www. calahotels.com. 68 units. £70 ($105) double. Rates include Scottish breakfast. AE, MC, V. **Amenities:** Restaurant, bar, nightclub; babysitting; laundry service. *In room:* TV, coffeemaker, hair dryer.

DINING

Park Guest House BRITISH   In a century-old stone house about a 10-minute walk north of the ferry terminal, this is the best dining room in town, with a country-house decor and a fireplace in the style of Charles Rennie Mackintosh. Menu items feature seasonal game, such as venison in port-wine sauce, and seafood choices like oysters raw or au gratin, pan-fried scallops in lemon butter and herbs, and turbot filet grilled with herb butter. The restaurant is fully licensed and at its most elegant between 7 and 9pm.

Nine simple guest rooms go for £42 to £58 ($63 to $87) double, including breakfast. Each unit comes with a TV and hair dryer.

30 James St., Stornoway, Lewis, Outer Hebrides H51 2QN. ℂ 01851/702-485. Reservations required. Main courses £11.95–£17.95 ($17.95–$26.95); fixed-price 2-course early-bird dinner (5:30–6:45pm) £11.95 ($17.95). MC, V. Tues–Sat 5:30–9pm.

STORNOWAY AFTER DARK

Most of the pubs lining the waterfront have live music on weekends, usually traditional Celtic or Scottish performers. There's generally no cover. **Clachan Bar,** North Beach Street (ℂ **01851/703-653**), boasts none of the quaintness of a traditional pub, but locals and visitors alike come on Friday and Saturday for live bands downstairs or for the disco upstairs. Another updated bar with live music is **Lewis Bar,** South Beach Street (ℂ **01851/704-567**). On Saturday, the stage might hold anything from a rock band to a traditional Scottish group.

An Lanntair Gallery, Town Hall, South Beach Street (ℂ **01851/703-307**), stages musical and theatrical events with a strong emphasis on Gaelic culture. The center also has jazz, folk, and traditional music concerts, plus classic and contemporary drama, comedy, and children's shows. Tickets are £6 to £7 ($9 to $10.50) for adults. Productions take place in either the gallery space, which seats 55, or the town hall, which holds 350.

10 Harris ✦

218 miles (351km) NW of Glasgow, 56 miles (90km) NW of Mallaig, 246 miles (396km) NW of Edinburgh, 34 miles (55km) S of Stornoway

Harris, south of Lewis but really part of the same island, has a different geography. North Harris is full of mountains, dominated by the **Clisham,** which at 2,600 feet (789m) is the highest peak in the Outer Hebrides. Harris may not have as many ancient relics as Lewis, but most visitors agree that the mountains, beaches, and scenic vistas make up for it. The beaches in the west are good for strolling, swimming (if you're hearty), or camping; the bays in the east are ideal for fishing and sailing.

The locals, some 3,000 in all, are called Hearach, and they're different from the people of Lewis, even speaking with a different accent. If you've arrived in Lewis, you can drive to Harris, as the two islands are connected by a small single-lane road. As you go along the rugged terrain, you might meet another car. If you do, "passing places" have been provided. In any case, you should drive slowly, as sheep might suddenly scamper in front of your wheels. The distance from Stornoway, the capital of Lewis, to Tarbert, the capital of Harris, is 34 miles (55km).

Many visitors prefer to take the ferry from the little port of Uig on the Isle of Skye; it heads for Harris Monday through Saturday. Even in the busiest season, Harris isn't overrun. From Harris you can also make connections to Lochmaddy on North Uist (see "North & South Uist," below).

Harris has long been known for its hand-weaving and tweed. Although that industry has now passed to Stornoway (see "Lewis: Island of Heather," above), you can still buy Harris tweed jackets in Harris. In summer, you'll see them displayed on the walls of sheds along the road, selling for very good prices.

The main village is one-street **Tarbert.** The island is bisected by two long sea lochs that meet at Tarbert, which is surrounded by rocky hills. Whatever you need in the way of supplies, you should pick up here—otherwise you'll be out of luck. If you're touring by car, also fill up with petrol (gas) here. Ask at the tourist center about the island bus tours conducted in summer. For an adventure, take the car ferry running regularly across the sound to the little fishing community of **Scalpay,** an offshore island.

ESSENTIALS
GETTING THERE   You can take a **ferry** to Tarbert, capital of Harris, from Uig on the Isle of Skye, Monday through Saturday. There are one or two ferries per day; a one-way ticket for the 1¾-hour trip costs £8.50 ($12.75). Call **Caledonian MacBrayne** (© **0990/650-000**) for schedules.

Buses run from Stornoway to Tarbert daily (a 70-min. trip). Call **Harris Coaches** (© **01859/502-441**) for schedules. At least five buses per day make the run Monday through Saturday.

If you're **driving** from Stornoway on Lewis in the north, head south along A859 to reach Tarbert.

VISITOR INFORMATION   A **tourist office** operates from the port at Tarbert (© **01859/502-011**). April to October, it's open Monday through Saturday from 9am to 5pm; November to March, it's open Monday through Saturday from 10am to 2pm.

EXPLORING THE ISLAND
Because of the lack of roads, you can't make a circular tour of the island. However, using Tarbert as your base, you can set out northwest along the coast of **West Loch Tarbert,** with the Forest of Harris to your north. Or you can go south from Tarbert, hugging the western coast road along the Sound of Taransay, with Rodel as your final destination.

Taking the northwesterly route first, you come to an **Old Whaling Station** at Bunavoneadar. Norwegians set up a whaling station here in the early 20th century, but because of dwindling profits it was abandoned in 1930. Continuing north along B887, you'll arrive at the **Amhuinnsuidhe Estate,** a Scottish baronial castle built in 1868. The river to the left has one of the most beautiful salmon leaps in Scotland. The road beyond the castle continues to **Hushinish Point,** where you can see the little island of Scarp, which was once inhabited.

Returning to Tarbert, you can take A859 south. Some of the South Harris coastline will remind you of Norway, with its sea lochs and fjord fingers. The main road to Rodel is mostly two lanes and well surfaced; however, if you take the east-coast road, you'll find it not only single lane but also winding. Along the way you'll pass the **Clach Mhicleoid** ("standing stone"). Locals call it MacLeod's Stone.

From here you can look out across the Sound of Taransay to the **Island of Taransay,** named after St. Tarran. It has several ancient sites, including the remains of St. Tarran's Chapel. Like Scarp, it was once populated, but now its grazing fields have been turned over to sheep. Continuing on the coastal road along the wild Atlantic—actually the Sound of Taransay—you'll see another ancient stone, the **Scarista Standing Stone.** Before reaching it, you'll pass **Borve Lodge,** the former home of Lord Leverhulme, the soap tycoon.

The road south passes the little promontory of Toe Head jutting into the Atlantic. An ancient chapel, **Rudhan Teampull,** stands about three quarters of a mile (1.2km) west of Northton, reached by a sand track. Many prehistoric sites were uncovered and excavated on the tiny machair-studded peninsula of Toe Head.

The next village is **Leverburgh,** named after Lord Leverhulme. He's credited with trying to bring the people of the area into the 20th century, but his efforts to rejuvenate the economy largely failed. From here you can take a small passenger ferry to North Uist and Berneray.

Finally, drive east to Rodel, where **St. Clement's Church** ☆ stands high in the village. Overlooking Loch Rodel, this church is one of the most important monuments in the Western Isles. Cruciform in plan, it has a western tower, a nave, and two cross aisles. Some of the masonry work in freestone is similar to that used at Iona Abbey. The church is believed to have been built in the late 15th century or very early 16th century.

In the Sound of Harris, separating Harris from North Uist, lie the islands of **Ensay, Killegray,** and **Pabbay.** They were once populated, but now have been turned over to grazing sheep.

The island has a 9-hole **Golf Club,** Sgarasta (© **01859/502-214**), an isolated, windswept course carved into the Hebridean moors. Greens fees are £12 ($18). You can rent clubs for around £5 ($7.50).

ACCOMMODATIONS & DINING

Ardvourlie Castle ☆ *Finds*   In 1860, the earl of Dunmore commissioned a substantial-looking hunting lodge here. It's now an elegant house filled with antiques. The lovely guest rooms overlook the Loch of Seaforth or an evocative tundra leading up to Harris's highest mountain. Most of the bathrooms contain combination tub/showers. The dining room features splendid food, such as honey-marinated crisp duck with orange-flavored Drambuie sauce and garlic potatoes. There's also a cocktail lounge and interesting libraries full of books.

Hwy. A859, Tarbert, Harris, Outer Hebrides HS3 3AB. © **01859/502-307.** Fax 01859/502-348. 4 units. £180–£230 ($270–$345) double. Rates include breakfast and dinner. No credit cards. Closed Oct–Mar. Drive 10 miles (16km) north of Tarbert or 27 miles (43.5km) south of Stornaway along A859. **Amenities:** Restaurant, bar. *In room:* No phone.

Harris Hotel ☆   This Queen Anne hotel, a landmark since it opened in 1904, is one of the most popular places in the Outer Hebrides. Each room has hot and cold running water and lots of old-fashioned comfort. Some family rooms are available, many overlooking the garden. The pub is the social center for locals. You can order pub grub throughout the day; a more formal restaurant offers moderately priced dinners.

Tarbert, Harris, Outer Hebrides HS3 3DL. ℂ **01859/502-154.** Fax 01859/502-281. www.harrishotel.com. 24 units, 16 with private bathroom. £67 ($100.50) double without bathroom; £77 ($115.50) double with bathroom. Rates include Scottish breakfast. MC, V. **Amenities:** Restaurant, bar. *In room:* TV, hair dryer, no phone.

Leachin House ℛ *(Finds*   On the north shore of the loch, this house was built of Berneray granite (a form of gneiss) with Victorian gingerbread trim. Its original owner was Norman McLeod, the fisherman and entrepreneur credited as the father of the Harris tweed industry. The house is now loaded with antiques and paintings. The comfortable, high-ceilinged guest rooms will make you think you're staying in a friend's home, while the rather pricey dinners have the feel of a private dinner party. The food is based on modern Scottish cuisine.

Tarbert, Isle of Harris HS3 3AH. ℂ and fax **01859/502-157.** www.leachin-house.com. 2 units, 1 with private bathroom. £90 ($135) double with or without bathroom. MC, V. From Tarbert, follow A859 for 1 mile (1.6km), signposted to Stornoway. **Amenities:** Restaurant; activities arranged by staff; laundry service. *In room:* TV, coffeemaker, hair dryer, no phone.

Scarista House ℛℛ   Built long ago as a Georgian vicarage, this is now a lovely hotel with handsome guest rooms and two self-catering apartments. Most of the bathrooms are equipped with tub/shower combinations. Some summer guests enjoy a bracing dip in the icy water of Scarista Beach, while others prefer to read in the well-stocked library. Here you get the best breakfast around: freshly squeezed orange juice, compote of fresh and dried fruits, organic oatmeal porridge with cream, Lewis kippers, Stornoway black pudding, bacon, sausage, fresh eggs, and fresh herring rolled in oatmeal. There's also a variety of baked goods. If you plan to burn off this morning feast on a hike, a packed lunch will be provided. Most guests return for a drink by the fireplace, and then at 8:15pm enjoy an upscale four-course dinner featuring local shellfish and heather-fed lamb.

On A859, about 15 miles (24km) southwest of Tarbert, Scarista, Harris, Outer Hebrides HS3 3HX. ℂ **01859/ 550-238.** Fax 01859/550-277. www.scaristahouse.com. 7 units. £130 ($195) double; £275–£550 ($412.50–$825) apt. Room rates include Scottish breakfast. MC, V. Closed Oct–Apr. **Amenities:** Restaurant; babysitting; laundry service. *In room:* Hair dryer.

11 North & South Uist

90–100 miles (145–161km) NW of Glasgow

Standing stones, chambered cairns, ruins, and fortresses tell of a history-rich past on North Uist and South Uist, connected by the smaller island of Benbecula.

ESSENTIALS
GETTING THERE   British Airways flies Monday through Saturday to **Benbecula Airport** (the nearest connection for North Uist) from Glasgow, a 1-hour trip. Phone ℂ **0141/887-1111** at the Glasgow Airport for flight information.

Lochboisdale is the site of the ferry terminal providing a link between South Uist and the mainland at Oban, taking 5½ hours. Monday through Saturday, one ferry per day runs from Oban to Lochboisdale, costing £18.75 ($28.15) one-way. Some of these ferries stop at Castlebay on Barra. Other ferries run from Uig on the Isle of Skye to Lochmaddy, North Uist, once or twice daily. The most popular connection, this ferry trip takes anywhere from 2 to 4 hours and costs £8.50 ($12.75) one-way. For information, consult **Caledonian MacBrayne** (ℂ **01876/500-337** in Lochmaddy).

North Uist is linked to Benbecula and South Uist by causeways and bridges, so you can **drive** to or from either of these islands along A867, which becomes A865.

VISITOR INFORMATION   Consult the **Western Isles Tourist Board** in Stornoway (see "Lewis: Island of Heather," earlier in this chapter). There's also a **tourist office** at the pier in Lochmaddy, on North Uist (© **01876/500-321**), open Monday through Friday from 9am to 5pm, Saturday from 9:30am to 1pm and 2 to 5:30pm, and Monday, Wednesday, and Friday from 7:30 to 8:30pm. The staff can arrange accommodations if you've arrived without a reservation. On South Uist, a **tourist office** is found at the pier at Lochboisdale (© **01878/700-286**), open Easter to October only, Monday through Saturday from 9am to 5pm. It's also open for late ferry arrivals, usually Monday through Thursday and Saturday from 9 to 10pm and Friday from 7:30 to 8:30pm. Accommodations can be arranged through this office as well.

NORTH UIST

A real bogland where hardy crofters try to wrestle a living from a turbulent sea and disappointing ground, North Uist is one of the lesser-known islands in the Outer Hebrides, but it's beautiful nonetheless. Its antiquity is reflected in the brochs, duns, wheelhouses, and stark monoliths, all left by the island's prehistoric dwellers.

The population of North Uist is about 2,000, and the island is about 12½ miles (20km) wide by 35 miles (56km) at its longest point. North Uist is served by a circular road, usually a single lane variety with passing places, and several feeder routes that branch east and west.

The main village is **Lochmaddy,** on the eastern shore. Whatever you need, you're likely to find it here (if it's available on North Uist at all), from a post office to a petrol station. Lochmaddy is also the site of a ferry terminal. In addition to the ferries from Oban and Uig, a small private ferry runs from Newton Ferry, north of Lochmaddy, to Leverburgh on Harris. This isn't a car ferry, but it does allow small motorcycles and bikes. A small vehicular ferry will take you to the island of Berneray. In keeping with the strict religious tradition of these islands, the ferry doesn't operate on Sunday—and neither, seemingly, does anything else.

EXPLORING THE ISLAND

North Uist may be small, but its scenery is extremely varied. The eastern shores possess an untamed beauty. The coastline is dotted with trout-filled lochs, and everything is set against a backdrop of rolling heather-clad hills. Nights come on fast in winter; sunsets linger in summer. The western side of North Uist is a land of rich meadows filled with wildflowers. Here you find long white beaches, where Atlantic rollers attract the hardier surfers.

Heading northwest from Lochmaddy for 2½ miles (4km), you come to the hamlet of **Blashaval,** where you'll find the **Three Standing Stones of the False Men.** Local tradition has it that this trio of stones, known in Gaelic as *Na Fir Bhreige,* were actual men, wife deserters from Skye turned into stone by a witch.

Continuing along the road for 4 miles (6.5km), you approach uninhabited **Dun Torcuill Island,** rising above the west side of **Loch an Duin.** Access to the island is possible on foot only during low tide; exercise caution. On the island is a ruined but still fine example of a broch (circular fortified tower) that provided defense during the Middle Ages. Most visitors prefer to admire it from across the water.

Turning north on B893, you come to **Newton Ferry.** A 15-minute crossing will take you to the little offshore island of **Berneray,** which has some ancient sites, including the mysterious-looking **Borve Standing Stone.** There's a privately run hostel here. The 140 or so people who live on the island are mainly engaged in crofting and fishing and may regard *you* as a sightseeing attraction.

After you return to Newton Ferry, head south on the same road. A left-hand fork takes you to **Trumisgarry** to see the ruins of an old chapel where an early Christian settlement was founded. **St. Columba's Well** (*Tobar Chaluim Chille* in Gaelic) is named after the saint.

Return to the main road and head west toward Sollas. On both sides of the road are cairns and standing stones, many from 2000 B.C.—some hard to reach, including those on uninhabited islands. Pass through **Hosta,** site of the Highland Games, heading for the **Balranaid Nature Reserve,** 3 miles (5km) northwest of Bayhead. At a reception cottage at **Goulat,** near Hougharty, you can learn more about the birds inhabiting the Outer Hebrides. You can walk through the reserve at any time at no charge, but guided tours (£2.50/$3.75) are given at 2pm Tuesday and Friday.

Back on the main road, you'll pass through **Bayhead** heading southeast. Again, the area is filled with an astonishing number of ancient monuments. At the junction, take A867 back toward Lochmaddy. You'll see a sign pointing to **Ben Langass.** On the mountain slopes is a chambered cairn thought to be at least 3,000 years old, one of the best preserved on the island. Some historians believe a warrior chieftain was buried here, but others suggest it was a communal burial ground. Bones and pottery fragments removed from excavations were sent to the National Museum in Edinburgh.

Returning to the main road again, retrace your trail and head south for Carinish, a hamlet known for the **Carinish Stone Circle** and the **Barpa Carinish,** the site of the major attraction on the island, **Trinity Temple** (*Teampull na Trionad* in Gaelic), off A865 some 8 miles (13km) southwest of Lochmaddy. Admission is free and it's open at all times. The monastery is said to have been founded in the 13th century by Beathag, the first prioress of Iona, daughter of Somerland, an Irish mercenary and the founding father of the MacDonalds.

ACCOMMODATIONS & DINING

Langass Lodge ⚘ *Finds* This hotel's spaciousness and comfort come as a welcome surprise after the miles of windswept, barren countryside you traverse before reaching it. The nearby sycamores are cited by the staff as among the few trees on all North Uist. Built as a hunting lodge in 1876, the hotel today attracts hunters, anglers, and nature lovers. The guest rooms were completely refurbished in 1997, with solid furnishings and pleasant decor. Each has a small, shower-only bathroom and views of the nearby loch.

Locheport, North Uist, Outer Hebrides HS6 5HA. ⓒ and fax **01876/580-285.** 6 units. £60 ($90) double. Rates include Scottish breakfast. MC, V. Closed Feb. **Amenities:** Dining room, bar. *In room:* TV, coffeemaker, hair dryer.

Lochmaddy Hotel You can't miss the peaked gables of this white-walled hotel a few steps from the ferry terminal. Those who come to fish for the area's brown trout, sea trout, and salmon often stay here. (Guests are welcome to use the hotel's scales to weight the catch of the day.) This is one of the few places on the island where you can buy fishing permits; prices are £6 to £40 ($9 to $60) a day, according to what kind of fish you're seeking and the season. The guest rooms are tasteful, each with a small, shower-only bathroom. The bar offers about the best collection of single-malt whiskies in the Outer Hebrides. The dining room serves fresh local produce, lobster, king prawns, venison, and salmon.

Lochmaddy, North Uist, Outer Hebrides HS6 5AA. © 01876/500-331. Fax 01876/500-210. www. lochmaddyhotel.co.uk. 15 units. £65–£80 ($97.50–$120) double. Rates include Scottish breakfast. AE, MC, V. Amenities: 2 restaurants, 2 bars; watersports. In room: TV, coffeemaker, hair dryer.

SOUTH UIST

South Uist holds a rich treasure trove of antiquity. A number of ecclesiastical remains are scattered along its shores, and Clan Ranald left many ruins and fortresses known as *duns*. Ornithologists and anglers are attracted to this island. Part bogland, it's 20 miles (32km) long and 6 miles (10km) wide at its broadest. A main road, A865, bisects the island, with feeder roads branching off east and west.

EXPLORING THE ISLAND

The biggest village in South Uist is **Lochboisdale,** at the head of a deep-sea loch in the southeastern part of the island. It was settled in the 19th century by crofters who had been forced off their land in the notorious Land Clearances. The ruins of a small medieval castle can be seen at the head of the loch on the island of Calvay, one of the many places where Bonnie Prince Charlie hid out.

Leaving Lochboisdale, A865 goes west for 3 miles (5km) to Daliburgh, where you can pick up B888 south to Pollachar on the southern shore, a distance of 6 miles (10km). The village is named for the **Pollachar Standing Stone,** a jagged dolmen rising a few paces from the hamlet's center. Continue east along a minor road for 2½ miles (4km) to the Ludag jetty, where a private ferry goes to Eriskay and Barra.

The next stop is the **Klipheder Wheelhouse,** 2 miles (3km) west of A865, the meager ruins of a circular building from A.D. 200. Back on the main road again, you come to Askernish, site of a nine-hole **golf course.**

Three miles (5km) north from Daliburgh, at Airidh Mhuilinn, is a **Flora MacDonald memorial.** West of A865, about 200 yards (182m) up a little farm track half a mile (about 1km) north of Milton, a cairn atop a little hill marks the spot where this woman, so revered in legend, was born in 1722. Staying on the minor roads, you'll see the dramatic machair-fringed shoreline and pass through the hamlets of Bornish, Ormiclete, and Stoneybridge. At Ormiclete are the ruins of **Ormiclete Castle,** constructed by the Clan Ranald chieftains in the early 18th century.

Rejoin the main road at Howbeg. The part of the island directly north of Howbeg is rich in archaeological remains. Ruins of several **medieval chapels** are all that's left of a major South Uist ecclesiastical center.

Farther north, A865 passes the **Loch Druidibeg National Nature Reserve,** the most significant breeding ground in the country for the native grayleg goose. Attracting the dedicated bird-watcher, it's a setting of machair and brackish lochs. At Drimsdale lie the ruins of a big dun, a fortification in a loch where the villagers retreated when under attack. It continued as a stronghold for the Clan Ranald until the early 1500s.

The road continues past the Royal Artillery Rocket Range. On the flank of Reuval Hill stands **Our Lady of the Isles,** a 30-foot (9m) statue of the Virgin and Child. Erected in 1957, it's the largest religious statue in Britain. **Loch Bee,** inhabited by mute swans, nearly bisects the northern part of South Uist.

You'll find **Hebridean Jewelry,** Garrieganichy, Iochdar (© **01870/610-288**), signposted on the north end of the Iochdar Road. The shop produces silver and gold pendants and brooches featuring Celtic patterns. The artists here can create custom pieces on request.

If you'd like to explore the island by bike, head for **Rothan Cycles,** 9 Howmore (© **01870/620-283**).

ACCOMMODATIONS & DINING

Borrodale Hotel   Near the center of the island, 2½ miles (4km) west of Loch Boisdale along A865, this gabled hotel stands in a landscape of freshwater lakes, heather, and gorse. The hotel underwent extensive renovations in 1997, updating the guest rooms and common areas, which include an upscale restaurant. The owners will assist in arranging fishing and golf expeditions.

Daliburgh, South Uist, Outer Hebrides HS8 5SS. © **01878/700-444.** Fax 01878/700-446. www.witb.co.uk. 14 units, 13 with private bathroom. £60–£85 ($90–$127.50) double with bathroom. Rates include Scottish breakfast. MC, V. **Amenities:** Restaurant, 2 bars; babysitting. *In room:* TV, coffeemaker, hair dryer, iron.

Lochboisdale Hotel   This is the quintessential anglers' refuge. Solidly built of local stone in 1892, it's in the center of town by the ferry terminal and proudly displays tables and scales near its entrance for weighing and preparing the daily catch of its guests. Trophies and memorabilia decorate the half-paneled walls of the lounge and restaurant. Both have blazing fireplaces and a feeling of conviviality. The midsize guest rooms are outfitted in English country-house style, with chintz curtains and shower-only bathrooms. The hotel's public bar is the only one within 4 miles (6.5km) and is frequented by locals.

Lochboisdale, South Uist, Outer Hebrides HS8 5TH. © **01878/700-332.** Fax 01878/700-367. 17 units. £74–£86 ($111–$129) double with bathroom. Rates include Scottish breakfast. MC, V. **Amenities:** Restaurant, bar. *In room:* Coffeemaker, hair dryer (on request).

12 Barra ⊛: Garden of the Hebrides

118 miles (190km) NW of Edinburgh, 88 miles (142km) NW of Glasgow

Barra lies at the southern end of the Outer Hebrides. Locals claim it has some 1,000 varieties of wildflowers. The island is one of the most beautiful in the Hebridean chain, with heather-clad meadows, beaches, sandy grasslands, peaks, rocky bays, and lofty headlands. Since the days of the conquering Vikings, it has been associated with the Clan MacNeil.

Most of the 200 inhabitants of Barra are centered at **Castlebay,** its capital, a 19th-century herring port and the best place to stock up on supplies. In the background of the port rises **Ben Heaval,** at 1,250 feet (379m) the highest mountain on Barra. A circular road of 10 miles (16km) will take you around Barra, which is about 4 by 8 miles (6.5 by 13km) in size.

ESSENTIALS

GETTING THERE   At the northern end of Barra is **Cockle Strand,** the airport. A long and wide beach of white sand, it's the only runway in Britain washed twice daily by sea tides. The Scottish airline, **Loganair** (call British Airways at © **0345/222-111** in Glasgow for flight information), flies here from Glasgow or from Benbecula on Lewis.

From the mainland at Oban, Barra can be reached by **Caledonian MacBrayne** car ferry (© **0990/650-000** for information), which docks at Castlebay. Subject to weather conditions, departures from Oban are on Monday,

Wednesday, Thursday, and Saturday, with a return on Tuesday, Thursday, Friday, and Sunday. Sailing time is 5 hours, and a one-way ticket is £18.75 ($28.15).

VISITOR INFORMATION   The **Castlebay Tourist Information Centre** (© 01871/810-336) is near the pier where the ferry docks. From Easter to mid-October, it's open Monday through Saturday from 9am to 5pm. The staff will help you locate a room should you arrive on Barra without a reservation.

EXPLORING THE ISLAND

The most important attraction is in the bay: **Kismul Castle** (© 01871/810-313) was built for strategic purposes on a small islet, the longtime stronghold of the notorious MacNeils of Barra, a clan known for piracy and lawlessness. The oldest part of the castle is an 1120 tower. In 1938, the 45th chieftain, the late Robert Lister MacNeil of Barra, began restoration work on his ancestral home. From April to October, you can visit on Monday, Wednesday, and Saturday afternoons. A boatman will take you over and back from 2 to 4 or 5pm. Entrance is £3 ($4.50) for adults and £1 ($1.50) for children, including the boat ride.

To drive around the island, head west from Castlebay until you reach Kinloch. On the left is **Loch St. Clair,** reached by a tiny track road. In the loch, on an islet, stand the ruins of St. Clair Castle, called **MacLeod's Fort.**

Continuing north to Borve, you'll see the **Borve Standing Stones** on your left. At Borve, the north fork leads to a chambered cairn and the hamlet of **Craigston,** which has a church dedicated to St. Brendan, the Irish navigator who many cite as the discoverer of America. In the area are two interesting ruins: **Dun Bharpa,** a collection of stones encircled by standing stones, and **Tigh Talamhanta,** a ruined wheelhouse.

Continue north to Allasdale. **Dun Cuier** is one of the few excavated Hebridean Iron Age forts, better preserved than most. Opposite Allasdale is **Seal Bay,** a beauty spot where the seals do as much inspection of you as you of them.

At **Northbay** at Loch an Duin, the remains of an old dun protrude from the water. Continue north to Eoligarry, site of a small ferry terminal taking passengers to Ludag on South Uist. Eoligarry's proud possession is **St. Barr's Church,** named after St. Findbarr of Cork (A.D. 550–623), who's said to have converted the islanders to Christianity after finding many of them practicing cannibalism when he arrived. The original 12th-century chapel was restored by Fr. Callum MacNeil.

For bike rentals and advice on scenic routes, head for **Barra Cycle Hire,** 29 St. Brendans Rd. (© 01871/810-284).

ACCOMMODATIONS & DINING

Castlebay Hotel   Built around 1890, this gabled hotel overlooks the bay and the ferry terminal where most of the island's visitors disembark. The small guest rooms are simply but comfortably furnished, each with a neat, shower-only bathroom. Its cocktail bar has a quiet corner reserved for dining. Adjacent to the hotel and under the same management is the Castlebay Bar, the island's most popular gathering place.

Castlebay, Barra, Outer Hebrides HS9 5XD. © 01871/810-223. Fax 01871/810-455. 13 units. £65 ($97.50) double. Rates include Scottish breakfast. MC, V. Closed Dec 22–Jan 5. **Amenities:** Restaurant, bar. *In room:* TV, coffeemaker.

Isle of Barra Hotel 🏕 *Finds*   This low-slung seashore hotel is architecturally striking, and for the Outer Hebrides, it's a luxury choice. Its brick walls are adorned with nautical paraphernalia, and the hotel is a favorite with the yachting crowd. It commands a view of the tranquil, less-populated western shore of the island, and its pub, the most westerly in Scotland, is widely touted as the "last dram before America." From the dining room and many of the well-furnished guest rooms, you can see everything that's coming and going at sea. Most bathrooms have combination tub/showers. The best food on Barra is served here.

Tangusdale, Castlebay, Barra, Outer Hebrides HS9 5XW. ℭ 01871/810-383. Fax 01871/810-385. www. isleofbarra.com/iob.html. 30 units. £78–£84 ($117–$126) double with breakfast; £112 ($168) double with half-board. Rates include Scottish breakfast. MC, V. Closed Oct 18–Mar 20. Amenities: Restaurant, bar, lounge. In room: TV, no phone.

The Orkney & Shetland Islands

Northern outposts of civilization, the Orkney and Shetland archipelagos consist of around 200 islands, about 40 of which are inhabited. "Go to Shetland for scenery, Orkney for antiquities"—or so the saying goes. That doesn't mean the Orkneys don't have scenery too. They do, in abundance.

These far-flung and scattered islands are rich in a great Viking heritage. Ceded to Scotland by Norway as part of the 1472 dowry of Princess Margaret when she married James III, the islands were part of the great Norse earldoms. They were a gathering place for Norse fleets and celebrated in the Orkneyinga Saga, which detailed the exploits of the Viking warriors.

Before the Vikings, however, tribes of Stone Age people occupied both the Shetlands and the Orkneys. The Picts came later, and you can still see ruins of their round forts dotting the coastlines. The island chains aren't part of the Highlands and totally differ from both the Inner and the Outer Hebrides. Clans, Gaelic, and kilts were unfamiliar to the Orcadians and the Shetlanders—until the Scots arrived. At first these merchants and newcomer landlords were bitterly resented. Even today, the islanders are fiercely independent. They speak of themselves as Orcadians and Shetlanders rather than Scots. Not only are Orkney and Shetland different from the Highlands, they're different from each other, as you'll soon see.

Change, as was inevitable, has come to the Orkneys and Shetlands by the way of oil and modern conveniences, but tradition is still strong. It has a lot to do with climate and with ancestry.

P&O Ferries (© 01856/850-655) provides service from Scrabster (near Thurso) on Scotland's north coast to the Orkneys. The 2-hour trip is made two to three times per day (once a day on Sunday) in summer; in winter, service drops to one to two trips per day. While P&O accommodates both vehicles and pedestrians, **John o' Groats Ferries** (© 01955/611-353) accepts passengers only and operates from Easter to September two to four times daily; the trip takes about 45 minutes. **British Airways** (© 0345/222-111; www.british airways.co.uk) flies into the Orkneys, as it does to Sumburgh, 26 miles (42km) south of Lerwick, the most important center on the Shetlands. P&O Ferries provides overnight ferry service once daily, Monday through Friday, between Aberdeen in northeast Scotland and Lerwick. It also provides twice-weekly service from the Orkneys to Lerwick. Book in advance during July and August.

1 The Orkney Islands: An Archaeological Garden ★★

6 miles (10km) N of John o' Groats (mainland Scotland) across Pentland Firth, 280 miles (451km) N of Edinburgh

To visit the Orkney Islands, an archipelago extending about 50 miles (80.5km) north and northeast, is to look at 1,000 years of history. Orkney is a virtual

The Orkney Islands

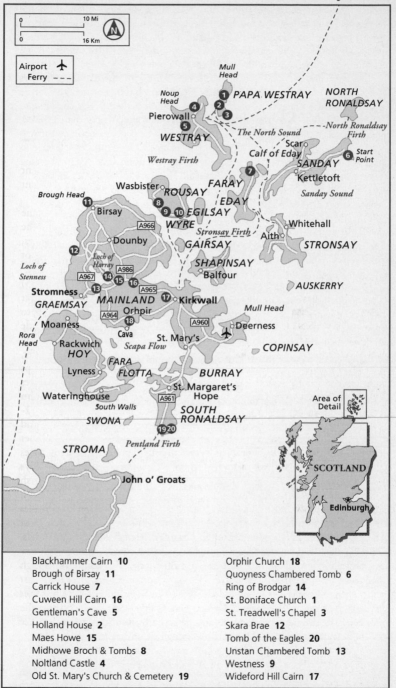

0 10 Mi
0 16 Km

N

Airport ✈
Ferry – – –

Mull
Head

Noup
Head

Pierowall

1 PAPA WESTRAY
2
4
3

NORTH
RONALDSAY

5

WESTRAY

The North Sound

North Ronaldsay
Firth

Scar

Westray Firth

Calf of Eday

SANDAY

6 Start
Point

Kettletoft

Wasbister

FARAY

7

Sanday Sound

Brough Head

ROUSAY

8

EDAY

Birsay

9 **10** EGILSAY

Whitehall

11

WYRE

Aith

Dounby

A966

Stronsay Firth

STRONSAY

12

Loch of
Harray

GAIRSAY

Loch of
Stenness

A986

SHAPINSAY

14

A967

Balfour

13 **15** **16**

AUSKERRY

Stromness

A965

17 Kirkwall

GRAEMSAY

MAINLAND

Orphir

Mull Head

18

A964

Deerness

Moaness

Cava

A960

Rora
Head

Rackwich

St. Mary's

COPINSAY

HOY

Scapa Flow

Lyness

FARA

FLOTTA

BURRAY

Wateringhouse

St. Margaret's
Hope

South Walls

A961

SOUTH

SWONA

RONALDSAY

19 20

STROMA

Pentland Firth

John o' Groats

Area of
Detail

SCOTLAND

Edinburgh

archaeological garden. Some 100 of the 500 known brochs—often called the "castles of the Picts"—are found here. Built by Orkney chiefs, they were fortified structures where islanders could find refuge from invaders, and wells inside provided water. The Orkneyinga Saga, written in the 9th or 10th century, is the record of the pomp and heraldry of Orkney's "golden age."

Covering a land area of 376 square miles (977.5sq km), the islands lie 6 miles (10km) north of the Scottish mainland. The terrain has lots of rich and fertile farmland but also dramatic scenery: Britain's highest perpendicular cliffs rise to 1,140 feet (346m). The population of the entire chain is less than 20,000, spread sparsely across about 29 inhabited islands. The people are somewhat suspicious of strangers, and if you meet an Orcadian in a local pub, you'll have to break the ice. The climate is far milder than the location would suggest because of the warming currents of the Gulf Stream. There are few extremes in temperature. From May to July, you'll be astonished by the sunsets, with the midsummer sun remaining over the horizon for 18¼ hours a day. The Orcadians call their midsummer sky "Grimlins" from the Old Norse word *grimla,* which means to twinkle or glimmer. There's enough light for golfers to play at midnight.

Who comes here other than golfers? Archaeologists, artists, walkers, climbers, bird-watchers, and more. Divers are drawn by the remains of the German Imperial Navy warships scuttled here on June 21, 1919, on orders of Rear Adm. Ludwig von Reuter. Most of the vessels have been salvaged, but there are still plenty down in the deep. From mid-March to the first week in October, anglers come in droves. Unlike other parts of Scotland, fishing is free in Orkney because of Old Norse law and ancient Udal tradition. The wild brown trout is said to be the best in Britain.

A large percentage of the world's gray seal population visits the Orkneys to breed and molt. The islanders call the seal a "selkie." Migrating from Iceland and northern Europe in winter are wildfowl such as the goldeneye, the red-throated diver (known locally as the "rain goose"), and the short-eared owl ("cattieface"), as well as such breeding seabirds as kittiwakes, puffins ("tammie-honies"), and guillemots. The resident bird of prey is the hen harrier. Some 300 species have been identified on the islands.

The Orkneys are also known for their flora, including the Scottish primrose, which is no more than 2 inches (5cm) in height and is believed to have survived the Ice Age by growing in small ice-free areas. The amethyst, with a pale-yellow eye, is found only in the Orkneys and parts of northern Scotland.

ORKNEY ESSENTIALS

GETTING THERE   Monday through Saturday, **British Airways** (℃ **0345/ 222-111;** www.britishairways.co.uk) offers service to Kirkwall Airport, on Mainland Orkney, from Glasgow, Inverness, and Aberdeen, with connections from London and Birmingham.

If you aren't driving, it's faster and cheaper to go from "end-of-the-line" John o' Groats to Burwick. The **John o' Groats Ferries** (℃ **01955/611-353**) operate from May to September, with departures twice daily. Round-trip fares are £25 ($37.50). **P&O Ferries** (℃ **01856/850-655** in Stromness) leaves Scabster at noon daily, with additional departures at 6am Monday through Saturday and at 5:45am Monday, Friday, and Saturday. A 5-day round-trip fare is £24 ($36) per person, £60 ($90) per car.

If you're driving over, head for Scrabster, near Thurso, in the northern province of Caithness. Here, P&O's *St. Ola* operates a roll-on/roll-off ferry service with 2-hour sailings to Stromness on Mainland Orkney. The ferry sails two or three times a day in summer. A 5-day round-trip fare is £60 ($90) for a car.

GETTING AROUND   Island-hopping is common in the north of Scotland. **Loganair** (call British Airways at © **0345/222-111** for reservations) operates flights from Kirkwall Airport on Mainland to the isles of Sanday, Stronsay, Westray, Eday, North Ronaldsay, and Papa Westray.

Orkney Ferries Ltd. (© **01856/872-044** in Kirkwall; www.orkneyferries. co.uk) operates scheduled service from Kirkwall to Orkney's north and south islands: Eday, Papa Westray, Sanday, Stronsay, Westray, North Ronaldsay, and Shapinsay. From Houton, there's service to the south isles: Flotta, Graemsay, and Hoy at Longhope and Lyness, and from Tingwall to Rousay, Egilsay, and Wyre. There's also a private ferry service to take you to Hoy, departing from Stromness. The tourist office will have details on departures.

The Churchill barriers, erected to impede enemy shipping in World War II, have been turned into a road link between the islands of Mainland and South Ronaldsay.

VISITOR INFORMATION   To find out what's going on during your visit, consult the *Orcadian,* a weekly published since 1854. There are tourist offices in Kirkwall and in Stromness (see below). You can also get information at **www.orkney.com**.

SPECIAL EVENTS   These sparsely populated islands generate quite a bit of cultural activity, especially in celebrating the region's music. A number of festivals draw both curious visitors and fans of Scottish and, more specifically, Orkney music. Information is available through the Kirkwall tourist office (see below), which publishes the yearly *Orkney Diary,* listing events and dates.

The season kicks off in February with the **Drama Festival,** which hosts traveling companies presenting an array of productions in venues spread across the islands. Ticket prices hover around £3 to £5 ($4.50 to $7.50). Early May brings the **Country and Irish Festival,** while late May finds the **Orkney Traditional Folk Festival** in full swing. Both feature ceilidhs and concerts of traditional music; tickets to most events are £4 to £6 ($6 to $9). June brings a change of pace in the form of the **St. Magnus Festival,** which celebrates classical music and the dramatic arts, as well as music and drama workshops. Tickets average £10 to £15 ($15 to $22.50).

TOURS   Bus tours operate throughout the year, but with limited schedules in winter. One reliable choice is **Wildabout Tours,** 5 Clouston Corner, Stenness (© **01856/851-011**). Its full- and half-day minibus tours (of no more than 15 passengers) take in prehistoric and Neolithic monuments and local wildlife. Prices range from £16 to £18 ($24 to $27). The tours are popular, particularly in summer, so it's wise to book seats in advance.

KIRKWALL

Kirkwall, established by Norse invaders on the island called Mainland, has been the capital of the Orkney Islands for at least 900 years. It used to be called Kirkjuvagr ("church bay"), after a church built around 1040 honoring the memory of King Olaf Harraldsson, later the patron saint of Norway. That church no longer stands.

The Old Norse streets of Kirkwall are very narrow, to protect the buildings from galelike winds. But don't get the idea they're pedestrian walkways: That myth is dispelled when a car comes roaring down the street.

The **tourist office** is at 6 Broad St. (© **01856/872-856;** www.orkney.com). It's open in April, Monday through Saturday from 9am to 5pm and Sunday from 10am to 4pm; May to September, daily from 8:30am to 8pm; and October to March, Monday through Saturday from 9:30am to 6pm.

SEEING THE SIGHTS

For the most scenic walk in town, providing views of Kirkwall and the North Isles, head up **Wideford Hill,** about 2 miles (3km) west of town. On the western slope of this hill, 2½ miles (4km) west of Kirkwall, is the **Wideford Hill Cairn,** a trio of concentric walls built around a passage and a megalithic chamber.

The "Pride of Orkney" is **St. Magnus Cathedral** 錄錄, on Broad Street (© **01856/874-894**). Jarl Rognvald, nephew of the martyred St. Magnus, the island chain's patron saint, founded the cathedral to honor him in 1137, and the remains of the saint and Rognvald were interred between the two large East Choir piers. The cathedral is a "Norman" building, constructed of gray and pinkish rose sandstone. Work went on over centuries, and additions were made in the transitional and very early Gothic styles. It's still in regular use as a church. You can visit from April to September, Monday through Saturday from 9am to 6pm and Sunday from 2 to 6pm; and October to March, Monday through Saturday from 9am to 1pm and 2 to 5pm.

Across from the cathedral are the ruins of a 12th-century **Bishop's Palace,** Broad Street (© **01856/871-918**), with a round tower from the 16th century. King Haakon came here to die in 1263, following the Battle of Largs and his attempt to invade Scotland. The palace was originally constructed for William the Old, a bishop who died in 1168. An easy scenic walk will take you to the impressive ruins of **Earl Patrick's Palace** 錄, on Watergate (© **01856/871-918**). Built in 1607, it has been called the most mature and accomplished piece of Renaissance architecture left in Scotland. Earl Patrick Stewart was the son of the illegitimate brother of Mary Queen of Scots, and the palace figured in Sir Walter Scott's *The Pirate.* Both the Bishop's Palace and Earl Patrick's Palace are open April through September, daily from 9:30am to 6:30pm. Admission covering both palaces is £2 ($3) for adults, £1.50 ($2.25) for seniors and students, and 75p ($1.10) for children 5 to 16.

Nearby is the 1574 **Tankerness House** (also known as the **Orkney Museum**), on Broad Street (© **01856/873-191**), an example of a merchant laird's mansion, with crow-stepped gables, a courtyard, and gardens. The museum depicts life in the Orkneys over the past 5,000 years. Exhibits range from the bones of the earliest prehistoric inhabitants and Neolithic pottery to Pictish stone symbols and domestic utensils. It's open Monday through Saturday from 10:30am to 12:30pm and 1:30 to 5pm (10:30am to 5pm May through September). Admission is free.

Orkney Wireless Museum, Kiln Corner, Junction Road (© **01856/871-400**), is a museum of wartime communications used at Scapa Flow, which was a major naval anchorage in both world wars. Today, this sea area, enclosed by Mainland and several other islands, has developed as a pipeline landfall and tanker terminal for North Sea oil. You can also see a large collection of early domestic radios. It's open from April to September, Monday through Saturday from 10am to 4:30pm and Sunday from 2:30 to 4:30pm. Admission is £2 ($3) for adults and £1 ($1.50) for children.

In the environs are the **Grain Earth Houses** at Hatson, near Kirkwall. This is an Iron Age souterrain (underground cellar), with stairs leading down to the chamber. Another Iron Age souterrain, **Rennibister Earth House,** is about 4½ miles (7km) northwest of Kirkwall. This excavation also has an underground chamber with supporting roof pillars.

SHOPPING

The **Longship,** 7–9 Broad St. (© **01856/873-251**), is the retail outlet of Ola Gorie for Orkney jewelry in Kirkwall. This family business has a wide range of high-quality pieces, including some inspired by stone carvings found at archaeological digs and others by the rich flora and fauna of the islands. A collection based on Charles Rennie Mackintosh designs has proved popular. The Longship also offers a variety of gifts, including fashion and furnishing accessories by Orkney-based Tait & Style.

Ortak Jewelry, 10 Albert St. (© **01856/873-536**), is the main shop of the famous jewelry studio that produces a wide range of silver and gold pieces featuring Celtic, traditional Arcadian, Victorian, and Art Nouveau designs. The shop also sells items like pottery, barometers, and crystal made by other local artists. The **Ortak Factory Shop,** Hatston Industrial Estate (© **01856/872-224**), is adjacent to the Ortak factory, and is the only shop that carries the complete Ortak line. A visitor center shows videos on jewelry making, and free factory tours are offered Monday through Friday in July and August. In winter, the shop and visitor center are open by appointment only.

Judith Glue, 25 Broad St. (© **01856/874-225**), produces hand- and machine-made knitwear for the entire family. The artisans tend to favor old-fashioned island patterns, handed down over the generations. Also available are wares of other local artists, along with an interesting selection of handmade pottery, jewelry, greeting cards, soaps, and island music.

ACCOMMODATIONS

You can also rent rooms at the **Foveran Hotel** (see "Dining," below).

Ayre Hotel   Midway between the town's copper-spired church and the harbor-front, this hotel consists of a 1792 stone core and a sprawling, uninspired 1970s addition. When it was first built, it was a social center for the town, hosting dances and bridge parties. Today, guests congregate in the popular bar. The small bedrooms are functionally modern and well appointed, each with a shower. The restaurant and bar serve moderately priced meals.

Ayre Rd., Kirkwall, Orkney KW15 1QX. © 01856/873-001. Fax 01856/876-289. www.ayrehotel.co.uk. 33 units. £90–£140 ($135–$210) double. Rates include Scottish breakfast and dinner. AE, MC, V. **Amenities:** Restaurant, bar. *In room:* TV, coffeemaker, hair dryer.

Royal Hotel   Although this hotel has been fully refurbished and the guest rooms modernized (with shower-only bathrooms), the overall style is traditional. The restaurant offers a moderately priced table d'hôte menu nightly as well as an extensive a la carte selection. There are also two well-stocked bars, both offering affordable food.

Victoria St., Kirkwall, Orkney KW15 1DN. © 01856/873-477. Fax 01856/872-767. www.orkneyhotel.co.uk. 30 units. £80 ($120) double. Rates include Scottish breakfast. MC, V. **Amenities:** Restaurant, 2 bars; business center; nearby golf. *In room:* TV, dataport, coffeemaker, hair dryer.

West End Hotel   This hotel offers simple comforts but is still among the top three or four places to stay in town. It was built just outside of Kirkwall in 1837 by a retired sea captain. Today, owners Jimmy and Isabelle Currie provide a warm welcome and comfortable guest rooms, each with shower-only bathroom.

The property has been refurbished in the past few years and is now fresh and inviting. Cost-conscious meals are served in a small restaurant and bar. The hotel is fully licensed to sell alcohol, attracting both locals and visitors.

14 Main St., Kirkwall, Orkney KW15 1BU. (©) **01856/872-368.** Fax 01856/876-181. www.westendhotel. org.uk. 16 units. £58 ($87) double. Rates include Scottish breakfast. AE, DC, MC, V. **Amenities:** Restaurant, bar; access to nearby health club. In room: TV, coffeemaker, hair dryer.

DINING

Foveran Hotel (ⓡ) SCOTTISH   Located on 34 acres (13.8 hectares) overlooking the Scapa Flow, where the German Imperial Fleet was sunk in 1919, the Foveran looks like a modern hotel of Scandinavian design. Fully licensed to sell alcohol, its restaurant offers the best cuisine in the area and emphasizes "taste of Scotland" menus. The catch of the day might turn out to be lobster, grilled salmon, deep-fried squid, giant crab claws (known locally as "partan toes"), or brown trout. Also offered are vegetarian meals, as well as succulent portions of Orkney Island beef, lamb, and farm-made cheeses.

The hotel rents eight pleasant guest rooms; doubles go for £70 ($105), which includes breakfast.

St. Ola (2 miles/3km west of Kirkwall), Kirkwall, Orkney KW15 1SF. (©) **01856/872-389.** Fax 01856/876-430. Reservations recommended. Main courses £9.95–£16 ($14.95–$24). MC, V. Daily 7–9pm.

EXPLORING MAINLAND FROM KIRKWALL TO STROMNESS

Heading south from Kirkwall along the southern coastal road toward Stromness, you come first to the hamlet of Orphir. **Orphir Church,** along A964, is 6 miles (10km) southwest of Kirkwall. The ruins are of the country's only circular medieval church, built in the first part of the 1100s and dedicated to St. Nicholas. At Orphir, you can see vast tracts of land set aside for bird-watching. This area is also ideal for scenic walks even if you aren't a "birdie." If you're an angler, the fishing is free on Kirbister Loch. Ferries leave the Houton Terminal for Hoy and Flotta five or six times a day.

In the area is the **Cuween Hill Cairn,** along A965, half a mile (1km) south of Finstown and 6 miles (10km) northwest of Kirkwall. The owner of a nearby farmhouse (look for the signs) has the key that opens a door to reveal a low mound over a megalithic passage tomb, probably dating from the 3rd millennium B.C. Ancient human bones, along with those of their oxen and dogs, were excavated here.

Bypassing Stromness for the moment, you can continue on a circular tour of the island. Near Stromness, lying off A965, is **Maes Howe,** 10 miles (16km) west of Kirkwall. Dating from 2700 B.C., this is a superb achievement of prehistoric architecture, constructed from single slabs more than 18 feet (5.5m) long and some 4 feet (1.2m) wide. There's a passageway that the sun shines through only at the winter solstice. It also contains the world's largest collection of Viking rune inscriptions, the work of marauding Norsemen who broke into the chambered cairn in search of buried treasure.

The **Ring of Brodgar** (ⓡ), between Lochand Stenness and Loch of Harray, is 5 miles (8km) northwest of Stromness. Dated to 1560 B.C., a circle of some 36 stones is surrounded by a deep ditch carved out of solid bedrock. While it has been suggested it was a lunar observatory, like Stonehenge, its exact purpose remains a mystery. In the vicinity, the **Stenness Standing Stones** are a quartet of four upright stones, all that's left of a stone circle from 3000 B.C.

The **Unstan Chambered Tomb** (ⓡ), 2 miles (3km) northeast of Stromness along A965, 10 miles (16km) west of Kirkwall, is a big (115 feet/35m in diameter) burial mound dating from 2500 B.C. For its type, it's unsurpassed in western Europe. There's a chambered tomb more than 6 feet (2m) high. It's open throughout the day, and admission is free. For information, call the **Tankerness House** (© 01856/873-191). Unstan Ware is the name given to pottery discovered in the tomb.

Last occupied about 2500 B.C., **Skara Brae** 𝕣𝕣 (© 01856/841-815), 7½ miles (12km) north of Stromness, was a collection of Neolithic village houses joined by covered passages. This colony, which was believed to have sheltered farmers and herders, remained buried in the sands for 4,500 years, until an 1850 storm revealed the ruins. You can see the remains of six houses and a workshop. The walls were made from flagstone rock and the roofs were skins laid on wooden or whalebone rafters. A fireplace was in the center; beds were placed against the side walls. The bed "linen" was bracken or heather, and the "quilts" were animal skins. This prehistoric village is the best preserved of its type in Europe. It's open from April to September, daily from 9:30am to 6:30pm; and October to March, Monday through Saturday from 9:30am to 4:30pm and Sunday from 2 to 4:30pm. Admission is £4.50 ($6.75) for adults, £3.30 ($4.95) for seniors, and £1.30 ($1.95) for children.

Brough of Birsay, in Birsay at the northern end of Mainland about 11 miles (18km) north of Stromness, is the ruin of a Norse settlement and Romanesque church on an islet that you can reach only at low tide. You can see a replica of a Pictish sculptured stone. (The original was removed to a museum for safekeeping.) The site is open daily year-round; admission is free. Nearby are the ruins of the **Earls' Palace** at Birsay, a mansion constructed in the 16th century for the earls of Orkney.

Click Mill, off B9057, 2 miles (3km) northeast of Dounby, is the only still-functioning example of an old horizontal water mill on the island.

If you'd like to explore the region described above on two wheels, stop by **Bobby's Cycle Centre,** Kirkwall (© 01856/873-097), with rates of £8 ($12) daily or £60 ($90) weekly. It's open Monday through Saturday from 9am to 5:30pm.

Every Wednesday night, the **Ayre Hotel,** in Kirkwall (© 01856/873-001), hosts the **Accordian and Fiddle Club.** On Thursday nights in winter, locals gather at the Town Hall to enjoy the music of the **Reel and Strathspey Society.** Admission to these events is about £3 to £5 ($4.50 to $7.50). Parish halls in the different communities host an erratic schedule of ceilidhs and concerts throughout the year. Check with the Kirkwall tourist office (see above)for details.

DINING

Scorrabrae Inn BRITISH   In an extension attached to a 19th-century grocer's shop, this simple but convenient restaurant also contains the town's only pub. The bar features whiskies distilled in the Orkneys. The menu offers a wide variety of choices, including several fish and chicken dishes, lasagna, salads, and vegetarian meals.

Orphir. © 01856/811-262. Reservations recommended. Main courses £6.50–£10 ($9.75–$15). No credit cards. May–Aug Mon–Thurs 6–11pm, Fri 5pm–1am, Sat noon–2pm and 5pm–1am, and Sun 12:30–10pm; Sept–April Mon–Sat 6–10pm, Sat noon–2pm, Sun noon–10pm. Bar open year-round to at least 11:30pm.

STROMNESS

Set on the west coast of Mainland against a hill, Brinkie's Brae, Stromness was once known as Hamnavoe ("haven bay") in Old Norse. With its sheltered anchorage, it's the main port of Orkney, and the stone-flagged main street is said to "uncoil like a sailor's rope." The ferry *St. Ola* arrives here from Scrabster on the mainland. Fishing boats find shelter here from storms in the North Atlantic.

With its waterfront gables, nousts (slipways), and jetties, Stromness strikes many visitors as more interesting than Kirkwall. It's an ideal place to walk about, exploring whatever captures your fancy. In the old days, you could see whaling ships in port, along with vessels belonging to the Hudson's Bay Company. Some young men of Orkney left with them to man lonely fur stations in the far outposts of Canada. For many transatlantic vessels, Stromness was the last port of call before the New World. At Login's Well, many ships were outfitted for Arctic expeditions.

Stromness has a **tourist office** in the ferry terminal building (✆ **01856/ 850-716**), open from April to October, Monday through Friday from 8am to 4pm, Saturday from 9 to 4pm, and Sunday from 10am to 3pm (also opens to greet all incoming ferries, too, as late as 9pm; July and August, also open Sunday from 9am to 4pm); and November to March, Monday through Friday from 8am to 5pm and Saturday from 9am to 4pm.

A small but well-planned bookshop, **Stromness Books and Prints,** 1 Graham Place (✆ **01856/850-565**), specializes in books about Orkney and has in-stock copies of the Orkneyinga Saga. It's open Monday through Saturday from 10am to 6pm and sometimes during ferry arrival times in the evening.

The **Pier Arts Centre,** Victoria Street (✆ **01856/850-209**), has dazzled Orcadians with its "St. Ives school" of art, including works by Barbara Hepworth and Ben Nicholson. Admission is free; it's open Tuesday through Saturday from 10:30am to 5pm (closed from 12:30 to 1:30pm in winter).

At the **Stromness Museum,** 52 Alfred St. (✆ **01856/850-025**), you can see a collection of artifacts relating to the history of the Orkneys, especially a gallery devoted to maritime subjects, such as the Hudson's Bay Company and the sinking of the German Imperial Fleet. The section on natural history has excellent collections of local birds and their eggs, fossils, shells, and butterflies. It's open from May to September, daily from 10am to 5pm; and October to April, Monday through Saturday from 11am to 3:30pm. Admission is £2.50 ($3.75) for adults, £2 ($3) for students, 50p (75¢) for children under 14, and £5 ($7.50) per family.

If you want to rent a bike, head for **Orkney Cycle Hire,** 52 Dundas St. (✆ **01856/850-255**), which charges rates of £5 to £6.50 ($7.50 to $9.75) daily and £30 to £35 ($45 to $52.50) weekly. Summer hours are daily from 8:30am to dusk.

ACCOMMODATIONS & DINING

Ferry Inn   As its name implies, this modernized hotel is near the ferry. The small guest rooms are simple and a bit utilitarian. Affordable meals are served at lunch and dinner; look for typical Scottish fare like haggis, smoked salmon, and steak pie. To finish, try a clootie dumpling with cream.

John St., Stromness, Orkney KW16 3AA. ✆ 01856/850-280. Fax 01856/851-332. www.ferryinn.com. 17 units, 16 with private bathroom. £42 ($63) double without bathroom; £50 ($75) double with bathroom. AE, MC, V. Metered daytime parking available. **Amenities:** Restaurant, bar. *In room:* TV, coffeemaker, hair dryer, no phone.

Stromness Hotel   Behind an elaborate Victorian facade of symmetrical bay windows and beige sandstone blocks, this is the most important hotel in the Orkneys' second most important community. It was once a bit dowdy, but was extensively renovated in 1997. The small guest rooms are outfitted with old-fashioned furniture and shower-only bathrooms; many offer views of the water.

Lunch and dinner, simple but hearty, are served in the lounge; the moderately priced restaurant focuses on seafood and steaks from Orkney.

Victoria St. (about 100 yards/91m from the ferry terminal), Stromness, Orkney KW16 3AA. © 01856/850-298. Fax 01856/850-610. www.stromnesshotel.com. 40 units. £78 ($117) double. Rates include Scottish breakfast. MC, V. **Amenities:** Restaurant, 2 bars; bike rental. *In room:* TV, coffeemaker.

BURRAY

Burray and South Ronaldsay (see below) are two of the most visited of the southeastern isles, lying within an easy drive of Kirkwall on Mainland. Both are connected to Mainland by the Churchill Barriers causeway linking the islands of Glims Holm, Burray, and South Ronaldsay. The Vikings called the island Borgarey ("broch island").

You come to Burray for scenic drives, coastal views, lush pastures, and rugged grandeur. A center for watersports in summer, it also boasts several sandy beaches. You can inquire locally about the possibilities, as everything is casually run. But many Scots come here for canoeing, diving, sailing, swimming, and water-skiing.

The island is an ornithologist's delight, with a **bird sanctuary** filled with a wide range of species, including grouse, lapwing, curlew, and the Arctic tern. Look also for the puffin, the cormorant, and the oystercatcher. You can see gray seals along various shorelines. Their breeding ground is Hesta Head.

Burray is one of the major dive centers of the Orkneys. **Scapa Flow** is the best dive site in the northern hemisphere, for here lay the remnants of the German High Seas fleet scuttled on June 21, 1919. Seven warships range from battleships to light cruisers. Many block ships were sunk before the building of the Churchill Barriers, which were constructed to prevent enemy ships from coming into British waters. Marine life, including some rare sponges, enhances the variety of the dives. If you'd like a diving adventure, call the **European Technical Dive Center,** Garlise, Burray (© **01856/731-269**).

ACCOMMODATIONS & DINING

Watersound Restaurant/Sands Motel   One of the island's most prominent structures, this building was originally a fish-processing plant. The hostelry sits in the center of Burray Village, 8 miles (13km) north of the passenger ferry at Burwick, on South Ronaldsay. There are four upper-story flats, each containing three rooms and a kitchenette. These can be rented for less than a week if not fully booked (most likely in low season).

The reputable restaurant contains the island's only pub. Lunch and dinner choices may include preparations of local trout as well as other Orkney products.

Burray Village, Burray, Orkney KW17 2SS. © **01856/731-298.** Fax 01856/731-298. 4 units. £280–£300 ($420–$450) per week for 1–6 occupants. MC, V. **Amenities:** Restaurant, bar. *In room:* TV, kitchenette, refrigerator, coffeemaker, iron.

SOUTH RONALDSAY

Also joined by the Churchill Barriers, the island of South Ronaldsay is unspoiled fertile countryside. The hamlet St. Margaret's Hope was named after the young Norwegian princess, the "Maid of Norway," who was Edward II's child bride. Had she lived, she was slated to become queen of England, which at the time laid claim to Scotland. South Ronaldsay is the nearest Orkney island to mainland Scotland, 6½ miles (10.5km) north of the port of John o' Groats. It's separated from the British mainland by the waters of Pentland Firth.

The island offers some of the best **sea angling** waters in the world. Record-breaking catches, particularly in halibut and skate, have been caught, and you can hire local boats on a daily basis. There's also excellent shore fishing from local shores and rocks.

Tomb of the Eagles, south of Windwick Bay at the southern tip of the island, is a fine chambered tomb dating from 3000 B.C. Nearby is a recently excavated mound dating from 1500 B.C. Mr. R. Simison of Liddle Farm, who has excavated the area, will be happy to explain the mound and tomb. Please call at the farm before visiting the tomb and mound (℃ **01856/831-339**). Admission is £3 ($4.50) for adults, £2.50 ($3.75) for seniors, and £1.50 ($2.25) for children under 13. Open daily from 10am to 8pm.

In the southwest corner of the island, on the opposite side from the Tomb of Eagles, stands **Old St. Mary's Church and Cemetery.** This ancient church is stone-carved with the shape of two feet. Other stones of similar type have been found, and they're thought to be coronation stones for tribal chiefs or petty kings.

The Workshop, Front Road (℃ **01856/831-587**), is a craft producers' cooperative in the center of the village of St. Margaret's Hope. It sells a wide range of locally produced crafts, including pottery, jewelry, baskets, rugs, and fine-quality handknits.

DINING

Creel Restaurant ℛ SCOTTISH   This cozy restaurant, a winner of the "Taste of Scotland" award, overlooks the bay and uses a large variety of local products. Specialties include Orkney crab soup and roasted monkfish tails with sweet-pepper dressing. For a change from the traditional clootie dumpling you may have sampled elsewhere, the clootie dumpling parfait is a lighter version. The strawberry shortcake, made with homemade shortbread, cream, and fresh Orkney strawberries in season, is also a treat.

The restaurant rents three guest rooms costing £75 ($112.50) double, which includes a Scottish breakfast.

Front Rd., St. Margaret's Hope, Orkney KW17 2SL. ℃ 01856/831-311. Reservations recommended. All main dishes £15.80 ($23.70). MC, V. April–Oct daily 7–9pm; open some weekends in winter (call first).

SHAPINSAY

Visitors come here mainly for the secluded beaches, the many walking trails, and the wildlife, including seals. Getting here is fairly easy if you're based on Kirkwall, for the **Orkney Ferries Ltd.,** Shore Street (℃ **01856/872-044; www. orkneyferries.co.uk**), comes here six times a day. The round-trip passage is £15.80 ($23.70) for vehicles, £5.30 ($7.95) for adults, and £2.60 ($3.90) for children.

The island was the seat of the Balfours of Trenabie. John Balfour was a nabob, making his fortune in India before becoming the member of Parliament for Orkney and Shetland in 1790. He launched the Scottish baronial castle Balfour. There are several Neolithic sites on the island, but most remain unexcavated.

ACCOMMODATIONS & DINING

Balfour Castle ℛ (Finds   There is no more unusual accommodation in all the Orkney Islands. The region's most important benefactors were the Balfour family, worldwide shipping magnates. John Balfour began work on this castle in the southwest corner of Shapinsay, but it was completed by his heir in 1847. In the 1950s, when the last Balfour died without an heir, the castle and estate were bought by a former Polish officer, Tadeusz Zawadski, and his Scottish wife, Catherine. Today, the place is run by the widow Catherine and her family. It accepts no more than 12 guests at a time, and the family treats them to conversation and entertainment. The guest rooms boast antique or semi-antique furniture and lots of character.

The cuisine relies on such tempting ingredients as local wild duck and fresh scallops, crabmeat, and lobster. Guests who catch their own dinner will have it cheerfully prepared for them.

The estate shelters the only forest in the Orkney Islands, planted in the 19th century by the Balfours and composed chiefly of sycamores. In its center, a 12-foot (3.5m) stone wall surrounds the kitchen gardens, where greenhouses produce peaches, figs, and grapes; strawberries, cabbages, and salad greens grow well within the shelter of the wall. The estate is still a working farm, involved with beef cattle, sheep, and grain production. The hosts will take the time to tour the property with guests and also arrange fishing trips or bird-watching tours, as well as photographic and ornithological trips with guide and boat. Between May and July, the bird life is unbelievably profuse. Guests may also be taken to the family's 100-acre (40.5-hectare) uninhabited island, where colonies of gray seals and puffins like to say hello.

Balfour Village, Shapinsay, Orkney KW17 2DY. (© 01856/711-282. Fax 01856/711-283. www.balfourcastle. co.uk. 6 units. £100 ($150) per person. Rates include 3 meals. Discount of 30% for children under 13. V. **Amenities:** Restaurant, bar. *In room:* Coffeemaker, hair dryer, iron, no phone.

ROUSAY

Called the "Egypt of the North," the island of Rousay lies off the northwest coast of Mainland. Almost moon-shaped and measuring about 6 miles (10km) across, the island is known for its trout lochs, which draw anglers from all over Europe. Much of the land is heather-covered moors. Part of the island has hills, including **Ward Hill,** which many people walk up for a panoramic sweep of Orcadian seascape. In the northwestern part of the island is **Hellia Spur,** one of Europe's most important seabird colonies. As you walk about, you can see the much-photographed puffin.

But where does the bit about Egypt come in? Rousay boasts nearly 200 prehistoric monuments, including one of the most significant, the Iron Age **Midhowe Broch and Tombs** ✶, in the west of the island, excavated in the 1930s. The walled enclosure on a promontory is cut off by a deep rock-cut ditch. The cairn is more than 75 feet (23m) long and was split among a dozen stalls or compartments. The graves of some two dozen settlers, along with their cattle, were found inside. One writer called the cairn the "great ship of death." The other major sight, the **Blackhammer Cairn,** lies north of B9064 on the southern coast. This megalithic burial chamber is believed to date from the 3rd millennium B.C. It was separated into about half a dozen compartments for the dead.

Excavation began in 1978 on a Viking site at **Westness,** which figured in the Orkneyinga Saga. A farmer digging a hole to bury a dead cow came across an Old Norse grave site. Three silver brooches, shipped to the National Museum of Scotland at Edinburgh, were discovered among the ruins; the earliest one dated from the 9th century. Die-hard archaeology buffs might like to know that a mile-long (1.6km) archaeological trail begins here; a mimeographed map (not very precise) is sometimes available from the tourist office. The trail is clearly marked with placards and signs describing the dusty-looking excavations that crop up on either side.

To reach Rousay, you can rely on the service provided by the **Orkney Ferries Ltd.,** in Kirkwall (© **01856/872-044;** www.orkneyferries.co.uk). The trip is made six times daily; round-trip passage is £15.80 ($23.70) for vehicles, £5.30 ($7.95) for adults, and £2.60 ($3.90) for children.

EDAY

Called the "Isthmus Isle of the Norsemen," Eday is the center of a hardworking and traditional crofting community that ekes out a living among the heather and peat bogs of this isolated island.

Life isn't easy here, for most of this north isle is barren, with heather-clad and hilly moorlands that often lead to sheer cliffs or give way to sand dunes with long sweeping beaches. Chambered cairns and standing stones speak of ancient settlements. In the 18th and 19th centuries, the island was a major supplier of peat.

Today, most of the population derives its income from cattle and dairy farming, although other products include hand-knit sweaters, cheese, and a highly rated beer brewed in individual crofts by local farmers and their families.

People come to this almost-forgotten oasis today for bird-watching, beachcombing, and sea angling. Others prefer the peaceful scenic walks to the Red Head cliffs, likely to be filled with guillemots and kittiwakes. The cliffs rise to a height of 200 feet (61m), and on a clear day you can see Fair Isle.

On its eastern coastline, Eday opens onto Eday Sound, where pirate John Gow was captured. After a trial in London, he was hanged in 1725; his exploits are detailed in Sir Walter Scott's *The Pirate.* Following his capture, Gow was held prisoner at **Carrick House,** discreetly signposted on the northern part of the island. Carrick House was built in 1633 by James Stewart, the second son of Robert Stewart, who had been named earl of Carrick. It's now the home of **Mrs. Joy** (© 01857/622-260), but if you're polite and have a flexible schedule, she might open her house to a visit. There may or may not be a fee—about £5 ($7.50) per person "feels right." She's most amenable to visitors between late June and mid-September, and Sundays are an especially good time to test your luck. Despite the sale of various parcels of land to the island's 130 to 140 inhabitants, most of the island is owned by the laird of Eday, Mrs. Rosemary Hebdon Joy, whose link to the island dates to around 1900, when her grandfather bought it from his London club. The circumstances surrounding the island's inheritance have made it one of the few matriarchal lairdships in Scotland—its ownership has passed from mother to daughter for several generations.

Because of limited accommodations, Eday is most often visited on a day trip. **Loganair,** in Kirkwall (call British Airways at © 0345/111-222 for reservations), offers service to Eday every Wednesday. **Orkney Ferries Ltd.,** Shore Street in Kirkwall (© 01856/872-044; www.orkneyferries.co.uk), crosses to Eday about twice daily. The round-trip fare is £23.50 ($35.25) for vehicles and £10.50 ($15.75) for adults.

ACCOMMODATIONS

There's no formal tourist office in Eday. However, **Mrs. Popplewell** (© 01857/622-248) from Little Croft House (see "Dining," below) provides an information service and can assist you with finding accommodations or organizing any activities.

Skaill Farm ℛ *Finds*   Operated by a pair of English expatriates fleeing the congestion of the London suburbs, Skaill is the centerpiece for the island's third-largest farm. Set on 800 acres (324 hectares) of windswept grazing land, midway along the length of the island near its narrowest point, 5 miles (8km) from both Calfsound and Backaland, it's in a stone building whose 18th-century core was constructed on the foundations of Orkney's medieval skaill. (A skaill is the honorific home of an earl, designed to shelter him during his visits from other parts of his realm.) Michael and Dee Cockram welcome you to their home, providing well-prepared dinners and simple but comfortable guest rooms. Meals might include fresh vegetables from the family garden, lobsters, scallops, lamb, and beef.

Skaill, Eday, Orkney KW17 2AA. ℂ and fax **01857/622-271**. 2 units, none with private bathroom. £58 ($87) double. No credit cards. Rates include half-board. **Amenities:** Dining room, lounge. *In room:* No phone.

DINING

Little Croft House ☆ *Value* SCOTTISH   One of the most charming possibilities for a meal on Eday is provided by Emma Popplewell, who, if notified in advance, will prepare fixed-price lunches and dinners. Meals are often served to a loyal following of "off-island" yacht owners enjoying the nautical challenges of the local waters. The setting is a croft cottage whose 30-inch-thick (76cm) stone walls were built around 1900. Its flower and vegetable gardens slope down to the edge of the sea, source of some of the kelp and seaweed Mrs. Popplewell uses to flavor her succulent versions of Orkney lamb. Depending on what's available, menu items may include grilled halibut with scallops and local dill and fennel, salads made with wild greens gathered from the hills, homemade raspberry bramble sorbet, locally made cheeses and beers, and aromatic crusty bread that's freshly baked every morning.

In one of the croft's outbuildings (a former boathouse), Mrs. Popplewell sells sweaters, accessories, and caftans that are handknit on Eday by local women. Also for sale are paintings and sculpture by island artists.

Mrs. Popplewell also rents four comfortably furnished rooms containing TVs; the two doubles are £48 ($72), including half-board.

Isle of Eday, Orkney KW17 2AB. ℂ **01857/622-248**. Reservations required as far in advance as possible. About £10 ($15) per person. No credit cards. Time to be arranged when making reservations.

SANDAY

The name of Sanday means "sand island," which is appropriate; the island's long white beaches have grown as tides have changed over the last century. With few residents or visitors, the stretches of seashore are often deserted—perfect for long, solitary walks. One of the largest of the North Isles, some 16 miles (26km) in length, Sanday is part of the eastern archipelago.

On the Elsness Peninsula, jutting southeast from the bulk of Sanday Island, you'll find one of the most spectacular chambered cairns found in the Orkneys: the **Quoyness Chambered Tomb** ☆. The tomb and its principal chamber date from around 2900 B.C., reaching a height of some 13 feet (4m). Access is by key, which is available at the local post office in Lady Village. Other ancient monuments, including Viking burial grounds and broch sites, have been found on Sanday.

You can see rare migrant birds and terns at the **Start Point Lighthouse,** near the extreme tip of Start Point, a tidal peninsula jutting northward from the rest of Sanday. The early-19th-century lighthouse is one of the oldest in the country, but since the 1960s has been on "automatic pilot," without a permanent resident to tend the machinery except for a part-time warden (ℂ **01857/600-385**) who may or may not be here at the time of your visit. The number of ships wrecked off Sanday's shore is topped only by North Ronaldsay; you can see the wreck of a German destroyer on the Sand of Langamay. If you want to see this monument, know that only specialized vehicles can drive across the tidal flats and only at low tide. Locals, however, are aware of the times when a trekker can safely walk across the kelp-strewn sandy flats. If you feel adventurous, ask a local how to get here or phone the warden for advice.

414 CHAPTER 12 · THE ORKNEY & SHETLAND ISLANDS

Loganair flies in from the Kirkwall Airport (© **01856/872-494**) twice a day Monday through Friday and once on Saturday at a cost of £31 ($46.50). **Orkney Ferries Ltd.,** Shore Street, Kirkwall (© **01856/872-044;** www.orkneyferries. co.uk), crosses to the island about two times daily. Round-trip fares are £10.50 ($15.75) for adults and £23.50 ($35.25) for vehicles.

ACCOMMODATIONS & DINING
Accommodations are extremely limited, so book your room in advance.

Belsair Hotel In the village of Kettletoft, site of about 15 buildings and the most central of the island's four communities, this hotel contains the island's only restaurant. It's located about 8 miles (13km) northeast of Sanday's roll-on–roll-off ferry pier. The ancestors of Belsair's present owners built it of stone and clapboards in 1879. The owner and manager, Mrs. Joy Foubister, is the island's postmistress, and her husband, Kenneth, is the postman. The functionally furnished guest rooms were upgraded and renovated back in 1992. Gardens across the road produce many of the vegetables served in the dining room, where moderately priced dishes include straightforward but flavorful preparations of fish, beef, and lamb.

Kettletoft, Sanday, Orkney KW17 2BJ. © 01857/600-206. 6 units, 3 with private bathroom. £37 ($55.50) double without bathroom; £50 ($75) double with bathroom. Rates include full Scottish breakfast. No credit cards. **Amenities:** Restaurant. *In room:* TV, coffeemaker, no phone.

WESTRAY
One of the biggest of the North Isles, Westray is a fertile island with a closely knit community, many of whom are said to have Spanish blood, owing to shipwrecks of the Armada off its stormy shores. The western shoreline is the steepest, rising in parts to some 200 feet (61m), from which you can enjoy panoramic vistas. You can see seabirds like guillemots around Noup Head, with its red-sandstone cliffs. The island is a bird-watcher's paradise. Along the lochs are many sandy beaches.

Below the cliffs is the so-called **Gentleman's Cave.** A Balfour of Trenabie is said to have found refuge in this cave, along with his comrades, after the defeat at Culloden in 1746. As winter winds howled outside, they drank to the welfare of the "king over the water," Bonnie Prince Charlie. A hike to the remote cave is recommended only for the hardy and only after you've talked to locals first about how to access it. A knowledgeable guide is **Mr. Alex Costie** (© **01857/ 677-355**), who gives hiking tours of the island for around £22 ($33) per person.

At **Pierowall,** the major hamlet, you can see **Pierowall Church,** a ruin with a chancel and a nave. There are also some finely lettered grave slabs.

The most famous attraction is **Noltland Castle,** a former fortress overlooking Pierowall. A governor of the island, Thomas de Tulloch, had this castle built in 1420. Eventually it was occupied by Gilbert Balfour of Westray, who had it redesigned as a fortress in a "three-stepped" or Z plan. This would have provided complete all-around visibility against attack—but it was never finished. The castle's present ruins date from around the mid-1500s. It was destroyed in part by a fire in 1746. A kitchen, a stately hall, and a winding staircase are still standing.

Orkney Ferries Ltd. (© **01856/872-044** in Kirkwall; www.orkneyferries. co.uk) sails to Pierowall, Westray, two to three times daily. Bookings are required for cars; the cost is £23.50 ($35.25) round-trip. Adult passengers pay £10.50 ($15.75). **Loganair** flies to Westray one to two times Monday through Saturday at a cost of £31 ($46.50). Phone © **01856/872-494** in Kirkwall for information; for reservations, call British Airways at © **0345/222-111.**

ACCOMMODATIONS & DINING

Because accommodations are very limited, make reservations in advance.

Pierowall Hotel   Built a century ago as a manse (clergyman's residence) for a nearby Presbyterian church, this cozy hotel, 7¼ miles (12km) north of the roll-on-roll-off ferry terminal, is the domain of Mrs. Jean Fergus. The pub offers affordable food and drink to anyone who stops in.

Pierowall Village, Westray, Orkney KW17 2BZ. (℃ **01857/677-208.** Fax 01857/677-707. 5 units, 2 with private bathroom. £20 ($30) double without bathroom; £26 ($39) double with bathroom. Rates include Scottish breakfast. MC, V. **Amenities:** Restaurant, 2 bars. *In room:* TV, coffeemaker, hair dryer, no phone.

PAPA WESTRAY

Both bird-watchers and students of history are drawn to Papa Westray, which was believed to have been settled by at least 3500 B.C. One of the most northerly isles in the Orkneys, it's rich in archaeological sites. In the fertile farmland around Holland, the **Knap of Howar** was discovered, the earliest standing dwelling house in northwestern Europe, dating from before 3000 B.C.

On the eastern shore of Loch Treadwell, on a peninsula jutting southeast from the bulk of Papa Westray, you can visit the ruins of **St. Treadwell's Chapel,** believed to have marked the arrival of Christianity in the Orkney Islands. The chapel, now in ruins, was dedicated to Triduana, a Celtic saint. When a Pictish king, Nechtan, admired her lovely eyes, she is said to have plucked them out and sent them by messenger to the king—she hoped he'd learn it was foolish to admire physical beauty. For many decades, the chapel was a place of pilgrimage for those suffering from eye problems.

On the island's western edge, about 2 miles (3km) from St. Treadwell's Chapel, north of the airport, is **St. Boniface Church,** also a Celtic site. Stone Celtic crosses were found here, as well as a series of much-eroded grave slabs carved from red sandstone. This is believed to have been a Christian Viking burial ground, now exposed to the howling winds and bleak sunlight of this rocky peat-clad island.

A major attraction here is **Holland House,** formerly the home of the Traills of Holland. Dating from the 17th century, the house is a fine example of a circular "Horse Engine House," which was driven by 11 horses and a dovecote. The house is now owned by farmer John Rendall (℃ **01857/644-251**); you might be able to see inside if you're polite and Mr. Rendall is feeling sociable.

The northern end of the island has been turned into a **nature reserve,** which is the best place to go for scenic walks. Along with colonies of guillemots and kittiwakes, **North Hill** is the site of one of the largest breeding colonies of the Arctic tern.

Twice-daily flights to Papa Westray from Kirkwall on Mainland are offered by **Loganair** (℃ **01856/872-494,** or call British Airways at ℃ 0345/222-111 for reservations). **Orkney Ferries Ltd.,** Shore Street, Kirkwall (℃ **01856/872-044;** www.orkneyferries.co.uk), sails to Papa Westray direct on Tuesdays and Fridays; on other days, the ferry stops at Westray, where you catch a smaller ferry service to Papa Westray. Round-trip fares are £23.50 ($35.25) for vehicles and £10.50 ($15.75) for adult passengers.

ACCOMMODATIONS & DINING

Beltane House   Built in 1983 about 2 miles (3km) from the island's main pier, this all-purpose accommodation is run by the local farm cooperative. A row of stone-sided farmworkers' cottages was renovated to form a complex of shops, a guesthouse, and a bare-bones youth hostel containing two dorms (male and female) with bunk beds. June and July are the busiest months, requiring advance reservations. No meals are provided in the hostel, but there's a self-catering kitchen. Hostel guests sometimes choose to join the guests of the main house for the affordable nightly dinner.

Papa Westray, Orkney KW17 2BU. © **01857/644-267**. 4 units in guesthouse. £80 ($120) double. Rates include Scottish breakfast and dinner. For youth hostel: £8 ($12) per adult; £7 ($10.50) per child under 18. (Rates are set by the Scottish Youth Hostel Association and change frequently.) MC, V. **Amenities:** Restaurant. *In room:* No phone.

2 Fair Isle ⟨★

27 miles (43.5km) S of Lerwick, Shetland Islands

Called the "most isolated inhabited part of Britain," Fair Isle lies on the same latitude as Bergen, Norway. It measures only about 1 mile by 3½ miles (1.6km by 6km) and sits about midway between the Orkneys and the Shetlands, administered by the latter. Relentless seas pound its 20-mile (32km) coast in winter and powerful westerly winds fling Atlantic spray from one side of the island to the other. It's home to fewer than 100 rugged, self-reliant souls.

An important staging point for migrating birds, Fair Isle is even better known for its patterned pullovers, which greatly aid the island's economy. In stores around the world, you'll see these intricately patterned garments retailing at high prices. The homegrown product is sold on Fair Isle at half the price. Fair Isle knitting is even a part of the curriculum at all primary schools, and many jobless men have turned to knitting.

Originally the fame of the sweaters was spread in the 1920s by the prince of Wales. The pattern is of mysterious origin. Some suggest it was derived from Celtic sources, others that it came from the island's Viking heritage. A more daring theory maintains the themes were Moorish, learned from Spanish sailors shipwrecked off Fair Isle from the Armada in 1588.

In 1954, the island was acquired by the National Trust for Scotland. The bird observatory installed here is the most remarkable in the country. Since work began in 1948, some 200 species have been ringed. Fair Isle is an important breeding ground for everything from the puffin and the Arctic skua to the razorbill and the storm petrel.

GETTING THERE

Loganair operates scheduled service in a seven-seat "Islander"; flight time is 25 minutes. From Sumburgh Airport, there's a flight on Saturday only, which links with incoming Loganair flights from both Glasgow and Edinburgh. From Lerwick Airport, flights are once or twice a day from Monday to Saturday. Call Loganair at © **01856/872-494** or British Airways at © **0345/222-111** for more information.

The mailboat *Good Shepherd* sails on Tuesday, Thursday, and Saturday from Grutness Pier, Sumburgh Head, on Shetland. It's advisable to check sailing times from Grutness by phoning before 9:30am on the morning of the scheduled departure for Fair Isle, in case of weather delay. Bookings for the trips to Fair Isle can be made through **J. W. Stout**, Skerryholm, Fair Isle (© **01595/760-222**). A one-way fare is £2.20 ($3.30); the trip takes 2½ hours.

ACCOMMODATIONS & DINING

Fair Isle Lodge and Bird Observatory ★ *(Finds*   Even if you're not a birdwatcher, you might want to stay at this low-slung, big-windowed building in the shelter of treeless hillsides, near the sea at the northern end of the island. It was the dream of a well-respected ornithologist, George Waterston, who bought the lodge in 1948 and created the observatory. It's now administered by the Fair Isle Bird Observatory Trust. The place is most popular during the spring and autumn bird migrations. It's always wise to reserve well in advance, especially during those seasons. Sometimes the wardens will take guests on before-breakfast tours of bird traps, which, for tagging purposes, are placed in strategic points along the stone dikes surrounding the island.

Adjacent accommodations were constructed to provide housing for visitors. There are 33 beds for rent. It's also possible to stay in a dorm room, with four to six beds.

Fair Isle, Shetland ZE2 9JU. © and fax **01595/760-258.** www.fairislebirdobs.co.uk. 17 units, none with private bathroom. £74 ($111) double; £30 ($45) dorm bed. Rates include full board. MC, V. Closed Nov to mid-April. **Amenities:** Bar; ranger service providing guided walks and other activities.

3 The Shetland Islands: A Land of Stark Beauty (*

60 miles (97km) N and NE of the Orkneys

The northernmost part of the British Isles, the archipelago of the Shetland Islands includes some 100 islands that make up 50 square miles (130sq km) of land. Many are merely islets or rocks, but 17 are inhabited. The major island is called Mainland, as in the Orkneys. This island, on which the capital, Lerwick, is located, is about 55 miles (88.5km) long and 20 miles (32km) wide. It has been turned into what some critics have called "a gargantuan oil terminal." The Shetlands handle about half of Britain's oil.

The islands have been called "that long string of peat and gneiss that stands precariously where three seas—the Atlantic Ocean, the North Sea, and the Arctic Ocean—meet." Shetland's fjordlike voes (sheer rock cliffs) make the islands beautiful in both seascape and landscape. But it's a stark beauty, wild and rugged, with windswept moors. Because there are few trees, the landscape at first looks barren. After a while, it begins to take on a fascination, especially when you come on a typical Shetlander, in his sturdy Wellington boots and thick woolen sweater, cutting peat along a bog as his ancestors did before him. Shetlanders are proud, warm, and often eager to share the treasures of their island chain with you. At no point in Shetland are you more than 3 miles (5km) from the sea—the coastline stretches for some 3,000 miles (4,830km).

The major airport is at **Sumburgh,** on the southern tip of the southernmost island of Mainland. The far-northern outpost is **Muckle Flugga Lighthouse,** an advanced achievement of engineering. Standing poised on near-vertical rock, it's the "last window on the world" through which Great Britain looks out to the north. It's not as cold here as you might think: The Shetland archipelago benefits from the warming influence of the Gulf Stream, but even in summer the weather tends to be chilly. Shetland has less than half the annual rainfall recorded in the western Highlands. In summer, there's almost continuous daylight. The Shetlanders call it "Simmer Dim." In midwinter, there are no more than 5 hours of daylight.

Civilization here dates back some 5,000 years. The Shetlands were inhabited more than 2,000 years before the Romans, who called them "Ultima Thule." These islands paraded Neolithic people, followed by the people of the Iron and Bronze Ages, who gave way to the Picts and the Celts. But the most enduring influence came from the Vikings, who ruled the Shetlands until some 500 years ago. The Norse established an influence that lasted for centuries and is still evident today in language, culture, and customs.

The Vikings held the islands from A.D. 800 until they were given to Scotland in 1469 as part of the wedding dowry of Princess Margaret of Norway when she married James III. Scotland's takeover of the Shetlands marked a sad period in the life of the islanders, who found themselves under the sway of often cruel and unreasonable feudal barons. One of the most hated of rulers was Earl Patrick Stewart, who was assigned the dubious task of imposing Scottish customs on a people who had known only Viking law. His son matched him in cruelty, and eventually both earls were executed in Edinburgh for their crimes. Shetlanders still think of themselves as separate from Scots.

The impact of the North Sea oilmen on this traditionally straitlaced community is noticeable, in overcrowding and other ways. However, away from all the oil activity, life in the Shetlands goes on much as it always did, except for the profusion of modern conveniences and imported foodstuffs—you'll notice that food on Shetland tastes better when it's from Shetland; for example, try the Reestit mutton, salted and smoked, with a distinctive flavor.

The islands are famous for their ponies and wool. Shetland ponies roam freely among the hills and common grazing lands in the island chain. Some are shipped south to England, where they're popular as children's mounts. The Shetlands also have 10% of all the seabirds in the British Isles, and several of the smaller islands or islets have nature reserves. Seals are protected and welcomed here—you can see them drifting among the waves, sliding down in pursuit of a fish dinner, or lounging about on the rocks and beaches. You'll recognize most of them as the Atlantic gray seal, with its big angular head. The common seal, with a dog-shaped head, is most often found on the islet of Mousa. And if you want to see otters, you have a better chance in Shetland than anywhere else in Britain.

Anglers find some 200 freshwater lochs in Shetland, and deep-sea angling makes for a memorable sport. Many world fishing records have been set in Shetland. "Ton-up" fish are common.

The island craftspeople are noted for their creativity, reflected in their handcrafts, jewelry, and knitware. In some places, you can watch these items being made in the workshops of the artists. Hand-knitted sweaters are still produced in great numbers, and anyone contemplating a visit might want to return with at least one.

Note: It's imperative to have advance reservations if you're considering a trip to the Shetlands, especially in midsummer.

SHETLAND ESSENTIALS

GETTING THERE   Shetland is a 2½-hour flight from London. By air or sea, Aberdeen is the major departure point from Scotland. **British Airways** (© 800/ 247-9297 in the U.S., or 0345/222-111) flies from Aberdeen four times per day Monday through Friday, with reduced service on Saturday and Sunday. The flight takes less than an hour.

Roll-on–roll-off car ferries operate from Aberdeen to Shetland Monday through Friday, carrying up to 600 passengers and 240 cars. For information, contact **P&O Ferries,** Jamieson's Quay, Aberdeen (© 01224/572-615). The trip takes about 14 hours and costs £120 to £200 ($180 to $300) per person. On-board facilities include restaurants, cafeterias, bars, lounges, and gift shops.

P&O offers year-round ferry service once a week, departing on Sunday at noon and Tuesday at 10pm from Stromness, Orkney, heading for Lerwick in the Shetlands. For information, call © 01856/850-655 in Stromness.

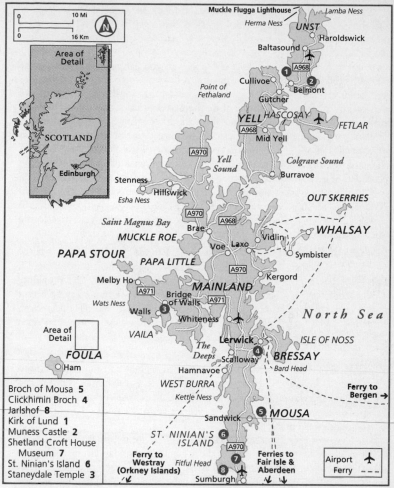

The Shetland Islands map, including:

0 — 10 Mi / 0 — 16 Km

Area of Detail — SCOTLAND, Edinburgh

Muckle Flugga Lighthouse • Lamba Ness • Herma Ness • UNST • Haroldswick • Baltasound • A968 • Cullivoe • **1** • **2** Belmont • Gutcher • Point of Fethaland • YELL • HASCOSAY • FETLAR • A968 • Mid Yell • Yell Sound • Colgrave Sound • Burravoe • A970 • Stenness • Hillswick • OUT SKERRIES • Esha Ness • A970 • A968 • Brae • Vidlin • WHALSAY • Saint Magnus Bay • Voe • Laxo • MUCKLE ROE • Symbister • PAPA STOUR • PAPA LITTLE • A970 • Melby Ho • Kergord • MAINLAND • A971 • Bridge of Walls • North Sea • Wats Ness • A971 • Walls • **3** • Whiteness • Area of Detail • VAILA • Lerwick • ISLE OF NOSS • FOULA • The Deeps • **4** • BRESSAY • Ham • Scalloway • Bard Head • Hamnavoe • WEST BURRA • Ferry to Bergen • Kettle Ness • **5** MOUSA • Sandwick • ST. NINIAN'S ISLAND • **6** • Ferry to Westray (Orkney Islands) • Fitful Head • A970 • **7** • Ferries to Fair Isle & Aberdeen • Airport • Ferry • **8** • Sumburgh

Broch of Mousa **5**
Clickhimin Broch **4**
Jarlshof **8**
Kirk of Lund **1**
Muness Castle **2**
Shetland Croft House Museum **7**
St. Ninian's Island **6**
Staneydale Temple **3**

GETTING AROUND If you have a problem with transportation either to or around the islands, you can always check with the tourist office in Lerwick (see below).

Loganair (© **01595/840-246**) provides daily and weekly service to the islands of Whalsay, Fetlar, Foula, and Out Skerries. Although flying is a bit more expensive than taking a ferry, the bonus is that you can go and return on the same day as opposed to spending 2 or possibly 3 days on a rather small island.

Most of the inhabited islands are reached from the Shetland Mainland, and passenger fares are nominal because they're heavily subsidized by the government. Service is 13 to 16 times a day to the islands of Unst, Yell, Whalsay, Fetlar, and Bressay. Passenger and cargo vessels service the islands of Fair Isle, Foula, the Skerries, and Papa Stour. Scheduled services to the little-visited places operate only once or twice a week, however. Boat trips to the islands of Mousa and Noss can be arranged in summer. Call the **Shetland Islands Tourism office** (© **01595/693-434**) for more information.

In summer, buses travel around Mainland to all the major places of interest. Call the leading bus company, **John Leask & Son** (© **01595/693-162**), or pick up a copy of the *Inter-Shetland Transport Timetable*, costing 75p ($1.15) at the tourist office.

It's easier to drive around the Shetlands than you'd think, as there are some 500 miles (805km) of passable roads—no traffic jams, no traffic lights. Many of the islands are connected by road bridges, and for those that aren't, car ferries provide service. Renting a car might be the best solution if you want to cover a lot of ground in the shortest time. You can either bring a car from mainland Scotland or pick one up in Lerwick. No major international car rental firm as yet maintains an office in the Shetlands. However, Avis and Europcar have as their on-island agents **Bolts Car Hire**, 26 North Rd., Lerwick (© **01595/693-636**); a competitor is **Grantsfield Garage**, North Road, Lerwick (© **01595/692-709**).

If you want to bike your way around, **Grantsfield Garage,** North Road (© **01595/692-709**), rents bikes for £7.50 ($11.25) per day and £45 ($67.50) per week. If you're planning on renting a bike for several days, reserve at least a day in advance.

VISITOR INFORMATION The **Shetland Islands Tourism office** is at the Market Cross in Lerwick (© **01595/693-434;** www.shetland-tourism.co.uk). The helpful staff does many things, such as arranging rooms and providing information on ferries, boat trips, car rentals, and local events—they even rent fishing tackle. It's open from April to September, Monday through Friday from 8am to 6pm and Saturday from 8am to 4pm (May to August, also Sunday from 10am to 1pm); and October to March, Monday through Friday from 9am to 5pm.

SPECIAL EVENTS Festivals and a festive atmosphere surround the communities of these remote islands, where the slightest excuse will kick off music and revelry. Pubs and community centers regularly schedule music and dancing, and on most weekend nights, all you have to do is go in search of a pint of beer to find live traditional music.

The **Shetland Folk Festival** (© **01595/694-757** for information) takes place at Lerwick around the end of April and the beginning of May. Young fiddlers on the island take part, and international artists fly in for 4 days of concerts, workshops, and informal jam sessions, climaxed by what is called the "Final Foy." Concerts, usually incorporating dinner and dancing, and are held in local halls throughout the islands, with most events costing about £7 to £13 ($10.50 to $19.50). Often festival entertainers will convene at the pubs and join local performers.

January also finds Lerwick hosting **Up Helly Aa,** its famous **Fire Festival,** on the last Tuesday of the month, when a thousand locals, torches held high, are cheered on as they storm an effigy of a Viking longboat and set it aflame. These heroes and their witnesses follow this with 2 straight days of eating, drinking, playing music, and dancing. The celebrations spread out from here, and more remote communities hold their local versions of the event over the next 3 months (see "Up Helly Aa!," below).

Summer months are marked by artistic and cultural **exchange programs** with Norway, Holland, and Sweden. Highlights during these events are musical and dramatic performances by the visiting artists. You can get information about the varying dates, venues, and prices by contacting the tourist office in Lerwick (see "Visitor Information," above). Summer weekends also bring regularly scheduled local **regattas,** in which different communities compete in sailing and rowing competitions. Afterward, there are celebratory dinners, music, and dancing in local venues.

LERWICK

The capital of the Shetlands since the 17th century, Lerwick, on the eastern coast of Mainland, is sheltered by the little offshore island of Bressay. In the 19th century, it was the herring capital of northern Europe, and before that, a haven for smugglers. The fishing fleet of the Netherlands put in here after combing the North Sea. Even before Victoria came to the throne in 1837, Lerwick had a bustling, cosmopolitan atmosphere. That's even truer today, with the influx of foreign visitors.

Ⓒ Up Helly Aa!

The farther north you travel in Scotland, the stronger are the undercurrents of pagan myth and pageantry, culminating in the vivid Norse traditions of the Shetlands. On the moss-covered rocky surface of the 100 or so islands, the collective unconscious of the locals is sometimes startlingly revealed as something other than Anglo-Saxon or Celtic.

Ask anyone in a local pub, and he or she will tell you the islands are Scottish only because of the fiscal embarrassment of a Norwegian king who sold the Shetlands to the Scottish monarchs in 1469 with the tacit understanding they'd eventually be returned to Scandinavia. Although for many generations the Shetlanders retained their Norse dialect and allegiance to Viking ways, the switch back to Norway never happened. Perhaps in reaction to their medieval role as bartered chattel between the two northern kingdoms, the Shetlands remained dourly outside Scottish culture, with a populace who, for many generations, used "the mainland" to refer to the provincial capital of Lerwick and not to the mainland of Scotland.

How do the Shetlanders celebrate their Nordic heritage? By brightening up the midwinter darkness with the Up Helly Aa festival, held—in fair weather, snow, or storm—every year on the last Tuesday in January. The festival's centerpiece is a meticulously crafted re-creation of a Viking longboat. The people of Lerwick parade by torchlight through the streets in Viking costume, and the highlight of the evening comes when the longboat is set alight and its dragon-head prow is engulfed in flames. Presiding over the ritual is an elected master of ceremonies, the Guizer Jarl (a significant honor bestowed only on a longtime resident male of proven civic worth and integrity).

This ancient ritual celebrates the death of winter and the return of the sun and the earth's rebirth with the coming of spring. The ceremony is based on an ancient Viking death ritual when the body of a dead earl (Jarl) would be set ablaze at sea. An essential part of the ritual is the almost immediate removal of all traces of the burned-out hulk of the longboat after the cremation is over. The morning after the ceremony, even the ashes of the celebration have been carted off, and Lerwick resumes its outwardly Christian and Scottish demeanor—until the Viking tradition of the Up Helly Aa is revived again the following year.

Believe it or not, Lerwick is sometimes the sunniest place in Britain, experiencing some 12 hours of sunshine a day in early summer. Commercial Street is the town's principal artery, and it's said that beneath the steep and narrow lanes runs a network of passages used by smugglers. Lerwick today is the main port and shopping center of Shetland.

EXPLORING THE TOWN

Your first stop should be at the tourist office (see above). The helpful staff members are used to unusual requests: Sometimes visitors from Canada or the United States drop in here wanting their ancestors traced.

Shetland Library and Museum, Lower Hillhead Road, a 5-minute walk west of Lerwick's center (© **01595/695-057;** www.shetland-museum.org.uk), has, in addition to a reading room, four galleries devoted to exhibits covering art and textiles, shipping, archaeological digs, and oil exploration. Admission is free. It's open Monday, Wednesday, and Friday from 10am to 7pm and Tuesday, Thursday, and Saturday from 10am to 5pm.

Entered via both Market Street and Charlotte Street, pentagonal **Fort Charlotte** (© **01595/693434**), built in 1665, contains high walls with gun slits pointing, naturally, at the sea. Eight years after it was constructed, it was burned by the Dutch. Restoration came in 1781. It's open daily from 9am to 10pm; admission is free.

Clickhimin Broch, about a quarter of a mile (0.4km) southwest of Lerwick beside A970, was fortified at the beginning of the Iron Age. Excavated in the 1950s, the site revealed 1,000 years of history. It was at one time turned into a broch, rising 17 feet (5m) and built inside the fort. Admission is free; it's open daily with no set hours. It's a great place to go for a scenic walk.

A 40-foot (12m) replica of a Viking longboat, *Dim Riv* ("Morning Light"), is available for a tour of the harbor on summer evenings. The boat was constructed by Lerwick craftsmen in 1980. Ask at the tourist office (see above).

Of the many shops in Lerwick, you may want to drop in at **Anderson & Co.,** Shetland Warehouse, Commercial Street (© **01595/693-714**), which sells handmade crofter and designer sweaters as well as other cottage-industry goods. **G. Rae,** 92 Commercial St. (© **01595/693-686**), sells silver and gold jewelry featuring Celtic motifs and images based on Norse mythology and Shetland legends. Gold- and silversmith Rosalyn Thompson produces the jewelry sold at **Hjaltasteyn,** 161 Commercial St. (© **01595/696-224**), where you'll find a selection of sterling silver and gold items, some of which are set with garnets and amethysts.

ACCOMMODATIONS

Glen Orchy House   Near the top of a brae (gently sloping hill) and not far from a nine-hole golf course that's free to the public, Glen Orchy House is a 4-minute walk from the center of town. The building was constructed in 1904 as an Episcopalian nunnery; the most recent modifications to it were in 1997, when a new wing was added. In addition to singles and doubles, there are now four family rooms. The hosts will provide an affordable evening meal to those who request it.

20 Knab Rd., Lerwick, Shetland ZE1 0AX. © and fax **01595/692-031.** www.guesthouselerwick.com. 22 units. £66 ($99) double. Rates include Scottish breakfast. MC, V. **Amenities:** Bar. *In room:* A/C, TV, coffeemaker, hair dryer.

Grand Hotel   A grander hotel would be hard to find anywhere in Shetland. With pointed turrets, weather vanes, crow's-step gables, and solid stone walls, it lies a block from the waterfront, in the town center. The guest rooms are conservative yet comfortable, each with a shower-only bathroom. The extensively modernized hotel has two lounge bars, a dining room, and a nightclub open Wednesday, Friday, and Sunday. The Grand shares its reservations facilities and some of its staff with the Queens Hotel (see below).

149 Commercial St., Lerwick, Shetland ZE1 0AB. © **01595/692-826.** Fax 01595/694-048. www.kgqhotels. co.uk. 24 units. £90 ($135) double; £120 ($180) family room. Rates include Scottish breakfast. AE, DC, MC, V. Free parking in nearby public lot. **Amenities:** Restaurant, 2 bars, nightclub. *In room:* TV, coffeemaker, hair dryer.

Lerwick Hotel ⚐ This is one of the biggest and most up-to-date hotels in the Shetlands, sprawling beside a gravel- and kelp-covered beach. Its simply furnished guest rooms offer various amenities and small, shower-only bathrooms; half have views over the water toward Bressay. The upscale restaurant offers at least one seafood and one vegetarian choice as well as chicken or wild game. In summer, dinner dances that combine hearty meals with traditional Scottish fun are frequently held.

South Rd., Shetland ZE1 0RB. © **01595/692-166.** Fax 01595/694-419. www.shetlandhotels.com. 35 units. £89.75 ($134.65) double; £115 ($172.50) suite. Rates include Scottish breakfast. AE, DC, MC, V. Take Scalloway Rd. west from the center for 5 min. **Amenities:** Restaurant, brasserie, bar; nearby health club; room service; laundry service. *In room:* TV, coffeemaker, hair dryer.

Queens Hotel ⚐ Its foundations rise directly from the sea at the harborfront, so on blustery nights, fine sprays of saltwater sometimes coat the windowpanes of the lower floors. Built of natural stone around 1900, the Queens rivals the nearby Grand Hotel (see above) as the most prestigious hotel in Lerwick. They share the same reservations staff. The small guest rooms are conservatively and comfortably furnished, each with shower. Inexpensive bar lunches are offered in the cocktail lounge, and more formal dinners are served in the dining room (see below).

24 Commercial St., Lerwick, Shetland ZE1 0AB. © **01595/692-826.** Fax 01595/694-048. www.kgqhotels. co.uk. 26 units. £90 ($135) double; £120 ($180) family room. Rates include Scottish breakfast. AE, DC, MC, V. **Amenities:** Restaurant, 2 bars. *In room:* TV, coffeemaker, hair dryer.

Shetland Hotel Built in 1984, this four-story brick, stone, and concrete structure is one of the most modern hotels in the Shetlands. It's opposite the ferry terminal, with a good view of the harbor. The guest rooms are well furnished, each with a small bathroom with shower. The two on-site restaurants offer local fish and vegetarian items.

Holmsgarth Rd., Lerwick, Shetland ZE1 0PW. © **01595/695-515.** Fax 01595/695-828. www.shetlandhotels. com. 67 units. £89.90 ($134.85) double; £99.75 ($149.65) suite. Rates include Scottish breakfast. AE, DC, MC, V. **Amenities:** 2 restaurants (see Oasis Bistro, below), bar, lounge; room service; laundry service. *In room:* TV, coffeemaker, hair dryer.

DINING

Golden Coach CHINESE One of the two Chinese restaurants in the Shetlands, this intimate place is softly lit and contemporary in decor. Try the barbecued Peking duck or deep-fried shredded beef in sweet-and-sour sauce. Malaysian chicken comes in a peanut sauce, or you can order king prawns Peking with garlic sauce.

17 Hillhead. © **01595/693-848.** Reservations required Sat–Sun. Main courses £6.80–£8 ($10.20–$12); fixed-price lunch £5 ($7.50); dinner menu £18 ($27). MC, V. Mon–Fri noon–2pm and 5:30–11pm; Sat–Sun noon–11pm.

Oasis Bistro SCOTTISH   This eatery is a good choice for a light snack at odd hours; salads and sandwiches are served all day. The restaurant also offers hot meals at lunch and dinner. Emphasis is on fresh fish and vegetarian fare straight from Shetland gardens.

In the Shetland Hotel, Holmsgarth Rd. ℂ 01595/695-515. Main courses £6–£13 ($9–$19.50). AE, DC, MC, V. Daily 11am–9:30pm; hot meals noon–2pm and 5–9:30pm.

Queens Hotel *Kids* BRITISH   On the lobby level of this previously recommended hotel, this pink-and-white dining room overlooks the sea, the wharves, and the many fishing boats bobbing at anchor. It caters to families, many of whom seem to arrive in groups as part of reunions. Many locals consider it the best restaurant in Lerwick, a staple on the island's culinary scene. Specialties include goujons of haddock with tartar sauce, roast beef sirloin with Yorkshire pudding, chicken Caribbean with pineapple sauce, braised lamb cutlets, and conservative preparations of fish dishes.

24 Commercial St. ℂ 01595/692-826. Reservations recommended. Main courses £9.50–£12.50 ($14.25–$18.75); fixed-price 3-course dinner £16.50 ($24.75). AE, DC, MC, V. Daily noon–2pm and 6–9:30pm.

LERWICK AFTER DARK

From May to September, the **Islesburgh Community Centre,** King Harold Street (ℂ **01595/692-114**), hosts dancing to Shetland fiddle music called the Summer Exhibition on Wednesdays and Fridays from 7 to 9:30pm. Admission is £2.50 ($3.75). The **Lounge Bar,** Mounthooly Street (ℂ **01595/692-231**), hosts an informal evening of traditional fiddle music on Wednesdays, usually starting around 9:30pm. There's also live music on Friday nights and often on Saturday afternoons. There's no cover.

SCALLOWAY

On the western coast, 6 miles (10km) west of Lerwick, Scalloway was once the capital of Shetland. This town was the base for rescue operations in Norway during the darkest days of World War II. Still an important fishing port, Scalloway has changed because of the oil boom. New businesses have opened, attracting more and more people to the area, which has emerged after a long slumber into a prosperous and lively place in this remote corner of the world.

Dominating the town are the ruins of corbel-turreted medieval **Scalloway Castle** (ℂ **01595/880-243**), commissioned by the dreaded Earl Patrick Stewart at the beginning of the 17th century and built with forced (slave) labor culled from the island's residents. After it was built, he imposed exorbitant taxes and fines on the islanders. In 1615, the Earl and all his sons were executed in Edinburgh, partly as a means of placating the islanders, partly because he rebelled against the powers of the central Scottish-British government. Admission is free; hours are those of the Shetland Woollen Company (see below), from which you must get the key to enter.

The **Shetland Woollen Company** (ℂ **01595/880-243**) is open Monday through Friday from 9am to 5pm (in summer, also Saturday from 9am to 5pm). You can see the processing and finishing of Shetland knitware, and then visit the showroom where a selection of garments is sold.

To escape to a beautiful area, ideal for long walks or drives, follow B9075 east off A970 to the top of a small sea inlet that will lead you to the surprisingly lush **Kergord.** This green valley contains forests ideal for long strolls.

WEST MAINLAND

It's said you can see more of Shetland from the **Scord of Weisdale** than from any other vantage point in the archipelago.

Shetland's only stone-polishing business operates at **Hjaltasteyn**, Whiteness, 9 miles (14.5km) west of Lerwick. Here gemstones are turned out from raw materials in fetching hand-wrought silver settings. Alas, the workshop isn't currently open to visitors. You can, however, visit the showroom at 161 Commercial St., Lerwick (© **01595/696-224**). It's open in summer only, Thursday through Saturday, Monday, and Tuesday from 9:15am to 4:45pm, and Wednesday from 10am to 4pm (closed daily from 1 to 2pm for lunch).

Continuing north, you can watch high-quality jewelry being made at **Shetland Jewelry,** Soundside, Weisdale (© **01595/830-275**), where the artisans base many of their designs on ancient Celtic and Viking patterns. It's open Monday through Friday from 9am to 1pm and 2 to 5pm.

You can continue your tour of West Mainland by heading west along A971 toward Walls. You come first to **Staneydale Temple,** 2¾ miles (4.5km) outside Walls. This early Bronze Age (perhaps Neolithic) hall once had a timbered roof. It's called a temple because it bears a remarkable resemblance to similar sites on Malta, lending support to the theory that the early settlers of Shetland came from the Mediterranean.

Continuing past several lochs and sea inlets, you come to **Walls,** a hamlet built on the periphery of two voes (a local term for inlet). Its natural harbor is sheltered by the offshore islet of Vaila.

ACCOMMODATIONS & DINING

Burrastow House *ꝭꝭ (Finds* This is the most tranquil, idyllic retreat in the Shetlands. About 3 miles (5km) southwest of Walls, a 40-minute drive northwest of Lerwick, this simple but comfortable building was constructed in 1759 as a *haa* (home of the farm manager of a laird's estate). Set amid lands still used for grazing sheep, it lies at the widest section of a windswept peninsula with views of a cluster of rocky and sparsely inhabited islands. The well-furnished guest rooms evoke country-house living. There's one family suite, consisting of a double room and a twin room connected by a bathroom.

The food is the best on the island. The daily menu in the oak-paneled dining room is likely to include nettle-and-oatmeal fritters, mussel brose (a stew of mussels thickened with oatmeal), and monkfish with anchovy stuffing, lamb, and Scottish beef. Lunch, high tea, and upscale dinners are served daily. The proprietors ask that you call ahead if you want a hot meal, but they'll accommodate you with fresh-baked bread, cheese, and homemade soup if you just drop in. They offer a good vegetarian selection. The restaurant is closed Sunday and Monday to nonguests.

Walls, West Mainland, Shetland ZE2 9PD. © **01595/809-307.** Fax 01595/809-213. www.bustahouse.com. 6 units. £176 ($264) double; £86 ($129) per person in family room. Rates include half-board. AE, MC, V. Closed Jan–Feb. **Amenities:** Restaurant. *In room:* TV (on request), coffeemaker, no phone.

PAPA STOUR

The "great island of priests," in the shape of a large starfish, Papa Stour lies off the west coast of Mainland, 25 miles (40km) northwest of Lerwick. As its name indicates, it was an early base for monks. Two centuries ago there was a leper colony here on the little offshore islet of Brei Holm.

Legend has it that its profusion of wildflowers had such a strong scent that old fishermen could use the perfume—borne far out on the wind—to fix their positions. Papa Stour is very isolated, and once it was feared the island might be depopulated, but about 26 settlers live here now.

In the darkest days of winter, bad weather can cut it off for days. But if you see it on a sunny day, it's striking. Encircled by pillars of rock and reefs, its sea caves, sculpted by turbulent winds and raging seas, are among the most impressive in Britain. The largest of these is **Kirstan's Hole,** extending some 80 yards (73m).

Boats go to Papa Stour about seven times per day, 5 days a week, from West Burrafirth on Mainland, at a cost of £5 ($7.50). Call **Mr. Clark** at ℂ **01595/ 810-460** for information on these constantly changing details.

ACCOMMODATIONS & DINING

Northouse *Finds* Within walking distance of the island's only pier, just outside Housa Voe (the only hamlet, with seven buildings), this stone croft is an unusual building. The foundations are Viking, and Dutch coins from the 1620s have been unearthed here. It's the domain of Andrew and Sabina Holt-Brook, who moved from the mainland of Scotland more than 20 years ago. Now owners of 30 acres (12.2 hectares) of windswept peninsula, they offer the only accommodations and meals on the island. The rooms are comfortable and inviting, and the "garden room" has its own entrance. Meals are served to both guests and nonguests, but for just a meal, call in advance. The working farm supplies the Holt-Brooks with free-range eggs and fresh vegetables. The inexpensive lunches are brown-bag affairs (homemade sandwiches and cakes) to be taken along while you enjoy the island's wild landscapes.

North-house, Papa Stour, Shetland ZE2 9PW. ℂ 01595/873-238. 4 units, 1 with private bathroom. £56 ($84) double. Rates include full board. No credit cards. **Amenities:** Dining room. *In room:* No phone.

FOULA

This tiny, remote island is only 3 miles (5km) wide by 5 miles (8km) long, with five high peaks. Called the "Island West of the Sun," Foula may have been the Romans' legendary Thule. In local dialect, *foula* means "bird island"—and the name fits. Uncountable numbers of birds haunt the isle. Its towering sea cliffs include the second-highest cliff face in Britain, the **Kame,** at 1,220 feet (370m). About 3,000 pairs of the world's great skuas, known as "bonxie," live here. You'll hear many stories about the rock-climbing prowess of locals who go in search of gulls' eggs.

The island lies 27 miles (43.5km) west of Scalloway on the west coast of Mainland, where the locals are vastly outnumbered by sheep. Until the beginning of the 19th century, Old Norse was the language spoken. Its 400 people remain very traditional. If you're very lucky, you might see them dance the Foula reel, a classic dance in Shetland.

If the weather's right, a weekly mailboat sails to Foula from Walls on Mainland. Even in summer, the seas are likely to be turbulent, and in winter, Foula has been known to be cut off from the rest of Britain for weeks. The trip takes 2½ hours. **Loganair** also operates a summer service from Tingwall on Monday, Wednesday, and Friday; trip time is 15 minutes.

ACCOMMODATIONS & DINING

Because of the interest by visitors in recent years, some islanders have taken to offering accommodations that include half-board.

Mrs. Marion Taylor   Owners Bryan and Marion run this cozy modern farmhouse near the geographical center of the island, within walking distance of everything. The comfortable rooms in the main house have easy access to the large kitchen, whose brick hearth is the focal point of the farm. The cottage has two bedrooms, a sitting room, and a kitchen. There are no food shops on the island, so you'll have to bring your own supplies, as the rates for the cottage don't include meals. The Taylor's 7 acres (2.8 hectares) are a sheep farm, and they extend their income by knitting and spinning—you can order a custom-made, hand-knit sweater.

Leraback, Isle of Foula, Shetland ZE2 9PN. ℭ 01595/753-226. 3 units, none with private bathroom; 1 cottage. £50 ($75) double; £25 ($37.50) per day in cottage (sleeps up to 4). No credit cards. *In room:* TV, refrigerator, microwave, no phone.

NORTH MAINLAND

The most rugged scenery Shetland has to offer is in the northern part of the island of Mainland. Some visitors have found the area reminds them of Norway, and we agree. That's especially true in the tiny village of **Voe,** with its little wooden houses.

Heading north from Voe along A970, you'll reach the eastern junction of B9071, which will take you to **Vidlin,** where the **Lunna Kirk,** one of the oldest churches in the archipelago, is still used by its congregation. Construction began in 1753. The church has a "leper hole," from which the poor victims could listen to the sermon without being seen.

Heading west back to A970, continue north to **Mavis Grind,** a narrow isthmus marking the point where the North Mainland is at its most narrow. The touristy thing to do in North Mainland is to pause at Mavis Grind, take a couple of stones, and throw one to your right into the North Sea and the other to your left into the Atlantic Ocean.

Near the villages of **Brae** and **Busta,** you'll find some of the best food and hotels in Shetland. Oil contractors, helicopter pilots, and shipping executives sent by mainland companies to service the nearby Sullom Voe, site of the largest oil terminal in Europe, often stay in this area.

If you head north along A970, we suggest you take the secondary road going west to **Esha Ness,** where you'll come upon the most dramatic cliff scenery not only in Shetland but in all Britain. This is a simply gorgeous area for hiking. On the way, 15 miles (24km) northwest of Brae, you'll pass the little fishing hamlet of **Hillswick,** opening onto the bay in Ura Firth.

ACCOMMODATIONS & DINING

Brae Hotel   Built in 1979, this modern building lies in the center of Brae, 28 miles (45km) north of Lerwick beside A970 about a mile (1.6km) south of the narrow isthmus that separates North from South Mainland. The small, pastel-toned guest rooms are reassuringly warm. Each comes with a small, shower-only bathroom. The restaurant serves affordable meals.

Brae, North Mainland, Shetland ZE2 9QJ. ℭ 01806/522-456. Fax 01806/522-459. 36 units. £55 ($82.50) double. Rates include Scottish breakfast. Discounts offered for stays of 4 or more days. AE, DC, MC, V. **Amenities:** Restaurant, bar; bank; billiard room; hair salon. *In room:* TV, coffeemaker.

Busta House 𝕬𝕬   Busta House is the oldest continuously inhabited house in the Shetlands. Built in 1580, with ample extensions added in 1714 and 1983, it was the original *busta* (homestead) of the medieval Norwegian rulers of the island. Later inhabited by the island's laird, it once welcomed Elizabeth II at tea during her tour of the Shetlands on the royal yacht *Britannia.* The estate's long and tormented history includes episodes of multiple drownings, a handful of resident ghosts, and some of the most famous lawsuits in Britain. Some literary enthusiasts claim the house in all its drama was the inspiration for Dickens's *Bleak House.*

In recent times, the important economic agreement that paved the way for the construction of the massive Sullom Voe oil terminal (the Busta House Agreement) was signed here between the local government and Britain's multinational oil companies.

Rising above its own small harbor a short drive from A970, a 10-minute drive south of the village of Sullom, 1½ miles (2.5km) from Brae, the hotel has crow's-foot gables, stone walls measuring 6 feet (2m) thick, and an appearance of a fortified manor house. The proprietors maintain the antique charm of the public rooms and the chintz-filled guest rooms, and prepare upscale dinners as well. (There's also a more affordable bar menu.)

Busta, near Brae, North Mainland, Shetland ZE2 9QN. © 01806/522-506. Fax 01806/522-588. www. bustahouse.com. 20 units. £91 ($136.50) double. Rates include Scottish breakfast. Discounts offered for stays of 4 or more days. AE, DC, MC, V. **Amenities:** Restaurant, bar; room service; laundry service; business center. *In room:* TV, dataport, coffeemaker, hair dryer.

SOUTH MAINLAND

This part of Shetland, reached by heading south along A970, is both ancient and modern. On the one hand, there's the gleaming **Sumburgh Airport,** which has played a major role in the North Sea oilfields development and services many of the offshore rigs today. On the other hand, you'll stumble on the ruins of **Jarl-shof** (see below), which may have been inhabited for some 3,000 years.

EXPLORING THE AREA

As you go down the "long leg" of Shetland, as it's called, heading due south, passing a peaty moorland and fresh meadows, the first attraction is not on Mainland at all but on an offshore island called Mousa: the famous **Broch of Mousa** 🎯🎯, a Pictish defense tower that guarded the islet for some 2,000 years. It reached the then-incredible height of some 40 feet (12m) and was constructed of local stones, with two circular walls, one within the other. They enclosed a staircase leading to sleeping quarters. It's the best-preserved example of an Iron Age broch in Britain. The village of **Sandwick,** 7 miles (11km) south of Lerwick, is the ferry point for reaching Mousa. There's daily bus service between Lerwick and Sandwick. A local boatman, Mr. Jamieson, will take you across to Mousa; it takes about 15 minutes. From April to September only, you can visit Mousa Monday through Saturday. The cost is £7.50 ($11.25) for adults and £3.50 ($5.25) for children. For boat schedules, call the tourist office in Lerwick at © **01595/693-434.**

South of Sandwick, you reach the parish of Dunrossness. At Boddam is the **Shetland Croft House Museum** (© **01595/695-057**), east of A970 on an unmarked road 25 miles (40km) south of Lerwick. Rural Shetland life comes alive here in this thatched croft house from the mid-1800s. The museum also has some outbuildings and a functioning water mill. It's open from May to September. Admission is free.

Continuing south, you reach the outstanding man-made attraction in Shetland, **Jarlshof** 🎯, Sumburgh (© **01950/460-112**), near the Sumburgh Airport. It has been called the most remarkable archaeological discovery in Britain. A violent storm in 1897 performed the first archaeological dig. Washing away sections of the large mound, it revealed huge stone walls. Excavations that followed turned up an astonishing array of seven distinct civilizations. The earliest was from the Bronze Age, but habitation continued at the site through the 1500s, from wheel-house people to Vikings, from broch builders to medieval settlers. A manor house was built here in the 16th century by the treacherous Patrick Stewart, but it was sacked in 1609. The site is open April through September, daily from 9:30am to 6:30pm. Admission is £2.80 ($4.20) for adults, £2 ($3) for seniors, and £1 ($1.50) for children.

Also nearby is the **Sumburgh Lighthouse,** one of the many Scottish light-houses constructed by the grandfather of Robert Louis Stevenson. The lighthouse is now fully automated. The property offers a self-catering four-bedroom cottage, costing £350 ($525) per week. Built in 1821, it can be visited by the public, but you must phone the Lerwick tourist office (ⓒ **01595/693-434**) for an appointment; reservations for the cottage can also be made with the owner, Mr. Johnston-Ferguson, at ⓒ **01387/372-240.** Reserve at least 3 months in advance.

On the coast at the tip of Scatness, about a mile (1.6km) southwest of Jarl-shof at the end of the Mainland, is the **Ness of Burgi,** which was a defensive Iron Age structure related to a broch.

Heading back north toward Lerwick, you can veer west for a trip to **St. Ninians Island** in the southwestern corner of Shetland. It's reached by going along B9122. The island is approached by what's called a *tombolo* (bridging sandbar). An early monastery once stood on this island, but it wasn't uncovered until 1958. Puffins often favor the islet, which has a pure white sandy beach on each side. The island became famous in 1958 when a group of students from Aberdeen came upon a rich cache of Celtic artifacts, mainly silverware, includ-ing brooches and other valuable pieces. Monks are believed to have hidden the treasure trove, fearing a Viking attack. The St. Ninian treasure is in the National Museum of Scotland at Edinburgh.

ACCOMMODATIONS & DINING

Sumburgh Hotel This is an old favorite. Its turrets and towers were built in 1857 for the laird of Virkie, the Victorian descendant of Robert the Bruce. Set on 12 barren acres (4.9 hectares) of land jutting dramatically out to sea, it lies at the southernmost end of the Shetland Islands, at the end of A970. A modern addition completed in the 1960s doubled the size of the place, which contains the Voe Room restaurant (offering affordable dinners nightly) and two popular bars. Recent refurbishments have made the bedrooms more inviting.

Sumburgh Head, Virkie Parish, Shetland ZE3 9JN. ⓒ **01950/460-201.** Fax 01950/460-394. www.sumburgh-hotel.zetnet.co.uk. 32 units. £60 ($90) double. Rates include Scottish breakfast. AE, MC, V. **Amenities:** Restaurant; 2 bars; room service; laundry service. *In room:* TV, coffeemaker, hair dryer.

UNST

The northernmost point of Britain, remote and beautiful Unst is easy to reach. After crossing over to Yell, you can drive along A968 to the little harbor at Gutcher, northeast of Yell. The **Shetland Island Coastal Marine Operations** (ⓒ **01957/722-259** for schedules) operates a ferry crossing from here fairly fre-quently every day. The cost is £3.10 ($4.65) for a car and driver, £1.30 ($1.95) for each extra adult, and 20p (30¢) per child. **Loganair** (ⓒ **01595/840-246**) flies to Unst from both Lerwick and Sumburgh, once a day from Monday to Friday.

Robert Louis Stevenson stayed on Unst for a time. His father, Alan Stevenson, was designing and building the Muckle Flugga Lighthouse on an outermost skerry, which is even farther north than Labrador.

Unst is steeped in folklore and legend. An **Old Norse longhouse,** believed to date from the 9th century, was excavated at Underhoull. The best beach is at **Skaw,** set against the backdrop of **Saxa Vord,** legendary home of the giant Saxi. A drive to the top will reward you with a view of the Burra Firth. Visitors go to Haroldswick to mail their cards and letters in the northernmost post office in the British Isles.

The roll-on–roll-off car ferry from Yell comes into Belmont. Nearby is **Muness Castle,** constructed in 1598 by Laurence Bruce, a relative of the notorious Earl Patrick Stewart who ruled Shetland so harshly. Adam Crawford, who designed Scalloway Castle for the ruling earls on Mainland, also drew up the plans for Muness. Built with rubble and known for its fine architectural detail, the castle was inhabited for less than a century. Normally it's open April through September, daily from 9am to 7pm. If it's closed, ask for the key at Mrs. Peterson's cottage across the way. For information, call © **01957/755-215.**

The ruins of the **Kirk of Lund,** dating from the Middle Ages, can also be seen on Unst. Like Lunna Kirk in Vidlin, it, too, had a "leper hole" through which victims could hear the service.

Unst is home of the **Hermaness Bird Reserve,** one of the most important ornithological sites in Britain. Ideal for scenic walks, its 600-foot (182m) cliffs are filled with kittiwakes, razorbills, guillemots, and the inevitable puffins.

ACCOMMODATIONS & DINING

Baltasound Hotel *(Finds* Built 150 years ago for the local laird and converted into a hotel in 1939, this granite house sits in isolation beside the sea about a quarter mile (0.5m) from the hamlet of Baltasound. Many of the guests are bird-watchers and geologists. The simple, uncluttered bedrooms are in what locals call a "Scandinavian extension" jutting out to the building's side, sheathed with blackened wood siding. In 1992, the hotel was enlarged with a series of motel-like "chalet" rooms attached to the main building. The bars serve lunch and inexpensive dinners; the restaurant offers moderately priced dinners, which you should book in advance.

Baltasound, Unst, Shetland ZE2 9DS. © **01957/711-334.** 25 units, 22 with private bathroom. £64 ($96) double with or without bathroom. Rates include Scottish breakfast. MC, V. **Amenities:** Restaurant, 2 bars. *In room:* TV, coffeemaker, hair dryer (on request).

Appendix: Scotland in Depth

A small nation ("Tis a wee country, aye—but a bonny one"), Scotland is only 275 miles (443km) long and some 150 miles (241.5km) wide at its broadest. No Scot lives more than 40 miles (64.5km) from saltwater. But despite the small size of their country, the Scots have extended their influence around the world. And in this land of bagpipes and clans and kilts, you'll find some of Europe's grandest scenery.

Inventor Alexander Graham Bell and explorers Mungo Park and David Livingstone came from Scotland. This country gave the world entrepreneur Andrew Carnegie, poet Robert Burns, novelist Sir Walter Scott, actor Sean Connery, singer Sheena Easton, and comedian/actor Billy Connelly. But, curiously, for a long time its most famous resident has been neither man nor woman but Nessie, the Loch Ness Monster.

The border is just a line on a map; you'll hardly be aware of crossing out of England into Scotland. Yet even though the two countries have been joined constitutionally since 1707, Scotland is very different from England and is very much its own country. (In fact, on July 1, 1999, Scotland was granted greater independence when a reform instituted by Prime Minister Tony Blair brought back regional government and a new Scottish Parliament was opened by Queen Elizabeth in Edinburgh.)

In Scotland, you'll discover mountains and glens, lochs and heather-covered moors, skirling bagpipes and twirling kilts, and rivers and streams filled with trout and salmon. Lush meadowlands are filled with sheep, and rocky coves and secret harbors wait for the adventurous. You can hear the sounds of Gaelic, admire the misty blue hills, and attend a Highland Gathering. You can schedule quiet contemplation or an activity-filled calendar. And in Scotland, you'll find one of Europe's biggest welcomes.

1 History 101

Much of the history of the Scots has been shaped by their country's location in a remote corner of northwestern Europe. Amazingly, Scotland encompasses 787 islands (although only about a fourth are inhabited). Its 6,214 miles (10,004.5km) of coastline are deeply penetrated by the Atlantic Ocean on the west and the often turbulent North Sea on the east. Most places lie only 60 miles (96.6km) inland. In fact, the sea has shaped Scotland's destiny more than any other element and bred a nation of seafarers, many of whom still earn their living on the water.

Dateline

- 6000 B.C. The earliest known residents of Scotland establish settlements on the Argyll Peninsula.
- 3000 B.C. Celtic tribes invade, making the use of Gaelic widespread.
- A.D. 82 Roman armies directed by Agricola push into southern Scotland; the Roman victories, however, are short-lived.
- A.D. 90 Romans abandon the hope of conquering Scotland, retreating to England and the relative safety of Hadrian's Wall.

continues

Scotland is a world apart, a distinctly unique nation within the United Kingdom. Just more than half the size of England, with only a tenth of England's population, it boasts more open spaces and natural splendor than England ever did. The Scots are hard to classify: They're generous yet have a reputation for stinginess, eloquent yet dour at times, and romantic at heart yet brutally realistic in their appraisals (especially of the English). Even the Romans couldn't subdue these Caledonians, and they remain Braveheart proud and fiercely independent.

But how did it all begin?

EARLY HISTORY Scotland was a melting pot in its early history. Standing stones, brochs, cromlechs, cairns, and burial chambers attest to its earliest occupation, but we know little about these first tribes and invaders. When the Roman armies decided to invade in A.D. 82, the land was occupied by a people the Romans called the Picts (Painted Ones). Despite spectacular bloodletting, the Romans were unsuccessful, and the building of Hadrian's Wall effectively marked the northern limits of their influence.

Parts of Hadrian's Wall still stand, but in England, not Scotland. The wall extends for 73 miles (117.5km) across the north of England, from the North Sea to the Irish Sea, its most interesting stretch consisting of 10 miles (16km) west of the town of Housesteads. If you're driving north from England into Scotland, you might want to stop and see the remains of this wall before penetrating the Border Country of Scotland.

By A.D. 500, the Picts were again attacked, this time by the Dalriad Irish called Scots, who were successful. They established themselves on the Argyll Peninsula and battled and intermarried with the Picts. Britons emigrated from the south and Norsemen from the east, creating new

- **500** Newcomers from Ireland, identified as Scots, invade from the west, mingling their bloodlines with Norse, Pictish, Celtic, and Teutonic tribes.
- **563** St. Columba establishes a mission on Iona, accelerating the movement established by earlier ecclesiastics to Christianize Scotland.
- **843** Kenneth MacAlpin unifies the Picts and the Scots.
- **1005–34** Malcolm II unites the four major tribes of Scotland into one roughly cohesive unit.
- **1124–53** David I builds monasteries, consolidates royal power and prestige, and imports clearly defined Norman values.
- **1266** The Hebrides and the coast of western Scotland are released from Norse control; the Donald clan consolidates power here into a semi-autonomous state within Scotland.
- **1272** Edward I of England embarks on an aggressive campaign to conquer both Wales and Scotland but is deflected by Robert the Bruce, among others.
- **1314** The victory of the Scots over the English armies at Bannockburn leads to the Treaty of Northampton (1328), formally recognizing Scotland's independence from England.
- **1468** The Orkney and the Shetland Islands are given to Scotland as part of the marriage dowry of a Norse princess to a Scottish king.
- **Late 1400s** The Auld Alliance with France, a cynical arrangement based mostly on mutual distrust of England, is born.
- **1535** At the urging of Henry VIII of England, Parliament officially severs all ties with the Catholic Church, legally sanctioning the Reformation.
- **1559–64** John Knox lays out the rough outline of the Scottish Presbyterian Church.
- **1561** Queen Mary returns to Scotland from France.
- **1568** Mary is defeated and flees to England.
- **1572** John Knox dies; his work is continued by Andrew Melville.
- **1587** Mary Queen of Scots is executed.

continues

bloodlines and migratory patterns. Druidism, a little-understood mystical form of nature worship whose most visible monuments are runic etchings and stone circles, flourished at this time. Languages of the era included a diverse array of Celtic and Norse dialects with scatterings of Low German and Saxon English.

The power of the Scotians, entrenched in western Scotland, was cemented when a missionary named Columba (later canonized) arrived from Ireland in 563. The rocky Hebridean island of Iona became the base for his Christian mission. Christianity, already introduced by Sts. Ninian and Mungo to Strathclyde and Galloway, became widespread.

If you have an interest in this early part of Scottish history, visit remote Iona, part of the Hebrides (see chapter 11, "The Hebridean Islands," for more information). More than any dull recitation of history, a visit here, especially to Iona Abbey, can recapture some of this land's dim, often unrecorded history.

THE MIDDLE AGES The Scots and the Picts were united in 843 under the kingship of an early chieftain named Kenneth MacAlpin, but it was the invasionary pressures from England and Scandinavia and the unifying force of Christianity that molded Scotland into a relatively coherent unit. Under Malcolm II (1005–34), the British and the Angles, who occupied the southwest and southeast of the Scottish mainland, merged with the Scots and the Picts. Malcolm's son and heir, Duncan, was murdered by Macbeth of Moray, and this event fueled the plotline of Shakespeare's famous "Scottish play." Glamis Castle, outside Dundee, contains Duncan's Hall, where the Victorians imagined Macbeth killed Duncan. See chapter 9, "Aberdeen & the Tayside & Grampian Regions," for details on Glamis.

- **1603** Mary's son, James VI of Scotland, accedes to the throne of England as James I and unifies the two countries.
- **1689** Parliament strips the uncompromising Catholic James II of his crown and imports the Protestant William and Mary from Holland to replace him.
- **1746** Bonnie Prince Charlie's attempt to reclaim his grandfather's throne ends in defeat at the Battle of Culloden, destroying any hope of a Stuart revival.
- **1750–1850** England and Scotland experience rapid industrialization; the Clearances strip many crofters of their farms, creating epic bitterness and forcing new patterns of Scottish migrations.
- **1789** The French Revolution ignites; British monarchists tighten their grip on civil unrest in Scotland.
- **Late 19th century** An astonishing success in the sciences propels Scotland into the role of arbiter of industrial know-how around the globe.
- **Mid–20th century** The decline of traditional industries, especially shipbuilding, painfully redefines the nature of Scottish industry.
- **1970** The discovery of North Sea oil deposits brings new vitality to Scotland.
- **1973** Scotland, as part of the United Kingdom, becomes a member of the Common Market.
- **1974** The old counties or shires are reorganized; many regions are renamed.
- **1979** Scots vote on devolution (separation from England): 33% vote yes, 31% vote no, and 36% don't vote at all.
- **1981** The largest oil terminal in Europe is launched at Sullom Voe in the Shetland Islands.
- **1988** Scottish nationalism revives under the marching cry of "Scotland in Europe"; Pan Am Flight 103 from London crashes at Lockerbie, killing all passengers, including some locals.
- **1992** The Scots continue to express dissatisfaction with English rule: Polls show one out of two favor independence.

continues

Malcolm III's marriage to an English princess, Margaret, furthered the Anglicization of the Scottish Lowlands. A determined woman of strong ideas, she imported English priests into Scotland and carried out church reforms that soon replaced St. Columba's Gaelic form of Christianity. Her Anglicization efforts and introduction of the English language as a teaching tool laid important groundwork for making Scotland into a potential English kingdom. She led a life of great piety and was canonized as St. Margaret in 1251.

While Europe's feudal system was coming to full flower, Scotland was

- **1996** A psychopath guns down 16 kids and a teacher in one of Britain's greatest mass-murder sprees.
- **1997** A sheep is cloned for the first time; Scotland votes to establish a legislature of its own for the first time since 1707.
- **1999** British Prime Minister Tony Blair holds off threats from the Nationalist Party as his own Labour Party triumphs in national elections; on July 1, Queen Elizabeth opens a new Scottish Parliament for the first time in 300 years.
- **2001** Scottish Parliament opens to a bad press—goes from the so-called "silly season to the totally absurd."

preoccupied with the territorial battles of clan allegiances and the attempt to define its borders with England. Cultural assimilation with England continued under David I (1081–1153), who made land grants to many Anglo-Norman families, providing Scotland with a feudal aristocracy and bringing in ancient names like Fraser, Seton, and Lindsay. He also embarked on one of the most lavish building sprees in Scottish history, erecting many abbeys, including Jedburgh, Kelso, Melrose, and Dryburgh. You can still see these abbeys or their ruins.

In 1266, after about a century of Norse control, the foggy and windswept Western Isles were returned to Scotland following the Battle of Largs. Despite nominal allegiance to the Scottish monarch, this region's inhabitants quickly organized themselves around the Donald (or MacDonald) clan, which for nearly 100 years was one of the most powerful, ruling its territory almost as an independent state. The honorary title of their patriarch, Lord of the Isles, is still one of the formal titles used on state occasions by Britain's Prince of Wales. To learn more about what may be the most important clan in Scottish history, you can visit the Clan Donald Visitor Centre at Armadale on the Isle of Skye (see chapter 11).

In the meantime, real trouble was brewing in the south. Edward I, ambitious Plantagenet king of England, yearned to rule over an undivided nation incorporating England, Scotland, and Wales. Successful at first, he set up John de Balliol as a vassal king to do homage to him for Scotland. Many of Scotland's legendary heroes lived during this period: Sir William Wallace (1270–1305), who drove the English out of Perth and Stirling; Sir James Douglas, the Black Douglas (1286–1330), who terrorized the English borders; and Robert the Bruce (1274–1329), who finally succeeded in freeing Scotland from England. Crowned Robert I at Scone in 1306 in defiance of the English, Robert the Bruce decisively defeated Edward II of England at the 1314 Battle of Bannockburn. Scotland's independence was formally recognized in the 1328 Treaty of Northampton, inaugurating a heady but short-lived separation from England.

For more legend and lore about those towering Scottish heroes William Wallace and Robert the Bruce, see chapter 8, "Fife & the Central Highlands." You can also visit Stirling Castle, which loomed so large in Scottish history. If you'd rather see where the crucial Battle of Bannockburn took place, you can visit the Bannockburn Heritage Centre outside Stirling (see chapter 8).

In 1468, the Orkneys and the Shetlands, Norse to the core, were brought into the Scottish web of power as part of the marriage dowry of the Norse princess Margaret to James III. This acquisition was the last successful expansion of Scottish sovereignty during the period when Scottish power and independence were at their zenith. It was at this time the Scots entered with the French into an alliance that was to have far-reaching effects. The line of Stuart (or Stewart) kings, so named because the family had become powerful as stewards of the English king, were generally accepted as the least troublesome of a series of potential evils. Real power, however, lay with Scotland's great lords, patriarchs of the famous clans. Jealous of both their bloodlines and their territories, they could rarely agree on anything other than their common distrust of England.

THE REFORMATION The passions of the Reformation burst on an already turbulent Scottish scene in the person of John Knox, a devoted disciple of the Geneva Protestant John Calvin and a bitter enemy of both the Catholic Church and the Anglican Church. Knox became famous for the screaming insults he heaped on ardently Catholic Queen Mary and for his absolute lack of a sense of humor. His polemics were famous—in his struggle against Queen Mary, he wrote his *First Blast of the Trumpet Against the Monstrous Regiment of Women*. His was a peculiar mixture of piety, conservatism, strict morality, and intellectual independence that's still a pronounced feature of the Scottish character.

Knox's teachings helped shape the democratic form of Scottish government and set the Scottish Church's austere moral tone for generations to come. He focused on practical considerations as well as religious ones: church administration and funding, and the relationship between church and state. Foremost among the tenets were provisions for a self-governing congregation and pure allegiance to the Word of God as contained in meticulous translations of the Old and New Testaments. In Edinburgh, you can still visit the John Knox House, where the reformer lived (see chapter 4, "Edinburgh & the Lothian Region," for more information).

On Knox's 1562 death, his work was continued by Scots-born, Geneva-trained Andrew Melville, who hated ecclesiastical tyranny even more (if that were possible) than Knox himself. Melville reorganized the Scottish universities and emphasized classical studies and the study of the Bible in its original Hebrew and Greek. Under his leadership emerged a clearly defined Scottish Presbyterian Church whose elected leaders were responsible for practical as well as spiritual matters.

Later, the Church of Scotland's almost obsessive insistence on self-government led to endless conflicts, first with the Scottish and then, after unification, with the British monarchs.

MARY QUEEN OF SCOTS When Mary Stuart, Queen of Scots (1542–87), took up her rule, she was a Roman Catholic of French upbringing trying to govern an unruly land to which she was a relative newcomer. Daughter of Scotland's James V and France's Mary of Guise, she became queen when 6 days old. She was sent to be educated in France and at age 15 married the heir to the French throne; she returned to Scotland only after his death. Mary then set out on two roads that were anathema to the Scots—to make herself absolute monarch in the French style and to impose Roman Catholicism. The first alienated the lords who held the real power, and the second made her the enemy of John Knox and the Calvinists. After a series of disastrous political and romantic alliances and endless abortive episodes of often indiscreet intrigue, her life was ended by the headsman's ax in England. The execution order was reluctantly issued by her cousin Elizabeth I, who considered Mary's presence an incitement to civil unrest and a threat to the stability of the English throne.

Of all the towering figures in Scottish history, only Mary Queen of Scots left an extensive trail of palaces and castles that you can still visit. Begin in the Borders at Mary Queen of Scots House (see chapter 5, "The Borders & Galloway Regions," for more information) and go on to the Palace of Holyroodhouse in Edinburgh (see chapter 4), where her Italian secretary, David Rizzio, was stabbed 56 times in front of her. The queen used to come to Falkland Palace for hunting and hawking and lived at Stirling Castle as an infant monarch for the first 4 years of her life (see chapter 8).

The power of the great lords of Scotland was broken only in 1603, when Mary's son, James VI of Scotland, assumed the throne of England as James I, Elizabeth's heir. James succeeded where his doomed mother had failed. He was the first of the Stuarts to occupy the English throne, and his coronation effectively united England and Scotland.

UNION WITH ENGLAND   Despite the hopes for peace that accompanied the union, religion almost immediately became a prime source of discontent. From their base in England, the two Stuart kings attempted to promote a Church of Scotland governed by bishops, in opposition to the Presbyterian Church's self-ruling organization. So incensed were the Scots that in 1638 they signed the National Covenant, which not only reasserted the Reformation's principles but also questioned the king's right to make laws, a role the Covenanters believed should be filled by Parliament. However, the monarch was still allowed a role, unlike the position the Puritans took in England.

Charles I, king of England from 1625 to 1649, believed strongly in the divine right of kings. When Parliament stripped away much of his authority in 1642, Charles fled north to organize an army against the Parliamentary forces centered in London. A civil war ensued, and the forces of Parliament were led to victory by Oliver Cromwell (1599–1658). Charles fled to Scotland, but the Scots turned him over to Parliament, and in 1649 he was convicted of treason and beheaded. Under the Commonwealth set up, Cromwell assumed a dominant political role and became Lord Protector in 1653. King in all but name, he ruled England until his death.

But trouble brewed in Scotland. The death of Charles I led to deep divisions in the country, which finally openly defied Cromwell, proclaiming Charles II king. The Scots even launched abortive invasions of England. Cromwell's forces finally defeated the Scots at Dunbar in 1650. For nearly 9 years (1651–60), Scotland was under Commonwealth military occupation, although the result of that invasion had virtually nothing to do with what you'll see as a visitor today.

Tips A Scot Is Not a Scotch

Remember one thing: Scotch is a whisky and not the name of the proud people who inhabit the country. They're called **Scots,** and the adjective is **Scottish.** Even if you forget and call them Scotch, they'll forgive you. What they won't forgive is calling them English.

Religious friction continued, however, after the restoration of Charles II to the English throne.

THE JACOBITES In 1689, when the English Parliament stripped Catholic James II of his crown and imported Protestant monarchs William and Mary from Holland, the exiled ex-king and then his son James Edward (the Old Pretender) became focal points for Scottish unrest. The Jacobites (the name comes from *Jacobus*, the Latin form of James) attempted unsuccessfully in 1715 to place the Old Pretender on the English throne and restore the Stuart line. Although James died in exile, his son Charles Edward (the Young Pretender), better known as Bonnie Prince Charlie, carried on his father's dream. Charismatic but with an alcohol-induced instability, he was the central figure of the 1745 Jacobite uprising. For more legend and lore about Bonnie Prince Charlie, see chapter 11.

Although the revolt was initially promising because of the many Scottish adherents who crossed religious lines to rally to the cause, the Jacobite forces were crushed at the Battle of Culloden, near Inverness, by a larger English army led by the duke of Cumberland. Many supporters of the Pretender's cause were killed in battle, some were executed, and others fled to the United States and other safe havens. Fearing a rebirth of similar types of Scottish nationalism, the clan system was rigorously suppressed; clans that supported the Jacobite cause lost their lands, and, until 1782, the wearing of Highland dress was made illegal. Six miles southeast of Inverness, you can still visit the historic battlefield at Culloden (see chapter 10, "Inverness & the West Highlands," for more information).

The Young Pretender himself was smuggled unglamorously out of Scotland, assisted by Flora MacDonald, a resident of the obscure Hebridean island of South Uist. One of the era's most visible Scottish heroines, she has ever since provided fodder for the Scottish sense of romance. The Bonnie Prince dissipated himself in Paris and Rome, and the hopes of an independent Scotland were buried forever.

ECONOMIC GROWTH & THE INDUSTRIAL REVOLUTION During the 18th century, the Scottish economy underwent a radical transformation of growth and diversification. The British government, fearing civil unrest, commissioned one of its most capable generals to build roads and bridges throughout the country, presumably to increase military access from London in the event of a revolt—however, they actually encouraged business and commerce.

As trade with British overseas colonies, England, and Europe increased, the great ports of Aberdeen, Glasgow, and Leith (near Edinburgh) flourished. The merchants of Glasgow grew rich on a nearly monopolistic tobacco trade with Virginia and the Carolinas, until the outbreak of the Revolution sent American tobacco elsewhere. Other forms of commerce continued to enrich a battalion of shrewd Scots.

The 1789 outbreak of the French Revolution engendered so much Scottish sympathy for the cause that a panicked government in London became more autocratic than ever in its attempts to suppress antimonarchical feelings.

The infamous Clearances (1750–1850) changed forever Scotland's demographics. Small farmers, or crofters, were expelled from their ancestral lands to make way for sheep grazing. Increased industrialization, continued civil unrest, migration into urban centers, and a massive wave of emigration to the United States, Canada, Australia, South Africa, and New Zealand all contributed to a changing national demographic and a dispersal of the Scottish ethic throughout the world.

ℓ The Stone of Destiny, Home at Last

After a rocky journey, the Stone of Scone or Stone of Destiny has finally been returned to Scotland. The stone is physically only a block of sandstone, measuring 26 inches long and 16 inches wide and weighing 336 pounds. But it's not just a stone: Revered for centuries as a holy relic, it allegedly came from the Middle East, and in biblical times Jacob is said to have used the stone as a pillow.

The stone was used at Dunadd, Iona, and Dunstaffnage for enthroning the Dalriad Irish Monarchs called Scots. Later it was moved to Scone, and in 1292 John Balliol became the last king to be crowned on the stone in Scotland. So powerful was its legend that Edward I took it to England in 1296, believing possession of the stone gave him sovereignty over Scotland. There it stayed, under the coronation chair in Westminster Abbey. In 1328, the Treaty of Northampton recognizing Scotland's independence returned the stone to Scotland, but the English reneged on the promise and the stone never moved from Westminster Abbey.

On Christmas Day 1950, the stone was taken from the abbey by a group of Scottish Nationalists. No one knows where it went then, but it was found about 4 months later in Arbroath Abbey and returned to Westminster. A rumor went around that the found stone was actually a replica and that the replica—and not the real stone—was carted back to London, but this has never been proved.

In 1996, the Stone of Destiny left Westminster Abbey by Land Rover, crossing from England into Scotland at the border town of Coldstream, where a small but moving ceremony was held. On November 30 of that year, the stone proceeded with pomp and circumstance up the Royal Mile in Edinburgh to its permanent home beside the Scottish Crown Jewels in Edinburgh Castle, where you can see it today (see chapter 4).

Scots hailed the return of the stone after 700 years in English captivity. Yet not all are pleased with the return of the stone. Some have denounced it as a "cheap political ploy," especially as the Queen claims she's "lending" it to her Scottish subjects—the idea is that after 7 centuries, possession is nine tenths of the law, and it can be called back to London for a future coronation.

Some Scots want to see the stone returned to Scone. "Edinburgh has no claim, legally, morally, or whatever, to the Stone of Scone," said Andrew R. Robinson, administrator of Scone Castle. "It's not called the Stone of Edinburgh, is it?"

Meanwhile, rapid progress in the arts, sciences, and education and the new industrial age meshed neatly with the Scottish genius for thrift, hard work, shrewdness, and conservatism. The 19th century produced vast numbers of prominent Scots who made broad and sweeping contributions to all fields of endeavor. Many of the inventions that altered the history of the developing world were either invented or installed by Scottish genius and industry.

THE 20TH CENTURY   Scotland endured bitter privations during the Great Depression and the two world wars. In the 1960s and 1970s, Scotland found that, like the rest of Britain, its aging industrial plants couldn't compete with more modern commercial competition from abroad. The most visible decline occurred in the shipbuilding industries. The vast Glasgow shipyards that once produced some of the world's great ocean liners went bankrupt. The companies that produced automobiles were wiped out during the 1930s. Many commercial enterprises once controlled by Scots had been merged into English or multinational conglomerates.

However, all wasn't bleak on the Scottish horizon. The 1970 discovery of North Sea oil by British Petroleum boosted the economy considerably and provided jobs for thousands of workers. Oil has continued to play a prominent role in the Scottish economy. In 1981, the largest oil terminal in Europe opened at Sullom Voe in the remote Shetland Islands.

As part of the United Kingdom, Scotland became a member of the European Common Market in 1973, although many Scots—perhaps owing to their long-time isolationism—opposed entry. Some voters expressed a fear that membership would take away hunks of their rights of self-government and determination. In 1974, Scotland underwent a drastic revision of its counties, and many regions were renamed. Tayside, for example, was carved out of the old counties of Perth and Angus.

A landmark scientific breakthrough occurred in 1997. The Scots had always contributed almost disproportionately to the world's sciences and technology. Now the land that gave us Sir Alexander Fleming, Nobel Prize winner as discoverer of penicillin, gave us the first cloned sheep. The issue of *Nature* for February 27, 1997, reported the event, the work of scientists in Roslin. Dolly was the first lamb to be produced by cloning the udder cells of an adult sheep. In the summer of 1997, another major step was taken, and Polly was created, a lamb that has a human gene in every cell of its body. The work was hailed as a milestone. Animals with human genes (at least in theory) could be used to produce hormones or other biological products to treat human diseases or even to produce organs for human transplant.

In May 1999, national election results gave Prime Minister Tony Blair a victory over the Nationalist Party of Scotland. Labour, however, failed to win outright control of the Scottish Parliament; but Blair said he felt the results represented an endorsement of his reform of British politics. Because it came in nine seats short of a majority in the new 129-seat Parliament (the first legislature Scotland had since its 1707 union with England), Labour became obliged to enlist the centrist Liberal Democrats in a coalition, a form of governing not seen in Britain since World War II.

The new Scottish legislature has authority to pursue such matters as health, education, public transportation, and public housing. Unlike the new Welsh Parliament, the Scottish Parliament will also have taxing powers and can make laws. The main Parliament, of course, will remain in London, where Scotland will be widely represented. The country will bow to the greater will of Britain in matters like foreign policy, national defense, and economic and fiscal policies, and may one day become part of euroland, the new umbrella of single-currency countries (France, Germany, Italy, and so on). So far, Britain has decided to stick with the pound sterling as its time-honored form of currency.

The Scottish Parliament got off to a bad start in 2000, with Scotland's 21 robustly competitive newspapers writing of "the silly season" or the "totally absurd." The press noted that members of Parliament awarded lawmakers with commemorative medals before they had done anything, granted bonuses, and fretted about parking spaces and vacation grants instead of tackling some of the country's more serious problems, such as a feudal landowning system. Some lawmakers found themselves heckled in the streets, and they had to endure the bite of such popular comics as Billy Connolly, who dismissed the body "as a wee pretendy Parliament."

On a more optimistic front, Scotland is turning a strong face to the world, with its abundant natural resources in oil, water, gas, and coal. Its high-tech industries have played an important role in the technological revolution, and today the country produces 13% of Europe's personal computers, 45% of Europe's workstations, and 50% of Europe's automated banking machines. Everything in the country is loosening up—blue laws are giving way, later hours are being kept, nightlife is looking up, and ecotourism is being developed. Scotland's time-tested crafts (woolen tweeds and knitwear) are thriving, the market for Scotch whisky has burgeoned all around the world, and tourists are visiting in record numbers.

As Scotland goes deeper into the 21st century, there's a new esprit in the land. Scots are on a roll, declaring that their country is not a mere tartan theme park.

And speaking of tartans, nothing has shaken up the identity of Scotland more than the new kilts designed by Howie Nicholsby of Edinburgh. To model his new kilt design, Howie secured tough rugby star Chris Capaldi. The kilt is transparent—and in pink, no less.

Is nothing sacred?

2 A Portrait of the Scots

LANGUAGE   In Scotland's earliest history, its prevailing tongue was the Celtic language, Gaelic, along with a smattering of Norse dialects. When English was introduced and Scottish English developed, it borrowed heavily not only from Gaelic but also from Scandinavian, Dutch, and French. In the 15th and 16th centuries, when Scotland had close ties to France, French was a literary language of precision and grace, and it was the language of Mary Queen of Scots, who spoke no Gaelic at all. After the Scottish court moved to England in 1603, Scottish English was looked on as a rather awkward dialect.

As the centuries progressed, the ancient and complex Gaelic diminished in importance, partly because the British government's deliberate policy was to make English the language of all Britain. By the 1980s, less than 2% of the Scottish population understood Gaelic. Most of those who still speak it live in the northwestern Highlands and in the Hebridean Islands—especially the Isle of Skye, where about 60% of the population still uses Gaelic.

Scottish English never developed the linguistic class divisions that exist so strongly in England among upper-, middle-, and lower-class speech patterns. Throughout most of its English-speaking history, the hardships of Scotland were suffered in common by a society that was well knit and had few barriers between the classes. Social snobbery was relatively unknown and the laird (estate owner) and his man conversed as equals.

At the end of the 20th century, the great leveling effects of TV and radio had begun to even out some of the more pronounced burrs and lilts of the Scottish tongue. However, the dialect and speech patterns of the Scots are still rich and evocative. Today, after years of struggle, Scottish students are rewarded with approval by pro-Scots educators when they say, "Whos all comin tae the jiggin?"

("Who's coming to the dance?"). This increasing pride in the Scottish language is in direct contrast to what happened in classrooms back in, say, the 1950s. At that time, students were under a constant threat of a whack from a tawse (leather strap) if they blurted out a single *aye*.

HIGHLAND GAMES & GATHERINGS   Highland Gatherings or Games have their origins in the fairs organized by the tribes or clans for the exchange of goods. At these gatherings, there were often trials of strength among the men, and the strongest were selected for the chief's army.

The earliest games were held more than 1,000 years ago. The same tradition is maintained today: throwing hammers, putting rounded stones found in the rivers, tossing tree trunks, and running in flat races and up steep hillsides. Playing the bagpipes and performing dances have always been part of the gatherings. The Heavies, a breed of gigantic men, draw the most attention with their prowess. Of all the events, the most popular and most spectacular is the tossing of the caber (the throwing of a great tree trunk).

Queen Victoria, who had a deep love for Scotland (which was dramatized in the film *Mrs. Brown*), popularized the Highland Games, which for many decades had been suppressed after the failure of the 1745 rebellion. In 1848, the queen and her consort, Prince Albert, attended the Braemar Gathering and saw her ghillie, Duncan, win the race up the hill of Craig Choinnich, as she recorded in her journal.

The most famous gathering nowadays is at Braemar, held in late August or early September and patronized by the royal family. When that chief of chiefs takes the salute, Queen Elizabeth is fulfilling a role assumed by a predecessor of hers in the 11th century.

Other major games are held at Ballater (Grampian), Aberdeen, Elgin, and Newtonmore.

CLANS, TARTANS & KILTS   To the outsider, Scotland's deepest traditions appear to be based on the clan system of old with all the familiar paraphernalia of tartans and bagpipes. However, this is a romantic memory, and in any case, a good part of the Scots—the 75% of the population that live in the central Lowland, for example—have little or no connection with the clansmen of earlier times.

The clan tradition dates from the tribal units of the country's earliest Celtic history. Power was organized around a series of chieftains who exacted loyalties from the inhabitants of a particular region in exchange for protection against exterior invasions. The position of chieftain wasn't hereditary, and land was owned by the clan, not by the chieftain. Clan members had both rights and duties. Rigidly militaristic and paternalistic—the stuff with which Scottish legend is imbued—the clan tradition is still emphasized today, albeit in a much friendlier fashion than when claymores and crossbows threatened a bloody death or dismemberment for alleged slights on a clan's honor.

Chieftains were absolute potentates, with life and death power over members and interlopers, although they were usually viewed as patriarchs actively engaged in the perpetuation of the clan's bloodlines, traditions, and honor. The entourage of a chieftain always included bodyguards, musicians (harpers and pipers), a spokesman (known as a tatler), and—perhaps most important to latter-day students of clan traditions—a bard. The bard's role was to sing, to exalt the role of the clan and its heroes, to keep a genealogical record of births and deaths, and to compose or recite epic poems relating to the clan's history.

C How the Scots Say It

aber   river mouth
ach   field
aird   promontory
alt   stream
auch   field
auld   old
baillie   magistrate
bal   hamlet or tiny village
ben   peak, often rugged
birk   birch tree
brae   hillside, especially along a river
brig   bridge
broch   circular stone tower
burn   stream
cairn   heap of stone piled up as memorial or landmark
ceilidh   Scottish hoedown with singing, music, and tall tales
clach   stone
clachan   hamlet
close   narrow passage leading from the street to a court or tenement
craig   rock
creel   basket
croft   small farm worked by a tenant, often with hereditary rights
cromlech, dolmen   prehistoric tomb or monument consisting of a large flat stone laid across upright stones
dram   ⅛ fluid ounce
drum   ridge
dun   fortress, often in a lake, for refuge in times of trouble
eas   waterfall
eilean   island
factor   manager of an estate
fell   hill
firth   arm of the sea reaching inland

Most of the clans were organized during two distinctly different eras of Scottish history. One of the country's oldest and largest is Clan Donald, whose original organization occurred during the early mists of the Christianization of Scotland and whose headquarters has traditionally been Scotland's northwestern coast and western islands. The fragmentation of Clan Donald into subdivisions (which include the Sleat, the Dunyveg, the Clanranald, and the Keppoch clans) happened after the violent battles of succession over control of the clan in the 1400s. These feuds so weakened the once powerful unity of the MacDonalds that a new crop of former vassal tribes in northwestern Scotland declared their independence and established new clans of their own. These included the Mackintoshes, the Macleans, the MacNeils, the Mackinnons, and the MacLeods.

Meanwhile, the giant Celtic earldoms of eastern Scotland disintegrated and Norman influences from the south became more dominant. Clans whose earliest

gait street (in proper names)
gil ravine
glen a small valley
haugh water meadow
how burial mound
howff meeting place
inver mouth of a river
kil, kin, kirk church
kyle narrows of ancient or unknown origin
land house built on a piece of ground considered as property
larig mountain pass
links dunes
loch lake
machair sand dune, sometimes covered with sea grass
mon hill
muir moor
mull cape or promontory
ness headland
neuk nose
pend vaulted passage
provost mayor
reek smoke
ross cape
schist highly compact crystalline rock formation
strath broad valley
tarbert isthmus
tolbooth old town hall (often with prison)
uig sheltered bay
uisge water
uisge beatha water of life, whisky
way bay
wynd alley

makeup might have been heavily influenced by Norman bloodlines include Clan Frasier (from the French *des fraises,* because of the strawberry leaves on the family's coat of arms), de Umfraville, and Rose. Other clans adapted their Celtic names, like Clan Robertson (Celtic Clan Donnachaidh) and Clan Campbell (Celtic Diarmid).

Simultaneously, in the Borders between England and Scotland, families and clans with differing sets of traditions and symbols held a precarious power over one of Britain's most heavily contested regions, enduring or instigating raids on their territories from both north and south. But despite the rich traditions of the Lowland and Border clans, it's the traditions of the Highland clans (with their costumes, bagpipes, speech patterns, and grandly tragic struggles) that have captured the imagination of the world.

🖉 Garb o' the Gods

A memorable photograph from the handover of Hong Kong may spare the First Battalion of the Black Watch from having to answer the question most frequently put to men in kilts. As the flags were being lowered at the Cenotaph, a rush of wind lifted the tartan fabrics from the backside of Lance Cpl. Lee Wotherspoon and revealed nothing at all but his backside. He received a lot of mail and an admiring review from a gay publication in France.

—Warren Hoge, *New York Times*(1998)

Although not every visitor to Scotland is descended from a clan, almost all are familiar with plaids and the traditions associated with them. Over the centuries, each clan developed a distinctive pattern to be worn by its members, presumably to better identify its soldiers in the heat of battle. (Today, *tartan* is used interchangeably with *plaid*, but the word *tartan* originally referred specifically to a mantle of cloth draped over the back and shoulders.)

Kilts enjoy an ancient history. Checkered tartans were first mentioned in a 1471 English inventory. The clans developed special dyeing and weaving techniques, with colors and patterns reflecting their flair and imagination. The craft of dyeing was raised to an art that was a point of pride for the clan: Alder bark, steeped in hot water, produces a black dye; gorse, broom, and knapweed produce shades of green; cup moss produces purple; dandelion leaves produce magenta; bracken and heather produce yellow; white lichens produce red; and indigo had to be imported for blue.

When Bonnie Prince Charlie launched his abortive rebellion in 1745, he used tartans as a symbol of his army, and this threatened the English enemy so much that public display of tartans was banned for a period after his defeat. Tartans came into high fashion in Queen Victoria's day,

The clans had broken down long before Sir Walter Scott wrote his romantic novels about them and long before Queen Victoria made Scotland socially fashionable. The clans today represent a cultural rather than a political power. The best place to see the remnants of their tradition in action is at any traditional Highland gathering, although battalions of bagpipers seem to show up at everything from weddings and funerals to political rallies, parades, and civic events throughout Scotland.

3 A Taste of Scotland

FROM ANGUS BEEF TO HAGGIS   For many years, restaurants in Scotland were known mainly for their modest prices, watery overcooked vegetables, and boiled meats. But you need no longer expect a diet of oats, fried fish, and greasy chips—in the past 20 or so years, there has been a significant improvement in Scottish cookery. There was a time when the Scot going out for dinner would head for the nearest hotel, but independent restaurants are now opening everywhere, often by newly arrived immigrants, along with bistros and wine bars.

when she and her kilt-wearing German consort, Albert, made all things Scottish popular.

Today, there are at least 300 tartans, each subtly distinct from its neighbor and all available for sale in Scotland's shops and markets. If you're not fortunate enough to be of Scottish extraction, Queen Victoria long ago authorized two Lowland designs as suitable garb for Sassenachs (the English and, more remotely, the Americans).

Few people realize that from 7 to 10 yards of tartan wool cloth goes into the average kilt. Even fewer non-Scots know what's actually worn beneath those folds strapped over the muscular thighs of a parading Scotsman. For a Highlander, the answer to that question is nothing, an answer that goes along with such defenders of ancient tradition who hold that only a Stewart can wear a Stewart tartan, only a Scotsman looks good in a kilt, and only a foreigner would stoop to wearing anything under it.

Alas, commercialism has reared its head with the introduction of undershorts to match the material making up bagpipe players' kilts. A story is told of a colonel who heard a rumor that the soldiers of his elite Highland Light Infantry regiment were mollycoddling themselves with undershorts. The next day, his eyebrows bristling, he ordered the entire regiment to undress in front of him. To his horror, half a dozen of his soldiers had disgraced the regiment by putting on what only an Englishman would wear. He publicly ordered the offending garments removed, and when he gave the order the next day to drop your kilts, not a soldier in the regiment had on the trews (close-cut tartan shorts).

Even In today's general decline of standards, the mark of a man in the Highlands is still whether he can abide the drafts up his thighs and the feel of wool cloth against his tender flesh.

More and more restaurants are offering "Taste of Scotland" menus of traditional dishes prepared with the freshest local ingredients, a culinary program initiated by the Scottish Tourist Board. Scotland's culinary strength is in its fresh raw ingredients, ranging from seafood, beef, and game to vegetables and native fruits.

One of Scotland's best-known exports is pedigree **Aberdeen Angus beef.** In fact, ye olde roast beef of England often came from Scotland. Scottish **lamb** is known for its tender, tasty meat. A true connoisseur can taste the difference in lamb by its grazing grounds, ranging from the coarse pastureland and seaweed of the Shetlands to the heather-clad hills of the mainland.

Game plays an important role in the Scottish diet, ranging from woodcock, red deer, and grouse to the rabbit and hare in the crofter's kitchen. And **fish** in this land of seas, rivers, and lochs is a mainstay, from salmon to the pink-fleshed brown trout to the modest herring that's transformed into the elegant kipper (the best are the Loch Fyne kippers). Scottish smoked salmon is, of course, a delicacy known worldwide.

The good news is that the word "eclectic" now describes many restaurants in Scotland. To cite only an example or two, fresh salads are often given a Thai kick with lime leaves and chile, and stir-fries and chargrill are standard features. Scots today can eat better than ever before. Robert Burns would be shocked at some of the new taste sensations creative chefs are devising. But he would be happy to learn that alcohol—especially whisky—is still a favored ingredient in many dishes and sauces.

Of course, it takes a wise chef to leave well enough alone, and many Scottish cooks know the simplest dishes have never lost their appeal, especially if that means **Lismore oysters** or **Loch Etive mussels.** The Scots have always been good bakers, and many small tearooms still bake their own **scones** and buttery **shortbread.** Heather honey is justly celebrated, and jams make use of Scotland's abundant harvest of soft fruit. Scottish raspberries, for example, are said to be among the finest in the world.

You'll most definitely want to try some of Scotland's excellent **cheeses.** The mild or mature cheddars are the best known. A famous hard cheese, Dunlop, comes from the Orkney Islands as well as Arran and Islay. One of the best-known cheeses from the Highlands is Caboc, creamy and rich, formed into cork shapes and rolled in pinhead oatmeal. Many varieties of cottage cheese are flavored with herbs, chives, or garlic.

And, yes, **haggis** is still Scotland's national dish—it's perhaps more symbolic than gustatory. One wit described it as a "castrated bagpipe." Regardless of what you might be told facetiously, haggis isn't a bird. Therefore, you should turn down invitations (usually offered in pubs) to go on a midnight haggis hunt. Cooked in a sheep's paunch (nowadays more likely a plastic bag), it's made with bits and pieces of the lung, liver, and heart of sheep mixed with suet and spices, along with onions and oatmeal. Haggis is often accompanied by single-malt whisky—then again, what isn't?

SINGLE MALT OR BLEND?   "It's the only liquor fit for a gentleman to drink in the morning if he can have the good fortune to come by it . . . or after dinner either." Thus wrote Sir Walter Scott of the drink of his country—**Scotch whisky.** Of course, if you're here or almost anywhere in Britain or Europe, you don't have to identify it as *Scotch* whisky when you order. That's what you'll get. In fact, in some parts of Scotland, England, and Wales, they look at you oddly if you order Scotch as you would in the States.

The true difference in the Scotch whiskies you may have become accustomed to seeing in bars or liquor stores at home is whether they're blends or single-malt whiskies. Many connoisseurs prefer single malts, whose tastes depend on their points of origin: Highlands, Lowlands, Islay, or Campbeltown on Kintyre. These are usually seen as sipping whiskies, not to be mixed with water (well, maybe soda) and not to be served with ice. Many have come to be used as after-dinner drinks, served in a snifter like cognac.

The blended Scotches came into being both because the single malts were for a long time too harsh for delicate palates and because they were expensive and time-consuming to produce. A shortcut was developed: The clear and almost tasteless alcohol produced in the traditional way could be mixed with such ingredients as American corn, Finnish barley, Glasgow city tap water, and caramel coloring with a certain percentage of malt whiskies that flavored the entire bottle. Whichever you prefer, both the single malts and the blends must be made within the borders of Scotland and then aged for at least 3 years before they can legally be called Scotch whisky.

Two after-dinner drinks are Scotch-based liqueurs—**Drambuie** and **Glayva.** The recipe for Drambuie, better known to Americans than Glayva, is supposed to have been given to its first producers, the Mackinnons of Strath on the Isle of Skye, by an impecunious guest, Bonnie Prince Charlie. The name of the drink is derived from the Gaelic *an dram buidheach,* meaning "a dram that satisfies."

The making of Scottish **beer**—the ales drunk by the common folk in earlier days—almost died out when palates became more adapted to Scotch whisky and when a malt tax was levied in the 18th century, followed in the 19th century by beer duty. The brewing industry has made a comeback in the last quarter of a century, and Scottish beer, or Scotch ale, is being produced. Real **ale** is beer made from malted barley, hop flowers, yeast, and water, with a fining process (use of an extract from the swim bladders of certain fish) to complete the brewing. Ales are fermented in casks in a series of steps. Scottish ale, either dark or light, is malty and full of flavor.

4 Recommended Books

BIOGRAPHY & AUTOBIOGRAPHY   *Burns: A Biography of Robert Burns,* by James MacKay, is one of the best works devoted to Scotland's national poet (1759–96). The life of Burns is portrayed against the historical framework of 18th-century Scotland. A Burns scholar, MacKay defends the author of *Tam O'Shanter* and "Auld Lang Syne" against previously published charges that he was a drunkard and a rake.

Robert Louis Stevenson: A Biography, by Frank McLynn, maintains that the frail adventurer and author of *The Strange Case of Dr. Jekyll and Mr. Hyde* was Scotland's greatest writer. The book documents the tragic life of the writer who suffered from "bloody jack" (a hemorrhaging consumptive) and died at 44.

Today's most famous Scot is revealed in the biography *Sean Connery: From 007 to Hollywood Icon,* by Andrew Yule. It traces the legendary actor's rise from humble origins in Edinburgh to later success "escaping bondage" in such films as *Rising Sun.* Like all true Scotsmen, Connery is said to have a fascinated interest in golf (playing it) and money (not spending it). Scottish-American readers may find the early years of growing up in Edinburgh during the Depression the most interesting.

In Muriel Spark's autobiography *Curriculum Vitae,* the gifted writer sets the record straight about her first 39 years, up to 1957 and the publication of her novel *The Comforters.* The best parts are about her life as a child in Edinburgh. She tells how at 5 she was sent to Gillespie's, an Edinburgh day school, where she became a pupil of Miss Christina Kay—in time, she'd appear in Ms. Spark's fiction as the immortal Miss Jean Brodie.

FICTION & POETRY   Scotland's most celebrated literary figure remains Robert Burns (1759–96), whose "Auld Lang Syne" is still sung the world over on New Year's Eve. All bookstores in Scotland sell volumes of his poems, plus numerous biographies. Although not read with the fervor as in days of yore, poet and novelist Sir Walter Scott (1771–1832) was one of Scotland's top literary figures. The list of his works is so long it would take up a full printed page, everything from *Ivanhoe* in 1820 to *The Fair Maid of Perth* in 1828.

Another great name in Scottish literature, poet and novelist Robert Louis Stevenson (1850–94), became famous in 1883 after the publication of his first novel, *Treasure Island.* He went on to produce memorable works like *Kidnapped* in 1885 and *The Strange Case of Dr. Jekyll and Mr. Hyde* in 1886. (The story was based on an Edinburgh man, Deacon Brodie, but set in London.)

In modern times, Scotland hasn't turned out the big names in literature that it had previously. A Communist, poet Hugh MacDiarmid (1892–1978), produced an enormous output of poetry and essays as his international stature grew. His *Complete Poems* was published in two volumes in 1978. *Morning Tide,* by Neil Gunn, was written in the 1930s and helps explain why Gunn (1891–1973) is considered the master of modern Scottish fiction. It's a straightforward account of a boy's coming of age in a small fishing village in Scotland in the last years of Victoria's reign.

Glaswegian Alistair MacLean (1922–87) has also achieved acclaim. His novel *HMS Ulysses,* drawing heavily on his experiences with Russian convoys, became one of the most successful British novels of all time and was followed by *The Guns of Navarone,* which earned a worldwide audience. Many readers became familiar with the works of Muriel Spark (b. 1918) through her most famous book, *The Prime of Miss Jean Brodie,* which was made into a successful film starring Maggie Smith. With numerous works still in print, including *Symposium* and *The Ballad of Peckham Rye,* Ms. Spark remains a giant of contemporary fiction.

The 1995 film *Braveheart* inspired a book of the same name by Randall Wallace, who also wrote the screenplay. Most critics found it an entertaining read "if you don't mind the complete bastardization of Scottish history."

HISTORY   Good historical overviews of Scotland, beginning with its earliest prehistory, are provided by Michael Jenner's *Scotland Through the Ages,* Rosalind Mitchison's *A History of Scotland,* and *A New History of Scotland,* by W. Croft Dickinson and George S. Pryde. Also insightful, perhaps because of its authorship by a famous Scots novelist, is Alistair Maclean's *Alistair Maclean Introduces Scotland.*

Dealing in detail with the famous personalities of the 16th century is Alison Plowden's *Elizabeth Tudor and Mary Stewart: Two Queens in One Isle.* Antonia Fraser's *Mary, Queen of Scots* is highly readable. (Also by Antonia Fraser is a short, subjective, and exceedingly charming anthology, *Scottish Love Poems: A Personal Anthology.*)

Other historical eras are analyzed by Iain Moncreiffe in *The Highland Clans* and by Richard B. Sher and Jeffrey R. Smitten in *Scotland and America in the Age of Enlightenment.* Also interesting are David Daiches's *A Hotbed of Genius: The Scottish Enlightenment 1730–1790* and Henry Hamilton's *The Industrial Revolution in Scotland.* For U.S. citizens of Scots descent, a richly evocative book, much applauded in the American South, is Duane Gilbert Meyer's *The Highland Scots of North Carolina.*

The more recent Scottish experience, particularly the events engendered by the flow of black gold from the North Sea, is carefully described in *North Sea Oil and Scotland's Economic Prospects,* by T. M. Lewis and J. H. McNicoll. In the same vein is *The Renaissance of the Scottish Economy,* by Charlotte Lythe and Madhavi Mamjudar. Appropriate for anyone interested in European history just before, during, and after World War II is T. Christopher Smout's *A History of the Scottish People 1930–1950.*

CLANS & THEIR SYMBOLS   Finally, on a purely decorative and symbolic level, but with rich interest for anyone tracing genealogical roots, is Robert Bain's *The Clans and Tartans of Scotland,* enlarged and re-edited by Margaret MacDougall, with heraldic advice supplied by P. E. Stewart-Blacker. Somewhat more succinct is *Tartans,* edited and published by the Belvedere Editions of Rizzoli International.

Index

FROMMER'S® COMPLETE TRAVEL GUIDES

Alaska
Amsterdam
Argentina & Chile
Arizona
Atlanta
Australia
Austria
Bahamas
Barcelona, Madrid & Seville
Beijing
Belgium, Holland & Luxembourg
Bermuda
Boston
British Columbia & the Canadian
    Rockies
Budapest & the Best of Hungary
California
Canada
Cancún, Cozumel & the Yucatán
Cape Cod, Nantucket &
    Martha's Vineyard
Caribbean
Caribbean Cruises & Ports of Call
Caribbean Ports of Call
Carolinas & Georgia
Chicago
China
Colorado
Costa Rica
Denmark
Denver, Boulder & Colorado Springs
England
Europe
European Cruises & Ports of Call
Florida
France

Germany
Great Britain
Greece
Greek Islands
Hawaii
Hong Kong
Honolulu, Waikiki & Oahu
Ireland
Israel
Italy
Jamaica
Japan
Las Vegas
London
Los Angeles
Maryland & Delaware
Maui
Mexico
Montana & Wyoming
Montréal & Québec City
Munich & the Bavarian Alps
Nashville & Memphis
Nepal
New England
New Mexico
New Orleans
New Zealand
Nova Scotia, New Brunswick &
    Prince Edward Island
Oregon
Paris
Philadelphia & the Amish Country
Portugal
Prague & the Best of the Czech
    Republic

Provence & the Riviera
Puerto Rico
Rome
San Antonio & Austin
San Diego
San Francisco
Santa Fe, Taos & Albuquerque
Scandinavia
Scotland
Seattle & Portland
Shanghai
Singapore & Malaysia
South Africa
South America
Southeast Asia
South Florida
South Pacific
Spain
Sweden
Switzerland
Texas
Thailand
Tokyo
Toronto
Tuscany & Umbria
USA
Utah
Vancouver & Victoria
Vermont, New Hampshire
    & Maine
Vienna & the Danube Valley
Virgin Islands
Virginia
Walt Disney World & Orlando
Washington, D.C.
Washington State

FROMMER'S® DOLLAR-A-DAY GUIDES

Australia from $50 a Day
California from $70 a Day
Caribbean from $70 a Day
England from $75 a Day
Europe from $70 a Day

Florida from $70 a Day
Hawaii from $80 a Day
Ireland from $60 a Day
Italy from $70 a Day
London from $85 a Day

New York from $90 a Day
Paris from $80 a Day
San Francisco from $70 a Day
Washington, D.C., from $80
    a Day

FROMMER'S® PORTABLE GUIDES

Acapulco, Ixtapa & Zihuatanejo
Alaska Cruises & Ports of Call
Amsterdam
Aruba
Australia's Great Barrier Reef
Bahamas
Baja & Los Cabos
Berlin
Big Island of Hawaii
Boston
California Wine Country
Cancún
Charleston & Savannah
Chicago
Disneyland

Dublin
Florence
Frankfurt
Hong Kong
Houston
Las Vegas
London
Los Angeles
Maine Coast
Maui
Miami
New Orleans
New York City
Paris

Phoenix & Scottsdale
Portland
Puerto Rico
Puerto Vallarta, Manzanillo &
    Guadalajara
San Diego
San Francisco
Seattle
Sydney
Tampa & St. Petersburg
Vancouver
Venice
Virgin Islands
Washington, D.C.

FROMMER'S® NATIONAL PARK GUIDES

Family Vacations in the National
    Parks
Grand Canyon

National Parks of the American
    West
Rocky Mountain
Yellowstone & Grand Teton

Yosemite & Sequoia/
    Kings Canyon
Zion & Bryce Canyon

FROMMER'S® MEMORABLE WALKS

Chicago	New York	San Francisco
London	Paris	

FROMMER'S® GREAT OUTDOOR GUIDES

Arizona & New Mexico	Northern California	Vermont & New Hampshire
New England	Southern New England	

SUZY GERSHMAN'S BORN TO SHOP GUIDES

Born to Shop: France	Born to Shop: Italy	Born to Shop: New York
Born to Shop: Hong Kong, Shanghai & Beijing	Born to Shop: London	Born to Shop: Paris

FROMMER'S® IRREVERENT GUIDES

Amsterdam	Los Angeles	San Francisco
Boston	Manhattan	Seattle & Portland
Chicago	New Orleans	Vancouver
Las Vegas	Paris	Walt Disney World
London	Rome	Washington, D.C.

FROMMER'S® BEST-LOVED DRIVING TOURS

Britain	Germany	New England
California	Ireland	Scotland
Florida	Italy	Spain
France		

HANGING OUT™ GUIDES

Hanging Out in England	Hanging Out in France	Hanging Out in Italy
Hanging Out in Europe	Hanging Out in Ireland	Hanging Out in Spain

THE UNOFFICIAL GUIDES®

Bed & Breakfasts and Country Inns in:	Florida with Kids	New Orleans
California	Golf Vacations in the Eastern U.S.	New York City
New England	The Great Smokey & Blue Ridge Mountains	Paris
Northwest	Inside Disney	San Francisco
Rockies	Hawaii	Skiing in the West
Southeast	Las Vegas	Southeast with Kids
Beyond Disney	London	Walt Disney World
Branson, Missouri	Mid-Atlantic with Kids	Walt Disney World for Grown-ups
California with Kids	Mini Las Vegas	Walt Disney World for Kids
Chicago	Mini-Mickey	Washington, D.C.
Cruises	New England & New York with Kids	World's Best Diving Vacations
Disneyland		

SPECIAL-INTEREST TITLES

Frommer's Adventure Guide to Australia & New Zealand
Frommer's Adventure Guide to Central America
Frommer's Adventure Guide to India & Pakistan
Frommer's Adventure Guide to South America
Frommer's Adventure Guide to Southeast Asia
Frommer's Adventure Guide to Southern Africa
Frommer's Britain's Best Bed & Breakfasts and Country Inns
Frommer's France's Best Bed & Breakfasts and Country Inns
Frommer's Italy's Best Bed & Breakfasts and Country Inns
Frommer's Caribbean Hideaways

Frommer's Exploring America by RV
Frommer's Gay & Lesbian Europe
Frommer's The Moon
Frommer's New York City with Kids
Frommer's Road Atlas Britain
Frommer's Road Atlas Europe
Frommer's Washington, D.C., with Kids
Frommer's What the Airlines Never Tell You
Israel Past & Present
The New York Times' Guide to Unforgettable Weekends
Places Rated Almanac
Retirement Places Rated

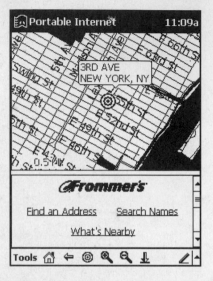